Alison Balter

W9-BTK-664

Alison Balter's Mastering Access 2002 Enterprise Development

SAMS

201 West 103rd Street, Indianapolis, Indiana 46290

Alison Balter's Mastering Access 2002 Enterprise Development

International Standard Book Number: 0-672-32113-0

Library of Congress Catalog Card Number: 00-110541

Printed in the United States of America

First Printing: June 2002

05   04   03   02   4   3   2   1

Trademarks

Warning and Disclaimer

Executive Editor
Michael Stephens

Acquisitions Editor
Kim Spilker
Sondra Scott

Development Editor
Audrey Doyle

Managing Editor
Charlotte Clapp

Project Editor
Elizabeth Finney

Copy Editors
Krista Hansing
Karen A. Gill

Indexer
Sandra Henselmeier

Proofreader
Jessica McCarty

Technical Editors
Jon Price
Shimon Mordzynski

Team Coordinator
Lynne Williams

Media Developer
Dan Scherf

Interior Designer
Gary Adair

Cover Designer
Alan Clements

Page Layout
Brad Lenser

Contents at a Glance

Table of Contents

About the Author

Alison Balter is the president of InfoTechnology Partners, Inc., a computer consulting firm based in Camarillo, California. Alison is a highly experienced independent trainer and consultant specializing in Windows applications training and development. During her 19 years in the computer industry, she has trained and consulted with many corporations and government agencies. Since Alison founded InfoTechnology Partners, Inc. (formerly Marina Consulting Group) in 1990, its client base has expanded to include major corporations and government agencies such as Shell Oil, Accenture, Northrop, the Drug Enforcement Administration, Prudential Insurance, Transamerica Insurance, Fox Broadcasting, the United States Navy, and others.

InfoTechnology Partners, Inc. is a Microsoft Certified Partner, and Alison is a Microsoft Certified Professional. Alison was one of the first professionals in the computer industry to become a Microsoft Certified Solutions Developer (MCSD).

Alison is the author of more than 300 internationally marketed computer training videos, including 7 Access 2.0 videos, 11 Access 95 videos, 13 Access 97 videos, 18 Access 2000 videos, and 35 Access 2002 videos. These videos are available by contacting Alison's company, InfoTechnology Partners, Inc. Alison travels throughout North America giving training seminars in Microsoft Access, Visual Basic, Microsoft SQL Server, Visual Studio .NET, Visual InterDev, and Visual Basic for Applications. She is also featured in several live satellite television broadcasts for National Technological University.

Alison is a regular contributing columnist for *Access/Office/VB Advisor* as well as other computer publications. She is also a regular on the Access, Visual Basic, SQL Server, and Visual InterDev national speaker circuits. She was one of four speakers on the Visual Basic 4.0 and 5.0 World Tours seminar series cosponsored by Application Developers Training Company and Microsoft.

Alison is also a coauthor of three other Access books published by Sams Publishing: *Essential Access 95*, *Access 95 Unleashed*, and *Access 97 Unleashed*.

An active participant in many user groups and other organizations, Alison is a past president of the Independent Computer Consultants Association of Los Angeles and of the Los Angeles Clippers Users' Group.

On a personal note, Alison keeps herself busy skiing, ice skating, horseback riding, running, lifting weights, hiking, traveling, and dancing. She most enjoys spending time with her husband, Dan, their daughter Alexis, and their son Brendan.

Alison's firm, InfoTechnology Partners, Inc., is available for consulting work and onsite training in Microsoft Access, Visual Basic, SQL Server, Visual Studio .NET, and Visual InterDev, as well as for Windows NT, Windows 95/98, Windows 2000, Windows XP, Windows .NET Server, PC networking, and Microsoft Exchange Server. Contact Alison by electronic mail at Alison@InfoTechnologyPartners.com, or visit InfoTechnology Partners' Web site at www.InfoTechnologyPartners.com.

Dedication

I dedicate this book to my husband Dan, my daughter Alexis, my son Brendan, my parents Charlotte and Bob, and to my real father, Herman. Dan, you are my partner in life and the wind beneath my wings. You are a true partner in every sense of the word. I am so lucky to be traveling the path of life with such a spectacular person. Alexis, you are the sweet little girl that I always dreamed of. You are everything that I could have ever wanted and so very much more. You make every one of my days a happy one! Brendan, you are the one who keeps me on my toes. There is never a dull moment with you around. I wish I had just a small portion of your energy. I thank you for the endless laughter that you bring to our family and for reminding me about all of the important things in life. Mom and Dad, without all that you do to help out with life's chores, the completion of this book could never have been possible. Words cannot express my gratitude!

To my real father, Herman, I credit my ability to soar in such a technical field to you. I hope that I inherited just a small part of your intelligence, wit, and fortitude. I am sorry that you did not live to see this accomplishment. I hope that you can see my work and that you are proud of it. I also hope that in some way you share in the joy that Dan, Alexis, and Brendan bring to me. More than anyone else, I dedicate this book to you.

Finally, I want to thank God for giving me the gift of gab, a wonderful career, an incredible husband, two beautiful children, a very special home, and an awesome life. Through your grace, I am truly blessed.

Acknowledgments

Writing a book is a monumental task. Without the support and understanding of those close to me, my dreams for this book would have never come to fruition. Special thanks go to the following special people who helped to make this book possible:

Dan Balter (my incredible husband) for his ongoing support, love, encouragement, friendship, and for, as usual, being patient with me while I wrote this book. Dan, words cannot adequately express the love and appreciation that I feel for all that you are and all that you do for me. You treat me like a princess! Thank you for being the phenomenal person you are. I enjoy sharing not only our career successes, but even more I enjoy sharing the life of our beautiful children, Alexis and Brendan. I look forward to continuing to reach highs we never dreamed of. There is no one I'd rather spend forever with than you.

Alexis Balter (my precious daughter) for giving life a special meaning. Your intelligence, compassion, caring, and perceptiveness are far beyond your years. Alexis, you make all my hard work worth it. No matter how bad my day, when I look at you, sunshine fills my life. You are the most special gift that anyone has ever given me.

Brendan Balter (my adorable son) for showing me the power of persistence. Brendan, you are small, but boy are you mighty! I have never seen such tenacity and fortitude in such a little person. I never imagined that one little guy could render hours of expensive baby-proofing worthless! Thank you for your sweetness, your sensitivity, and your unconditional love. Most of all, thank you for reminding me how important it is to have a sense of humor.

Charlotte and Bob Roman (Mom & Dad) for believing in me and sharing in both the good times and the bad. Mom and Dad, without your special love and support, I never would have become who I am today. Without all your help, I could never get everything done. Words can never express how much I appreciate all that you do!

Sue Terry for being the most wonderful best friend anyone could possibly have. You inspire me with your music, your love, your friendship, and your faith in God. Whenever I am having a bad day, I picture you singing "Dear God" or "Love Thy Neighbor Blues," and suddenly my day gets better. Thank you for the gift of friendship. Thanks also to Kim (Sue's better half) for all of your love and support.

Roz, Ron, and Charlie Carriere for supporting my endeavors and for encouraging me to pursue my writing. It means a lot to know that you guys are proud of me for what I do. I enjoy our times together as a family. Charlie, I am *very* proud of the man that you are becoming.

Steven Chait for being a special brother. I want you to know how much you mean to me. When I was a little girl, I was told about your gift to write. You may not know this, but my desire to write started as a little girl wanting to be like her big brother.

Sonia Aguilar for being the best nanny that anyone could ever dream of having. You are a person far too special to describe in words. I can't tell you how much it means to know that Alexis and Brendan have someone so loving and caring with whom to spend their days. You are an amazing model of love, kindness, and charity. Hugo, Claudia, Gaby, and Hugito, you are all special, too. Dan, Alexis, Brendan, and I are so very lucky to have you in our family.

Doug and Karen Sylvester for being the best neighbors and friends a couple could have. You are loads of fun to be with and are always there when we need you. We are so glad you are such an integral part of our lives. We look forward to watching Alexis, Brendan, Nathaniel, and Noah grow up together.

Greggory Peck from Blast Through Learning for his contribution to my success in this industry. I believe that the opportunities you gave me early on have helped me reach a level in this industry that would have been much more difficult for me to reach on my own.

Edie Swanson for being a great assistant. You did a great job keeping all my other responsibilities to a minimum so that I could focus on the completion of this book. Thanks for making my day-to-day work life easier.

Diane Dennis, Shell Forman, Joyce Milner, Chuck Hinkle, Scott Barker, and all of the other wonderful friends that I have in my life. Diane, you have been my soul mate in life since we were four! Shell, my special "sister," I am lucky to have such a special friend as you. Joyce, miles can't keep our hearts apart. I only wish that we could see more of each other. Chuck, you have a special place in my heart. Scott, you have always been a great business and personal support.

Jack Gupton, Lisa Dosch, Ellen McCrea, David Cummins, Bob Hess, and all of the other special clients and work associates that I have in my life. Although all of you started out as clients, I feel that our relationship goes much deeper than that. I am *very* lucky to have people in my work life like you. Thank you all for your patience with my schedule as I wrote this book.

Kim Spilker, Sondra Scott, Audrey Doyle, Elizabeth Finney, Krista Hansing, Karen Gill, Jon Price, Chris Thibodeaux, Shimon Mordzynski, and Rosemarie Graham for making my experience with Sams a positive one. I know that you all worked very hard to ensure that this book came out on time and with the best quality possible. Without you, this book wouldn't have happened. I have *really* enjoyed working with *all* of you over these past several months. I appreciate your thoughtfulness and your sensitivity to my schedule and commitments outside of this book. It is nice to work with people who appreciate me as a person, not just as an author.

Tell Us What You Think!

As the reader of this book, *you* are our most important critic and commentator. We value your opinion and want to know what we're doing right, what we could do better, what areas you'd like to see us publish in, and any other words of wisdom you're willing to pass our way.

As an Executive Editor for Sams Publishing, I welcome your comments. You can fax, email, or write me directly to let me know what you did or didn't like about this book—as well as what we can do to make our books stronger.

Please note that I cannot help you with technical problems related to the topic of this book, and that due to the high volume of mail I receive, I might not be able to reply to every message.

When you write, please be sure to include this book's title and author as well as your name and phone or fax number. I will carefully review your comments and share them with the author and editors who worked on the book.

Fax: 317-581-4770

Email: feedback@samspublishing.com

Mail: Michael Stephens
            Executive Editor
            Sams Publishing
            201 West 103rd Street
            Indianapolis, IN 46290 USA

Introduction

Many people believe that Microsoft Access is not an appropriate tool for enterprise development. I have many happy large corporate clients whose real-life experiences strongly contradict that opinion. The problem with many people's attempts at enterprise development with Access is that their approach is completely inappropriate.

New clients often call me out to their site because their client/server Access application is not only slow, but it also is bringing the entire network to a crawl. These clients are often convinced that we must immediately rewrite the application in Visual Basic, PowerBuilder, Active Server Pages (ASP), or some other tool. Sometimes they are correct, but most of the time the problem is that the developer of the application has architected it improperly. Usually, the forms and reports return all of the data over the network wire whether the user needs it or not. After redesigning the application so that it brings only the necessary data over the network (a much less expensive proposition than rewriting the application in another environment), my clients are thrilled with the results. Empirical evidence proves over and over again that Microsoft Access *can* play in the enterprise arena.

This book picks up where *Alison Balter's Mastering Access 2002 Desktop Development* left off. It begins by discussing a strategy for developing Access applications. It talks about Access's strengths and weaknesses, as well as when it is appropriate to use Access as a development tool and when it is not. Chapter 2, "Developing Multiuser Applications," continues by talking about how you can write applications that transition easily from the single-user environment through the enterprise client/server environment. You learn about multiuser issues such as multiuser design strategies, linking to external tables, and record locking. Whereas Chapter 2 focuses on multiuser issues, Chapter 3, "Introduction to Client/Server Development Techniques," covers client/server techniques. You learn when to move an application to the client/server environment and how to upsize an application to a client/server environment. You also learn about the various client/server techniques available to you.

Chapter 4, "SQL Server Basics," begins a section of the book that focuses on Microsoft SQL Server. Within Chapter 4, you learn all of the basics of working with SQL Server 2000. The chapter tours Enterprise Manager, Query Analyzer, Performance Monitor, and data-transformation services (DTS). Within Chapter 4, you also learn how to create a SQL Server database. With all of that information under your belt, you are ready to move on to Chapter 5, "SQL Server Tables and Database Diagrams," where you learn how to create and modify the design of tables and diagrams. Then, in Chapter 6, "Mastering T-SQL," I discuss all of the basics of working with the Transact-SQL (T-SQL) language. This information is necessary so that you can effectively build SQL Server views, stored procedures, functions, and triggers, which are an integral part of any client/server application and an important part of any client/server developer's arsenal. Chapter 7, "Working with SQL Server Views," covers the process of building SQL Server views, and Chapter 8, "Designing SQL Server Stored Procedures, User-Defined Functions, and Triggers," covers the process of building SQL Server stored procedures, functions, and triggers. It is important to secure the SQL Server database and components that you build. Even a secured Access application is useless if the user can access the SQL Server directly and destroy the data that your application so carefully maintains. Chapter 9, "SQL Server Security," covers SQL Server security. You learn how to set up logins and roles and the basics of securing all of the objects in your database.

After you have read Chapters 4 through 9, you are ready to start thinking about building your client/server applications. Chapter 10, "ADO and SQL Server," covers ActiveX data objects (ADO). It focuses on how you can use ADO to work with SQL Server data and objects. Chapter 11, "Developing an MDB Client/Server Application with Linked Tables," shows you how to build an MDB client/server application with linked tables and bound forms. Chapter 12, "Developing an ADP Application," transitions you to the process of building an Access Data Project (ADP) client/server application. Because there are times when you will need to develop parts of your application with unbound forms, Chapter 13, "Building Unbound Applications," covers the ins and outs of unbound forms. For the real hard-core developers and applications, Access can participate in a multitier environment. Chapter 14, "Building N-Tier Applications," shows you how you can build applications in which all of the data access code resides in middle-tier business objects, written in a development environment such as Visual Basic. You can use these components with your Access applications as well as with Visual Basic, ASP, and any other applications that support the Component Object Model (COM).

After you have completed Chapter 14, you have not only covered all of the basics of SQL Server, but you have also covered all of the important client/server development techniques. You are ready to move on to special topics that make your life as a client/server enterprise developer easier. Chapter 15, "Configuring, Maintaining, and Tuning SQL Server," covers the process of configuring and maintaining your SQL Server. Included in the chapter are important topics such as backing up and restoring, SQL Server configuration options, and troubleshooting performance problems. Although you can leave these techniques to your company's database administrator (DBA), it is a good idea to have a general understanding of all of the topics covered in the chapter.

Chapters 16, "Transaction Processing," 17, "Access Replication Made Easy," and 18, "Taking Advantage of the Microsoft Office XP Developer," move the focus off SQL Server and back onto Access. In Chapter 16, you learn how to implement transaction processing in the applications that you build. Chapter 17 covers Access replication. You learn what replication is and when it's appropriate. You also learn how to implement replication in your own Access databases. Chapter 18 covers the Microsoft

Office XP Developer. You learn what the XP Developer is and the tools within it that you will probably want to take advantage of. Chapter 19, "Source Code Control," covers Visual SourceSafe. This powerful tool is a must in a multideveloper environment. It offers versioning control, as well as the capability to keep track of who modified what and when. If you have purchased the Microsoft Office XP Developer, you can integrate this powerful product into the Access development environment.

Well, it seems as if every book these days has to include coverage of the Internet and intranet. This book is no exception. Chapters 20–23 focus on Access, SQL Server, and their integration with the Internet. Chapter 20, "Publishing Data on the Web," begins the discussion by covering how you can publish your Access and SQL Server data to the Web from within Microsoft Access. You learn not only how to create Hypertext Markup Language (HTML) documents from your Access objects, but also how you can use HTX/IDC files and ASP files to dynamically publish data to the Web. Chapter 21, "XML Support in Microsoft Access," covers XML support within Microsoft Access. In that chapter, you learn how to publish XML from your database objects, as well as how to generate schema (XSD) and style sheets (XSL). Chapter 22, "Data Access Pages," continues the Web coverage with the creation of data access pages. Data access pages allow you to display your application data in a browser. Using data access pages, you can view, analyze, or update data. These Web forms can provide a great means to get you up and running quickly with an intranet application. The final chapter, Chapter 23, "SQL Server and the Internet," covers SQL Server and the Internet. Certain Web features are stronger in SQL Server than in Access. For example, you can configure SQL Server to automatically republish an HTML document each time data in certain fields changes. Chapter 23 shows you where SQL Server 2000 shines in the Internet and intranet world.

The Access development environment is robust and exciting. It is in no way limited to simple desktop applications. With the keys to deliver all that Access 2002 offers, you can produce enterprise applications that provide satisfaction as well as financial rewards. After poring over this hands-on guide and keeping it nearby for handy reference, you, too, can become masterful at enterprise development with Access 2002. This book is dedicated to demonstrating how you can fulfill the promise of making Access 2002 perform up to its lofty capabilities. As you will see, you have the ability to really make Access 2002 shine in the enterprise development world!

PART I

Client/Server Development

IN THIS PART

1

A Strategy for Developing Access Applications

Why This Chapter Is Important

In talking to users and developers, I find that Access is a very misunderstood product. Many people think that it is just a toy to be used by managers or secretaries wanting to play with data. Others feel that it is a serious developer product intended for no one but experienced application developers. This chapter dispels the myths of Access. It helps you to decipher what Access is and what it isn't. After reading the chapter, you will know when Access is the tool for you and when it makes sense to explore other products.

When you are clear on whether Access is the tool for you, you are ready to learn the several tricks of the trade that can save you a lot of time in the development process and help to ensure that your applications are as optimized as possible for performance. This chapter addresses these strategies and also explains several commonly misunderstood aspects of the Jet Engine (Access's database engine), the Access Runtime Engine, and security. You should keep all the topics covered in this chapter in mind when developing your Access applications. When reading this chapter, think of the general strategy outlined rather than the details of each topic. Other chapters of the book cover each topic in depth.

Access as a Development Tool

Access is a very flexible product. You can use Access to develop a personal application or to develop an enterprise-wide corporate application. Access offers a variety of features for different database needs. You can use Access to develop six general types of applications:

- Personal applications

- Small-business applications

- Departmental applications

- Corporation-wide applications

- A front end for enterprise-wide client/server applications

- Intranet/Internet applications

Access as a Development Platform for Personal Applications

At its most basic level, you can use Access to develop simple personal database-management systems. I caution people against this idea, though. People who buy Access hoping to automate everything from their exercise history to their home finances are often disappointed. The problem is that Access is deceptively easy to use. Its wonderful built-in wizards make Access look like a product that anyone can use. After answering a series of questions, you have finished applications—switchboards, data-entry screens, reports, and the underlying tables that support them. In fact, when Microsoft first released Access, many people asked if I was concerned that my business as a computer programmer and trainer would diminish because Access seemed to let absolutely anyone write a database application. The problem is that most people are not satisfied with the functionality that the wizards provide. Although it's true that you can produce the simplest of Access applications without any thought of design and without writing a single line of code, most applications require at least some designing and custom code.

As long as you're satisfied with a wizard-generated personal application with only minor modifications, no problems should occur. It's when you want to substantially customize a personal application that problems develop. The bottom line is that most real-life applications require a level of customization that requires significant knowledge, time, and effort.

Access as a Development Platform for Small-Business Applications

Access is an excellent platform for developing an application that can run a small business. Its wizards let developers quickly and easily build the application's foundation. The capability to build code modules allows developers to create code libraries of reusable functions, and the capability to add code behind forms and reports allows them to create powerful custom forms and reports.

The main limitation of using Access for developing a custom small-business application is the time and money involved in the development process. Many people use Access wizards to begin the development process but find that they need to customize their application in ways they can't accomplish on their own. Small-business owners often experience this problem on an even greater scale. The demands of a small-business application are usually much higher than those of a personal application. Many doctors, attorneys, and other professionals call me after they reach a dead end in the development process. They're always dismayed at how much money it will cost to make their applications usable.

Access as a Development Platform for Departmental Applications

Access is perfect for developing applications for departments in large corporations. It's relatively easy to upgrade departmental users to the appropriate hardware—for example, it's much easier to buy additional RAM for 15 users than it is for 4,000! Furthermore, Access's performance is adequate for most departmental applications without the need for client/server technology. Finally, most departments in large corporations have the development budgets to produce well-designed applications.

Fortunately, most departments usually have a PC guru who is more than happy to help design forms and reports. This gives the departments a sense of ownership because they have contributed to the development of their applications. It also makes my life as a developer much easier. I can focus on the hard-core development issues, leaving some of the form and report design tasks to the local talent.

Access as a Development Platform for Corporation-wide Applications

Although Access might be best suited for departmental applications, it can also be used to produce applications that are distributed throughout the organization. How successful this endeavor is depends on the corporation. There's a limit to the number of users who can concurrently share an Access application while maintaining acceptable performance, and there's also a limit to the number of records that each table can contain without a significant performance drop. These numbers vary depending on factors such as the following:

- How much traffic already exists on the network?

- How much RAM and how many processors does the server have?

- How is the server already being used? For example, are applications such as Microsoft Office being loaded from the server or from local workstations?

- What types of tasks are the users of the application performing? Are they querying, entering data, running reports, and so on?

- Where are Access and your Access application run (from the server or the workstation)?

- What network operating system is in place?

My general rule of thumb for an Access application that's not client/server–based is that poor performance generally results with more than 10–15 concurrent users and more than 100,000 records. Remember, these numbers vary immensely depending on the factors mentioned, as well as on the definition of acceptable performance by you and your users. The details of how to develop multiuser and enterprise applications are covered in Chapter 2, "Developing Multiuser Applications."

Developers often misunderstand what Access is and what it isn't when it comes to being a client/server database platform. I'm often asked, "Isn't Access a client/server database?" The answer is that Access is an unusual product because it's a file server application out of the box, but it can act as a front end to a client/server database. In case you're lost, here's an explanation: If you buy Access and develop an application that stores the data on a file server in an Access database, Access performs all data processing on the workstation. This means that every time the user runs a query or report, Access brings all the data over to the workstation and runs the query on the workstation machine. It displays the results in a datasheet or on a report. This process generates a significant amount of network traffic, particularly if multiple users are running reports and queries at the same time on large Access tables. In fact, such operations can bring the entire network to a crawl.

Access as a Development Platform for Enterprise-wide Client/Server Applications

A client/server database, such as Microsoft SQL Server or Oracle, processes queries on the server machine and returns results to the workstation. The server software itself can't display data to the user, so this is where Access comes to the rescue. Acting as a front end, Access can display the data retrieved from the database server in reports, datasheets, or forms. If the user updates the data in an Access form, Access sends the update to the back-end database. You can accomplish this either by linking to these external databases so that they appear to both you and the user as Access tables (although you cannot modify their structure from within Microsoft Access) or by using techniques that access client/server data directly.

Using Access Project files (not to be confused with Microsoft Project files), you can build an application specifically for a client/server environment. These project files, known as Access Data Projects (ADP) files, contain the program's forms, reports, macros, modules, and data access pages. The project is connected to the back-end database that contains the tables, stored procedures, views, and database diagrams that the program accesses. From within a project file, you can easily modify and manipulate objects stored on the server, using Access's friendly graphical user interface. ADP files help to bring rapid application development to the process of building client/server applications. Because Access 2002 ships with an integrated data store (the SQL Server 2000 Desktop Engine), you can develop a client/server application on the desktop and then easily deploy it to an enterprise SQL Server database. The alternatives and techniques for developing client/server applications are covered throughout this text.

NOTE

Access Data Projects (ADPs) were introduced in Access 2000. They were considered by many to be version 1.0 technology in that product. Microsoft did significant work with ADP files in Access 2002, and today they are a very viable solution for client/server application development.

When you reduce the volume of network traffic by moving the processing of queries to the back end, Access becomes a much more powerful development solution. It can handle huge volumes of data and a large number of concurrent users. These main issues are usually faced by developers who want to deploy such a widescale Access application:

- The variety of operating systems used by each user

- Difficulties with deployment

- The method by which each user is connected to the application and data

- The type of hardware each user has

Although Access processes queries in a client/server application at the server, which significantly reduces network traffic, the application itself still must reside in the memory of each user's PC. This means that each client machine must be capable of running the appropriate operating system and the correct version of Access. Even when the correct operating system and version of Access are in place, your problems are not over. Dynamic Link Library Dynamic Link Library (DLL) conflicts often result in difficult-to-diagnose errors and idiosyncrasies in an Access application. Furthermore, Access is not the best solution for disconnected users who must access an application and its data over the Internet. Finally, Access 2002 is hardware hungry! The bottom line is that, before you decide to deploy a widescale Access application, you need to know the hardware and software configurations of all your system's users. You must also decide whether the desktop support required for the typical Access application is feasible given the number of people who will use the system that you are building.

Access as a Development Platform for Intranet/Internet Applications

Using data access pages, intranet and Internet users can update your application data from within a browser. Data access pages are HTML documents that are bound directly to data in a database. They are stored outside your database and are used just like standard Access forms, except that they are designed to run in Microsoft Internet Explorer 5.5 or higher rather than in Microsoft Access. Data access pages use dynamic HTML to accomplish their work. Because they are supported only in Internet Explorer 5.5 or higher, data access pages are much more appropriate as an intranet solution (where you can often control the browser that users use) than an Internet solution. In addition to using data access pages, you can publish your database objects as either static or dynamic Hypertext Markup Language (HTML) pages. Static pages are standard HTML. You can view them in any browser. You can dynamically publish database objects either to the HTX/IDC file format or to the Active Server Page (ASP) file format. The Web server dynamically publishes HTX/IDC files. The resulting HTML is browser independent. ASP files published by Microsoft Access are also published dynamically by the Web server but require Internet Explorer 4.0 or higher on the client machine.

New to Access 2002 is the capability to create Extensible Markup Language (XML) data and schema documents from Jet or SQL Server structures and data. You can also import data and data structures into Access from XML documents. You can accomplish this either using code or via the user interface. The last section of this book covers all of the Internet and intranet features of Access 2002 in detail.

Access as a Scalable Product

One of Access's biggest strong points is its scalability. An application that begins as a small-business application running on a standalone machine can be scaled to an enterprise-wide client/server application. If you design your application properly, scaling can be done with little or no rewriting of your application. This feature makes Access an excellent choice for growing businesses, as well as for applications being tested at a departmental level with the idea that they might eventually be distributed corporation-wide.

The great thing about Access is that, even acting as both the front end and the back end with data stored on a file server in Access tables, it provides excellent security and the capability to establish database rules previously available only on back-end databases. You can assign security to every object in a database at either a user or a group level. You can apply referential integrity rules at the database level, ensuring that (for example) orders aren't entered for customers who don't exist. You can enforce data validation rules at either a field or a record level, maintaining the integrity of the data in your database. In other words, many of the features previously available only on high-end database servers are now available by using Access's own proprietary data-storage format.

Splitting Databases into Tables and Other Objects

When earlier versions of Access ran in a multiuser environment, it was imperative to place the system's tables in one database and the rest of the system objects in another database. With Access 95 and the advent of replication, you could either split the tables from the other objects or use replication to deploy design changes without comprising live data. Access 2000 and Access 2002 take this a step further with the Access Data Project (ADP), in which tables, views, stored procedures, and data diagrams are stored in a SQL Server database or by the SQL Server 2000 Desktop Engine (formerly the Microsoft Data Engine, or MSDE). Forms, reports, macros, and modules are stored in the ADP file.

As mentioned earlier, splitting tables from other system objects is still a very viable solution. For simplicity, I'll refer to the database containing the tables as the Table database and the database with the other objects as the Application database. Linking from the Application database to the Table database connects the two databases. This strategy enhances the following:

- Maintainability

- Performance

- Scalability

Assume for a moment that you distribute your application as one MDB file. Your users work with your application for a week or two, writing down all problems and changes. It's time for you to make modifications to your application. Meanwhile, the users have entered live data into the application for two weeks. You make a copy of the database (which includes the live data) and make all the fixes and changes. This process takes a week. You're ready to install your copy of the database on the network. Now what? The users of the application have been adding, editing, and deleting records all week. Data replication, which is covered in Chapter 17, "Access Replication Made Easy," could help you with this problem, but replication isn't always feasible.

The simplest solution is to split the database objects so that the tables containing your data are in one MDB file and the rest of your database objects (your application) are in a second MDB file. When you're ready to install the changes, all you would need to do is copy the Application database to the file server. You could then install the new Application database on each client machine from the file server. In this way, users could run new copies of the application from their machines. The database containing your data tables would remain intact and would be unaffected by the process. (Of course, this is possible only if you finalize your table structure before splitting the database.)

The second benefit of splitting the database objects is performance. Your Table database obviously needs to reside on the network file server so that the data can be shared among the system's users; however, there's no good reason why the other database components need to be shared. Access gives you optimal performance if the Application database is stored on each local machine. This method also significantly reduces network traffic, and it decreases the chance of database corruption. If the Application database is stored on the file server, Access will need to send the application objects and code over the network each time the user opens an object in the database. If the Application database is stored on each local machine, then Access will only need to send the data over the network. The only complication to this scenario is that, each time you update the Application database, you will need to redistribute it to the users. On an already overtaxed network, this is a small inconvenience compared to the performance benefits gained from this structural split.

The third benefit of splitting tables from the other database objects is scalability. Because you have already linked the tables, it's easy to change from a link to a table stored in Access's own proprietary format to any ODBC database, such as Microsoft SQL Server. This capability gives you quick-and-dirty access to client/server databases. If you have already thought through your system's design with linked tables and client/server in mind, the transition will be that much easier. Don't be fooled, though, by how easy this sounds. Many issues associated with using Access as a front end to client/server data go far beyond simply linking to the external tables. The book covers these issues in detail.

TIP

A few special types of tables should be stored in the Application database rather than the Table database. Tables that rarely change should be stored in the Application database on each user's local machine. For example, a state table rarely, if ever, changes, but it's continually accessed to populate combo boxes, participate in queries, and so on. Placing the state table on each local machine, therefore, improves performance and reduces network traffic. You should also place lookup tables containing localized information such as department codes in the Application database.

Temporary Access tables should also be placed on each local machine—this is more a necessity than an option. If two users are running the same process at the same time and that process uses temporary Access tables, a conflict occurs when one user overwrites the other's temporary tables. Placing temporary tables on each local machine improves performance and eliminates the chance of potentially disastrous conflicts. It is important to note that an alternative to temporary Access tables are temporary SQL Server tables. These are covered in Chapter 8, "Designing SQL Server Stored Procedures, User-Defined Functions, and Triggers."

If you have already designed your application and included all the tables in the same database as the rest of your database objects, don't despair; Access 2002 includes the Database Splitter Wizard. You can find this valuable tool by choosing Tools, Database Utilities, Database Splitter. *Alison Balter's Mastering Access 2002 Desktop Development* covers both the Database Splitter and linked tables.

Understanding the Access Runtime Engine

Many developers don't understand what Access has to offer out of the box and what the Microsoft Office XP Developer (MOD) tools can add to the picture. They often tell me, "I can't develop applications in Access because my company refuses to buy each user a copy of Access," or "I'm going to buy the MOD so that I can compile my applications with the MOD tools." These are just two of the many misconceptions about exactly what the MOD tools do and don't have to offer.

Features of the MOD

You do not need to buy a separate product to create runtime versions of your Access applications. As a developer, you will likely buy the MOD edition of Office, which includes Office Premium and a host of additional components. An important feature of the MOD edition of Office is a royalty-free distribution license. It allows you to distribute unlimited copies of your Access application; your users don't have to own separately licensed copies of Access. By using the MOD tools, you can create applications and distribute them to your users along with the necessary runtime engine. The MOD edition includes numerous additional tools that are covered in Chapter 18, "Taking Advantage of the Microsoft Office XP Developer."

Differences Between the Standard and Runtime Versions of Access

It's important to understand the differences between the standard and runtime versions of Access. The following differences have definite implications for the way you develop any applications that you expect to run from the runtime version:

- The Database, Macro, and Module windows aren't available in the runtime environment.

- No Design views are available in the runtime environment.

- No built-in toolbars are available in the runtime environment.

- Many windows, menus, and commands are invisible in the runtime environment. For example, the Window, Hide and Window, Unhide commands are invisible. Although these and other commands aren't visible, their functions are generally accessible by using code.

- You must build error handling into your runtime applications. If you don't, when an error occurs, the application displays a standard Access dialog box indicating an irrecoverable error and then exits to the desktop.

- You must build your own custom help files for each runtime application.

- Some keystrokes aren't available in the runtime application.

Some of the disabled features protect your applications. For example, the absence of the Database and Design windows means that your users can't modify your application while running it under Access's runtime version. Other disabled features translate into additional coding chores for you, such as the absence of command bars. If you want your application to offer toolbars, you have to build your own and then assign them to the forms and reports in your database.

Steps for Preparing an Application for Distribution

With all the features absent from the runtime version of Access, it's not surprising that you must take some special steps to prepare your application for distribution. Most are steps you'll probably want to take so that your application seems professional to the user. The following are preparations specific to running Access from the runtime version:

- Base your application on forms.

- Add startup options to your database.

- Secure the objects in your application.

- Build error handling into your application.

- Add some level of custom help.

- Build custom command bars to be associated with your application's forms and reports.

Basing Your Application on Forms

Your application should be based on and controlled through forms. It should generally begin with a main switchboard that lets the user get to the other components of your application. Or, it can start with a core data-entry form on which the rest of the application is based. If you opt to go with an application switchboard, the main switchboard can direct the user to additional switchboards, such as a data-entry switchboard, a report switchboard, or a maintenance switchboard. You can build switchboards with an add-in called the Switchboard Manager. Alternately, you can design them as custom dialog boxes. *Alison Balter's Mastering Access 2002 Desktop Development* covers these techniques. The main advantage of using the Switchboard Manager is that it lets you quickly and easily create a polished application interface. The primary advantage of custom switchboards is the flexibility and freedom they offer.

An alternative to the switchboard approach is to build the application around a core data-entry form, such as a contact-management application based on a contacts form. All other forms and reports that make up the application are accessed via custom menu bars and toolbars on the contacts form.

Adding Startup Options to Your Database

Regardless of the approach that you take, you designate a form as the starting point for your application by modifying the database's startup options. Choose Tools, Startup to open the Startup dialog box. (See Figure 1.1.) In this dialog box, you can set options, such as a startup form, an application title, and an icon that appears when the user minimizes your application. *Alison Balter's Mastering Access 2002 Desktop Development* covers these options.

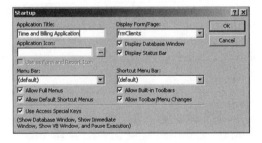

FIGURE 1.1   The Startup dialog box lets you control many aspects of your application environment.

NOTE

If Startup does not initially appear on the Tools menu, go to Tools, Customize and click to select Always Show Full Menus.

Securing Your Application

As you will learn in the next section, a database isn't secure just because you're running it from a runtime version of Access. Without security, anyone with a full copy of Access can modify your application. Therefore, securing your database objects is an important step in preparing your application for distribution. Security is covered in *Alison Balter's Mastering Access 2002 Desktop Development*.

Access 2000 and Access 2002 also offer you the capability to remove the source code from your applications. This protects your intellectual property and improves the performance of your application. The resulting database is called an MDE.

Building Error Handling into Your Applications

If you don't build error handling into your application and an error occurs while your user is running your application from Access's runtime version, Access will rudely exit the user from the program. She won't get an appropriate error message and will be left wondering what happened. Hence, it's essential that you add error handling to your application's procedures. Error handling is covered in *Alison Balter's Mastering Access 2002 Desktop Development*. The VBA Error Handler, included with the Microsoft Office XP Developer (MOD), can also assist in building error handling into your application.

Adding Custom Help

In most cases, you want your users to have at least some level of custom help specific to your application. You can use the ControlTip Text property of controls and the Description property of fields to add the most basic level of help to your application. The ControlTip Text property provides a description of a control when a user hovers his mouse pointer over the control. The Description property of a field appears on the status bar when a control based on that field has the focus. If you are more ambitious, and if the scope and budget for the application warrant it, you can build a custom help file for your application. To add custom help to your application, you must build a help file and then attach parts of it to application's forms and controls.

Building Custom Command Bars

Finally, because built-in toolbars aren't available in the runtime version of Access and most of the features on the standard built-in menus are disabled, you should build your own command bars associated with specific forms and reports. Creating custom command bars adds both polish and functionality to your application.

After you complete these steps, you'll be ready for the final phase of preparing your application for distribution, which includes the following steps:

1. Test your application by using the /Runtime switch.

2. Create setup disks or perform a network install with the Packaging Wizard.

3. Install your application on a machine that has never run a copy of either the standard or runtime version of Access.

4. Test your application on the machine; make sure it runs as expected.

Before you bother running the Packaging Wizard (a somewhat lengthy process), it's best that you run your application with the /Runtime switch. This switch simulates the runtime environment, allowing you to mimic user actions under the runtime version of Access. Taking this step saves you a lot of time and energy. It will find most, if not all, of the problems associated with the runtime version.

After you test your application with the /Runtime switch, you're ready to run the Packaging Wizard (covered in Chapter 18). It lets you create setup disks or perform a network install. Selecting A:Setup (or the appropriate network drive and path) provides a professional-looking, familiar setup program similar to those included with most Microsoft products.

After you run the Packaging Wizard, you must test your application by running the install on a machine that has never contained a copy of either the standard or the runtime version of Access. The whole idea is to test your application on a machine containing no Access-related files. This ensures that all the required files are included on your setup disks.

I suggest that you use a "ghosting" utility such as Symantec Ghost to create a complete image of your operating system and application drives. Install and fully test your application; make sure you experiment with every feature. When you're done testing, restore the original machine from the ghost image so that you can use it to test your next installation.

TIP

Symantec Ghost allows you to restore individual files, selected directories, or entire hard drives as needed. When you create a backup image file, you can compress it by up to 70%, greatly reducing transfer times and storage requirements. Among its many other uses, Symantec Ghost greatly facilitates the testing process by allowing you to easily restore a test machine to its pretesting state. Learn more about Symantec Ghost at http://www.ghostsoft.com.

The Access Runtime Engine: Summing It Up

You have just read an overview of the differences between the full and runtime versions of Access. The process of preparing an application for distribution with the runtime version of Access is covered in detail in *Alison Balter's Mastering Access 2002 Desktop Development*. If you plan to distribute an application with the runtime version of Access, remember which features will be available to your users; otherwise, you and your users will be in for some big surprises.

Using an EXE Versus Access Database: What It Means to You

Many developers mistakenly think that distributing an application with the runtime version of Access is equivalent to distributing an EXE. An unsecured database distributed with the runtime version of Access can be modified just like any other database.

Users can run your application using Access's runtime version, and all the rules of running an application under the runtime version apply. This means that users can't go into Design view, can't create their own objects, don't have access to the built-in toolbars, and so on.

Using their own copies of the standard version of Access, users can open the same database. If the objects in the database haven't been secured, users can modify the application at will.

In short, a database prepared with the Packaging Wizard is no different from any other database. The wizard doesn't modify an MDB file in any way. It simply compresses all the files needed to run your application, including the database and runtime engine, and creates a network install folder or distribution disks containing the compressed files. Two ways to protect the design of your application are to set up security and to distribute your application as an MDE file.

Understanding the Importance of Securing Your Database

By now, you should understand the importance of securing your application. Setting up security is a complex but worthwhile process that can be done at either a group or a user level. You can assign rights to objects, and those rights can be assigned to either individual users or a group of users. Figure 1.2 shows the User and Group Permissions dialog box. As you can see, rights can be assigned for each object. For a table, you can assign the user or group rights to read, insert, update, and delete data, as well as to read, modify, or administer the table's design. You can assign different groups of users different rights to an object. For example, you can assign one group rights to add, edit, and delete data. You can assign another group rights to edit only and another group rights to view only, and you can deny another the right to even view the data.

FIGURE 1.2   The User and Group Permissions dialog box lets you assign user and group rights to each database object.

Available rights differ for tables, queries, forms, reports, macros, and modules. The types of rights that you can assign are appropriate to each particular type of object. When you properly invoke security, it is difficult to violate, no matter how someone tries to access the database objects (including using the runtime version of Access, a standard copy of Access, programming code, or even a Visual Basic application). If properly secured, the database is as difficult to illegally access as an executable file.

NOTE

Web site businesses exist that remove Access security for a fee. Although Access security protects you against "honest" people, it doesn't completely protect you against those who are out to get you, your application, or the data that your application stores.

Using Access as a Front End

If you're planning to use Access as a front end to other databases, you need to consider a few issues. In fact, the whole design methodology of your system will differ depending on whether you plan to store your data in an Access database or on a back-end database server.

In a system in which your data is stored solely in Access tables, the Jet Engine supplies all data-retrieval and management functions and handles security, data validation, and enforcement of referential integrity.

In a system in which Access acts as a front end to client/server data, the server handles the data-management functions. It's responsible for retrieving, protecting, and updating data on the back-end database server. In this scenario, the local copy of Access is responsible only for sending requests and getting either data or pointers to data back from the database server. If you're creating an application in which Access acts as a front end, capitalizing on the strengths of both Access and the server can be a challenging endeavor.

Things You Need to Worry About in Converting to Client/Server

The transition to client/server technology isn't always a smooth one. You need to consider the following factors if you're developing a client/server application or planning to eventually move your application from an Access database to a back-end Structured Query Language (SQL) database server:

- Not all field types supported in Access are supported in every back-end database.

- Any security that you set up in Access won't be converted to your back-end database.

- Many of the validation rules that you set up in Access need to be re-established on the back end.

- Referential integrity isn't supported on all back ends. If it is on yours, it may not be automatically carried over from Access.

- Some queries involving joins that could be updated in Access can't be updated on the back-end server.

This list is just an overview of what you need to think about when moving an application from an Access database with linked tables to a back-end server or when developing an application specifically for a back end. Many of these issues have far-reaching implications. For example, if you set up validation rules and validation text in your application, the rules will need to be rewritten as triggers on the back end. If a validation rule is violated on the back end, you will get a returnable error code. You have to respond to this code by using error handling in your application, displaying the appropriate message to your user. You can't use the Validation Text property.

TIP

The Access 2000 and Access 2002 Upsizing Wizards address most of the transitioning issues covered in this chapter. These tools, included as part of Access 2000 and Access 2002, respectively, automate the migration of data from the native Access data format to Microsoft SQL Server. The Upsizing Wizard is covered in Chapter 3, "Introduction to Client/Server Development Techniques."

Benefits and Costs of Client/Server Technology

With all the issues discussed in the previous section, you might ask, "Why bother with client/server?" In each case, you need to evaluate whether the benefits of client/server technology outweigh its costs. The major benefits include the following:

- Greater control over data integrity
- Increased control over data security
- Increased fault tolerance
- Reduced network traffic
- Improved performance
- Centralized control and management of data

These are some of the major expenses:

- Increased development costs
- Hardware costs for the server machine
- Setup costs for the server database
- The cost of employing a full- or part-time database administrator (DBA)

These and other issues are covered in more detail throughout this book.

Your Options When Using Access as a Front End

Client/server applications are not an all-or-none proposition, nor is there only one way to implement them through Access. One option is to use Access as a true front end, which means that all data and all queries are stored on the server. With this model, you use stored procedures rather than stored Access queries throughout the application. Stored procedures are SQL statements that are stored on the back end. You can execute them for an Access application using data access objects (DAO) or ActiveX data objects (ADO) code.

Another alternative is to use pass-through queries to communicate to the back end. With pass-through queries, a back end–specific SQL statement is passed to the back end. With this model, you ensure that the back end executes the query.

To make Access a true front end, you must also disable its natural capability to bind data to forms and reports. Doing so, however, eliminates all the features that make Access a strong product in the first place. Unfortunately, you haven't eliminated all the overhead associated with the functionality you removed. If you want to use this approach, you're better off developing the entire application in a lower-overhead environment, such as Visual Basic, or instead developing a Web-based solution.

Yet another alternative is to use linked tables and stored Access queries to communicate with the back-end database. In this scenario, your queries are stored in Access SQL. They are translated to ODBC and then by the appropriate driver to back end–specific SQL. Although this model requires the least knowledge and the fewest application modifications on your part, it does have its disadvantages. Some SQL statements are translated poorly. Furthermore, although most properly designed Access queries execute on the back end, there are several situations in which Access processes the queries on the front end. In those situations, performance is severely affected. Finally, using linked tables, you cannot take advantage of proprietary back end–specific functionality that is not available within Access.

Another approach is a hybrid method in which you use a combination of linked tables, SQL pass-through queries, stored procedures, and local Access tables. The idea is that you take advantage of Access's features and strong points whenever possible. You use pass-through queries and stored procedures to perform functions that are done more efficiently by communicating directly to the back end or that aren't available at all with Access SQL. To further improve performance, many tasks can be performed locally and then communicated to the server as one transaction, after any initial validation has been done. Access Project files, introduced in Access 2000, allow you to communicate with the back-end database without loading the Microsoft Jet Engine. With Access Projects, commonly referred to as ADP files, you can improve both the performance and the functionality of a client/server application. Several chapters in this book cover ADP files. In addition to the solutions just discussed, data can be downloaded to Access in bulk so that additional processing can be done locally. Many possibilities exist, and each is appropriate in different situations. It takes experience and experimentation to determine the combination of methods that will optimize performance in a given situation.

What Are the Considerations for Migrating to a Client/Server Environment?

The preceding sections have given you an overview of the issues you need to consider when building a client/server application or considering moving to a client/server environment in the future. The remainder of the book contains more detailed information about client/server development and its implications.

Summary

It's important that you have a strategy before you begin the application-development process. This chapter introduced many strategic issues, such as Access's role in the application design model and the processes of splitting a database into tables and other objects and using Access as a front end.

Many people don't fully understand the Access runtime engine, so this chapter explained what it is and what it isn't. It also explained what you need to be concerned about when preparing an application for distribution, including the importance of properly securing your databases.

Finally, the chapter covered converting to a client/server environment, explored the benefits and costs involved in such a conversion, and discussed the different options available to you. The chapter provided you with ideas of what you can do to prepare your applications for future growth.

2

Developing Multiuser Applications

Why This Chapter Is Important

Many people forge right into the application-development process with little worry about the scalability of the application. Even a simple application that begins as a single-user application can develop into a multiuser application. You can even use it throughout the enterprise. Unfortunately, the techniques that you can get away with in the single-user application can wreak havoc in a network or client/server environment. It is therefore necessary to think about the future when you design any application. Although the initial development process might be more complex, if written properly, the application will survive any growth that it experiences. This chapter focuses on writing applications that transition easily from the single-user environment through the enterprise client/server environment.

Designing Your Application with Multiuser Issues in Mind

When you develop applications that multiple users will access over the network, you must make sure that they effectively share data and other application objects. Many options are available for developers when they design multiuser applications, and this chapter covers the pros and cons of these options.

Multiuser issues revolve around locking data; they include deciding where to store database objects, when to lock data, and how much data to lock. In a multiuser environment, having several users simultaneously trying to modify the same data can cause conflicts. As a developer, you need to handle these conflicts. Otherwise, your users will experience unexplainable errors.

Strategies for Installing Access

Many methods, such as sharing the entire database, sharing tables only, or replicating databases, exist for handling concurrent access to data and other application objects by multiple users; each one offers both advantages and limitations. It's important to select the best solution for your particular environment.

Two strategies exist for installing Access:

- Run Access from a file server across a network.

- Run a separate copy of Access on each workstation.

The advantages of running Access from a file server are that it provides for the following:

- Allows for central administration of the Access software

- Reduces hard-disk requirements

- Potentially reduces the licensing requirements

- Allows Access applications to be installed on diskless workstations

---

NOTE

The Access software takes up a significant amount of disk space. Although using the Access runtime engine can reduce disk-space requirements by a small amount, local hard-disk space can definitely be a problem. Installing Access on the file server at least partially eliminates this problem. It can totally eliminate the problem if Dynamic Link Libraries (DLLs) are also installed on the file server.

Serious drawbacks also are associated with a file server installation. Every time the user launches an Access application, the Access EXE, DLLs, and any other files required to run Access are *all* sent over the network wire to the local machine. Obviously, this generates a significant volume of network traffic. Thus, performance is generally degraded to unacceptable levels.

Because the disadvantages of running Access from a file server are so pronounced, I strongly recommend that Access, or at least the runtime engine, be installed on each user's machine.

Strategies for Installing Your Application

Just as there are different strategies for installing Access, there are various strategies for installing your application, such as the following:

- Install both the application and the data on a file server.

- Install the data on the file server and the application on each workstation.

- Install the application and the data on a machine running Windows 2000 Terminal Services.

In other words, after you have created an application, you can place the entire application on the network, which means that all the tables, queries, forms, reports, macros, and modules that make up the system reside on the file server. Although this method of shared access keeps everything in the same place, you will see many advantages to placing only the database's data tables on the file server. The remaining objects are placed in a database on each user's machine, and each local application database is linked to the tables on the network. In this way, users share data but not the rest of the application objects.

The advantages of doing this are as follows:

- Because each user has a copy of the local database objects, load time and network traffic are both reduced.

- It's very easy to back up data without having to back up the rest of the application objects.

- When redistributing new versions of the application, you don't need to worry about overwriting the application's data.

- Multiple applications can all be designed to use the same centrally located data.

- Users can add their own objects (such as their own queries) to their local copies of the database.

In addition to storing the queries, forms, reports, macros, and modules that make up the application in a local database, I recommend that you store the following objects in each local database:

- Temporary tables

- Static tables

- Semistatic tables

Temporary tables should be stored in the database that's on each workstation because if two users are performing operations that build the same temporary tables, you don't want one user's process to interfere with the other user's process. You can eliminate the potential conflict of one user's temporary tables overwriting the other's by storing all temporary tables in each user's local copy of the database.

You should also place static lookup tables, such as state tables, on each workstation. Because the data doesn't change, maintenance isn't an issue. The benefit is that Access doesn't need to pull that data over the network each time it's needed.

Semistatic tables—tables that are rarely updated—can also be placed on the local machine. As with static tables, having these tables in a local database means reduced network traffic and better performance, not only for the user needing the data but also for anyone sharing the same network wire. You can transport the changes made to the semistatic tables to each workstation by using replication (covered in Chapter 17, "Access Replication Made Easy").

Figure 2.1 illustrates the configuration described throughout this section.

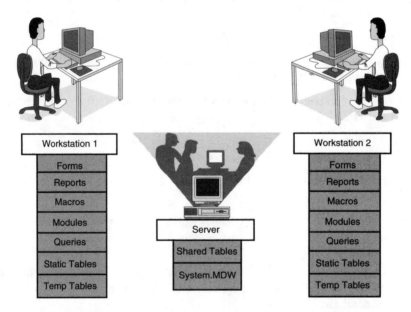

FIGURE 2.1   An example of a configuration with database objects split, storing temporary and static tables locally and shared tables remotely (on the file server).

A final option has recently emerged as a viable alternative for deployment of an Access application. It addresses both bandwidth and centralization issues. With this option, a Windows 2000 machine runs Windows 2000 Terminal Services. Client machines then access the server machine using the Terminal Server Client Utility. In this scenario, you install Access, your application, and the data that it accesses, all on the Windows 2000 Server machine. All other machines access the application via user sessions created on the server machine. The Terminal Server Client Utility sends keystrokes and mouse events from the client machines to the server machine. It returns the resulting screen image to the client machine. This configuration addresses many of the problems inherent in both the Access database on the file server scenario and also the Access database being installed locally on the client computer.

> **NOTE**
>
> Another alternative is somewhat of a compromise. It involves splitting the application objects (forms, reports, and so on) from the data (tables). The difference is that, in this scenario, both the application database and the data database reside on the file server. This scenario affords you the advantages of easy backup, simple redeployment, and many of the benefits achieved when the application database resides on each workstation. Its downside is that Access must still transfer the application objects over the network wire. The major advantage of this scenario over storing the application database on each workstation is that when you update the application database, you need to redeploy it only to the file server (rather than to each workstation).

The Basics of Linking to External Data

Linking to external data, including data not stored in another Access database, is covered extensively in *Alison Balter's Mastering Access 2002 Desktop Development.* Three options are available to you:

- Design the databases separately from the start.

- Include all objects in one database; then split them manually when you're ready to distribute your application.

- Include all objects in one database; then split them by using the Database Splitter Wizard.

Alison Balter's Mastering Access 2002 Desktop Development covers the first two options. The last option, the Database Splitter Wizard, is covered here. To split the objects in a database into two separate .MDB files, follow these steps:

1. Open the database whose objects you want to split.

2. Choose Tools, Database Utilities, Database Splitter to open the Database Splitter dialog box, shown in Figure 2.2.

3. Click Split Database; this opens the Create Back-End Database dialog box. (See Figure 2.3.)

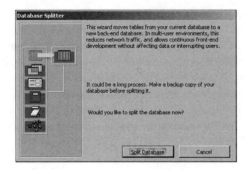

FIGURE 2.2   The Database Splitter Wizard helps you split the data tables that should reside on the server.

FIGURE 2.3   Entering a name for the new, shared database.

4. Enter the name for the database that will contain all the tables. Click Split. The Database Splitter Wizard creates a new database holding all the tables. It creates links between the current database and the database containing the tables. (See Figure 2.4.)

CAUTION

Be aware that, when you're distributing an application using linked tables, you must write code to make sure that Access can locate the data tables from each application database on the network. This is because Access hard-codes the location of linked tables into the application database. If each user has the same path to the file server, this isn't a problem. However, if the path to the file server varies, you need to write a routine that makes sure the application can successfully relink the tables. If the routine can't relink the tables, it prompts the user for the data's location. *Alison Balter's Mastering Access 2002 Desktop Development* covers this routine in detail. The section that follows, titled "Automating the Process of Linking to Tables," provides an example.

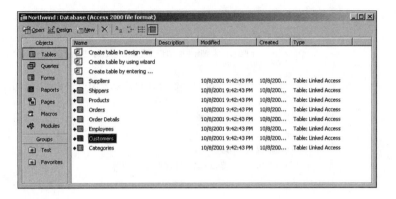

FIGURE 2.4   The database has been split.

Automating the Process of Linking to Tables

Access hard-codes locations for table links. This means that if you install your application on another machine, the tables will not link successfully unless the other machine has exactly the same folder structure as you do on your machine. The code shown in Listing 2.1 checks to see whether the required tables are available. If the routine does not find the tables in the expected location, it attempts to locate them in the same folder as the application database. If it still cannot locate them, the user is given an opportunity to locate the files. If the user cannot locate the tables, the application terminates.

LISTING 2.1   The LinkTables Routine

```
Function LinkTables() As Boolean
    On Error GoTo LinkTables_Err:

        Dim objFileDialog As FileDialog
        Dim strFileName As String

        'Determine if links are ok
        If Not VerifyLink Then

            'If links not ok, attempt to link with default file name
            'in the current folder
            If Not ReLink(CurrentProject.FullName, True) Then

                'If still unsuccessful, allow user to locate the data database
                MsgBox "You Must Locate Tables to Proceed" & vbCrLf & _
                    "The Tables are Located in the Chap02EXData Database" _
```

LISTING 2.1   Continued

```
                        & vbCrLf & _
                        "in the Directory Where You Placed the Sample Files"

                Set objFileDialog = Application.FileDialog(msoFileDialogOpen)

                With objFileDialog
                    .Show
                    .AllowMultiSelect = False
                    strFileName = .SelectedItems(1)
                End With

                'Attempt to relink with the database the user selected
                If Not ReLink(strFileName, False) Then

                    'If still unsuccessful, display message to the user and
                    'return false from this routine
                    MsgBox "You Cannot Run This App Without " & _
                    "Locating Data Tables"
                    LinkTables = False
                Else

                    'User successfully designated new location; return True
                    LinkTables = True

                End If
            Else

                'Data database located with default name in the same location
                'as the application database; return True
                LinkTables = True

            End If
        Else

            'Table links not broken; return True
            LinkTables = True

        End If

    Exit Function

LinkTables_Err:
    MsgBox "Error # " & Err.Number & ": " & Err.Description
    Exit Function

End Function
```

NOTE

This code—and the rest of the code in this chapter—can be found in Chap02Ex.MDB on this book's CD-ROM.

NOTE

The code in this example requires references to both the Office 10.0 Object Library and the Microsoft ADO Ext 2.6 for DDL and Security Library.

The routine begins by executing a function called `VerifyLink`. Listing 2.2 shows the `VerifyLink` function found in the Chap02Ex.MDB file on the sample code CD. It first creates an ADOX `Catalog` object. It sets the `ActiveConnection` property of the `Catalog` object to the `Connection` property of the `CurrentProject` object. The `CurrentProject` object returns a reference to the database using the library rather than to the library itself. The heart of the routine is the `For...Next` loop. It loops through each `Table` object in the `Tables` collection of the `Catalog` object. If the table is linked, it attempts to reference the first field in the table. If an error occurs, the table link must be broken. The error number is nonzero, and the routine exits the `For...Next` loop. Because the function returns whether or not the error number is equal to 0, it returns `False` if an error occurs and `True` if no error occurs.

LISTING 2.2   The `VerifyLink` Function

```
Function VerifyLink() As Boolean
    'Verify connection information in linked tables.

    'Declare Required Variables
    Dim cat As ADOX.Catalog
    Dim tdf As ADOX.Table
    Dim strTemp As String

    'Point Database object variable at the current database
    Set cat = New ADOX.Catalog

    With cat
        Set .ActiveConnection = CurrentProject.Connection

        'Continue if links are broken.
        On Error Resume Next

        'Open one linked table to see if connection
        'information is correct.
        'For Each tdf In .Tables
```

LISTING 2.2 Continued

```
'       If tdf.Type = "LINK" Then
'           strTemp = tdf.Columns(0).Name
'           If Err.Number Then
'               Exit For
'           End If
'       End If

'Next tdf

'If code above is too slow, this is the
'less conservative alternative
For Each tdf In .Tables

    If tdf.Type = "LINK" Then
        strTemp = tdf.Columns(0).Name
        Exit For
    End If

Next tdf



End With

VerifyLink = (Err.Number = 0)


End Function
```

If the `VerifyLink` function returns `False`, the code executes the `Relink` function. Listing 2.3 shows the `Relink` function. It receives two parameters. The first parameter is the name of the database that the function will attempt to link to. The second parameter is a Boolean variable that the code uses to designate whether the database is considered the default database.

The function begins by modifying the status bar. It then creates a `Catalog` object and an instance of a custom class called `DBInfo`. The `ActiveConnection` property of the `Catalog` object is set equal to the `Connection` property of the current project. Next, the `FullName` property of the `DBInfo` class is set equal to the name of the file that it receives as a parameter. The `DBInfo` class extracts the path and the filename from the full filename. Just as with the `VerifyLink` function, the `ReLink` function uses a `For..Next` loop to loop through all the tables in the database. As it loops through each table, it attempts to establish a link to a database with the name passed as a parameter to the `Relink` function.

This is where the DefaultData parameter comes into play. The first time that the LinkTables routine calls the Relink function, it passes the name and path of the application database as the first parameter, and it passes True as the second parameter. The Relink function then attempts to link to a database located in the same folder as the application database, but with the word *Data* appended to the end of the filename. For example, if the application database is named Membership, the Relink function looks for a database called MembershipData in the same location as the application database. If it is successful, it returns True; if it is unsuccessful, it returns False. I use this method to attempt to re-establish the link because I commonly place both the application and data databases on a client's network, both in the same folder. When I do this, I employ a naming convention in which the data database has the same name as the application database, but with the word *Data* appended to it.

If the code does not find a data database with the expected filename in the folder where the application database is located (False was returned from the Relink function), the LinkTables routine uses the FileDialog object to display a File Open dialog box. This gives the user the opportunity to locate the data database. The code passes the filename and path that the user selects in the dialog box to the Relink routine, along with False as the second parameter. Because the user has selected the file that he believes contains the data, there is no reason to append the word *Data* to the filename. Again, the Relink routine loops through the tables collection of the Catalog object, attempting to re-establish the broken links. If successful, it returns True; if unsuccessful, it returns False. If False is returned from the second call to the Relink function, the LinkTables routine exits the Access application.

LISTING 2.3   The Relink Function

```
Function ReLink(strDir As String, DefaultData As Boolean) _
    As Boolean

    Dim cat As ADOX.Catalog
    Dim tdfRelink As ADOX.Table
    Dim oDBInfo As DBInfo
    Dim strPath As String
    Dim strName As String
    Dim intCounter As Integer
    Dim vntStatus As Variant

    'Update status bar
    vntStatus = SysCmd(acSysCmdSetStatus, "Updating Links")

    Set cat = New ADOX.Catalog
    Set oDBInfo = New DBInfo

    With cat
```

LISTING 2.3   Continued

```
        'Use File Information class to extract the application
        'database file name
        .ActiveConnection = CurrentProject.Connection
        oDBInfo.FullName = strDir
        strPath = oDBInfo.FilePathOnly
        strName = Left(oDBInfo.FileName, InStr(oDBInfo.FileName, ".") - 1)

        'Disable error handling
        On Error Resume Next

        'Update progress meter
        Call SysCmd(acSysCmdInitMeter, "Linking Data Tables", .Tables.Count)

        'Loop through each table, attempting to relink
        For Each tdfRelink In .Tables
            intCounter = intCounter + 1
            Call SysCmd(acSysCmdUpdateMeter, intCounter)
            If .Tables(tdfRelink.Name).Type = "LINK" Then
                tdfRelink.Properties("Jet OLEDB:Link Datasource") = _
                    strPath & strName & IIf(DefaultData, "Data.Mdb", ".mdb")
            End If

            'If an error occurs, exit the loop
            If Err.Number Then
                Exit For
            End If
        Next tdfRelink
    End With

    'Remove the progress meter
    Call SysCmd(acSysCmdRemoveMeter)

    'Clear the status bar
    vntStatus = SysCmd(acSysCmdClearStatus)

    'Return whether or not an error occurred
    ReLink = (Err = 0)

End Function
```

Understanding Access's Locking Mechanisms

Although the preceding tips for designing network applications reduce network traffic, they in no way reduce locking conflicts. To protect shared data, Access locks either a record or a page of data as the user edits a record. In this way, multiple users can read the data, but only one user can make changes to it. You can lock data through a form or through a recordset that isn't bound to a form.

Here are the methods of locking for an Access application:

- Record locking

- Page locking

- Table and recordset locking

- Opening an entire database with Exclusive access

With record locking, Access locks only the record that the user is editing. With page locking, Access locks only the 4K page with the edited record. On the other hand, in table and recordset locking, Access locks the entire table or recordset containing the edited record. With database locking, Access locks the entire database, unless the user opening the database has opened it for read-only access. In that case, other users can also open the database for read-only access. The capability to get exclusive use of a database can be restricted through security.

It's important to note that the locking scheme you adhere to depends on the source providing the data. If you're using client/server data, you inherit the locking scheme of the particular back end you're using. If you're manipulating ISAM data over a network, you get the type of data locking that the particular ISAM database supports. For example, if you're working with a FoxPro database, you can use record locking or any other locking scheme that FoxPro supports.

Locking and Refreshing Strategies

Access has several tools for controlling locking methods in datasheets, forms, and reports. To configure the global multiuser settings, choose Tools, Options, and then click the Advanced tab. The dialog box shown in Figure 2.5 appears.

You can configure the following multiuser settings from this dialog box:

- Default Record Locking

- Record-Level Locking

- Default Open Mode

- Number of Update Retries

- ODBC Refresh Interval

- Refresh Interval

- Update Retry Interval

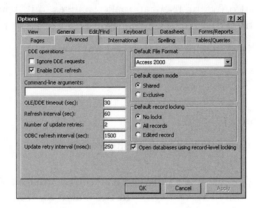

FIGURE 2.5   The Advanced tab of the Options dialog box.

Default Record Locking

The Default Record Locking option lets you specify the default record locking as No Locks (optimistic), All Records (locks entire table or dynaset), or Edited Record (pessimistic). This dialog box is where you can affect settings for all the objects in your database. Modifying this option doesn't affect any existing queries, forms, or reports, but it does affect any new queries, forms, and reports. Because they apply to forms and recordsets, the record-locking options are discussed later in this chapter.

Prior to Access 2000, I *always* recommended the use of optimistic locking. This was because pessimistic locking locked too many records for long periods of time, causing a high incidence of locking contentions. With the introduction of row-level locking in Access 2000, I began to utilize pessimistic locking. I feel that the optimal solution for today's applications is a combination of record locking and pessimistic locking. This ensures that Access locks rows only while users edit them and that only one user can edit a row at a time.

Determining the Locking Mechanism for a Query

If you want to determine the locking method for a particular query, you can do this by modifying the Record Locks query property. Again, the options are No Locks, All Records, and Edited Record. You can view and modify query properties by clicking a blank area of the Query design window with the Properties window open. Figure 2.6 shows the Query Properties window.

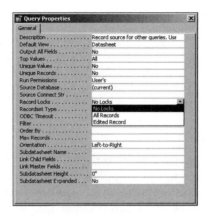

FIGURE 2.6   Setting the locking method for a query.

Determining the Locking Mechanism for a Form or Report

Just as you can configure the locking mechanism for a query, you can configure the locking mechanism for each form and report. Forms and reports have Record Locks properties. (See Figure 2.7.) Changing these properties modifies the locking mechanism for that particular form or report.

FIGURE 2.7   Setting the locking method for a form.

NOTE

Reports don't offer the choices for locking because the user can't modify report data.

Record-Level Locking

Regardless of the default record locking that you have chosen, the Open Databases Using Record-Level Locking check box allows you to designate whether Access locks only one record or locks a page of records. For example, if you select the No Locks option, Access uses optimistic locking, but the locking occurs at the record level rather than at the page level.

Default Open Mode

The Default Open Mode allows you to configure the default open mode for databases. By encouraging users to set this option in their own copies of Access, you prevent people from inadvertently opening a database exclusively. Take a good look at the options available under the Open command button within the Access File Open dialog box, shown in Figure 2.8. This is where you can override the default open mode and open a database with the locking method you desire.

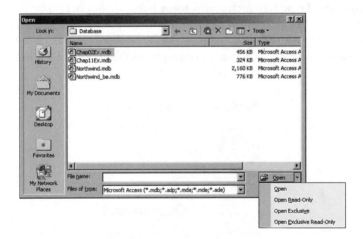

FIGURE 2.8   The Open command button in the File Open dialog box allows you to specify the open mode for a database.

Number of Update Retries

The number of update retries specifies how many times Access will try to save data to a locked record. The higher this number is, the greater the chance is that the update will succeed. The downside is that the user has to wait while Access continues trying to update the data, even when there's no hope that the update will be successful. The default for this setting is 2; the value can range from 0 to 10.

ODBC Refresh Interval

The ODBC Refresh Interval determines how often Access updates your form or datasheet with changes made to data stored in ODBC data sources. For example, assume that two users are viewing the same data stored in a back-end Microsoft SQL Server database. User 1 makes a change to the data, and the ODBC Refresh Interval determines how long it is before User 2 sees the change. The higher this number is, the less likely it is that User 2 will see the current data. The lower this number is, the more network traffic will be generated. The default for this setting is 1500 seconds (just over 25 minutes), and the value can range from 1 to 32,766 seconds.

Refresh Interval

The Refresh Interval specifies how long it takes for Access to update a form or datasheet with changed data from an Access database. This is very similar to the ODBC Refresh Interval. However, the ODBC Refresh Interval applies only to ODBC data sources, and the Refresh Interval applies only to Access data sources. As with the ODBC Refresh Interval, the higher this number is, the lower the chance is that the data seen by the user is current. The lower this number is, the more network traffic is generated. The default for this setting is 60 seconds; the value can range from 1 to 32,766 seconds.

NOTE

Access automatically refreshes the data in a record whenever the user tries to edit the record. The benefit of a shorter Refresh Interval is that the user sees that another user has changed or locked the record before he tries to edit it.

Update Retry Interval

The Update Retry Interval determines how many seconds Access waits before again trying to update a locked record. The default for this setting is 250 milliseconds, and the value can range from 0 to 1,000 milliseconds (1 second).

Refreshing Versus Requerying Data

It's important to understand the difference between refreshing and requerying a recordset. *Refreshing* a recordset updates changed data and indicates any deleted records. It doesn't try to bring a new recordset over the network wire; instead, it *refreshes* the data in the existing recordset. This means that Access doesn't reorder the records, new records don't appear, and deleted records aren't removed from the display. The record pointer remains on the same record. You cannot refresh all recordset types.

Requerying, on the other hand, gets a new set of records. This means that Access runs the query again, and all the resulting data is sent over the network wire. Access reorders the data, new records appear, and deleted records are no longer displayed. Access moves the record pointer to the first record in the recordset.

Form-Locking Strategies

Earlier in the chapter, you learned about the locking strategies for forms: No Locks, All Records, and Edited Record. Using the three locking strategies, as appropriate, you can develop a multiuser application with little or no multiuser programming. You won't gain the same power, flexibility, and control that you get out of recordsets, but you can quickly and easily implement multiuser techniques. In this section, you will see how all three of these strategies affect the bound forms in your application.

No Locks

The No Locks option means that Access won't lock the page of data with the edited record until it tries to write the changed data to disk. This happens when there's movement to a different record or the user explicitly saves the data in the record. If page locking is in place, the No Locks option is the least restrictive locking option for forms.

Several users can be editing data in the same 4K page of data at the same time, but the conflict occurs when two users try to modify the same record. Say, for example, that User 1 tries to modify data in the record for customer ABCDE, and User 2 tries to modify the *same* record. No error occurs because you specified the No Locks option for the form both users are accessing. Next, User 1 makes a change to the address, and User 2 makes a change to the contact title. User 1 moves off the record, saving her changes. No error occurs because Access has no way of knowing that User 2 is modifying the record. Now User 2 tries to move off the record, and the Write Conflict dialog box, shown in Figure 2.9, appears. User 2 has the choice of saving her changes, thereby overwriting the changes that User 1 made; copying User 1's changes to the Clipboard so that she can make an educated decision on what to do; or dropping her own changes and accepting the changes User 1 made.

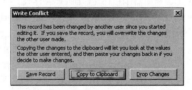

FIGURE 2.9   The Write Conflict dialog box appears when two users edit the same record.

Many developers and users do not like the dialog box shown in Figure 2.9. They feel that it is confusing or that it provides users with too many choices. The good news is that you can easily design and implement your own custom dialog box. Figure 2.10 provides an example. Listing 2.4 shows the code required to implement a custom dialog box.

LISTING 2.4   Example of Custom Optimistic Locking

```
Private Sub Form_Error(DataErr As Integer, Response As Integer)
    On Error GoTo Form_Error_Err:
    Dim intAnswer As Integer

    'If data has changed error occurs, display a message to the user
    'and suppress the standard dialog
    If DataErr = 7787 Then
        intAnswer = MsgBox("Another User Has Modified This Record " & vbCrLf & _
        "Since You Began Editing It. " & vbCrLf & vbCrLf & _
        "Click OK to Cancel Your Changes", _
        vbOK, "Locking Conflict")
        Response = acDataErrContinue
    End If

    Exit Sub

Form_Error_Err:
    MsgBox "Error # " & Err.Number & ": " & Err.Description
    Exit Sub
End Sub
```

FIGURE 2.10   You can create a custom Write Conflict dialog box to appear when two users edit the same record.

This code, found in frmCustomers, is located in the `Error` event of the form. It evaluates to see whether a data change error has occurred. If so, it displays an appropriate message to the user and suppresses the standard error message. In addition to suppressing the standard error message, the `acDataErrContinue` parameter also discards the current user's changes and refreshes the record.

All Records

The All Records locking option is the most restrictive. When All Records is in effect, other users can only view the data in the tables underlying the form. They can't make any changes to the data, regardless of their own locking options. When they open the form, they see a quick status bar message that they can't update the data. If they try to modify data in the form, the computer beeps and displays a message in the status bar.

Edited Record

You use the Edited Record option when you want to prevent the conflicts that happen when the No Locks option is in place. With page-level locking, instead of getting potential conflicts for changed data, users are much more likely to experience locking conflicts because every time a user begins editing a record, the entire 4K page of data surrounding the record is locked. If you use row-level locking, this is not an issue because only the record actually being edited is locked.

Consider this scenario with page-level locking. User 1 begins editing a record, and User 2 tries to modify the same record. The computer beeps and a lock symbol appears in the form's record selector. (See Figure 2.11.) Now User 2 moves to another record. If the other record is in the same 4K page as the record User 1 has locked, the locking symbol appears and User 2 can't edit that record either until User 1 has saved the record she was working on, thereby releasing the lock.

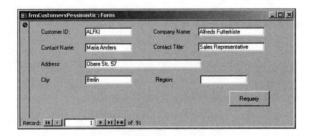

FIGURE 2.11   The lock symbol on an edited record.

NOTE

If you want to override any of the default locking error dialog boxes that appear when you're in a form, you must code the form's `Error` event. Although you can use this method to replace any error message that appears, you can't trap for the situation with pessimistic locking when another user has the record locked. Users are cued that the record is locked only by viewing the locking symbol and hearing the beep when they try to edit the record. If you want to inform users that the record is locked before they try to edit it, you need to place code in the form's `Timer` event that checks whether the record is locked. The later section of this chapter titled "Testing a Record for Locking Status" covers this technique.

One alternative when using pessimistic locking (Edited Record) is to limit the amount of time that the user locks the data. The code in Listing 2.5 accomplishes this task.

LISTING 2.5   Limiting the Amount of Time a User Can Lock a Record

```
Private mboolSecondTime As Integer

Private Sub Form_AfterUpdate()
    'Disable the timer
    Me.TimerInterval = 0

    'Reset the flag
    mboolSecondTime = False

    'Remove the warning message
    Me.lblStatus.Caption = ""
End Sub


Private Sub Form_Current()
    'Remove the warning message
    Me.lblStatus.Caption = ""
End Sub


Private Sub Form_Dirty(Cancel As Integer)
    'Form is dirty; Start the timer
    Me.TimerInterval = 20000
End Sub


Private Sub Form_Timer()
    'If second time, undo changes and inform user
    If mboolSecondTime Then
        Me.Undo
        Me.lblStatus.Caption = "Timeout Period Exceeded" & vbCrLf & _
            "Unsaved Changes Have Been Undone!!!"

    'If first time, warn user, and change flag value
    Else
        Me.lblStatus.Caption = _
            "You Have Locked the Data for Too Long!" & vbCrLf & _
            "You Have 20 Seconds to Save Your Changes " & _
            "or You Will Lose Them!!!"
        mboolSecondTime = True
    End If
End Sub
```

The form's Dirty event activates the form's timer and sets the timer interval to the amount of time that occurs before it warns the user of a problem. The form's Timer event executes after the timer interval has passed. The first time that it occurs for a dirty record, it warns the user that he has 20 seconds to save his changes. The mboolSecondTime flag is set to True. The second time the Timer event executes, it undoes the user's changes to the record and alerts the user that it has done so. When a user saves changes to a dirty row, the AfterUpdate event executes. It disables the timer, resets the flag, and removes any warning message. Finally, when the user moves from row to row, the code in the Current event removes any message displayed to the user from another record.

Recordset Locking

Recordset locking locks pages of data found in a recordset. By using recordset locking, you can control when and for how long Access locks the data. This is different from locking data through bound forms, which gives you little control over the specifics of the locking process.

When you're traversing through a recordset, editing and updating data, locking occurs regardless of whether you intervene, so you must understand when the locking occurs and whether you need to step in to intercept the default behavior. If you do nothing, Access locks a record, or possibly an entire page of records, each time you begin editing data from your VBA code. This page level lock is 4096 bytes (4K) and surrounds the record being edited. If Access finds an OLE object in the record being edited, it isn't locked with the record because it occupies its own space.

Pessimistic Locking

VBA lets you determine when and for how long Access locks a page of data. The default behavior is *pessimistic locking*, which means that Access locks the record or page when the first field is updated. Listing 2.6 illustrates this process.

LISTING 2.6   Utilizing Pessimistic Locking

```
Sub PessimisticLock(strAuthorID As String)
    Dim cnn As ADODB.Connection
    Dim rst As ADODB.Recordset
    Dim strCriteria As String

    Set cnn = New ADODB.Connection
    cnn.ConnectionString = " Provider=sqloledb;" & _
        "Data Source=(local);Initial Catalog=pubs;uid=sa;pwd="
```

LISTING 2.6   Continued

```
    cnn.Open

    Set rst = New ADODB.Recordset
    rst.ActiveConnection = cnn
    rst.CursorType = adOpenKeyset
    rst.LockType = adLockPessimistic 'Invoke Pessimistic Locking
    rst.CursorLocation = adUseServer
    rst.Open "Select * from Authors Where Au_ID ='" _
        & strAuthorID & "'", _
        Options:=adCmdText

    rst!City = "Thousand Oaks" 'Lock occurs here
    Stop
    rst.Update 'Lock Released Here
End Sub
```

NOTE

Listing 2.6 requires the use of SQL Server. The example in Listing 2.6 uses the Pubs database on the local server.

NOTE

Many of the locking examples in this chapter contain Stop statements. To properly test the examples, you must open two copies of Access (one read-only). Run the routine in each copy until you reach the Stop statement. Step once in the first copy and then once in the second copy. You will receive an error in the second copy.

NOTE

Not all database providers support all lock types. To determine the functionality available for a particular Recordset object, use the Supports method with adUpdate and adUpdateBatch. Furthermore, the adLockPessimistic setting is not supported when the CursorLocation property is set to adUseClient. Whether the provider does not support the locking type or the cursor location does not support the locking type, no error results. Instead, the closest available locking type is used.

NOTE

ADO recordsets using CurrentProject.Connection do not support pessimistic locking. For this reason, the code shown in Listing 2.5 creates a new connection.

In this scenario, although the lock occurs for a very short period of time, it's actually being issued when the data is first edited; then it's released at the update.

The advantage of this method of locking is that you can make sure that the user does not make any changes to the data between the time the edit process begins and the time you issue the Update method. Furthermore, when the edit process begins successfully, you are ensured write access to the record. The disadvantage is that the time between the edit and the update might force the lock to persist for a significant period of time, locking other users out of that record. Furthermore, if you use page locking, Access locks the entire page of records where the edited record is located.

This phenomenon is exacerbated when transaction processing (covered in Chapter 16, "Transaction Processing") is invoked. Basically, transaction processing ensures that when you make multiple changes to data, Access successfully makes all changes or no changes occur. Listing 2.7 illustrates how pessimistic record locking affects transaction processing.

LISTING 2.7   Pessimistic Record Locking and Its Effect on Transaction Processing

```
Sub PessimisticTrans(strOldCity As String, strNewCity As String)
    Dim cnn As ADODB.Connection
    Dim rst As ADODB.Recordset
    Dim strCriteria As String

    Set cnn = New ADODB.Connection
    cnn.ConnectionString = " Provider=sqloledb;" & _
        "Data Source=(local);Initial Catalog=pubs;uid=sa;pwd="
    cnn.Open

    Set rst = New ADODB.Recordset
    rst.ActiveConnection = cnn
    rst.CursorType = adOpenKeyset
    rst.LockType = adLockPessimistic 'Invoke Pessimistic Locking
    rst.CursorLocation = adUseServer
    rst.Open "SELECT * FROM Authors WHERE City = '" & strOldCity & "'", _
        Options:=adCmdText

    cnn.BeginTrans
    Do Until rst.EOF
        rst!City = strNewCity 'Lock occurs here
        rst.Update
        rst.MoveNext
    Loop
    cnn.CommitTrans  'Lock released here
End Sub
```

Here you can see that the lock is in place from when the code edits the city of the very first record until the code issues the CommitTrans. This means that no one can update any records, or possibly pages of data, involving the edited records until the code issues the CommitTrans. This can take a prohibitive amount of time during a long process.

Optimistic Locking

Optimistic locking delays the time at which Access locks the record. Access issues the lock upon update rather than when the first field is edited. Listing 2.8 shows the code.

LISTING 2.8   Utilizing Optimistic Locking

```
Sub OptimisticLock(strAuthorID As String)
    Dim cnn As ADODB.Connection
    Dim rst As ADODB.Recordset
    Dim strCriteria As String

    Set cnn = New ADODB.Connection
    cnn.ConnectionString = " Provider=sqloledb;" & _
        "Data Source=(local);Initial Catalog=pubs;uid=sa;pwd="
    cnn.Open

    Set rst = New ADODB.Recordset
    rst.ActiveConnection = cnn
    rst.CursorType = adOpenKeyset
    rst.LockType = adLockOptimistic 'Invoke Optimistic Locking
    rst.CursorLocation = adUseServer
    rst.Open "Select * from Authors Where Au_ID = '" & _
        strAuthorID & "'", _
        Options:=adCmdText

    Stop
    rst!City = "Thousand Oaks"
    Stop
    rst.Update 'Lock occurs and is Released Here
End Sub
```

NOTE

It is important to note that to keep the examples simple, much of the code in this chapter is devoid of error handling. For example, if you pass an invalid AuthorID to the subroutine shown in Listing 2.8, the code will fail.

As you can see, the lock doesn't happen until the code issues the Update method. The advantage of this method is that Access locks the page or record for a very brief period. However, the disadvantage occurs when two users grab the record for editing at the same time. When one user tries to update, no error occurs. When the other user tries to update, she gets an error indicating that the data has changed since the code issued her edit. Handling this error message is covered in the section "Coding Around Optimistic Locking Conflicts," later in this chapter.

Optimistic locking with transaction handling isn't much different from pessimistic locking. As the code reaches the Update method for each record, Access locks the page containing that record. It remains locked until the code commits the transaction. The code appears in Listing 2.9.

LISTING 2.9   Optimistic Record Locking and Its Effect on Transaction Processing

```
Sub OptimisticTrans(strOldCity As String, strNewCity As String)
    Dim cnn As ADODB.Connection
    Dim rst As ADODB.Recordset
    Dim strCriteria As String

    Set cnn = New ADODB.Connection
    cnn.ConnectionString = " Provider=sqloledb;" & _
        "Data Source=(local);Initial Catalog=pubs;uid=sa;pwd="
    cnn.Open

    Set rst = New ADODB.Recordset
    rst.ActiveConnection = cnn
    rst.CursorType = adOpenKeyset
    rst.LockType = adLockOptimistic 'Invoke Optimistic Batch Locking
    rst.CursorLocation = adUseServer
    rst.Open "SELECT * FROM Authors WHERE City = '" & strOldCity & "'", _
        Options:=adCmdText

    cnn.BeginTrans
    Do Until rst.EOF
        rst!City = strNewCity
        rst.Update 'Lock occurs here
        rst.MoveNext
    Loop
    cnn.CommitTrans   'Lock released here
End Sub
```

NOTE

You use the constant `adLockBatchOptimistic` when you desire batch updates rather than immediate updates. The updates do not occur until you use the `UpdateBatch` method of the `Recordset` object. In the case of batch optimistic locking, Access does not lock the records until the code issues the `UpdateBatch` method.

Effectively Handling Locking Conflicts

If a user has a page or record locked and another user tries to view data in the record or on that page, no conflict occurs. On the other hand, if other users try to edit data on that same page, they get an error.

You won't always want Access's own error handling to take over when a locking conflict occurs. For example, rather than having Access display its generic error message indicating that a record is locked, you might want to display your own message and then try to lock the record a couple of additional times. To do something like this, you must learn to interpret each locking error generated by VBA so that you can make a decision about how to respond.

Locking conflicts happen in the following situations:

- A user tries to edit a record that's already locked.

- A record has changed or been deleted since the user first started to edit it.

These errors can occur whether you're editing bound data through a form or accessing the records through VBA code.

Errors with Pessimistic Locking

To begin the discussion of locking conflicts, take a look at the types of errors that occur when pessimistic locking is in place. With pessimistic locking, you generally need to code for the following errors:

- The current record is locked by another user. Usually, you can just wait a short period of time and then try the lock again.

- Someone deleted the record since the code retrieved the recordset. In this case, it's best to refresh the data.

NOTE

The error numbers that occur differ based on which provider you use. The examples in this chapter therefore use sample error numbers. Refer to online help for trappable Microsoft Jet errors, ADO error codes, and ADO provider errors. As an alternative to the VBA error code, you can use the `Errors` collection of the `Connection` object to view properties of the error that occurred.

Coding Around Pessimistic Locking Conflicts

It's fairly simple to write code to handle pessimistic locking conflicts. Your code should look like Listing 2.10.

LISTING 2.10　Handling Pessimistic-Locking Errors

```
Sub PessimisticRS(strAuthorID As String)
    On Error GoTo PessimisticRS_Err
    Dim cnn As ADODB.Connection
    Dim rst As ADODB.Recordset
    Dim strCriteria As String
    Dim intChoice As Integer

    Set cnn = New ADODB.Connection
    cnn.ConnectionString = "Provider=sqloledb;" & _
        "Data Source=(local);Initial Catalog=pubs;uid=sa;pwd="
    cnn.Open

    Set rst = New ADODB.Recordset
    rst.ActiveConnection = cnn
    rst.CursorType = adOpenKeyset
    rst.LockType = adLockPessimistic 'Invoke Pessimistic Locking
    rst.CursorLocation = adUseServer
    rst.Open "Select * from Authors Where Au_ID = '" & _
        strAuthorID & "'",  _
        Options:=adCmdText

    Stop
    rst!City = "Thousand Oaks" 'Lock occurs here
    rst.Update 'Lock Released Here
    Exit Sub

PessimisticRS_Err:
    Select Case Err.Number
        Case 3197
            rst.Move 0
            Resume
        Case -2147217887, -2147467259
          intChoice = MsgBox(Err.Description, vbRetryCancel + vbCritical)
          Select Case intChoice
              Case vbRetry
                  Resume
```

LISTING 2.10   Continued

```
            Case Else
                MsgBox "Couldn't Lock"
            End Select
        Case 3021
            MsgBox "Record Has Been Deleted"
        Case Else
            MsgBox Err.Number & ": " & Err.Description
        End Select


End Sub
```

The error-handling code for this routine handles the errors that can happen with pessimistic locking. If a "–2147217887 Record Is Locked" error or a "–2147467259 Timeout Expired" error occurs, the code asks the user whether she wants to try again. If she responds affirmatively, the edit process resumes; otherwise, the code informs the user that the lock failed. If the record being edited has been deleted, an error 3021 occurs and the user is informed that the record has been deleted. The situation looks like Listing 2.11 when transaction processing is involved.

LISTING 2.11   Handling Pessimistic-Locking Errors in Transactions

```
Sub PessimisticRSTrans(strOldCity as string, strNewCity as string)
    On Error GoTo PessimisticRSTrans_Err
    Dim cnn As ADODB.Connection
    Dim rst As ADODB.Recordset
    Dim strCriteria As String
    Dim intCounter As Integer
    Dim intTry As Integer
    Dim intChoice As Integer

    Set cnn = New ADODB.Connection
    cnn.ConnectionString = "Provider=sqloledb;" & _
        "Data Source=(local);Initial Catalog=pubs;uid=sa;pwd="
    cnn.Open

    Set rst = New ADODB.Recordset
    rst.ActiveConnection = cnn
    rst.CursorType = adOpenKeyset
    rst.LockType = adLockPessimistic 'Invoke Pessimistic Locking
    rst.CursorLocation = adUseServer
    rst.Open "SELECT * FROM Authors WHERE City = '" & strOldCity & "'", _
```

LISTING 2.11   Continued

```
        Options:=adCmdText

    cnn.BeginTrans
    Do Until rst.EOF
        rst!City = strNewCity 'Lock occurs here
        rst.Update
        rst.MoveNext
    Loop
    cnn.CommitTrans  'Lock released here

PessimisticRSTrans_Exit:
    Exit Sub

PessimisticRSTrans_Err:
    Select Case Err.Number
        Case 3197
            rst.Move 0
            Resume
        Case -2147217887
            intCounter = intCounter + 1
            If intCounter > 2 Then
                intChoice = MsgBox(Err.Description, vbRetryCancel + vbCritical)
                Select Case intChoice
                    Case vbRetry
                        intCounter = 1
                    Case vbCancel
                        Resume CantLock
                End Select
            End If
            DoEvents
            For intTry = 1 To 100: Next intTry
            Resume
        Case Else
            MsgBox "Error: " & Err.Number & ": " & Err.Description
    End Select

CantLock:
    cnn.RollbackTrans
    Exit Sub
End Sub
```

This code tries to lock the record. If it's unsuccessful (that is, if an error –2147217887 or –2147467259 is generated), it tries three times; then it prompts the user for a response. If the user selects Retry, the process repeats. Otherwise, a rollback occurs and the code exits the subroutine. If any other error occurs, the code issues a rollback and none of the updates is accepted.

TIP

When using a database server such as Microsoft SQL Server, you can much more effectively accomplish the task of updating records using a stored procedure.

Errors with Optimistic Locking

Now that you have seen what happens when a conflict occurs with pessimistic locking, see what happens when optimistic locking is in place. These are the two most common error codes generated by locking conflicts when optimistic locking is in place:

- An error occurs when you use the Update method to save a locked record or a record on a locked page. This error can occur when you use optimistic locking and a user tries to update a record on the same page as a record that another machine has locked. You can usually just wait a short period of time and then try the lock again.

- An error occurs with optimistic locking when someone else has updated a record since you first started viewing it.

Coding Around Optimistic Locking Conflicts

Remember that with optimistic locking, VBA tries to lock the page when the code issues an Update method. There's a chance that a "Data Has Changed" error could occur. You need to handle this in your code, so modify the preceding subroutine for optimistic locking with the code in Listing 2.12.

LISTING 2.12   Handling Optimistic-Locking Errors

```
Sub OptimisticRS(strAuthorID)
    On Error GoTo OptimisticRS_Err
    Dim cnn As ADODB.Connection
    Dim rst As ADODB.Recordset
    Dim strCriteria As String
    Dim intChoice As Integer

    Set cnn = New ADODB.Connection
```

LISTING 2.12   Continued

```
    cnn.ConnectionString = " Provider=sqloledb;" & _
        "Data Source=(local);Initial Catalog=pubs;uid=sa;pwd="
    cnn.Open

    Set rst = New ADODB.Recordset
    rst.ActiveConnection = cnn
    rst.CursorType = adOpenKeyset
    rst.LockType = adLockOptimistic 'Invoke Optimistic Locking
    rst.CursorLocation = adUseServer
    rst.Open "Select * From Authors Where Au_ID = '" & _
        strAuthorID & "'", _
        Options:=adCmdText

    rst!City = "Thousand Oaks"
    Stop
    rst.Update 'Lock occurs and is Released Here

OptimisticRS_Exit:
    Exit Sub

OptimisticRS_Err:
    Select Case Err.Number
    Case -2147217885
        If rst.EditMode = adEditInProgress Then  'Data has Changed
            MsgBox "Another User has Edited Record Since You Began " & _
                "Modifying It"
        End If
    Case -2147217871   'Locked or ODBC Timeout
        intChoice = MsgBox(Err.Description, vbRetryCancel + vbCritical)
            Select Case intChoice
                Case vbRetry
                    Resume
                Case vbCancel
                    MsgBox "Update Cancelled"
            End Select
    Case Else
        MsgBox "Error: " & Err.Number & ": " & Err.Description
    End Select
    Resume OptimisticRS_Exit
End Sub
```

As with pessimistic error handling, this routine traps for all potential errors that can occur with optimistic locking. In the case of a "Data Has Changed" conflict, the code warns the user of the problem. In the case of a locking conflict, the code asks the user whether she wants to try again. Listing 2.13 shows what it looks like with transaction processing involved.

LISTING 2.13 Handling Optimistic-Locking Errors in Transactions

```
Sub OptimisticRSTrans()
    On Error GoTo OptimisticRSTrans_Err
    Dim cnn As ADODB.Connection
    Dim rst As ADODB.Recordset
    Dim strCriteria As String
    Dim intChoice As Integer
    Dim boolInTrans As Boolean

    Set cnn = New ADODB.Connection
    cnn.ConnectionString = " Provider=sqloledb;" & _
        "Data Source=(local);Initial Catalog=pubs;uid=sa;pwd="
    cnn.Open

    Set rst = New ADODB.Recordset
    rst.ActiveConnection = cnn
    rst.CursorType = adOpenKeyset
    rst.LockType = adLockOptimistic 'Invoke Optimistic Locking
    rst.CursorLocation = adUseServer
    rst.Open "tblCustomers", _
        Options:=adCmdTable

    cnn.BeginTrans
    boolInTrans = True
    Do Until rst.EOF
        rst!CompanyName = rst!CompanyName & 1 'Lock occurs here
        rst.Update
        rst.MoveNext
    Loop
    cnn.CommitTrans  'Lock released here
    Exit Sub

OptimisticRSTrans_Err:
    Select Case Err.Number
        Case -2147217885 'Data has Changed
            If rst.EditMode = adEditInProgress Then
```

LISTING 2.13   Continued

```
                MsgBox "Another User has Edited Record" & _
                " Since You Began " & _
                  "Modifying It"
            End If
        Case -2147217871    'Locked or ODBC Timeout
            intChoice = MsgBox(Err.Description, _
                vbRetryCancel + vbCritical)
                Select Case intChoice
                    Case vbRetry
                        Resume
                    Case vbCancel
                        MsgBox "Update Cancelled"
                End Select
        Case Else
            MsgBox "Error: " & Err.Number & ": " & Err.Description
    End Select

    If boolInTrans Then
        cnn.RollbackTrans
    End If

    Exit Sub
End Sub
```

If a "Data Has Changed" conflict occurs, the code cancels the entire processing loop
(a rollback occurs). If a locking error occurs, the code retries the lock several times. If
it's still unsuccessful, the code rolls back the entire transaction.

Testing a Record for Locking Status

Often you want to determine the locking status of a record *before* you attempt an
operation with it. By utilizing pessimistic locking and trying to modify the record,
you can determine whether someone has locked the current row. The code looks like
Listing 2.14.

LISTING 2.14   Determining Whether a Record Is Locked Before Editing It

```
Sub TestLocking()

    Dim cnn As ADODB.Connection
    Dim rst As ADODB.Recordset
```

LISTING 2.14   Continued

```
    Dim boolLocked As Boolean

    Set cnn = New ADODB.Connection
    cnn.ConnectionString = " Provider=sqloledb;" & _
        "Data Source=(local);Initial Catalog=pubs;uid=sa;pwd="
    cnn.Open

    Set rst = New ADODB.Recordset
    rst.ActiveConnection = cnn
    rst.CursorType = adOpenKeyset
    rst.LockType = adLockPessimistic 'Invoke Pessimistic Locking
    rst.CursorLocation = adUseServer
    rst.Open "Authors", Options:=adCmdTable

    boolLocked = IsItLocked(rst)
    MsgBox boolLocked

End Sub

Function IsItLocked(rstAny As ADODB.Recordset) As Boolean
    On Error GoTo IsItLocked_Err
    IsItLocked = False

    With rstAny
        .Update
    End With
    Exit Function

IsItLocked_Err:
    If Err = -2147467259 Then
        IsItLocked = True
        Exit Function
    End If
End Function
```

The TestLocking routine sends its recordset to the IsItLocked() function, which receives the recordset as a parameter. It then issues an Update method on the recordset. If an error occurs, someone has locked the record. The error handler sets the return value for the function to True.

Using Code to Refresh or Requery

In this section, you'll see how to requery by using code. The Requery method makes sure that the user gets to see any changes to existing records as well as any added records. It also ensures that deleted records are removed from the recordset. It's easiest to understand the Requery method by looking at the data underlying a form:

```
Private Sub cmdRequery_Click()
    If Me.RecordsetClone.Restartable Then
        Me.RecordsetClone.Requery
    Else
        MsgBox "Requery Method Not Supported on this Recordset"
    End If
End Sub
```

This code first tests the Restartable property of the recordset underlying the form. If the Restartable property is True, the recordset supports the Requery method that's performed on the form's recordset. Of course, the Restartable property and the Requery method work on any recordset, not just the recordset underlying a form. The only reason a recordset might not be restartable is that you cannot restart some back-end queries.

Before running this code, new records don't appear in the recordset and deleted records appear with #Deleted. (See Figure 2.12.) After you issue the Requery method, all new records appear and deleted records are removed.

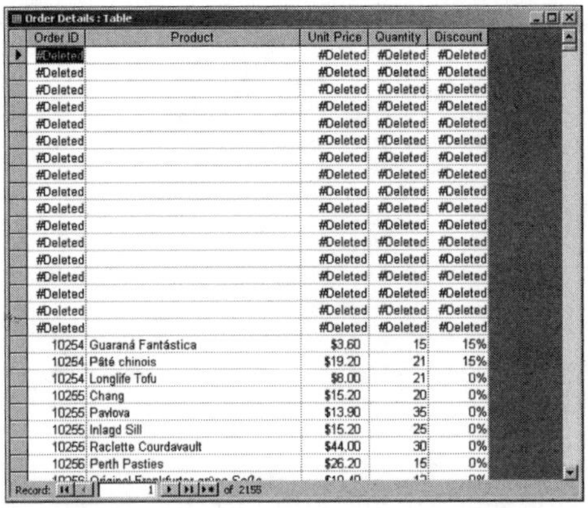

FIGURE 2.12   A recordset that hasn't been requeried yet.

Understanding the .LDB File

Every database opened for shared use has a corresponding .LDB file, a locking file created to store computer and security names and to place byte-range locks on the recordset. The .LDB file always has the same name and location as the databases whose locks it's tracking. Access deletes the .LDB file when the last user exits the database file. Twice, Access does not delete the .LDB file:

- When the database is marked as damaged (politically correct term)

- When the last user out doesn't have delete rights in the folder with the database and .LDB files

The Jet Engine writes an entry to the .LDB file for every user who opens the database. The entry is 64 bytes; the first 32 bytes contain the user's computer name, and the last 32 bytes contain his security name. Because the maximum number of users for an Access database is 255, the .LDB file can't get larger than 16K. The .LDB file information prevents users from writing data to records or pages that other users have locked and determines who has the records or pages locked.

The User Roster

Access 2000 introduced the user roster. The user roster allows you to programmatically determine who is logged on to a database. The OpenSchema method of the Connection object provides this information.

The OpenSchema method receives three parameters. They include Query Type, Restrictions, and Schema ID. Listing 2.15 illustrates the use of the OpenSchema method to identify the user roster.

LISTING 2.15   Determining Who Is Using a Database

```
Public Const JET_SCHEMA_USERROSTER = _
    "{947bb102-5d43-11d1-bdbf-00c04fb92675}"


Sub UserRoster()
    Dim cnn As ADODB.Connection
    Dim rst As ADODB.Recordset

    Set cnn = New ADODB.Connection
    cnn.ConnectionString = "Provider=Microsoft.Jet.OLEDB.4.0;" & _
    "Data Source=C:\My Documents\Test.mdb"
```

LISTING 2.15　Continued

```
    cnn.Open

    Set rst = cnn.OpenSchema(adSchemaProviderSpecific, _
        , JET_SCHEMA_USERROSTER)
    Debug.Print rst.GetString
End Sub
```

The code begins by declaring and instantiating a Connection object. It opens the connection using a connection string to the database for which you want to obtain the user roster. It executes the OpenSchema method on the Connection object. The parameters passed to the OpenSchema method designate that you want to return a user roster. The code returns the roster into the Recordset object.

Creating Custom Counters

Access offers an AutoNumber field type that can be set to automatically generate sequential or random values. Although the AutoNumber field type is adequate for most situations, you might want to home-grow your own AutoNumber fields for any of the following reasons:

- You don't like the AutoNumber field discarding values from canceled records.

- The primary key value needs to be some algorithm of the other fields in the table (the first few characters from a couple of fields, for example).

- The primary key value needs to contain an alphanumeric string.

To generate your own automatically numbered sequential value, you should probably build a table that holds the next available value for your custom AutoNumber field. You must lock this table while a user is grabbing the next available sequential value, or the code might assign two users the same value.

Using Unbound Forms

One solution to locking conflicts is to use unbound forms. By doing this, you can greatly limit the amount of time a record is locked and fully control when Access tries to secure the lock. Unbound forms require significantly more coding than bound forms, so you should make sure that the benefits you get from using unbound forms outweigh the coding and maintenance involved. With improvements to both forms and the Jet Engine in Access 2000, the reasons to use unbound forms with Access data are less compelling. Unbound forms are covered in more detail in Chapter 13, "Building Unbound Applications."

Using Replication to Improve Performance

You can use replication, covered in Chapter 17, to improve performance in a multi-user application. Using replication, you can place multiple copies of the database containing the tables on the network, each on a different file server. Different users can be set up to access data from the different file servers, thereby better distributing network traffic. Using the Replication Manager, which ships with the Microsoft Office Developer Edition (MOD), you can synchronize the databases at regular intervals. Although this isn't a viable solution when the data users are viewing needs to be fully current, this type of solution might be adequate in many situations. It's often the only solution when limited resources don't allow migrating an application's data to a client/server database.

NOTE

The Replication Manager comes only with Microsoft Office XP Developer.

Summary

VBA offers several alternative locking strategies for the developer, ranging from locking the entire database to locking one record at a time. In addition, VBA lets you control how long you lock data. You use this feature through the techniques of optimistic and pessimistic locking, as well as deciding on page locking versus record locking. The developer must select which combination of strategies to use in each particular application. The decision about which method to use is influenced by many factors, including the volume of traffic on the network and the importance of making sure that collisions never happen.

3

Introduction to Client/Server Development Techniques

Why This Chapter Is Important

The previous chapter covered the basics of using Access in a multiuser environment. This chapter takes things a step further by discussing client/server applications. *One* of the hot computing terms introduced in the 1990s, *client/server* refers to distributed processing of information. A client/server model involves the storage of data on database servers dedicated to the tasks of processing data and storing it.

The chapter begins by explaining the client/server model. It talks about the roles that Access can play in the design model and about when it is appropriate to utilize the client/server model. You learn the important client/server buzz words and then see how you can upsize your existing Access databases. Finally, the chapter talks about the various ways that you can connect to client/server data.

Understanding the Client/Server Model

The client/server model introduces a separation of functionalities. The *client*, or front end, is responsible for presenting the data and doing some processing. The *server*, or back end, is responsible for storing, protecting, and performing the bulk of the data processing.

With its tools that assist in the rapid development of queries, forms, and reports, Access provides an excellent front end for the presentation of back-end data.

For years, most information professionals worked with traditional programming languages to process and maintain data integrity in the application. With traditional programming languages, data-validation rules were embedded in the programming code. Furthermore, these types of applications are record oriented—that is, all records are read into memory and processed. This scenario has several drawbacks:

- If the underlying data structure changes, every application that uses the data structure must be changed.

- Data-validation rules must be placed in *every* application that accesses a data table.

- Presentation, processing, and storage are handled by one program.

- Record-oriented processing results in an extraordinary amount of unnecessary network traffic.

Deciding Whether to Use the Client/Server Model

Client/server technology was not as necessary when there was a clear delineation between mainframe applications and personal computer applications. Today, the line of demarcation has blurred. Personal computer applications have taken over many applications that had been relegated to mainframe computers in the past. The problem is that users still are very limited by the bandwidth of network communications. This is one place where client/server technology can really help.

However, many developers are confused about what client/server architecture really is. Some mistakenly believe that an Access MDB database file stored on a file server acts as a database server. This is not the case. (In fact, I have participated in many debates in which other developers have insisted that Access itself is a database server application. Well, it's not.) Access is a front-end application that can process data stored on a back end. In this scenario, the Access application runs on the client machine accessing data stored on a database server running software such as Microsoft SQL Server. Access does an excellent job acting as the client-side, front-end software in this scenario. The confusion is about Access's capability to act as a database server.

The key factor is the way that Access retrieves data when it acts as the front end to a database server versus when the data is stored in an Access MDB file. Suppose that you have a table with 500,000 records. A user runs a query based on the 500,000-record table stored in an Access database on a file server. Suppose that the user wants to see a list of all the Californians who make more than $75,000 per year. With the data stored on the file server in the Access MDB file format, Access sends all records over the network to the workstation and performs the query on the workstation. (See Figure 3.1.) This results in significant network traffic.

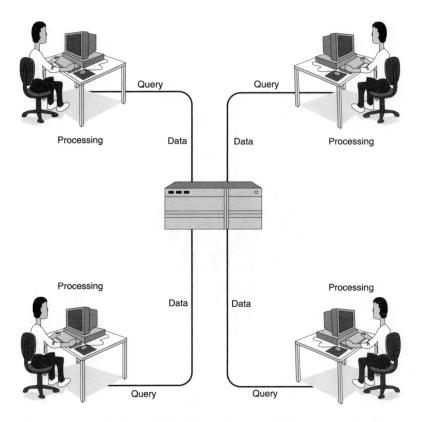

FIGURE 3.1   Access as a front end utilizing data stored in an Access database.

On the other hand, assume that these 500,000 records were stored on a database server such as Microsoft SQL Server. If user runs the same query, SQL Server sends only the names of the Californians who make more than $75,000 per year over the network. In this scenario, SQL Server retrieves only the specific fields requested. (See Figure 3.2.)

What does this mean to you? When should you become concerned with client/server technology and what it can offer you? The following sections present some guidelines on why you might want to upsize from an Access back end to a SQL Server back end.

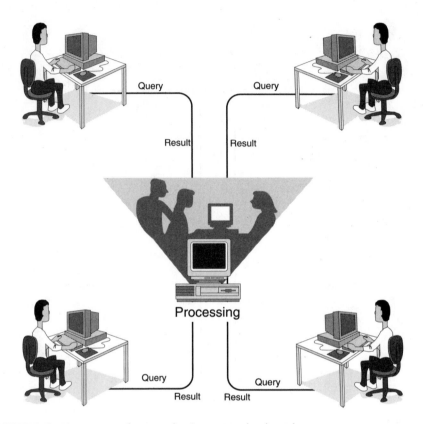

FIGURE 3.2   Access as a front end using a true back end.

Dealing with a Large Volume of Data

As the volume of data in your Access database increases, you probably will notice a degradation in performance. Many people say that 100MB is the magical number for the maximum size of an Access database, but many back-end database servers can handle databases containing multiple gigabytes of data. Although a maximum size of 100MB for an Access database is a good general guideline, it is *not* a hard-and-fast rule. You might find that the need to upsize occurs when your database is significantly larger or smaller than 100MB. The magic number for you depends on all the factors discussed in the following sections, as well as on how many tables are included in the database. Generally, Access performs better with large volumes of data stored in a single table rather than in multiple tables.

Dealing with a Large Number of Concurrent Users

Just as a large volume of data can be a problem, so can a large number of concurrent users. In fact, more than 10 users concurrently accessing an Access database can degrade performance. As with the amount of data, this is not a magic number. I have seen applications with fewer than 10 users whose performance is awful, and I have seen applications with significantly more than 10 users whose performance is acceptable. It often depends on the design of the application as well as what tasks the users are performing.

Demanding Faster Performance

Certain applications demand better performance than other applications. An online transaction processing (OLTP) system generally requires significantly better performance than a decision support system (DSS), for example. Suppose that 100 users are simultaneously taking phone orders. It would not be appropriate for the users of the system to ask their customers to wait 15 seconds between entering each item that is ordered. On the other hand, asking users to wait 60 seconds to process a management report that users run once each month is not a lot to ask (although many still will complain about the minute).

Most back-end database servers can use multithreaded operating systems with multiple processors to handle large volumes of user demand; Access cannot.

Handling Increased Network Traffic

As a file server in an organization experiences increasing demands, the Access application simply might exacerbate an already growing problem. By moving the application data to a database server, the overall reduced demands on the network might provide all users on the network with better performance, regardless of whether they are using the Access application.

Probably one of the most exaggerated situations I have seen is one in which all the workstations were diskless. Windows and all application software were installed on a file server. All the users were concurrently loading Microsoft Word, Microsoft Excel, and Microsoft PowerPoint over the network. In addition, they had large Access applications with many database objects and large volumes of data. All this was stored on the file server as well. Needless to say, performance was abysmal. You can't expect an already overloaded file server to handle sending large volumes of data over a small bandwidth. The benefits offered by client/server technology can help alleviate this problem.

Implementing Backup and Recovery

The backup and recovery options offered with an Access MDB database stored on a file server simply do not rival the options for backup and recovery on a database server. Any database server worth its salt sports very powerful uninterruptible power sources (UPSs). Many have hot-swappable disk drives with disk mirroring, disk duplexing, or disk striping with parity (RAID Level 5). With disk mirroring and duplexing, data can be written to multiple drives at one time, providing instantaneous backups. Furthermore, some database server tape-backup software enables you to complete backups while users are accessing the system. Many offer automatic transaction logging. All these options mean less chance of data loss or downtime. With certain applications, this type of backup and recovery is overkill. With other applications, it is imperative. Although you can mimic some of what database servers have to offer in backup and recovery by using code and replication, it is nearly impossible to get the same level of protection from an Access database stored on a file server that you can get from a database stored on a database server.

Focusing on Security

Access offers what can be considered the best security for a desktop database. However, it cannot compare with the security provided by most database servers. Database server security often works in conjunction with the network operating system. This is the case, for example, with Microsoft SQL Server and Windows NT Server or Windows 2000. The user is given no direct rights to the physical database file; it can be accessed only via an Open Database Connectivity (ODBC) data source or an ADO connection. Remember that, no matter how much security you place on an Access database, this does not prevent a user from seeing or even deleting the entire MDB file from the network disk.

It is very easy to offer protection from this potential problem and others on a database server. Furthermore, many back-end application database server products offer field-level security not offered within an Access MDB file. Finally, many back ends offer integrated security with one logon for both the network and the database.

Sharing Data Among Multiple Front-End Tools

The Access MDB file format is proprietary. Very few other products can read data stored in the Access database format. With a back-end database server that supports ODBC or OLE DB, developers can write front-end applications in a variety of front-end application software, all concurrently using the same back-end data.

Understanding What It All Means

You must evaluate the specific environment in which your application will run:

- How many users are there?
- How much data exists?
- What is the network traffic already like?
- What type of performance is required?
- How disastrous is downtime?
- How sensitive is the data?
- What other applications will use the data?

After you answer these and other questions, you can begin to decide whether the benefits of the client/server architecture outweigh the costs involved.

The good news is that it is not an all-or-nothing decision. Various options are available for client/server applications using Access as a front end. Furthermore, if you design your application with upsizing in mind, moving to client/server technology will not require you to throw out what you have done and start again. In fact, Microsoft provides an upsizing wizard that makes upsizing to a SQL Server database a relatively painless process. How painless depends on numerous factors, including how complex your queries are, whether your queries include VBA functions, and other factors that are covered later in this chapter and throughout the book.

The Roles Access Plays in the Application Design Model

This section takes a look at the many different roles Access can take in an application design.

The Front End and Back End as Access MDB Files

Earlier in this book, you learned about using Access as both the front end and the back end. The Access database is not acting as a true back end because it is not doing any processing. Figure 3.3 shows the architecture in this scenario. The Access application resides on the workstation. Access uses the Microsoft Jet Engine to communicate with data stored in an Access MDB database file stored on the file server.

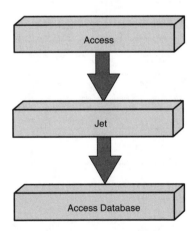

FIGURE 3.3   Access as a front end using an MDB file for data storage.

The Front End as an MDB File Using Links to Communicate to a Back End

In the second scenario, back-end tables can be linked to the front-end application database (.MDB). The process of linking to back-end tables is almost identical to that of linking to tables in other Access databases or to external tables stored in FoxPro, Paradox, or dBASE. And you can treat the linked tables just like any other linked tables. Access uses ODBC to communicate with the back-end tables. (See Figure 3.4.) Your application sends an Access Structured Query Language (SQL) statement to the Access Jet Engine, which translates the statement into ODBC SQL. Access sends this ODBC SQL statement to the ODBC Manager, which locates the correct ODBC driver and passes it the ODBC SQL statement. Supplied by the back-end vendor, the driver translates the statement into the back end's specific dialect. The ODBC Manager sends the now back end–specific query to the SQL Server and to the appropriate database. As you might imagine, all this translation takes quite a bit of time. Furthermore, ODBC is becoming a technology of the past; the ADO/OLE DB technology is quickly replacing the ODBC older technology. That is why one of the two alternatives that follow might be a better solution.

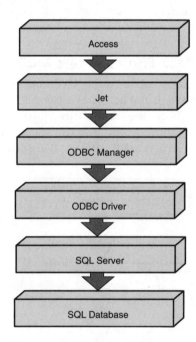

FIGURE 3.4   Access as a front end using links to back-end tables.

The Front End Using SQL Pass-Through to Communicate to a Back End

One of the bottlenecks of using linked tables is waiting for all the translation to happen. Because of this and for the following reasons, you want to bypass the translation process:

- Access SQL might not support some operation that the native query language of the back end supports.

- Either the Jet Engine or the ODBC driver produces a SQL statement that is not optimized for the back end.

- You want a process performed in its entirety on the back end.

As an alternative, you can execute a pass-through query written in the syntax specific to the back-end database server. Although the query does pass through the Jet Engine, Jet does not perform any translation on the query. Neither does ODBC. The ODBC Manager sends the query to the ODBC driver, which passes the query to the back end without performing any translation. In other words, exactly what Access sends is what the SQL database receives. Figure 3.5 illustrates this scenario. Notice that the Jet Engine, the ODBC Manager, and the ODBC driver are not eliminated entirely. They are still there, but they have much less impact on the process than they do with attached tables. Pass-through queries are covered in more detail in the "Using Pass-Through Queries" section later in this chapter.

As you will see later in this chapter, pass-through queries are not a panacea, although they are very useful. The results of a pass-through query are not updateable, for example. Furthermore, because you write pass-through queries in the back end's specific SQL dialect, you must rewrite them if you swap out your back end. For these reasons and others, you generally use pass-through queries along with other solutions.

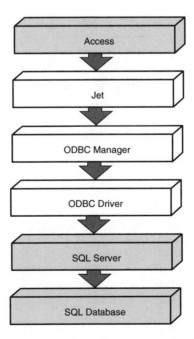

FIGURE 3.5   Access sending a pass-through query to a back-end database.

The Front End Executing Procedures Stored on a Back End

A *stored procedure* is compiled SQL code stored on a back end. You generally execute stored procedures using ADO or DAO code. You can also execute a stored procedure using a pass-through query. Regardless of what you call it, you write the code in a stored procedure in the SQL native to the back end on which it is stored, and SQL Server executes the stored procedure in its entirety on the back end. Stored procedures can return results or can simply execute on the back end without returning any data.

The Front End as a Microsoft Access Data Project Communicating Directly to a Back End

An additional, very viable solution is available when working with a back-end database server. This involves using a Microsoft Access Data Project (.adp), which was introduced with Access 2000. By using a Microsoft Access Data Project (.adp), you bypass the Jet Engine entirely. An Access project contains only code-based objects such as forms, reports, data access pages, macros, and modules. All tables, views, database diagrams, functions, and stored procedures are stored in a SQL Server database. After you have connected with a SQL Server database, you can easily view, create, modify, and delete SQL Server objects. Figure 3.6 illustrates this scenario. Notice that neither the Jet Engine nor ODBC is involved in the scenario.

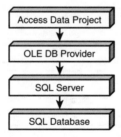

FIGURE 3.6   Access using a Microsoft Access Data Project to communicate to a back end.

Learning the Client/Server Buzzwords

People who talk about client/server technology use many terms that are unfamiliar to the average database developer. To get a full appreciation of client/server technology and what it offers, you must have at least a general understanding of the terminology. Table 3.1 lists the most commonly used terms.

TABLE 3.1   Client/Server Terms

Term	Definition
Column	A field.
DDL	A data definition language used to define and describe the database structure.
Foreign key	A value in one table that must be looked up in another table for validation.
Jet	The native database engine used by Microsoft Access.
Open Database Connectivity (ODBC)	A standard proposed by Microsoft that provides access to a variety of back-end databases through a common interface. In essence, ODBC is a translator.
OLE DB	A new standard for connecting to relational and nonrelational data sources.
Data access objects (DAO)	A method of manipulating data. It is being replaced by ADO and was optimized for accessing Jet databases.
ActiveX data objects (ADO)	A COM-based object model that allows you to easily manipulate OLE DB data sources. It is the data access methodology that replaces DAO.
Primary key	A set of fields that uniquely identifies a row.
Row	A record.
Schema	A blueprint of the entire database. Includes table definitions, relationships, security, and other important information about the database.
Structured Query Language (SQL)	A type of data-manipulation language commonly used to talk to tables residing on a server.
Stored procedures	Compiled SQL statements, such as queries, stored on the database server. Can be called by an application.
Transaction	A set of actions that must be performed on a database. If any one action fails, all the actions are discarded.
Triggers	Pieces of code that execute in response to an action occurring on a table (insert, edit, or delete).

Many books are devoted solely to client/server technology. Most magazines targeted at developers contain numerous articles on client/server technology. *Access/VB/SQL Advisor* always offers excellent articles on client/server development. Many of the articles are specifically about client/server connectivity using Access as a front end. *Visual Studio Magazine* often contains useful articles as well. Another excellent source of information is the Microsoft Developer Network CD. Offered by Microsoft as a subscription, it includes numerous articles and whitepapers on client/server technology, ODBC, and the use of Access as a front end to a database server.

Upsizing: What to Worry About

Suppose that your database is using Microsoft Access as both the front end and the back end. Although an Access database on a file server might have been sufficient for a while, the need for better performance, enhanced security, or one of the other benefits that a back-end database provides compels your company (or your client's company) to upsize to a client/server architecture. You have already created the Access tables. Those tables may even contain volumes of data. In this scenario, it might make sense to upsize.

Because you designed all the tables as Access tables, they must be upsized to the back-end database server. Upsizing involves moving tables from a local Access database (or from any PC database) to a back-end database server that usually runs on Unix, Windows 2000, Windows NT Server, and OS/2 LAN Server or as a Novell NetWare NLM.

Another reason why tables are upsized from Access to a back-end server is that many developers prefer to design their tables from within the Access environment. Access offers a more user-friendly environment for table creation than most server applications.

Because of the many caveats involved when moving tables from Access to a back end, many people opt to design the tables directly on the back end. If you do design your tables in Access, you can export them to the back end and then link them to your local database, or you can use the Upsizing Wizard (covered later in the chapter) to greatly facilitate this process. Regardless of the method that you choose, as you export your tables to the database server, you need to be aware of the issues covered in the following sections.

> **NOTE**
>
> If you are updating to a SQL Server database, the upsizing wizards included as part of Microsoft Access 2000 and Microsoft Access 2002 handle most of the concerns involving upsizing.

Indexes

When exporting a table to a server without the use of the Upsizing Wizard, no indexes are created. You need to re-create all indexes on the back-end database server. If your database server is running Microsoft SQL Server, you can use the Access Upsizing Wizard for Access 2000 or Access 2002. These wizards create indexes for server tables in the place where the indexes exist in your Access tables.

AutoNumber Fields

AutoNumber fields are exported as Long integers. Because some database servers (other than Microsoft SQL Server) do not support autonumbering, you have to create an insert trigger on the server that provides the next key value. You also can achieve autonumbering by using form-level events, but this is not desirable. If other applications access the data, the numbering is not enforced. If you are upsizing to Microsoft SQL Server, the Upsizing Wizard for Access 2000 and Access 2002 converts all AutoNumber fields to Identity fields.

Default Values

Default values are not automatically moved to the server, even if the server supports them. You can set up default values directly on the server, but these values do *not* automatically appear when the user adds new records to the table unless the record is saved without data being added to the field containing the default value. As with autonumbering, you can implement default values at the form level, with the same drawbacks. If you use the Upsizing Wizard for Access 2000 or Access 2002 to move the data to Microsoft SQL Server, default values are exported to your server database.

Validation Rules

Validation rules are not exported to the server. They must be re-created using triggers on the server. "No Access-defined" error messages are displayed when a server validation rule is violated. You should code your application to provide the appropriate error messages. You also can perform validation rules at the form level, but they are not enforced if the data is accessed by other means. The upsizing wizards for Access 2000 and Access 2002 export validation rules to the SQL Server database.

Relationships

Relationships need to be enforced using server-based triggers. Access's default error messages do not appear when the data violates referential integrity rules. You need to respond to and code for these error messages in your application. You can enforce relationships at the form level, but, as with other form-level validations, this method of validation does not adequately protect your data. If you use the Upsizing Wizard for Access 2000 or Access 2002 to move the data to Microsoft SQL Server, all relationships and referential integrity that you have set up in your Access database are set up within the server database.

Security

Security features that you have set up in Access do not carry forward to the server. You need to re-establish table security on the server. After security is set up on the server, Access is unaware that the security exists until the Access application attempts to violate the server's security. Then error codes are returned to the application. You must handle these errors by using code and displaying the appropriate error message to users.

Table and Field Names

Servers often have much more stringent rules than Access does regarding the naming of fields. When you export a table, all characters that are not alphanumeric are converted to underscores. Most back ends do not allow spaces in field names. Furthermore, many back ends limit the length of object names to 30 characters or fewer. If you already have created queries, forms, reports, macros, and modules that use spaces and very long field and table names, these database objects might become unusable when you move your tables to a back-end database server.

Reserved Words

Most back ends have many reserved words. It is important to be aware of the reserved words of your specific back end. It is quite shocking when you upsize a table to find that field names you have been using are reserved words on your database server. If this is the case, you need to rename all the fields in which a conflict occurs. Again, this means modifying all the queries, forms, reports, macros, and modules that reference the original field names.

Case Sensitivity

Many back-end databases are case sensitive. If this is the case with your back end, you might find that your queries and application code don't process as expected. Queries or code that refer to the field or table name by using the wrong case are not recognized by the back-end database and do not process correctly.

Visual Basic Code

Certain properties and methods that work on Access tables might not work on remote tables. This might necessitate some coding changes after you export your tables.

Proactively Preparing for Upsizing

If you set up your tables and code modules with upsizing in mind, you can eliminate many of the pitfalls discussed previously. Despite any of the problems that upsizing can bring, the scalability of Access is one of its strongest points. Sometimes resources are not available to implement client/server technology in the early stages of an application. If you think through the design of the project with the possibility of upsizing in mind, you will be pleased at how relatively easy it is to move to client/server technology when the time is right. With the Access 2000 and Access 2002 Upsizing Wizards, which are designed to upsize an Access application to

Microsoft SQL Server, the process is relatively simple. The upsizing tools for Access 2000 and Access 2002 perform a lot of the work involved in upsizing a database, with just the click of a few buttons.

CAUTION

Although the upsizing tools for Access 2000 and Access 2002 are both excellent, they do have their drawbacks. For example, they do not always map the Access field type to the desired SQL Server field type. For this reason, you can opt not to use the wizards. If, despite their shortcomings, you decide to use the upsizing wizards, make sure that you carefully review both the upsizing report and the structure of each table after it is upsized.

Using the Upsizing Wizard

As mentioned in the previous sections, the Upsizing Wizard, included with Access 2002, greatly facilitates the process of upsizing to a SQL Server database. To invoke the Upsizing Wizard, follow these steps:

1. Select Tools, Database Utilities, Upsizing Wizard. The Upsizing Wizard appears (see Figure 3.7). Here you can opt to upsize to an existing SQL Server database or to create a new database.

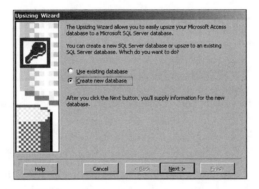

FIGURE 3.7 The first step of the Upsizing Wizard allows you to create a new SQL Server database or to use an existing database.

2. Make the appropriate selection and click Next. If you opt to create a new database, the Upsizing Wizard appears, as in Figure 3.8.

3. Select the server where you want the database to reside.

4. Enter a login ID and password with privileges to create a database.

5. Enter a name for the new database. Click Next. The Upsizing Wizard appears, as in Figure 3.9.

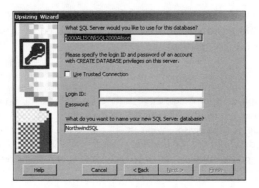

FIGURE 3.8   The second step of the Upsizing Wizard allows you to designate the server, a login ID, a password, and other important information required when creating a new database.

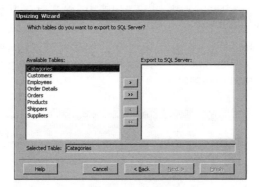

FIGURE 3.9   The third step of the Upsizing Wizard allows you to select the tables that you want to upsize.

6. Select the tables that you want to export to SQL Server and click Next.

7. The next step of the Upsizing Wizard, shown in Figure 3.10, allows you to specify important information about what is included in the upsized tables. You can designate whether indexes, validation rules, defaults, and table relationships are upsized. You can also determine whether timestamps are added to the tables. Finally, you must designate whether table structures only or table structures and data are upsized. Make your selections and click Next.

8. In the next step of the Upsizing Wizard, pictured in Figure 3.11, you can opt for Access to modify your database to create links to the new tables. If you prefer, Access will create an Access Data Project (ADP). Otherwise, you can opt

for no application changes to be made. If you specify that you want access to create a new Access client/server application (ADP), you must specify the ADP filename. Click Next after making your selection.

FIGURE 3.10   The fourth step of the Upsizing Wizard allows you to designate whether indexes, validation rules, defaults, and table relationships are upsized.

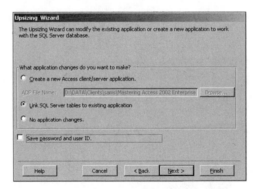

FIGURE 3.11   In the fifth step of the Upsizing Wizard, you specify whether the wizard establishes table links or creates an Access Data Project file as part of the upsizing process.

9. Click Finish. The database is upsized. Access produces an Upsizing Wizard report (see Figure 3.12). You should review this report because it contains important information about the status of the upsizing process. Figure 3.13 shows the result of upsizing the Northwind database.

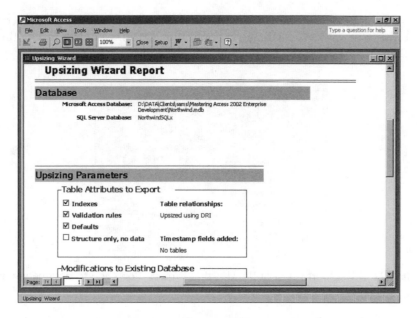

FIGURE 3.12   The Upsizing Wizard report provides important information about the upsizing process.

FIGURE 3.13   The Northwind database after upsizing.

Defining an ODBC Data Source

If you plan to link to ODBC tables, you must load the appropriate ODBC drivers. These drivers come with Access and are installed with the product. You also need to load drivers for the specific back-end database servers to which you want to connect. These drivers usually are purchased from the back-end database vendor and often come with a per-seat charge. This means that you must purchase a client license for each user who will connect to the remote data.

An ODBC *data source* is a user-defined name that points to a remote source of data. It contains all the properties of the data source that are necessary to communicate with data stored on a database server.

Before you can access a remote table from Access, you must define it by using the ODBC Data Source Administrator. If you do not define that data source, or if it is not defined correctly, you will be unable to access the data.

You set up ODBC data sources in the ODBC Data Source Administrator. (See Figure 3.14.) Depending on your installation, the ODBC Data Source Administrator could be a standalone application, or it could appear as a Control Panel icon. By default, this icon appears as ODBC Data Sources. It enables you to create, modify, and delete data sources and to obtain information about existing drivers. Remember that a data source is simply a user-definable name that stores settings that can be used to access a back end located on a particular server using a specified driver.

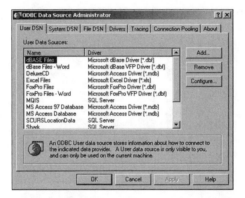

FIGURE 3.14   The User Data Sources window in the ODBC Data Source Administrator.

The ODBC Data Source Administrator is a tabbed dialog box. Table 3.2 describes how you use these tabs.

TABLE 3.2   Using the ODBC Data Source Administrator

Tab	Function
User DSN	Enables you to add, delete, and set up data sources that are local to a computer and can be used only by the current user.
System DSN	Enables you to add, delete, and set up data sources that are local to a computer but are not specific to a particular user.
File DSN	Enables you to add, delete, and set up data sources that are file-based and can be shared between all users who have the same drivers installed. File DSNs are not limited to a specific machine.
Drivers	Displays information about installed ODBC drivers.

TABLE 3.2   Continued

Tab	Function
Tracing	Enables you to specify how the ODBC Driver Manager traces calls to ODBC functions. The available options are when to trace, the log file path, and the custom trace Dynamic Link Library (DLL).
Connection Pooling	Allows you to designate settings that enable you to reuse open connection handles, saving round trips to the server.
About	Gives information about core components such as the location of files and version numbers.

After you enter the ODBC Data Source Administrator, you probably should set up a new data source. To define a new data source, click the Add button on the User DSN or System DSN tabs, or click Add on the File DSN tab of the dialog box. The Create New Data Source dialog box appears, from which you must select the name of the driver that the data source will use. (See Figure 3.15.)

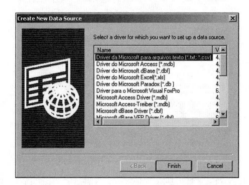

FIGURE 3.15   The Create New Data Source dialog box.

The list of available drivers varies, depending on which client drivers have been installed on the machine. After you select a data source and click Finish, a wizard appears, which varies depending on which driver you selected. You use this wizard to define specific information about the data source you are creating. An example is the Create a New Data Source to SQL Server Wizard, shown in Figure 3.16.

1. The first step of this wizard (shown in Figure 3.16) allows you to specify the data source name, a description for the data source, and the name of the SQL Server you want to connect to. Click Next when you are finished specifying the desired options.

2. The second step of the Create a New Data Source to SQL Server Wizard appears in Figure 3.17. It allows you to specify login information for the ODBC data source. Select the appropriate choices and click Next.

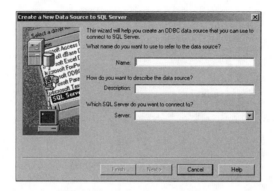

FIGURE 3.16   The first step of the Create a New Data Source to SQL Server Wizard allows you to specify the data source name, a description, and the name of the database server.

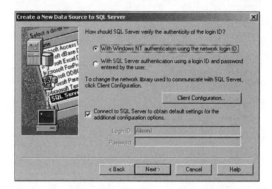

FIGURE 3.17   In the second step of the wizard, you specify login information for the ODBC data source.

3. The third step of the wizard, pictured in Figure 3.18, allows you to specify information about the database that you are linking to. In Figure 3.18, the default database is designated as Northwind. Click Next when you are ready to continue.

4. The fourth and final step of the Create a New Data Source to SQL Server Wizard allows you to further refine the connection to the SQL Server data source (see Figure 3.19). When you're finished specifying all options, click Finish.

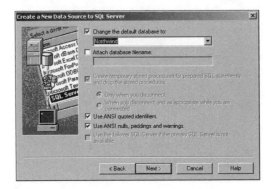

FIGURE 3.18   The third step of the wizard allows you to specify information for the database you are linking to.

FIGURE 3.19   In the fourth step of the wizard, you can specify additional attributes of the data source.

5. The ODBC Microsoft SQL Server Setup dialog box appears (see Figure 3.20). This dialog box provides you with information about the data source and allows you to test the data source. It is a good idea to test the data source to confirm that all the specified settings are valid. A successful test appears in Figure 3.21. Click OK when you're finished.

NOTE

You might be wondering how you can possibly go through the process of defining data sources on thousands of user machines in a large installation. Fortunately, you can automate the process of defining data sources by using DLL functions. It is a matter of using the ODBC Data Source Administrator DLL function calls to set up the data source by using code. The alternative is to set up file DSNs that are available to all your users.

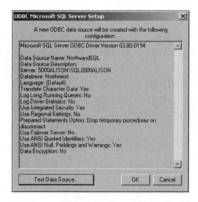

FIGURE 3.20   The ODBC Microsoft SQL Server Setup dialog box provides you with information about the data source and allows you to test the data source.

FIGURE 3.21   An example of a successful test of an ODBC data source.

Connecting to a Database Server

After you define a data source, you are ready to connect to it. You can use these methods to access server data:

- Link to tables residing on the server

- Link to views residing on the server

- Use pass-through queries to send SQL statements directly to the server

- Use VBA code to open the server tables directly

- Create an Access Data Project (with this option, you do not define an ODBC data source)

Working with Linked Tables

The easiest method of accessing data on the server is to link to the external tables. These linked tables act almost exactly like native Access tables. When you link to remote tables, Access analyzes the fields and indexes contained in the tables so that it can achieve optimal performance. It is important to relink the tables if the structures of the remote tables change. You can use the following techniques to link to external tables:

- Linking to external tables via the user interface

- Linking to external tables using code

Linking to Views Rather Than Tables

Views on a database server are similar to Access queries. Views provide a form of security by limiting which rows and columns a user can see. You give access to the view rather than directly to the underlying table. By default, views are not updateable. You can make a view updatable by including all the fields that compose the primary key in the view and building a unique index on the primary key. You can create views in one of three ways:

- Using the SQL Server Enterprise Manager for SQL 7.0 or SQL 2000 (or the equivalent option for your back-end database server)

- Using the `Create View` statement in Access

- Using the View tab of an ADP file

> **NOTE**
>
> Chapter 11, "Developing an MDB Client/Server Application with Linked Tables," covers the process of working with linked tables in detail.

Using Pass-Through Queries

Ordinarily, store and execute a query in Access, even if it is running on remote data, Access compiles and optimizes the query. In many cases, this is exactly what you want. On other occasions, however, it might be preferable for you to execute a pass-through query because these queries are not analyzed by Access's Jet Engine. These queries are passed directly to the server, and this reduces the time Jet needs to analyze the query and enables you to pass server-specific syntax to the back end. Furthermore, pass-through queries can log informational messages returned by the server. Finally, bulk update, delete, and append queries are faster using pass-through queries than they are using Access action queries based on remote tables.

Pass-through queries do have their downside. They always return a snapshot, rendering them not updatable. You also must know the exact syntax the server requires, and you must type the statement into the Query window instead of painting it graphically. Finally, you cannot parameterize a query so that it prompts the user for a value.

Creating a Pass-Through Query in an MDB File Using the User Interface

To create a pass-through query, you can build the query in the Access query builder. Choose Query, SQL Specific, Pass-Through. You are presented with a text-editing window where you can enter the query statement. The SQL statement that you enter must be in the SQL flavor specific to your back end.

Executing a Pass-Through Query Using Code

You also can perform a pass-through query by using VBA code. In fact, you must create the pass-through query by using VBA code if you want the query to contain parameters that you will pass to the server.

NOTE

Chapter 11 covers the process of working with pass-through queries in detail.

Executing and Creating Stored Procedures

You can execute stored procedures on a back-end database server. A stored procedure is similar to a query or program stored on the back end, and it performs some action.

Executing a Stored Procedure

An example is the SQL Server 2000 stored procedure named sp_columns. This stored procedure returns information on the fields in a particular table. Figure 3.22 shows how you would execute the sp_columns stored procedure from the Query Design window. You simply type the name of the stored procedure and any parameters it must receive. Take a good look at the Query Properties window shown in Figure 3.22. If you enter a valid ODBC connect string, the user is not prompted to log on at runtime. The Return Records property is another important property. In this case, you want to set the value of the property to Yes so that you can see the results of the stored procedure. If the stored procedure does not return records, it is important to set this property to No. Otherwise, you receive an error message indicating that no rows were returned. Figure 3.23 shows the results of running the stored procedure.

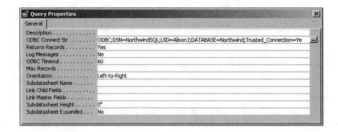

FIGURE 3.22   If you enter a valid ODBC connect string in the Properties window, Access does not prompt the user to log in at runtime.

TABLE_QUALIF	TABLE_OWNE	TABLE_NAME	COLUMN_NAM	DATA_TYPE	TYPE_NAME	PRECISION	LENG
Northwind	dbo	Customers	CustomerID	-8	nchar	5	
Northwind	dbo	Customers	CompanyName	-9	nvarchar	40	
Northwind	dbo	Customers	ContactName	-9	nvarchar	30	
Northwind	dbo	Customers	ContactTitle	-9	nvarchar	30	
Northwind	dbo	Customers	Address	-9	nvarchar	60	
Northwind	dbo	Customers	City	-9	nvarchar	15	
Northwind	dbo	Customers	Region	-9	nvarchar	15	
Northwind	dbo	Customers	PostalCode	-9	nvarchar	10	
Northwind	dbo	Customers	Country	-9	nvarchar	15	
Northwind	dbo	Customers	Phone	-9	nvarchar	24	
Northwind	dbo	Customers	Fax	-9	nvarchar	24	

Record: 14 | 1 | ▶ ▶I ▶* of 11

FIGURE 3.23   The result of running the `sp_columns` stored procedure.

Creating a Stored Procedure

If your application is an ADP file, you can create stored procedures directly from the Access environment. If your application is an MDB file, you can create a stored procedure using a pass-through query. In either case, you can create a stored procedure using the SQL Server Query Analyzer or the SQL Server Enterprise Manager.

NOTE

Chapter 8, "Designing SQL Server Stored Procedures, User-Defined Functions, and Triggers," and Chapter 11 cover the process of creating and working with stored procedures in detail.

Using a Microsoft Access Data Project to Access Client/Server Data

As mentioned earlier in this chapter,   Access projects (ADP files) enable you to work with SQL Server databases without loading the Microsoft Jet Engine. Access projects have the following advantages over the other methods of accessing client/server data covered in this chapter:

- They provide you direct access to a Microsoft SQL Server database.

- You can easily create and modify SQL Server tables, views, database diagrams, and stored procedures all from the Access development environment.

- You can build forms, reports, data access pages, and modules that access SQL Server data, without involving Jet.

- Fewer resources are required on the client side.

- The server is responsible for all query processing.

- You can access functionality not available when accessing ODBC via Jet.

- You can execute asynchronous queries. This means that you don't have to wait for a query to complete execution before you begin another operation.

- You can perform batch updates. This means that you can cache changes locally and then submit them to the server as a batch.

- You can run queries that return multiple resultsets.

- You easily can limit the number of records returned in a resultset.

- You easily can monitor messages and errors generated by the remote data source.

The disadvantages of Access Data Project files follow:

- You cannot create local tables.

- You cannot create local queries.

- There is a learning curve associated with the process of becoming proficient in working with ADP files.

- The process of creating tables, views, database diagrams, and stored procedures involves a learning curve.

NOTE

Chapter 12, "Developing an ADP Application," covers the process of working with ADP files in detail.

Summary

In this chapter, you learned to be concerned with client/server technology when dealing with large volumes of data, large numbers of concurrent users, a demand for faster performance, problems with increased network traffic, backup and recovery, security, and a need to share data among multiple front-end tools. You also learned the roles Access can play in the application design model. In particular, you learned about upsizing and the various ways you can interface with a client/server database, including using Access Data Projects (ADPs). ADP files were introduced with Access 2000. They allow you to connect directly to a Microsoft SQL Server database. Many client/server buzzwords and concepts also were introduced in the chapter.

4

SQL Server Basics

Why This Chapter Is Important

Now that you have explored strategy, as well as the basics of both client/server and multiuser development, you are ready to launch into the specifics of Microsoft SQL Server 2000. The chapter begins by talking about the various editions of SQL Server available and the appropriate uses of each edition. After reading the chapter, you will know which edition is appropriate for you. Next the chapter previews the various SQL Server components. It introduces you to each component and its uses. The text delves into the more commonly used components in detail. After reading the chapter, you will be comfortable with the SQL Server 2000 environment and will have a general understanding of the tools that you can utilize to manage your databases.

Editions of SQL Server Available

You can select from one of many different editions of SQL Server. In fact, the number of editions is so immense that it can be confusing to determine the appropriate edition for you. The following are the editions available and a description of the capabilities of each edition. The list also includes a description of the intended audience for each edition.

- **Enterprise Edition**—This edition supports all SQL Server features and scales up to a very large number of concurrent users. Microsoft intends large workgroups and corporate enterprises to use this edition of SQL Server.

- **Standard Edition**—This edition of SQL Server lacks several of the analysis tools included in the Enterprise Edition. It does not support clustering multiple servers together. Furthermore, it cannot take full advantage of parallel processing. This edition of SQL Server is ideal for small workgroups and departmental databases.

- **Personal Edition**—This edition replaces the Desktop Edition in SQL 7.0. In addition to running on the more robust operating systems, such as Windows 2000 Server, the Personal Edition runs on Windows 95, Windows 98, and Windows Me. Microsoft limits this edition of SQL Server to five concurrent batches (connections). The Personal Edition is therefore ideal for standalone and disconnected users.

- **Developer Edition**—This edition of SQL Server sports all of the features of the Enterprise Edition. The main limitation is its licensing, which prohibits use as a production server. Microsoft intends for those developing and testing SQL Server applications to use this edition of SQL Server.

- **Desktop Engine**—This edition of SQL Server was formerly known as Microsoft Data Engine (MSDE). It is a redistributable edition of SQL Server. Microsoft intends this to be the edition of SQL Server that software vendors distribute with their applications. This edition of SQL Server contains no graphical management tools, support for clustering, support for parallel processing, or any analysis services. Because of SQL Server's instancing capabilities, this edition of SQL Server can easily coexist with other versions and editions of SQL Server. Like the Personal Edition of SQL Server 2000, the Desktop Engine limits you to five concurrent batches or connections.

- **Windows CE Edition**—Microsoft designed this edition of SQL Server for use on Windows CE and Pocket PC devices. The engine is different from the engine used for the other editions of SQL Server. Microsoft specifically designed it with a low memory footprint. It supports most standard queries and is capable of synchronizing with data stored in the Enterprise and Standard editions of SQL Server.

- **Enterprise Evaluation Edition**—This special version of SQL Server is identical to the Enterprise Edition. Its only limitation is that it terminates after 120 days. Microsoft allows you to download this version of SQL Server from its Web site and intends for you to use it for evaluation purposes only.

Overview of the SQL Server Components

SQL Server 2000 is composed of several important components. Each plays its own important role in the database management process. The components include:

- **Enterprise Manager**—The Enterprise Manager, pictured in Figure 4.1, is a graphical tool that you can use to manage almost every aspect of SQL Server. As you can see in Figure 4.1, the Enterprise Manager provides you with a hierarchical view of your database server. Using the Enterprise Manager, you can create and drop databases, tables, views, stored procedures, and database diagrams. You can also schedule jobs, back up your databases, and perform other management tasks. The section of this chapter titled "Introduction to the Enterprise Manager" and other chapters in this book cover the various aspects of the Enterprise Manager.

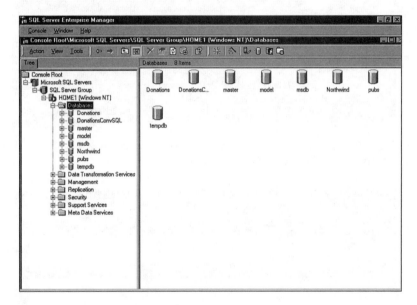

FIGURE 4.1   The Enterprise Manager is a graphical tool that allows you to manage almost every aspect of your SQL Server.

- **Query Analyzer**—The Query Analyzer, pictured in Figure 4.2, provides a graphical environment within which you can interactively create, run, and debug Transact-SQL (T-SQL) statements. The section of this chapter titled "Introduction to the Query Analyzer" and other chapters in this book teach you how to harness the power of this easy-to-use tool.

- **Profiler**—The SQL Profiler, pictured in Figure 4.3, provides a graphical environment within which you can capture SQL Server events. Using the Profiler, you can diagnose performance and locking problems, perform security audits, and troubleshoot various other problems with your server. The section of this chapter titled "Introduction to the Profiler" and other chapters in this book cover the various aspects of the Profiler.

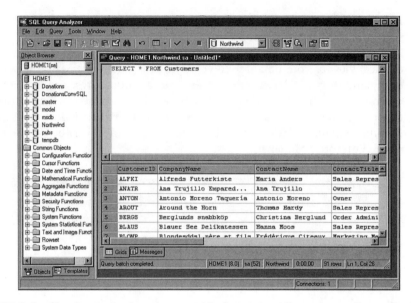

FIGURE 4.2   The Query Analyzer is a graphical tool that allows you to interactively create, run, and debug Transact-SQL statements.

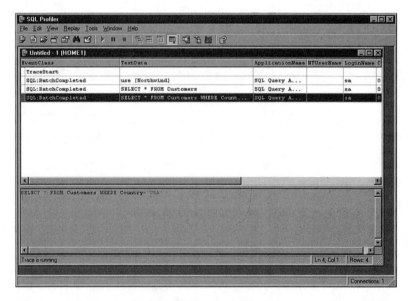

FIGURE 4.3   The Profiler is a graphical tool that allows you to capture SQL Server events.

- **Analysis Services**—In previous versions of SQL Server, Microsoft referred to Analysis Services as OLAP Services. The standard installation process does not install Analysis Services. The Analysis Services allow you to perform online analytical processing, data warehousing, and data mining. This text does not cover Analysis Services; they are covered in SQL Server 2000 books such as *Microsoft SQL Server 2000 DBA Survivor Guide*, available from Sams.

- **English Query**—English Query is a powerful tool that allows you to design applications that enable users to enter queries in English rather than T-SQL. Like Analysis Services, the standard installation process does not include English Query. This text does not cover English Query; it is covered in SQL Server 2000 books such as *Microsoft SQL Server 2000 DBA Survivor Guide*, available from Sams.

- **Client Network Utility**—Primarily, network administrators use the Client Network Utility. This graphical tool allows you to start and stop the SQL Server service, as well as to manage the client Net-Libraries and to define server alias names. Using this tool, you can also set the default options used by DB-Library applications. Figure 4.4 shows the Client Network Utility. It is covered in SQL Server 2000 books such as *Microsoft SQL Server 2000 DBA Survivor Guide*, available from Sams.

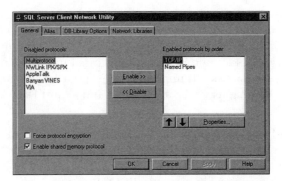

FIGURE 4.4   The Client Network Utility is a graphical tool that allows you to start and stop the SQL Server service and to perform other administrative tasks.

- **Configure SQLXML support in IIS**—This utility (shown in Figure 4.5) assists you with the process of setting up a virtual directory on your Internet Information Server (IIS). Chapter 21, "XML Support in Microsoft Access," covers this utility.

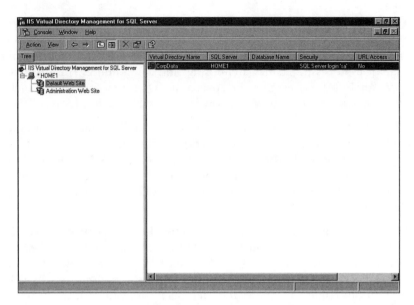

FIGURE 4.5   The Configure SQLXML support in the IIS utility assists you with the process of setting up a virtual directory on your Internet Information Server (IIS).

- **Import and Export Data**—The Import and Export Data option launches the Data Transformation Services Import/Export Wizard. Using this tool, you can easily import OLE DB data into or export OLE DB data from SQL Server 2000. This powerful tool also provides a sophisticated means for transforming data (modifying the data as it is imported). The "Data Transformation Services" portion of this chapter covers the Import and Export Data feature in more detail.

- **Server Network Utility**—The Server Network Utility, pictured in Figure 4.6, provides a graphical user interface for managing the server Net-Libraries that SQL Server uses. This tool is necessary only if you want to modify the options that you designated when you installed SQL Server. It allows you to designate the network protocol stacks on which an instance of SQL Server listens for client requests and the order in which the SQL Server evaluates network libraries when establishing connections. It also allows you to create new network addresses that SQL Server listens to. The Server Network Utility is covered in SQL Server 2000 books such as *Microsoft SQL Server 2000 DBA Survivor Guide*, available from Sams.

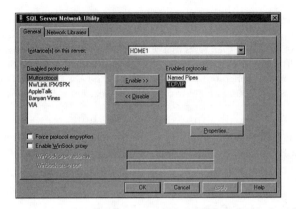

FIGURE 4.6   The Server Network Utility is a graphical tool for managing the server Net-Libraries that SQL Server uses.

- **Service Manager**—You use the Service Manager to start, stop, and pause the SQL Server components. Figure 4.7 shows the Service Manager. You can launch it by double-clicking the appropriate icon in the system tray or by selecting Programs, Microsoft SQL Server, Service Manager from the Start menu.

FIGURE 4.7   The Service Manager allows you to start, stop, and pause the SQL Server components.

- **Books On-line**—Books On-line is the help system for SQL Server 2000. Within this comprehensive help system, you can easily obtain help on *any* aspect of SQL Server or the T-SQL language.

NOTE

Transact-SQL, otherwise known as T-SQL, is the language that you use to query and manipulate a SQL Server database. Even tasks that you perform in Enterprise Manager are executing T-SQL statements under the covers. T-SQL is based on standard SQL (the Structured Query Language). Although it adheres to the SQL defined by the ANSI standards board, the T-SQL included in SQL Server 2000 includes many language features specific to SQL Server.

The sections that follow cover the more commonly used components. Books dedicated to Microsoft SQL Server 2000, such as *Microsoft SQL Server 2000 DBA Survival Guide*, cover the remainder of the components.

Introduction to the Enterprise Manager

Most database administrators (DBAs) spend much of their time within the Enterprise Manager.

The Wizards

The Enterprise Manager contains many wizards that facilitate the process of setting up and managing a SQL Server. These wizards include the Create Database Wizard, the DTS Export Wizard, the Backup Wizard, the Web Assistant Wizard, and *many* more. To invoke the Select Wizard dialog box, select Tools, Wizards from the Enterprise Manager. The Select Wizard dialog box appears, as shown in Figure 4.8. Select the appropriate wizard and click OK. The resulting steps depend on the particular wizard selected.

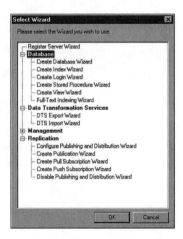

FIGURE 4.8   The Select Wizard dialog box allows you to easily launch the appropriate wizard.

The Databases

The SQL Server installation process creates several important databases on your server. These appear in Figure 4.9. It is important to understand what each of these databases is and what role each database serves.

FIGURE 4.9   SQL Server 2000 creates several databases automatically.

Master

I refer to the Master database as the database of all databases. It stores information about all of the other objects (such as databases) on the server. It keeps track of login accounts and configuration settings. The Master database also contains all system-stored procedures and extended stored procedures. SQL Server 2000 uses the system-stored procedures, written in T-SQL, to perform administration and informational tasks. Extended stored procedures are written in another programming language, such as C or C++. SQL Server dynamically loads them and runs them directly in its address space. The Master database and its contents are so critical that if Master is corrupted, deleted, or in some other way damaged, you will not even be able to boot the server!

Model

Model is a very useful database. It acts as a template for all the databases that you create on a particular server. Each time that you create a new database, SQL Server copies all of the objects within Model to the new database that you create. You can add generic tables, views, stored procedures, functions, user-defined data types, and database options to Model. These objects appear in each database that you create. For example, each database that you create may require a state table. If you add a state table to Model and add a list of states to it, SQL Server adds the table, any details of its structure (such as indexes), *and* the data that it contains to each new database that you create.

Tempdb

Although it's important, you don't need to think much about Tempdb. SQL Server creates Tempdb each time that it starts. It removes Tempdb each time that it shuts down. Tempdb holds all temporary tables and stored procedures. It also provides any temporary workspace required by complex queries. Nothing in Tempdb is permanent.

MSDB
MSDB is responsible for keeping track of all scheduled jobs. It also contains a log of all backup and restore activity, including when the backup or restore was performed and who performed it.

Distribution
The Distribution database appears only if you have set up your server for replication. It contains all pertinent data regarding replication such as transactions, synchronization status, and replication history. It does not appear in Figure 4.9 because the server used to shoot the figure was not set up for replication.

Pubs
Pubs is a sample database that has shipped with many versions of SQL Server. It contains information about books and publishers. As with Northwind, you can utilize Pubs to practice creating and working with views and stored procedures.

Northwind
The Northwind database is a copy of its well-known Microsoft Access counterpart. It contains all of the same tables that appear in the Microsoft Access version of the database. You can utilize the Northwind database to practice creating and working with views and stored procedures.

Data Transformation Services
Data Transformation Services (DTS) is an extremely powerful tool that you can use to import data into and export data from SQL Server. Using DTS, you can transfer data to or from another SQL Server as well as to or from any OLE DB data source. Figure 4.10 shows the Data Transformation Services portion of the Enterprise Manager tree. Among other tasks, here you can create and modify DTS packages. A DTS package contains a series of steps that run when you execute the package. Steps include connecting to a data source, copying data or objects, transforming data, and performing notification of processes or events. This section of this chapter titled "Introduction to Data Transformation Services" covers DTS in more detail.

Management
The Management node of the Enterprise Manager tree (see Figure 4.11) allows you to perform a host of administrative tasks required by your SQL Server. It contains nodes for the SQL Server Agent, Backup, Current Activity, Database Maintenance Plans, and SQL Server Logs. The sections that follow outline each of these tasks.

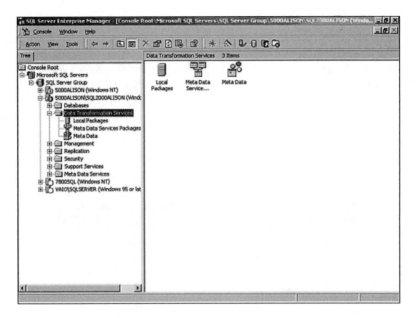

FIGURE 4.10 Data Transformation Services (DTS) is an extremely powerful tool that you can use to import data into and export data from SQL Server.

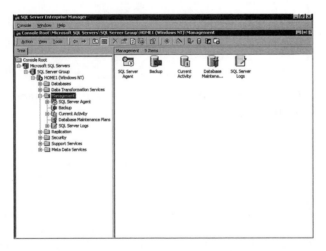

FIGURE 4.11 The Management node of the Enterprise Manager tree allows you to perform a host of administrative tasks required by your SQL Server.

SQL Server Agent

The SQL Server Agent is responsible for running automated maintenance tasks. Tasks performed by the SQL Server Agent include executing jobs, firing alerts, and notifying operators. The jobs are scheduled tasks that SQL Server Agent executes. SQL Server Agent is a separate program from SQL Server. For the jobs to run, the DBA must start the SQL Server Agent. The DBA starts the SQL Server Agent either by using the Service Manager or by right-clicking the SQL Server Agent and selecting Start.

As Figure 4.12 illustrates, the SQL Server Agent node contains three subnodes. These include Alerts, Operators, and Jobs. These nodes allow you to maintain and monitor information about the tasks that the SQL Server Agent is responsible for.

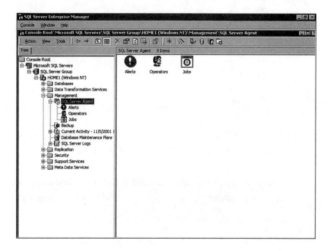

FIGURE 4.12   The SQL Server Agent is responsible for running automated maintenance tasks. It includes Alerts, Operators, and Jobs nodes.

Backup

The Backup node of the Enterprise Manager displays information about backup devices. Backup devices include tape devices as well as disk directories. Right-click the Backup node to create a new backup device or to back up a database. If you opt to back up a database, the SQL Server Backup dialog box appears (see Figure 4.13). This is where you designate the specifics of the backup that you are performing. Chapter 15, "Configuring, Maintaining, and Tuning SQL Server," covers backups in more detail.

FIGURE 4.13   The SQL Server Backup dialog box allows you designate the specifics of the backup that you are performing.

Current Activity

The Current Activity node (shown in Figure 4.14) displays information about the current SQL Server activity. It contains information about the current users and locks. Using this node of the Enterprise Manager, you can easily see who is using the system and what objects they are working with.

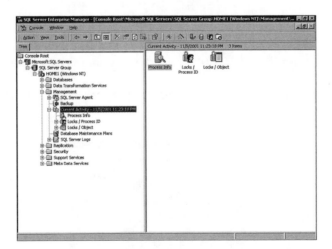

FIGURE 4.14   The Current Activity node displays information about the current SQL Server activity.

Database Maintenance Plans

The Database Maintenance Plans node allows you to create and modify database maintenance plans. Database maintenance plans greatly simplify the process of performing all of the tasks necessary to properly maintain your databases. A database maintenance plan can update database statistics, back up your databases, perform integrity checks, and even ship transaction logs to another server (if you have the Enterprise edition of SQL Server).

Microsoft provides an excellent wizard to assist you with the process of creating a database maintenance plan. The following are the steps involved:

1. To invoke the wizard, right-click Database Maintenance Plans and click New Maintenance Plan.

2. Click Next after reading the introductory screen.

3. Select the database(s) for which you want to create maintenance plans (see Figure 4.15). Click Next.

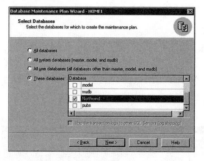

FIGURE 4.15   Select the database(s) for which you want to create maintenance plans.

4. Select the optimizations that you want SQL Server to perform (see Figure 4.16), and click Next.

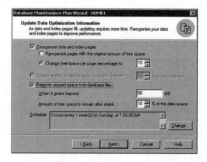

FIGURE 4.16   Select the optimizations that you want SQL Server to perform.

5. Select the database integrity checks that you want SQL Server to perform (see Figure 4.17), and click Next.

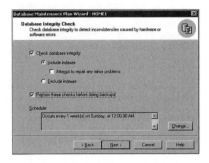

FIGURE 4.17 Select the database integrity checks that you want SQL Server to perform.

6. Specify information about the backup step of the maintenance plan (see Figure 4.18), and click Next.

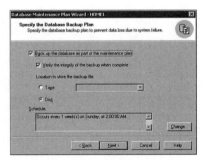

FIGURE 4.18 Specify information about the backup step of the maintenance plan.

7. Designate location information for the backup (see Figure 4.19), and click Next.

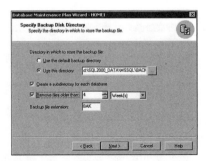

FIGURE 4.19 Designate location information for the backup.

8. Indicate whether you want to back up the log file (see Figure 4.20), and click Next.

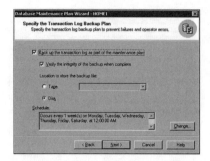

FIGURE 4.20   Indicate whether you want to back up the log file.

9. Designate location information for the log file, and click Next.

10. Designate the reports that you want SQL Server to generate (see Figure 4.21), and click Next.

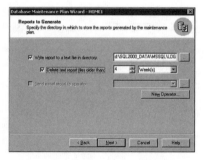

FIGURE 4.21   Designate the reports that you want SQL Server to generate.

11. Specify information about the maintenance plan history (see Figure 4.22), and click Next.

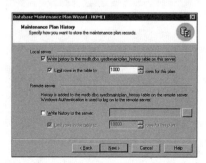

FIGURE 4.22   Specify information about the maintenance plan history.

12. SQL Server displays the designated options in a dialog box (see Figure 4.23). Click Finish to create the maintenance plan.

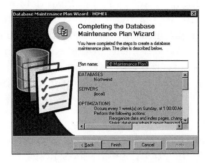

FIGURE 4.23   The last step of the wizard displays information about the selected options.

NOTE

Chapter 15 covers the process of creating database maintenance plans in more detail.

SQL Server Logs

The SQL Server Logs node provides you with information about processes that have run. By viewing a log, you can determine whether each task completed successfully. Each time you start the server, SQL Server creates a new log file. It keeps the last six logs. SQL Server stores logs as text files. The most recent log has an extension of .1. The next most recent has an extension of .2, and so on (see Figure 4.24). Chapter 15 covers SQL Server logs in more detail.

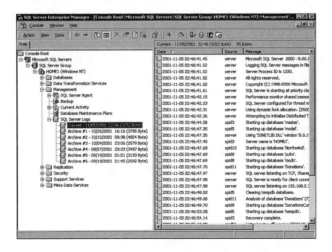

FIGURE 4.24   The SQL Server Logs node displays the logs found on the server.

Replication

The Replication node of the Enterprise Manager allows you to create and manage replication tasks. Replication allows you to publish data to other databases or servers. SQL Server includes wizards to assist you with the replication process. The Publication subnode of the replication node allows you to define a set of objects that you want to replicate. The Subscription subnode allows you to request a publication from another database or server. Books devoted to SQL Server, such as *Microsoft SQL Server 2000 DBA Survival Guide*, cover replication in more detail.

Security

The Security node of the Enterprise Manager allows you to manage security for the server. The Security node includes Logins, Server Roles, Linked Servers, and Remote Servers subnodes. The text that follows briefly discusses each of these subnodes. Chapter 9, "SQL Server Security," covers SQL Server security in additional detail.

Logins

You must grant a user a login so that he can gain access to the server or any of its objects. The Logins subnode of the Security node allows you to manage the logins for the server. After you establish a login, you can then assign the login to roles or grant permissions to that login.

Server Roles

SQL Server contains built-in server roles. These server roles possess predefined rights. You can add users to the predefined server roles. Those users obtain the rights that the role possesses.

Linked Servers

Using linked servers, you can gain access to any OLE DB data source. The Link Servers subnode of the Security node allows you to create and manage linked servers.

Remote Servers

Whereas linked servers access other data sources, the Remote Servers subnode of the Security node allows you to access other SQL Servers. Using this subnode, you can create and manage remote servers.

Support Services

The Support Services node contains child nodes for the Distributed Transaction Coordinator, Full-Text Search, and SQL Mail. The text that follows discusses each of these subnodes.

Distributed Transaction Coordinator

The Microsoft Distributed Transaction Coordinator (MS DTC) manages transactions that span data sources. This allows you to create client applications that include data from multiple data sources while ensuring the integrity of that data. The MS DTC coordinates the proper completion of the transactions on all of the involved servers, ensuring that all of the updates on all of the servers are completed successfully; if not, the entire process is rolled back.

Full-Text Search

The Full-Text Search subnode allows you to create full-text indexes for word searches in character string data. To accomplish its work, this subnode stores word information for a certain column. That information is used to complete full-text queries that search for a particular word or for a combination of words.

> **NOTE**
>
> The default SQL Server installation process does not install the Full-Text Search feature. You might need to run the SQL Server install to add this feature.

SQL Mail

SQL Mail is a service that enables the SQL Server to utilize e-mail functionality via any MAPI-compliant e-mail host. Using SQL Mail, you can connect to Microsoft Exchange Server, Windows NT mail, or any POP3 server. You can then generate messages using stored procedures, triggers, jobs, and alerts. SQL Server books such as *Microsoft SQL Server 2000 DBA Survival Guide* cover SQL Mail in more detail.

Meta Data Services

Microsoft referred to Meta Data Services as the Repository in SQL 7.0. Meta Data Services stores SQL Server metadata. *Metadata* refers to data about data. This service stores data needed by DTS, OLAP, and other tools.

Introduction to the Query Analyzer

The Query Analyzer is probably the second-most-used tool that ships with SQL Server (the first is Enterprise Manager). The SQL Server 2000 Query Analyzer is both robust and easy to use. Figure 4.25 shows the SQL Server 2000 Query Analyzer. This powerful tool provides a graphical user interface for interactively creating, running, and debugging T-SQL statements. The Query Analyzer allows you to:

- View existing SQL Server objects in an object browser

- View T-SQL in a color-coded environment

- Use templates to create T-SQL statements

- Execute statements from multiple connections

- Easily debug your stored procedures

- View a graphical diagram of your query execution plans

- Load the Index Tuning Wizard, a tool that determines whether the process of adding indexes will improve the performance of a query

FIGURE 4.25   The Query Analyzer provides a graphical user interface for interactively creating, running, and debugging Transact-SQL statements.

You can launch the Query Analyzer from the Start menu or from within the Enterprise Manager. Here's the process:

1. To launch from the Start menu, select Start, Programs, Microsoft SQL Server, Query Analyzer. To launch Query Analyzer from within Enterprise Manager, select Tools, Query Analyzer. If you launch Query Analyzer from the Start menu, the Connect to SQL Server dialog box appears (see Figure 4.26).

2. Select a server from the SQL Server drop-down menu, or type **SERVERNAME\Instance name.**

3. Designate whether you want to connect using Windows NT authentication or SQL Server authentication. If you select SQL Server authentication, you must enter a valid login name and case-sensitive password. Click OK. The SQL Query Analyzer appears, as in Figure 4.25.

FIGURE 4.26 The Connect to SQL Server dialog box allows you to log on to the designated server.

If the login fails, the message in either Figure 4.27 or Figure 4.28 appears. The message in Figure 4.27 indicates that the user supplied an invalid login. The message in Figure 4.28 indicates that the SQL Server service for the specified server is not running or that you typed the server name incorrectly.

FIGURE 4.27 The error message that appears when you type the username or password incorrectly.

FIGURE 4.28 The error message that appears when the specified server is not found or when the SQL Server service for the specified server is not running.

When you have successfully connected to the server, you are ready to run SQL queries. You can either type SQL statements in the Query window or click the Load SQL Script tool to open an existing SQL script file. When you are ready to execute the SQL statement(s), simply click the Execute button. If the Query window contains multiple statements, you can highlight the statements that you want to execute. Here's an example of how you can execute a simple SQL statement:

1. Click the New Query tool to create a new query.

2. Select Northwind from the Database drop-down menu.

3. Type the following in the Query window:

    `SELECT CustomerID, CompanyName, ContactTitle FROM Customers`

4. Click the Execute button. The results appear in Figure 4.29.

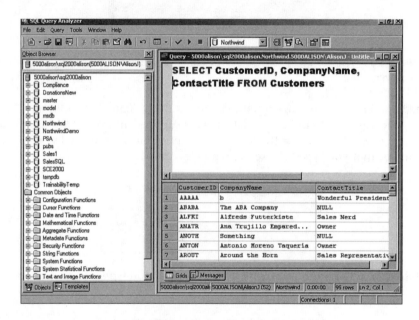

FIGURE 4.29   The SQL Query Analyzer after running a simple query.

Introduction to the Profiler

The SQL Server Profiler (pictured in Figure 4.30) is a tool that you can use to capture SQL Server events. It allows you to:

- Diagnose bottlenecks in slow-running queries

- Determine the cause of deadlocks or blocking

- Troubleshoot problems between client and server applications

- Run security audits to record login attempts

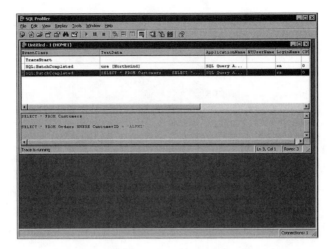

FIGURE 4.30   The SQL Server Profiler allows you to capture SQL Server events.

To launch the Profiler, select Tools, SQL Profiler while in Enterprise Manager, or select Profiler under the Microsoft SQL Server program group on the Start menu. To create a trace that keeps track of everything important to SQL Server events:

1. Select File, New, Trace. The Connect to SQL Server dialog box appears.

2. Enter login information and click OK. The Trace Properties dialog box appears (see Figure 4.31).

FIGURE 4.31   The General tab of the Trace Properties dialog box allows you to designate general properties for the trace.

3. Enter a name for the trace on the General tab.

4. Click the Events tab and designate the event classes that you want to trace (see Figure 4.32).

FIGURE 4.32   The Events tab allows you to designate the event classes that you want to trace.

5. Click the Data Columns tab and specify the columns that you want to capture (see Figure 4.33).

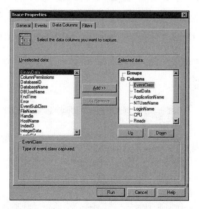

FIGURE 4.33   The Data Columns tab allows you to specify the columns that you want to capture.

6. Click the Filters tab and designate the criteria for the events that you want to capture (see Figure 4.34).

7. After you have designated all of the appropriate options, click Run. The Trace window then shows you all activity for the selected trace (see Figure 4.35).

FIGURE 4.34   The Filters tab allows you to designate the criteria for the events that you want to capture.

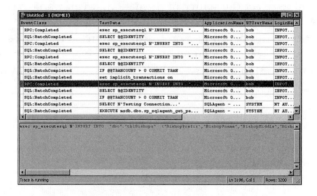

FIGURE 4.35   The Trace window shows you all activity for the selected trace.

NOTE

Chapter 15 covers the SQL Server Profiler in more detail.

Introduction to Data Transformation Services

Data Transformation Services is more commonly known as DTS. It is SQL Server's tool for importing, exporting, and transforming data. In addition to its ability to transfer data, DTS is also capable of transferring indexes, triggers, rules, defaults, constraints, views, stored procedures, and user-defined data types.

When using DTS, you can either run the wizard to perform an isolated import or export, or you can save the import or export specification as a package. A package contains collections of connections, DTS tasks, DTS transformations, and workflow constraints. It is made up of one or more steps that DTS executes when it runs the package. You can schedule a package to run at specified periods of time. Furthermore, DTS exposes a COM object model, allowing you to easily run a DTS package from your application code.

To run the DTS Import/Export Wizard:

1. Right-click the Data Transformation Services node of the Enterprise Manager tree and select All Tasks. Select either Import Data or Export Data, depending on the task that you want to perform. The Data Transformation Services Import/Export Wizard launches. This example illustrates the process of import-ing data.

2. Click Next. The Choose a Data Source step of the wizard appears. This step allows you to select the source of the data that you want to copy (see Figure 4.36). Enter the appropriate information and click Next. Note that the required information varies depending on the data source selected. Figure 4.36 shows this step of the wizard when you select SQL Server as the data source. Figure 4.37 shows this step of the wizard when you select Microsoft Access as the data source.

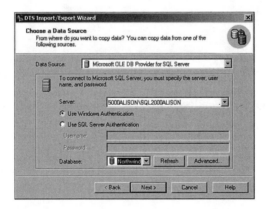

FIGURE 4.36   The first step of the Import/Export Wizard allows you to select the source of the data that you want to copy.

3. The next step of the wizard allows you to designate all of the destination infor-mation for the data (see Figure 4.38). As with the Choose a Data Source step, the required information varies depending upon the data source that you select. Supply all of the required information and click Next.

4. The next step of the wizard prompts you to designate what you want to copy (see Figure 4.39). Designate the appropriate option and click Next.

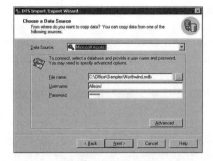

FIGURE 4.37   The first step of the wizard looks like this when you select Microsoft Access as the data source.

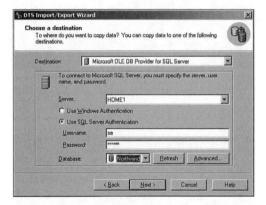

FIGURE 4.38   The next step of the wizard allows you to designate all of the destination information for the data.

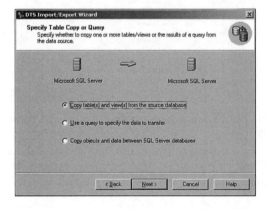

FIGURE 4.39   The next step of the wizard prompts you to designate what you want to copy.

5. The next step varies quite a bit depending upon which option you selected. If you opt to copy a table(s) and view(s) from the source database, the wizard appears as in Figure 4.40. This is where you can select source and destination tables as well as define data transformations (see Figure 4.41).

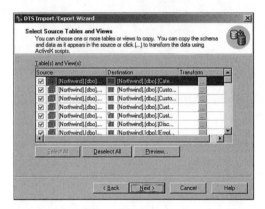

FIGURE 4.40 If you opt to copy a table(s) and view(s) from the source database, the wizard appears like this.

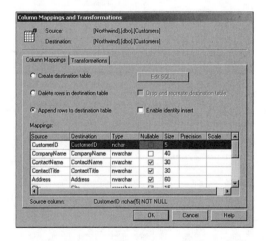

FIGURE 4.41 If you opt to define data transformations, the wizard looks like this.

If you opt to use a query to specify the data to transfer, the wizard appears as in Figure 4.42, allowing you to create a SQL statement that is used as criteria for the transfer.

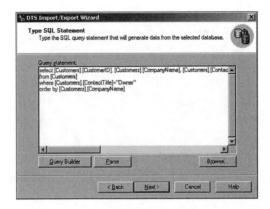

FIGURE 4.42 If you opt to use a query to specify the data to transfer, the wizard appears like this.

Finally, if you opt to copy objects and data between SQL Server databases (available only if you are copying from one SQL Server database to another), the wizard appears, as in Figure 4.43. After you have entered the required information, click Next.

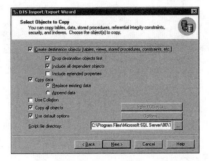

FIGURE 4.43 If you opt to copy objects and data between SQL Server databases, the wizard looks like this.

6. The next step of the wizard allows you to determine when the transfer occurs (see Figure 4.44). You can also opt to create a DTS package. Enter the required information and click Next.

7. The final step of the wizard presents you with all of the information that you entered (see Figure 4.45). After verifying the information, click Finish. DTS executes the package.

FIGURE 4.44   This next step of the wizard allows you to determine when the transfer occurs.

FIGURE 4.45   The final step of the wizard presents you with all of the information that you entered.

Configuring the Server

Many server properties are available. These properties allow you to determine various aspects of how the server behaves. To configure the server:

1. From with the Enterprise Manager, expand the list of servers until you can see the server that you want to configure (see Figure 4.46).

2. Right-click the name of the server that you want to configure and select Properties. The SQL Server Properties dialog box appears (see Figure 4.47).

3. Click the appropriate tab to configure the desired options.

4. Click OK when done.

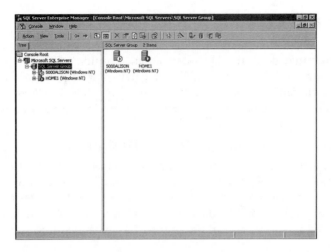

FIGURE 4.46   Expand the list of servers until you can see the server that you want to configure.

FIGURE 4.47   The SQL Server Properties dialog box allows you to designate configuration options for the server.

NOTE

Chapter 15 covers the process of configuring the server in more detail.

Designing and Creating a SQL Server Database

Many people believe that database tools are so easy to use that database design is something that they don't need to worry about. I couldn't disagree more! Just as a house without a foundation will fall over, a database with poorly designed tables and relationships will fail to meet the needs of the users. Therefore, before you learn how to create a SQL Server database, you must first learn database design principles.

The History of Relational Database Design

Dr. E.F. Codd first introduced formal relational database design in 1969 while he was at IBM. He based it on set theory and predicate logic. Relational theory applies to both databases and database applications. Codd developed 12 rules that determine how well an application and its data adhere to the relational model. Since Codd first conceived these 12 rules, the number of rules has expanded into the hundreds!

Goals of Relational Database Design

The number one goal of relational database design is to, as closely as possible, develop a database that models some real-world system. This involves breaking the real-world system into tables and fields and determining how the tables relate to each other. Although this might on the surface appear to be a trivial task, it can be an extremely cumbersome process to translate a real-world system into tables and fields.

A properly designed database has many benefits. A properly designed database greatly facilitates the process of adding, editing, deleting, and retrieving table data. Reports are easy to build. Most important, the database becomes easy to modify and maintain.

Rules of Relational Database Design

You must follow certain rules if you want to adhere to the relational model. These rules determine what is stored in a table and how the tables are related.

The Rules of Tables

Each table in a system must store data about a single entity. An entity usually represents a real-life object or event. Examples of objects are customers, employees, and inventory items. Examples of events include orders, appointments, and doctor visits.

The Rules of Uniqueness and Keys

Tables are composed of rows and columns. To adhere to the relational model, each table must contain a unique identifier. Without a unique identifier, it becomes programmatically impossible to uniquely address a row. You guarantee uniqueness in a table by designating a *primary key*, which is a single column or a set of columns that uniquely identifies a row in a table.

Each column or set of columns in a table that contains unique values is considered a *candidate key*. One candidate key becomes the *primary key*. The remaining candidate keys become *alternate keys*. A primary key made up of one column is considered a simple key. A primary key comprising multiple columns is considered a *composite key*.

It is generally a good idea to pick a primary key that is:

- Minimal (has as few columns as possible)
- Stable (rarely changes)
- Simple (is familiar to the user)

Following these rules greatly improves the performance and maintainability of your database application, particularly if you are dealing with large volumes of data.

Consider the example of an employee table. An employee table is generally composed of employee-related fields such as Social Security number, first name, last name, hire date, salary, and so on. You could consider the combination of the first name and the last name fields a primary key. This choice might work until the company hires two employees with the same name. Although you could combine the first and last names with additional fields to constitute uniqueness (for example, hire date), this would violate the rule of keeping the primary key minimal. Furthermore, an employee might get married, and her last name might change.

Using a name as the primary key violates the principle of stability. The Social Security number might be a valid choice, but a foreign employee might not have a Social Security number. This is a case where a derived rather than natural primary key is appropriate. A derived key is an artificial key that you create. A natural key is one that is already part of the database.

I suggest adding an EmployeeID as an AutoNumber field. Although the field would violate the rule of simplicity (because an employee number is meaningless to the user), it is both small and stable. Because it is numeric, it is also efficient to process. In fact, I use AutoNumber fields (an identity field in SQL Server) as primary keys for most of the tables that I build.

Foreign Keys and Domains

A *foreign key* in a table is the field that relates to the primary key in a second table. For example, the CustomerID is the primary key in the Customers table. It is the foreign key in the Orders table.

A *domain* is a pool of values from which columns are drawn. A simple example of a domain is the specific data range of employee hire dates. In the case of the Order table, the domain of the CustomerID column is the range of values for the CustomerID in the Customers table.

Normalization and Normal Forms

One of the most difficult decisions that you face as a developer is what tables to create and what fields to place in each table, as well as how to relate the tables that you create. *Normalization* is the process of applying a series of rules to ensure that your database achieves optimal structure. Normal forms are a progression of these rules. Each successive normal form achieves a better database design than the previous form did. Although there are several levels of normal forms, it is generally sufficient to apply only the first three levels of normal forms. The following sections describe the first three levels of normal forms.

First Normal Form

To achieve first normal form, all columns in a table must be atomic. This means, for example, that you cannot store the first name and last name in the same field. The reason for this rule is that data becomes very difficult to manipulate and retrieve if multiple values are stored in a single field. Using the full name as an example, it would become impossible to sort by first name or last name independently if both values are stored in the same field. Furthermore, you must perform extra work to extract just the first name or the last name from the field.

Another requirement for first normal form is that the table must not contain repeating values. An example of repeating values is a scenario in which Item1, Quantity1, Item2, Quantity2, Item3, and Quantity3 fields are all found within the Orders table (see Figure 4.48). This design introduces several problems. What if the user wants to add a fourth item to the order? Furthermore, finding the total ordered for a product requires searching several columns. In fact, all numeric and statistical calculations on the table become extremely cumbersome. The alternative, shown in Figure 4.49, achieves first normal form. Notice that each item ordered is located in a separate row.

OrderID	CustomerID	OrderDate	Item1	Quantity1	Item2	Quantity2	Item3	Quantity3
1	1	5/1/2001	Widget	2	Hammer	5	Diskette	7
2	2	5/1/2001	Horn	4	Car	8	Computer	2
3	1	5/7/2001	Calendar	8	Painting	2	Book	3
4	3	5/18/2001	Boat	2	Leaf	3	Hat	8
(AutoNumber)	0			0		0		0

FIGURE 4.48   This table contains repeating groups. Repeating groups make it difficult to summarize and manipulate table data.

Second Normal Form

To achieve second normal form, all nonkey columns must be fully dependent on the primary key. In other words, each table must store data about only one subject. Notice the table shown in Figure 4.49. It includes information about the order (OrderID, CustomerID, and OrderDate) and information about the items that the customer is ordering (Item and Quantity). To achieve second normal form, this data must be broken into two tables: an orders table and an order detail table. The process of breaking the data into two tables is called *decomposition*. It is considered to be *nonloss* decomposition because no data is lost during the decomposition process. After the data is broken into two tables, you can easily bring the data back together by joining the two tables in a query. Figure 4.50 shows the data broken up into two tables. These two tables achieve second normal form.

OrderID	OrderItemID	CustomerID	OrderDate	Item	Quantity
1	1	1	5/1/2001	Widget	2
2	2	1	5/1/2001	Horn	4
3	3	1	5/1/2001	Calendar	8
4	1	2	5/18/2001	Boat	2
5	2	2	5/18/2001	Car	1
6	1	1	6/2/2001	Horse	2
7	2	1	6/2/2001	Computer	5
8	3	1	6/2/2001	Chair	6
9	1	3	7/4/2001	Book	2
10	2	3	7/4/2001	Chair	3
11	3	3	7/4/2001	Widget	2
12	4	3	7/4/2001	Painting	3
(AutoNumber)	0	0			0

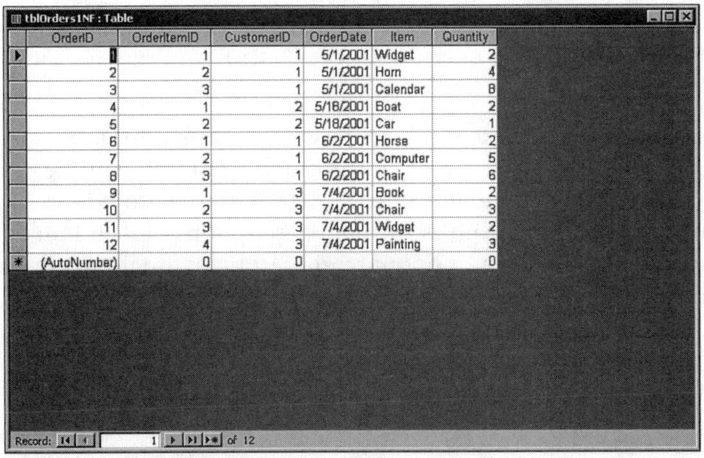

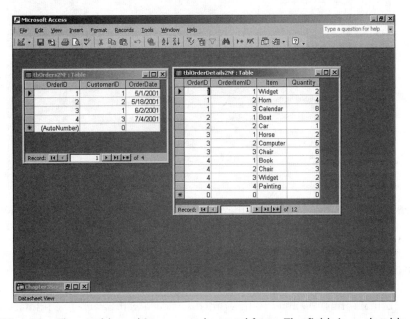

FIGURE 4.49 This table achieves first normal form. Notice that all fields are atomic and that the table contains no repeating groups.

OrderID	CustomerID	OrderDate
1	1	5/1/2001
2	2	5/18/2001
3	1	6/2/2001
4	3	7/4/2001
(AutoNumber)	0	

OrderID	OrderItemID	Item	Quantity
1	1	Widget	2
1	2	Horn	4
1	3	Calendar	8
2	1	Boat	2
2	2	Car	1
3	1	Horse	2
3	2	Computer	5
3	3	Chair	6
4	1	Book	2
4	2	Chair	3
4	3	Widget	2
4	4	Painting	3
0	0		0

FIGURE 4.50 These tables achieve second normal form. The fields in each table pertain to the primary key of the table.

Third Normal Form

To attain third normal form, a table must meet all of the requirements for first and second normal form, and all nonkey columns must be mutually independent. This means that you must eliminate any calculations, and you must break out data into lookup tables.

An example of a calculation stored in a table is the product of price multiplied by quantity. Rather than storing the result of this calculation in the table, you would generate the calculation in a query, or in the control source of a control on a form or a report.

The example in Figure 4.50 does not achieve third normal form because the description of the inventory items is stored in the order details table. If the description changes, the user needs to modify all rows with that inventory item. The order detail table, shown in Figure 4.51, shows the item descriptions broken into an inventory table. This design achieves third normal form. All fields are mutually independent. The user can modify the description of an inventory item in one place.

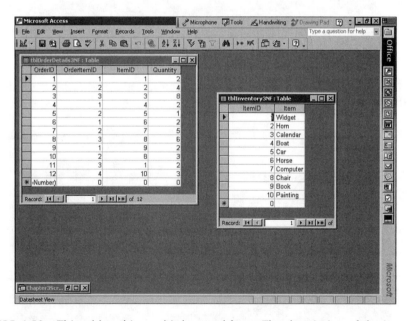

FIGURE 4.51   This table achieves third normal form. The description of the inventory items is moved to an inventory table, and the ItemID is stored in the order details table.

Denormalization—Purposely Violating the Rules

Although the developer's goal is normalization, many times it makes sense to deviate from normal forms. We refer to this process as *denormalization*. The primary reason for applying denormalization is to enhance performance.

An example of when denormalization might be the preferred tact could involve an open invoices table and a summarized accounting table. It might be impractical to calculate summarized accounting information for a customer when the user needs it. The system maintains summary calculations in a summarized accounting table so that the system can easily retrieve them as needed. Although the upside of this scenario is improved performance, the downside is that the system must update the summary table whenever changes are made to the open invoices. This imposes a definite trade-off between performance and maintainability. You must decide whether the trade-off is worth it.

If you decide to denormalize, document your decision. Make sure that you make the necessary application adjustments to ensure that the system properly maintains denormalized fields. Finally, test to ensure that performance is actually improved by the denormalization process.

Integrity Rules

Although integrity rules are not part of normal forms, they are definitely part of the database design process. Integrity rules are broken into two categories. They include overall integrity rules and database-specific integrity rules.

Overall Rules

The two types of overall integrity rules are referential integrity rules and entity integrity rules. Referential integrity rules dictate that a database does not contain any orphan foreign key values. This means that:

- Child rows cannot be added for parent rows that do not exist. In other words, an order cannot be added for a nonexistent customer.

- A primary key value cannot be modified if the value is used as a foreign key in a child table. This means that a CustomerID cannot be changed if the orders table contains rows with that CustomerID.

- A parent row cannot be deleted if child rows are found with that foreign key value. For example, a customer cannot be deleted if the customer has orders in the orders table.

Entity integrity dictates that the primary key value cannot be null. This rule applies not only to single-column primary keys, but also to multicolumn primary keys. In fact, in a multicolumn primary key, no field in the primary key can be null. This makes sense because, if any part of the primary key can be null, the primary key can no longer act as a unique identifier for the row. Fortunately, SQL Server does not allow a field in a primary key to be null.

Database-Specific Rules

The other set of rules applied to a database are not applicable to all databases, but, instead, are dictated by business rules that apply to a specific application. Database-specific rules are as important as overall integrity rules. They ensure that the user enters only valid data into a database. An example of a database-specific integrity rule is that the delivery date for an order must fall after the order date.

Creating Databases

Now that you know the theory behind database design, you are ready to build your first database. Although you can use T-SQL to create a database, the Enterprise Manager provides the easiest way to create a database. Here are the steps involved:

1. Expand the server node to view the Databases node.

2. Right-click the Databases node and select New Database. The Database Properties dialog box appears (see Figure 4.52).

FIGURE 4.52   The General tab of the Database Properties dialog box allows you to enter the name of the database.

3. Enter a name for the database on the General tab. The name must be unique for that server.

4. Select a collation name. The collation name dictates the language and sort order for the data. Although the collation name defaults to the collation that you designated when you installed SQL Server, you can designate a different collation name for each database on a server. Click the Data Files tab (see Figure 4.53).

5. Enter the name, location, initial size, and filegroup information.

6. Designate the File Properties for the file (for example, the maximum size). Notice that you can have SQL Server automatically grow the file as needed to accommodate the data within the database.

FIGURE 4.53   The Data Files tab of the Database Properties dialog box allows you to enter the name, location, initial size, and filegroup information for the database.

7. Click the Transaction Log tab (see Figure 4.54) and designate the name, location, initial size, and filegroup information for the log file.

FIGURE 4.54   The Transaction Log tab of the Database Properties dialog box allows you to designate the name, location, initial size, and filegroup information for the log file.

8. Click OK to create the database.

The transaction log is an integral part of SQL Server. Each time that you create a new database, SQL Server automatically creates a transaction log. As users access the database, SQL Server records all database activity in the transaction log. Here's how it works:

1. The user makes a change.

2. SQL Server records the change in the transaction log.

3. The data pages that SQL Server will modify are read into the in-memory storage cache.

4. SQL Server makes the changes to the cached pages.

5. A checkpoint process occurs in which SQL Server writes the changes to disk.

If a system failure occurs, you perform the following process:

1. Restore the backup file.

2. Apply transactions from the transaction log.

With this process, you are easily restored to the condition that you were in just before the crash.

NOTE

You should always place the transaction log on a different device from that of the primary data files. The main reason for this philosophy is that if the device containing the data fails, the transaction log does you no good if you place it on the same device as the data.

Configuring Database Properties

After you create the database, you can modify many of its properties. Simply right-click the database and select Properties. The Database Properties dialog box appears, this time with three additional tabs: Filegroups, Options, and Permissions (see Figure 4.55).

FIGURE 4.55   The Database Properties dialog box with three additional tabs: Filegroups, Options, and Permissions.

The Filegroups tab allows you to create and modify filegroup information (see the section "Files and Filegroups" for more information). To add a filegroup, simply type its name on a new line of the Filegroups tab. Click OK to close the dialog box. Figure

4.56 shows a filegroup called MyNewFileGroup being added. You must then select the filegroup from the Filegroup drop-down list on the Data Files tab.

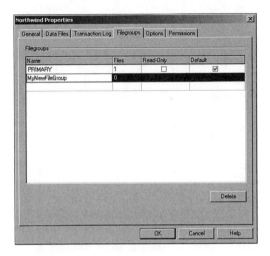

FIGURE 4.56 To add a filegroup, simply type its name on a new line of the Filegroups tab.

Figure 4.57 shows the new filegroup being selected from the Data Files tab. The Options tab allows you to modify important database options (see Figure 4.58). Finally, the Permissions tab allows you to designate the permissions that each role has for the database (see Figure 4.59).

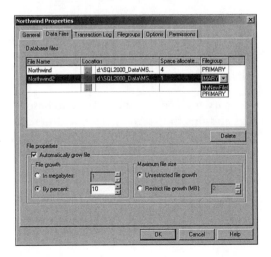

FIGURE 4.57 After you add a filegroup, you must then select it from the Filegroup drop-down on the Data Files tab.

FIGURE 4.58   The Options tabFilegroups allows you to modify important database information.

FIGURE 4.59   The Permissions tab allows you to designate the permissions that each role has for the database.

Files and Filegroups

SQL Server creates a primary file when you create a database. You have the option of creating additional files and filegroups. You place the different files and filegroups on different devices. This serves to improve the performance of the database because multiple hardware devices can access the data simultaneously.

Summary

SQL Server is a very powerful database tool. Many editions are available. This chapter helped you to determine the appropriate edition for you. A major component of SQL Server is the Enterprise Manager. Using this powerful tool, you can manage most aspects of SQL Server. The chapter gave you a tour of Enterprise Manager, highlighting the components that are most frequently used by Access developers. It also introduced you to the Query Analyzer, Profiler, and Data Transformation Services, all tools that can help you to get your job done more effectively. Finally, you learned how to configure the server and how to create SQL Server databases.

5

SQL Server Tables and Database Diagrams

Why This Chapter Is Important

Once you have created a database, you are ready to add other objects to it. Generally, the first objects that you add to a database are the tables that it contains. After you add the tables, you establish relationships between them. This chapter shows you how to create tables. When you understand how to create tables, you will want to refine the properties of those tables. The chapter shows you how to create defaults and how to add and modify constraints. You will also learn how to create your own data types and how to add and modify indexes. Finally, you will learn how to use database diagrams to establish relationships between the tables contained in your databases.

Creating SQL Server Tables

Tables in a SQL Server database are similar to tables in Microsoft Access. Each table is made up of rows and columns. As with Access, we refer to columns as fields. Each field has a unique name and contains a specific piece of information about the row. Each table in a SQL Server database must have a unique name.

To create a table:

1. Within Enterprise Manager, right-click the Tables node of the database to which you want to add a table and select New Table. The Table Designer appears (see Figure 5.1).

2. Enter the column names, data types, and length for each field in the table.

3. Designate whether each field allows null.

4. Enter the other properties for the table.

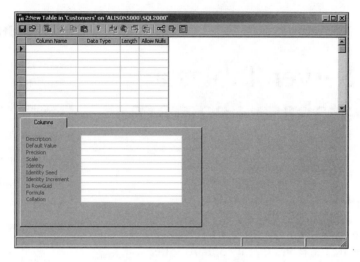

FIGURE 5.1 The Table Designer allows you to enter the column names, data types, length, and other properties for each field in the table.

One of the most important properties of a column in a table is the data type. If you do not select the correct data type for a field, the rest of your design efforts will be futile. This is because the data type determines what data you can store in the field. Table 5.1 outlines the available field types and the type of information that each data type can contain.

TABLE 5.1 Field Types and Appropriate Uses

Field Type	Description	Storage
Bigint	New to SQL Server 2000. Can hold numbers ranging from -2^{63} to $2^{63} - 1$.	8 bytes.
Binary	Holds from 1 to 8,000 bytes of fixed-length binary data.	Whatever is in the column, plus 4 additional bytes.
Bit	Can hold a value of either 1 or 0. Nulls not allowed.	8-bit fields take up 1 byte of data.
Char	Holds from 1 to 8,000 bytes of fixed-length non-Unicode characters.	The number of bytes corresponds to the length of the field (regardless of what is stored in it).
DateTime	Holds valid dates from January 1, 1753 to December 31, 9999.	4 bytes.
Decimal	Used for numbers with fixed precision and scale. When maximum precision is used, values can range from $-10^{38} - 1$ to $10^{38} - +1$. Scale must be less than or equal to the precision.	Depends on the precision.

TABLE 5.1   Continued

Field Type	Description	Storage
Float	Can hold positive and negative numbers from −1.79E + 308 to 1.79E + 308. It offers binary precision up to 15 digits.	8 bytes.
Image	Consists of linked data pages of binary data. It can contain up to 2,147,483,647 bytes of binary data.	Depends on what is stored in it.
Int	Can store *whole* numbers from −2,147,483,648 to 2,147,483,647.	4 bytes.
Money	Can store decimal data ranging from −263 to 263 − 1, scaled to four digits of precision. It offers accuracy to 1/10,000 of a monetary unit.	8 bytes.
NChar	Can contain from 1 to 4,000 Unicode characters.	Twice the amount of bytes of Char. Corresponds to the length of the field (regardless of what is stored in it).
NText	Can hold data up to 1,073,741,823 Unicode characters.	Each character takes 2 bytes of storage.
Numeric	Used for numbers with fixed precision and scale. When maximum precision values can range from $−10^{38} − 1$ to $10^{38} − +1$.	Depends on the precision.
NVarChar	Can contain from 1 to 4,000 Unicode characters.	2 bytes per character stored.
Real	A smaller version of float. Contains a single-precision floating-point number from −3.40E + 38 to 3.40E + 38.	4 bytes.
SmallDateTime	Consists of two 2-byte integers. Can store dates only between 1/1/1900 and 6/6/2079.	4 bytes.
SmallInt	A smaller version of int. Can store values between −32,768 and 32,767.	2 bytes.
SmallMoney	A smaller version of money. Can store decimal data scaled to four digits of precision. Can store values from −214,748.3648 to +214,748.3647.	4 bytes.

TABLE 5.1   Continued

Field Type	Description	Storage
SQL_Variant	New to SQL 2000. Can store `int`, `binary`, and `char` values. Is a very inefficient data type.	Varies.
Text	Stores up to 2,147,483,647 characters of non-Unicode data.	1 byte for each character of storage.
TimeStamp	Generates a unique binary value that SQL Server automatically creates when a row is inserted and that SQL Server updates every time that the row is edited.	8 bytes.
TinyInt	Stores whole numbers from 0 to 255.	1 byte.
UniqueIdentifier	A globally unique identifier (GUID) that is automatically generated using the `NEWID( )` function.	16 bytes.
VarBinary	Can hold variable-length binary data from 1 to 8000 bytes.	Varies from 1 to 8000 bytes.
VarChar	A variable-length string that can hold 1 to 8,000 non-Unicode characters.	1 byte per character stored.

Working with Constraints

Constraints limit or control the types of data that can be entered into your tables. There are seven main categories of constraints. They include primary key constraints, foreign key constraints, default constraints, not null constraints, check constraints, rules, and unique constraints. The text that follows covers each of these constraint types in detail.

Primary Key Constraints

A primary key constraint is a column or a set of columns that uniquely identify a row in the table. Although you can designate more than one field as the primary key, each table can have only one primary key.

Every table in your database should have a primary key constraint. Furthermore, it is best if your primary key meets the following criteria:

- Short

- Stable

- Simple

Short means that it should be composed of as few fields as possible and the smaller the field type is, the better. In fact, the optimal primary key is a single int field. *Stable* means that the data within the field never changes. A great candidate for a primary key is an identity column. The "Identity Columns" section of this chapter covers identity columns in detail. *Simple* means that it is easy to remember and deal with. For example, an int field is simple, whereas a char field containing a long string of complex characters is not.

To add a primary key to a table:

1. Use the gray selectors on the left side of the Table Designer to select the fields that comprise the primary key (see Figure 5.2).

2. Click the Set Primary Key tool on the toolbar. The columns appear with a Key icon on the record selector (see Figure 5.3).

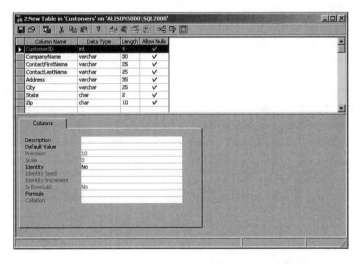

FIGURE 5.2   Use the gray selectors on the left side of the Table Designer to select the fields that comprise the primary key.

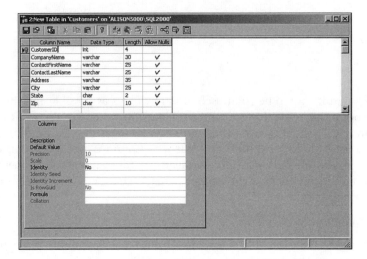

FIGURE 5.3   The columns included in the primary key appear with a Key icon on the record selector.

Foreign Key Constraints

A foreign key constraint consists of a column or of a set of columns that participates in a relationship with a primary key table. The primary key is on the *one side* of the relationship, whereas the foreign key is on the *many side* of the relationship. Whereas a table can have only one primary key, it can have multiple foreign keys. Each foreign key relates to a different primary key in a separate table. SQL Server looks up the foreign key value in the primary key table to ensure that only valid data is included in the table. The section of this chapter titled "Working with Database Diagrams" covers foreign key constraints in additional detail.

Default Constraints

A default constraint is a value that SQL Server automatically places in a particular field in a table. A default value can be a constant, null, or a function. All fields except identity and time stamp fields can contain default values. Each column can have one default constraint. You enter the default constraint in the properties for the desired field (see Figure 5.4).

Table 5.2 shows examples of default constraints.

TABLE 5.2   Examples of Default Constraints

Expression	Result
GetDate()	Sets the default value to the current date
Null	Sets the default value to null
7	Sets the default value to the number 7
'Hello'	Sets the default value to the string "Hello"

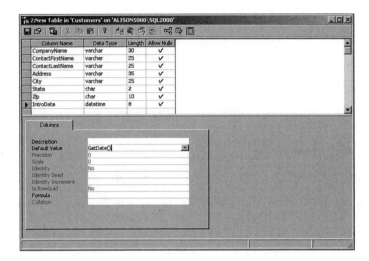

FIGURE 5.4   You enter the default constraint in the properties for the desired field.

Not Null Constraints

In certain situations, you will want to require the user to enter data into a field. The Not Null constraint allows you to accomplish this task. To set a Not Null constraint, ensure that you uncheck the Allow Nulls check box (see Figure 5.5).

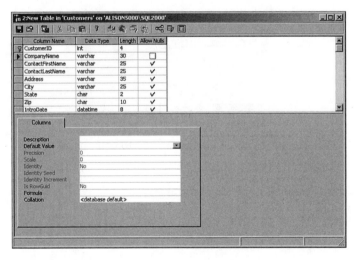

FIGURE 5.5   To set a Not Null constraint, ensure that the Allow Nulls check box is unchecked.

Check Constraints

Check constraints limit the range of values that a user can enter into a column. You can enter as many check constraints as you want for a particular column. SQL Server evaluates the check constraints in the order in which you entered them. To enter a check constraint:

1. Click the Manage Constraints tool on the toolbar. The Properties dialog box appears with the Check Constraints tab selected.

2. Click New to add a new constraint.

3. Provide a constraint name and a constraint expression.

4. Designate other options as necessary. The completed dialog box appears as in Figure 5.6.

5. Click Close to close the dialog box and add the constraint.

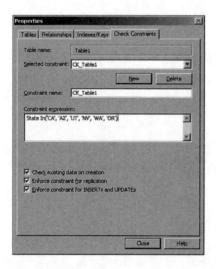

FIGURE 5.6   The Properties dialog box allows you to enter check constraints for the table.

Table 5.3 shows examples of check constraints.

TABLE 5.3   Examples of Check Constraints

Expression	Result
`@State In('CA', 'AZ', 'UT', 'CO')`	Limits the value entered to CA, AZ, UT, and CO
`DateEntered <= GetDate()`	Limits the value entered to a date on or before the current date
`CreditLimit Between 0 and 10000`	Limits the value entered to a value between 0 and 10,000

Rules

Whereas check constraints apply only to the table that you enter them for, you can apply rules to multiple tables. To create a rule:

1. Right-click the Rules node for the database and select New Rule. The Rule Properties dialog box appears (see Figure 5.7).

2. Enter the name for the rule and the text for the rule.

3. Click OK.

4. Right-click the rule and select Properties.

5. Click Bind UDTs to bind the rule to user-defined types. The Bind Rule to User-Defined Data Types dialog box appears (see Figure 5.8). Alternately, click Bind Columns to bind the rule to columns in your tables. The Bind Rule to Columns dialog box appears (see Figure 5.9).

6. Click OK when done.

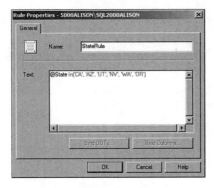

FIGURE 5.7   The Rule Properties dialog box allows you to enter rules that you can apply to multiple tables.

FIGURE 5.8   The Bind Rule to User-Defined Data Types dialog box allows you to bind a rule to a data type.

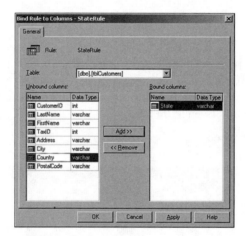

FIGURE 5.9   The Bind Rule to Columns dialog box allows you to bind a rule to one or more columns in your database.

Table 5.4 shows examples of rules.

TABLE 5.4   Examples of Rules

Expression	Result
`@State In('CA', 'AZ', 'UT', 'CO')`	Limits the value entered to CA, AZ, UT, and CO
`@DateEntered <= GetDate()`	Limits the value entered to a date on or before the current date
`@CreditLimit Between 0 and 10000`	Limits the value entered to a value between 0 and 10,000

Unique Constraints

A unique constraint requires that each entry in a particular column be unique. Each table can have 249 unique constraints. You create a unique constraint by creating a unique index. The process of creating unique constraints is covered in the section of this chapter titled "Adding and Modifying Indexes."

Identity Columns

Identity columns provide an autoincrementing value for a table. You should use an identity column as the primary key field for any table that has no natural primary key that is short, stable, and simple. Identity columns are often the int data type. You use the properties of the field to designate a column as an identity column (see Figure 5.10). Notice that once you designate a column as an identity column, you can designate both the identity seed and the identity increment. The identity seed is the starting value for the field. The identity increment is the value by which each automatically assigned value is incremented. For example, an identity field with an identity seed of 100 and an identity increment of 5 will assign the values 100, 105, 110, and so on.

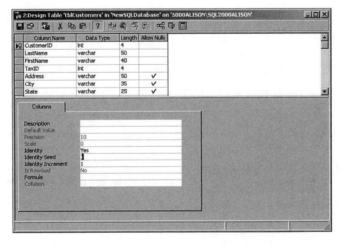

FIGURE 5.10   You use the properties of the field to designate a column as an identity column.

Working with Computed Columns

With computed columns, you can create a column that is based on data in other columns. SQL Server automatically updates the computed column when the columns that it depends on are updated. An example is an extended total that you base on the product of the price and quantity columns. To create a computed column, simply enter the desired formula into the Formula property of the column (see Figure 5.11).

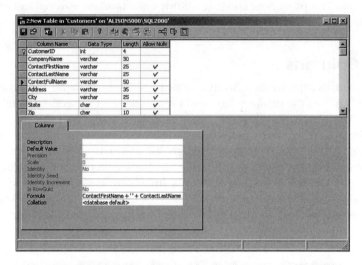

FIGURE 5.11   To create a computed column, simply enter the formula into the Formula property of the column.

Table 5.5 shows examples of computed columns.

TABLE 5.5   Examples of Computed Columns

Expression	Result
Price * Quantity	Calculates the product of the price times the quantity
(Price * Quantity) * (1 - Discount)	Calculates the discounted price
FirstName + ' ' + LastName	Combines the contents of the first and last name fields, separated by a space

Working with User-Defined Data Types

User-defined data types allow you to further refine the data types provided by SQL Server. A user-defined data type is a combination of a data type, length, null constraint, default value, and rule. Once you define a user-defined data type, you can use it in any tables that you build. To create a user-defined data type:

1. Right-click the User-Defined Data Types node and select New User-Defined Data Type. The User-Defined Data Type Properties dialog box appears (see Figure 5.12).

2. Enter the required information and click OK.

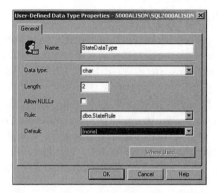

FIGURE 5.12 The User-Defined Data Type Properties dialog box allows you to create or modify a user-defined data type.

To apply a user-defined data type to a field:

1. Go into the design of the table whose field you want to apply the data type to.

2. Open the Data Type drop-down for the field to which you want to apply the data type (see Figure 5.13).

3. Select the user-defined data type.

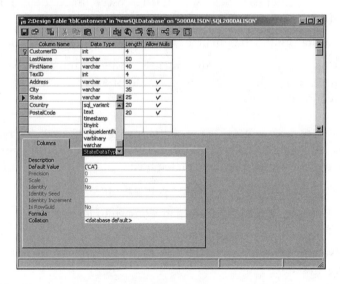

FIGURE 5.13 You can select a user-defined data type as the data type for a field.

As mentioned previously, you can include a rule as part of a user-defined data type. By doing so, you can easily apply the rule to many of the fields that you create. You must first create the rule. You can then select it from the Rule drop-down list in the User-Defined Data Type Properties dialog box.

Adding and Modifying Indexes

You use indexes to improve performance when the user searches a field. Although it's generally best to include too many indexes rather than too few, indexes do have downsides. Indexes speed up searching, sorting, and grouping data. The downside is that they take up hard disk space and slow the process of editing, adding, and deleting data. Although the benefits of indexing outweigh the detriments in most cases, you should not index every field in each table. Create indexes only for fields or combinations of fields on which the user will search or sort. Do not create indexes for fields that contain highly repetitive data. A general rule is to provide indexes for all fields regularly used in searching and sorting, and as criteria for queries.

To create and modify indexes:

1. Modify the design of the table.

2. Click the Manage Indexes/Keys tool on the toolbar. The Properties window appears with the Indexes/Keys tab selected (see Figure 5.14).

3. Click New to create a new index.

4. Enter a name for the index.

5. Select the field or fields on which you want to base the index.

6. Designate whether each field is included in ascending or descending order in the index.

7. Click Create Unique to designate the index as a unique constraint.

8. Click Clustered to designate the index as clustered. You can have only one clustered index per table. The data is physically stored based on the order of the clustered index.

Another way to manage indexes is to use the Manage Indexes dialog box. The Manage Indexes dialog box allows you to easily manage all indexes associated with a table. To invoke the Manage Indexes dialog box:

1. Right-click the table whose indexes you want to manage.

2. Select All Tasks, Manage Indexes. The Manage Indexes dialog box appears (see Figure 5.15).

3. Click New to create a new index, Edit to modify an existing index, or Delete to remove an index.

4. Click Close after making the desired changes.

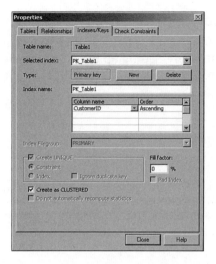

FIGURE 5.14   The Properties window allows you to manage table indexes.

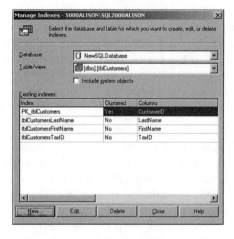

FIGURE 5.15   The Manage Indexes dialog box allows you to manage table indexes.

An Introduction to Triggers

A trigger is a T-SQL statement that SQL Server executes in response to data being edited, inserted, or deleted. Triggers provide you with another way to enforce business rules. They also allow you to perform tasks such as inserting data into an audit log when the user modifies important fields. Chapter 8, "Designing SQL Server Stored Procedures, User-Defined Functions, and Triggers," covers triggers in detail.

An Introduction to Relationships

Three types of relationships can exist between tables in a database: one-to-many, one-to-one, and many-to-many. Setting up the proper type of relationship between two tables in your database is imperative. The right type of relationship between two tables ensures:

- Data integrity

- Optimal performance

- Ease of use in designing system objects

This chapter discusses many reasons behind these benefits. Before you can understand the benefits of relationships, though, you must understand the types of relationships available.

One-to-Many

A one-to-many relationship is by far the most common type of relationship. In a *one-to-many relationship*, a record in one table can have many related records in another table. A common example is a relationship set up between a Customers table and an Orders table. For each customer in the Customers table, you want to have more than one order in the Orders table. On the other hand, each order in the Orders table can belong to only one customer. The Customers table is on the *one side* of the relationship, and the Orders table is on the *many side*. For this relationship to be implemented, the field joining the two tables on the one side of the relationship must be unique.

In the Customers and Orders tables example, the CustomerID field that joins the two tables must be unique within the Customers table. If more than one customer in the Customers table has the same customer ID, it is not clear which customer belongs to an order in the Orders table. For this reason, the field that joins the two tables on the one side of the one-to-many relationship must be a primary key or must have a unique index. In almost all cases, the field relating the two tables is the primary key of the table on the one side of the relationship. The field relating the two tables on the many side of the relationship is called a *foreign key*.

One-to-One

In a one-to-one relationship, each record in the table on the one side of the relationship can have only one matching record in the table on the many side of the relationship. This relationship is not common and is used only in special circumstances. Usually, if you have set up a one-to-one relationship, you should have combined the fields from both tables into one table. The following are the most common reasons why you should create a one-to-one relationship:

- The number of fields required for a table exceeds the number of fields allowed in a SQL Server table.

- Certain fields that are included in a table need to be much more secure than other fields included in the same table.

- Several fields in a table are required for only a subset of records in the table.

The maximum number of fields allowed in a SQL Server table is 1,024. There are very few reasons (if any) why a table should ever have more than 1,024 fields. In fact, before you even get close to 1,024 fields, you should take a close look at the design of your system. On the *very* rare occasion when having more than 1,024 fields is appropriate, you can simulate a single table by moving some of the fields to a second table and creating a one-to-one relationship between the two tables.

The second reason to separate into two tables data that logically would belong in the same table involves security. An example is a table containing employee information. Many users of the system might need to access certain information, such as employee name, address, city, state, ZIP code, home phone, and office extension. Other fields, including the hire date, salary, birth date, and salary level, might be highly confidential. Although you can easily solve this problem using views, in which you create a view with only those fields that all of the users can see, you may opt instead to store the secure fields in a table separate from the less-secure fields.

The last situation in which you would want to define one-to-one relationships occurs when certain fields in a table will be used for only a relatively small subset of records. An example is an Employee table and a Vesting table. Certain fields are required only for vested employees. If only a small percentage of a company's employees are vested, it is not efficient in terms of performance or disk space to place all the fields containing information about vesting in the Employee table. This is especially true if the vesting information requires a large volume of fields. By breaking the information into two tables and creating a one-to-one relationship between them, you can reduce disk-space requirements and improve performance. This improvement is particularly pronounced if the Employee table is large.

Many-to-Many

In a *many-to-many relationship*, records in both tables have matching records in the other table. You cannot directly define a many-to-many relationship; you must develop this type of relationship by adding a table called a *junction table*. You relate the junction table to each of the two tables in one-to-many relationships. An example is an Orders table and a Products table. Each order probably will contain multiple products, and each product is found on many different orders. The solution is to create a third table called Order Details. You relate the Order Details table to the Orders table in a one-to-many relationship based on the OrderID field. You relate the Order Details table to the Products table in a one-to-many relationship based on the ProductID field.

Establishing Relationships Between SQL Server Tables

You can use three methods to create relationships between the tables in your database. The easiest method is to use a database diagram. A database diagram allows you to graphically establish the relationships between the tables in your database. The second method is via the Properties window for a table. Using the Relationships tab of the Properties window, you can easily add, modify, and remove relationships between the tables in your database. Finally, you can establish and maintain relationships using T-SQL code.

Working with Database Diagrams

As mentioned previously, one way that you can establish and maintain relationships between SQL Server tables is to create a database diagram. It is important to understand how to create a database diagram, add tables to it, edit the diagram, and remove tables from the diagram. The sections that follow cover these topics.

Creating a Database Diagram

To create a database diagram:

1. Right-click the Diagrams node and select New Database Diagram. The Create Database Diagram wizard launches. Click Next.

2. Designate the tables that you want to add to the database diagram (see Figure 5.16).

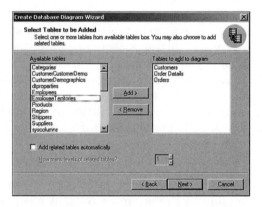

FIGURE 5.16   Designate the tables that you want to add to the database diagram.

3. Indicate whether you want SQL Server to automatically add related tables to the diagram.

4. Designate how many levels of relationships you want SQL Server to include.

5. Click Next and then click Finish to complete the process. The selected tables appear in a database diagram (see Figure 5.17).

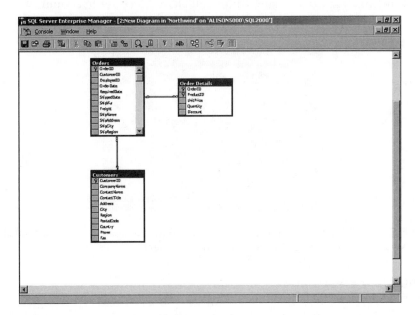

FIGURE 5.17   The completed database diagram shows you the relationship between the included tables.

6. Click and drag from the field(s) in the Primary Key table that you want to relate to the field(s) in the Foreign Key table. The Create Relationship dialog box appears (see Figure 5.18).

FIGURE 5.18   The Create Relationship dialog box allows you to designate the specifics of the relationship that you are creating.

7. When you close the database diagram, SQL Server first prompts you for a name for the diagram. Then the Save dialog box appears (see Figure 5.19), letting you know what tables the relationships will affect. Click Yes to commit the changes to the underlying tables.

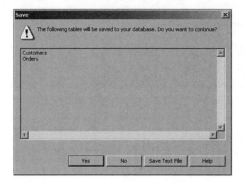

FIGURE 5.19   When you close the database diagram, the Save dialog box appears, letting you know what tables the relationships will affect.

Editing a Database Diagram

To edit the relationship between two tables in a database diagram:

1. Right-click the line between any two tables on the diagram and select Properties.

2. Modify any of the desired properties.

3. Click Close.

Adding Tables to a Database Diagram

To add tables to the database diagram:

1. Click the Add Table on Diagram tool on the toolbar. The Add Table dialog box appears (see Figure 5.20).

FIGURE 5.20   The Add Table dialog box allows you to add additional tables to the database diagram.

2. Select the tables that you want to add to the diagram and click Add.

3. Click Close. SQL Server adds the requested tables to the diagram.

Removing Tables from a Database Diagram
To remove tables from the database diagram:

1. Right-click the table that you want to remove and select Remove Table from Diagram.

2. It is important to note that SQL Server removes the table from the diagram but does not remove the relationship from the database.

NOTE

It is important to understand the correlation between the database diagram and the actual relationships that you have established within the database. A database can contain multiple database diagrams. Each database diagram lets you view and modify the existing relationships. When you establish relationships, SQL Server creates the actual relationship between the tables. You can delete the tables from the database diagram (by right-clicking and selecting Remove Table from Diagram), but the relationships still will exist (permanently removing relationships is covered in the section "Using the Properties Window to Delete a Relationship," later in this chapter). The Database Diagram window provides a visual blueprint of the relationships that you have established. If you modify the layout of the diagram by moving around tables, adding tables to the diagram, or removing tables from the diagram without changing any relationships, SQL Server *still* prompts you to save the changes to the diagram when you close the diagram window. In that case, SQL Server is not asking whether you want to save the relationships that you have established; it is simply asking whether you want to save the visual layout of the window.

Working with the Relationships Tab of the Properties Window
The Relationships tab of the Properties window allows you to maintain relationships between the current table and the other tables in the database. Using the Relationships tab, you can add, edit, and delete table relationships.

Using the Properties Window to Add a Relationship
To use the Properties window to add a relationship:

1. While viewing the design of the table for which you want to establish a relationship, click Manage Relationships. The Properties window appears with the Relationships tab selected (see Figure 5.21).

2. Click New.

3. Provide a name for the relationship.

4. Select the Primary Key table and the Foreign Key table included in the relationship.

5. Designate all of the desired options for the relationship.

6. When you close the table, the Save dialog box appears, letting you know what tables the relationships will affect. Click Yes to commit the changes to the underlying tables.

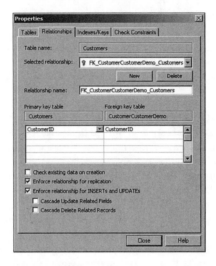

FIGURE 5.21   The Relationships tab of the Properties window allows you to add, modify, and remove table relationships.

Using the Properties Window to Modify a Relationship

You can also use the Relationships tab of the Properties window to modify an existing relationship:

1. While viewing the design of the table for which you want to establish a relationship, click Manage Relationships. The Properties window appears with the Relationships tab selected.

2. Change the primary and/or foreign keys, or modify any of the properties.

3. Click Close to close the Properties window.

4. When you close the table, the Save dialog box appears, letting you know what tables the relationships will affect. Click Yes to commit the changes to the underlying tables.

Using the Properties Window to Delete a Relationship

To use the Properties window to delete a relationship:

1. While viewing the design of the table for which you want to establish a relationship, click Manage Relationships. The Properties window appears with the Relationships tab selected.

2. Use the Selected Relationship drop-down list to select the relationship that you want to delete.

3. Click Delete. You are asked if you really want to delete the relationship. Click Yes.

4. When you close the table, the Save dialog box appears, letting you know what tables the relationships will affect. Click Yes to commit the changes to the underlying tables.

> **TRY IT** Create a new database and add a table called tblCustomers, another called tblOrders, and another called tblOrderDetails. The table should have the following fields:

tblCustomers: CustomerID, CompanyName, Address, City, State, ZipCode

tblOrders: OrderID, CustomerID, OrderDate, ShipVIA

tblOrderDetails: OrderID, LineNumber, ItemID, Quantity, Price

1. In the tblCustomers table, set the CustomerID field as the primary key. Set the type of the field to char. Set the size of the field to 5. All other fields can be left with their default properties.

2. In the tblOrders table, make OrderID the int data type and create an identity column with a seed of 1 and an increment of 1. Make the OrderID the primary key field. Set the type of the CustomerID field to char and the length of the CustomerID field to 5. Set the field type of the OrderDate field to DateTime.

3. In the tblOrderDetails table, set the field type of the OrderID field to int. Set the type of the LineNumber field to int. The primary key of the table should be based on the combination of the OrderID and LineNumber fields. The ItemID and Quantity fields should be the int data type. The Price field should be the money type.

4. Right-click the Diagrams node and select New Database Diagram. Click Next. Add the tblCustomers, tblOrders, and tblOrderDetails tables to the diagram. Click Next and then click Finish. SQL Server adds all three tables to the diagram. Click and drag from the CustomerID field in the tblCustomers table to the CustomerID field in the tblOrders table. After the Create Relationship dialog box appears, click OK. Repeat the process, clicking and dragging the OrderID field from the tblOrders table to the OrderID field in the tblOrderDetails table.

Establishing Referential Integrity

As you can see, establishing a relationship is quite easy. Establishing the right kind of relationship is a little more difficult. When you attempt to establish a relationship between two tables, SQL Server makes some decisions based on a few predefined factors:

- A one-to-many relationship is established if one of the related fields is a primary key or has a unique index.

- A one-to-one relationship is established if both the related fields are primary keys or have unique indexes.

- A relationship cannot be created if neither of the related fields is a primary key and neither has a unique index.

As covered earlier in this chapter, *referential integrity* consists of a series of rules that SQL Server applies to ensure that the relationships between tables are maintained properly. At the most basic level, referential integrity rules prevent the creation of orphan records in the table on the many side of the one-to-many relationship. After establishing a relationship between a Customers table and an Orders table, for example, all orders in the Orders table must be related to a particular customer in the Customers table. Before you can establish referential integrity between two tables, the following conditions must be met:

- The matching field on the one side of the relationship must be a primary key field or must have a unique index.

- The matching fields must have the same data types. They also must have the same size. Number fields on both sides of the relationship must have the same size (int, for example).

- Both tables must be part of the same database.

- If you select the Check Existing Data on Creation check box, existing data within the two tables cannot violate any referential integrity rules. All orders in the Orders table must relate to existing customers in the Customers table, for example.

After referential integrity is established between two tables, the following rules are applied:

- You cannot enter a value in the foreign key of the related table that does not exist in the primary key of the primary table. For example, you cannot enter a value in the CustomerID field of the Orders table that does not exist in the CustomerID field of the Customers table.

- You cannot delete a record from the primary table if corresponding records exist in the related table. For example, you cannot delete a customer from the Customers table if related records exist in the Orders table (records with the same value in the CustomerID field) unless you select the Cascade Delete Related Records check box in the Properties dialog box for the relationship (see "Try It" section that follows).

- You cannot change the value of a primary key on the one side of a relationship if corresponding records exist in the related table. For example, you cannot change the value in the CustomerID field of the Customers table if corresponding orders exist in the Orders table unless you select the Cascade Update Related Fields check box in the Properties dialog box for the relationship (see "Try It" section that follows).

If any of the previous three rules is violated and referential integrity is being enforced between the tables, an appropriate error message is displayed, as shown in Figure 5.22.

FIGURE 5.22   An appropriate error message appears if referential integrity is violated.

SQL Server's default behavior is to prohibit the deletion of parent records that have associated child records and to prohibit the change of a primary key value of a parent record when that parent has associated child records. You can override these restrictions by using the two check boxes available in the Relationships dialog box when you establish or modify a relationship.

> **TRY IT**   The following example enforces referential integrity between the tblCustomers table and the tblOrders table. It illustrates how this affects the process of adding and deleting records.

1. To open the database diagram, select the Diagrams node. Double-click the diagram that you created earlier. Right-click the join line between tblCustomers and tblOrders, and select Properties. Enable the Enforce Relationship for Inserts and Updates check box (if it is not already selected). Click OK. Repeat the process for the relationship between tblOrders and tblOrderDetails.

2. Go into tblCustomers and add a couple of records. Take note of the customer IDs. Go into tblOrders. Add a couple of records, taking care to assign customer IDs of customers that exist in the tblCustomers table. Now try to add an order for a customer whose customer ID does not exist in tblCustomers. You should get an error message.

3. Attempt to delete a customer from tblCustomers who does not have any orders. You should be allowed to complete the process. Now try to delete a customer who does have orders. SQL Server should prohibit you from deleting the customer. Attempt to change the customer ID of a customer who has orders. You should not be able to do this.

Cascade Update Related Fields

The Cascade Update Related Fields option is available only if you have established referential integrity between the tables. With this option selected, the user can change the primary key value of the record on the one side of the relationship. When the user makes an attempt to modify the field joining the two tables on the one side of the relationship, the change is cascaded down to the Foreign Key field on the many side of the relationship. This is useful if the primary key field is modifiable. For example, a purchase number on a purchase order master record may be updateable. If the user modifies the purchase order number of the parent record, you would want to cascade the change to the associated detail records in the purchase order detail table.

NOTE

There is no need to select the Cascade Update Related Fields option when the related field on the one side of the relationship is an identity field. An identity field can never be modified. The Cascade Update Related Fields option has no effect on identity fields.

Cascade Delete Related Records

The Cascade Delete Related Records option is available only if you have established referential integrity between the tables. With this option selected, the user can delete a record on the one side of a one-to-many relationship, even if related records exist in the table on the many side of the relationship. The user can delete a customer even if the customer has existing orders, for example. Referential integrity is maintained between the tables because SQL Server automatically deletes all related records in the child table.

If you attempt to delete a record from the table on the one side of a one-to-many relationship and no related records exist in the table on the many side of the relationship, you are able to delete the record. On the other hand, if you attempt to delete a record from the table on the one side of a one-to-many relationship and related records exist in the child table, you will delete the record from the parent table as well as any related records in the child table.

TIP

The Cascade Delete Related Records option is not always appropriate. It is an excellent feature, but you should use it prudently. Although it is usually appropriate to cascade delete from an Orders table to an Order Details table, for example, it generally is not appropriate to cascade delete from a Customers table to an Orders table. This is because you generally do not want all your order history deleted from the Orders table if for some reason you want to delete a customer. Deleting the order history causes important information, such as your profit and loss history, to change. It therefore is appropriate to prohibit this type of deletion and handle the customer in some other way, such as marking him as inactive or archiving his data. On the other hand, if you delete an order because it was canceled, you probably want the corresponding order detail information to be removed as well. In this case, the Cascade Delete Related Records option is appropriate. You need to make the appropriate decision in each situation, based on business needs. The important thing is to carefully consider the implications of each option before making your decision.

TRY IT   With the Cascade Update feature enabled, you can update the primary key value of a record that has associated child records. With the Cascade Delete feature enabled, you can delete a parent record that has associated child records. This exercise illustrates the use of the Cascade Update and Cascade Delete features.

1. Modify the relationship between tblCustomers and tblOrders. Enable the Cascade Update Related Fields check box. Modify the relationship between tblOrders and tblOrderDetails. Enable the Cascade Delete Related Records check box. There is no need to enable Cascade Update Related Fields because the OrderID field in tblOrders is an Identity column.

2. Attempt to delete a customer who has orders. You still should be prohibited from doing this because you did not enable Cascade Delete Related Records. Change the customer ID in tblCustomers of a customer who has orders. This change should be allowed. Take a look at the tblOrders table. The customer ID of all corresponding records in the table now should be updated to reflect the change in the parent record.

3. Add some order details to the tblOrderDetails table. Try to delete any order that has details within the tblOrderDetails table. You should be allowed to complete the process.

Looking at the Benefits of Relationships

The primary benefit of relationships is the data integrity they provide. Without the establishment of relationships, users are free to add records to child tables without regard to entering required parent information. After you establish referential integrity, you can enable Cascade Update Related Fields or Cascade Delete Related Records, as appropriate, which will save you quite a bit of code in maintaining the integrity of the data in your system. Many relational database-management systems require that you write the code to delete related records when a parent record is deleted or to update the foreign key in related records when the primary key of the parent is modified. By enabling the Cascade Update and Cascade Delete check boxes, you are sheltered from having to write a single line of code to perform these tasks when they are appropriate.

Relationships automatically are carried into your queries. This means that each time you build a new query, the relationships between the tables within it automatically are established, based on the relationships that you have set up in the Relationships window. Furthermore, each time you build a form or report, relationships between the tables included on the form or report are used to assist with the design process. Whether you delete or update data using a datasheet or a form, all referential integrity rules automatically apply, even if the relationship is established after the form is built.

Examining Indexes and Relationships

The field that joins two tables on the one side of a one-to-many relationship must be a primary key field or must have a unique index so that referential integrity can be maintained. If the index on the one side of the relationship is not unique, there is no way to determine to which parent a child record belongs. It is also necessary for you to create an index for the field on the many side of the relationship. If you fail to do this, the performance of the application suffers.

Summary

Tables and the relationships between them are the foundation for any application that you build. It is therefore important that you set up your tables with all of the necessary properties and then establish the proper relationships between them. This chapter began by covering all of the important aspects of designing database tables. You learned about important topics such as constraints, identity columns, and indexes. After exploring the various ways that you can refine the tables that you build, you learned how to use database diagrams to relate the tables in your database.

6

Mastering T-SQL

Why This Chapter Is Important

T-SQL, or Transact-SQL, is the dialect of the Structured Query Language (SQL) incorporated in SQL Server. To work effectively as a SQL Server developer, you must have a strong grasp of T-SQL.

Introduction to T-SQL

Fortunately, T-SQL is easy to learn. When retrieving data, you simply build a SELECT statement. SELECT statements are composed of clauses that determine the specifics of how the data is selected. When they're executed, SELECT statements select rows of data and return them as a recordset.

NOTE

In the examples that follow, keywords appear in uppercase. Values that you supply appear italicized. Optional parts of the statement appear in square brackets. Curly braces, combined with vertical bars, indicate a choice. Finally, ellipses are used to indicate a repeating sequence.

The SELECT Statement

The SELECT statement is at the heart of the SQL language. You use the SELECT statement to retrieve data from one or more tables. Its basic syntax is:

```
SELECT column-list FROM table-list WHERE where-clause
➥ORDER BY order-by-clause
```

The SELECT Clause

The SELECT clause specifies what columns you want to retrieve from the table that SQL Server returns to the recordset. The basic syntax for a SELECT clause is:

```
SELECT column-list
```

The simplest SELECT clause looks like this:

```
SELECT *
```

This SELECT clause retrieves all columns from a table. Here's another example that retrieves only the CustomerID and CompanyName columns from a table:

```
SELECT CustomerID, CompanyName
```

Not only can you include columns that exist in your table, but you also can include expressions in a SELECT clause. Here's an example:

```
SELECT CustomerID, City + ', ' + Region + ' ' + PostalCode AS Address FROM
➥Customers
```

This SELECT clause retrieves the CustomerID column as well as an alias called Address, which includes an expression that concatenates the City, Region, and PostalCode columns (see Figure 6.1).

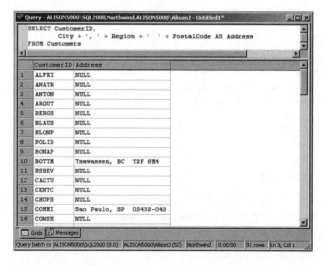

FIGURE 6.1   A SELECT clause that retrieves the CustomerID column as well as an alias called Address, which includes an expression that concatenates the City, Region, and PostalCode columns.

The FROM **Clause**

The FROM clause specifies the tables or views from which the records should be selected. It can include an alias that you use to refer to the table. The FROM clause looks like this:

```
FROM table-list [AS alias]
```

Here's an example of a basic FROM clause:

```
FROM Customers
```

In this case, the name of the table is Customers. If you combine the SELECT clause with the FROM clause, the SQL statement looks like this:

```
SELECT CustomerID, CompanyName FROM Customers
```

This SELECT statement retrieves the CustomerID and CompanyName columns from the Customers table.

Just as you can alias the fields included in a SELECT clause, you can also alias the tables included in the FROM clause. The alias is used to shorten the name and to simplify a cryptic name, as well as for a variety of other reasons. Here's an example:

```
SELECT CustomerID, CompanyName FROM Customers AS Clients
```

The WHERE **Clause**

The WHERE clause limits the records retrieved by the SELECT statement. A WHERE clause can include columns combined by the keywords AND and OR. The syntax for a WHERE clause looks like this:

```
WHERE expression1 [{AND|OR} expression2 [...]]
```

A simple WHERE clause looks like this:

```
WHERE Country = 'USA'
```

Using an AND to further limit the criteria, the WHERE clause looks like this:

```
WHERE Country = 'USA' AND ContactTitle Like 'Sales%'
```

This WHERE clause limits the records returned to those in which the country is equal to USA and the ContactTitle begins with Sales. Notice that T-SQL uses the percent (%) sign as a wildcard. Using an OR, the SELECT statement looks like this:

```
WHERE Country = 'USA' OR Country = 'Canada'
```

This WHERE clause returns all records in which the country is equal to either USA or Canada. Compare that with the following example:

```
WHERE Country = 'USA' OR ContactTitle Like 'Sales%'
```

This WHERE clause returns all records in which the country is equal to USA or the ContactTitle begins with Sales. For example, the salespeople in China will be returned from this WHERE clause because their ContactTitle begins with Sales. The WHERE clause combined with the SELECT and FROM clauses looks like this (see also Figure 6.2):

```
SELECT CustomerID, CompanyName FROM Customers
    WHERE Country = 'USA' OR Country = 'Canada'
```

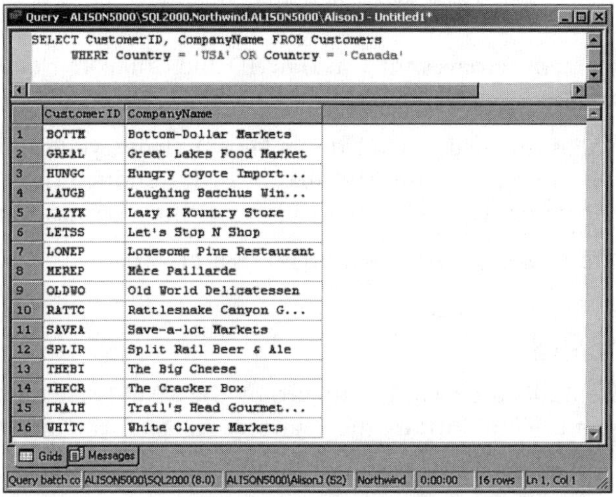

FIGURE 6.2   A SELECT clause that retrieves the CustomerID and CompanyName columns for all of the customers in the USA and Canada.

You must follow several rules when building a WHERE clause. You must enclose the text strings that you are searching for in apostrophes. You must also surround dates with apostrophes. Finally, you must include the keyword LIKE when utilizing wildcard characters. Remember that T-SQL uses the percent symbol as the wildcard for zero or more characters. The underscore (_) is the wildcard for a single character.

The ORDER BY Clause

The ORDER BY the order in which SQL Server sorts the returned rows. It's an optional clause and looks like this:

```
ORDER BY column1 [{ASC|DESC}], column2 [{ASC|DESC}] [,...]]
```

Here's an example:

```
ORDER BY CustomerID
```

The ORDER BY clause can include more than one field:

```
ORDER BY Country, CustomerID
```

When you specify more than one field, SQL Server uses the leftmost field as the primary level of sort. Any additional fields are the lower sort levels. Combined with the rest of the SELECT statement, the ORDER BY clause looks like this:

```
SELECT CustomerID, CompanyName FROM Customers
    WHERE Country = 'USA' OR Country = 'Canada'
    ORDER BY CompanyName
```

The results appear in order by *CompanyName* (see Figure 6.3).

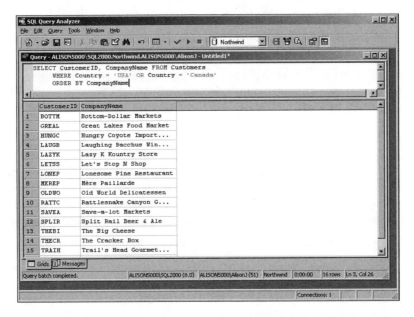

FIGURE 6.3 A SELECT clause that retrieves the CustomerID and CompanyName columns for all of the customers in the USA and Canada. SQL Server orders the results by CompanyName.

The ORDER BY clause allows you to determine whether the sorted output appears in ascending or descending order. By default, output appears in ascending order. To switch to descending order, use the optional keyword DESC. Here's an example:

```
SELECT CustomerID, CompanyName FROM Customers ORDER BY CustomerID DESC
```

This example selects the CustomerID and CompanyName fields from the Customers table, ordering the output in descending order by the CustomerID field (see Figure 6.4).

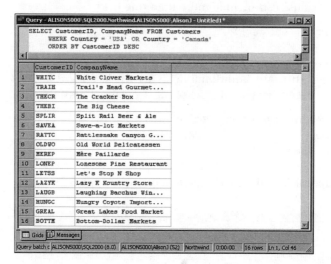

FIGURE 6.4   A SELECT clause that retrieves the CustomerID and CompanyName columns for all of the customers in the USA and Canada. SQL Server orders the results in descending order by CustomerID.

The JOIN Clause

Often you'll need to build SELECT statements that retrieve data from more than one table. When building a SELECT statement based on more than one table, you must join the tables with a JOIN clause. The JOIN clause differs depending on whether you join the tables with an INNER JOIN, a LEFT OUTER JOIN, or a RIGHT OUTER JOIN.

The SQL-89 and SQL-92 syntax for joins differs. The basic SQL-89 syntax is:

```
SELECT column-list FROM table1, table2 WHERE table1.column1 = table2.column2
```

Most people prefer the SQL-92 syntax because it renders the sole purpose of the WHERE clause for specifying criteria. It is:

```
SELECT column-list FROM table1 {INNER|LEFT [OUTER]|RIGHT [OUTER]} JOIN table2
    ON table1.column1 = table2.column2
```

Note that the keyword OUTER is optional.

Here's an example of a simple INNER JOIN:

```
SELECT Customers.CustomerID,
    Customers.CompanyName, Orders.OrderID,
    Orders.OrderDate
    FROM Customers
    INNER JOIN Orders ON Customers.CustomerID = Orders.CustomerID
```

Notice that SQL Server returns four columns in the query result. Two columns are from Customers and two are from Orders. The SELECT statement uses an INNER JOIN from Customers to Orders based on the CustomerID field. This means that SQL Server displays only customers who have orders in the query result (see Figure 6.5).

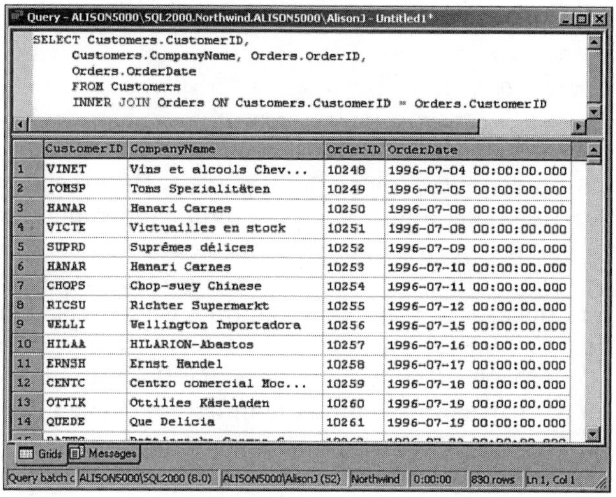

FIGURE 6.5   A SELECT clause that returns four columns in the query result, two from Customers and two from Orders.

Compare this with the following SELECT statement:

```
SELECT Customers.CustomerID,
    Customers.CompanyName, Orders.OrderID,
    Orders.OrderDate
    FROM Customers
    LEFT JOIN Orders ON Customers.CustomerID = Orders.CustomerID
```

This SELECT statement joins the two tables using a LEFT JOIN from Customers to Orders based on the CustomerID field. All clients are included in the resulting records, whether they have projects or not.

NOTE

The word OUTER is assumed in the LEFT JOIN clause used when building a left outer join.

At times you will need to join more than two tables in a SQL statement. The ANSI-92 syntax is:

```
FROM table1 JOIN table2 ON condition1 JOIN table3 ON condition2
```

The following example joins the Customers, Orders, and OrderDetails tables:

```
SELECT Customers. CustomerID, Customers.CompanyName,
    Orders.OrderID, Orders.OrderDate
    FROM (Customers
    INNER JOIN Orders
    ON Customers.CustomerID = Orders.CustomerID)
    INNER JOIN [Order Details]
    ON Orders.OrderID = [Order Details].OrderID
```

In the example, the order of the joins is unimportant. The exception to this is when you combine inner and outer joins. When combining inner and outer joins, the SQL Server engine applies two specific rules. First, the nonpreserved table in an outer join cannot participate in an inner join. The nonpreserved table is the one whose rows may not appear. In the case of a left outer join from Customers to Orders, the Orders table is considered the nonpreserved table. Therefore, it cannot participate in an inner join with OrderDetails. The second rule is that the nonpreserved table in an outer join cannot participate with another nonpreserved table in another outer join.

The DISTINCT Keyword

The DISTINCT keyword ensures uniqueness of values in the column or combination of columns included in the query result. Consider the following SQL statement:

```
SELECT Country FROM Customers
```

This statement returns one row for each customer (see Figure 6.6). The same country appears multiple times in the output.

Contrast the statement with:

```
SELECT DISTINCT Country FROM Customers
```

This statement returns a list of unique countries from the list of customers (see Figure 6.7).

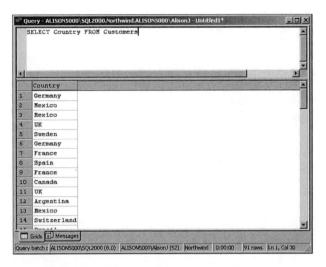

FIGURE 6.6   A SELECT statement that returns one row for each customer. The same country appears multiple times in the output.

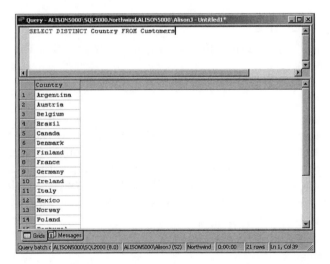

FIGURE 6.7   A SELECT statement that returns a list of unique countries from the list of customers.

The statement that follows returns a unique list of country and city combinations (see Figure 6.8):

```
SELECT DISTINCT Country, City FROM Customers
```

FIGURE 6.8   A SELECT statement that returns a list of unique country and city combinations from the list of customers.

The GROUP BY **Clause**

You can use the GROUP BY clause to calculate summary statistics. The syntax of the GROUP BY clause is:

```
GROUP BY group-by-expression1 [,group-by-expression2 [,...]]
```

You use the GROUP BY clause to dictate the fields on which SQL Server groups the query result. When you include multiple fields in a GROUP BY clause, they are grouped from left to right. SQL Server automatically outputs the fields in the order designated in the GROUP BY clause. In the following example, the SELECT statement returns the country, city, and total freight for each country/city combination. The results are displayed in order by country and city (see Figure 6.9):

```
SELECT Customers.Country, Customers.City,
    Sum(Orders.Freight) AS SumOfFreight
    FROM Customers
    INNER JOIN Orders ON Customers.CustomerID = Orders.CustomerID
    GROUP BY Customers.Country, Customers.City
```

The GROUP BY clause indicates that SQL Server doesn't display the detail for the selected records. Instead, it displays the fields indicated in the GROUP BY uniquely. One of the fields in the SELECT statement must include an aggregate function. SQL Server displays this result of the aggregate function along with the fields specified in the GROUP BY clause.

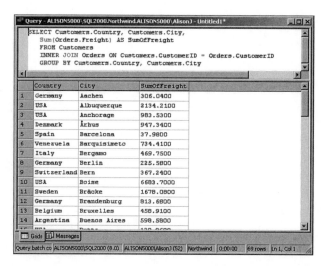

FIGURE 6.9 A SELECT statement that returns the country, city, and total freight for each country/city combination.

Aggregate Functions

You use aggregate functions to summarize table data. The aggregate functions available include COUNT, COUNT_BIG, SUM, AVG, MIN, and MAX. The following sections discuss each of these aggregate functions. You can find additional aggregate functions in Books On-line (online help for SQL Server).

COUNT

You use the COUNT function to count the number of rows in a table. It looks like this:

```
SELECT COUNT(*) AS CountOfCustomers FROM Customers
```

The example counts the number of rows in the Customers table (see Figure 6.10).

As an alternative, you can count values in a particular column. It looks like this:

```
SELECT COUNT(Region) AS CountOfCustomers FROM Customers
```

This example counts the number of regions found in the Customers table (see Figure 6.11).

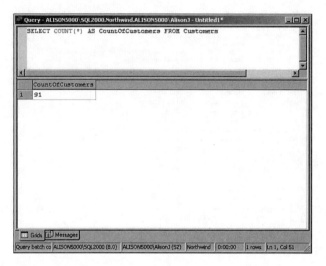

FIGURE 6.10   A SELECT statement that counts the number of rows in the Customers table.

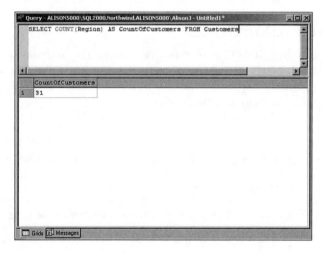

FIGURE 6.11   A SELECT statement that counts the number of regions found in the Customers table.

COUNT_BIG

The COUNT_BIG function is identical to the COUNT function, except that it returns a bigint data type. It looks like this:

```
SELECT COUNT_BIG(Region) AS CountOfCustomers FROM Customers
```

SUM

The SUM function is available only for numeric columns. It adds the data in the columns. Here's an example:

```
SELECT SUM(Freight) FROM Orders
```

The example totals the Freight column for all rows in the Orders table. When used with the GROUP BY clause, the SUM function can easily total values for each grouping.

```
SELECT ShipVia, SUM(Freight) FROM Orders GROUP BY ShipVia
```

The example totals the freight for each shipper (see Figure 6.12).

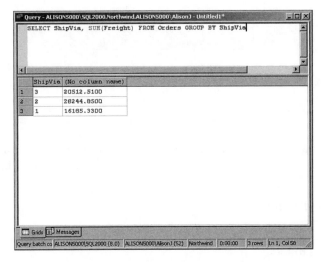

FIGURE 6.12   A SELECT statement that totals the freight for each shipper found in the Orders table.

AVG

Just as you can easily total data, you can average data. The following statement finds the average freight for all orders in the Orders table:

```
SELECT AVG(Freight) FROM Orders
```

When used with the GROUP BY clause, the AVG function can easily average values in each grouping.

```
SELECT ShipVia, AVG(Freight) FROM Orders GROUP BY ShipVia
```

The result provides the average freight for each shipper (see Figure 6.13).

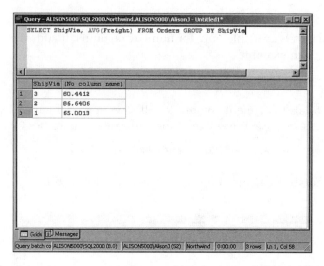

FIGURE 6.13   A SELECT statement that provides the average freight for each shipper found in the Orders table.

MIN

Another important aggregate function is MIN. You use the MIN function to find the minimum value in a column. This statement finds the minimum freight in the Orders table:

```
SELECT MIN(Freight) FROM Orders
```

When used with the GROUP BY clause, the MIN function can easily find the minimum values in each grouping.

```
SELECT ShipVia, MIN(Freight) FROM Orders GROUP BY ShipVia
```

The result provides the minimum freight for each shipper (see Figure 6.14).

MAX

A related aggregate function is MAX (see Figure 6.15). You use the MAX function to find the maximum value in a column.

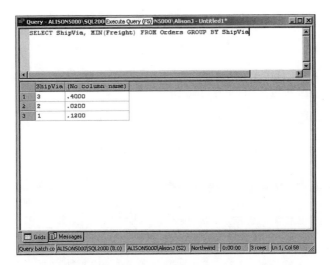

FIGURE 6.14 A SELECT statement that provides the minimum freight for each shipper found in the Orders table.

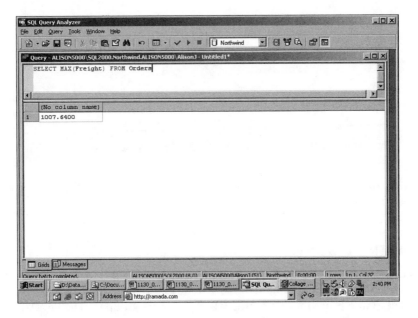

FIGURE 6.15 You use the MAX function to find the maximum value in a column.

This statement finds the maximum freight in the Orders table:

SELECT MAX(*Freight*) FROM *Orders*

When used with the GROUP BY clause (see Figure 6.16), the MAX function can easily find the maximum values in each grouping.

SELECT *ShipVia*, MAX(*Freight*) FROM *Orders* GROUP BY *ShipVia*

The result provides the maximum freight for each shipper.

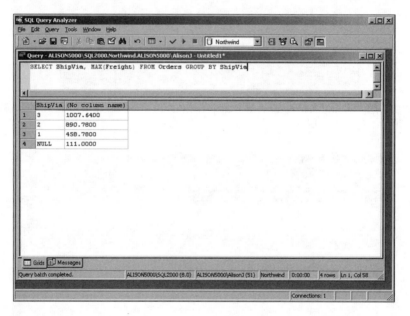

FIGURE 6.16 When used with the GROUP BY clause, the MAX function can easily find the maximum values in each grouping.

The HAVING Clause

A HAVING clause is similar to a WHERE clause, but it differs in one major respect: SQL Server applies it after it summarizes the data rather than beforehand. In other words, the WHERE clause is used to determine which rows are grouped. The HAVING clause determines which groups are included in the output. A HAVING clause looks like this:

HAVING *expression1* [{AND|OR} *expression2*[...]]

In the following example, SQL Server applies the criteria > 1000 after it applies the aggregate function SUM to the grouping. Therefore, SQL Server includes only country/city combinations with total freight greater than 1000 in the output (see Figure 6.17).

```
SELECT Customers.Country, Customers.City,
    Sum(Orders.Freight) AS SumOfFreight
    FROM Customers
    INNER JOIN Orders ON Customers.CustomerID = Orders.CustomerID
    GROUP BY Customers.Country, Customers.City
    HAVING (((Sum(Orders.Freight))>1000))
```

FIGURE 6.17 A SELECT statement that includes country/city combinations with total freight greater than 1000 in the output.

Top Values Queries

You use the TOP clause to limit the number of rows that SQL Server includes in the output. Here's an example:

```
SELECT TOP 10 OrderDate, Sum(Freight) FROM Orders
    GROUP BY OrderDate
    ORDER BY SUM(Freight) DESC
```

This example shows the 10 order dates with the highest total freight (see Figure 6.18).

In addition to allowing you to select the top number of rows, T-SQL also allows you to select the top percent of rows. Here's an example:

```
SELECT TOP 10 PERCENT OrderDate, Sum(Freight) FROM Orders
    GROUP BY OrderDate
    ORDER BY SUM(Freight) DESC
```

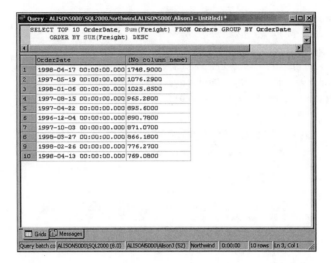

FIGURE 6.18   A SELECT statement that shows the 10 order dates with the highest total freight.

Here the top 10 percent of freight amounts appear in the query result.

Join Types

When you build a system based on normalized table structures, you must join the tables back together to see the data in a useable format. For example, if you have separated customers, orders, and order details, you will need to join these tables in a query to see the name of the customer who placed an order for a particular item. Several types of joins are available. They include inner joins, outer joins, full joins, and self-joins. The sections that follow cover each of these join types.

Inner Joins

An inner join is the most common type of join. When you use an inner join, only rows on the one side of the relationship that have matching rows on the many side of the relationship are included in the output. Here's an example:

```
SELECT Customers.CustomerID,
    Customers.CompanyName, Orders.OrderID,
    Orders.OrderDate
    FROM Customers
    INNER JOIN Orders ON Customers.CustomerID = Orders.CustomerID
```

This example includes only those customers who have orders.

Outer Joins

An outer join allows you to include rows from one side of the join in the output, regardless of whether matching rows exist on the other side of the join. Two types of outer joins exist: left outer joins and right outer joins. With a left outer join, SQL Server includes in the output all rows in the first table specified in the SELECT statement. Here's an example:

```
SELECT Customers.CustomerID,
    Customers.CompanyName, Orders.OrderID,
    Orders.OrderDate
    FROM Customers
    LEFT OUTER JOIN Orders ON Customers.CustomerID = Orders.CustomerID
```

In the previous example, customers are included regardless of whether they have orders. With the right outer join shown next, orders are included whether or not they have associated customers. If you have properly enforced referential integrity, this scenario should never exist.

```
SELECT Customers.CustomerID,
    Customers.CompanyName, Orders.OrderID,
    Orders.OrderDate
    FROM Customers
    RIGHT OUTER JOIN Orders ON Customers.CustomerID = Orders.CustomerID
```

Full Joins

A full join combines the behavior of the left and right outer joins. It looks like this:

```
SELECT Customers.CustomerID,
    Customers.CompanyName, Orders.OrderID,
    Orders.OrderDate
    FROM Customers
    FULL JOIN Orders ON Customers.CustomerID = Orders.CustomerID
```

In this example, all customers appear in the output regardless of whether they have orders, and all orders appear in the output whether or not they are associated with customers.

Self-Joins

A self-join involves joining a table to itself. Although it is not the most common type of join, this join type is very valuable. Imagine the scenario in which an Employee table contains a field called EmployeeID and another field called ReportsTo. The ReportsTo field must contain a valid EmployeeID. It would not make sense to have separate Employee and Supervisor tables because supervisors are employees. This is where the self-join comes in. A self-join looks like this:

```
SELECT Employees.EmployeeID, Employees.LastName, Employees.FirstName,
    Supervisors.EmployeeID as SupervisorID,
    Supervisors.LastName as SupervisorLastName,
    Supervisors.FirstName as SupervisorFirstName
    FROM Employees INNER JOIN Employees as Supervisors
    ON Employees.ReportsTo = Supervisors.EmployeeID
```

In this example, the EmployeeID from the Employees table is joined to an alias of the ReportsTo field of an alias of the Employees table (called Supervisors). The resulting employee and supervisor information is output from the query (see Figure 6.19).

```
SELECT Employees.EmployeeID, Employees.LastName, Employees.FirstName,
    Supervisors.EmployeeID as SupervisorID,
    Supervisors.LastName as SupervisorLastName,
    Supervisors.FirstName as SupervisorFirstName
    FROM Employees INNER JOIN Employees as Supervisors
    ON Employees.ReportsTo = Supervisors.EmployeeID
```

	EmployeeID	LastName	FirstName	SupervisorID	SupervisorLastName	Supervisor
1	1	Davolio	Nancy	2	Fuller	Andrew
2	3	Leverling	Janet	2	Fuller	Andrew
3	4	Peacock	Margaret	2	Fuller	Andrew
4	5	Buchanan	Steven	2	Fuller	Andrew
5	6	Suyama	Michael	5	Buchanan	Steven
6	7	King	Robert	5	Buchanan	Steven
7	8	Callahan	Laura	2	Fuller	Andrew
8	9	Dodsworth	Anne	5	Buchanan	Steven

FIGURE 6.19   A SELECT statement that shows the result of joining the Employee table to itself.

Union Queries

Union queries allow you to combine rather than join data from more than one table. A typical example of a union query is one that combines data from a Products table and a DiscontinuedProducts table. Another example is a query that combines data from a Customers table and a CustomerArchive table. Here's an example of a union query:

```
SELECT ProductID, ProductName, UnitPrice FROM Products
UNION ALL
SELECT ProductID, ProductName, UnitPrice FROM DiscontinuedProducts
```

This example outputs all rows from the Products table as well as from the DiscontinuedProducts table (see Figure 6.20).

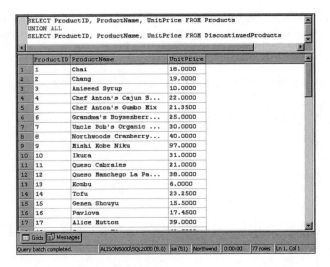

```
SELECT ProductID, ProductName, UnitPrice FROM Products
UNION ALL
SELECT ProductID, ProductName, UnitPrice FROM DiscontinuedProducts
```

	ProductID	ProductName	UnitPrice
1	1	Chai	18.0000
2	2	Chang	19.0000
3	3	Aniseed Syrup	10.0000
4	4	Chef Anton's Cajun S...	22.0000
5	5	Chef Anton's Gumbo Mix	21.3500
6	6	Grandma's Boysenberr...	25.0000
7	7	Uncle Bob's Organic ...	30.0000
8	8	Northwoods Cranberry...	40.0000
9	9	Mishi Kobe Niku	97.0000
10	10	Ikura	31.0000
11	11	Queso Cabrales	21.0000
12	12	Queso Manchego La Pa...	38.0000
13	13	Konbu	6.0000
14	14	Tofu	23.2500
15	15	Genen Shouyu	15.5000
16	16	Pavlova	17.4500
17	17	Alice Mutton	39.0000

Grids / Messages

Query batch completed.   ALISON5000\SQL2000 (8.0)   sa (51)   Northwind   0:00:00   77 rows   Ln 1, Col 1

FIGURE 6.20   A SELECT statement that outputs all rows from the Products table as well as from the DiscontinuedProducts table.

NOTE

The NorthWind database does not contain a DiscontinuedProducts table. To follow along with this example, you will need to create a table with the same structure as the Products table, except the primary key field should not be an IDENTITY column.

If you want to order the results, you must place the ORDER BY statement after the second SELECT statement:

```
SELECT ProductID, ProductName, UnitPrice FROM Products
UNION ALL
SELECT ProductID, ProductName, UnitPrice FROM DiscontinuedProducts
ORDER BY UnitPrice DESC
```

In this example, SQL Server combines the results of both SELECT statements in descending order by UnitPrice.

Subqueries

A subquery is a query that SQL Server evaluates before it evaluates the main query. Here's an example:

```
SELECT CustomerID, CompanyName, City, Country FROM Customers WHERE
    CustomerID Not In(Select CustomerID FROM Orders)
```

In this example, SQL Server executes the statement that selects data from the Orders table *before* it evaluates the statement that selects data from the Customers table (see Figure 6.21).

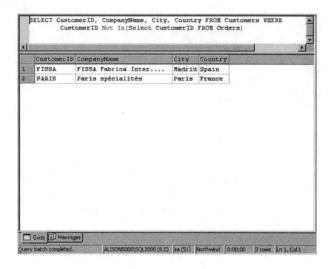

FIGURE 6.21   A SELECT statement that selects data from the Orders table *before* it evaluates the statement that selects data from the Customers table.

This is *not* a very efficient method of accomplishing the task of finding all of the customers without orders. A better solution would be to use an outer join to solve this problem. You could modify the SQL statement to look like this:

```
SELECT Customers.CustomerID, CompanyName, City, Country
    FROM Customers LEFT JOIN Orders ON Customers.CustomerID = Orders.CustomerID
    WHERE Orders.CustomerID Is Null
```

This example uses a left outer join to select all customers who do not have orders. Because this uses a left outer join, customers are included whether or not they have orders. Because the criteria designate that only rows with a null CustomerID appear in the output, only Customers without orders are included (see Figure 6.22).

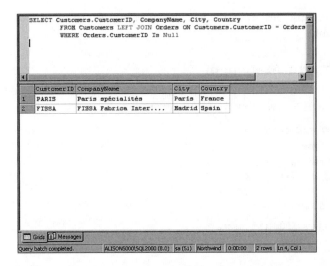

FIGURE 6.22 A SELECT statement that uses a left outer join to select all customers who do not have orders.

Modifying Data with Action Queries

The queries that we have explored thus far are all SELECT queries. This means that they *select* data from one or more tables. The queries that we will discuss now are action queries. They are queries that modify data. The five types of action queries that we will discuss are INSERT, UPDATE, SELECT INTO, DELETE, and TRUNCATE.

The INSERT Statement

You use the INSERT statement to insert data into an *existing* table. The INSERT statement has the following format:

```
INSERT [INTO] table_or_view [(col1, col2...)] VALUES (value1, value2)
```

Here's an example:

```
INSERT INTO Customers
(CustomerID, CompanyName, ContactName,
ContactTitle, City, Country)
VALUES
('INFO', 'InfoTechnology Partners, Inc.',
'Alison Balter', 'President',
'Camarillo', 'USA')
```

In this example, the designated values are inserted into the specified fields in the Customers table.

The SELECT INTO **Statement**

Whereas the INSERT statement inserts data into an existing table, the SELECT INTO statement creates a new table. Here's an example:

```
SELECT Customers.CustomerID,
Customers.CompanyName,
Customers.ContactName,
Customers.ContactTitle,
Customers.City,
Customers.Country
INTO USACustomers FROM Customers
WHERE Country = 'USA'
```

In this example, all customers with a country of USA are inserted into a new table called USACustomers.

The UPDATE **Statement**

As its name implies, an UPDATE statement updates table data. The format of the UPDATE statement is:

```
UPDATE tablename SET column1=value1, [column2=value2....]
```

The example that follows updates the contents of the Customers table, changing the city to Oak Park for all rows in which the city is Westlake Village.

```
UPDATE Customers
SET City = 'Oak Park'
WHERE City = 'Camarillo'
```

The DELETE **Statement**

You use the DELETE statement to remove rows from a table. The format of the DELETE statement is:

```
DELETE [FROM] table-name [WHERE search_conditions]
```

Here's an example:

```
DELETE FROM USACustomers WHERE ContactTitle = 'Owner'
```

This example removes all rows from the USACustomers table in which the contact title is Owner.

The TRUNCATE Statement

The TRUNCATE statement removes all rows from a table. It executes more quickly than a DELETE statement without a WHERE clause. Unlike the DROP statement, the TRUNCATE statement retains the structure of the table. It looks like this:

```
TRUNCATE TABLE USACustomers
```

T-SQL Functions

The T-SQL language contains numerous functions that you can incorporate into the T-SQL statements that you build. These functions perform a variety of important tasks. The text that follows covers some of the commonly used numeric, string, date/time, and null-related functions. For additional information on the plethora of T-SQL functions available, consult Books On-line.

Numeric Functions

Important numeric functions include IsNumeric and ROUND. The sections that follow example these functions and provide examples of their uses.

The IsNumeric Function

The IsNumeric function returns information on whether a value is numeric. Here's an example:

```
SELECT CustomerID, PostalCode, IsNumeric(PostalCode) FROM Customers
```

The SELECT statement returns each customer's CustomerID, PostalCode, and information on whether the postal code is numeric (see Figure 6.23).

The ROUND Function

As its name implies, the ROUND function rounds an expression to a specified length. Here's an example:

```
SELECT OrderID, Freight, Round(Freight, 0) FROM Orders
```

This SQL statement returns the OrderID, Freight, and the Freight rounded to whole numbers from the Orders table (see Figure 6.24).

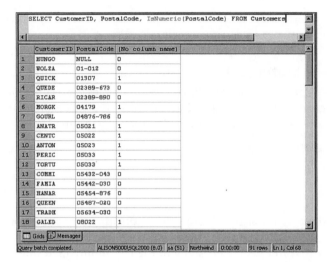

FIGURE 6.23 A SELECT statement that uses the IsNumeric function to determine whether the postal code is numeric.

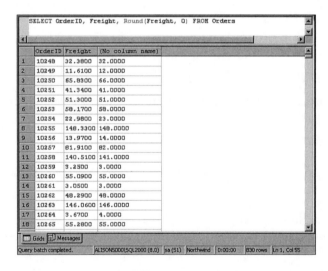

FIGURE 6.24 A SELECT statement that returns the OrderID, Freight, and the Freight rounded to whole numbers from the Orders table.

String Functions

Important string functions include LEFT, RIGHT, LEN, REPLACE, STUFF, SUBSTRING, LOWER, UPPER, LTRIM, and RTRIM.

The LEFT Function

The LEFT function extracts a designated number of characters from the left of a string:

```
SELECT CustomerID, LEFT(CompanyName, 5) FROM Customers
```

This example selects the CustomerID and the five leftmost characters from the Customers table (see Figure 6.25).

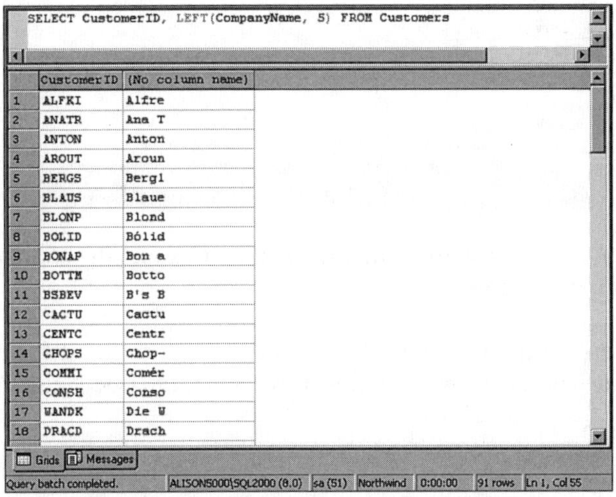

FIGURE 6.25   A SELECT statement that selects the CustomerID and the five leftmost characters from the Customers table.

The RIGHT Function

The RIGHT function works similarly but extracts the designated rightmost characters from a string. The same example using the RIGHT function looks like this:

```
SELECT CustomerID, RIGHT(CompanyName, 5) FROM Customers
```

This example returns the CustomerID and the five rightmost characters from the CompanyName (see Figure 6.26).

The SUBSTRING Function

The SUBSTRING function extracts specified characters from a string. Here's an example:

```
SELECT CustomerID, ContactTitle, SUBSTRING(ContactTitle, 5, 3) FROM Customers
```

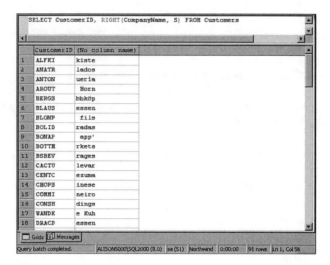

FIGURE 6.26   A SELECT statement that returns the CustomerID and the five rightmost characters from the CompanyName.

This example returns the CustomerID, ContactTitle, and the fifth through seventh characters of the ContactTitle from the Customers table (see Figure 6.27).

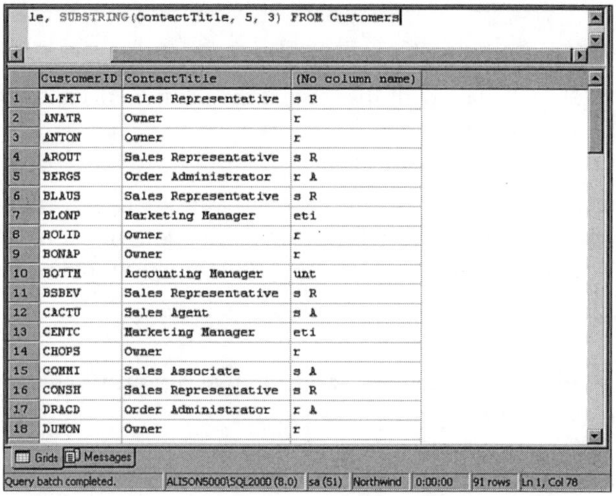

FIGURE 6.27   A SELECT statement that returns the CustomerID, ContactTitle, and the fifth through seventh characters of the ContactTitle from the Customers table.

The LEN Function

The `LEN` function returns the length of a string. It looks like this:

```
SELECT CustomerID, CompanyName, LEN(CompanyName) FROM Customers
```

This example returns the CustomerID, CompanyName, and the length of the company name for each row in the Customers table (see Figure 6.28).

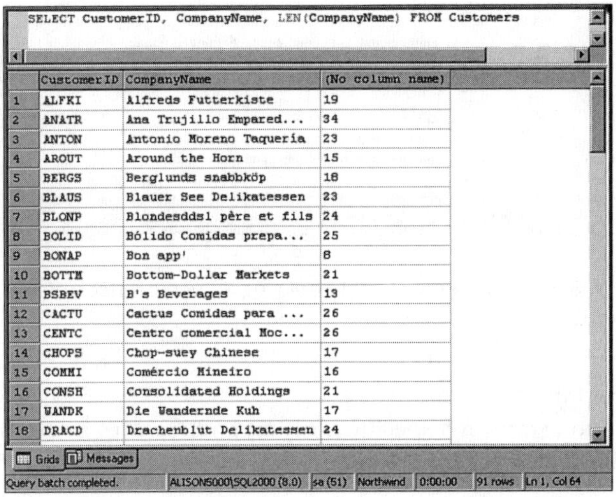

SELECT CustomerID, CompanyName, LEN(CompanyName) FROM Customers

	CustomerID	CompanyName	(No column name)
1	ALFKI	Alfreds Futterkiste	19
2	ANATR	Ana Trujillo Empared...	34
3	ANTON	Antonio Moreno Taquería	23
4	AROUT	Around the Horn	15
5	BERGS	Berglunds snabbköp	18
6	BLAUS	Blauer See Delikatessen	23
7	BLONP	Blondesddsl père et fils	24
8	BOLID	Bólido Comidas prepa...	25
9	BONAP	Bon app'	8
10	BOTTM	Bottom-Dollar Markets	21
11	BSBEV	B's Beverages	13
12	CACTU	Cactus Comidas para ...	26
13	CENTC	Centro comercial Moc...	26
14	CHOPS	Chop-suey Chinese	17
15	COMMI	Comércio Mineiro	16
16	CONSH	Consolidated Holdings	21
17	WANDK	Die Wandernde Kuh	17
18	DRACD	Drachenblut Delikatessen	24

FIGURE 6.28 A `SELECT` statement that returns the CustomerID, CompanyName, and the length of the company name for each row in the Customers table.

The REPLACE Function

The `REPLACE` function replaces all occurrences of one string with another. Here's an example:

```
SELECT CustomerID, ContactTitle,
    REPLACE(ContactTitle, 'Sales', 'Marketing' )
    FROM Customers
```

This example selects the CustomerID and ContactTitle from the Customers table. It includes an additional column that replaces all occurrences of the word `Sales` with the word `Marketing` (see Figure 6.29).

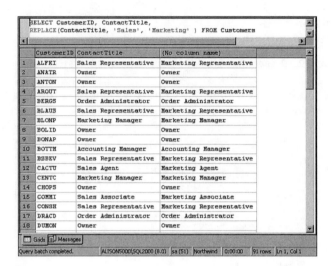

FIGURE 6.29 A SELECT statement that replaces all occurrences of the word Sales with the word Marketing.

The STUFF Function
The STUFF function starts at a specific position and replaces a specified number of characters with other specified characters. Here's an example:

```
SELECT CustomerID, ContactTitle,
    STUFF(ContactTitle, 5, 3, '***' )
    FROM Customers
```

This example selects the CustomerID and ContactTitle from the Customers table. It includes an additional column that replaces the fifth through seventh characters with asterisks (see Figure 6.30).

The LOWER Function
The LOWER function returns the lowercase version of a string. It looks like this:

```
SELECT CustomerID, LOWER(CompanyName) FROM Customers
```

The example returns the contents of the CustomerID field and then the lowercase version of the contents of the CompanyName field (see Figure 6.31).

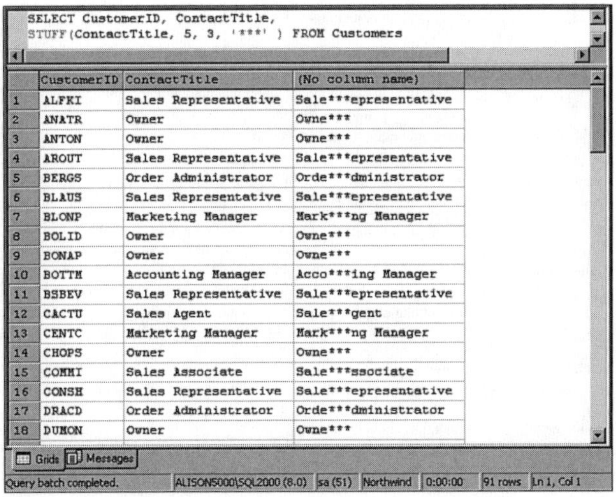

```
SELECT CustomerID, ContactTitle,
STUFF(ContactTitle, 5, 3, '***' ) FROM Customers
```

	CustomerID	ContactTitle	(No column name)
1	ALFKI	Sales Representative	Sale***epresentative
2	ANATR	Owner	Owne***
3	ANTON	Owner	Owne***
4	AROUT	Sales Representative	Sale***epresentative
5	BERGS	Order Administrator	Orde***dministrator
6	BLAUS	Sales Representative	Sale***epresentative
7	BLONP	Marketing Manager	Mark***ng Manager
8	BOLID	Owner	Owne***
9	BONAP	Owner	Owne***
10	BOTTM	Accounting Manager	Acco***ing Manager
11	BSBEV	Sales Representative	Sale***epresentative
12	CACTU	Sales Agent	Sale***gent
13	CENTC	Marketing Manager	Mark***ng Manager
14	CHOPS	Owner	Owne***
15	COMMI	Sales Associate	Sale***ssociate
16	CONSH	Sales Representative	Sale***epresentative
17	DRACD	Order Administrator	Orde***dministrator
18	DUMON	Owner	Owne***

Grids Messages
Query batch completed.   ALISON5000\SQL2000 (8.0) sa (51) Northwind 0:00:00 91 rows Ln 1, Col 1

FIGURE 6.30 A SELECT statement that replaces the fifth through seventh characters with asterisks.

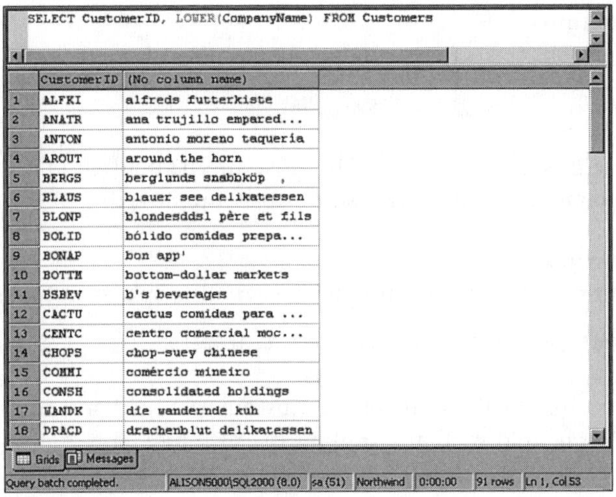

```
SELECT CustomerID, LOWER(CompanyName) FROM Customers
```

	CustomerID	(No column name)
1	ALFKI	alfreds futterkiste
2	ANATR	ana trujillo empared...
3	ANTON	antonio moreno taqueria
4	AROUT	around the horn
5	BERGS	berglunds snabbköp ,
6	BLAUS	blauer see delikatessen
7	BLONP	blondesddsl père et fils
8	BOLID	bólido comidas prepa...
9	BONAP	bon app'
10	BOTTM	bottom-dollar markets
11	BSBEV	b's beverages
12	CACTU	cactus comidas para ...
13	CENTC	centro comercial moc...
14	CHOPS	chop-suey chinese
15	COMMI	comércio mineiro
16	CONSH	consolidated holdings
17	WANDK	die wandernde kuh
18	DRACD	drachenblut delikatessen

Grids Messages
Query batch completed.   ALISON5000\SQL2000 (8.0) sa (51) Northwind 0:00:00 91 rows Ln 1, Col 53

FIGURE 6.31 A SELECT statement that returns the lowercase version of the contents of the CompanyName field.

The UPPER Function

The UPPER function returns the uppercase version of a string. It looks like this:

```
SELECT CustomerID, UPPER(CompanyName) FROM Customers
```

The example returns the contents of the CustomerID field and then the uppercase version of the contents of the CompanyName field (see Figure 6.32).

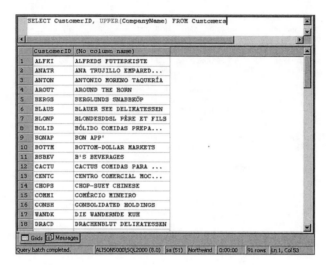

```
SELECT CustomerID, UPPER(CompanyName) FROM Customers
```

	CustomerID	(No column name)
1	ALFKI	ALFREDS FUTTERKISTE
2	ANATR	ANA TRUJILLO EMPARED...
3	ANTON	ANTONIO MORENO TAQUERÍA
4	AROUT	AROUND THE HORN
5	BERGS	BERGLUNDS SNABBKÖP
6	BLAUS	BLAUER SEE DELIKATESSEN
7	BLONP	BLONDESDDSL PÈRE ET FILS
8	BOLID	BÓLIDO COMIDAS PREPA...
9	BONAP	BON APP'
10	BOTTM	BOTTOM-DOLLAR MARKETS
11	BSBEV	B'S BEVERAGES
12	CACTU	CACTUS COMIDAS PARA ...
13	CENTC	CENTRO COMERCIAL MOC...
14	CHOPS	CHOP-SUEY CHINESE
15	COMMI	COMÉRCIO MINEIRO
16	CONSH	CONSOLIDATED HOLDINGS
17	WANDK	DIE WANDERNDE KUH
18	DRACD	DRACHENBLUT DELIKATESSEN

Grids Messages

Query batch completed.   ALISON5000\SQL2000 (8.0) sa (51) Northwind 0:00:00 91 rows Ln 1, Col 53

FIGURE 6.32   A SELECT statement that returns the uppercase version of the contents of the CompanyName field.

The LTRIM Function

The LTRIM function returns the string *without leading spaces*. It looks like this:

```
SELECT CustomerID, LTRIM(CompanyName) FROM Customers
```

The example returns the contents of the CustomerID field and then the contents of the CompanyName field with any leading spaces removed.

The RTRIM Function

The RTRIM function returns the string *without* trailing spaces. It looks like this:

```
SELECT CustomerID, RTRIM(CompanyName) FROM Customers
```

The example returns the contents of the CustomerID field and then the contents of the CompanyName field with any trailing spaces removed.

Date/Time Functions

Important date/time functions include GETDATE, MONTH, DAY, YEAR, DATEPART, DATENAME, DATEADD, and DATEDIFF. The sections that follow cover these functions.

The GETDATE Function

The GETDATE function returns the system date and time. It looks like this:

```
SELECT GETDATE()
```

The MONTH Function

The MONTH function returns the month portion of a date. It looks like this:

```
SELECT OrderID, OrderDate, MONTH(OrderDate) FROM Orders
```

This SQL statement returns the OrderID, the OrderDate, and the month of the order date from the Orders table (see Figure 6.33).

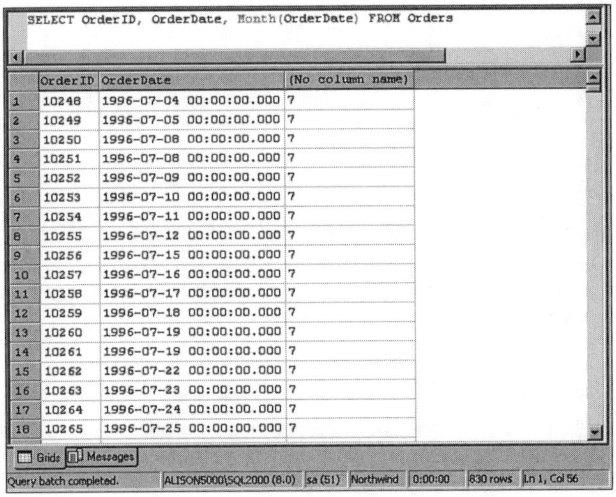

FIGURE 6.33 A SELECT statement that returns the OrderID, OrderDate, and month of the order date from the Orders table.

The DAY Function

The DAY function returns the day portion of a date. It looks like this:

```
SELECT OrderID, OrderDate, DAY(OrderDate) FROM Orders
```

This SQL statement returns the OrderID, the OrderDate, and the day of the order date from the Orders table (see Figure 6.34).

The YEAR Function

The YEAR function returns the year portion of a date. It looks like this:

```
SELECT OrderID, OrderDate, YEAR(OrderDate) FROM Orders
```

This SQL statement returns the OrderID, the OrderDate, and the month of order date from the Orders table (see Figure 6.35).

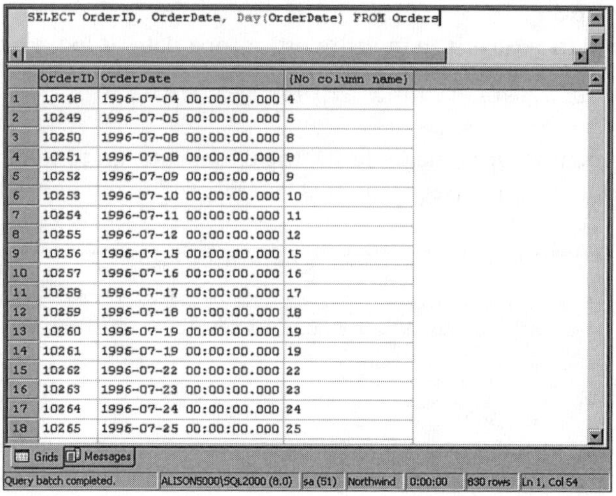

FIGURE 6.34   A SELECT statement that returns the OrderID, OrderDate, and day of the order date from the Orders table.

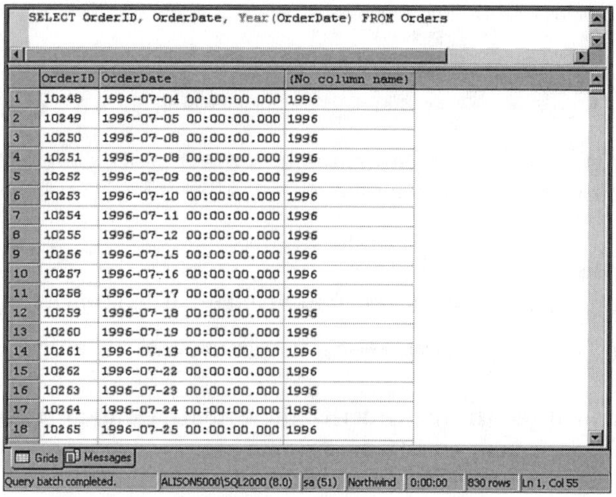

FIGURE 6.35   A SELECT statement that returns the OrderID, OrderDate, and year of order date from the Orders table.

The DATEPART Function

You use the DATEPART function to extract a part of a date. The first parameter to the DATEPART function is an abbreviation designating the part of the date that you want to extract. The second parameter is the date that you want to extract it from. Here's an example:

```
SELECT OrderID, OrderDate, DATEPART(qq, OrderDate) FROM Orders
```

This example selects the OrderID, the OrderDate, and the quarter of the OrderDate from the Orders table (see Figure 6.36).

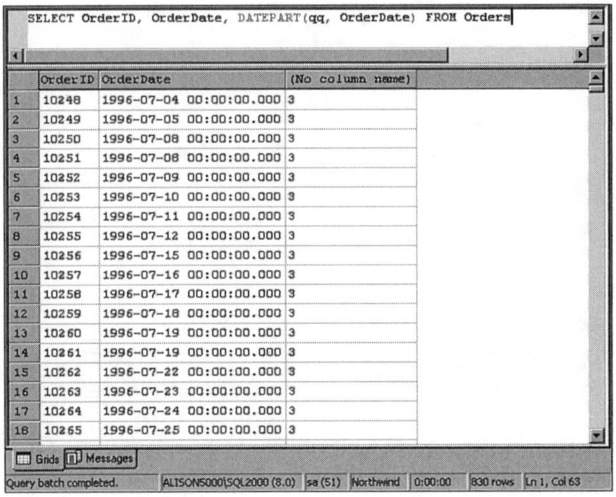
SELECT OrderID, OrderDate, DATEPART(qq, OrderDate) FROM Orders

	OrderID	OrderDate	(No column name)
1	10248	1996-07-04 00:00:00.000	3
2	10249	1996-07-05 00:00:00.000	3
3	10250	1996-07-08 00:00:00.000	3
4	10251	1996-07-08 00:00:00.000	3
5	10252	1996-07-09 00:00:00.000	3
6	10253	1996-07-10 00:00:00.000	3
7	10254	1996-07-11 00:00:00.000	3
8	10255	1996-07-12 00:00:00.000	3
9	10256	1996-07-15 00:00:00.000	3
10	10257	1996-07-16 00:00:00.000	3
11	10258	1996-07-17 00:00:00.000	3
12	10259	1996-07-18 00:00:00.000	3
13	10260	1996-07-19 00:00:00.000	3
14	10261	1996-07-19 00:00:00.000	3
15	10262	1996-07-22 00:00:00.000	3
16	10263	1996-07-23 00:00:00.000	3
17	10264	1996-07-24 00:00:00.000	3
18	10265	1996-07-25 00:00:00.000	3

FIGURE 6.36 A SELECT statement that selects the OrderID, OrderDate, and quarter of the OrderDate from the Orders table.

The DATENAME Function

The DATENAME function returns a string representing a part of a date. It also receives two parameters. The first is the abbreviation indicating the part of the date that you want to extract. The second is the date that you want to extract it from. Here's an example:

```
SELECT OrderID, OrderDate, DATENAME(dw, OrderDate) FROM Orders
```

This example returns the OrderID, the OrderDate, and a text description of the day of the week of the OrderDate (see Figure 6.37).

The DATEADD Function

You use the DATEADD function to add or subtract time from a date. The first parameter is the time period that you want to add or subtract. The second parameter is the number of that time period that you want to add or subtract. The final parameter is the date that you want to add it to or subtract it from. Here's an example:

```
SELECT OrderID, OrderDate, DATEADD(mm, 1, OrderDate) FROM Orders
```

This returns the OrderID, the OrderDate, and the date one month greater than the order date (see Figure 6.38).

```
SELECT OrderID, OrderDate, DATENAME(dw, OrderDate) FROM Orders
```

	OrderID	OrderDate	(No column name)
1	10248	1996-07-04 00:00:00.000	Thursday
2	10249	1996-07-05 00:00:00.000	Friday
3	10250	1996-07-08 00:00:00.000	Monday
4	10251	1996-07-08 00:00:00.000	Monday
5	10252	1996-07-09 00:00:00.000	Tuesday
6	10253	1996-07-10 00:00:00.000	Wednesday
7	10254	1996-07-11 00:00:00.000	Thursday
8	10255	1996-07-12 00:00:00.000	Friday
9	10256	1996-07-15 00:00:00.000	Monday
10	10257	1996-07-16 00:00:00.000	Tuesday
11	10258	1996-07-17 00:00:00.000	Wednesday
12	10259	1996-07-18 00:00:00.000	Thursday
13	10260	1996-07-19 00:00:00.000	Friday
14	10261	1996-07-19 00:00:00.000	Friday
15	10262	1996-07-22 00:00:00.000	Monday
16	10263	1996-07-23 00:00:00.000	Tuesday
17	10264	1996-07-24 00:00:00.000	Wednesday
18	10265	1996-07-25 00:00:00.000	Thursday

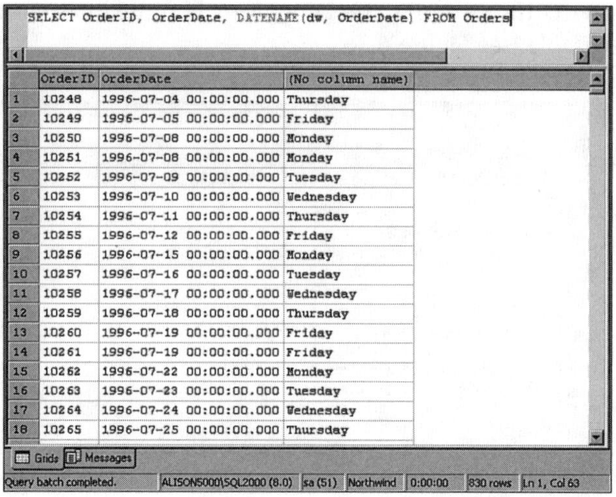

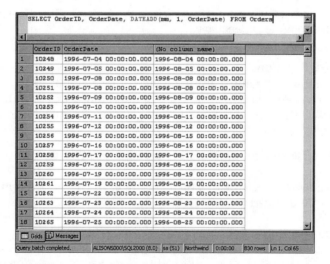

FIGURE 6.37 A SELECT statement that returns the OrderID, the OrderDate, and a text description of the day of the week of the OrderDate.

```
SELECT OrderID, OrderDate, DATEADD(mm, 1, OrderDate) FROM Orders
```

	OrderID	OrderDate	(No column name)
1	10248	1996-07-04 00:00:00.000	1996-08-04 00:00:00.000
2	10249	1996-07-05 00:00:00.000	1996-08-05 00:00:00.000
3	10250	1996-07-08 00:00:00.000	1996-08-08 00:00:00.000
4	10251	1996-07-08 00:00:00.000	1996-08-08 00:00:00.000
5	10252	1996-07-09 00:00:00.000	1996-08-09 00:00:00.000
6	10253	1996-07-10 00:00:00.000	1996-08-10 00:00:00.000
7	10254	1996-07-11 00:00:00.000	1996-08-11 00:00:00.000
8	10255	1996-07-12 00:00:00.000	1996-08-12 00:00:00.000
9	10256	1996-07-15 00:00:00.000	1996-08-15 00:00:00.000
10	10257	1996-07-16 00:00:00.000	1996-08-16 00:00:00.000
11	10258	1996-07-17 00:00:00.000	1996-08-17 00:00:00.000
12	10259	1996-07-18 00:00:00.000	1996-08-18 00:00:00.000
13	10260	1996-07-19 00:00:00.000	1996-08-19 00:00:00.000
14	10261	1996-07-19 00:00:00.000	1996-08-19 00:00:00.000
15	10262	1996-07-22 00:00:00.000	1996-08-22 00:00:00.000
16	10263	1996-07-23 00:00:00.000	1996-08-23 00:00:00.000
17	10264	1996-07-24 00:00:00.000	1996-08-24 00:00:00.000
18	10265	1996-07-25 00:00:00.000	1996-08-25 00:00:00.000

FIGURE 6.38 A SELECT statement that returns the OrderID, the OrderDate, and the date one month greater than the order date.

The DATEDIFF Function

The DATEDIFF function returns the difference between two dates. It receives three parameters. The first is the time period that you want the difference to appear in (days, months, and so on). The second and third parameters are the dates whose difference you want to evaluate. Here's an example:

```
SELECT OrderID, OrderDate, ShippedDate,
DATEDIFF(dd, OrderDate, ShippedDate) FROM Orders
```

This example returns the OrderID, OrderDate, ShippedDate, and number of days between the OrderDate and the ShippedDate (see Figure 6.39).

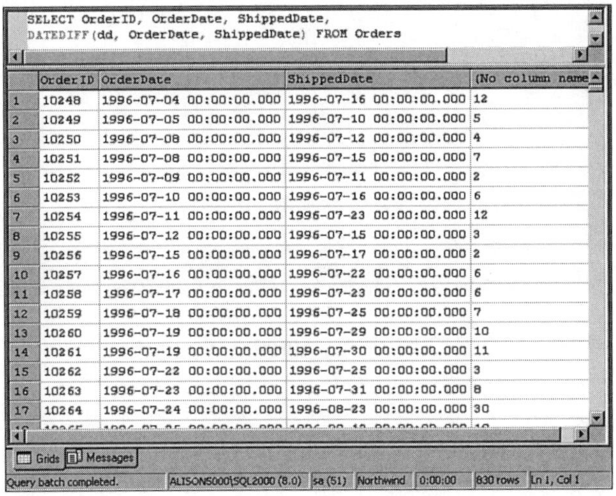

```
SELECT OrderID, OrderDate, ShippedDate,
DATEDIFF(dd, OrderDate, ShippedDate) FROM Orders
```

	OrderID	OrderDate	ShippedDate	(No column name)
1	10248	1996-07-04 00:00:00.000	1996-07-16 00:00:00.000	12
2	10249	1996-07-05 00:00:00.000	1996-07-10 00:00:00.000	5
3	10250	1996-07-08 00:00:00.000	1996-07-12 00:00:00.000	4
4	10251	1996-07-08 00:00:00.000	1996-07-15 00:00:00.000	7
5	10252	1996-07-09 00:00:00.000	1996-07-11 00:00:00.000	2
6	10253	1996-07-10 00:00:00.000	1996-07-16 00:00:00.000	6
7	10254	1996-07-11 00:00:00.000	1996-07-23 00:00:00.000	12
8	10255	1996-07-12 00:00:00.000	1996-07-15 00:00:00.000	3
9	10256	1996-07-15 00:00:00.000	1996-07-17 00:00:00.000	2
10	10257	1996-07-16 00:00:00.000	1996-07-22 00:00:00.000	6
11	10258	1996-07-17 00:00:00.000	1996-07-23 00:00:00.000	6
12	10259	1996-07-18 00:00:00.000	1996-07-25 00:00:00.000	7
13	10260	1996-07-19 00:00:00.000	1996-07-29 00:00:00.000	10
14	10261	1996-07-19 00:00:00.000	1996-07-30 00:00:00.000	11
15	10262	1996-07-22 00:00:00.000	1996-07-25 00:00:00.000	3
16	10263	1996-07-23 00:00:00.000	1996-07-31 00:00:00.000	8
17	10264	1996-07-24 00:00:00.000	1996-08-23 00:00:00.000	30

FIGURE 6.39 A `SELECT` statement that returns the OrderID, OrderDate, ShippedDate, and number of days between the OrderDate and the ShippedDate.

Working with Nulls

Several functions help you deal with nulls in your table data. They include `ISNULL`, `NULLIF`, and `COALESCE`. The sections that follow cover these functions.

The `ISNULL` Function

The `ISNULL` function returns information on whether the value in an expression is null. It receives two parameters. The first parameter is the expression that you want to evaluate. The second is the value that you want to return if the expression is null. The `ISNULL` function looks like this:

```
SELECT CustomerID, Region,
ISNULL(Region, 'No Region')
FROM Customers
```

This example returns the CustomerID and Region fields from the Customers table. If the region is null, the third column contains the words `No Region`. Otherwise, the third column contains the value for the region (see Figure 6.40).

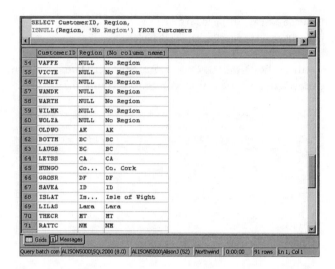

FIGURE 6.40   A SELECT statement that handles nulls in the Region field.

The NULLIF Function

The NULLIF function replaces specified values with nulls. It receives two parameters. The first is the name of the expression that you want to replace. The second is the value that you want to replace with nulls. Here's an example:

```
SELECT AVG(NULLIF(Freight, 0)) FROM Orders
```

This example calculates the average freight amount in the Orders table, eliminating 0 values from the calculation (see Figure 6.41).

The COALESCE Function

The COALESCE function returns the first non-null expression in a series of expressions. SQL Server evaluates the first expression. If it is null, it evaluates the second expression. If the second expression is null, it evaluates the third expression. This continues until the function reaches the last expression. Here's an example:

```
SELECT CustomerID,
COALESCE(Region, PostalCode, Country)
FROM Customers
```

This example returns the CustomerID. It then returns the Region if it is not null. If the region is null, it evaluates the PostalCode. If it is non-null, the PostalCode is returned. Otherwise, it evaluates the country (see Figure 6.42).

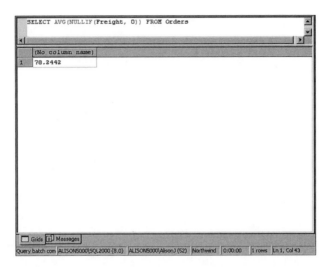

FIGURE 6.41   A SELECT statement that calculates the average freight amount in the Orders table, eliminating 0 values from the calculation.

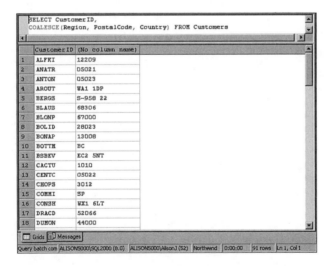

FIGURE 6.42   A SELECT statement that uses the COALESCE function to appropriately handle nulls in the Region and PostalCode fields.

Summary

The T-SQL language is the foundation for most of what you do in SQL Server. It is therefore necessary that you have a strong understanding of the T-SQL language constructs. This chapter covered all of the basics of the T-SQL language. We will cover T-SQL in additional detail throughout the remainder of the book.

7

Working with SQL Server Views

Why This Chapter Is Important

A view is a saved SELECT statement. A view can retrieve data from one or more tables. Once a view is created, you can select data from a view just as you can select it from a table. Views allow you to select data; they cannot update data (although you can update the data in the result of a view). For example, a T-SQL UPDATE statement in a stored procedure updates data. Although you cannot use a T-SQL UPDATE statement in a view, you can update the results returned from a SELECT statement.

Views have several advantages. They allow you to:

- Join data so that users can easily work with it

- Aggregate data so that users can easily work with it

- Customize data to users' needs

- Hide underlying column names from users

- Limit the columns and rows that a user works with

- Easily secure data

Although a normalized database is easy to work with and maintain from a programmer's viewpoint, it is not always easy for the user to work with. For example, if the user looks at the NorthWind Orders table, he sees only the customer ID associated with the order. If he wants to see the customer's name, he must join the two tables. This is not a particularly easy task for the user to accomplish. Using a view, you can join the Customers and Orders table. You provide the view to the user. The user can build forms, queries, and reports that are based on the view without having to understand how to join the underlying tables.

Just as a view can join data, it can aggregate data. You can very easily create a view that contains the total order amounts for each customer. The user can use the view as the foundation for forms, queries, and reports that he builds. Again, it is not necessary for the user to understand the syntax required to aggregate the data.

Another advantage of views is their capability to customize data to users' needs. For example, a column in a view can combine the first name and last name of a customer, or it can combine the customer's city, state, and ZIP code. The user does not need to understand how to combine this information. Instead, he uses the view as the foundation for the forms, queries, and reports that he needs. Just as a view can combine fields, it can also contain calculations, once again facilitating the data retrieval process for the user.

Developers often use column names that are not particularly intuitive for users. This is another situation in which views come to the rescue. You can easily build a view that aliases column names. The user will never see the underlying column names. You simply provide him with access to the view, and he can easily build the forms, queries, and reports that he needs.

The number of fields in a table can be overwhelming to a user. Most of the time, the user needs certain fields for the majority of the work that he does. You can create views containing only the critical fields. This simplifies the process when the user builds forms, queries, and reports based on the table data.

A major advantage of views is the security that they provide. You can grant logins and roles the rights to views *without* granting them rights to the underlying tables. An example is an employee table. You can create a view that includes the EmployeeID, FirstName, LastName, Extension, and other nonsensitive fields. You can then grant rights to the view. Although the users have no rights to the Employee table—and, therefore, have no access to fields such as the employee salary—they gain rights to the rows and columns included in the view.

Earlier versions of SQL Server imposed several limitations on the capabilities of views. You could not parameterize views. Furthermore, you could not include an ORDER BY clause within a view. Views could not contain triggers, nor could you index views. As you'll see in this chapter, SQL Server 2000 does away with all of these limitations. Using user-defined functions, you can parameterize views. Using the TOP syntax, you can order view results. SQL Server 2000 allows you to create INSTEAD OF triggers. Finally, SQL Server 2000 introduces indexed views. All of these new features make SQL Server 2000 views more powerful than ever!

Creating a Simple View

A view is actually a SELECT statement with a CREATE VIEW statement that causes SQL Server to save it as a view. You can use several different methods to create a SQL Server view:

- You can use the Create View Wizard to create a view.

- You can use the Enterprise Manager Query Builder to create a view.

- You can create a view from within an Access Project.

- You can use the Query Analyzer to create a view.

- You can use T-SQL to create a view.

The sections that follow cover each of these options.

Using the Create View Wizard to Create a View

The Create View Wizard facilitates the process of creating a view. To create a view
with the Create View Wizard:

1. Select Tools, Wizards from within the Enterprise Manager. The Select Wizard
   dialog box appears.

2. Expand the Database node. Select Create View Wizard and click OK. The Create
   View Wizard appears. Click Next.

3. The Select Database step of the wizard appears. Select the database that will
   contain the view and click Next.

4. The Select Objects step of the wizard appears (see Figure 7.1). Use the Include
   in View check box to select the objects that the view will reference, and click
   Next.

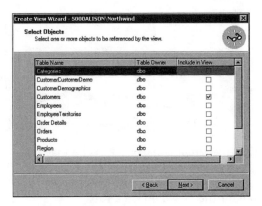

FIGURE 7.1   The Select Objects step of the wizard allows you to designate the objects
that the view will reference.

5. The Select Columns step of the wizard appears (see Figure 7.2). Select the columns that you want to include in the view and click Next.

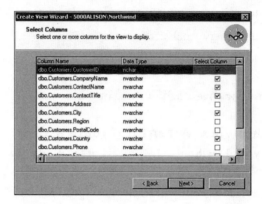

FIGURE 7.2   The Select Columns step of the Columns step of wizard allows you to select the columns that you want to include in the view.

6. Enter an Columns step ofoptional WHERE clause that limits the data displayed in the view (see Figure 7.3), and click Next.

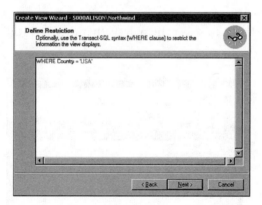

FIGURE 7.3   You can enter an optional WHERE clause that limits the data displayed in the view.

7. Provide a name for the view and click Next.

8. The Create View Wizard displays the SQL for the CREATE VIEW statement (see Figure 7.4). Click Finish.

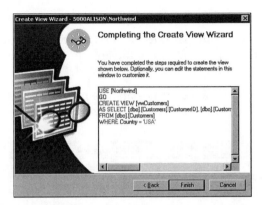

FIGURE 7.4   The final step of the Create View Wizard displays the SQL for the CREATE VIEW statement.

9. You should receive a message that SQL Server successfully created the view. Click OK. After closing and saving the view, it appears as in Figure 7.5.

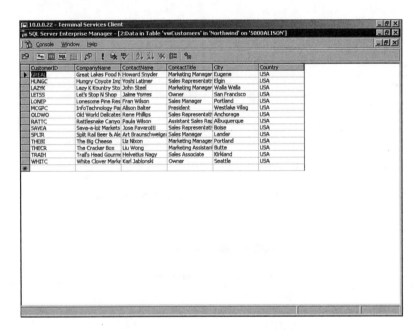

FIGURE 7.5   An example of a view created with the Create View Wizard.

Using the Enterprise Manager Query Builder to Create a View

Although it requires very little knowledge, the Create View Wizard is not very flexible. For that reason, you may opt to use the Enterprise Manager Query Builder to create a view. Here are the steps involved:

1. Right-click the Views node of the database in which you want the view to appear, and select New View. The New View window appears (see Figure 7.6).

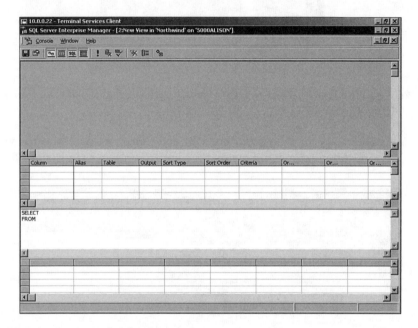

FIGURE 7.6   An example of a new view.

2. Click the Add Table tool on the toolbar. The Add Table dialog box appears (see Figure 7.7).

FIGURE 7.7   The Add Table dialog box allows you to add tables, views, and functions to your view.

3. Click each table, view, and function that you want to add to the view, and click Add. In the example shown in Figure 7.8, the Customers and Orders tables are included in the view.

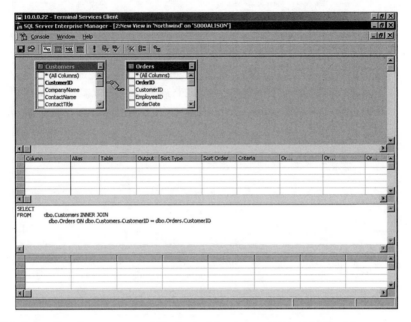

FIGURE 7.8 The Customers and Orders tables appear joined in the view.

4. Click the check boxes to the left of the field names to select the fields that you want to add to the view. If you prefer, you can drag and drop fields to the column list on the query grid. Figure 7.9 shows a view with the CustomerID, CompanyName, Country, OrderID, OrderDate, and Freight fields included.

5. Specify any criteria that you want to apply to the view. To add criteria, enter the desired criteria in the Criteria column of the appropriate field on the query grid. Adding criteria limits the records returned when you execute the view. Figure 7.9 shows criteria limiting the selected records to those in USA and Canada.

6. Test the view using the Run button. SQL Server prompts you to save changes to the view.

7. The view appears in the list of views under the View node. You can treat it much like a table.

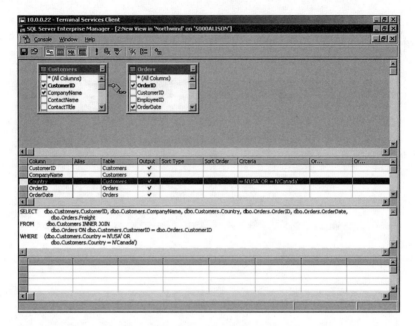

FIGURE 7.9   A view with selected fields and criteria.

NOTE

The Query Builder offers fours panes. These are the diagram pane, the grid pane, the SQL pane, and the results pane. The diagram pane shows you the tables included in the view. The grid pane graphically presents you with the columns, aliases, tables, groupings, and criteria for the data in the view. The SQL pane shows you the actual SQL statement that underlies the view. The results pane provides you with the results of executing the view. You can easily hide and show each of these panes using the Show/Hide Diagram Pane tool, the Show/Hide Grid Pane tool, the Show/Hide SQL Pane tool, and the Show/Hide Results Pane tool, respectively.

TIP

You can easily drag and drop tables to the diagram pane of the view. Simply resize the View and Console windows so that you can see both windows simultaneously, and then drag and drop the tables from the Tables node of the appropriate database to the diagram pane of the view.

Creating a View from an Access Project

Another option is to create a view from within an Access project. After you launch the View Designer, you will see that the process is identical to that of creating a view from within the Enterprise Manager. The process is:

1. Select Queries from the Objects list.

2. Double-click Create View in Designer. The View window appears.

3. Define the columns, criteria, and other attributes of the view, as covered in the section of this chapter titled "Using the Enterprise Manager Query Builder to Create a View."

4. The view appears in the Database window. You can treat it much like a table (see Figure 7.10).

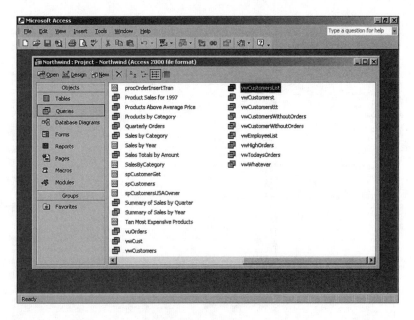

FIGURE 7.10 An Access Data Project (ADP) with a view.

Creating a View from the Query Analyzer

The Query Analyzer facilitates the process of creating a view by providing you with a template for views. Creating a view with the Query Analyzer is not as easy or intuitive as creating a view with the Create View Wizard or the Enterprise Manager Query Builder. Its advantage is in its flexibility; it allows you to include syntax unsupported in the graphical tools. To create a view from the Query Analyzer:

1. Open the Query Analyzer.

2. Use the Database drop-down list to select the database that will contain the view.

3. Click to select the Templates tab of the Object Browser (see Figure 7.11).

4. Expand the Create View node of the Object Browser.

5. You can create a view with a basic template, create a view with CHECK OPTION, or create a view with schema binding. Double-click the appropriate option. A window appears with the basic syntax required to create the view (see Figure 7.12).

6. Modify the syntax to customize it for your needs (see Figure 7.13).

7. Click the Execute Query button to create the view.

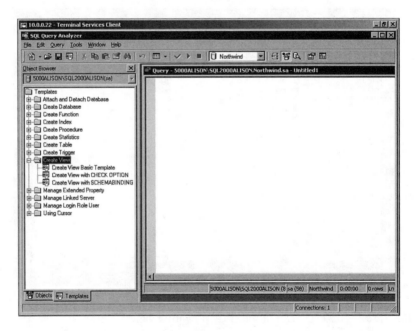

FIGURE 7.11   The Templates tab of the Object Browser allows you to create a view based on a template.

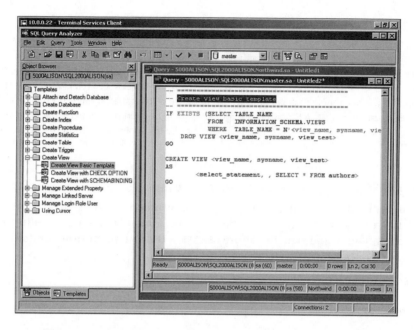

FIGURE 7.12   When you double-click the appropriate template, a window appears with the basic syntax required to create the view.

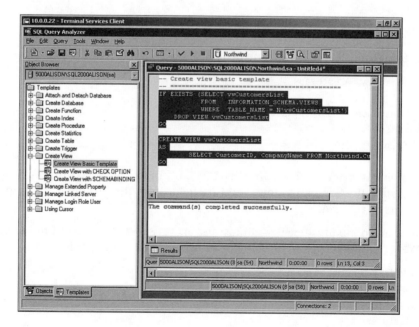

FIGURE 7.13   You must customize the template to create the view that you need.

Using T-SQL to Create or Modify a View

In addition to all of the alternatives that we have discussed thus far, you can use T-SQL to create a view. Rather than starting with a template, as outlined in the previous section, you would type the entire CREATE VIEW statement from scratch. The syntax for a CREATE VIEW statement is:

```
CREATE VIEW [DatabaseName] [<owner>] ViewName
    [(column [,...n])]
    [WITH <ViewAttribute> [,...n]]
AS
SelectStatement
[WITH CHECK OPTION]


<ViewAttribute> :: = [ENTCRYPTION|SCHEMASBINDING|VIEW_METADATA]
```

An example of a CREATE VIEW statement is:

```
CREATE VIEW vwUSACustomers
AS
SELECT CustomerID, CompanyName, City
FROM Customers
WHERE Country = 'USA'
```

The statement creates a view named vwUSACustomers that selects the contents of the CustomerID, CompanyName, and City fields from the Customers table for all customers in the USA.

If you want to modify a view, you must use an ALTER VIEW statement rather than a CREATE VIEW statement. An example of an ALTER VIEW statement is:

```
ALTER VIEW vwUSACustomers
AS
SELECT CustomerID, CompanyName, ContactName, City
FROM Customers
WHERE Country = 'USA'
```

This example modifies the vwUSACustomers view, adding the ContactName field to the view.

Creating Complex Views

Views can contain complex joins and subqueries. The sections that follow cover these and other advanced topics.

Creating Views Based on Data in Multiple Tables

Creating a view based on data from multiple tables is quite simple. While in the View Builder, you use the Add Table tool on the toolbar to add additional tables to the view. SQL Server automatically joins the tables based on relationships established in the database.

Views and Subqueries

Just as a T-SQL statement can contain a subquery (see Chapter 6, "Mastering T-SQL"), a view can contain a subquery. The syntax looks like this:

```
CREATE VIEW vwCustomersWithoutOrders
AS
    SELECT CustomerID, CompanyName, ContactName
    FROM Customers
    WHERE NOT EXISTS
    (SELECT CustomerID FROM Orders WHERE
    Customers.CustomerID = Orders.CustomerID)
```

This example selects all customers that do not have orders. You would simply call the view like this:

```
SELECT * FROM vwCustomersWithoutOrders
```

An alternative to the subquery is a LEFT JOIN. A LEFT JOIN is almost always more efficient than a subquery. The section that follows covers views and outer joins.

Views and Outer Joins

As discussed in the preceding section, views, like T-SQL statements, can contain outer joins. Here's the subquery example rewritten as:

```
CREATE VIEW vwCustomersWithoutOrders2
AS
    SELECT Customers.CustomerID, CompanyName, ContactName
    FROM Customers LEFT JOIN Orders
    ON Customers.CustomerID = Orders.CustomerID
    WHERE Orders.CustomerID Is Null
```

This example uses a `LEFT JOIN` from the Customers table to the Orders table to accomplish its task. Because only orders with a Null CustomerID appear in the result, the view returns only customers without orders.

Views and Top Values

SQL Server 7.0 introduced the `TOP` syntax. It is available for both T-SQL statements and views. The `TOP` syntax for views works the same way as it does for tables. It looks like this:

```
SELECT TOP 100 Percent OrderID, OrderDate, Freight
FROM Orders
```

This example shows only that the `TOP` clause is available for views. The following section, "Sorting View Results," provides practical examples of the `TOP` clause.

Sorting View Results

Prior to SQL Server 7.0, you could not sort a view. Instead, you could sort the output only from a view. The syntax looked like this:

```
SELECT * FROM vwCust ORDER BY Country, CustomerName
```

SQL Server 7.0 introduced the capability to sort a view. The syntax is a little bit different than you might expect and, in fact, violates the ANSI SQL-92 standard. It looks like this:

```
CREATE VIEW vwHighOrders
AS
SELECT TOP 100 Percent OrderID, OrderDate, Freight
FROM Orders
ORDER BY Freight DESC
```

The combination of the `TOP` clause and the `ORDER BY` clause allows you to sort the view result. Of course, you can use similar syntax to return only the top values in the result:

```
CREATE VIEW vwHighOrders
AS
SELECT TOP 5 Percent OrderID, OrderDate, Freight
FROM Orders
ORDER BY Freight DESC
```

Although ANSI SQL-92 purists may argue that the nonstandard syntax should not be used, I don't see any reason why you should not use it.

Views and Functions

Prior to SQL Server 2000, a major limitation of views in SQL Server was that you could not parameterize them. SQL Server 2000 handles this limitation with the introduction of user-defined functions. User-defined functions allow you to pass parameters to functions as if they were stored procedures but allow you to work with the results as if they were views.

Two types of functions are available in SQL Server 2000. The first is built-in functions. You can use built-in functions within the views that you build. Here's an example:

```
ALTER VIEW vwTodaysOrders
AS
SELECT OrderID, OrderDate, Freight
FROM Orders
WHERE OrderDate = Convert(VarChar(10),GetDate(),101)
```

In this example, SQL Server returns only orders placed on the current day. The GetDate() function returns the current date and time. The Convert function converts this to the mm/dd/yyyy format so that the current date and time can be compared to the order date.

The second type of function available in SQL Server is user-defined functions. For more information on user-defined functions, see Chapter 8, "Designing SQL Server Stored Procedures, User-Defined Functions, and Triggers."

You can use built-in functions within the views that you build. Here's an example:

```
ALTER VIEW vwTodaysOrders
AS
SELECT OrderID, OrderDate, Freight
FROM Orders
WHERE OrderDate = Convert(VarChar(10),GetDate(),101)
```

In this example, SQL Server returns only orders placed on the current day. The GetDate() function returns the current date and time. The Convert function converts the date to the mm/dd/yyyy format so that the current date and time can be compared to the order date.

Views and Triggers

One of the limitations of views is that you cannot update the data in a view based on multiple joined tables. Fortunately, you can use INSTEAD OF triggers to overcome this limitation. Using an INSTEAD OF trigger, you can perform inserts, updates, and deletes on other tables. You can also use complex logic to update fields such as computed columns and time stamps. Chapter 8 covers INSTEAD OF triggers in detail.

Using Views to Secure Data

One of the major benefits of a view is the security that it provides. Consider the following view:

```
CREATE VIEW vwEmployeeList
AS
SELECT EmployeeID, FirstName, LastName, Extension
FROM Employees
```

This view selects the EmployeeID, FirstName, LastName, and Extension fields from the Employees table. In this scenario, you would grant no rights to certain users for the Employees table. Instead, you would grant them rights to the view. Figure 7.14 shows the Permissions dialog box for a view. Notice that the permissions available for a view are similar to those available for the table. As long as the owner of the table and the owner of the view are the same, the user will be able to interact with the table based on the permissions granted to the view.

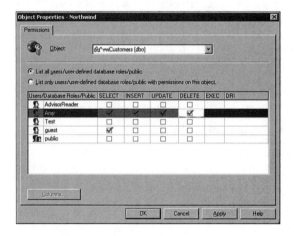

FIGURE 7.14   The permissions available for a view are similar to those available for the table.

Modifying Data in a View

With a few exceptions, the results of views are updateable. Recognize that a view is not a table and does not contain any data. Therefore, when you are modifying the data in a view, you are modifying the underlying table. You cannot violate any rules, check constraints, referential integrity rules, or any other rules that govern the data that can be contained in the tables. The following are limitations to the updateability of a view:

- If a view joins multiple tables, you can insert and update data in only one table at a time in the view result.

- The results of a view that aggregates data are not updateable.

- The results of a view that unions data without the UNION ALL clause are not updateable.

- The results of a view that contains a DISTINCT statement are not updateable.

- Text and image columns cannot be updated via a view.

Modifying Views

Modifying a view is similar to modifying a table.

1. Select Views from the Objects list.

2. Select the view whose attributes you want to modify.

3. Click Design. The design of the existing view appears.

4. Modify the attributes of the view.

5. Close the window and save your changes when you are done.

Renaming Views

Renaming a view is a relatively simple process.

1. Right-click the view that you want to rename and select Rename.

2. Enter a new name for the view. The dialog box shown in Figure 7.15 appears.

3. If you click Yes, the view is renamed. If you click No, the view returns to its original name. If you click View Dependencies, the Dependencies dialog box appears (see Figure 7.16).

FIGURE 7.15 When renaming a view, you are prompted for whether you want to rename the view and whether you want to look at its dependencies.

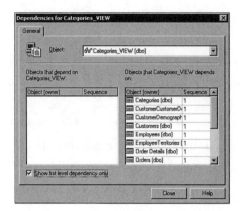

FIGURE 7.16 The Dependencies dialog box shows you what other objects a view depends on.

Deleting Views

Deleting a SQL Server view is simple:

1. Select Views from the Objects list.

2. Right-click the view that you want to delete.

3. Select Delete from the pop-up menu. The Drop Objects dialog box appears (see Figure 7.17).

4. If you want to look at the view's dependencies, click Show Dependencies. The Dependencies dialog box appears (see Figure 7.18).

5. Click Close when you are done viewing dependencies.

6. If you want to drop the view, click Drop All. SQL Server deletes the view.

FIGURE 7.17 The Drop Objects dialog box allows you to drop a view.

FIGURE 7.18   The Dependencies dialog box shows you what other objects a view depends on.

As with tables, it is important to remember that deleting a view from an ADP removes it from the SQL Server database. Again, this highlights the need for establishment of proper security on the SQL Server database.

Indexed Views

SQL Server 2000 introduced indexed views. They provide you with greatly improved performance by allowing you to create a unique clustered index for a view. Here's the reason why. SQL Server does not store the result set of a standard view in the database. Each time a query references the view, SQL Server dynamically creates the result set. The overhead of building the result set can be substantial, particularly for complex views. You can greatly improve performance by creating a unique clustered index for the view. When you create a unique clustered index, SQL Server stores the data that exists at the time you create the view. SQL Server then reflects all modifications to table data within the stored view. This improves the efficiency of data retrieval. Once you create a unique clustered index for the view, you can then create additional nonclustered indexes. An example of the syntax to create a unique clustered index is:

```
CREATE UNIQUE CLUSTERED INDEX [vwCustomerInfoCustomerID]
ON [dbo].[vwCustomerInfo] ([CustomerID])
```

This example creates a clustered index for the view called vwCustomerInfo based on the CustomerID field. The index is called vwCustomerInfoCustomerID and is based on the CustomerID field. Another example is:

```
CREATE INDEX [vwCustomerInfoCountry] ON [dbo].[vwCustomerInfo] ([Country])
```

It is easy to use the SQL Enterprise Manager to create an indexed view. Here are the steps:

1. Create the view.

2. Within the design of the view, click Properties.

3. Click to select the Bind to Schema property (see Figure 7.19).

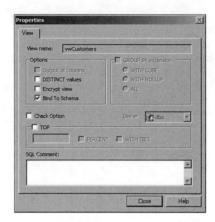

FIGURE 7.19   You must select the Bind to Schema property when creating an indexed view.

4. Close and save the view.

5. Right-click the view and select All Tasks, Manage Indexes (this feature is available only after you select the Bind to Schema property). The Manage Indexes dialog box appears (see Figure 7.20).

FIGURE 7.20   The Manage Indexes dialog box allows you to add, edit, and delete indexes.

6. Click New to create a new index. The Create New Index dialog box appears (see Figure 7.21).

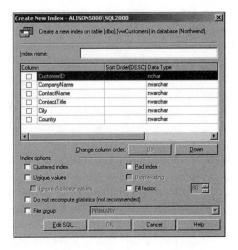

FIGURE 7.21   The Create New Index dialog box allows you to designate the specifics of a new index.

7. Enter a name for the index.

8. Click to select the column(s) included in the index.

9. Specify index options, such as whether the index is clustered and whether it is unique. Figure 7.22 shows an index called vwCustomersCustomerID. It is based on the CustomerID field and is clustered and unique.

FIGURE 7.22   An example of a clustered, unique index called vwCustomersCustomerID based on the CustomerID field.

10. Click Edit SQL, if desired, to view the SQL statement that you will execute (see Figure 7.23).

FIGURE 7.23   The Edit SQL feature allows you to view the SQL statement that you will execute.

11. Click Execute to create the index. You should receive a message that the index was successfully created (see Figure 7.24).

12. Click OK to close the dialog box. You are returned to the Manage Indexes dialog box, where you can create additional indexes, modify existing indexes, or delete unwanted indexes.

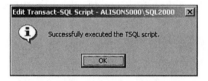

FIGURE 7.24   The message that appears indicating that an index created successfully.

NOTE

Indexed views are available only for the Enterprise Edition of SQL Server and the Developer Edition of SQL Server.

WARNING

If you add the Bind to Schema option to an already saved view, the Manage Indexes dialog box is unavailable until you refresh the table.

When to Use Indexed Views

Indexed views are not appropriate in all situations. Although indexed views speed up data retrieval, they slow data updates. You must therefore ascertain that the benefits of data retrieval performance outweigh the performance degradation experienced for data update operations.

Requirements for Indexed Views

Not all views can be indexed. A view must meet all of the following requirements for you to index it:

- The view cannot reference other views.
- The tables underlying the view must be in the same database as the view and must have the same owner as the view.
- You must set the ANSI_NULLS option to ON when you create the tables referenced by the view.
- You must set the ANSI_NULLS and QUOTED_IDENTIFIER options to ON before creating the view.
- You must create the view and any functions underlying the view with the SCHEMABINDING option. This means that you cannot modify or drop tables and other objects underlying the view without dropping the view first.

In addition to the limitations for the view, there are limitations for the syntax within the view. They are:

- You cannot use * to designate all columns.
- You cannot use the keyword UNION.
- You cannot use the keyword DISTINCT.
- You cannot include the keywords TOP or ORDER BY.
- You cannot use COUNT(*).
- You cannot include AVG, MAX, MIN, STDEV, STDEVP, VAR, or VARP.
- You cannot repeat a column in a view (for example, SELECT CustomerID, CompanyName, ContactName, CompanyName as Client).
- You cannot include derived tables or subqueries.

Optimizing the Views That You Build

The most important thing that you can do to improve the performance of your views is to design your indexes efficiently. The SQL Server query optimizer automatically selects the most efficient index for any query. It can select only from existing indexes. It is therefore necessary that you create all the indexes that your queries will need to execute. Here are the guidelines:

- Create indexes for any fields used in the criteria of queries.

- Create indexes for any fields that are included in the sorting or grouping of a query.

- Create indexes for all columns used in joins.

- *Do not* create indexes for columns that have very few unique values.

Displaying the Estimated Execution Plan

When in doubt about what indexes you need, the Query Analyzer can help you. Using the Query Analyzer, you can display the estimated execution plan for a query, perform index analysis, display the execution plan when the query executes, show a server trace, and show client statistics. Here's how:

1. Open Query Analyzer and enter the SQL statement underlying the view.

2. Select Query, Display Estimated Execution Plan (see Figure 7.25). The Query Analyzer appears as in Figure 7.26.

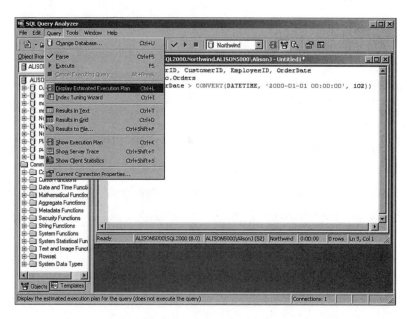

FIGURE 7.25   The Query Analyzer allows you to display the Estimated Execution Plan.

3. Hover your mouse pointer over each icon to show the statistics for that particular statement. In Figure 7.27, you can see that the search for the OrderDate uses an index seek. This is because an OrderDate index exists for the Orders table. Contrast this with Figure 7.28, in which SQL Server must perform an index scan. This is because no index exists for the ShipCountry field.

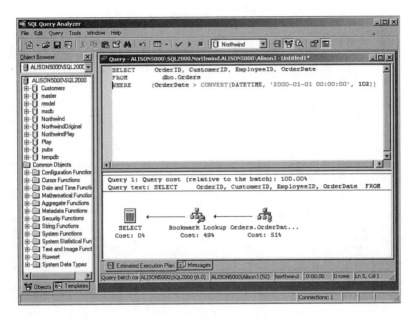

FIGURE 7.26 The Query Analyzer with the Estimated Execution Plan displayed.

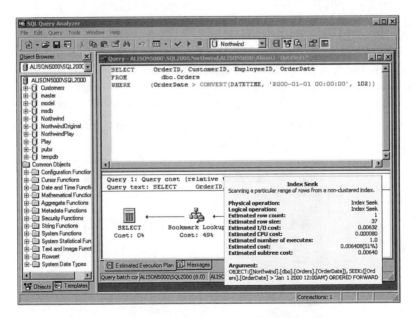

FIGURE 7.27 Because the necessary index is available, the search for the OrderDate uses an index seek.

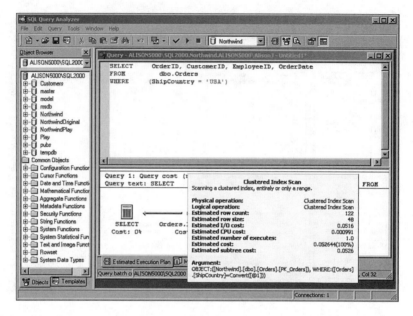

FIGURE 7.28   Because the necessary index is not available, the search for the ShipCountry uses an index scan.

Using the Index Tuning Wizard

Also available from the Query Analyzer is the capability to use the Index Tuning Wizard. The Index Tuning Wizard analyzes your database and the tables, views, stored procedures, functions, and other objects that it contains. It suggests the indexes that are necessary for the views and stored procedures that you build. Here's how:

1. Select Query, Index Tuning Wizard. The Index Tuning Wizard appears (see Figure 7.29). Click Next to continue.

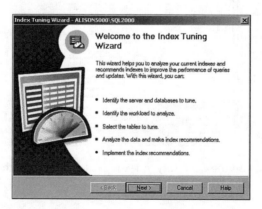

FIGURE 7.29   The Index Tuning Wizard suggests the indexes necessary for the views and stored procedures that you build.

2. Select the server and the database that you want to analyze, as well as whether you want to add indexed views. Also designate the tuning mode as Fast, Medium, or Thorough (see Figure 7.30). Click Next.

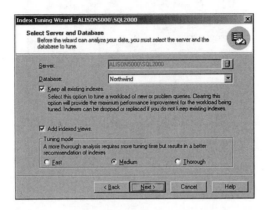

FIGURE 7.30   The Index Tuning Wizard allows you to select the server and the database that you want to analyze, as well as whether you want to add indexed views. You also can designate the tuning mode as Fast, Medium, or Thorough.

3. Specify a workload (see Figure 7.31).

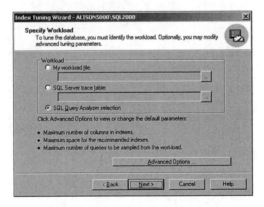

FIGURE 7.31   The Index Tuning Wizard allows you to specify a workload.

4. Click Advanced Options to designate additional tuning parameters (see Figure 7.32). Click OK when done, and Next to continue with the next step of the wizard.

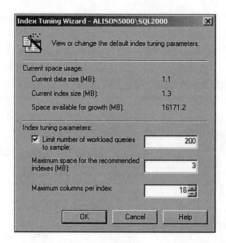

FIGURE 7.32   Click Advanced Options to designate additional tuning parameters.

5. Click to select the tables that you want to tune (see Figure 7.33). Click Next.

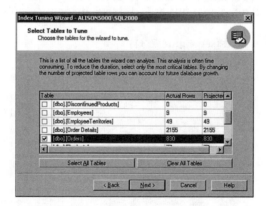

FIGURE 7.33   Click to select the tables that you want to tune.

6. SQL Server provides you with index recommendations (see Figure 7.34).

7. Click Analysis to see an analysis of indexes for the selected tables (see Figure 7.35).

8. Click Save to save the report or Close to close it. Click Next to go to the next step of the wizard, in which SQL Server asks you whether you want to apply the changes or save them to a script file (see Figure 7.36). Click Finish to complete the wizard.

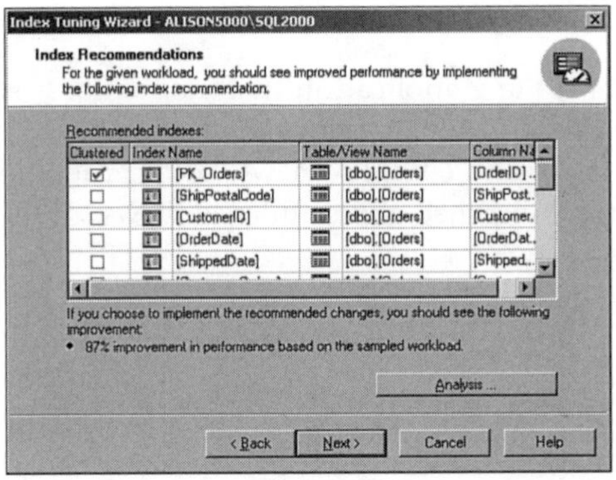

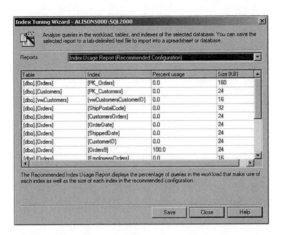

FIGURE 7.34   SQL Server provides you with index recommendations.

FIGURE 7.35   Click Analysis to see an analysis of indexes for the selected tables.

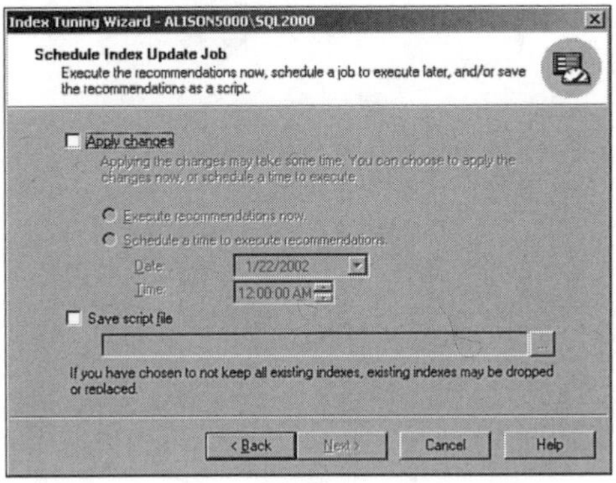

FIGURE 7.36   SQL Server asks you whether you want to apply the changes or save them to a script file.

Summary

Views are a critical part of any application that you build. It is therefore important that you understand how to create and work with views. This chapter showed you how to create both simple and complex views. You learned how to modify, rename, and delete views. You also learned about indexed views.

8

Designing SQL Server Stored Procedures, User-Defined Functions, and Triggers

Why This Chapter Is Important

Stored procedures are at the heart of any client/server application. This is because, using stored procedures, you can guarantee that processing is completed on the server. Stored procedures have many other benefits as well:

- Stored procedures help you to separate the client application from the structure of the database.

- Stored procedures help you to simplify client coding.

- Stored procedures process at the server (reducing required bandwidth).

- Stored procedures allow you to create reusable code.

- Stored procedures allow you to perform error handling at the server.

- Stored procedures facilitate the security of data.

- Because stored procedures are precompiled, they execute more quickly.

- Stored procedures improve the stability of the application.

- Stored procedures reduce network locking.

- When you build a stored procedure, a query plan is created. This query plan contains the most efficient method of executing the stored procedure given available indexes and so on.

This chapter covers the ins and outs of stored procedures. First, you learn about the basics of working with stored procedures. You then learn how to work with variables and how to control the flow of the stored procedures that you build. Next, we delve into more advanced techniques such as working with parameters, updating data, handling errors, and working with transactions.

Finally, you will learn about user-defined functions and triggers, two other important SQL Server objects. You will learn about the types of user-defined functions available. You will also learn how to include triggers in the applications that you build. All of the techniques covered in this chapter are integral to your success as a client/server developer.

Stored Procedure Basics

You can create stored procedures in the following manners:

- With the Create Stored Procedure Wizard
- From the Enterprise Manager
- Using the Query Analyzer
- From an Access ADP file
- Using T-SQL

Using the Create Stored Procedure Wizard to Create a Stored Procedure

The Create Stored Procedure Wizard facilitates the process of creating a stored procedure. To create a stored procedure with the Create Stored Procedure Wizard:

1. Select Tools, Wizards from within the Enterprise Manager. The Select Wizard dialog box appears.

2. Expand the Database node. Select Create Stored Procedure Wizard and click OK. The Create Stored Procedure Wizard appears. Click Next.

3. The Select Database step of the wizard appears. Select the database that will contain the stored procedure and click Next.

4. The Select Stored Procedures step of the wizard appears (see Figure 8.1). Use the Insert, Update, and Delete check boxes to select the objects that you want the wizard to build the stored procedures for and what actions you want the stored procedures to perform. Click Next.

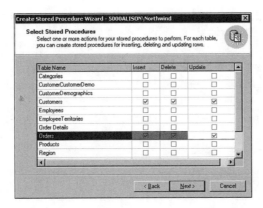

FIGURE 8.1   The Select Stored Procedures step of the wizard allows you to select the objects that you want the wizard to build the stored procedures for.

5. The final step of the wizard appears (see Figure 8.2). To modify a stored procedure, click the stored procedure that you want to modify and click Edit. The Edit Stored Procedure Properties dialog box appears (see Figure 8.3).

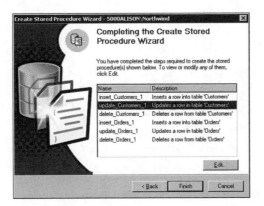

FIGURE 8.2   The final step of the wizard allows you to edit any of the stored procedures that the wizard is about to create.

6. Modify the name of the stored procedure, if desired, and select the columns that you want to include in the stored procedure.

7. Click Edit to edit the T-SQL behind the stored procedure, if desired. The Edit Stored Procedure SQL dialog box appears (see Figure 8.4).

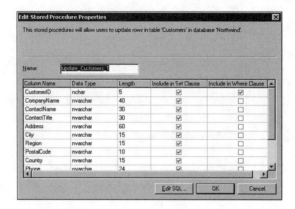

FIGURE 8.3   The Edit Stored Procedure Properties dialog box allows you to modify the name of the stored procedure and select the columns that you want to include in the stored procedure.

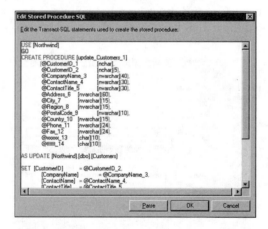

FIGURE 8.4   The Edit Stored Procedure SQL dialog box allows you to modify the T-SQL statement.

8. Modify the T-SQL as desired. Click Parse to check the syntax, and click OK to return to the wizard.

9. Click Finish to complete the process.

10. You should receive a message that SQL Server successfully created the stored procedures. Click OK. The resulting stored procedures appear in the Stored Procedures node of the Enterprise Manager (see Figure 8.5).

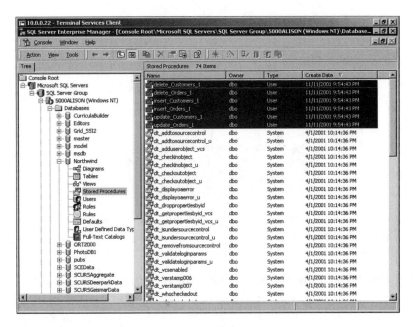

FIGURE 8.5 The stored procedures that the wizard creates appear in the Stored Procedures node of Enterprise Manager.

Using the Enterprise Manager to Create a Stored Procedure

To create a stored procedure from the Enterprise Manager:

1. Right-click the Stored Procedures node of the database to which you want to add the stored procedure.

2. Select New Stored Procedure. The Stored Procedure Properties dialog box appears (see Figure 8.6).

3. Type the T-SQL for the stored procedure.

4. Click Check Syntax to ensure that the syntax that you entered is correct.

5. Click OK to close the Stored Procedure Properties dialog box and save the stored procedure.

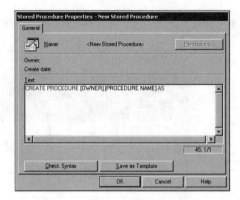

FIGURE 8.6   The Stored Procedure Properties dialog box allows you to type the T-SQL that the stored procedure will contain.

Using the Query Analyzer to Create a Stored Procedure

The Query Analyzer facilitates the process of creating a stored procedure by providing you with a template for stored procedures. Creating a stored procedure with the Query Analyzer is not as easy or intuitive as creating a stored procedure with the Create Stored Procedure Wizard. Its advantage is in its flexibility. To create a stored procedure from the Query Analyzer:

1. Open the Query Analyzer.

2. Use the Database drop-down list to select the database that will contain the stored procedure.

3. Click to select the Templates tab of the Object Browser (see Figure 8.7).

4. Expand the Create Procedure node of the Object Browser.

5. You can create a stored procedure with a basic template, with the CURSOR OUTPUT parameter, or with the OUTPUT parameter. Double-click the appropriate option. A window appears with the basic syntax required to create the stored procedure (see Figure 8.8).

6. Modify the syntax to customize it for your needs (see the example in Figure 8.9).

7. Click the Execute Query button to create the stored procedure.

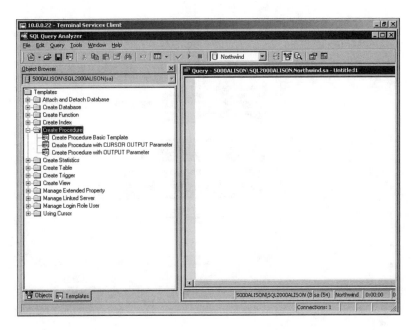

FIGURE 8.7   The Templates tab of the Object Browser allows you to create a stored procedure based on a template.

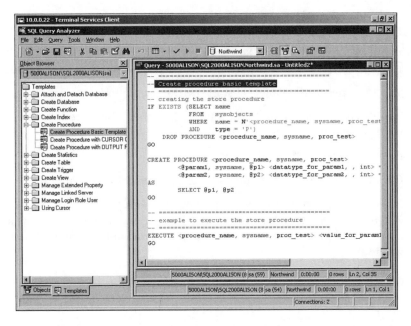

FIGURE 8.8   When you double-click the appropriate template, a window appears with the basic syntax required to create the stored procedure.

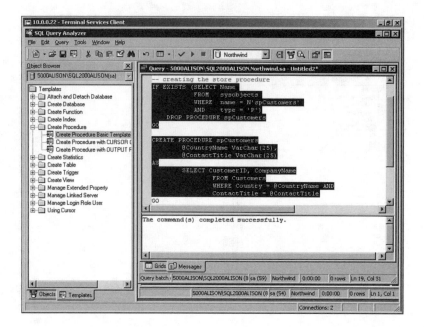

FIGURE 8.9   You must customize the template to create the stored procedure that you need.

Creating a Stored Procedure from an ADP File

If your application is an Access Data Project (ADP) file, you can create stored procedures directly from the Access environment. The following steps are required:

1. Select Queries in the Objects list of the Database window.

2. Double-click Create Stored Procedure in Designer. The Stored Procedure window appears (see Figure 8.10).

3. Enter the text for the stored procedure.

4. Click the Save tool on the toolbar. The Save As dialog box appears.

5. Enter the name for the stored procedure and click OK. The stored procedure is added to the database associated with the Access Data Project. It appears in the list of stored procedures in the Database window and can be modified from within Access.

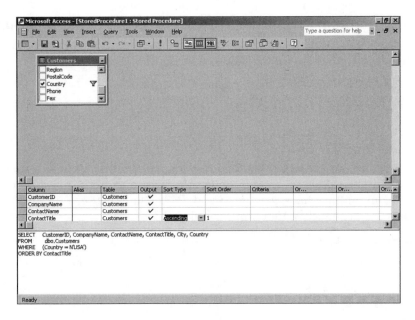

FIGURE 8.10   The Stored Procedure dialog box allows you to build a stored procedure on a database server.

Using T-SQL to Create a Stored Procedure

The following is the syntax required to create a stored procedure:

```
(CREATE or ALTER) Procedure ProcName
[@ParameterName datatype (length)],
[@ParameterName datatype (length)]
AS
[BEGIN]
stored procedure code goes here...
[END]
```

An example is:

```
CREATE PROCEDURE procGetCustomers
AS
SELECT CompanyName, ContactName,
    ContactTitle, City
FROM Customers
ORDER BY City, CompanyName
```

This example creates a procedure called `procGetCustomers`. The procedure selects the contents of the CompanyName, ContactName, ContactTitle, and City fields from the Customers table, ordering the results by the City and CompanyName fields.

Including Comments in the Stored Procedures That You Build

Many people fail to add comments to the stored procedures that they build. Comments are important for the following reasons:

- They allow you to document complex processes.
- They allow you to enter the creation date and author.
- They allow you to easily track revisions.

Comments are easy to implement. To add a comment within a line of a stored procedure, you use two dashes (- -). This renders the remainder of the line as a comment. To comment multiple lines, you use /* and */. The lines between the /* and the */ are considered comments. Here's an example:

```
CREATE Procedure MyProc
AS
BEGIN    --This is a comment
   SELECT * from Orders
   /*  This comment
   spans for multiple
   lines in the stored procedure
   */
END
```

Notice the difference between the single-line comment and the block comment.

Calling the Stored Procedures That You Build

You can use three methods to execute a stored procedure:

- procGetCustomers
- EXECUTE procGetCustomers
- EXEC procGetCustomers

Although in many situations you can get away with omitting the keyword EXEC, it is generally a good idea to get into the habit of using it.

Declaring and Working with Variables

Just as you can create variables within the subroutines and functions that you build, you can declare variables in your stored procedures. You use the keyword DECLARE to create a variable. The syntax looks like this:

```
DECLARE @VariableName DataType [(length)], @VariableName DataType [(length)]
```

Here's an example:

```
DECLARE @FirstName VarChar(35)
```

Uninitialized variables are assigned the value Null. You use a SELECT statement to assign a value to a variable. It looks like this:

```
SELECT @FirstName = 'Alexis'
```

The following is a stored procedure that illustrates the use of a variable:

```
DECLARE @strCompany varchar (50)
SELECT @strCompany = Upper(CompanyName)
FROM Customers
WHERE CustomerID = 'ALFKI'
SELECT @strCompany
```

The example declares a variable called @strCompany. The code stores the uppercase version of the CompanyName associated with the customer ALFKI in the variable. The procedure returns the variable in a SELECT. Figure 8.11 illustrates the result of executing the sample stored procedure.

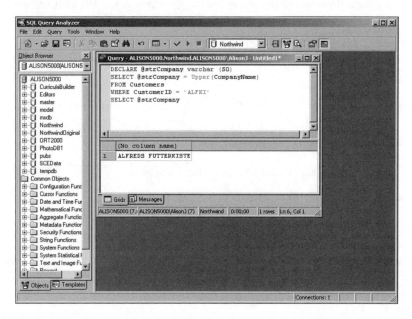

FIGURE 8.11   An example of a variable used in a stored procedure.

Controlling the Flow

Often you want specified statements in your stored procedure to execute only if certain conditions are true. T-SQL contains several constructs that allow you to control the flow of your stored procedures. These include BEGIN...END, IF...ELSE, GOTO, RETURN, CASE, and WHILE. The sections that follow cover each of these constructs.

IF...ELSE

You use the IF...ELSE construct to make a decision within the stored procedure. This decision is generally based on parameters supplied to the stored procedure. The IF...ELSE construct works like this:

```
IF (SomeCondition)
    BEGIN
        --Execute multiple statements
    END
```

With this version of the IF...ELSE construct, certain statements execute only if the condition is true. No special statements execute if the condition is false. The construct that follows accommodates for the scenario when the condition is false:

```
IF (SomeCondition)
    BEGIN
        --Execute multiple statements
    END
ELSE
    BEGIN
        --Execute multiple statement
    END
```

Here's an example of an IF...THEN construct in action:

```
DECLARE @Locale VarChar(20), @Country VarChar(30)

SELECT @Country = Country
    FROM Customers
    WHERE CustomerID = 'ALFKI'

IF @Country    = 'USA'
    BEGIN
        SELECT @Locale = 'Domestic'
    END
```

```
ELSE
    BEGIN
        SELECT @Locale= 'Foreign'
    END

SELECT CustomerID, @Locale
    FROM Customers
    WHERE CustomerID = 'ALFKI'
```

The code begins by declaring two variables: @Locale and @Country. It stores the contents of the Country field for the customer ALFKI in the @Country variable. It then evaluates the contents of the @Country variable, storing the appropriate locale in the @Locale variable. Finally, it returns the CustomerID and the contents of the @Locale variable for the customer with the CustomerID ALFKI. Figure 8.12 provides an example of executing the stored procedure.

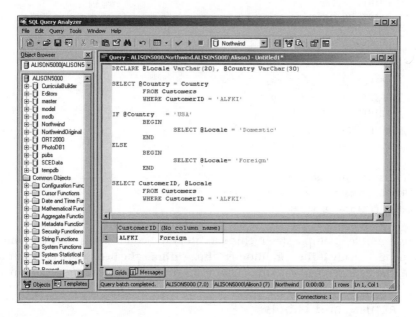

FIGURE 8.12   An example of executing a stored procedure that includes an IF...ELSE construct.

NOTE

It is important to note that if you want to execute more than one statement under a specific condition, you must enclose the statements within the BEGIN...END construct (as explained in the next section).

BEGIN...END

The BEGIN...END construct allows you to group a series of statements together. Without the BEGIN...END construct, only the first statement after the IF or the ELSE executes. Consider the following example:

```
DECLARE @Locale VarChar(20), @Country VarChar(30)

SELECT @Country = Country
    FROM Customers
    WHERE CustomerID = 'ALFKI'

IF @Country   = 'USA'
    BEGIN
        SELECT @Locale = 'Domestic'
        PRINT 'This is domestic'
        PRINT ' '
        PRINT 'Hello there'
    END
ELSE
    BEGIN
        SELECT @Locale= 'Foreign'
        PRINT 'This is foreign'
        PRINT ' '
        PRINT 'Hello there'
    END

SELECT CustomerID, @Locale
    FROM Customers
    WHERE CustomerID = 'ALFKI'
```

In this example, multiple statements execute if the condition is true, and multiple statements execute if the condition is false. Without the BEGIN...END construct after the IF, the code renders an error. Figure 8.13 shows this stored procedure in action.

GOTO, RETURN, and Labels

You use the GOTO statement to jump to a label in your stored procedure. Most programmers use this statement most commonly in error handling. The RETURN statement unconditionally exits the stored procedure without executing any other statements. A Label is a named area of code in your stored procedure. These three keywords are covered together because they generally work as a group. Consider the following examples:

FIGURE 8.13   An example of executing a stored procedure that includes a BEGIN...END construct.

```
IF Month(GetDate()) > 6
    BEGIN
        PRINT 'In IF Statement'
        GOTO MyLabel
    END
SELECT CustomerID, CompanyName FROM Customers

MyLabel:
    SELECT  OrderID, OrderDate FROM Orders
```

This example evaluates to see if the month associated with the current date is greater than the value 6. If it is, the statement In IF Statement prints and code execution jumps to the label MyLabel. The procedure then selects data from the Orders table. If the month associated with the current date is less than or equal to the value 6, the procedure first selects data from the Customers table. Code execution then falls into the label where the procedure selects data from the Orders table. Figure 8.14 shows an example of executing the code when the month associated with the current date is greater than 6. Figure 8.15 shows the sample procedure in which the month associated with the current date is less than or equal to 6.

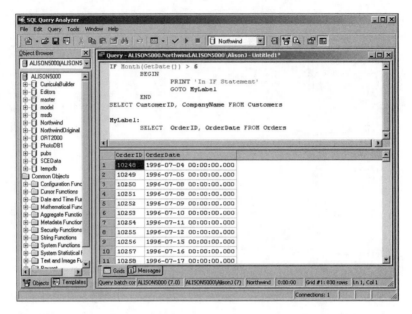

FIGURE 8.14   An example of executing a stored procedure that includes GOTO and a label.

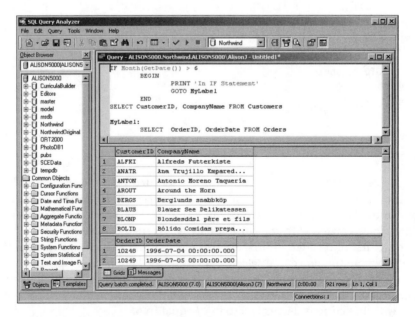

FIGURE 8.15   An example of executing the same stored procedure with a different value for the month of the current date.

As mentioned, a RETURN statement unequivocally exits from the procedure. Take a look at the procedure that follows:

```
IF Month(GetDate()) > 6
    BEGIN
        PRINT 'In IF Statement'
        GOTO MyLabel
    END
SELECT CustomerID, CompanyName FROM Customers
RETURN

MyLabel:
    SELECT  OrderID, OrderDate FROM Orders
```

In this example, if the month associated with the current date is greater than the value 6, the In IF Statement message appears and then the procedure returns data from the Orders table. If the month associated with the current date is less than or equal to the value 6, the code selects data from the Customers table and then exits the procedure. Because of the RETURN statement, the procedure does not select data from the Orders table. Figure 8.16 shows an example of executing the code when the month associated with the current date is greater than 6. Figure 8.17 shows the sample procedure in which the month associated with the current date is less than or equal to 6.

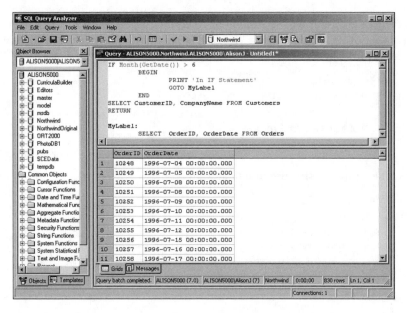

FIGURE 8.16 An example of executing a stored procedure that includes the RETURN statement.

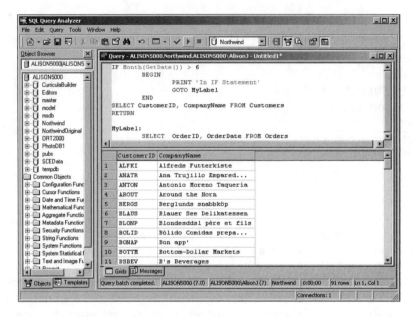

FIGURE 8.17   An example of executing the same stored procedure with a different value for the month of the current date.

CASE

Most developers use the CASE statement to compare a result from a SQL statement against a set of simple responses. The CASE statement replaces a table value with an alternate value. The CASE statement looks like this:

```
CASE InputExpression
    WHEN WhenExpression THEN ResultExpression
        [...n]
    [ELSE ElseResultExpression]
END
```

Here's an example of this use of a CASE statement:

```
SELECT OrderID, OrderDate,
    CASE ShipVIA
        WHEN 1 THEN 'UPS'
        WHEN 2 THEN 'FedEx'
        WHEN 3 THEN 'U.S. Mail'
    END AS Shipper,
    Freight FROM Orders
```

The expression selects the OrderID, OrderDate, and Freight fields from the Orders table. The CASE statement evaluates the contents of the ShipVIA field. It returns an appropriate string depending on the value in the ShipVIA field. Figure 8.18 illustrates this example.

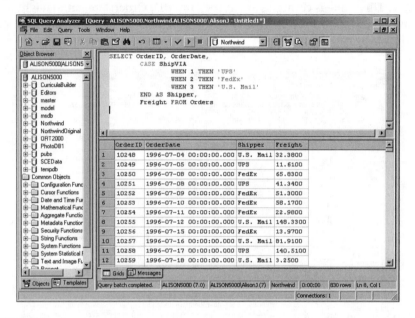

FIGURE 8.18 An example of executing a CASE statement that replaces a table value with an alternate value.

The second use of the CASE construct looks like this:

```
CASE
    WHEN Expression THEN TruePart
    ELSE FalsePart
END
```

Here's an example:

```
DECLARE @AverageFreight Money
SELECT @AverageFreight = AVG(Freight) FROM Orders

SELECT OrderID, OrderDate, Freight,
    CASE
        WHEN FREIGHT <= @AverageFreight
        THEN 'Low Freight'
        ELSE 'High Freight'
    END AS Shipper,
    Freight FROM Orders
```

The example first declares the @AverageFreight variable. It sets the variable equal to the average freight amount from the Orders table. The CASE statement evaluates whether the freight of the current row is less than or equal to the average freight amount. If so, the statement returns Low Freight. Otherwise, it returns High Freight. This value is combined with the OrderID, OrderDate, and Freight amounts that are also selected from the table. Figure 8.19 shows this use of the CASE statement in action.

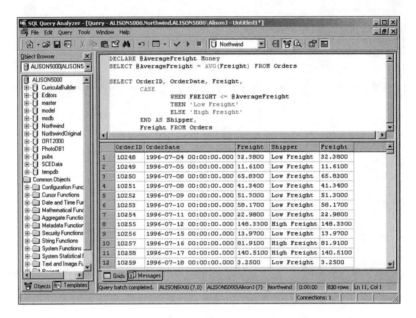

FIGURE 8.19   An alternative use of the CASE statement.

WHILE

You use the WHILE statement when you want to set up a loop. The loop continues to execute until the specified condition is met. The WHILE construct looks like this:

```
WHILE BooleanExpression
    (SQLStatement | SQLBlock)
```

Here's an example:

```
CREATE TABLE MyTable
(
LoopID INT,
LoopText VarChar(25)
)


DECLARE @LoopValue INT
```

```
DECLARE @LoopText CHAR(25)

SELECT @LoopValue = 1

WHILE (@LoopValue < 100)
BEGIN
    SELECT @LoopText = 'Iteration #' + Convert(VarChar(25), @LoopValue)
    INSERT INTO MyTable(LoopID, LoopText)
        VALUES (@LoopValue, @LoopText)
    SELECT @LoopValue = @LoopValue + 1
END

SELECT * FROM MyTable
```

The routine first creates a table called MyTable. The table contains two fields, an INT field and a CHAR field. The routine then declares two variables, an INT variable and a CHAR variable. It sets the value of the @LoopValue variable to 1. The code then loops from 1 to 100. As it loops, it sets the CHAR variable equal to the text Iteration # combined with the contents of the @LoopValue variable converted to a VarChar. Next it inserts the contents of the @LoopValue and @LoopText variables into the table. Finally, it increments the value of the @LoopValue variable. Figure 8.20 shows the results of executing the WHILE statement.

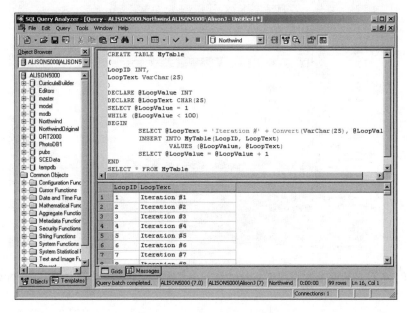

FIGURE 8.20 With a WHILE statement, the loop continues to execute until the specified condition is met.

The SET NOCOUNT Statement

The SET NOCOUNT statement, when set to ON, eliminates the "*xx* row(s) affected" message in the Query Analyzer window. It also eliminates the DONE_IN_PROC communicated from SQL Server to the client application. For this reason, the SET NOCOUNT ON statement, when included, improves the performance of the stored procedure. Here's an example:

```
CREATE PROCEDURE procGetCustomersNoCount AS
SET NOCOUNT ON
SELECT CompanyName, ContactName, ContactTitle, City
FROM Customers
ORDER BY City, CompanyName
```

If you execute this stored procedure from the Query Analyzer, you'll notice that the "*xx* row(s) affected" message does not appear (see Figure 8.21). You might wonder how with SET NOCOUNT ON you essentially can return the number of rows affected to the client application. Fortunately, this is easily accomplished using the @@RowCount system variable. The following section covers the @@RowCount system variable as well as other system variables.

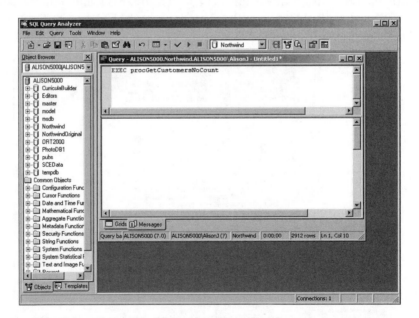

FIGURE 8.21   With a NOCOUNT statement, the "*xx* row(s) affected" message does not appear.

Using the `@@Functions`

Developers often refer to the `@@Functions` as global variables. In fact, they don't really behave like variables. You cannot assign values to them or work with them as you would work with normal variables. Instead, they behave as functions that return various types of information about what is going on in SQL Server.

`@@RowCount`

The `@@RowCount` variable returns the number of rows returned by a selected statement or affected by a statement that modifies data. It returns 0 if no values are returned by the SELECT statement or modified by the action query. Here's an example:

```
SELECT CustomerID, CompanyName
FROM Customers
WHERE Country = 'USA'
SELECT @@RowCount as NumUSACusts
```

The example selects all customers in the country of USA from the Customers table. If returns the number of rows selected (see Figure 8.22).

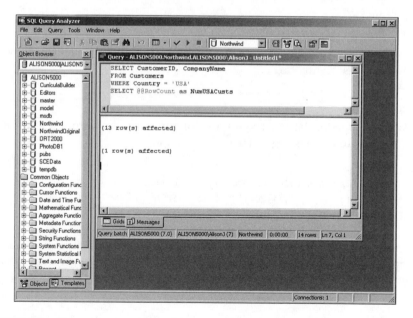

FIGURE 8.22   The `@@RowCount` variable returns the number of rows returned by a selected statement or affected by a statement that modifies data.

@@TranCount

The @@TranCount function is applicable when you are using explicit transactions. Transactions are covered later in this chapter. The BEGIN TRAN statement sets the @@TranCount to 1. Each ROLLBACK TRAN statement decrements @@TranCount by one. The COMMIT TRAN statement also decrements @@TranCount by one. When you use nested transactions, @@TranCount helps you keep track of how many transactions are still pending.

@@Identity

The @@Identity function retrieves the new value inserted into a table that has an identity column. Here's an example:

```
INSERT INTO Orders
    (CustomerID, EmployeeID, OrderDate, RequiredDate)
    VALUES ('ALFKI', 1, '1/1/2001', '1/15/2001')
    SELECT @@Identity
```

NOTE

The results of this procedure vary depending on the data contained in your copy of the Orders table.

The example inserts a row into the Orders table. It returns the identity value of the inserted row (see Figure 8.23).

@@Error

The @@Error function returns the number of any error that occurred in the statement immediately preceding it. Here's an example:

```
INSERT INTO Orders
    (CustomerID, EmployeeID, OrderDate, RequiredDate)
    VALUES ('xxxxx', 1, '1/1/2001', '1/15/2001')
    SELECT @@Error
```

This example attempts to insert a row into the Orders table. If it is successful, @@Error returns 0. If you attempt to insert an order for a customer that doesn't exist, it returns 547, a referential integrity error (see Figure 8.24).

FIGURE 8.23   The @@Identity function retrieves the new value inserted into a table that has an identity column.

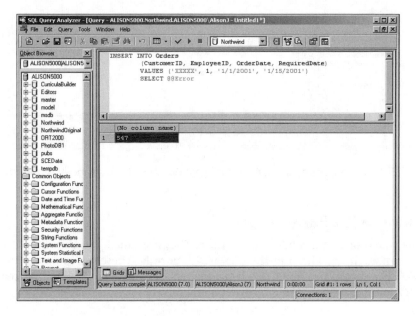

FIGURE 8.24   The @@Error function returns the number of any error that occurred in the statement immediately preceding it.

It is important to note that @@Error returns the error number associated with the line of code *immediately* preceding it. Consider this example:

```
INSERT INTO Orders
    (CustomerID, EmployeeID, OrderDate, RequiredDate)
    VALUES ('ALFKJ', 1, '1/1/2001', '1/15/2001')
    SELECT @@Identity
    SELECT @@Error
```

Although the INSERT statement renders an error, the @@Error function returns 0 (see Figure 8.25). This is because the SELECT @@Identity statement executes without error.

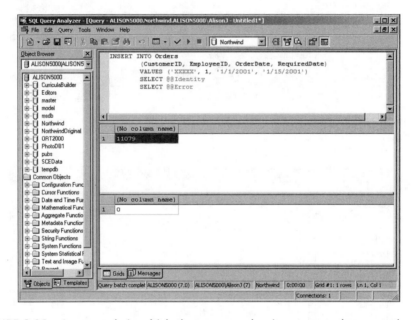

FIGURE 8.25   An example in which the error number is not properly reported.

Working with Parameters

Some stored procedures have no interface. They are called, but they do not receive or return anything. Other procedures are input only. These stored procedures have INPUT parameters but no OUTPUT parameters. A third type of stored procedure has both input parameters and OUTPUT parameters.

Input Parameters

Here is an example of a stored procedure that has neither INPUT nor OUTPUT parameters:

```
CREATE PROCEDURE procGetCustomersUSAOwners
AS
SELECT CompanyName, ContactName, ContactTitle, City
FROM Customers
WHERE Country = 'USA' AND
ContactTitle = 'Owner'
ORDER BY City, CompanyName
```

Contrast that stored procedure with the following:

```
CREATE PROCEDURE procGetCustomersByCountryAndTitle
    @CountryName VarChar(50),
    @ContactTitle VarChar(50)
AS
SELECT CompanyName, ContactName, ContactTitle, City
FROM Customers
WHERE Country = @CountryName AND
ContactTitle = @ContactTitle
ORDER BY City, CompanyName
```

The previous procedure receives two input parameters, @CountryName and @ContactTitle. The procedure uses these input parameters as variables for the WHERE clause for country and city. Here's how you execute the procedure:

```
procGetCustomersByCountryAndTitle 'USA', 'Owner'
```

The parameters in the previous stored procedure are required. If you do not supply them when you call the procedure, an error results (see Figure 8.26).

The following is the same procedure with Country set up as an optional parameter:

```
CREATE PROCEDURE procGetCustomersByCountryAndTitleOpt
    @CountryName VarChar(50) = NULL,
    @ContactTitle VarChar(50)
AS
If @CountryName IS Null
    SELECT CompanyName, ContactName, ContactTitle, City
    FROM Customers
    WHERE ContactTitle = @ContactTitle
ELSE
    SELECT CompanyName, ContactName, ContactTitle, City
    FROM Customers
    WHERE ContactTitle = @ContactTitle AND
    Country = @CountryName
```

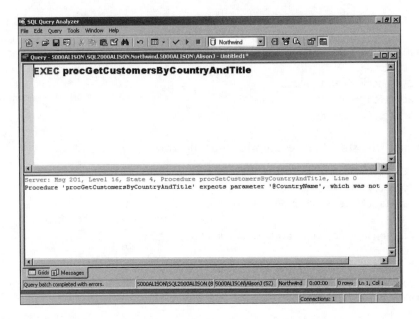

FIGURE 8.26   An error occurs if you omit a required parameter.

You establish an optional parameter by supplying SQL Server with a default value for the parameter. In this example, @CountryName is an optional parameter, but @ContactTitle is required. If you opt to omit the @CountryName parameter, you would call the stored procedure like this:

```
procGetCustomersByCountryAndTitleOpt @ContactTitle = 'Owner'
```

Notice that the example supplies the @ContactTitle parameter as a named parameter. If you omit the @CountryName parameter when you call the procedure, the procedure sets its value to Null. The stored procedure evaluates the value of the @CountryName variable. If it is Null (it wasn't supplied), the WHERE clause omits the country from the selection criteria. If the user of the stored procedure supplies the @CountryName parameter, the procedure uses the @CountryName parameter in the criteria for the WHERE clause.

OUTPUT Parameters

So far we have looked only at INPUT parameters, parameters that the user of the stored procedure supplies to the procedure. You can also declare OUTPUT parameters in the stored procedures that you build. SQL Server returns OUTPUT parameters to the caller (as their name implies). Here's an example:

```
CREATE PROCEDURE procGetCustomersByCountryAndTitleOutput
    @CountryName VarChar(50) = NULL,
    @ContactTitle VarChar(50),
    @MyMessage VarChar(50) = NULL OUTPUT
AS
IF @CountryName IS Null
    BEGIN
    SELECT CompanyName, ContactName, ContactTitle, City
    FROM Customers
    WHERE ContactTitle = @ContactTitle
    SELECT @MyMessage = 'No Country'
    END
ELSE
    BEGIN
    SELECT CompanyName, ContactName, ContactTitle, City
    FROM Customers
    WHERE ContactTitle = @ContactTitle AND
    Country = @CountryName
    SELECT @MyMessage = 'Country Supplied'
    END
SELECT @MyMessage
```

In addition to receiving two parameters, this procedure has an OUTPUT parameter called@MyMessage. The IF statement within the procedure sets the value of @MyMessage to the appropriate string (see Figure 8.27). You will see additional examples of OUTPUT parameters and their uses as we move through the rest of the book. In particular, you will see examples of ADO code that utilizes the OUTPUT parameters within the client/server applications that you build.

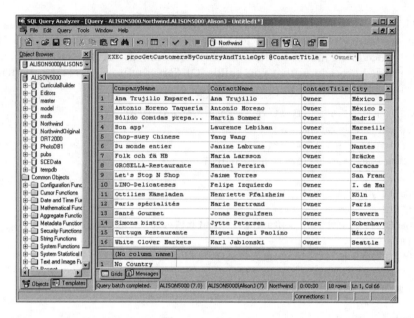

FIGURE 8.27   The IF statement within the procedure sets the value of @MyMessage to the appropriate string.

Modifying Data with Stored Procedures

Probably the most common use of a stored procedure is to modify the data in your database. You can easily design stored procedures to insert, update, and delete data. The sections that follow cover stored procedures that perform each of these tasks.

Inserting Data

Stored procedures are very effective at inserting data into your databases. Stored procedures that insert data generally contain several input parameters, one that corresponds with each field in the underlying table. They often contain OUTPUT parameters containing status or error information. Take a look at the following stored procedure:

```
CREATE PROCEDURE procAddCustomer
@CustomerID char(5),
@CompanyName varchar(40),
@ContactName varchar(30),
@ContactTitle varchar(30),
@City varchar(15),
```

```
@Country varchar(15)
AS
INSERT INTO Customers
(CustomerID, CompanyName, ContactName, ContactTitle, City, Country)
VALUES
(@CustomerID, @CompanyName, @ContactName, @ContactTitle, @City, @Country)
```

The procedure receives six INPUT parameters, one for each field in the Customers table that the procedure inserts data into. The INSERT INTO statement uses the INPUT parameters as values to insert into the table. As you can see, the previous example contains no OUTPUT parameters. The following procedure, which inserts data into the Orders table, contains an OUTPUT parameter called @OrderID.

```
CREATE PROCEDURE procOrderInsert
@CustomerID char(5),
@EmployeeID int = Null,
@OrderDate datetime = Null,
@RequiredDate datetime = Null,
@Freight money = 0,
@OrderID int = 0 OUTPUT
AS
INSERT INTO Orders
(CustomerID, EmployeeID, OrderDate, RequiredDate, Freight)
VALUES
 (@CustomerID, @EmployeeID, @OrderDate, @RequiredDate, @Freight)
SET @OrderID = @@IDENTITY
```

NOTE

If the procOrderInsert procedure exists in your database, the code in the previous example will render an error. By changing the keyword CREATE to ALTER, you will be able to modify the procedure if it exists.

In addition to receiving four input parameters, this procedure uses the OUTPUT parameter to house the identity value of the inserted row. Notice that the code populates the @OrderID OUTPUT parameter with the value of the system function @@IDENTITY. The client application can use the OUTPUT parameter via ADO code that you write.

Updating Data

Stored procedures are also excellent in their capability to update data. Here's an example:

```
CREATE PROCEDURE procCustomerUpdate
@CustomerID char (5),
@NewCity varchar (15) AS
UPDATE Customers
SET City = @NewCity
WHERE CustomerID = @CustomerID
```

The procedure receives two input parameters. One is for the CustomerID of the
customer whose city you want to modify. The other parameter contains the new
value for the city. Notice that the UPDATE statement sets the city to the @NewCity
value, where the CustomerID matches the customer passed in as the @CustomerID
parameter. Consider this more complex example:

```
CREATE PROCEDURE procCustomerEdit
@CustomerID char(5),
@CompanyName varchar(40),
@ContactName varchar(30),
@ContactTitle varchar(30),
@City varchar(15) = Null,
@Country varchar(15) = Null,
@ResultCode int = Null Output,
@ResultMessage varchar(20) = Null Output
AS
Update Customers
Set CompanyName = @CompanyName,
    ContactName = @ContactName,
    ContactTitle = @ContactTitle,
    City =@City,
    Country = @Country
    WHERE CustomerID = @CustomerID

SET @ResultMessage =
    Convert(varchar(20),  @@RowCount) +
    ' Records Affected'
SET @ResultCode = 0
```

This example is more similar to the INSERT example. It receives one INPUT parameter for each field in the Customers table that you want to modify. It updates the
fields in the Customers table with the values of the INPUT parameters for the
customer with the CustomerID designated in the @CustomerID parameter. It then sets
the @ResultMessage OUTPUT parameter to a string containing the @@RowCount value.
Finally, it sets the @ResultCode OUTPUT parameter to 0.

Deleting Data

Stored procedures are also very effective at deleting data. Here's an example:

```
CREATE PROCEDURE procCustomerDelete
@CustomerID char (5)
AS
DELETE FROM Customers
WHERE CustomerID = @CustomerID
```

This example receives one parameter, the CustomerID of the customer that you want to delete. Notice that the DELETE statement contains a WHERE clause that references the @CustomerID INPUT parameter.

Errors and Error Handling

So far, the examples in this chapter have contained no error handling. This means that they leave what happens when an error occurs up to chance. Although T-SQL provides a means of handling errors, the error-handling model in T-SQL is not as powerful as that in VBA. Because there's no ON ERROR GOTO statement, you must handle errors as they occur.

Handling Runtime Errors

One alternative to handling errors as they occur is to prevent errors from occurring in the first place. The Orders table in the Northwind database requires that data be entered for the OrderID and RequiredDate fields. The OrderID field is an IDENTITY column, so this is not of concern. Here's the error that occurs if a value is not supplied for the required date field:

```
Server: Msg 515, Level 16, State 2, Procedure procOrderInsert, Line 8
Cannot insert the value NULL into column 'RequiredDate', table
'Northwind.dbo.Orders';
column does not allow nulls. INSERT fails.
The statement has been terminated.
```

Here's an example of how you can prevent this error message from occurring:

```
CREATE PROCEDURE procOrderInsert
@CustomerID char(5),
@EmployeeID int = Null,
@OrderDate datetime = Null,
@RequiredDate datetime = Null,
@Freight money = 0,
@OrderID int = 0 OUTPUT
```

```
AS

IF @RequiredDate Is Null
    BEGIN
        PRINT 'RequiredDate MUST be Filled In'
        RETURN
    END

INSERT INTO Orders
(CustomerID, EmployeeID, OrderDate, RequiredDate, Freight)
VALUES
(@CustomerID, @EmployeeID, @OrderDate, @RequiredDate, @Freight)
SET @OrderID = @@IDENTITY
```

> **NOTE**
>
> As mentioned previously, if the procOrderInsert procedure exists in your database, the code in the previous example will render an error. By changing the keyword CREATE to ALTER, you will be able to modify the procedure if it exists.

In the example, the @RequiredDate parameter is optional. The procedure begins by testing to see if the value of the @RequiredDate is Null. If it is, a message is printed and the RETURN statement exits the procedure. This prevents the error message from occurring. Of course, you could add an OUTPUT parameter that would report the problem back to the client application. The section that follows discusses this technique. Chapter 10, "ADO and SQL Server," covers it in detail.

Returning Success and Failure Information from a Stored Procedure

As discussed in the previous section, it is important for the server to communicate to the client application the success or failure information about what happened within the stored procedure. You can select between two techniques to accomplish this task. The first method involves returning a recordset with status information. Here's an example:

```
CREATE PROCEDURE procOrderInsert
@CustomerID char(5),
@EmployeeID int,
@OrderDate datetime,
@RequiredDate datetime = Null,
@Freight money
AS
```

```
DECLARE @OrderID int, @LocalError int, @LocalRows int
INSERT INTO Orders
(CustomerID, EmployeeID, OrderDate, RequiredDate, Freight)
VALUES
(@CustomerID, @EmployeeID, @OrderDate, @RequiredDate, @Freight)
SELECT @OrderID = @@Identity, @LocalError = @@Error, @LocalRows = @@RowCount
SELECT @OrderID, @LocalError, @LocalRows
```

NOTE

Remember that you can change the keyword CREATE to ALTER, to prevent an error from occurring if the procOrderInsert procedure already exists.

The procedure first declares three variables: @OrderID, @LocalError, and @LocalRows. It then inserts an order into the Orders table. The statement immediately following the INSERT statement populates the three variables with the identity value, error number (if any), and number of rows affected. The alternative to this technique is to use OUTPUT parameters. Here's an example:

```
CREATE PROCEDURE procOrderInsert
@CustomerID char(5),
@EmployeeID int,
@OrderDate datetime,
@RequiredDate datetime = NULL,
@Freight money,
@OrderID int = 0 OUTPUT,
@LocalError int = 0 OUTPUT,
@LocalRows int = 0 OUTPUT
AS
INSERT INTO Orders
(CustomerID, EmployeeID, OrderDate, RequiredDate, Freight)
VALUES
(@CustomerID, @EmployeeID, @OrderDate, @RequiredDate, @Freight)
SELECT @OrderID = @@Identity, @LocalError = @@Error, @LocalRows = @@RowCount
```

Notice that the procedure does not declare any variables. Instead, it contains three output parameters, one for the OrderID, another for the error information, and the last for the number of rows affected. The procedure populates the OUTPUT parameters just as it populated the variables, with a SELECT statement immediately following the INSERT statement.

Stored Procedures and Transactions

It is a good idea to place transactions in all of the stored procedures that you build. Transactions ensure that a piece of work is completed in its entirety or not at all. One of the classic examples is a banking transaction. You want all the debits and credits to complete properly or not at all. This is where transactions come in.

You might have used the BEGINTRANS, COMMITTRANS, and ROLLBACK methods in data access objects (DAOs) going against Access data. These DAO methods are appropriate when going against an Access back end. When using a SQL Server back end, you should instead place all transaction processing inside the stored procedures that you build.

Types of Transactions

Two types of transactions exist: implicit transactions and explicit transactions. Implicit transactions happen regardless of what you do in your programming code. Each time that you issue an INSERT, UPDATE, or DELETE statement, SQL Server invokes an implicit transaction. If any piece of an INSERT, UPDATE, or DELETE statement fails, the entire statement is rolled back. For example, if your DELETE statement attempts to delete all of the inactive customers and somewhere in the process a record fails to delete (for example, for referential integrity reasons), SQL Server does not delete any of the records. Explicit transactions, on the other hand, are transactions that you define and control. Using explicit transactions, you package multiple statements within BEGIN TRANSACTION and COMMIT TRANSACTION statements. In your error handling, you include a ROLLBACK TRANSACTION statement. This ensures that all the statements complete successfully or not at all.

Implementing Transactions

As mentioned, you use the BEGIN TRANSACTION, COMMIT TRANSACTION, and ROLLBACK TRANSACTION statements to implement transactions. The following is a stored procedure that utilizes a transaction:

```
CREATE PROCEDURE procOrderInsertTran
@CustomerID char(5),
@EmployeeID int,
@OrderDate datetime,
@RequiredDate datetime,
@Freight money
AS
SET NOCOUNT ON
DECLARE @OrderID int, @LocalError int, @LocalRows int
BEGIN TRANSACTION
```

```
INSERT INTO Orders
(CustomerID, EmployeeID, OrderDate, RequiredDate, Freight)
VALUES
(@CustomerID, @EmployeeID, @OrderDate, @RequiredDate, @Freight)
SELECT @LocalError = @@Error, @LocalRows = @@RowCount
IF NOT @LocalError = 0 or @LocalRows = 0
    BEGIN
    ROLLBACK TRANSACTION
    SELECT OrderID = Null, Error = @LocalError, NumRows = @LocalRows
    END
ELSE
    BEGIN
    COMMIT TRAN
    SELECT @OrderID = @@Identity
    SELECT OrderID = @OrderID, Error = 0, NumRows = @LocalRows
    END
```

In the example, the BEGIN TRANSACTION starts the transaction. The procedure attempts to insert a row into the Orders table. It populates the @LocalError variable with the value returned from the @@Error function, and it populates the @LocalRows variable with the value returned from the @@RowCount function. An IF statement evaluates whether either @LocalError is 0 or @LocalRows is 0. If either variable contains 0, the procedure was unsuccessful at inserting the row. The ROLLBACK TRANSACTION statement is used to terminate the transaction, and the procedure returns error information to the caller. If neither variable equals 0, we can assume that the process completed successfully. The COMMIT TRANSACTION statement commits the changes, and the procedure returns the status and identity information to the caller.

Stored Procedures and Temporary Tables

SQL Server creates temporary tables in a special system database called TempDB. SQL Server creates TempDB each time it starts and destroys it each time it shuts down. SQL Server uses TempDB to house many temporary objects that it needs to run. You can use TempDB to share data between procedures or to help you accomplish complex tasks. Many times you will need to incorporate temporary tables into the stored procedures that you write. Here's an example of how you create and use a temporary table:

```
CREATE PROCEDURE procCustomersGetTemp AS
BEGIN
CREATE TABLE #TempCustomers
(CompanyName varchar (50) NOT NULL PRIMARY KEY,
```

```
ContactName varchar(50),
ContactTitle varchar (50),
City varchar (50))
INSERT INTO #TempCustomers
(CompanyName, ContactName, ContactTitle, City)
EXEC procCustomersGetByCountryAndTitle 'USA', 'Owner'
SELECT CompanyName, ContactName, ContactTitle, City
FROM #TempCustomers
ORDER BY City, CompanyName
END
```

This procedure uses a second procedure called procCustomersGetByCountryAndTitle. It looks like this:

```
CREATE PROCEDURE procCustomersGetByCountryAndTitle
    @CountryName VarChar(50),
    @ContactTitle VarChar(50)
AS
SELECT CompanyName, ContactName, ContactTitle, City
FROM Customers
WHERE Country = @CountryName AND
ContactTitle = @ContactTitle
ORDER BY City, CompanyName
```

The procCustomersGetByCountryAndTitle procedure receives two parameters. It uses those parameters for the WHERE clause for Country and ContactTitle. The procCustomersGetTemp procedure creates a temporary table that holds customer information. It inserts into the temporary table the results of executing the procCustomersGetByCountryAndTitle procedures, passing it USA and Owner as the country and title values. Finally, the procedure selects data from the temporary table, ordering the result by City and CompanyName.

Stored Procedures and Security

Like views, stored procedures provide an excellent tool for securing your application's data. This is because you can grant rights to a stored procedure without providing any rights to the underlying table(s). Consider the following scenario. Imagine that you create an unbound Access form by which users can select various customers. You then execute stored procedures to insert, update, and delete data. In this scenario, you can grant users view rights to the Customers table. You do not need to grant them insert, update, or delete rights to the table. Instead, you grant them execute rights to the appropriate stored procedures. In this way, you can allow your users to easily create queries and reports that use the Customer data (you granted them view rights to the table). They can only insert, update, and delete data via the stored procedures that you call from your application code.

Debugging the Stored Procedures That You Build

It is not always easy to determine what is wrong with a stored procedure. Fortunately, SQL Server 2000 includes a very good debugger that allows you to easily step through the stored procedures that you build. To debug a stored procedure:

1. Launch Query Analyzer.

2. Open the Object Browser.

3. Locate the stored procedure that you want to debug.

4. Right-click and select Debug. The Debug Procedure dialog box appears (see Figure 8.28).

5. Click each parameter and type the appropriate value in the Value text box.

6. Click Execute to execute the stored procedure. The T-SQL Debugger window appears (see Figure 8.29). Here, you can step through the stored procedure, watch the value of variables, set breakpoints, and more.

FIGURE 8.28 The Debug Procedure dialog box allows you to set the values of the parameters in your stored procedure.

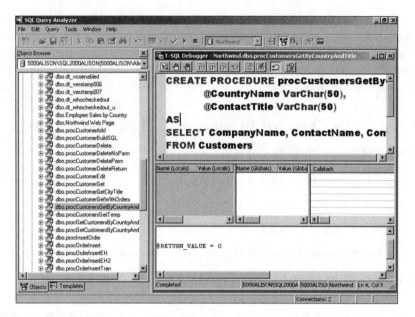

FIGURE 8.29 The T-SQL Debugger allows you to step through the stored procedure, watch the value of variables, set breakpoints, and more.

Building and Working with User-Defined Functions

SQL 2000 introduced user-defined functions. User-defined functions add power and flexibility that was previously unavailable with views and stored procedures. Three types of user-defined functions exist: scalar, inline table-valued, and multistatement table-valued. The sections that follow cover each of these types of user-defined functions in detail.

Scalar Functions

Scalar functions return a single value of the type defined in the RETURNS clause. The body of the function is between a BEGIN and an END block. Scalar functions can return any data type *except* text, ntext, image, cursor, or timestamp. Here's an example of a scalar function:

```
CREATE FUNCTION dbo.FullName
    (@FirstName nVarChar(10),
    @LastName nVarChar(20))
RETURNS nVarChar(35)
BEGIN
    RETURN (@LastName + ', ' + @FirstName)
END
```

This function receives two parameters: @FirstName and @LastName. It returns an nVarChar(35) value. The return value is the combination of the @LastName and @FirstName input parameters combined with a comma and a space. You could call the function like this:

```
SELECT FirstName, LastName, dbo.FullName(FirstName, LastName) FROM Employees
```

The example displays the FirstName, LastName, and result of the FullName function (see Figure 8.30).

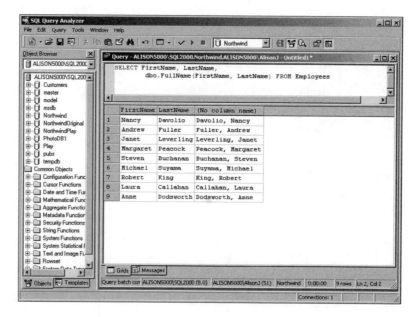

FIGURE 8.30   Scalar functions return a single value of the type defined in the RETURNS clause.

Inline Table-Valued Functions

As their name implies, inline table-valued functions return a table. Inline table-valued functions have no body. They simply return the result of a simple SELECT statement. Here's an example:

```
CREATE FUNCTION dbo.CustGetByTitle
    (@Title nVarChar(30))
RETURNS Table
AS
RETURN SELECT CustomerID, CompanyName, ContactName, City, Region
FROM Customers WHERE ContactTitle = @Title
```

This example receives a parameter called @Title. It returns a table containing selected fields from the Customers table in which the ContactTitle equals the @Title parameter value. You would call the function like this:

```
SELECT * FROM dbo.CustGetByTitle('Owner')
```

The example selects all fields from the table returned from the CustGetByTitle function. Because the example passes Owner as a parameter, only the owners are included in the result set (see Figure 8.31).

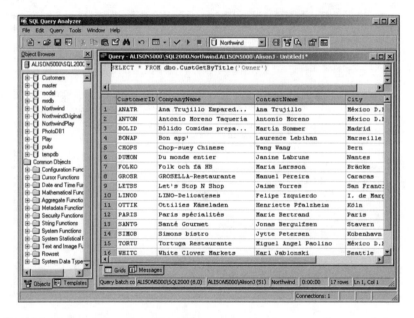

FIGURE 8.31   Inline table-valued functions return a table.

Multistatement Table-Valued Functions

Multistatement table-valued functions are similar to inline table-valued functions. The main difference is that, like scalar functions, they have a body defined by a BEGIN...END block. Like inline table-valued functions, they return a table.

Creating and Working with Triggers

A trigger is like an event procedure that runs when data changes. You can create triggers that execute in response to inserts, updates, and deletes. Developers use triggers to enforce business rules and even to perform tasks such as inserting data into an audit log.

Creating Triggers

To create or modify a trigger:

1. Right-click the table that you want to create the trigger for, and select Task, Manage Triggers. Another option is to click the Triggers toolbar button while in the design of the table. In either case, the Trigger Properties dialog box appears (see Figure 8.32).

2. The Name drop-down list shows the triggers already defined for the table. To modify an existing trigger, select it from the drop-down list. To create a new trigger, type the trigger code into the text window (see Figure 8.33).

3. Click Check Syntax to ensure that the trigger is syntactically correct.

4. Click OK to close the dialog box and create the trigger.

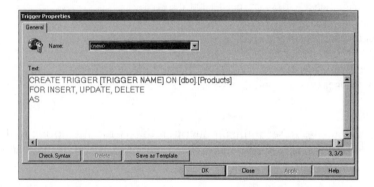

FIGURE 8.32   The Trigger Properties dialog box allows you to define and modify triggers.

FIGURE 8.33   To create a new trigger, type the trigger code into the text window.

The syntax for a trigger is:

```
CREATE TRIGGER TriggerName
    On TableName
    FOR [INSERT], [UPDATE], [DELETE]
    AS
    --Trigger Code
```

Here's an example:

```
CREATE TRIGGER NoDeleteActive ON [dbo].[Products]
FOR DELETE
AS

DECLARE @Discontinued Bit
SELECT @Discontinued = Discontinued FROM deleted

IF @Discontinued = 0
    BEGIN
        ROLLBACK TRAN
        RAISERROR('Active Product Cannot Be Deleted', 16,1)
    END
```

This trigger evaluates to see if the product that the user is attempting to delete is discontinued. If it is, SQL Server aborts the delete process and displays an error message.

The following is an example of a trigger that inserts data into an audit log whenever the user updates a row:

```
CREATE TRIGGER InsertProductAudit ON dbo.Products
FOR UPDATE
AS
DECLARE  @ProductID int, @ProductName NVarChar(40),
        @UnitPrice Money, @UnitsInStock SmallInt
SELECT @ProductID = ProductID, @ProductName = ProductName,
        @UnitPrice = UnitPrice, @UnitsInStock = UnitsInStock FROM inserted
INSERT ProductsAudit VALUES (@ProductID, @ProductName, @UnitPrice,@UnitsInStock)
```

This example inserts data into an audit log whenever the user modifies data in the Products table.

INSTEAD OF **Triggers**

An INSTEAD OF trigger fires in place of the triggering action. It executes after SQL Server creates the inserted and deleted tables, but before SQL Server takes any other actions. SQL Server executes INSTEAD OF triggers *before* constraints are applied. This allows you to perform preprocessing that supplements existing constraints.

Downsides of Triggers

Many developers avoid triggers entirely. Probably the biggest disadvantage of triggers is that they get buried in your database and are difficult to debug and troubleshoot. They also slow database operations. Furthermore, they often lock data for relatively long periods of time, increasing the chance of concurrency problems. For these reasons, most developers opt to utilize stored procedures or even middle-tier components to replace the role of triggers in the applications that they build.

Summary

SQL Server stored procedures, user-defined functions, and triggers are at the heart of any database application. In this chapter, you learned all about these three important database components. You saw examples of how you can use each component, and you learned about how each component can help you to create a robust and powerful database application.

9

SQL Server Security

Why This Chapter Is Important

Security is necessary to prohibit access to unauthorized users and to ensure that authorized users have only the rights that you want them to have. SQL Server security is very robust and offers you several alternatives for your security model. This chapter begins by introducing you to SQL Server security. It talks about both authentication and permissions validation. It then talks about a special option available for SQL Server security referred to as an application role. Finally, you'll learn how Access Security interacts with SQL Server security in the applications that you build.

Security Introduced

Access security is very limited and does not provide you with a lot of protection. This is because you must grant read, write, and delete permissions to the users of an Access database for the network share on which the database resides. This makes the database vulnerable to hackers as well as the inadvertent actions of users (for example, accidentally moving or deleting a file). Furthermore, you cannot integrate Access security with the operating system. This means that users must log on to both the operating system and Microsoft Access. Furthermore, operating system features such as password aging, the logging of user activity, and the logging of invalid login attempts are all unavailable with Microsoft Access.

As mentioned in the chapter introduction, SQL Server offers a very robust and flexible security model. SQL Server 2000 security is tightly integrated with Windows NT 4 and Windows 2000 security. This means that SQL Server can utilize the users and roles that you set up at the operating system level. Within SQL Server, you determine the rights that the users and roles have for the various SQL Server objects. Not only are Windows users and roles available, but you can also take advantage of operating system features such as password expiration and the logging of login attempts and database activities.

We refer to the process of validating a user as authentication. We refer to the process of determining what a user can do as permissions validation. This chapter covers both of these topics.

Authentication

Authentication involves ensuring that a user is who he says he is. After SQL Server authenticates a user, the user can perform any actions specifically granted to his login, as well as actions granted to any roles that the user is a member of.

Types of Authentication

Two types of authentication exist:

- SQL Server and Windows (mixed authentication)
- Windows Only

With SQL Server and Windows authentication, SQL Server supports both SQL Server and Windows NT/Windows 2000 logins. With Windows Only authentication, SQL Server supports only Windows NT/Windows 2000 logins. When you install SQL Server, you can configure the type of authentication that SQL Server will use. To modify the type of authentication that you want to use:

1. Launch Enterprise Manager.

2. Right-click the server whose authentication mode you want to modify and select Properties. The SQL Server Properties dialog box appears.

3. Click the Security tab.

4. Modify the authentication, as pictured in Figure 9.1.

Windows NT/Windows 2000 authentication has several advantages over SQL Server authentication. These advantages include:

- Requirement for the user to log on only once
- Central administration of logins
- Password expiration
- Enforceable minimum password length

- Account lockout after unsuccessful login attempts

- More secure validation

- Encryption of passwords

- Auditing features

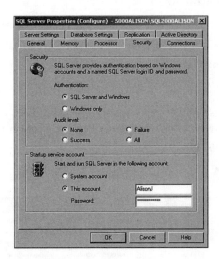

FIGURE 9.1 The Security tab of the SQL Server Properties dialog box allows you to modify the authentication type of the server.

SQL Server authentication does have a few advantages over Windows NT/Windows 2000 authentication. They include:

- You can use SQL Server logins on the Windows 9*x* platform.

- SQL Server authentication does not require you to have organized Windows domains on Windows systems.

- SQL Server authentication allows you to support non-Windows users such as Novell users.

Creating Logins

If you select Windows authentication, SQL Server assumes a trust relationship with your Windows NT or Windows 2000 server. It assumes that the user has already successfully logged on. Regardless of the authentication mode that you select, you must still create SQL Server logins.

To add a Windows NT/Windows 2000 login:

1. Click to expand the Security node for the server (see Figure 9.2).

2. Right-click Logins and select New Login. The SQL Server Login Properties dialog box appears (see Figure 9.3).

3. Type the name for the login.

4. Make sure that Windows Authentication is selected, and select the user's domain from the Domain drop-down.

5. Specify the default database for the user.

6. Click the Server Roles tab to grant the user membership to server roles.

7. Click the Database Access tab to designate which databases the user has rights to. The "Granting Database Access to Logins" section later in this chapter covers database access.

8. Click OK to close the dialog box and add the user.

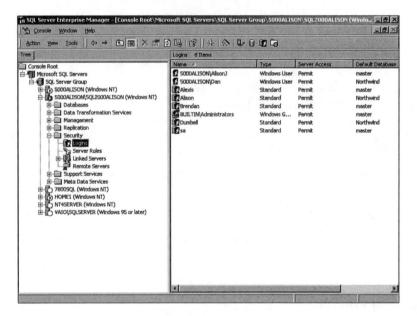

FIGURE 9.2 To add a Windows NT/Windows 2000 login, click to expand the Security node for the server.

FIGURE 9.3   The SQL Server Login Properties dialog box allows you to create a new login.

To add a SQL Server login:

1. Click to expand the Security node for the server.

2. Right-click Logins and select New Login. The SQL Server Login Properties dialog box appears.

3. Type the name for the login.

4. Make sure that you select SQL Server Authentication. Type a password for the user (see Figure 9.4). This case-sensitive password can contain from 1 through 128 characters, including letters, symbols, and digits.

5. Specify the default database for the user.

6. Click the Server Roles tab to grant the user membership to server roles.

7. Click the Database Access tab to designate which databases the user has rights to. The "Granting Database Access to Logins" section later in this chapter covers database access.

8. Click OK. SQL Server prompts you to confirm the password (see Figure 9.5).

9. Type the password and click OK.

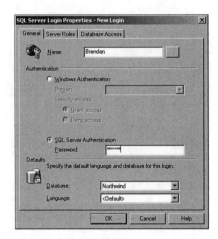

FIGURE 9.4   When using SQL Server authentication, the SQL Server Login Properties dialog box prompts you to type a password for the user.

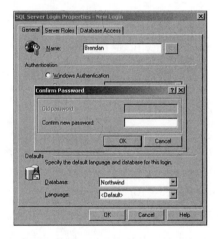

FIGURE 9.5   After you click OK, SQL Server prompts you to confirm the password.

Granting Database Access to Logins

Whether you use Windows NT/Windows 2000 authentication or SQL Server authentication, you will need to determine which databases the user has rights to and to which fixed database and user-defined database roles the user belongs. You can grant database access for a login when adding the login (see previous text). To grant database access for an existing login:

1. Click to expand the Security node for the server.

2. Click Logins in the left pane. The available logins appear in the right pane. Right-click the login that you want to affect and select Properties. The SQL Server Login Properties dialog box appears.

3. Click to select the Database Access tab. The dialog box appears, as in Figure 9.6.

4. Click the Permit check box next to each database to which you want the user to have access.

5. Click to select each database role (system- and user-defined) to which you want the user to belong.

6. Click OK to commit your changes.

FIGURE 9.6   The Database Access tab of the SQL Server Login Properties dialog box allows you to designate the databases to which you want the user to have access.

The SA Login

The SA login is a special login within the SQL Server environment. If you install SQL Server in mixed mode (Windows NT/Windows 2000 and SQL Server authentication), the SA login has unlimited powers. With mixed-mode authentication, there is no way to modify or delete the SA account. It is therefore *imperative* that you assign a password to the SA account. Failure to do so renders any other security that you apply to the server futile.

Creating Roles

Roles are the equivalent of Windows NT/Windows 2000 groups. You create roles and then grant users membership to those roles. Users who are members of a role inherit the permissions assigned to that role. The process of creating roles and assigning permissions to those roles greatly facilitates the process of administering security. This is because, rather than having to assign specific rights to each user of a system, you can instead assign rights to groups of users.

Types of Roles

SQL Server offers four types of roles. These include:

- Fixed server roles
- Fixed database roles
- User-defined database roles
- Application roles

Each of these types of roles serves a specific purpose. Generally, you will use several types of roles in combination. The sections that appear later in the chapter discuss each type of role in detail.

Fixed Server Roles

Fixed server roles are built into SQL Server and are in no way user-definable (you cannot add them, modify them, or delete them). They allow their members to perform server-level administrative tasks. The fixed server roles include:

- **Bulk Insert Administrators (bulkadmin)**—Can execute bulk insert statements.

- **Database Creators (dbcreator)**—Can create and alter databases.

- **Disk Administrators (diskadmin)**—Can manage disk files.

- **Process Administrators (processadmin)**—Can manage SQL Server processes.

- **Security Administrators (securityadmin)**—Can manage server logins.

- **Server Administrators (serveradmin)**—Can configure server-wide settings.

- **Setup Administrators (setupadmin)**—Can install replication and can manage extended properties.

- **System Administrators (sysadmin)**—Can perform *any* activity on that SQL Server instance. This includes all activities of the other roles. In fact, if a user is a member of the sysadmin role, you cannot prohibit him from performing *any* tasks on the server.

Server roles greatly facilitate the process of managing security. They accomplish this by allowing you to compartmentalize the administrative tasks that users can perform and to grant them rights to perform only those specific tasks.

> **NOTE**
>
> When you install SQL Server, the installation process adds the Windows NT/Windows 2000 Administrators group to the sysadmin role. This means that all members of the Administrators group instantly become members of sysadmin. Fortunately, you can remove this mapping from Administrators to the sysadmin role. To remove the mapping, you must deny the Administrators group from logging on to the SQL Server. You then grant the individual users membership to the sysadmin role.

To assign a user to a fixed server role:

1. Expand the Security node until you can see the Server Roles subnode (see Figure 9.7).

2. Right-click the role to which you want to grant users membership and select Properties. The Server Role Properties dialog box appears (see Figure 9.8).

3. Click Add to add a user to the role. The Add Members dialog box appears (see Figure 9.9).

4. Select the logins that you want to add, and click OK. SQL Server adds the selected users to the role.

Fixed Database Roles

Whereas fixed server roles allow you to assign rights to users that apply at the server level, fixed database roles allow you to assign rights at the database level. Because fixed server roles apply at the server level, they are found under the Security node. Because fixed database roles apply at a database level, they are located under the specific database node of the database that they apply to.

As with fixed server roles, you cannot add, remove, or modify the rights granted to fixed database roles. Fixed database roles facilitate the process of assigning permissions for a database. The fixed database roles include:

- **db_accessadmin**—Can add and remove Windows NT/Windows 2000 users and groups and SQL Server users for the database.

- **db_backupoperator**—Can back up the database.

- **db_datareader**—Can view data in all user tables in the database.

- **db_datawriter**—Can add, edit, and delete data in all user tables in the database.

- **db_ddladmin**—Can add, modify, and drop database objects.

- **db_securityadmin**—Can manage role membership and statement and object permissions for the database.

- **db_denydatareader**—Cannot see any data in the database.

- **db_denydatawriter**—Cannot modify any data in the database.

- **db_owner**—Can perform the activities of any of the other roles. Can also perform all database maintenance and configuration tasks.

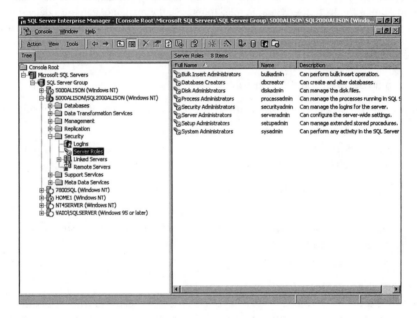

FIGURE 9.7   The Server Roles subnode of the Security node allows you to assign users to a fixed server role.

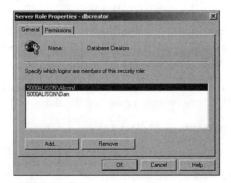

FIGURE 9.8   The Server Role Properties dialog box allows you to add users to a role.

FIGURE 9.9   The Add Members dialog box allows you to select the users that you want to add to a role.

To assign a user to a fixed database role:

1. Expand the Database node of the desired database until you can see the Roles subnode (see Figure 9.10).

2. Right-click the role to which you want to grant users membership and select Properties. The Database Role Properties dialog box appears (see Figure 9.11).

3. Click Add to add a user to the role. The Add Role Members dialog box appears (see Figure 9.12).

4. Select the logins that you want to add and click OK. SQL Server adds the selected users to the role.

The Public role is a special built-in fixed database role that every user is a member of. When you grant a user access to a database, SQL Server adds the user to the Public database role. You can't remove the Public role, nor can you remove users of a database from the Public role. Any rights that you grant to the Public role are automatically granted to all users of the database. The Public role therefore provides an excellent means of easily granting all users rights to a particular object. On the other hand, if you accidentally grant the Public role rights, those rights apply to all users of the database.

User-Defined Database Roles

At a database level, you are not limited to the predefined roles. In addition to the predefined roles, you can add your own roles. SQL Server offers two types of user-defined roles. They are:

- **Standard role**—Custom role that you use to facilitate the task of assigning rights to users of the database.

- **Application role**—Role used by an application. Application roles are covered later in this chapter.

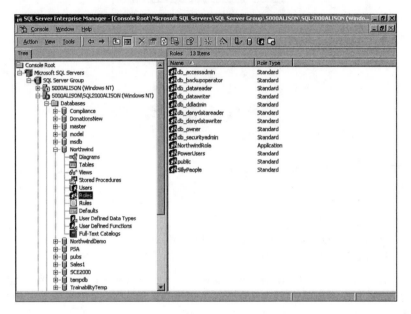

FIGURE 9.10   The Roles subnode of the Database node allows you to work with roles for that database.

FIGURE 9.11   The Database Role Properties dialog box allows you to add users to a database role.

FIGURE 9.12   The Add Role Members dialog box allows you to select the users that you want to add to a role.

To create a user-defined role:

1. Expand the Database node of the desired database until you can see the Roles subnode (see Figure 9.13).

2. Right-click the Roles subnode and select New Database Role. The Database Role Properties dialog box appears, prompting you to enter the name of the new role (see Figure 9.14).

3. Type the name of the role in the Name text box.

4. Click Add to add a user to the role. The Add Role Members dialog box appears.

5. Select the logins that you want to add and click OK. SQL Server adds the selected users to the role.

Ownership

It is important to understand what ownership is and what the implications of ownership are. SQL Server designates the creator of an object as its owner. The owner of an object has *full* permissions for that object. Furthermore, the name of the object is actually `owner.objectname` —for example, `alexis.tblCustomers`.

You cannot remove a user from a database as long as he owns objects within it. Ownership of an object is implied. This means that you cannot directly administer the owner of an object.

dbo is a special user account within each database. SQL Server maps the dbo to the sysadmin fixed server role. This means that if you are a member of the sysadmin group and you create an object, SQL Server flags the object as owned by dbo, not by you. You can refer to the object as `dbo.objectname`.

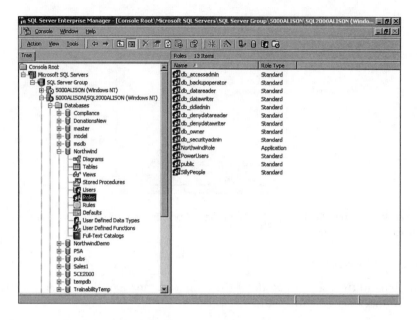

FIGURE 9.13   The Roles subnode of the Database node allows you to create and work with user-defined database roles.

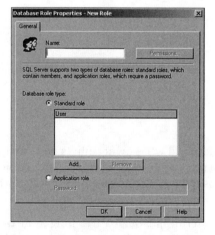

FIGURE 9.14   The Database Role Properties dialog box allows you to enter the name of the new role.

The `sp_changeobjectowner` system-stored procedure allows you to change the owner of an object. Only members of the sysadmin fixed server role, the db_owner fixed database role, or a member of *both* the db_ddladmin and db_securityadmin fixed database roles can execute the sp_changeobjectowner stored procedure. It looks like this:

```
EXEC sp_changeobjectowner 'tblCustomers', 'Brendan'
```

When you change the owner of an object, SQL Server drops all permissions for the object. To change the owner back to dbo, you must fully qualify the owner name and object name. The syntax looks like this:

```
EXEC sp_changeobjectowner 'Brendan.tblCustomers', 'dbo'
```

Permissions Validation

When a user logs in to the server, SQL Server first authenticates him to ensure that he is a valid user. SQL Server then grants the user permission to perform any task assigned to the user or to any roles that the user is a member of.

Types of Permissions

SQL Server offers three types of permissions. They include:

- **Object permissions**—Permissions set for objects such as tables and views. These include SELECT, INSERT, UPDATE, and DELETE permissions.

- **Statement permissions**—Permissions applied to statements such as the CREATE VIEW statement. These permissions define what rights the user has to the specified statement.

- **Inherited or implied permissions**—These permissions refer to rights that a user has to an object because he is a member of a role that has rights to that object, or because the user is the owner of the object.

Adding Database Users

If you want a user to have access to a database, you must first create a user account in the database. Here's how:

1. Expand the Database node of the desired database until you can see the Users subnode (see Figure 9.15).

2. Right-click the Users subnode and select New Database User. The Database User Properties dialog box appears, prompting you to enter the login name and username of the new user (see Figure 9.16).

3. Select the login name from the Login Name drop-down. Type the user name in the User Name text box.

4. Click to select the database role memberships for the user.

5. Click OK to add the user.

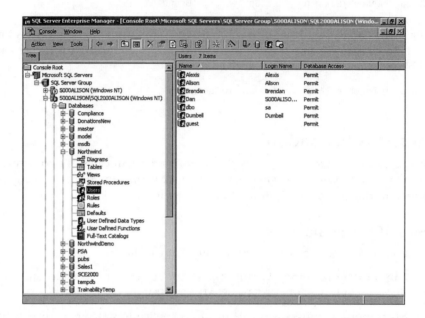

FIGURE 9.15   The Users subnode allows you to manage the users of a database.

FIGURE 9.16   The Database User Properties dialog box prompts you to enter the login name and username of the new user.

Permission Statements

You can execute three different permission statements for the objects in your database. They include:

- **GRANT**—Grants permission.

- **REVOKE**—Revokes permission. If you revoke permission for a user to an object, the user still possesses any permissions implied by the roles that the user is a member of.

- **DENY**—Revokes permission so that permission for that object cannot be inherited.

Administering Object Permissions

You can administer permissions for an object in one of two ways. The first way is via the object. This method shows you the rights for all users and roles for a particular object. It works like this:

1. Right-click the object and select Properties. The Properties dialog box appears.

2. Click Permissions. The Object Properties dialog box appears (see Figure 9.17). Here you can assign users and roles rights for the object.

3. Use the Object drop-down list to assign permissions for other database objects.

4. Click OK when done.

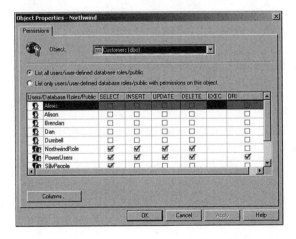

FIGURE 9.17 The Object Properties dialog box allows you to assign users and roles rights for the object.

As an alternative, you can assign rights for all objects to a user or role. The process works like this:

1. Right-click the user or role and select Properties. The Properties dialog box appears.

2. Click Permissions. Either the Database User Properties dialog box or the Database Role Properties dialog box appears (see Figure 9.18). Here you can see a particular user or role and manage rights to all objects for the user or role.

3. Use the Object drop-down list to assign permissions for other users or roles.

4. Click OK when done.

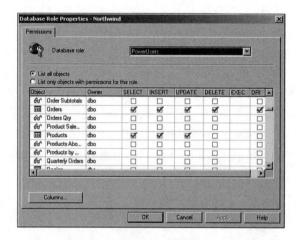

FIGURE 9.18   The Database User Properties and Database Role Properties dialog boxes let you see a particular user or role and manage rights to all objects for the user or role.

Table Permissions

You can grant SELECT, INSERT, UPDATE, DELETE, and DRI rights for a table. These are each described here.

- **SELECT permissions**—Allow the user to view the data in a table.

- **INSERT permissions**—Allow the user to add data to the table.

- **UPDATE permissions**—Allow the user to update the data in the table.

- **DELETE permissions**—Allow the user to delete table data.

- **DRI permissions**—Grant a user declarative referential integrity rights for an object. To assign permissions for a table:

1. Right-click the table that you want to assign permissions for and select Properties. The Properties dialog box appears.

2. Click Permissions. The Object Properties dialog box appears (see Figure 9.19).

3. Click to assign SELECT, INSERT, UPDATE, DELETE, and DRI permissions, as required.

4. Click OK when done.

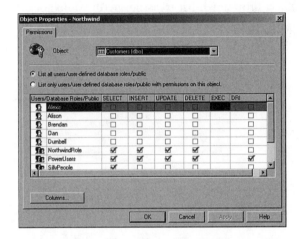

FIGURE 9.19   The Object Properties dialog box allows you to assign the appropriate rights to an object.

NOTE

EXEC permissions are not applicable to tables. They are applicable only for stored procedures and are therefore covered later in this chapter, in the section, "Stored Procedure Permissions."

Implementing Column-Level Security

SQL Server 2000 allows you to easily assign column-level permissions. Column-level permissions enable you to determine on a column-by-column basis whether the user has SELECT and UPDATE rights for that particular column. INSERT and DELETE rights cannot be assigned at a column level because they affect the entire row. The process looks like this:

1. Right-click the table that you want to assign permissions for and select Properties. The Table Properties dialog box appears.

2. Click Permissions. The Object Properties dialog box appears.

3. Select the table to which you want to apply column-level permissions.

4. Click Columns. The Column Permissions dialog box appears (see Figure 9.20). Indicate the SELECT and UPDATE rights for the individual columns as desired.

5. Click OK to close the Column Permissions dialog box and return to the Object Properties dialog box.

6. Use the Object drop-down list to assign permissions for other database objects.

7. Click OK when done.

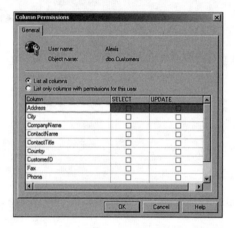

FIGURE 9.20 The Column Permissions dialog box lets you determine on a column-by-column basis whether the user has SELECT and UPDATE rights for that particular column.

View Permissions

Permissions for a view override those for the underlying tables. Using views, you can very easily apply both row-level and column-level security. You can achieve column-level security by limiting the columns included in the view. You can implement row-level security by adding a WHERE clause to the view. Because the results of most views are updateable, the process of applying security for a view is similar to that for a table:

1. Right-click the view that you want to assign permissions for and select Properties. The View Properties dialog box appears.

2. Click Permissions. The Object Properties dialog box appears (see Figure 9.21).

3. Click to assign SELECT, INSERT, UPDATE, DELETE, and DRI permissions, as required.

4. Click OK when done.

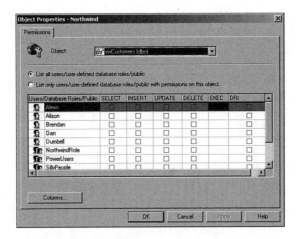

FIGURE 9.21   The Object Properties dialog box allows you to assign SELECT, INSERT, UPDATE, DELETE, and DRI permissions for a view, as required.

Stored Procedure Permissions

As with rights for a view, rights assigned for a stored procedure override rights assigned for the underlying tables and views. This is the case as long as the stored procedure has the same owner as the tables referenced with it. Stored procedures have only one permission, the EXECUTE permission. To assign rights for a stored procedure:

1. Right-click the stored procedure that you want to assign permissions for and select Properties. The Stored Procedure Properties dialog box appears.

2. Click Permissions. The Object Properties dialog box appears (see Figure 9.22).

3. Click to assign EXECUTE permissions, as required.

4. Click OK when done.

Function Permissions

As with rights assigned for views and stored procedures, rights assigned for a user-defined function that returns a table override rights assigned for the underlying tables and views. This is the case as long as the function has the same owner as the tables referenced with it. Functions have the same permissions as tables. The main limitation of functions is that they return read-only results. To assign rights for a function:

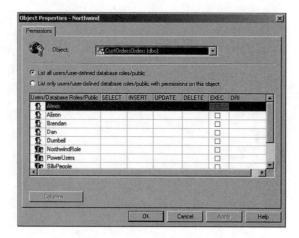

FIGURE 9.22   The Object Properties dialog box allows you to designate EXECUTE permissions for a stored procedure.

1. Right-click the function that you want to assign permissions for and select Properties. The Properties dialog box appears.

2. Click Permissions. The Object Properties dialog box appears.

3. Click to assign permissions as desired.

4. Click OK when done.

Administering Statement Permissions

Statement-level permissions allow you to determine what rights a user or role has to a specified statement. To assign statement-level permissions:

1. Right click the database to which you want to assign statement-level permissions and select Properties. Click to select the Permissions tab (see Figure 9.23).

2. Click to assign the appropriate statement permissions to each user and/or role.

Creating and Working with Application Roles

An application role is a special type of role that allows an application to log in to SQL Server, regardless of the user who is running the application. An application such as Microsoft Access activates the role. SQL Server then grants users of the application whatever rights were given to the role. To create an application role:

1. Expand the Database node until you can see the Roles subnode.

2. Right-click the Roles subnode and select New Database Role. The Database Role Properties dialog box appears.

3. Enter the name for the role.

4. Click Application Role as the Database role type.

5. Enter a password for the application role (see Figure 9.24).

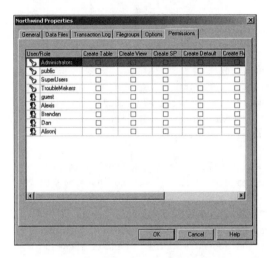

FIGURE 9.23 The Permissions tab of the Properties window allows you to assign the appropriate statement permissions to each user or role.

FIGURE 9.24 The Database Role Properties dialog box allows you to set up an application role.

After you have established an application role, you are ready to use it. You must take these steps:

1. You must set permissions for the role. You set permissions for an application role in the same way you would establish them for any other role.

2. Ensure that the application role can log on to SQL Server. If you are using SQL Server authentication, this involves creating a login for the application role.

3. Use code to connect to the server using the application role.

The code necessary to connect to the server using the application role is:

```
Sub AppRole()
    Dim cnn As Connection
    Set cnn = New ADODB.Connection
    cnn.ConnectionString = "Provider=SQLOLEDB.1;" & _
        "Data Source=5000Alison\SQL2000Alison;Initial Catalog=Northwind;" & _
        "User ID=alexis;PWD=alexis"
    cnn.Open
    'The following line will fail if the user designated
    'in the connection string above does not have rights to the
    'underlying table
    cnn.Execute "SELECT * FROM Customers"
    cnn.Execute "sp_setapprole 'NorthwindRole', 'password'"
    'After setting the app role, this line will succeed
    cnn.Execute "SELECT * FROM Customers"
End Sub
```

This code connects the local server to a database called NorthWind. It executes the SQL Server stored procedure called sp_setapprole, passing it the name of the role and the password for the role. You can then use the connection to perform tasks that the application role has the rights to perform.

Access Security and Its Role in a Client/Server Application

When you upsize an Access database, the security that you have established on the Access database is *not* upsized. Microsoft leaves it up to you to establish security on the SQL Server. You can write code to read the security in the Access .MDB and create it on the SQL Server. If you opt not to use code, you must go through the tedious process of establishing security on each object in the SQL Server database.

When you upsize the data, you still may opt to secure the Access .MDB. This serves to secure your forms, reports, and macros. You can secure your programming code by placing a password on the Visual Basic for Applications(VBA) project. Another option is to distribute your application as an .MDE. This distributes your application without source code. Because the data is secured by SQL Server, this option may be sufficient for you and greatly simplifies the security process.

> **NOTE**
>
> The creation of .MDE files and their implications is covered in *Alison Balter's Mastering Access 2002 Desktop Development.*

If you are using an Access Data Project (ADP), you are not able to individually secure the objects in your database (forms, reports, and macros). If you want to prevent people from modifying these objects, you will have to distribute your application as an .ADE. Of course, if your goal is to secure your programming code, you can simply apply a password to the VBA project.

Summary

SQL Server security is far more powerful than Access security. In this chapter, you learned about the two authentication modes available. You learned about object permissions and application roles. Finally, you learned about Access security and how it interacts with SQL Server security. Unless there is no need to secure the data that your application interacts with, all of these techniques are vital to the success of your application.

10

ADO and SQL Server

Why This Chapter Is Important

You use ActiveX data objects (ADO) to create, modify, and remove Jet Engine, SQL Server, or other OLE DB objects via code. ADO gives you the flexibility to move beyond the user interface to manipulate data stored in the Jet Engine and other formats. Some of the many tasks that you can perform with ADO include:

- Analyzing the structure of an existing database
- Adding or modifying tables and queries
- Creating new databases
- Changing the underlying definitions for queries by modifying the SQL on which the query is based
- Traversing sets of records
- Administrating security
- Modifying table data

A History of Data Access

Microsoft has had a series of data-access technologies that have evolved over the past several years. They include:

- DAO (data access objects)
- RDO (relational data objects)
- ADO (ActiveX data objects)
- ADO.NET (version of ADO for the .NET platform)

DAO was optimized for Jet (Microsoft Access) data. In response to DAO's limitations in dealing with client/server data, Microsoft introduced RDO. RDO was good at dealing with Open Database Connectivity (ODBC) data but was not good at dealing with JET data or nonrelational data. Microsoft introduced ADO to address the limitations of both DAO and RDO. ADO can handle relational *and* nonrelational data stores. It has a much simpler object model than either DAO or RDO. It is easier to use, has a lower memory footprint, and is much more flexible than its predecessors. Recently Microsoft introduced ADO.NET. This latest data-access technology has all the features of ADO but is excellent at dealing with disconnected and XML data.

ADO Quick Review

Figure 10.1 shows an overview of the Microsoft ADO model. Unlike the DAO model, the ADO object model is not hierarchical.

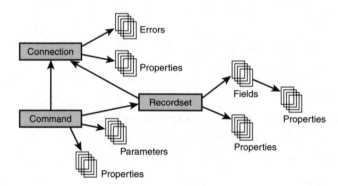

FIGURE 10.1   The ADO object model.

The Connection **Object**

The Connection object defines a session for a user for a data source. Although the ADO object model is not considered to be hierarchical, the Connection object is considered the highest-level ADO object. After you have established a Connection object, you can use it with multiple recordsets. This improves performance and greatly simplifies your programming code.

A Connection object must be declared before it is used. The declaration looks like this:

```
Dim cnn as ADODB.Connection
```

NOTE

Notice that the declaration specifies `ADODB.Connection` rather than just `Connection`. This process is called disambiguation. The process of disambiguating a reference ensures that the correct type of object is created. For example, both the ADO and DAO object libraries have `Recordset` objects. By disambiguating the reference, you explicitly designate the type of recordset object you want to create. If you do not disambiguate the reference, the object library with priority in Tools, References is assumed.

After you declare the `Connection` object, you must instantiate a new `Connection` object. The code looks like this:

```
Set cnn = New ADODB.Connection
```

The `Connection` must then be opened. The `Open` method of the `Connection` object receives a connection string—and optionally a user ID, password, and options—as a parameter. The following is an example of the simplest use of the `Open` method:

```
cnn.Open "Provider=SQLOLEDB.1;" & _
         "Data Source=(local); Initial Catalog=NorthWind;" & _
         "User ID=sa;PWD="
```

The connection string contains three pieces of information:

- The OLE DB provider that you want to use

- Standard ADO connection properties (for example, user ID)

- Provider-specific connection properties

The complete routine required to establish a connection appears in Listing 10.1.

LISTING 10.1   Creating a `Connection` Object

```
Sub CreateConnection()
    'Declare and instantiate the connection
    Dim cnn As ADODB.Connection
    Set cnn = New ADODB.Connection

    'Open the connection
    cnn.Open "Provider=SQLOLEDB.1;" & _
             "Data Source=(local); Initial Catalog=NorthWind;" & _
             "User ID=sa;PWD="

    'Close the connection
```

LISTING 10.1   Continued

```
    cnn.Close

    'Destroy the connection object
    Set cnn = Nothing
End Sub
```

TIP

All of the examples in this chapter first declare a variable using the keyword `Dim` and then instantiate it using the keyword `Set`. You can remove the `Set` statement by specifying the `New` keyword in the `Dim` statement. For example, you could use:

```
Dim rst as New ADODB.Recordset
```

Although this works, it is not considered desirable. This is because you have little control over when the object is placed in memory. For example, if the variable is public, Access places it in memory the moment anything in the module is referenced. Separating the `Dim` and `Set` statements allows you to declare the variable wherever you like and place it in memory when you need to. Another bad side effect of declaring a variable this way is that VBA wraps the statement with checks to see if the code already instantiated the object. This further slows down processing.

NOTE

Listing 10.1 and most code in this chapter is located in the CHAP10EX.MDB file included with this book's CD-ROM.

The `Recordset` Object

You use a `Recordset` object to look at records as a group. A `Recordset` object refers to the set of rows returned from a request for data. As with a `Connection` object, to use a `Recordset` object, you must first declare it. The code looks like this:

```
Dim rst as ADODB.Recordset
```

After you declare the `Recordset` object, you must instantiate it. The code looks like this:

```
Set rst = New ADODB.Recordset
```

As with a `Connection` object, the `Open` method is used to point the `Recordset` object at a set of records. The code looks like this:

```
rst.Open "Select * From tblClients", cnn
```

The first parameter of the Open method is the source of the data. The source can be a table name, a SQL statement, a stored procedure name, a Command object variable name, or the filename of a persisted recordset. In the example, the source is a SQL Select statement.

The second parameter of the Open method must be either a valid connection string or the name of a Connection object. In the example, cnn returns a reference to a Connection object referred to as cnn. The reference supplies the connection for the Recordset object. The completed code appears in Listing 10.2.

LISTING 10.2   Creating a Recordset Using a Connection String

```
Sub CreateRecordset1()

    'Declare and instantiate the connection
    Dim cnn As ADODB.Connection
    Set cnn = New ADODB.Connection

    'Declare and instantiate the recordset
    Dim rst As ADODB.Recordset
    Set rst = New ADODB.Recordset

    'Open the connection
    cnn.Open "Provider=SQLOLEDB.1;" & _
            "Data Source=(local); Initial Catalog=NorthWind;" & _
            "User ID=sa;PWD="

    'Open the recordset
    rst.Open "Select * From Customers", cnn

    'Print its contents
    Debug.Print rst.GetString

    'Close and destroy the recordset and the connection
    rst.Close
    Set rst = Nothing
    cnn.Close
    Set cnn = Nothing
End Sub
```

Notice that after the code opens the recordset, it prints the result of the GetString method of the Recordset object to the Immediate window. The GetString method of the Recordset object builds a string based on the data contained in the recordset. For now, this is a simple way of verifying that your code works as expected. Also, note that the code uses the Close method of the Recordset object to close the recordset. The Close method, when applied to either a Connection object or a Recordset object, has the effect of freeing the associated system resources. The Close method does *not* eliminate the object from memory. Setting the Recordset object equal to Nothing eliminates the object from memory.

Although this syntax works quite well, I prefer to set the parameters of the Open method as properties of the Recordset object before I issue the Open method. You will see that this makes your code much more readable as you add parameters to the Open method. The code appears in Listing 10.3.

LISTING 10.3   Creating a Recordset Using the ActiveConnection Property

```
Sub CreateRecordset2()

    'Declare and instantiate the connection
    Dim cnn As ADODB.Connection
    Set cnn = New ADODB.Connection

    'Declare and instantiate the recordset
    Dim rst As ADODB.Recordset
    Set rst = New ADODB.Recordset

    'Open the connection
    cnn.Open "Provider=SQLOLEDB.1;" & _
            "Data Source=(local); Initial Catalog=NorthWind;" & _
            "User ID=sa;PWD="

    'Use the ActiveConnection property of the recordset object
    'to supply the connection information
    rst.ActiveConnection = cnn

    'Open the recordset and print its contents
    rst.Open "Select * From Customers"
    Debug.Print rst.GetString

    'Close and destroy the recordset object and the connection object
    rst.Close
    Set rst = Nothing
    cnn.Close
    Set cnn = Nothing
End Sub
```

Finally, you can use a Connection object to provide a connection for the recordset. In fact, you can use the same Connection object for multiple recordsets. The code appears in Listing 10.4.

LISTING 10.4   Creating a Recordset Using a Connection Object

```
Sub CreateRecordset3()

    'Declare and instantiate one connection object
    'and two recordset objects
    Dim cnn As ADODB.Connection
    Dim rst1 As ADODB.Recordset
    Dim rst2 As ADODB.Recordset

    Set cnn = New ADODB.Connection
    Set rst1 = New ADODB.Recordset
    Set rst2 = New ADODB.Recordset

    'Open the connection
    cnn.Open "Provider=SQLOLEDB.1;" & _
            "Data Source=(local); Initial Catalog=NorthWind;" & _
            "User ID=sa;PWD="


    'Utilize the connection just opened as the connection for
    'two different recordsets
    rst1.ActiveConnection = cnn
    rst1.Open "Select * From Customers"
    rst2.ActiveConnection = cnn
    rst2.Open "Select * From Orders"

    'Retrieve data out of the recordsets
    Debug.Print rst1.GetString
    Debug.Print rst2.GetString

    'Close the recordsets and the connection and destroy the objects
    rst1.Close
    rst2.Close
    cnn.Close

    Set rst1 = Nothing
    Set rst2 = Nothing
    Set cnn = Nothing
End Sub
```

Notice that both rst1 and rst2 use the same Connection object.

The `Command` **Object**

The ADO `Command` object represents a query, SQL statement, or stored procedure that is executed against a data source. Although it is not always necessary, a `Command` object is particularly useful when executing parameterized queries and stored procedures. Just as with the `Connection` object and the `Recordset` object, you must declare the `Command` object before you use it:

```
Dim cmd as ADODB.Command
```

Next, you must instantiate the `Command` object:

```
Set cmd = New ADODB.Command
```

After you instantiate the `Command` object, you must set its `ActiveConnection` property and its `CommandText` property. As with a `Recordset` object, the `ActiveConnection` property can be either a connection string or a reference to a `Connection` object. The `CommandText` property is the SQL statement or stored procedure used by the `Command` object. The `ActiveConnection` and the `CommandText` properties look like this:

```
cmd.ActiveConnection = "Provider=SQLOLEDB.1;" & _
            "Data Source=(local); Initial Catalog=NorthWind;" & _
            "User ID=sa;PWD="
cmd.CommandText = "Select * from Customers"
```

The completed code appears in Listing 10.5.

LISTING 10.5   Using a Command Object

```
Sub CommandObject()

    'Declare a recordset and a command object
    Dim rst As ADODB.Recordset
    Dim cmd As ADODB.Command

    'Instantiate the command object
    Set cmd = New ADODB.Command

    'Designate where the data comes from
    cmd.CommandText = "Select * from Customers"

    'Establish the connection information
    cmd.ActiveConnection = "Provider=SQLOLEDB.1;" & _
            "Data Source=(local); Initial Catalog=NorthWind;" & _
            "User ID=sa;PWD="

    'Use the execute method to return a result set
```

LISTING 10.5   Continued

```
    'into the recordset object
    Set rst = cmd.Execute

    'Display the resulting data
    Debug.Print rst.GetString

    'Close the recordset and destroy the objects
    rst.Close

    Set cmd = Nothing
    Set rst = Nothing
End Sub
```

The code first instantiates the Command object. It sets the CommandText property to a
SQL Select statement, and it points the ActiveConnection property to the
NorthWind database on the local server. It then uses the Execute method of the
Command object to return the results of the SQL statement into the Recordset object.

Understanding ADO Recordset Types

Three parameters of the Open method of a Recordset object affect the type of recordset that ADO creates. They are the CursorType, the LockType, and the Options parameters. These parameters combine to determine the types of movements that can be
executed within a recordset, when changes that other users make to data underlying
the recordset will be seen, and whether the recordset's data is updateable.

The CursorType Parameter

By default, when you open a recordset, ADO sets the CursorType parameter to
adOpenForwardOnly. This means that you can only move forward through the
records in the recordset. You will not see any adds, edits, or deletions that other users
make. Furthermore, many properties and methods, such as the RecordCount property
and the MovePrevious method, are unavailable. Listing 10.6 illustrates this.

LISTING 10.6   The RecordCount Property Is Not Supported with a Forward-Only
Recordset

```
Sub ForwardOnlyRecordset()

    'Declare and instantiate a recordset object
    Dim rst As ADODB.Recordset
    Set rst = New ADODB.Recordset

    'Establish a connection and open a forward-only recordset
    rst.ActiveConnection = "Provider=SQLOLEDB.1;" & _
```

LISTING 10.6   Continued

```
            "Data Source=(local); Initial Catalog=NorthWind;" & _
            "User ID=sa;PWD="
    rst.Open "Select * from Customers", _
        CursorType:=adOpenForwardOnly

    'Attempt to retrieve the recordcount
    Debug.Print rst.RecordCount

    'Close and destroy the recordset
    rst.Close
    Set rst = Nothing
End Sub
```

The value ·1 will be displayed in the Immediate window because the `RecordCount` property is not supported with a forward-only recordset. Because you did not explicitly designate the cursor type, ADO created a forward-only recordset.

ADO offers three other values for the `CursorType`. They are `adOpenStatic`, `adOpenKeyset`, and `adOpenDynamic`. The `adOpenStatic` option allows forward and backward movement through the records in the recordset, but changes that other users make to the underlying data are not seen by the recordset. The `adOpenKeyset` option offers everything offered by the `adOpenStatic` option, but, in addition, edits that other users make are seen by the recordset. Finally, with the `adOpenDynamic` option, adds, edits, and deletions made by other users are seen by the recordset. Table 10.1 illustrates each of these options in further detail.

TABLE 10.1   Valid Choices for the `CursorType` Parameter

Value	Description
adOpenForwardOnly	Copies a set of records as the recordset is created. Therefore, it doesn't show changes made by other users. This is the fastest type of cursor, but it allows only forward movement through the recordset.
adOpenStatic	Copies a set of records as the recordset is created. Supports bookmarks and allows forward and backward movement through the recordset. Doesn't show changes made by other users. This is the only type of recordset allowed when using client-side cursors.
adOpenKeyset	Provides a set of pointers back to the original data. Supports bookmarks. Shows changes made by other users. Does not show new records, and provides no access to deleted rows.
adOpenDynamic	Provides access to a set of records. Shows all changes, including additions and deletions, made by other users.

You can set the CursorType property of the recordset in one of two ways. For instance, you can set it as a parameter of the Open method of the Recordset object. Listing 10.7 illustrates this.

LISTING 10.7   Supplying the CursorType as a Parameter of the Open Method

```
Sub StaticRecordset1()

    'Declare and instantiate a recordset object
    Dim rst As ADODB.Recordset
    Set rst = New ADODB.Recordset

    'Establish a connection and open a static recordset
    rst.ActiveConnection = "Provider=SQLOLEDB.1;" & _
            "Data Source=(local); Initial Catalog=NorthWind;" & _
            "User ID=sa;PWD="
    rst.Open "Select * from Customers", _
        CursorType:=adOpenStatic

    'Retrieve the recordcount
    Debug.Print rst.RecordCount

    rst.Close
    Set rst = Nothing
End Sub
```

Notice that, in Listing 10.7, the CursorType appears as a parameter of the Open method. Contrast Listing 10.7 with Listing 10.8.

LISTING 10.8   Supplying the CursorType as a Property of the Recordset Object

```
Sub StaticRecordset2()

    'Declare and instantiate a recordset object
    Dim rst As ADODB.Recordset
    Set rst = New ADODB.Recordset

    'Set the ActiveConnection and CursorType properties
    'of the recordset
    rst.ActiveConnection = "Provider=SQLOLEDB.1;" & _
            "Data Source=(local); Initial Catalog=NorthWind;" & _
            "User ID=sa;PWD="
```

LISTING 10.8   Continued

```
rst.CursorType = adOpenStatic

'Open the recordset
rst.Open "Select * from Customers"

'Retrieve the recordcount
Debug.Print rst.RecordCount

rst.Close
Set rst = Nothing

End Sub
```

Listing 10.8 set the CursorType as a property of the Recordset object prior to the execution of the Open method. Separating the properties from the Open method improves the readability of the code.

The LockType **Parameter**

Although the CursorType property of a Recordset object determines how movements can occur within the recordset and whether other users' changes are seen, the CursorType in no way affects the updateability of the recordset's data. In fact, when you open a recordset, ADO opens it as read-only by default. Only by changing the LockType property can you make the recordset updateable.

The options for lock type are adLockReadOnly, adLockPessimistic, adLockOptimistic, and adLockBatchOptimistic. The default, adLockReadOnly, does not allow changes to the recordset. The other options all provide updateability for the recordset's data. The difference lies in when ADO locks the records. With the adLockPessimistic option, locking occurs as soon as the editing process begins. With the adLockOptimistic option, ADO locks the record when you issue the Update method. Finally, with adLockBatchOptimistic, you can postpone locking until the code updates a batch of records.

As with the CursorType property, you can set the LockType property as a parameter of the Open method or as a property of the Recordset object. Listing 10.9 shows the configuration of the LockType as a property of the Recordset object.

LISTING 10.9   Configuration of the LockType Property

```
Sub OptimisticRecordset()

    'Declare and instantiate a recordset object
    Dim rst As ADODB.Recordset
```

LISTING 10.9   Continued

```
Set rst = New ADODB.Recordset

'Set the ActiveConnection and CursorType, and
'LockType properties of the recordset
rst.ActiveConnection = "Provider=SQLOLEDB.1;" & _
        "Data Source=(local); Initial Catalog=NorthWind;" & _
        "User ID=sa;PWD="
rst.CursorType = adOpenStatic
rst.LockType = adLockOptimistic

'Open the recordset
rst.Open "Select * from Customers"

'Modify the contents of the city field
rst("City") = "Westlake"
rst.Update
Debug.Print rst("City")

rst.Close
Set rst = Nothing

End Sub
```

In Listing 10.9, the code sets the LockType property to adLockOptimistic. The code locks the record when it issues the Update method of the Recordset object.

> **NOTE**
>
> Listing 10.9 references the field name in the format rst("City"). You can use any one of four syntactical constructs to reference a member of a collection. These include:
>
> Collection("Name")
> Collection(VariableName)
> Collection!Name
> Collection(Ordinal)
>
> You might wonder which is best. Although all are valid, I most prefer the Collection("Name") and Collection(VariableName) methods. I like the fact that the syntax is the same whether you are supplying a string or a variable. Furthermore, the same syntax works with Active Server Pages (ASP). The bang does not work with ASP, and you cannot rely on the ordinal position because it changes. One of the only instances when you must use a bang is when you are supplying a parameter for a query. Besides that, I use the Collection("Name") syntax in the ADO and DAO code that I write.

The Options Parameter

The Options parameter determines how the provider should evaluate the source argument. Table 10.2 illustrates the valid choices.

TABLE 10.2   Valid Choices for the Options Parameter

Value	Description
adCmdText	The provider evaluates the source as a command.
adCmdTable	A SQL query is generated to return all rows from the table named in the source.
adCmdTableDirect	The provider returns all rows in the table named in the source.
adCmdStoredProc	The provider evaluates the source as a stored procedure.
adCmdUnknown	The type of command in the source is unknown.
adCmdFile	The source is evaluated as a persisted recordset.
adAsyncExecute	The source is executed asynchronously.
adAsyncFetch	The initial quantity specified in the Initial Fetch Size property is fetched.
adAsyncFetchNonBlocking	The main thread never blocks when fetching.

The default for the Options parameter is adCmdUnknown. If you do not explicitly specify the Options parameter, the provider attempts to evaluate it while the code is running. This degrades performance. It is therefore important to specify the parameter. Listing 10.10 illustrates the use of the Options parameter of the Open method.

LISTING 10.10   The Options Parameter of the Open Method

```
Sub OptionsParameter()
    'Declare and instantiate a recordset object
    Dim rst As ADODB.Recordset
    Set rst = New ADODB.Recordset

    'Set the ActiveConnection and CursorType, and
    'LockType properties of the recordset
    rst.ActiveConnection = "Provider=SQLOLEDB.1;" & _
            "Data Source=(local); Initial Catalog=NorthWind;" & _
            "User ID=sa;PWD="
    rst.CursorType = adOpenStatic
    rst.LockType = adLockOptimistic

    'Open the recordset, designating that the source
    'is a command
    rst.Open "Select * from Customers", _
```

LISTING 10.10 Continued

```
        Options:=adCmdText

    'Modify the contents of the city field
    rst("City") = "Westlake"
    rst.Update
    Debug.Print rst("City")

    rst.Close
    Set rst = Nothing
End Sub
```

Listing 10.10 sets the Options parameter to adCmdText. This causes the source to be evaluated as a SQL command.

Selecting a Cursor Location

A cursor refers to the set of rows or row pointers that ADO returns when you open a recordset. With DAO, the location of the cursor is not an issue. On the other hand, ADO supports two cursor locations. As its name implies, the client manages a client-side cursor. The server manages a server-side cursor.

NOTE

If you are using Jet, the client machine always manages the cursor because Jet runs on only the client machine. You might think that this means that you should always designate a client-side cursor when working with Jet. Actually, the opposite is true. If you designate a client-side cursor when working with Jet, ADO caches the data twice on the client machine. When you specify a client-side cursor, the Microsoft Cursor Service for OLE DB requests all the data from the OLE DB provider and then caches it and presents it to the application as a static recordset. For this reason, when working with Jet, you should designate a client-side cursor only when you want to take advantage of functionality provided only by a client-side cursor.

Listing 10.11 illustrates how to designate the cursor location.

LISTING 10.11 Designating the Cursor Location

```
Sub CursorLocation()
    'Declare and instantiate a recordset object
    Dim rst As ADODB.Recordset
    Set rst = New ADODB.Recordset

    'Set the ActiveConnection and CursorType, and
    'LockType, and CursorLocation properties of the recordset
```

LISTING 10.11   Continued

```
    rst.ActiveConnection = "Provider=SQLOLEDB.1;" & _
           "Data Source=(local); Initial Catalog=NorthWind;" & _
           "User ID=sa;PWD="
    rst.CursorType = adOpenStatic
    rst.LockType = adLockOptimistic
    rst.CursorLocation = adUseServer

    'Open the recordset, designating that the source
    'is a SQL statement
    rst.Open Source:="Select * from Customers ", _
        Options:=adCmdText

    'Modify the contents of the city field
    rst("City") = "Old City"
    rst.Update
    Debug.Print rst("City")

    rst.Close
    Set rst = Nothing


End Sub
```

This example designates a server-side cursor.

Working with the Supports Method

Depending on which CursorType, LockType, CursorLocation, and Provider are used
to open a recordset, the functionality of the recordset varies. The Supports method
of a recordset determines which features a particular recordset supports. It returns a
Boolean value designating whether the selected feature is supported. Listing 10.12
provides an example.

LISTING 10.12   The Supports Method of the Recordset Object

```
Sub SupportsMethod()
    'Declare and instantiate a recordset object
    Dim rst As ADODB.Recordset
    Set rst = New ADODB.Recordset

    'Set the ActiveConnection and CursorType, and
    'LockType, and CursorLocation properties of the recordset
    rst.ActiveConnection = "Provider=SQLOLEDB.1;" & _
```

LISTING 10.12   Continued

```
                 "Data Source=(local); Initial Catalog=NorthWind;" & _
                 "User ID=sa;PWD="
      rst.CursorType = adOpenStatic
      rst.LockType = adLockOptimistic
      rst.CursorLocation = adUseServer

      'Open the recordset, designating that the source
      'is a SQL statement
      rst.Open Source:="Select * from Customers ", _
          Options:=adCmdText

      'Determine whether the recordset supports certain features
      Debug.Print "Bookmark " & rst.Supports(adBookmark)
      Debug.Print "Update Batch " & rst.Supports(adUpdateBatch)
      Debug.Print "Move Previous " & rst.Supports(adMovePrevious)
      Debug.Print "Seek " & rst.Supports(adSeek)
      rst.Close
      Set rst = Nothing

End Sub
```

ADO and Stored Procedures

One of ADO's strong points is its capability to execute SQL Server stored procedures. Using ADO, you can easily pass input parameters to stored procedures and retrieve the values of output parameters. The sections that follow cover the ins and outs of executing stored procedures and responding to the information that they output.

NOTE

The code examples that follow require you to create the associated stored procedures in the NorthWind database *prior* to running the code.

Executing a Stored Procedure

The easiest way to execute a stored procedure is to use the Command object. Listing 10.13 provides an example.

LISTING 10.13   Using the `Command` Object to Execute a Stored Procedure

```
Private Sub cmdNoParms_Click()
    Dim com As ADODB.Command
    Dim lngRowsAffected As Long

    Set com = New ADODB.Command
    With com
        .ActiveConnection = CONNSTRING
        .CommandText = "EXEC procCustomerDeleteNoParm"
        .Execute RecordsAffected:=lngRowsAffected
    End With

    MsgBox lngRowsAffected
End Sub
```

The code instantiates an ADODB `Command` object. The `CommandText` property of the `Command` object contains the name of the stored procedure that you want to execute (in this case, `procCustomerDeleteNoParm`). The `procCustomerDeleteNoParm` procedure looks like this:

```
CREATE PROCEDURE
    procCustomerDeleteNoParm AS
        DELETE FROM Customers
            WHERE CustomerID = 'AAAAA'
```

The stored procedure deletes the customer with the ID of AAAAA.

Executing a Parameterized Stored Procedure

Most stored procedures contain at least one input parameter. You can use three common methods when executing a stored procedure from a `Command` object. They include:

- Pass a single parameter immediately following the `EXEC` statement

- Pass one or more parameters as the `Parameters` parameter of the `Execute` method of the `Command` object

- Use the `Parameters` collection of the `Command` object

Listing 10.14 illustrates the process of passing a single parameter as part of the `EXEC` statement.

LISTING 10.14   Passing a Single Parameter as Part of the EXEC Statement

```
Private Sub cmdParameters_Click()
    Dim com As ADODB.Command
    Dim lngRowsAffected As Long

    Set com = New ADODB.Command
    With com
        .ActiveConnection = CONNSTRING
        .CommandText = "EXEC procCustomerDeleteParm '" & _
            Me.txtCustomerID & "'"
        .Execute RecordsAffected:=lngRowsAffected
    End With

    MsgBox lngRowsAffected

End Sub
```

The code declares and instantiates a `Command` object. It sets the `ActiveConnection` property of the `Command` object to a connection string stored in a constant called `CONNSTRING`. The important line of code is the one that sets the `CommandText` property of the `Command` object. Notice that after the keyword `EXEC` and the name of the stored procedure, the value code passes the value in the `txtCustomerID` textbox to the stored procedure. The example uses the `Execute` method of the `Command` object to execute the stored procedure designated in the `CommandText` property. The procedure returns the number of rows affected as the `RecordsAffected` parameter. This parameter contains a valid value only if the `SET NOCOUNT ON` statement is *not* included in the stored procedure. The `procCustomerDeleteParm` stored procedure looks like this:

```
CREATE PROCEDURE
    procCustomerDeleteParm
@CustomerID VarChar(5)
AS
DELETE FROM Customers
        WHERE CustomerID=@CustomerID
```

Notice that the stored procedure receives an input parameter that is the customer ID of the customer that you want to delete. The next method of executing the stored procedure involves passing an array to the `Parameters` parameter of the `Execute` method of the `Command` object. It appears in Listing 10.15.

LISTING 10.15   Passing an Array to the `Parameters` Parameter of the `Execute` Method of the `Command` Object

```
Private Sub cmdParameterArray_Click()
    Dim com As ADODB.Command
    Dim rst As ADODB.Recordset
    Dim varParamArray As Variant
    Dim lngRowsAffected As Long

    varParamArray = Array("London", "Sales Agent")

    Set com = New ADODB.Command
    With com
        .ActiveConnection = CONNSTRING
        .CommandText = "procCustomerGetCityTitle"
        .CommandType = adCmdStoredProc
        Set rst = .Execute(RecordsAffected:=lngRowsAffected, _
            Parameters:=varParamArray)
    End With

    If Not rst.EOF Then
        MsgBox rst("CustomerID")
    Else
        MsgBox "No Customers Found!"
    End If

End Sub
```

The code declares a `Command` object and a `Recordset` object. It populates an array called `varParamArray` with the values `London` and `Sales Agent`. After instantiating the `Command` object, the code sets the `ActiveConnection` property of the `Command` object to a string stored in the `CONNSTRING` constant. With this method of executing a parameterized stored procedure, you set the `CommandText` property to the name of the stored procedure. The example uses the `CommandType` property of the `Command` object to designate that `CommandText` is the name of a stored procedure. Finally, it's the `Execute` method of the `Command` object that receives the `varParmArray` as the `Parameters` parameter. The example stores the result of executing the stored procedure and returning the results into a recordset. The `If` statement uses the `EOF` property to evaluate whether the procedure returns any rows to the caller. The `procCustomerGetCityTitle` procedure looks like this:

```
CREATE PROCEDURE
    procCustomerGetCityTitle
```

```
@City nVarChar(150),
@ContactTitle nVarChar(30)
AS
SELECT * FROM Customers
WHERE Customers.City = @City AND
      Customers.ContactTitle = @ContactTitle
```

The procCustomerGetCityTitle stored procedure selects all fields from the Customers table for customers with the designated city and contact title.

The final method of executing a parameterized stored procedure is to use the Parameters collection of the Command object. You actually can use two different techniques to accomplish this task. The first two examples use a technique that is simpler but not as efficient as the third example (shown in Listing 10.16).

LISTING 10.16   Using the Parameters Collection of the Command Object

```
Private Sub cmdRecordset_Click()
    Dim com As ADODB.Command
    Dim rst As ADODB.Recordset

    Set com = New ADODB.Command
    With com
        .ActiveConnection = CONNSTRING
        .CommandText = "procCustomerGet"
        .CommandType = adCmdStoredProc
        .Parameters.Refresh
        .Parameters("@CustomerID") = Me.txtCustomerID
        Set rst = .Execute
    End With

    MsgBox rst("CompanyName")
End Sub
```

This routine creates a Command object and a Recordset object. It instantiates the Command object and then sets its ActiveConnection property to the value stored in the CONNSTRING constant. It sets the CommandText property to the name of the procedure that it executes (procCustomerGet). It sets the CommandType property to adCmdStoredProc, indicating to ADO that the CommandText contains the name of a stored procedure. It then uses the Parameters collection of the Command object to set the @CustomerID parameter to the value in the txtCustomerID textbox. Finally, it uses the Execute method of the Command object to execute the stored procedure, returning the result into the rst recordset. Here's the procCustomerGet procedure:

```
CREATE PROCEDURE
procCustomerGet
@CustomerID VarChar(5)
AS
      SELECT * FROM Customers
            WHERE CustomerID =
            @CustomerID
```

Listing 10.17 shows another example of this same technique. The differences in this example are that multiple parameters are passed, and the stored procedure that the code executes inserts data (rather than simply selecting it).

LISTING 10.17   Using the `Parameters` Collection of the `Command` Object to Pass Multiple Parameters

```
Private Sub cmdParametersCollection_Click()
    Dim com As ADODB.Command
    Set com = New ADODB.Command

    With com
        .ActiveConnection = CONNSTRING
        .CommandText = "procOrderInsert"
        .CommandType = adCmdStoredProc
        .Parameters.Refresh
        .Parameters("@CustomerID") = Me.txtCustomerID
        .Parameters("@Freight") = Me.txtFreight
        .Parameters("@OrderDate") = Now()
        .Execute
    End With

End Sub
```

The example declares and instantiates a `Command` object. It sets the `ActiveConnnection` property of the `Command` object to the value stored in the `CONNSTRING` constant. It sets the `CommandText` property of the `Command` object to the `procOrderInsert` stored procedure. Next it sets the `CommandType` property of the `Command` object to `acCmdStoredProc`, indicating that the value in the `CommandText` is the name of a stored procedure. Next it sets three input parameters of the stored procedure. The procedure sets the first two parameters, `@CustomerID` and `@Freight`, to the appropriate textbox values. It sets the `@OrderDate` parameter to the value returned from the built-in `GetDate` function. Finally, it executes the stored procedure. The `procOrderInsert` procedure looks like this:

```
CREATE PROCEDURE procOrderInsert
@CustomerID char(5),
@EmployeeID int = Null,
@OrderDate datetime,
@Freight money = 0,
@OrderID int OUTPUT
AS
INSERT INTO Orders
(CustomerID, EmployeeID, OrderDate, Freight)
VALUES
(@@CustomerID, @EmployeeID, @OrderDate, @Freight)
SET @OrderID = @@IDENTITY
```

Notice that the procedure receives four input parameters. It uses the values in the
input parameters to insert a row into the Orders table.

The disadvantage of both of the previous client-side examples is that they require a
round trip to the server to evaluate the Parameters collection of the stored procedure. A method that is more cumbersome to code but is a much more efficient way
of using the Parameters collection appears in Listing 10.18.

LISTING 10.18   A More Efficient Method of Using the Parameters Collection of the
Command Object

```
Private Sub cmdParametersAdd_Click()
    Dim com As ADODB.Command
    Dim parm As ADODB.Parameter

    Set com = New ADODB.Command

    With com
        .ActiveConnection = CONNSTRING
        .CommandText = "procOrderInsert"
        .CommandType = adCmdStoredProc

        .Parameters.Append .CreateParameter( _
            "CustomerID", adChar, adParamInput, 5, _
            Me.txtCustomerID)
        .Parameters.Append .CreateParameter( _
            "EmployeeID", adInteger, adParamInput, , 1)
        .Parameters.Append .CreateParameter( _
            "OrderDate", adDBTime, adParamInput, , _
            Now())
```

LISTING 10.18   Continued

```
        .Parameters.Append .CreateParameter( _
            "Freight", adInteger, adParamInput, , _
            Me.txtFreight)
        .Parameters.Append .CreateParameter( _
            "OrderID", adInteger, adParamOutput)
        .Execute
    End With


End Sub
```

The example uses the `Append` method of the `Parameters` collection of the `Command` object to append each parameter. The `CreateParameter` method of the `Command` object defines the name, data type, type (input versus output), and value of each parameter as the code adds it.

Handling Output Parameters

Many stored procedures contain output parameters. Output parameters allow you to pass status and other information from the stored procedure to the front end. The code in Listing 10.19 executes a stored procedure called `procOrderInsert`. The procedure contains an output parameter called `@OrderID`. Notice that the code uses the `Parameters` collection of the `Command` object to access the output parameter and retrieve its value.

LISTING 10.19   A More Efficient Method of Using the `Parameters` Collection of the `Command` Object

```
Private Sub cmdReturningParameters_Click()
    Dim com As ADODB.Command
    Set com = New ADODB.Command

    With com
        .ActiveConnection = CONNSTRING
        .CommandText = "procOrderInsert"
        .CommandType = adCmdStoredProc
        .Parameters.Refresh
        .Parameters("@CustomerID") = Me.txtCustomerID
        .Parameters("@Freight") = Me.txtFreight
        .Parameters("@OrderDate") = Now()
        .Execute
```

LISTING 10.19 Continued

```
        MsgBox "New OrderID = " & _
            .Parameters("@OrderID")
    End With

End Sub
```

Responding to Errors

It is important that you include error handling in both the VBA code and the stored procedures that you build. The code in Listing 10.20 executes the stored procedure called procOrderInsertEH. Notice that the routine displays two output parameters, @ReturnCode and @ReturnMessage. These parameters contain important information about the success or failure of the stored procedure. The VBA code also contains error handling to respond to a referential integrity error encountered by the stored procedure.

LISTING 10.20 Executing a Stored Procedure That Contains Important Information About the Success or Failure of the Procedure

```
Private Sub cmdErrorHandling_Click()

    On Error GoTo cmdErrorHandling_Err
    Dim com As ADODB.Command
    Set com = New ADODB.Command

    With com
        .ActiveConnection = CONNSTRING
        .CommandText = "procOrderInsertEH"
        .CommandType = adCmdStoredProc
        .Parameters.Refresh
        .Parameters("@CustomerID") = Me.txtCustomerID
        .Parameters("@EmployeeID") = 1
        .Parameters("@OrderDate") = Now()
        .Parameters("@Freight") = Me.txtFreight
        .Execute
        MsgBox "Result Code: " & _
            .Parameters("@ReturnCode") & _
            vbCrLf & _
            "Status: " & _
            .Parameters("@ReturnMessage")

    End With

cmdErrorHandling_Exit:
```

LISTING 10.20   Continued

```
    Exit Sub

cmdErrorHandling_Err:
    If Err.Number = -2147217873 Then 'Referential Integrity
        MsgBox "Invalid Customer, Try Again!"
    Else
        MsgBox Err.Number & ": " & Err.Description
    End If
    Resume cmdErrorHandling_Exit
End Sub
```

The procOrderInsertEH routine appears in Listing 10.21. The routine first tests to ensure that no null values are found in the input parameters that are associated with required fields. If it finds any null values, the code exits the procedure. If it finds all required values, the procedure attempts to insert a row into the Orders table. The code evaluates the @@RowCount function to see if any rows were affected. If one row was affected, it places the identity value in the @OrderID output parameter, it places a success code in the @ReturnCode parameter, and it places a message in the @ReturnMessage parameter. If no rows were affected, the @OrderID and @ReturnCode parameter values are set to 0 and the message "Insert Failed" is placed in the @ReturnMessage parameter.

LISTING 10.21   A Stored Procedure That Effectively Handles Errors

```
CREATE PROCEDURE procOrderInsertEH
@CustomerID char(5),
@EmployeeID int = Null,
@OrderDate datetime,
@Freight money = 0,
@OrderID int OUTPUT,
@ReturnCode int OUTPUT,
@ReturnMessage VarChar(50) OUTPUT
AS

IF @CustomerID Is Null
    SELECT @ReturnCode = 0,
      @ReturnMessage = @ReturnMessage +
      'Customer Required' + Char(13) + Char(10)

IF @EmployeeID Is Null
    SELECT @ReturnCode = 0,
```

LISTING 10.21   Continued

```
        @ReturnMessage = @ReturnMessage +
        'Employee Required' + Char(13) + Char(10)

IF @OrderDate  Is Null
    SELECT @ReturnCode = 0,
      @ReturnMessage = @ReturnMessage +
      'Order Date Required' + Char(13) + Char(10)

IF @Freight Is Null
    SELECT @ReturnCode = 0,
      @ReturnMessage = @ReturnMessage +
      'Freight Required' + Char(13) + Char(10)

IF @ReturnCode = 0
      RETURN

INSERT INTO Orders
(CustomerID, EmployeeID, OrderDate, Freight)
VALUES
(@CustomerID, @EmployeeID, @OrderDate, @Freight)

IF @@ROWCOUNT = 1
    SELECT @OrderID = @@IDENTITY,
      @ReturnCode = 1,
      @ReturnMessage = 'Order Number ' +
            Convert(VarChar, @@IDENTITY) + 'Added'
ELSE
    SELECT @OrderID = 0,
      @ReturnCode = 0,
            @ReturnMessage = 'Insert Failed'
```

An alternative to the previous procedure is the procOrderInsertEH2 routine shown in Listing 10.22. It is simplified for this example to eliminate the test for required parameters. It adds the use of the @@Error function after the code attempts to insert a row. If the @@Error function returns 0, the @OrderID parameter is set equal to the identity value of the inserted row, the @ReturnCode parameter is set to 1, and the @ReturnMessage parameter is set to a message that includes the identity value of the inserted row. If the @@Error function returns a nonzero value, @OrderID is set to 0, @ReturnCode is set to the value of @@Error, and @ReturnMessage is set to the appropriate error message.

LISTING 10.22   A Stored Procedure That Effectively Handles Errors by the Use of the
@@Error Function After the Code Attempts to Insert a Row

```
CREATE PROCEDURE procOrderInsertEH2
@CustomerID char(5),
@EmployeeID int = Null,
@OrderDate datetime,
@Freight money = 0,
@OrderID int OUTPUT,
@ReturnCode int OUTPUT,
@ReturnMessage VarChar(50) OUTPUT
AS
INSERT INTO Orders
(CustomerID, EmployeeID, OrderDate, Freight)
VALUES
(@CustomerID, @EmployeeID, @OrderDate, @Freight)

IF @@ERROR = 0
    SELECT @OrderID = @@IDENTITY,
       @ReturnCode = 1,
       @ReturnMessage = 'Order Number ' +
            Convert(VarChar, @@IDENTITY) + 'Added'
ELSE
    SELECT @OrderID = 0,
       @ReturnCode = @@ERROR,
                @ReturnMessage = 'Insert Failed'
```

Advanced ADO Techniques

ADO offers some additional advanced features that you should keep in your arsenal
of techniques. These include the capability to create a recordset without a data
source, to work with persisted recordsets, to work with hierarchical recordsets, and to
handle ADO events. The sections that follow cover these techniques.

Creating Recordsets Without a Data Source

Sometimes you will want to build your own cursors without connecting to a data
source. An example is a scenario in which you want to use the rich ADO cursor
engine to programmatically manipulate the files in a directory. Listing 10.23
provides an example.

LISTING 10.23   Creating a Cursor Without Connecting to a Data Source

```
Sub NoDataSource()

    Dim strFileName As String

    'Declare and instantiate the recordset
    Dim rst As ADODB.Recordset
    Set rst = New ADODB.Recordset

    With rst
        'Append to the Fields collection of the
        'recordset object
        With .Fields
            .Append "FileName", adVarChar, 255
            .Append "FileSize", adBigInt
        End With

        'Set the appropriate properties and open the recordset
        .CursorType = adOpenStatic
        .CursorLocation = adUseClient
        .Open

        'Loop through the directory entries, adding the
        'file names and file sizes to the recordset
        strFileName = Dir("c:\*.*")
        Do Until Len(strFileName) = 0
            .AddNew
                rst("FileName") = strFileName
                rst("FileSize") = FileLen("c:\" & strFileName)
            .Update
            strFileName = Dir()
        Loop

        'Sort the recordset by the FileName field
        .Sort = "FileName"

        'Loop through the recordset printing the
        'file names and file sizes
        Do Until .EOF
            Debug.Print rst("FileName"), rst("FileSize")
            .MoveNext
        Loop
    End With

End Sub
```

The code in the example begins by declaring and instantiating a recordset. It then adds fields to the recordset. Next it loops through the root of the C drive, adding the filenames and sizes to the recordset. It then sorts the resulting recordset by the FileName field. Finally, it loops through the recordset, displaying the contents in the Immediate window.

Persisted Recordsets

The ADO cursor engine allows you to save schema and data to various file formats and to retrieve the data later. Listing 10.24 provides an example.

LISTING 10.24   Working with a Persisted Recordset

```
Sub PersistedRecordset(strSaveFileName As String)
    Dim strFileName As String

    'Declare and instantiate the recordsets
    Dim rst As ADODB.Recordset
    Set rst = New ADODB.Recordset

    Dim rst2 As ADODB.Recordset
    Set rst2 = New ADODB.Recordset

    If Len(Dir(strSaveFileName)) <> 0 Then
        Kill strSaveFileName
    End If

    With rst
        'Append to the Fields collection of the
        'recordset object
        With .Fields
            .Append "FileName", adVarChar, 255
            .Append "FileSize", adBigInt
        End With

        'Set the appropriate properties and open the recordset
        .CursorType = adOpenStatic
        .CursorLocation = adUseClient
        .Open

        'Loop through the directory entries, adding the
        'file names and file sizes to the recordset
        strFileName = Dir("c:\*.*")
```

LISTING 10.24   Continued

```
        Do Until Len(strFileName) = 0
            .AddNew
                rst("FileName") = strFileName
                rst("FileSize") = FileLen("c:\" & strFileName)
            .Update
            strFileName = Dir()
        Loop

        'Sort the recordset by the FileName field
        .Sort = "FileName"

        'Save and close the recordset
        .Save strSaveFileName, adPersistADTG
        .Close

    End With

    With rst2

        'Set properties of the second recordset
        .CursorLocation = adUseClient
        .Source = strSaveFileName

        'Open the recordset
        .Open Options:=adCmdFile

        'Loop through the recordset printing the
        'file names and file sizes
        Do Until .EOF
            Debug.Print rst2("FileName"), rst2("FileSize")
            .MoveNext
        Loop
    End With

End Sub
```

The code declares and instantiates two ADO recordsets. If the file received as a para-
meter exists, the code deletes the file. It then adds two fields to the Recordset object.
It sets the CursorType property of the Recordset object to static and the
CursorLocation property to a client-side cursor.

Next, the code uses the `Dir` function to find the first file in the root of the C drive. It continually calls the `Dir` function until it finds no more files in the root of the C drive. As it loops through each file, it adds the filename to the FileName field of a new row and adds the file size to the FileSize field of the new row.

After the code loops through all the files, it sorts the resulting recordset. It then saves the recordset as a persisted recordset with the filename designated as the input parameter to the routine.

Finally, the code uses the second recordset to open and loop through the persisted file. It begins by designating the `CursorLocation` property as a client-side cursor. It sets the `Source` property to the name of the file designated as an input parameter to the routine (the one containing the persisted recordset). It opens the recordset and then loops through each row, printing the contents of the FileName and FileSize fields to the Immediate window.

One alternative when persisting a recordset is to save the data as XML. Listing 10.25 provides an example.

LISTING 10.25   Using a Persisted Recordset to Save Data as XML

```
Sub SaveToXML(strSaveFileName As String)

    'Declare and instantiate the recordset
    Dim rst As ADODB.Recordset
    Set rst = New ADODB.Recordset

    With rst

        'Set the appropriate properties and open the recordset
        .ActiveConnection = "Provider=SQLOLEDB.1;" & _
            "Data Source=(local); Initial Catalog=NorthWind;" & _
            "User ID=sa;PWD="
        .CursorType = adOpenStatic
        .LockType = adLockBatchOptimistic
        .CursorLocation = adUseClient
        .Source = "Customers"
        .Open

        'Save and close the recordset as XML
        If Len(Dir(strSaveFileName)) <> 0 Then
            Kill strSaveFileName
        End If
```

LISTING 10.25   Continued

```
        .Save strSaveFileName, adPersistXML
        .Close

    End With

End Sub
```

The routine declares and instantiates a `Recordset` object. It sets the `ActiveConnection` property of the `Recordset` object to point to the NorthWind database on the local server. It sets the `CursorType` property to a static cursor, the `LockType` property to adLockBatchOptimistic, and the `CursorLocation` property to adUseClient (a client-side cursor). The adLockBatchOptimistic choice is appropriate for this example because the example retrieves data from the Customer table of the SQL Server database, saves it as a file, allows the user to update the file, and then finally updates the SQL Server database with all changes made. The client-side cursor is appropriate because the code places the persisted recordset on the user's machine.

If the filename designated in the input parameter exists, the code uses the `Kill` statement to delete it. It then uses the `Save` method of the `Recordset` object to save the recordset as XML in a persisted recordset with the name supplied as the input parameter. The code shown in Listing 10.26 retrieves the data from the persisted recordset and updates its contents.

LISTING 10.26   Retrieving and Updating Data in a Persisted Recordset

```
Sub RetrieveFromXML(strSaveFileName As String)
    'Declare and instantiate the recordset
    Dim rst As ADODB.Recordset
    Set rst = New ADODB.Recordset

    With rst

        'Set the appropriate properties and open the recordset
        .CursorType = adOpenStatic
        .CursorLocation = adUseClient
        .LockType = adLockBatchOptimistic
        .Source = strSaveFileName
        .Open Options:=adCmdFile

        'Update the ContactName of the first row
        'and close the recordset
```

LISTING 10.26   Continued

```
        rst("ContactName") = "Alison Balter"
        .Save strSaveFileName, adPersistXML
        .Close

    End With

End Sub
```

This code declares and instantiates a Recordset object. As in the other examples, it sets the CursorType to static, the CursorLocation to a client-side cursor, and the LockType property to batch optimistic locking. It sets the Source property of the recordset to the name of the file designated as an input parameter to the routine. It opens the recordset and then updates the contents of the ContactName field of the first row. It uses the Save method of the recordset to save the changes back to the XML file. Listing 10.27 illustrates the final piece of the puzzle in which the code writes the data back to the SQL Server database.

LISTING 10.27   Saving Data from a Persisted Recordset Back to the SQL Server Database

```
Sub WriteBackToDB(strSaveFileName As String)
    'Declare and instantiate the recordset
    Dim rst As ADODB.Recordset
    Set rst = New ADODB.Recordset

    With rst

        'Set the appropriate properties and open the recordset
        .CursorType = adOpenStatic
        .CursorLocation = adUseClient
        .LockType = adLockBatchOptimistic
        .Source = strSaveFileName
        .Open Options:=adCmdFile
        .MarshalOptions = adMarshalModifiedOnly

        'Update the ContactName of the first row
        'and close the recordset
        .ActiveConnection = "Provider=SQLOLEDB.1;" & _
            "Data Source=(local); Initial Catalog=NorthWind;" & _
            "User ID=sa;PWD="
        .UpdateBatch adAffectAllChapters
```

LISTING 10.27   Continued

```
        .Close

    End With

End Sub
```

The code first declares and instantiates an ADO DB recordset. Again, it sets the CursorType to static, the CursorLocation to a client-side cursor, and the LockType property to batch optimistic locking. It sets the Source property of the recordset to the name of the file designated as an input parameter to the routine. It opens the recordset and then sets a property of the recordset called MarshalOptions to designate that it will marshal only modified rows to the SQL Server database. It then sets the ActiveConnection property of the recordset to point to the NorthWind database on the local server. Finally, it uses the UpdateBatch method of the recordset to update the SQL Server database with the changes made to the persisted recordset.

Working with Hierarchical Recordsets

Microsoft developed a variation of SQL that allows you to create hierarchical recordsets. Microsoft refers to these recordsets as "shaped" recordsets. Shaped recordsets contain special fields called chapters. These fields contain pointers to other recordsets, allowing a shaped recordset to handle hierarchies of information. Listing 10.28 provides an example.

LISTING 10.28   Example of a Hierarchical Recordset That Contains Customer and Order Information

```
Sub HierarchicalRecordset()
    'Declare and instantiate the recordset
    Dim rst As ADODB.Recordset
    Set rst = New ADODB.Recordset

    'Set the provider to the Shape provider and
    'the data provider to the SQL provider
    rst.ActiveConnection = "Provider=MSDataShape;" & _
        "Data Provider=SQLOLEDB.1;" & _
        "Data Source=(local);" & _
        "Initial Catalog=Northwind;" & _
        "Integrated Security=SSPI"

    'Set property to keep hierarchies in sync
```

LISTING 10.28   Continued

```
    rst.StayInSync = True

    'Open the recordset using the Shape syntax
    'Append the chapter (child) and relate the
    'linking fields together
    rst.Open "SHAPE {SELECT CustomerID, CompanyName " & _
        "FROM Customers}" & _
        "APPEND ({SELECT * FROM Orders} " & _
        "RELATE CustomerID TO CustomerID)"

    'Display the CustomerID of the first customer
    Debug.Print rst("CustomerID")

    'Display the OrderID of the first order associated
    'with the selected customer
    Debug.Print rst("Chapter1")("OrderID")
End Sub
```

The code declares and instantiates an ADO DB recordset. Notice that the `ActiveConnection` property designates the `Provider` attribute as `MSDataShape` and the `DataProvider` attribute as `SQLOLEDB.1`. The code uses the `StayInSync` property to ensure that the hierarchies remain in sync. The `Open` method uses a `SHAPE` statement to select data from the Customers table and the Orders table. It relates the CustomerID fields from the two tables. The Chapter1 field in the Customers table points to the filtered rows that match based on CustomerID (the orders for that customer). The code uses the syntax `rst("Chapter1")("OrderID")` to retrieve the order information for a particular customer.

Handling ADO Events

Several of the ADO objects support events. You can trap these events and respond to them as necessary. For example, you can easily determine when ADO successfully connects or executes a SQL statement.

The capability to trap events exists only within a class module (standalone, form, or report). You use the `WithEvents` keyword to react to an event. An example appears in Listing 10.29.

LISTING 10.29   Creating a Cursor Without Connecting to a Data Source

```
Private WithEvents mcnnEvents As ADODB.Connection

Private Sub cmdDoSomething_Click()
    Set mcnnEvents = New ADODB.Connection
    mcnnEvents.ConnectionString = "Provider=SQLOLEDB.1;" & _
            "Data Source=(local); Initial Catalog=NorthWind;" & _
            "User ID=sa;PWD="
    mcnnEvents.Open
    mcnnEvents.Execute "SELECT * FROM Customers WHERE Country = 'USA'"
End Sub

Private Sub mcnnEvents_ConnectComplete(ByVal pError As ADODB.Error, _
    adStatus As ADODB.EventStatusEnum, ByVal pConnection As ADODB.Connection)
    MsgBox "Hello, I Just Connected"
End Sub

Private Sub mcnnEvents_ExecuteComplete(ByVal RecordsAffected As Long, _
    ByVal pError As ADODB.Error, adStatus As ADODB.EventStatusEnum, _
    ByVal pCommand As ADODB.Command, ByVal pRecordset As ADODB.Recordset, _
    ByVal pConnection As ADODB.Connection)
    MsgBox "I Just Completed Executing Something!!!" & vbCrLf & _
        "and Affected " & RecordsAffected & " Rows "
End Sub
```

Notice that the code uses the general declarations section of the class module to declare the event. It uses the Private keyword along with a WithEvents statement to do so. After you add the private variable declaration with the WithEvents statement, the events available for the object appear as if they were events for a control on a form (see Figure 10.2). Listing 10.29 contains two event routines: one to respond to the ConnectComplete event and the other to respond to the ExecuteComplete event. If you run the frmAdvancedADO form and click the Command button, two messages display. The first indicates that the code established the connection. The second designates the number of rows affected by the Execute statement.

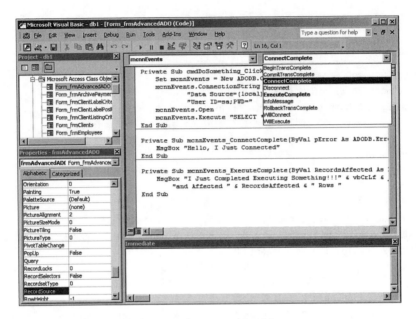

FIGURE 10.2   Events available for the Connection object.

Summary

Not everything can be done via the user interface or using Access queries. Furthermore, although something *can* be accomplished via the user interface, it is more efficient to use ADO code and stored procedures to accomplish the task at hand. This chapter covered the ins and outs of executing SQL Server stored procedures from the Access front ends that you build. A well-designed Access application will generally include a combination of bound forms, bound reports, and ADO code. The goal is to use Access and bound forms and reports to accomplish those tasks that Access can achieve efficiently. Mass updates and other tasks that involve large numbers of records should be performed using stored procedures.

11

Developing an MDB Client/Server Application with Linked Tables

Why This Chapter Is Important

Although in many cases the best solution for a client/server application is the Access Data Project (ADP) technology introduced with Access 2000, many successful client/server applications are running today as Access front ends linked to SQL Server back ends. I generally recommend that you do most *new* development in Access data projects. There are exceptions to this rule that involve difficulties in securing ADP applications (covered in Chapter 12, "Developing an ADP Application"). Because of the number of existing MDB (Jet database) applications and some of the security problems inherent in an ADP application, linked client/server applications are still a viable option today.

What Is a Linked Client/Server Application?

The easiest method of accessing data on the server is to link to the external tables. These linked tables act almost exactly like native Access tables. When you link to remote tables, Access analyzes the fields and indexes contained in the tables so that it can achieve optimal performance. It is important to relink the tables if the structures of the remote tables change. This chapter discusses how you can link to remote tables through the user interface and by using code.

How Linked Table Applications Work

When you include linked tables in your application, Access's Jet Engine uses Open Database Connectivity (ODBC) to communicate with the client/server database. When a user submits a query based on a table that is linked to a client/server database, Jet converts the Access SQL stored in the query to an ODBC-compliant dialect of SQL. It then submits the SQL statement, as well as connection information, to the ODBC Driver Manager. The ODBC Driver Manager loads the appropriate ODBC driver and passes the driver the instructions necessary to execute the SQL statement. The ODBC driver translates the ODBC-compliant SQL statement to DBMS-specific (database management system–specific) SQL that the particular back end understands.

To make the process simpler, a tool called the ODBC Data Source Administrator allows you to create an ODBC data source. The ODBC data source stores important information about the database in a neat package. An ODBC data source contains information such as the name of the database server, the name of the database that you are connecting to, and login and security information. Once created, many applications can share a data source. As you will see, this chapter covers many uses of the ODBC data source.

Working with Linked Tables

Several options are available when working with linked tables. These options are not mutually exclusive; they are generally used in combination within an application. This section covers linking to tables using the user interface and using VBA code. It also talks about linking to views rather than tables.

Linking to External Tables via the User Interface

To link to a remote table through the user interface, right-click within the Database window and then select Link Tables. From the Files of Type drop-down list, select ODBC Databases. The Select Data Source dialog box shown in Figure 11.1 appears. This dialog box has two tabs: File Data Source and Machine Data Source. You use the File Data Source tab to select from the file data source names (DSNs) that have been defined. These are the data sources available to all users on all machines. You use the Machine Data Source tab to select from the user and system data sources you have defined. User data sources are for a particular user on a particular machine, whereas system data sources are for any user on that particular machine.

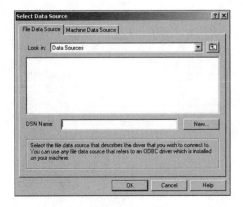

FIGURE 11.1   The Select Data Source dialog box.

You can select an existing data source or define a new data source directly from the Select Data Source dialog box. The section "Defining an ODBC Data Source" in Chapter 3, "Introduction to Client/Server Development Techniques," covers the details of defining an ODBC data source. After you select a data source, Access prompts you with a Login dialog. You can't obtain access to the server data unless you have a valid login ID and password. Figure 11.2 shows the SQL Server Login dialog box.

NOTE

The steps covered here apply when your ODBC data source points to a SQL Server database. The steps differ if you select another ODBC driver, such as Oracle.

FIGURE 11.2   The SQL Server Login dialog box.

If you successfully log on to the server, you are presented with a list of tables contained in the database that the data source is referencing. Here, you must select the table to which you want to link. Figure 11.3 shows the Link Tables dialog box.

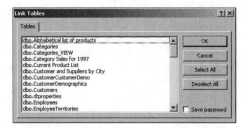

FIGURE 11.3   The Link Tables dialog box.

After you select one or more tables and click OK, you might be prompted with the Select Unique Record Identifier dialog box. Selecting a unique identifier for the table enables you to update records on the back-end data source. If prompted, select a unique identifier and click OK. The linked tables appear in the Database window, as shown in Figure 11.4. You can treat these tables like any other table (with a few exceptions that are covered later in this chapter).

FIGURE 11.4   The Database window with links to ODBC tables.

Linking to External Tables Using Code

You just learned how you can link to a remote table by using Access's user interface. Now take a look at how you can link to the same table by using code. The subroutine in Listing 11.1 accepts six parameters: the name of the Access table, the name of the server database, the name of the server table, the data source name, the user ID, and the password.

LISTING 11.1   VBA Code for Linking to an External Table

```
Sub LinkToSQL(strAccessTable, strDBName, strTableName, _
    strDataSourceName, strUserID, strPassWord)
    Dim cat As ADOX.Catalog
    Dim tbl As ADOX.Table

    Set cat = New ADOX.Catalog
    cat.ActiveConnection = CurrentProject.Connection

    Set tbl = New ADOX.Table
    tbl.Name = strAccessTable
    Set tbl.ParentCatalog = cat

    tbl.Properties("Jet OLEDB:Create Link") = True
    tbl.Properties("Jet OLEDB:Link Provider String") = "ODBC" & _
        ";DATABASE=" & strDBName & _
        ";UID=" & strUserID & _
        ";PWD=" & strPassWord & _
        ";DSN=" & strDataSourceName
    tbl.Properties("Jet OLEDB:Remote Table Name") = strTableName

    cat.Tables.Append tbl
End Sub
```

NOTE

This example requires that you use Tools, References to reference the Microsoft ADO Ext. 2.1 for DDL and Security library.

Here is an example of how you call the subroutine. The Access table that you are creating is named tblCustomers. The database name on the server is NorthWind. The table to which you are linking is named Customers, and the data source name is NorthWindData. You are logging in as SA (database system administrator) without a password. The user ID and password could have been supplied as the user logged on to your application and could have been stored in variables until needed for logging on to the server, as this code shows:

```
Call LinkToSQL("tblCustomers", "NorthWind", _
    "Customers", "NorthWindData", "SA", "")
```

NOTE

This code and most of the code found in this chapter is located in the CHAP11EX.MDB database on the sample code CD-ROM.

As an alternative, you can use NT Integrated security. In that case, there is no need to have the user log in. The code appears in Listing 11.2.

LISTING 11.2 VBA Code for Linking to an External Table Using Integrated Security

```
Sub LinkToSQLIntegrated(strAccessTable, strDBName, strTableName, _
    strDataSourceName)
    Dim cat As ADOX.Catalog
    Dim tbl As ADOX.Table

    Set cat = New ADOX.Catalog
    cat.ActiveConnection = CurrentProject.Connection

    Set tbl = New ADOX.Table
    tbl.Name = strAccessTable
    Set tbl.ParentCatalog = cat

    tbl.Properties("Jet OLEDB:Create Link") = True
    tbl.Properties("Jet OLEDB:Link Provider String") = "ODBC" & _
        ";DATABASE=" & strDBName & _
        ";Integrated Security = SSPI" & _
        ";DSN=" & strDataSourceName
    tbl.Properties("Jet OLEDB:Remote Table Name") = strTableName

    cat.Tables.Append tbl
End Sub
```

You no longer need to include the login information in the call to the procedure. It now looks like this:

```
Call LinkToSQLIntegrated("tblCustomers2", "NorthWind", "Customers", "NorthWind-
Data")
```

Linking to Views Rather Than Tables

Views on a database server are similar to Access queries. Views provide a form of security by limiting which rows and columns a user can see. You grant users or roles access to the view rather than directly to the underlying table. By default, views are not updateable from within Access. You can make a view updateable by including all the fields that compose the primary key in the view and by building a unique index on the primary key. You can create views in one of several ways. These include:

- Using the SQL Server Enterprise Manager for SQL 6.5, SQL 7.0, or SQL 2000 (or the equivalent option for your back-end database server)

- Using the SQL Server Query Analyzer for SQL 6.5, SQL 7.0, or SQL 2000 (or the equivalent option for your back-end database server)

- Using the Create View statement in Access

- Using the View tab of an ADP file

For more details about how to create views, see Chapter 7, "Working with SQL Server Views." After you create a view, you can link to it like any other table. If you link to the view, Access prompts you with the Select Unique Record Identifier dialog box, as shown in Figure 11.5. It is very important to supply Access with a unique index. Otherwise, the results of the view will not be updateable. The view then can be treated as though it were a link to a table.

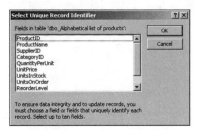

FIGURE 11.5   The Select Unique Record Identifier dialog box after selecting a view.

Using Pass-Through Queries

Ordinarily when you store and execute a query in Access, even if it is running on remote data, Access compiles and optimizes the query. In many cases, this is exactly what you want. On other occasions, however, it might be preferable for you to execute a pass-through query because these queries are not analyzed by Access's Jet Engine. These queries are passed directly to the server, and this reduces the time that Jet needs to analyze the query and enables you to pass server-specific syntax to the back end. Furthermore, pass-through queries can log informational messages returned by the server. Finally, bulk update, delete, and append queries are faster using pass-through queries than they are using Access action queries based on remote tables. This is because the server processes the action queries rather than sending the data back to the workstation to be processed.

Pass-through queries do have their downside. They always return a snapshot, which means that they are not updateable. You also must know the exact syntax that the server requires, and you must type the statement into the Query window instead of painting it graphically. Finally, you cannot parameterize a query so that it prompts the user for a value.

Creating a Pass-Through Query in an MDB File Using the User Interface

To create a pass-through query, you can build the query in the Access Query Builder:

1. Click Queries in the list of objects in the Database window.

2. Click Create Query in Design View.

3. Click Close when the Show Table dialog box appears.

4. Select Query, SQL Specific, Pass-Through. You are presented with a text-editing window where you can enter the query statement (see Figure 11.6). The SQL statement that you enter must be in the SQL dialect specific to your back end.

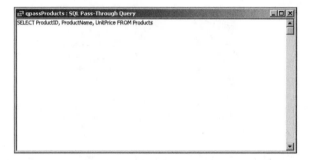

FIGURE 11.6   With a pass-through query, you must enter a SQL statement in the dialect that is specific to your back end.

5. With the query selected, click to select the ODBC Connect Str property in the Properties window (see Figure 11.7), and click Build (the ellipse). The Select Data Source dialog box appears.

6. Click the Machine Data Source tab (see Figure 11.8).

7. Select the appropriate data source, or define a new one, and click OK. You are prompted as to whether you want to save the password information.

8. After you make your selection, Access enters the appropriate connection string into the ODBC Connect Str property.

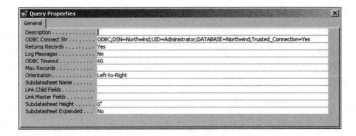

FIGURE 11.7   The ODBC Connect `Str` property allows you to designate connection information for the pass-through query.

FIGURE 11.8   The Machine Data Source tab of the Select Data Source dialog box allows you to select the data source upon which you want to base the pass-through query.

NOTE

To complete the preceding steps, you must understand how to set up an ODBC data source. Chapter 3 covers the process of creating an ODBC data source.

Executing a Pass-Through Query via the User Interface

You execute a pass-through query via the user interface much in the way that you execute a standard Access query. Double-click the query in the list of query objects in the Database window. If you did not store connection information with the query, Access prompts you with the Select Data Source dialog box. You must then select the appropriate data source before executing the query.

Executing a Pass-Through Query Using Code

You can also execute a pass-through query by using VBA code. In fact, you must execute the pass-through query by using VBA code if you want the query to contain parameters that you will pass to the server. Here's one way that you can execute a pass-through query by using VBA code:

1. Create a connection to the SQL Server database.

2. Use the `Execute` method of the `Connection` object to execute the SQL statement on the back-end database server. As with a SQL statement created by choosing Query, SQL Specific, Pass-Through, the statement that you create must be in the syntax specific to your particular back end.

Listing 11.3 shows the code for this procedure.

LISTING 11.3   Executing a Pass-Through Query Using Code

```
Sub PassThroughQuery(strDBName As String, _
                strDataSourceName As String, _
                strUserID As String, _
                strPassWord As String)

    Dim cnn As ADODB.Connection
    Dim strConnectString As String

    strConnectString = "ODBC" & _
        ";DATABASE=" & strDBName & _
        ";UID=" & strUserID & _
        ";PWD=" & strPassWord & _
        ";DSN=" & strDataSourceName

    Set cnn = New ADODB.Connection
    cnn.ConnectionString = strConnectString
    cnn.Open

    cnn.Execute "Update dbo.Products Set UnitPrice = UnitPrice + 1", _
        Options:=adCmdText
End Sub
```

You call the routine as shown in this code:

```
Call PassThroughQuery("NorthWind", "NorthWindData", "SA","" )
```

This subroutine uses a connect string that connects to a database named NorthWind, with a data source named NorthWindData, a user ID of SA, and no password. It then executes a pass-through query that updates the UnitPrice field of each record to UnitPrice+1.

As you saw, one method of executing a pass-through query is to create a connection to the database using the Open method of the Connection object and then execute the query using the Execute method of the database object. The limitation of this method is that the Execute method does not enable you to execute queries that return data. You can use another method of executing a pass-through query when you want to return records. It involves returning the result of the pass-through query in a recordset object. This is illustrated in Listing 11.4.

LISTING 11.4   Executing a Pass-Through Query That Returns Records

```
Sub PassThroughQueryResults(strDBName As String, _
            strDataSourceName As String, _
            strUserID As String, _
            strPassWord As String)

    Dim cnn As ADODB.Connection
    Dim rst As ADODB.Recordset
    Dim strConnectString As String

    strConnectString = "ODBC" & _
        ";DATABASE=" & strDBName & _
        ";UID=" & strUserID & _
        ";PWD=" & strPassWord & _
        ";DSN=" & strDataSourceName

    Set cnn = New ADODB.Connection
    cnn.ConnectionString = strConnectString
    cnn.Open

    Set rst = cnn.Execute("Select * from dbo.Products Where UnitPrice >5", _
        Options:=adCmdText)
    Do Until rst.EOF
        Debug.Print rst!ProductID, rst!UnitPrice
        rst.MoveNext
    Loop

End Sub
```

You call the code like this:

```
Call PassThroughQueryResults ("NorthWind", "NorthWindData", "SA", "")
```

This code uses an ADO Connection object to connect to the SQL Server. It uses the Execute method of the Connection object to execute a SQL statement that returns data to a recordset. It then loops through the recordset, printing the contents of the UnitPrice and Quantity fields.

Executing Stored Procedures

You can execute stored procedures using a pass-through query or using ADO code. The code that follows provides an example of how you can execute a stored procedure using a pass-through query. It is located in basStoredProcedures.

```
Sub SPWithPassThrough()
    DoCmd.OpenQuery ("qpassCustomers")
End Sub
```

This code executes a pass-through query called qpassCustomers that contains the SQL required to execute a stored procedure called procCustomerGetContactTitle. To run, the pass-through query must exist, it must contain a valid connection string, and it must contain SQL that looks something like this:

```
procCustomerGetContactTitle 'Marketing Manager'
```

In this example, the pass-through query executes a stored procedure called procCustomerGetContactTitle, passing it a parameter with the string "Marketing Manager." The stored procedure looks like this:

```
CREATE PROCEDURE procCustomerGetContactTitle @ContactTitle Varchar(30) AS
SELECT * FROM Customers
WHERE ContactTitle = @ContactTitle
```

NOTE

To run the example, you will need to create the procCustomerGetContactTitle stored procedure. Chapter 8, "Designing SQL Server Stored Procedures, User-Defined Functions, and Triggers," covers the process of creating the stored procedure.

As an alternative, you can use ADO code to execute the same stored procedure. The code appears in Listing 11.5.

LISTING 11.5   Executing a Stored Procedure Using ADO Code

```
Sub SPGetWithADOConnection()
    Dim cnn As ADODB.Connection
    Dim rst As ADODB.Recordset

    Set cnn = New ADODB.Connection

    'Establish a connection to the SQL Server
    cnn.ConnectionString = "Provider=SQLOLEDB.1;" & _
            "Data Source=(local); Initial Catalog=NorthWind;" & _
            "Integrated Security = SSPI"
    cnn.Open

    'Execute the stored procedure, returning the results int
    'a recordset
    Set rst = cnn.Execute("procCustomerGetContactTitle 'Owner'")

    'Loop through the resulting recordset, printing the
    'contents of the CompanyName field
    Do Until rst.EOF
        Debug.Print rst("CompanyName")
        rst.MoveNext
    Loop

    'Clean Up
    rst.Close
    cnn.Close


    Set cnn = Nothing
    Set rst = Nothing
End Sub
```

The code in the example executes the same stored procedure as in the previous example. It begins by establishing a connection to the SQL Server. Although the example uses integrated security, you could easily modify it to use SQL Server security. The example uses the Execute method of the Connection object to execute the stored procedure, returning the results in the recordset object. It then loops through the resulting recordset, printing the contents of the CompanyName field.

Building Client/Server–Friendly Forms

The goal of a client/server application is to reduce the amount of data that travels over the network wire. This involves carefully designing your forms and reports to ensure that only the required data is retrieved. An overview of the steps required to build such a client/server application using linked tables includes the following:

1. Link to the tables contained in the SQL Server database.

2. Build a tabbed form that will contain Customer, Order, and Order Detail tabs.

3. Add a combo box to the form that allows the user to locate data for a specific company.

4. Create a query that is used to populate the detail section of the form. The query retrieves data only for the selected customer.

5. Create a query that is used to populate the detail section of the order subform.

6. Create a query that is used to populate the detail section of the order details subform.

7. Hide the order and order detail subforms until the appropriate tab is selected.

8. Specify blank record sources for the subforms.

9. Designate the record source for the subforms, and make the subforms visible only when the appropriate tab is selected.

The following sections provide you with the details of each of the steps involved in creating the application.

Linking to Tables Contained in the SQL Server Database

Because this version of the application uses linked tables, the first step in the process is to link to the tables that are used by the application. The example uses the SQL Server version of the NorthWind database. Follow these steps to link to tables in the NorthWind database:

1. Right-click within the Database window and select Link Tables. The Link dialog box appears.

2. Select ODBC Databases in the Files of Type drop-down list. The Select Data Source dialog box appears.

3. Click the Machine Data Source tab (see Figure 11.9).

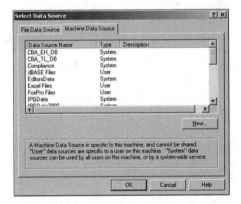

FIGURE 11.9   The Machine Data Source tab allows you to set up a machine data source.

4. Click New to create a new data source. The Create New Data Source dialog box appears (see Figure 11.10).

FIGURE 11.10   The Create New Data Source Wizard walks you through the steps of creating a new data source.

5. Select System Data Source and click Next.

6. Select the SQL Server driver from the list of drivers (see Figure 11.11). Click Next.

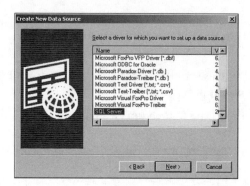

FIGURE 11.11   Select the SQL Server driver from the list of available drivers.

7. Click Finish. The Create a New Data Source to SQL Server dialog box appears (see Figure 11.12).

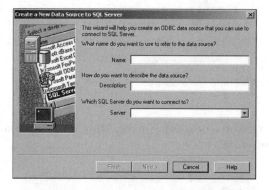

FIGURE 11.12   The Create a New Data Source to SQL Server dialog box walks you through the steps of establishing the new SQL Server data source.

8. Enter a name and optional description for the data source.

9. Select the SQL Server that you want to connect to. Click Next.

10. Select the appropriate security options and click Next (see Figure 11.13).

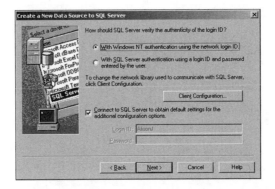

FIGURE 11.13   Enter the appropriate security options for the database.

11. Select the appropriate database options. These include how stored procedures
    are executed and how quotes and nulls are treated. Click Next (see Figure
    11.14).

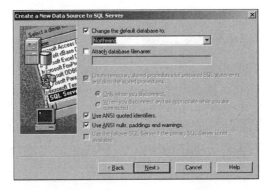

FIGURE 11.14   Select the appropriate database options.

12. Modify any of the remaining options (such as the type of encryption used) and
    click Finish.

13. A list of selected options appears (see Figure 11.15). Click Test Data Source to
    test the new data source. You should be notified that the test completed
    successfully.

14. Click OK to close the test dialog box. Click OK again to close the ODBC
    Microsoft SQL Server Setup dialog box. You are returned to the Select Data
    Source dialog box.

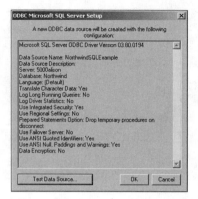

FIGURE 11.15   Click Test Data Source to test the data source with all the listed options.

15. Select the data source that you just created and click OK. You are prompted to log in to the SQL Server (see Figure 11.16). Enter a valid login ID and password, and click OK. The Link Tables dialog box appears (see Figure 11.17).

FIGURE 11.16   The SQL Server Login dialog box allows you to log in to the SQL Server.

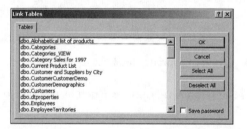

FIGURE 11.17   The Link Tables dialog box allows you to designate the SQL Server tables that you want to link to.

NOTE

The sample database includes links to the tables in the NorthWind database. If you want to practice linking, you can create links in a separate database, or you can delete the existing links in the sample database *before* completing these steps.

16. Click to select each table that you want to link to. Click OK when you're finished. The Database window, with the links established, appears in Figure 11.18.

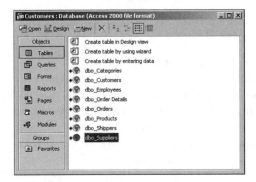

FIGURE 11.18   The Database window with links to the NorthWind database.

Building the Customer Form

The form that you will build is pictured in Figure 11.19. Notice that initially no data appears. This form is designed to display only one customer record at a time. It accomplishes this because the form is based on a query that retrieves data only for the customer selected in the Select a Company combo box. Furthermore, the application does not retrieve the data for the Orders and Order Details tabs until the user selects the tabs. This ensures that the application does not retrieve records on the many side of the one-to-many relationship unless the user needs them.

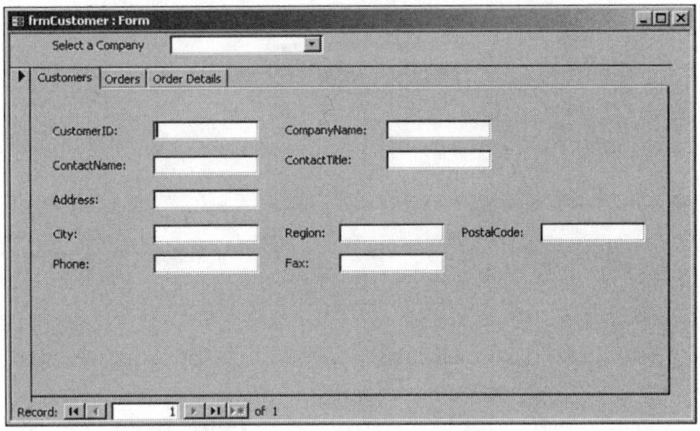

FIGURE 11.19   The completed customer form initially appears without any data.

To begin the process of designing the frmCustomer form, follow these steps:

1. Select Forms in the Objects list of the Database window.

2. Double-click Create Form in Design View.

3. Select View, Form Header/Footer to add a header and footer to the form.

Adding a Locate Combo Box to the Form

The first step required to build the form is to add a combo box to the form that allows the user to select the company whose information he wants to view. The form populates the combo box with the CustomerID and CompanyName of each company in the company table. When the user selects a company in the combo box, the code behind the form requeries the combo box to display data for the selected customer. Build the combo box using the Combo Box Wizard. Take the following steps:

1. Make sure that you select the Control Wizards tool in the toolbox.

2. Click to select the Combo Box tool in the toolbox, and then click and drag to add the combo box to the header of the form. The Combo Box Wizard launches.

3. Select I Want the Combo Box to Look Up the Values in a Table or Query. Click Next.

4. Select dbo_Customers (the linked table) from the list of tables (see Figure 11.20). Click Next.

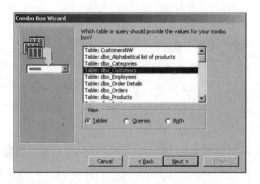

FIGURE 11.20   Select the dbo_Customers table from the list of available tables.

5. Select the CustomerID and CompanyName fields from the list of available fields (see Figure 11.21). Click Next.

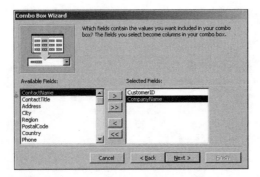

FIGURE 11.21   Select the CustomerID and CompanyName fields as the fields to be included in the combo box.

6. Double-click the right side of the CompanyName column to size the column to the largest entry (see Figure 11.22). Leave the Hide Key Column option checked. Click Next.

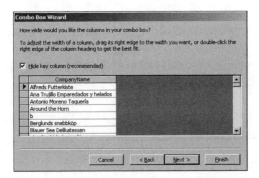

FIGURE 11.22   Double-click the right side of the CompanyName column to size the column to the largest entry.

7. Enter Select a Company as the label for the combo box. Click Finish. Access adds the combo box to the form (see Figure 11.23).

8. Click to select the combo box that you added.

9. Change the name of the combo box to cboSelectCompany.

10. Save the form as frmCustomer.

11. Test the form to make sure that the combo box displays a list of all the customers (see Figure 11.24).

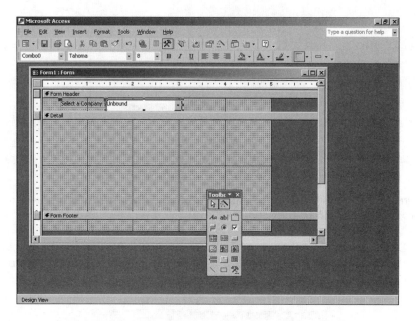

FIGURE 11.23 The combo box is added to the form.

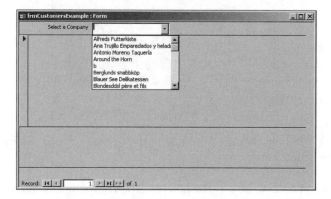

FIGURE 11.24 The completed combo box displays a list of customers.

Building the Query for the Customer Form

The next step is to design the query that underlies the frmCustomer form. The query will reference the CustomerID of the customer that the user selects in the cboSelectCompany combo box. Here are the steps involved:

1. Return to Design view, if necessary.

2. Select the Form.

3. Click the Data tab in the Properties window.

4. Click the RecordSource property (see Figure 11.25).

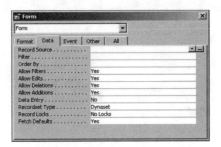

FIGURE 11.25   The RecordSource property allows you to designate the record source for the form.

5. Click Build. The Show Table dialog box appears.

6. Select dbo_Customers from the list of tables (see Figure 11.26). Click Add.

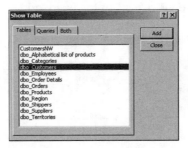

FIGURE 11.26   Select the dbo_Customers table from the Show Table dialog box.

7. Click Close.

8. Add the CustomerID, CompanyName, ContactName, ContactTitle, Address, City, Region, PostalCode, Phone, and Fax fields to the query (see Figure 11.27).

9. Enter **Forms!frmCustomer!cboSelectCompany** as the criteria for the CustomerID field (see Figure 11.28).

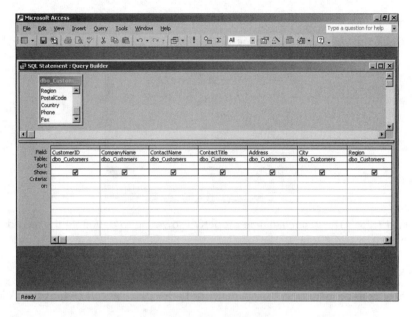

FIGURE 11.27   Add the desired fields to the query grid.

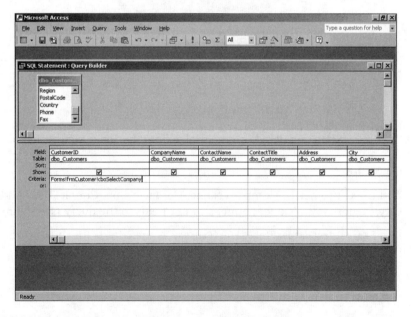

FIGURE 11.28   Selection criteria for the CustomerID field.

10. Close the SQL Statement Builder.

11. Click Yes to indicate that you want to save the changes made to the SQL statement and update the property.

Before you can add the fields to the form, you must design the tabs for the form. Take the following steps:

1. Select a tab control from the toolbox.

2. Click and drag to add it to the frmCustomer form.

3. Change the Caption property of the first tab to Customers.

4. Change the Name property of the first tab to pagCustomers.

5. Change the Caption property of the second tab to Orders.

6. Change the Name property of the second tab to pagOrders.

7. Right-click the page control and select Insert Page. A third page appears.

8. Change the Caption property of the third tab to Order Details.

9. Change the Name property of the third tab to pagOrderDetails.

10. Change the Name property of the tab control to tabDataEntry.

11. Add the fields to the Customers tab of the form, as shown in Figure 11.29.

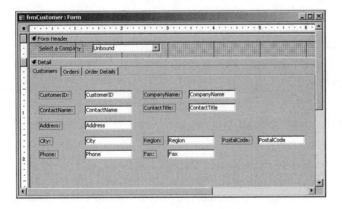

FIGURE 11.29 The Customers tab with the selected fields added.

Building the Query for the Orders Subform

The next step is to build the query that underlies the Orders subform. The query will select all orders where the CustomerID is that of the customer selected in the cboSelectCompany combo box. To create the query, follow these steps:

1. Select Queries from the list of objects in the Database window.

2. Double-click Create Query in Design View. The Show Tables dialog box appears.

3. Select dbo_Orders from the list of tables and click Add.

4. Click Close.

5. Add the OrderID, CustomerID, EmployeeID, OrderDate, RequiredDate, ShippedDate, ShipVia, and Freight fields to the query.

6. Enter `Forms!frmCustomer!cboSelectCompany` as the criteria for the CustomerID.

7. Save the query as qryOrders. The completed query appears in Figure 11.30.

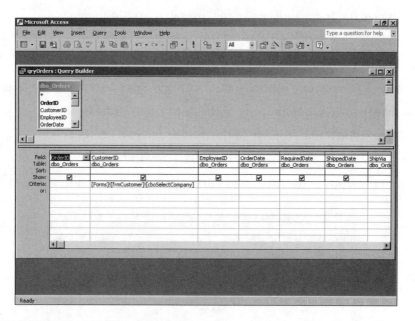

FIGURE 11.30   The completed qryOrders query.

Building the Query for the Order Details Subform
The next step is to build the query that underlies the OrderDetails subform. The query will select all order detail items in which the OrderID is that of the order selected in the fsubOrders subform. To create the query:

1. Select Queries from the list of objects in the Database window.

2. Double-click Create Query in Design View. The Show Tables dialog box appears.

3. Select dbo_OrderDetails from the list of tables and click Add.

4. Click Close.

5. Add the OrderID, ProductID, UnitPrice, Quantity, and Discount fields to the query.

6. Enter `Forms!frmCustomer.Form!fsubOrders!OrderID` as the criteria for the OrderID.

7. Save the query as qryOrderDetails. The completed query appears in Figure 11.31.

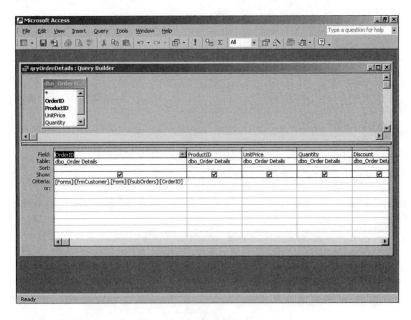

FIGURE 11.31   The completed qryOrderDetails query.

Creating the fsubOrders Subform

The fsubOrders subform will be used to display the orders associated with the selected customers. Take the following steps to create the fsubOrders subform and add it to the Orders page of the tab control:

1. Activate the frmCustomer form in Design view.

2. Click to select the Orders page of the tab control.

3. Make sure that the Control Wizards tool is selected.

4. Select the Subform/Subreport control.

5. Click and drag to add a subform control to the Orders tab. The SubForm Wizard appears (see Figure 11.32).

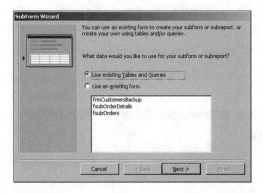

FIGURE 11.32 The SubForm Wizard assists you with the process of adding the Orders subform to the Orders tab.

6. Select Use Existing Tables and Queries and click Next.

7. Select qryOrders from the Tables/Queries drop-down list.

8. Add all fields in the query to the Selected Fields list (see Figure 11.33).

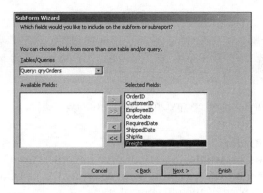

FIGURE 11.33   Add all fields from qryOrders to the list of selected fields.

9. Click Next.

10. Select None as the link between the main form and the subform (see Figure 11.34), and click Next.

11. Enter **fsubOrders** as the name of the subform and click Finish.

12. Size the subform control so that it appears as in Figure 11.35.

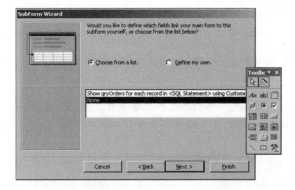

FIGURE 11.34   Select None as the link between the parent form and the subform.

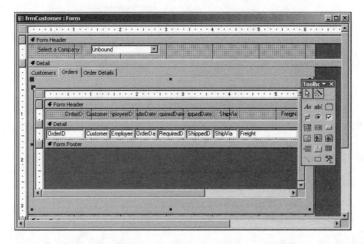

FIGURE 11.35   The fsubOrders subform after it has been added to the Orders tab.

Creating the fsubOrderDetail Subform

The fsubOrderDetails subform will be used to display the order detail items associated with the selected order. Take the following steps to create the fsubOrderDetails subform and add it to the Order Details page of the tab control:

1. Activate the frmCustomer form in Design view.

2. Click to select the Order Details page of the tab control.

3. Make sure that you select the Control Wizards tool.

4. Select the Subform/Subreport control.

5. Click and drag to add a subform control to the Order Details tab. The SubForm Wizard appears.

6. Select Use Existing Tables and Queries, and click Next.

7. Select qryOrderDetails from the Tables/Queries drop-down list.

8. Add all fields in the query to the list of Selected Fields.

9. Click Next.

10. You are prompted to define links between the main form and the subform (see Figure 11.36). Click Next without defining any links.

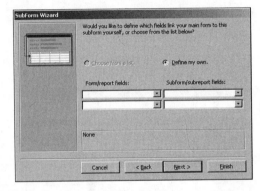

FIGURE 11.36   No links are created between the main form and the subform.

11. Enter **fsubOrderDetails** as the name of the subform and click Finish.

12. Size the subform control so that it appears as in Figure 11.37.

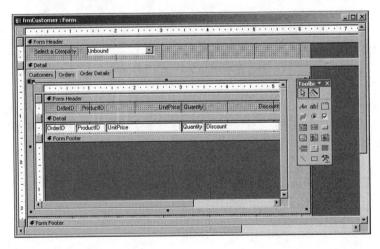

FIGURE 11.37   The fsubOrderDetails subform after it has been added to the Order Details tab.

Removing the SourceObject of the Order and Order Details Subforms Until the Appropriate Tab Is Selected

Probably the largest goal in client/server development is to limit the data that is transferred from the database server to the workstation. Many times a user will need to view the main customer information without needing to see the Order or Order Detail information. It is therefore unnecessary to retrieve the Order and Order Detail information unless the user explicitly requests it by clicking to select the Order or Order Details tabs. The code shown in Listing 11.6 handles the process of hiding and showing the appropriate subforms as the user clicks the various tabs on the form. As the code shows the subforms, it populates the RecordSource property of the subforms to display the appropriate data.

LISTING 11.6   The Change Event of the tabDataEntry Control

```
Private Sub tabDataEntry_Change()


    'Evaluate which page is selected
    Select Case Me.tabDataEntry.Pages. _
        Item(Me.tabDataEntry.Value).Name

        'If the Customers page, do nothing
        Case "pagCustomers"

        'If the orders page is selected, evaluate if the page has been
        'visited for that customer
        Case "pagOrders"

            'If Orders page not visited, set the source object
            'property to the fsubOrders subform and flip the flag
            If Not mboolOrdersVisited Then
                Me.fsubOrders.SourceObject = "fsubOrders"
                mboolOrdersVisited = True
            End If

        'If the order details page is selected, evaluate if the
        'page has been visited for that customer
        Case "pagOrderDetails"

            'If Order Details page not visited, set the source
            'object property to the fsubOrderDetails subform
            'and flip the flag
            If Not mboolOrderDetailsVisited Then
```

LISTING 11.6   Continued

```
            Me.fsubOrderDetails.SourceObject = "fsubOrderDetails"
            mboolOrderDetailsVisited = True

        'If the Order Details page has been visited,
        'simply requery the subform
        Else
            Me.fsubOrderDetails.Requery
        End If

    End Select
End Sub
```

The code begins by evaluating which page is selected. If the pagCustomers page is selected, nothing needs to be done.

If the pagOrders page is selected and the page has not been visited for that customer, the SourceObject property of the subform control is set to the fsubOrders subform and the mboolOrdersVisited variable is set to True.

If the pagOrderDetails page is selected and the page has not been visited for that customer, the SourceObject property of the subform is set to the fsubOrderDetails subform and the mboolOrderDetailsVisited variable is set to True. If the page has been visited for that customer, the code requeries the fsubOrderDetails subform.

Specifying Blank SourceObjects for the Subforms
It all comes together when the user selects a company from the cboSelectCompany combo box. The AfterUpdate event of the combo box executes. It is found in Listing 11.7.

LISTING 11.7   The AfterUpdate Event of the cboSelectCompany Combo Box

```
Private Sub cboSelectCompany_AfterUpdate()

    'Evaluate which page is active
    Select Case Me.tabDataEntry.Pages. _
        Item(Me.tabDataEntry.Value).Name

        'If the Customers page is selected,
        'set the SourceObjects of the Orders subform
        'and the Order Details subform to a zero-length string
        Case "pagCustomers"
            Me.fsubOrders.SourceObject = ""
```

LISTING 11.7   Continued

```
            Me.fsubOrderDetails.SourceObject = ""

        'If the Orders page is selected,
        'set the SourceObject of the Order Details
        'subform to a zero-length string
        Case "pagOrders"
            Me.fsubOrderDetails.SourceObject = ""

    End Select

    'Set visited flags to false because we are on a
    'different customer
    mboolOrdersVisited = False
    mboolOrderDetailsVisited = False

    'Requery the form to retrieve '
    'the data for the selected customer
    Me.Requery
End Sub
```

It begins by evaluating the name of the page that is selected. If the name of the page is pagCustomers, the `SourceObject` property of both the fsubOrders subform and the fsubOrderDetails subform is set to a zero-length string. If the name of the selected page is pagOrders, the `SourceObject` property of the fsubOrderDetails page is set to a zero-length string. In essence, the code ensures that when a different customer is selected, that customer's order and order detail records are not retrieved until the appropriate page is selected. This eliminates a lot of unnecessary network traffic.

Working with Local Tables

The use of local tables reduces the resources required on your SQL Server, therefore improving the scalability of your application. Any table whose data does not frequently change is a candidate for a local table. Excellent choices are tables that you use to populate combo boxes and list boxes. The form called fsubOrderDetails provides such an example. The cboProductID combo box uses a table called tblProducts_Local as its RowSource. To work with local tables, you need to be concerned with only creating them and then updating them from their SQL Server counterpart as needed.

Building the Local Table

The process of building the local table is quite simple. Here are the steps involved:

1. Build a query based on the SQL Server table that will have a local counterpart.

2. Select Query, Make Table from the menu. Name the new table with the name of the SQL Server table plus _Local—for example, tblProducts_Local.

3. Add all of the fields from the SQL Server table to the query grid.

4. Run the query.

5. Close the query without saving.

6. Open the local version of the table and set the primary key.

Updating the Local Table

When you use a local table, you must be concerned with ensuring that its data always reflects that of its SQL Server counterpart. The code in Listing 11.8 (located in the basRefresh module) provides a means of updating the tblProducts_Local table with data from the dbo_Products SQL Server table. You can call the code on demand from a command button or menu item, each time the application loads, or via an automated process that runs at night.

LISTING 11.8   Code That Updates a Local Table Based on Its SQL Server Counterpart

```
Public Sub RefreshLocalTables()
    Dim cnnAccess As ADODB.Connection
    Set cnnAccess = CurrentProject.Connection

    With cnnAccess
        .Execute ("DELETE * FROM tblProducts_Local")
        .Execute ("INSERT INTO tblProducts_Local ( ProductID, ProductName )" & _
            "SELECT dbo_Products.ProductID, dbo_Products.ProductName " & _
            "FROM dbo_Products")
    End With

End Sub
```

WARNING

To run the code in Listing 11.8, you will first need to use the Linked Table Manager to refresh the table link to dbo_Products.

The code relies on the fact that you are linked to the SQL Server version of the table. It first deletes the contents of the tblProducts_Local table and then inserts data into it based on the data stored on the dbo_Products linked table. In the absence of the linked table, you can use the results of a pass-through query to populate the local table, or you can use ADO code to accomplish the task. The pass-through query alternative appears in Listing 11.9.

LISTING 11.9   Using a Pass-Through Query to Update a Local Table Based on Its SQL Server Counterpart

```
Public Sub RefreshLocalTablesPassThrough()
    Dim cnnAccess As ADODB.Connection
    Set cnnAccess = CurrentProject.Connection

    With cnnAccess
        .Execute ("DELETE * FROM tblProducts_Local")
        .Execute ("qappProducts")
    End With

End Sub
```

This code first deletes all of the rows from the tblProducts_Local table. It then executes the append query called qappProducts. The append query looks like this:

```
INSERT INTO tblProducts_Local ( ProductID, ProductName )
SELECT qpassProducts.ProductID, qpassProducts.ProductName
FROM qpassProducts;
```

Notice that it appends to the tblProducts_Local table the results of the qpassProducts pass-through query. The qpassProducts pass-through query simply retrieves the contents of the Products table from the server.

Populating Combo Boxes and List Boxes Dynamically

Another important technique in building a client/server application is to make sure that combo boxes populate only with the necessary data. The form called frmReportTechniques contains two combo boxes. The first displays all of the contact titles. The second displays only those contacts with the selected contact title. The frmReportTechniques form appears in Figure 11.38.

The code that ensures that Access populates the cboSelectContact combo box only with those customers with the selected contact title appears here. It simply requeries the cboSelectContact combo box whenever the user selects a different contact title.

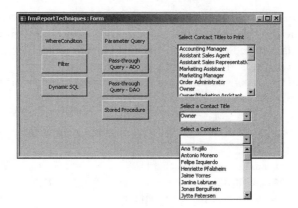

FIGURE 11.38   The form called frmReportTechniques allows the user to select a contact title and then populates the customer combo box with the customers that have that title.

```
Private Sub cboContactTitle_AfterUpdate()
    Me.cboSelectContact.Requery
End Sub
```

The SQL behind the cboSelectContact RowSource looks like this:

```
SELECT dbo_Customers.CustomerID, dbo_Customers.ContactName,
dbo_Customers.ContactTitle FROM dbo_Customers
WHERE dbo_Customers.ContactTitle=Forms!frmReportTechniques!cboContactTitle
ORDER BY dbo_Customers.ContactName;
```

Notice that the RowSource of the combo box includes only those customers who have a contact title that matches the contact title selected in the cboContactTitle combo box.

Building Client/Server–Friendly Reports

Most of the techniques that you saw with forms apply to reports as well. As with forms, the goal is to bring over as little data as possible. The following are techniques that you can use to limit the data sent over from SQL Server when you build MDB applications:

- Use the WhereCondition parameter of the DoCmd.OpenReport method
- Use the Filter property of the report
- Build the record source of a report dynamically
- Base the report on a parameter query

- Base the report on a view

- Base the report on a pass-through query

- Base the report on a stored procedure

The `WhereCondition` **Parameter**

When you use the `WhereCondition` parameter of the `DoCmd.OpenReport` method, Access includes the `WHERE` clause that you specify in the `WhereCondition` parameter as part of the SQL statement that it sends to SQL Server. This ensures that SQL Server returns only those rows specified in the `WhereCondition` parameter. Here's an example:

```
DoCmd.OpenReport "rptCustomers", View:=acPreview, _
    WhereCondition:="ContactTitle='Owner'"
```

Of course, you can base the `WhereCondition` on a value that the user selects in a combo box:

```
DoCmd.OpenReport "rptCustomers", View:=acPreview, _
    WhereCondition:="ContactTitle=" & Me.cboContactTitle
```

The form called frmReportTechniques (pictured in Figure 11.39) provides a more sophisticated example that allows the user to select contact titles from a multiselect list box. The code behind the WhereCondition command button appears in Listing 11.10.

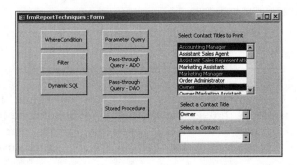

FIGURE 11.39   The form called frmReportTechniques allows the user to select contact titles from a multiselect list box.

LISTING 11.10   The `WhereCondition` Parameter of the `OpenReport` Method, Which Limits the Data Returned to the User

```
Private Sub cmdWhereCondition_Click()
    Dim varItem As Variant
    Dim strSQL As String

    'If no items are selected in the list box,
    'warn user and exit
    If Me.lstTitles.ItemsSelected.Count = 0 Then
        MsgBox "You Must Select at Least One Title Before " & _
            "Running this Report"
    Else

        'Loop through each item in the list box,
        'building an "In" clause
        strSQL = "ContactTitle In("
        For Each varItem In Me.lstTitles.ItemsSelected
            strSQL = strSQL & "'" & _
                Me.lstTitles.ItemData(varItem) & "',"
        Next varItem

        'Strip the trailing comma from the In clause
        strSQL = Mid(strSQL, 1, Len(strSQL) - 1) & ")"

        'Run the report, passing the Where Condition
        DoCmd.OpenReport "rptCustomers", acViewPreview, _
            WhereCondition:=strSQL
    End If

End Sub
```

The code begins by ensuring that the user has at least one contact title selected in the list box. It then loops through the selected items, building an In clause. The code uses the In clause as the `WhereCondition` parameter of the `OpenReport` method. This technique sends only the records that meet the specified criteria over the network wire.

The `Filter` **Property**

The `Filter` property of a report also limits the data that travels over the network wire. An example appears in Listing 11.11.

The code in Listing 11.11 requires that the form frmReportTechniques be open.

LISTING 11.11   The `Filter` Property of the Report Limits the Data Returned to the User

```
Private Sub Report_Open(Cancel As Integer)

    Dim varItem As Variant
    Dim strSQL As String

    'If no items are selected in the list box,
    'warn user and exit
    If Forms.frmReportTechniques.lstTitles.ItemsSelected.Count = 0 Then
        MsgBox "You Must Select at Least One Title Before " & _
            "Running this Report"
    Else

        'Loop through each item in the list box,
        'building an "In" clause to be used for the
        'report filter
        strSQL = "ContactTitle In("
        For Each varItem In Forms.frmReportTechniques.lstTitles.ItemsSelected
            strSQL = strSQL & "'" & _
                Forms.frmReportTechniques.lstTitles.ItemData(varItem) & "',"
        Next varItem

        strSQL = Mid(strSQL, 1, Len(strSQL) - 1) & ")"
    End If

    'Set the filter property of the report and turn filtering on
    Me.Filter = strSQL
    Me.FilterOn = True
End Sub
```

This code, placed in the `Open` event of the rptCustomersFiltered report, is invoked from the Cancel button on the frmReportTechniques form. It relies on the contact titles selected in the frmReportTechniques form. The code begins by ensuring that the user has at least one contact title selected in the list box. It then loops through the selected items, building an `In` clause that the code uses as the filter of the report. This technique sends only the records that meet the specified criteria over the network wire.

Building the `RecordSource` of the Report Dynamically

Another option is to build and set the `RecordSource` property of the report at runtime. An example appears in Listing 11.12.

LISTING 11.12   Building the `RecordSource` of the Report Dynamically

```
Private Sub Report_Open(Cancel As Integer)

    Dim varItem As Variant
    Dim strSQL As String

'If no items are selected in the list box,
    'warn user and exit
    If Forms.frmReportTechniques.lstTitles.ItemsSelected.Count = 0 Then
        MsgBox "You Must Select at Least One Title Before " & _
            "Running this Report"
    Else
        'Loop through each item in the list box,
        'building an "In" clause to be used for the
        'WHERE clause of the SELECT statement
        strSQL = "SELECT * FROM dbo_Customers WHERE ContactTitle In("
        For Each varItem In Forms.frmReportTechniques.lstTitles.ItemsSelected
            strSQL = strSQL & "'" & _
                Forms.frmReportTechniques.lstTitles.ItemData(varItem) & "',"
        Next varItem

        strSQL = Mid(strSQL, 1, Len(strSQL) - 1) & ")"
    End If

    'Set the RecordSource property of the report to the
    'SQL statement we just built
    Me.RecordSource = strSQL
End Sub
```

This code, found in the `Open` event of rptCustomersChangeRS, relies on the contact titles selected in the frmReportTechniques form. The code begins by ensuring that the user has at least one contact title selected in the list box. It then loops through the selected items, building an `In` clause that will become a SQL statement used as the `RecordSource` property of the report. This technique sends only the records that meet the specified criteria over the network wire.

Basing a Report on a Parameter Query

Another simple alternative is to base the report on a parameter query. The report called rptCustomersParameter provides such an example. The SQL statement in the record source of the report looks like this:

```
SELECT dbo_Customers.CustomerID, dbo_Customers.CompanyName, _
dbo_Customers.ContactName,
dbo_Customers.ContactTitle, dbo_Customers.Phone, dbo_Customers.Fax
FROM dbo_Customers
WHERE (((dbo_Customers.ContactTitle)= _
[Forms]![frmReportTechniques]![cboContactTitle]));
```

Notice that it relies on the user selecting a contact title from the cboContactTitle combo box on the frmReportTechniques form. It then uses the combo box value as the criteria for the ContactTitle.

Basing a Report on a View

Basing a report on a view is just like basing it on a table. The only difference is that, using a view, you easily limit the rows and columns returned over the network wire and displayed on the report. Furthermore, the user does not have to have rights to the tables underlying the view.

Basing a Report on a Pass-Through Query

Another excellent alternative is to base a report on a pass-through query. Listing 11.13 provides an example.

LISTING 11.13   Using ADO Code to Modify the SQL in a Pass-Through Query

```
Private Sub cmdPassThroughADO_Click()
    Dim varItem As Variant
    Dim strSQL As String
    Dim cat As ADOX.Catalog
    Dim cmd As ADOdb.Command

    'If no items are selected in the list box,
    'warn user and exit
    If Me.lstTitles.ItemsSelected.Count = 0 Then
        MsgBox "You Must Select at Least One Title Before " & _
            "Running this Report"
    Else
        'Loop through each item in the list box,
        'building an "In" clause
        strSQL = "SELECT * FROM Customers WHERE ContactTitle In("
```

LISTING 11.13   Continued

```
      For Each varItem In Me.lstTitles.ItemsSelected
          strSQL = strSQL & "'" & _
              Me.lstTitles.ItemData(varItem) & "',"
      Next varItem

      strSQL = Mid(strSQL, 1, Len(strSQL) - 1) & ")"

      'Instantiate a Catalog object and point its
      'connection at the current database
      Set cat = New ADOX.Catalog
      Set cat.ActiveConnection = CurrentProject.Connection

      'Point to and modify the SQL behind the
      'qpassCustomers pass-through query
      Set cmd = cat.Procedures("qpassCustomers").Command

      cmd.CommandText = strSQL
      Set cat.Procedures("qpassCustomers").Command = cmd

      'Run the report
      DoCmd.OpenReport "rptCustomersPassThrough", acViewPreview
  End If

End Sub
```

Notice that the code first builds an In clause with the contact titles that the user selects in the list box. It uses an ADOX catalog object and an ADODB command object to modify the SQL in the qpassCustomers pass-through query to reflect the contact titles that the user selects in the list box. It then runs the report called rptCustomersPassThrough. The record source of the report is the qpassCustomers pass-through query.

Listing 11.14 provides another example in which you use a pass-through query to limit the data that appears on a report. It uses DAO (rather than ADO) to accomplish its task.

LISTING 11.14   Using DAO Code to Modify the SQL in a Pass-Through Query

```
Private Sub cmdPassThroughDAO_Click()
    Dim varItem As Variant
    Dim strSQL As String
    Dim qdf As DAO.QueryDef

    'If no items are selected in the list box,
    'warn user and exit
    If Me.lstTitles.ItemsSelected.Count = 0 Then
        MsgBox "You Must Select at Least One Title Before " & _
            "Running this Report"
    Else
        strSQL = "SELECT * FROM Customers WHERE ContactTitle In("
        For Each varItem In Me.lstTitles.ItemsSelected
            strSQL = strSQL & "'" & _
                Me.lstTitles.ItemData(varItem) & "',"
        Next varItem

        strSQL = Mid(strSQL, 1, Len(strSQL) - 1) & ")"

        'Point at the query definition call qpassCustomers
        'and modify the SQL behind the query
        Set qdf = CurrentDb.QueryDefs("qpassCustomers")
        qdf.SQL = strSQL
        qdf.Close

        'Run the report
        DoCmd.OpenReport "rptCustomersPassThrough", acViewPreview
    End If


End Sub
```

The code uses a DAO `QueryDef` object to modify the SQL behind the pass-through query. Besides that, this example is identical to the ADO example.

Basing a Report on a Stored Procedure

The final alternative is to base the report on the results returned from a stored procedure. Listing 11.15 provides an example.

LISTING 11.15   Using ADO Code to Modify the SQL in a Pass-Through Query, Passing a Different Parameter to a Stored Procedure

```
Private Sub cmdStoredProcedure_Click()
    Dim varItem As Variant
    Dim strSQL As String
    Dim cat As ADOX.Catalog
    Dim cmd As ADOdb.Command

    'Build a SQL statement that includes a parameter for the
    'contact title
    strSQL = "procCustomerGetContactTitle '" & Me.cboContactTitle & "'"

    'Modify the pass-through query to reflect the name of the
    'stored procedure and the parameter you are passing it
    Set cat = New ADOX.Catalog
    Set cat.ActiveConnection = CurrentProject.Connection

    Set cmd = cat.Procedures("qpassCustomers").Command

    cmd.CommandText = strSQL
    Set cat.Procedures("qpassCustomers").Command = cmd

    'Run the report
    DoCmd.OpenReport "rptCustomersPassThrough", acViewPreview


End Sub
```

The example builds a `Where` clause based on the value selected in the cboContactTitle combo box. It uses ADO code to modify the SQL behind the `qpassCustomers` pass-through query to reflect the selected title. The example affects the same report, rptCustomersPassThrough, that we used in the previous examples.

The `procCustomerGetContactTitle` stored procedure looks like this:

```
CREATE PROCEDURE procCustomerGetContactTitle @ContactTitle Varchar(30) AS
SELECT * FROM Customers
WHERE ContactTitle = @ContactTitle
```

Notice that it includes a parameter for the ContactTitle. The pass-through query passes the parameter to the stored procedure.

Linked Table Gotchas

The main gotcha with linked tables is that it is way too easy to accidentally bring much more data over the network wire than is required. This is most commonly caused when a form is based on a table or on a query that brings back all of the rows from a table. Ensuring that you provide the user with a means for selecting only the data that he needs in each form and then basing the form on that criteria eliminates most of the problems inherent with linked tables.

Another gotcha with linked tables involves connections. Multiple combo boxes on a form utilize multiple connections. Basing static combo boxes on local tables greatly reduces the number of connections that each user consumes, thereby making your application more scalable.

Summary

Many successful production applications running today involve the use of linked tables. This chapter showed you how to link to tables using both the user interface and code. It then took you through the step-by-step process of building a successful client/server application by limiting the amount of data returned over the network wire.

12

Developing an ADP Application

Why This Chapter Is Important

Several alternatives are available for creating client/server applications in Microsoft Access. Access Projects are generally the best choice for client/server applications that you build today. This chapter begins by introducing you to Access Projects and telling how you and your users can benefit from them. It then goes on to show you how you can maintain a SQL Server database from within an Access Project. Next you'll learn how to properly design the forms and reports contained within your Access Projects. Finally, we'll talk about the ADP gotchas and how to avoid them.

What Are Access Projects?

Access 2000 introduced Access Projects (ADP). Whereas an Access database uses the Jet Engine and Open Database Connectivity (ODBC) to access client/server data, ADPs use OLE DB to access client/server data. This provides you with greatly enhanced functionality and performance when dealing with client/server data. The only caveat is that the client/server data must be stored in a Microsoft SQL Server 2000 database, a Microsoft SQL Server 7.0 database, the Microsoft Data Engine (MSDE) file format, or a Microsoft SQL Server 6.5 database with Service Pack 5 installed.

If you use an Access database to access client/server data, you must use linked tables, SQL pass-through queries, and ActiveX data object (ADO) code to manipulate the data. If you want to modify the structures of the client/server tables, you must do so within the SQL Server environment. With an Access Project, you can create and modify tables, views, database diagrams, and stored procedures directly from the Access environment.

Creating an Access Project

The process of creating an Access Project involves creating the ADP and designating the SQL Server database to which it is associated. To create an Access Project:

1. Click the New button on the toolbar. The New Task Pane appears (see Figure 12.1).

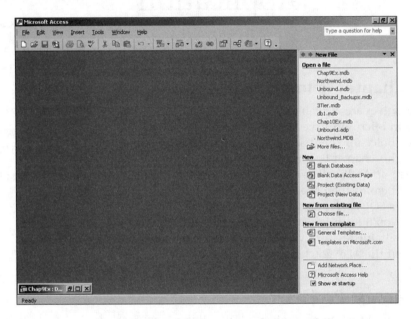

FIGURE 12.1 The New dialog box allows you to create an ADP based on a new or existing SQL Server database.

2. Two options allow you to build an ADP. The first allows you to create an ADP file using an existing SQL Server database. The second allows you to build an ADP file based on a new SQL Server database. If you click Project (Existing Data), Access creates an Access Project based on an *existing* SQL Server database. The File New Database dialog box appears. Enter the name and location of the ADP file, and click Create. The Data Link Properties dialog box appears (see Figure 12.2).

3. Enter the server name, the security information, and the name of the database that you want to connect to.

4. Click the Advanced tab to enter advanced options or the All tab to view or modify any connection options.

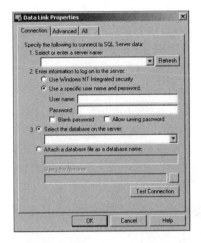

FIGURE 12.2 The Data Link Properties dialog box allows you to specify connection information about the SQL Server database that the ADP file is associated with.

5. When you're finished specifying all options, click the Connection tab and click Test Connection to ensure that you have correctly specified all of the settings.

6. Click OK to create the Access Project.

Figure 12.3 shows an ADP file based on the NorthWind sample database. Notice that the tables appear as if they were contained within the ADP file. In fact, they are stored in the SQL Server database. The important point here is that Access has not linked the tables! Because Access did not link the tables, they appear and you can manipulate them as if they are part of the ADP.

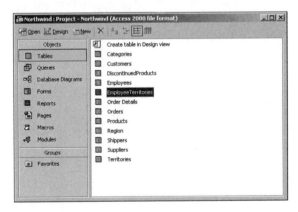

FIGURE 12.3 The ADP file shows you the tables, views, database diagrams, and stored procedures contained in the SQL Server database.

As you can see in Figure 12.3, the Database window is different for an ADP file than for an MDB file. The Objects list contains Tables, Views, Database Diagrams, and Stored Procedures rather than Tables and Queries. In fact, no local tables or queries can be stored in an ADP file.

To create an Access Project that builds a new SQL Server database:

1. Click the New button on the toolbar. The New Task Pane appears.

2. Click Project (New Data). Access creates an Access Project based on an *existing* SQL Server database. The File New Database dialog box appears. Enter the name and location of the ADP file and click Create. The Microsoft SQL Server Database Wizard appears (see Figure 12.4).

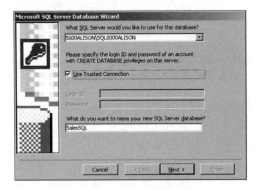

FIGURE 12.4   The Microsoft SQL Server Database Wizard allows you to create a SQL Server database from within Microsoft Access.

3. Select the server on which you want to create the database, enter login information, and provide a name for the new SQL Server database. Click Next and then click Finish. The ADP appears (see Figure 12.5). The ADP file for a new database contains only system objects and those objects found in the Model database.

NOTE

You can modify the connection associated with an ADP at any time. Simply select File, Connection. The Datalink Properties dialog box appears. Here you can change any connection information for the database.

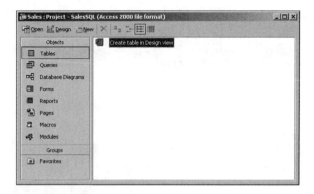

FIGURE 12.5   The ADP file for a new database contains only system objects and those objects found in the Model database.

Maintaining a SQL Server Database from an Access Project

One of the major benefits of Access Projects is that they allow you to easily administer the SQL Server database right from within Microsoft Access. This includes the capability to create, modify, rename, and delete SQL Server tables, views, stored procedures, user-defined functions, and database diagrams. This section shows you how to perform these various tasks. It is important to remember that any changes from within Access are immediately reflected within the associated SQL Server database.

Working with SQL Server Tables

As mentioned, you can create, modify, rename, and delete SQL Server tables directly from the Access environment. The designers available to you from within an ADP are the same as those available in SQL Server Enterprise Manager.

Creating a SQL Server Table

The SQL Server Table Designer allows you to create SQL Server tables from within Access. To create a table using the SQL Server Table Designer, do the following:

1. Select Tables from the Objects list.

2. Double-click Create Table in Design View. Access takes you to the SQL Server Table Designer, where you define the fields and their attributes (see Figure 12.6).

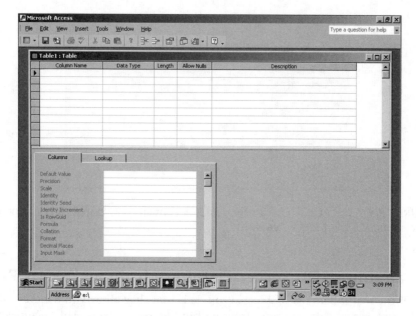

FIGURE 12.6   The SQL Server Table Designer allows you to enter the names of the columns and their attributes.

3. Enter the names of the columns and their attributes within the SQL Server Table Designer.

4. Close the window and save your changes when you are done.

Modifying a SQL Server Table

To modify the structure of an existing SQL Server table, do the following:

1. Select Tables from the Objects list.

2. Select the table whose structure you want to modify.

3. Click Design. The structure of the existing table appears. Figure 12.7 shows the NorthWind Customers table in Design view.

4. Modify the names and attributes of the desired columns.

5. Close the window and save your changes when you are done.

NOTE

Creating and working with SQL Server tables is covered in detail in Chapter 5, "SQL Server Tables and Database Diagrams."

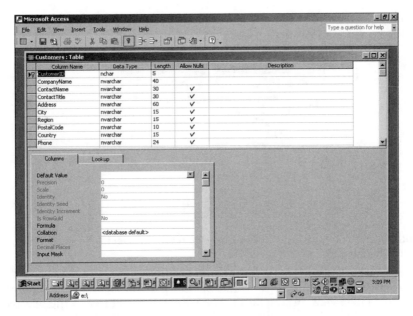

FIGURE 12.7   The NorthWind Customers table in Design view.

Deleting a SQL Server Table

Deleting a SQL Server table is very simple:

1. Select Tables from the Objects list.

2. Right-click the table that you want to delete.

3. Select Delete from the pop-up menu.

It is important to remember that deleting the table from the ADP removes it from the SQL Server database. The ease of deleting a SQL Server table via an ADP further necessitates that you establish proper security on the SQL Server database!

Working with SQL Server Views

SQL Server views are analogous to Access SELECT queries. The major difference is that SQL Server views do not support the use of parameters. (Stored procedures, covered later in the chapter, do accept parameters.)

Creating a SQL Server View

To create a SQL Server view, do the following:

1. Select Queries from the Objects list.

2. Double-click the Create View in Designer icon. The Add Table dialog box and the View Designer appear (see Figure 12.8).

FIGURE 12.8   The Add Table dialog box allows you to select the tables, views, or functions that you want to add to the view.

3. Select the Tables, Views, or Functions tab, depending on whether you want to add a table, view, or function to the view. Click Add to add the selected tables, views, and functions to the view (see Figure 12.9). Click Close when done.

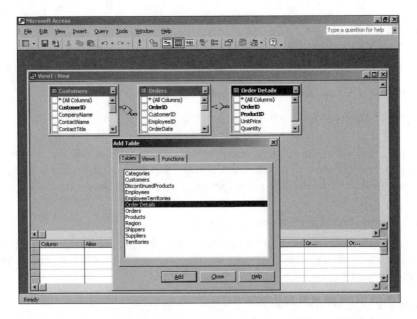

FIGURE 12.9   The Add Table dialog box and the View Designer, with the Customers and Orders tables added to the view.

4. Click the check boxes to the left of the field names to select the fields that you want to add to the view. If you prefer, you can drag and drop fields to the column list on the query grid. Figure 12.10 shows a view with the CustomerID, CompanyName, ContactName, Country, OrderID, and OrderDate fields included.

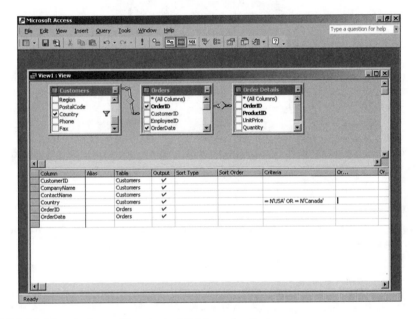

FIGURE 12.10   A view with selected fields and criteria.

5. Specify any criteria that you want to apply to the view. To add criteria, enter the desired criteria in the Criteria column of the appropriate field on the query grid. Adding criteria limits the records returned when you run the view. Figure 12.10 shows criteria limiting the selected records to those in the USA and Canada.

6. Click Properties to view or modify the properties of the view. The Properties dialog box appears (see Figure 12.11).

7. Test the view using the Run button. Access prompts you to save changes to the view.

8. The view appears in the Database window, and you can treat it much like a table.

FIGURE 12.11   The Properties dialog box allows you to view or modify the properties of the view.

NOTE

Creating and working with SQL Server views is covered in detail in Chapter 7, "Working with SQL Server Views."

Modifying a SQL Server View

Modifying a view is similar to modifying a table:

1. Select Queries from the Objects list.

2. Select the view whose attributes you want to modify.

3. Click Design. The design of the existing view appears.

4. Modify the attributes of the view.

5. Close the window and save your changes when you are done.

Deleting a SQL Server View

Deleting a SQL Server view is very simple:

1. Select Queries from the Objects list.

2. Right-click the view that you want to delete.

3. Select Delete from the pop-up menu.

As with tables, it is important to remember that deleting a view from an ADP removes it from the SQL Server database. Once again, this highlights the need for establishment of proper security on the SQL Server database.

Working with Database Diagrams

Database diagrams provide you with a visual method of managing and designing your database tables. Using a database diagram, you can establish and modify table relationships and edit table structures.

Creating a Database Diagram

To create a database diagram, follow these steps:

1. Select Database Diagrams from the Objects list.

2. Double-click Create Database Diagram in Designer. The Add Table dialog box appears (see Figure 12.12).

FIGURE 12.12   You add tables to the blank database diagram window to begin the process of creating a database diagram.

3. Double-click to add the desired tables to the database diagram and then click Close to close the dialog box.

4. To modify the structure of a table, right-click the table within the designer and select Column Properties. Properties changed in the database designer are immediately modified in the SQL Server database.

5. To modify a relationship, right-click the relationship line and select Properties. The Properties dialog box appears (see Figure 12.13). Here you can modify all the attributes of an existing relationship.

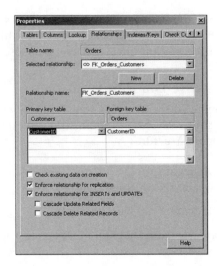

FIGURE 12.13   The Properties dialog box allows you to modify the attributes of an existing relationship.

6. To add a relationship, click and drag the field selector from one table to another. The Create Relationship dialog box appears (see Figure 12.14).

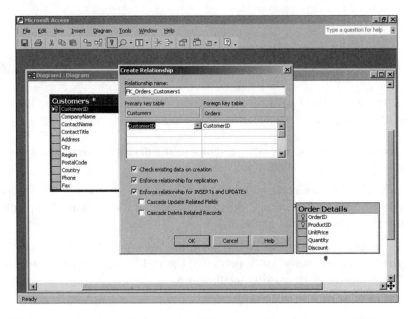

FIGURE 12.14   The Create Relationship dialog box allows you to establish the properties of a new relationship.

NOTE

Creating and working with SQL Server database diagrams is covered in detail in Chapter 5.

Modifying a Database Diagram

To modify an existing database diagram, do the following:

1. Select Database Diagrams from the Objects list.

2. Select the database diagram whose attributes you want to modify.

3. Click Design. The design of the database diagram appears. Figure 12.15 shows the database diagram associated with the NorthWindCS data project that ships with Microsoft Access.

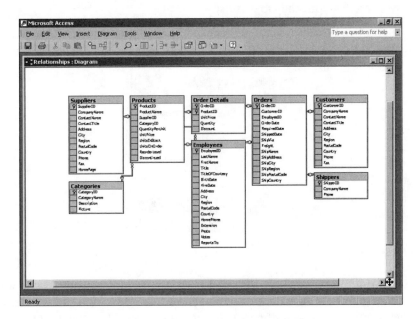

FIGURE 12.15   The database diagram window allows you to establish table relationships and modify the structure of tables.

4. Modify the attributes of the database diagram.

5. Close the window and save your changes when you are done.

Working with Stored Procedures

Although similar to views, stored procedures add two pieces of functionality unavailable within views. Stored procedures can include parameters. Therefore, a stored procedure can accept criteria at runtime. In addition, you can design stored procedures to edit table data.

There is a major distinction between executing an Access action query against a linked table and executing a stored procedure. In the case of an action query, all the data affected by the action query must travel over the network wire for Access to update at the workstation. On the other hand, a stored procedure updates data directly on the server, without requiring the data to travel over the network wire. This can result in major performance differences, especially when dealing with large volumes of data.

Creating a SQL Server Stored Procedure
To create a SQL Server stored procedure, do the following:

1. Select Queries from the Objects list.

2. Double-click the Create Stored Procedure in Designer icon. The Add Table dialog box and the Stored Procedure Designer appear (see Figure 12.16).

FIGURE 12.16   An example of a new stored procedure.

3. Select the Tables, Views, or Functions tab, depending on whether you want to add a table, view, or function to the view. Click Add to add the selected tables, views, and functions to the stored procedure. Click Close when done.

4. Click the check boxes to the left of the field names to select the fields that you want to add to the stored procedure. If you prefer, you can drag and drop fields to the column list on the stored procedure grid. Figure 12.17 shows a stored procedure with the CustomerID, CompanyName, ContactName, Country, OrderID, and OrderDate fields included.

5. Specify any criteria that you want to apply to the stored procedure. To add criteria, enter the desired criteria in the Criteria column of the appropriate field on the query grid. Adding criteria limits the records returned when Access runs the stored procedure. Figure 12.17 shows criteria limiting the selected records to those in the USA and Canada.

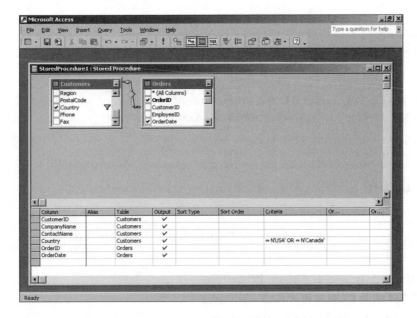

FIGURE 12.17   A stored procedure with selected fields and criteria.

6. Click Properties to view or modify the properties of the stored procedure. The Properties dialog box appears (see Figure 12.18).

FIGURE 12.18   The Properties dialog box allows you to view or modify the properties of the stored procedure.

7. Test the stored procedure using the Run button. Access prompts you to save changes to the view.

> **NOTE**
>
> Chapter 8, "Designing SQL Server Stored Procedures, User-Defined Functions, and Triggers," covers the details of creating and working with SQL Server stored procedures.

Modifying a SQL Server Stored Procedure

Modifying a stored procedure is similar to modifying a view:

1. Select Queries from the Objects list.

2. Select the stored procedure whose attributes you want to modify.

3. Click Design. The design of the existing stored procedure appears.

4. Modify the attributes of the stored procedure.

5. Close the window and save your changes when you are done.

Deleting a SQL Server Stored Procedure

Deleting a SQL Server stored procedure is very simple:

1. Select Queries from the Objects list.

2. Right-click the stored procedure that you want to delete.

3. Select Delete from the pop-up menu.

As with tables and views, it is important to remember that deleting a stored procedure from an ADP removes it from the SQL Server database. Once again, this highlights the need for establishment of proper security on the SQL Server database.

Working with User-Defined Functions

SQL 2000 introduced user-defined functions. User-defined functions add power and flexibility that were previously unavailable with views and stored procedures. In many ways, they combine the features of views and stored procedures. User-defined functions can receive parameters, and they can return single values or sets of rows.

Creating a SQL Server User-Defined Function

To create a SQL Server user-defined function, do the following:

1. Select Queries from the Objects list.

2. Double-click the Create Function in Designer icon. The Add table dialog box and the Function Designer appear (see Figure 12.19).

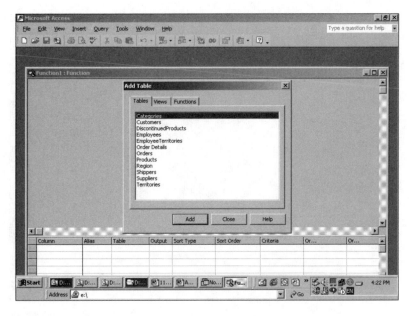

FIGURE 12.19   An example of a new user-defined function.

3. Select the Tables, Views, or Functions tab, depending on whether you want to add a table, view, or function to the user-defined function. Click Add to add the selected tables, views, and functions to the user-defined function. Click Close when done.

4. Click the check boxes to the left of the field names to select the fields that you want to add to the user-defined function. If you prefer, you can drag and drop fields to the column list on the user-defined function grid. Figure 12.20 shows a user-defined function with the CustomerID, CompanyName, ContactName, Country, OrderID, and OrderDate fields included.

5. Specify any criteria that you want to apply to the user-defined function. To add criteria, enter the desired criteria in the Criteria column of the appropriate field on the query grid. Adding criteria limits the records returned when you run the user-defined function. Figure 12.20 shows criteria limiting the selected records to those in the USA and Canada.

6. Click Properties to view or modify the properties of the user-defined function. The Properties dialog box appears (see Figure 12.21).

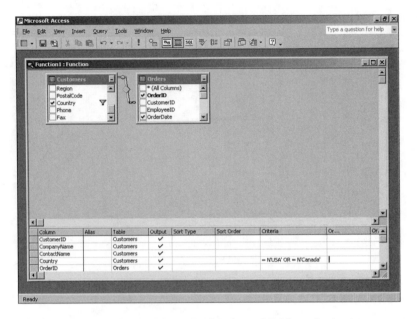

FIGURE 12.20   A user-defined function with selected fields and criteria.

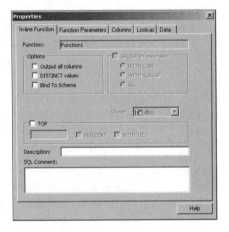

FIGURE 12.21   The Properties dialog box allows you to view or modify the properties of the user-defined function.

7. Test the user-defined function using the Run button. Access prompts you to save changes to the user-defined function.

Modifying a SQL Server User-Defined Function

Modifying a user-defined function is similar to modifying a view or stored procedure:

1. Select Queries from the Objects list.

2. Select the user-defined function whose attributes you want to modify.

3. Click Design. The design of the existing user-defined function appears.

4. Modify the attributes of the user-defined function.

5. Close the window and save your changes when you are done.

Deleting a SQL Server User-Defined Function

Deleting a SQL Server user-defined function is very simple:

1. Select Queries from the Objects list.

2. Right-click the user-defined function that you want to delete.

3. Select Delete from the pop-up menu.

As with tables and views, it is important to remember that deleting a user-defined function from an ADP removes it from the SQL Server database. Once again, this highlights the need for establishment of proper security on the SQL Server database.

Exploring Other Features Available with Access Projects

Besides providing you with the capability to maintain SQL Server tables, views, database diagrams, and stored procedures from within the Access environment, ADPs provide you with other benefits. From an ADP file, you can perform the following tasks:

- Back up the SQL Server database

- Restore the SQL Server database

- Transfer your SQL Server database to another SQL Server database

- Copy the SQL Server database file

- Drop the SQL Server database file

Building Access Project Forms

Chapter 11, "Developing an MDB Client/Server Application with Linked Tables," showed you how to properly build an application involving linked tables. As discussed in this chapter, the other alternative is to use an Access Project to solve the problem. Once again, the application will be built around the NorthWind client/server database.

To build the ADP file:

1. Click File, New.

2. Select Project (Existing Data).

3. Select a name and location for the Access Project (.adp). Click Create. The Data Link Properties dialog box appears.

4. In the Select or Enter a Server Name text box, enter the name of the server where the NorthWind database resides.

5. Specify how you will log on to the server.

6. Select the NorthWind database as the database on the server. The completed dialog box should appear similar to Figure 12.22.

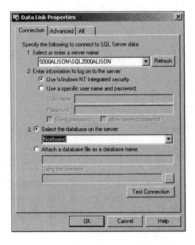

FIGURE 12.22 Use the Data Link Properties dialog box to specify information about the location of the data.

7. Click Test Connection to test the connection to the server and database. A dialog box should appear indicating that the test connection succeeded. Click OK to continue.

8. Click OK to close the Data Link Properties dialog box. The ADP file is built. The Database window should appear, as in Figure 12.23.

FIGURE 12.23   The Database window after the ADP file is built.

Designing the Customer Form

The form that you will build is pictured in Figure 12.24. Follow these steps to begin the process of designing the frmCustomer form:

1. Click Forms in the Objects list.

2. Double-click Create Form in Design View.

3. Select View, Form Header/Footer to add a header and footer to the form.

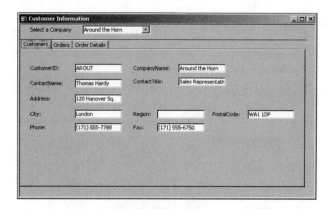

FIGURE 12.24   The completed frmCustomer form.

Adding a Locate Combo Box to the Form

As with the linked table application, the first step is to add a combo box to the form that allows the user to select the company whose information she wants to view. The combo box is populated with the CustomerID and CompanyName of each company in the company table. Build the combo box using the Combo Box Wizard. The steps are as follows:

1. If necessary, click the Control Wizards tool in the toolbox to turn on the Control Wizards.

2. Select a combo box from the toolbox and click and drag to add it to the header of the form. The Combo Box Wizard appears (see Figure 12.25).

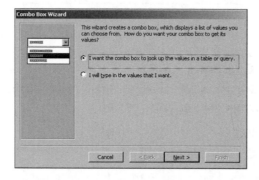

FIGURE 12.25   The Combo Box Wizard is used to add a combo box to the form.

3. Select I Want the Combo Box to Look Up the Values in a Table or View. Click Next.

4. Select the Customers table and click Next.

5. Select the CustomerID and CompanyName fields, and click Next (see Figure 12.26).

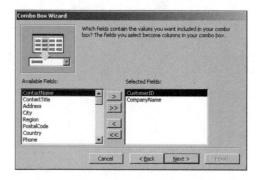

FIGURE 12.26   The CustomerID and CompanyName fields are added to the combo box.

6. Size the CompanyName column, if necessary, and click Next.

7. Enter the label **Select a Company** and click Finish.

8. Name the combo box **cboSelectCompany**.

Adding Pages and Controls to the Form

Before you can add the fields to the form, you must design the tabs for the form. Take the following steps:

1. Select a tab control from the toolbox.

2. Click and drag to add it to the frmCustomer form.

3. Change the Caption property of the first tab to Customers.

4. Change the Name property of the first tab to pagCustomers.

5. Change the Caption property of the second tab to Orders.

6. Change the Name property of the second tab to pagOrders.

7. Right-click the page control and select Insert Page. A third page appears.

8. Change the Caption property of the third tab to Order Details.

9. Change the Name property of the third tab to pagOrderDetails.

10. Change the Name property of the tab control to tabDataEntry.

11. Set the RecordSource property of the form to the Customers table.

12. Add the fields to the Customers tab of the form, as shown in Figure 12.27.

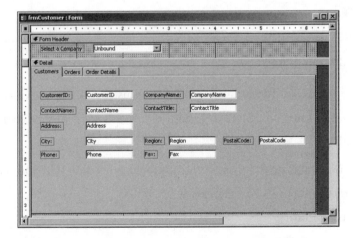

FIGURE 12.27   The Customers tab with the selected fields added.

Building the Stored Procedure to Underlie the Customer Form

The next step is to design the stored procedure that underlies the frmCustomer form. The stored procedure will reference the CustomerID of the customer that the user selects in the cboSelectCompany combo box. Here are the steps involved:

1. Return to the Database window.

2. Select Queries in the list of objects.

3. Double-click Create Stored Procedure in Designer. The Add Table dialog box appears.

4. Click Add to add the Customers table to the stored procedure, and click Close.

5. Click to add the CustomerID, CompanyName, ContactName, ContactTitle, Address, City, Region, PostalCode, Phone, and Fax fields to the stored procedure (see Figure 12.28).

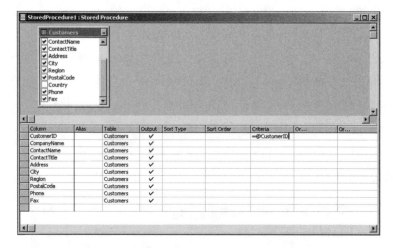

FIGURE 12.28   The stored procedure underlying the Customers form.

6. Enter =@CustomerID as the criteria for the CustomerID field (see Figure 12.28).

7. Close the stored procedure designating that you want to save changes to it. Name the stored procedure **spCustomerGetSelected**.

Now you must associate the form with the stored procedure that you have built.

1. Return to Design view, if necessary.

2. Select the form.

3. Click the Data tab in the Properties window.

4. Click the RecordSource property (see Figure 12.29).

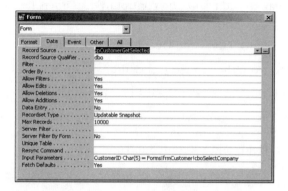

FIGURE 12.29   The RecordSource property allows you to designate the record source for the form.

5. Select the spCustomerGetSelected stored procedure.

6. Enter **CustomerID Char(5) = Forms!frmCustomer!cboSelectCompany** in the Input Parameters property of the form (see Figure 12.30).

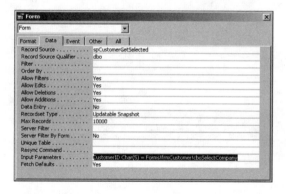

FIGURE 12.30   Use the Input Parameters property to designate the criteria for the form.

Creating the fsubOrders Subform

The fsubOrders subform will be used to display the orders associated with the selected customers. Take the following steps to create the fsubOrders subform and add it to the Orders page of the tab control:

1. Activate the frmCustomer form in Design view.

2. Click to select the Orders page of the tab control.

3. Make sure that the Control Wizards tool is selected.

4. Select the Subform/Subreport control.

5. Click and drag to add a subform control to the Orders tab. The SubForm Wizard appears.

6. Select Use Existing Tables and Queries, and click Next.

7. Select Orders from the Tables/Queries drop-down list.

8. Add all fields in the query to the list of Selected Fields.

9. Click Next. The SubForm Wizard asks you to define which fields link the subform to the main form (see Figure 12.31). Select the CustomerID for Form/Report Fields and Subform/Subreport Fields.

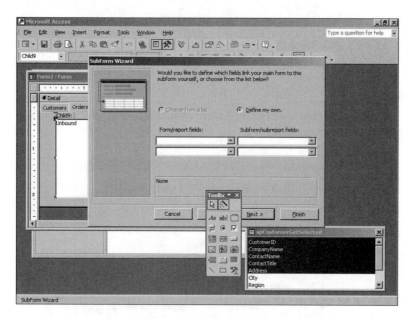

FIGURE 12.31   The SubForm Wizard asks you to define which fields link the subform to the main form.

10. Enter **fsubOrders** as the name of the subform, and click Finish.

11. Size the subform control as needed.

Creating the fsubOrderDetails Subform

The fsubOrderDetails subform will be used to display the order detail items associated with the selected order. Take the following steps to create the fsubOrderDetails subform and add it to the Order Details page of the tab control:

1. Activate the frmCustomer form in Design view.

2. Click to select the Order Details page of the tab control.

3. Make sure that the Control Wizards tool is selected.

4. Select the Subform/Subreport control.

5. Click and drag to add a subform control to the Order Details tab. The SubForm Wizard appears.

6. Select Use Existing Tables and Queries, and click Next.

7. Select OrderDetails from the Tables/Queries drop-down list.

8. Add all fields in the query to the list of Selected Fields.

9. Click Next. The Subform Wizard asks you to define which fields link the subform to the main form. Click Next without defining a link.

10. Enter **fsubOrderDetails** as the name of the subform, and click Finish.

11. Size the subform control as needed.

12. View the properties of the subform control.

13. Set the Link Child property to OrderID.

14. Set the Link Master property to Forms!frmCustomer!fsubOrders!OrderID.

Handling the AfterUpdate Event of the cboSelectCompany Combo Box

When a different customer is selected in the cboSelectCompany combo box, the recordset underlying the form must be re-created with the selected customer's information. The AfterUpdate event of the combo box appears in Listing 12.1.

LISTING 12.1 The AfterUpdate Event of the cboSelectCompany Combo Box

```
Private Sub cboSelectCompany_AfterUpdate()

    'Evaluate which page is active
    Select Case Me.tabDataEntry.Pages. _
        Item(Me.tabDataEntry.Value).Name

        'If Customers page is active,
```

LISTING 12.1   Continued

```
                'get rid of source object for Orders and
                'Order Details
                Case "pagCustomers"

                    Me.fsubOrders.SourceObject = ""
                    Me.fsubOrderDetails.SourceObject = ""

                'If Orders page is active,
                'requery the Orders subform and get rid
                'of the source object for Order Details
                Case "pagOrders"
                    Me.fsubOrderDetails.SourceObject = ""
                    Me.fsubOrders.Form.Requery

                'If OrderDetails page is active,
                'requery the Orders form and then the
                'Order Details form
                Case "pagOrderDetails"
                    Me.fsubOrders.Form.Requery
                    Me.fsubOrderDetails.Form.Requery

            End Select

            'Requery the form
            Me.Requery

            'Turn visited flag off for Order and
            'Order Details tabs
            mboolOrdersVisited = False
            mboolOrderDetailsVisited = False

End Sub
```

The case statement evaluates which tab of the form is selected. If the user selects the Customers tab, the source objects of the fsubOrders and fsubOrderDetails subform controls are set to zero-length strings. If the Orders tab is selected, the source object of the fsubOrderDetails subform is set to a zero-length string and the fsubOrders subform is requeried. If the user selects the Order Details tab, the code requeries the fsubOrders subform and then requeries the fsubOrderDetails subform.

Finally, the code requeries the form. This ensures that the input parameter is re-evaluated and the correct customer appears in the form.

Reacting to a User Who Is Clicking the Various Pages of the Form

The final piece of the puzzle is the code that reacts to the user who is selecting the various pages of the form. It appears in Listing 12.2.

LISTING 12.2   The Change Event of the tabDataEntry Tab Control As It Reacts to the User Selecting the Various Pages on the Form

```
Private Sub tabDataEntry_Change()
    'Evaluate which page is selected
    Select Case Me.tabDataEntry.Pages. _
        Item(Me.tabDataEntry.Value).Name

        'Do nothing if Customers page is selected
        Case "pagCustomers"

        'If Orders page is selected, set SourceObject
        'to Orders subform and requery the subform
        'Indicate that Orders was visited, but
        'Order Details was not
        Case "pagOrders"
            If Not mboolOrdersVisited Then
                Me.fsubOrders.SourceObject = "fsubOrders"
                mboolOrdersVisited = True
                mboolOrderDetailsVisited = False
            End If

        'If Order Details page is selected, if Orders has not been
        'visited for the Customer, set SourceObject to Orders subform
        'If Order Details page has not been visited for the Customer,
        'set the SourceObject to the Order Details subform
        'If Order Details page has been visited, simply requery the Order
        'Details subform
        Case "pagOrderDetails"

            If Not mboolOrdersVisited Then
                Me.fsubOrders.SourceObject = "fsubOrders"
            End If

            If Not mboolOrderDetailsVisited Then
                Me.fsubOrderDetails.SourceObject = "fsubOrderDetails"
```

LISTING 12.2   Continued

```
                mboolOrderDetailsVisited = True
        Else
                Me.fsubOrderDetails.Form.Requery
        End If

    End Select
End Sub
```

It begins by evaluating the selected page. If the user selects the Customers page, the code takes no special action.

If the user selects the Orders page and the user has not selected the Orders page for that customer, the SourceObject property of the fsubOrders subform control is set to fsubOrders. The code sets the mboolOrdersVisited flag to True and the mboolOrderDetailsVisited flag to False.

If the Order Details page is selected, and the user has not visited the orders tab for that customer, the SourceObject property of the fsubOrders form is set to fsubOrders. If the user has not visited the order details tab for that Order, the SourceObject property of the fsubOrderDetails subform control is set to fsubOrderDetails. The code sets the mboolOrderDetailsVisited flag to True. If the user has visited the Order Details tab for that customer, the code requeries the fsubOrderDetails subform.

Special Access Project Form Properties and Techniques

Access project forms have properties that are not available within MDB forms. These properties all help you to optimize your application for the client/server environment. Furthermore, there are techniques that you can employ with an ADP that are not available with an MDB. This section covers these properties and techniques.

Options for the RecordSource

Access project forms sport a variety of choices for the RecordSource property. You can select a table, view, stored procedure, or Transact-SQL statement as the record source of an Access project form. Creating a form based on a stored procedure is not an intuitive process. The steps are as follows:

1. Create a form without a record source.

2. Select the stored procedure from the form's RecordSource property (see Figure 12.32).

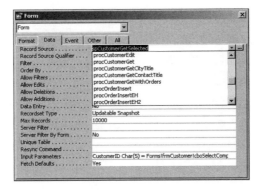

FIGURE 12.32   The form's RecordSource property allows you to select a stored procedure as the record source of the form.

In the past, forms based on stored procedures were not updateable. This is not true with ADP forms. When you base an ADP form on a stored procedure and you set the Recordset Type property to Updateable Snapshot (covered in the next section), Access allows you to update the data. This occurs because Access creates a static, client-side, optimistic recordset under the hood. Once the user makes changes to the form, Access generates a stored procedure to update the data on the server. The only caveat is that the user must have update rights on the underlying SQL Server tables.

Designating the Recordset Type

ADP forms offer two options for the RecordSet Type property: Snapshot and Updateable Snapshot (see Figure 12.33). Whereas the default, Updateable Snapshot, allows you to update the data underlying the form, the Snapshot option does not. Access project forms use ADO under the hood. When you select Updateable Snapshot, Access creates a recordset with the adOpenStatic, adLockOptimistic, and adUseClient options. The adOpenStatic option means that users do not see changes that other users make. The adLockOptimistic option means that Access does not lock the data until the user submits the update. The adUseClient option means that Access creates a client/side cursor. When you select the Updateable Snapshot option, Access caches information necessary to update the data on the server. Access does not maintain this information when you select the Snapshot option. It is therefore more efficient for you to select the Snapshot option in situations when users do not need to update the data.

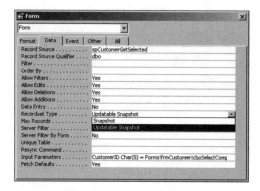

FIGURE 12.33   ADP forms offer two options for the RecordSet Type property: Snapshot and Updateable Snapshot.

The MaxRecords **Property**

Access project forms have a MaxRecords property. You use this property to limit the number of rows returned to the workstation. Although this property reduces network traffic, it also poses an issue that you should be aware of. Access does not warn you if the number of rows returned does not constitute a complete set of records. This means that the user may be completely unaware that the set of rows he is working with is not complete.

You can set the MaxRecords property either via the user interface or programmatically. Figure 12.34 shows how you can use the Max Records button on a form to limit the number of rows returned to the form. The Max Records button is located on the navigation bar. After you click the button, the Set Maximum Record Count dialog box appears. Enter the number of rows that you want to return and click OK.

FIGURE 12.34   The Set Maximum Record Count dialog box allows you to limit the number of rows returned to the form.

Listing 12.3 shows how you can programmatically set the MaxRecords property. It prompts the user for the maximum number of rows to display and sets the MaxRecords property prior to setting the record source of the form. You can find this code in frmOrders in the sample database.

LISTING 12.3   Programmatically Setting the MaxRecords Property of a Form

```
Private Sub Form_Load()
    Dim intRecords As Integer

    'Prompt the user for how many rows they wish to return
    intRecords = InputBox("How Many Orders to You Want to View?", _
        "Please Respond", 10)

    'Set the MaxRecords property of the form
    Me.MaxRecords = intRecords

    'Set the RecordSrouce property of the form
    Me.RecordSource = "Orders"
End Sub
```

The InputParameters Property

The InputParameters property of a form allows you to pass parameters to a form's record source. You can use the InputParameters property both with embedded SQL statements and with stored procedures. To use the InputParameters property with an embedded SQL statement, you must include at least one question mark in the statement. The question marks act as placeholders for the parameters.

```
SELECT * FROM Customers WHERE ContactTitle = ?
```

Notice that the ContactTitle included in the WHERE clause is variable. You then populate the parameter with the InputParameters property (see Figure 12.35).

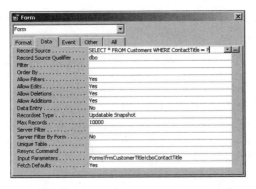

FIGURE 12.35   You use the InputParameters property to designate the parameter values for the form record source.

The code looks like this:

```
ContactTitle nvarchar(30)=Forms!frmCustomerTitle!cboContactTitle
```

This example requires only one line of code within the AfterUpdate event:

```
Private Sub cboContactTitle_AfterUpdate()
    Me.Requery
End Sub
```

The line of code is located in the AfterUpdate event of the cboContactTitle combo box. It simply requeries the form. This causes Access to re-evaluate the parameter value.

The ServerFilter Property

The Filter property, available for MDB forms, filters data *after* SQL Server returns it to the workstation. This is very inefficient in terms of network performance. ADP forms provide you with an alternative. SQL Server applies the filter designated in the ServerFilter property prior to returning data to the workstation. You must set the ServerFilter property *before* you set the RecordSource property of the form. Listing 12.4 provides an example:

LISTING 12.4   Using the ServerFilter Property of a Form to Limit the Data Returned to the Workstation

```
Private Sub Form_Open(Cancel As Integer)
    Dim strContactTitle As String
    strContactTitle = InputBox("Enter a Title", _
        "Please Respond", "Owner")

    Me.ServerFilter = "ContactTitle = '" & strContactTitle & "'"
    Me.RecordSource = "Customers"
End Sub
```

The Server Filter by Form Feature

The Server Filter by Form feature in an ADP is similar to the Filter by Form feature in an MDB. It allows users to define their own filter. The difference between the Filter by Form property and the Server Filter by Form property is that, whereas with the Filter by Form property Access applies the filter on the client, SQL Server applies the filter designated by the Server Filter by Form *before* it sends any data over the wire. To activate the Server Filter by Form feature, you simply set the Server Filter property of the form (see Figure 12.36).

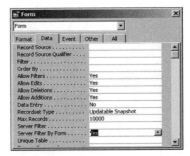

FIGURE 12.36   To activate the Server Filter by Form feature, you simply set the Server Filter property of the form.

After you set the Server Filter property of the form to True, Access opens the form in Filter view (see Figure 12.37). In the example, the user is filtering the form to display just the customers whose contact title is owner. To apply the filter, simply click the Apply Server Filter button. Access saves the WHERE clause that the user designated in the ServerFilter property of the form.

FIGURE 12.37   After you set the Server Filter property of the form to True, when you open the form, Access opens the form in Server Filter view rather than in regular view.

You must be familiar with a couple of properties when dealing with the Server Filter by Form feature. The first is the FilterLookup property of the control (see Figure 12.38).

You can set this property to Never, Database Default, or Always. This property controls what the user sees in the combo box when in Filter by Form view. When set to Never, the user sees only Is Null and Is Not Null as the choices in the combo box (see Figure 12.39). When set to Always, the user sees all choices for that field based on the available data (see Figure 12.40).

FIGURE 12.38   The FilterLookup property controls what the user sees in the combo box when in Filter by Form view.

FIGURE 12.39   When the FilterLookup property is set to Never, the user sees only Is Null and Is Not Null in the combo box.

FIGURE 12.40   When the FilterLookup property is set to Always, the user sees all choices for that field based on the available data.

This is not very efficient because it loads, for example, all company names into the combo box. The final choice, Database Default, is dictated by the choice that the user has made in the Edit/Find tab of Tools, Options (see Figure 12.41). When Records at Server is selected for the Show List of Values In option, Access populates controls that have their Filter Lookup property set to Database Default with all the data available for that field. When unchecked, only the Is Null and Is Not Null options appear. Notice the text box titled Don't Display Lists Where More Than This Number of Records Read; this text box allows you to limit the maximum number of rows returned when you check the Records at Server option.

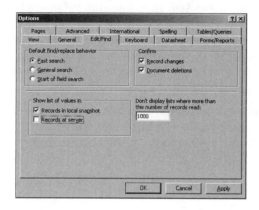

FIGURE 12.41   The Database Default option for `FilterLookup` is dictated by the choice that the user has made in the Edit/Find tab of Tools, Options.

The Unique Table Property

In an MDB form, you can update tables on both sides of the relationship in a one-to-many join. In an Access 2000 ADP form, you cannot update data on either side of the relationship unless you set the `UniqueTable` property of the form. In an Access 2002 ADP form, it is not necessary for you to set this property if you want to update data on the many side of a one-to-many relationship. Figure 12.42 shows the `UniqueTable` property.

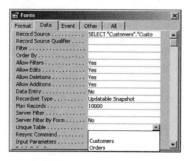

FIGURE 12.42   The `UniqueTable` property of the form allows you to designate the table in the form that you can update.

The `Resync` **Command**

The `Resync` command is a companion command to the `UniqueTable` property. In an Access MDB, if you have a form based on customer and order information and you modify the CustomerID associated with a particular order, Access automatically refreshes the customer information to reflect the selected customer when it saves the record. In an Access 2000 ADP, this is not the default behavior. You must use the `Resync` command for Access to update the customer information. You must set the Resync Command property to the same SQL statement that is used for the RecordSource of the form. The only difference is that you must add a question mark parameter placeholder for each key field in the unique table. For example, consider a form in which the SQL behind the form looks like this:

```
SELECT Orders.CustomerID, Customers.CompanyName, Customers.ContactName,
Customers.ContactTitle, Orders.OrderID, Orders.EmployeeID,
Orders.OrderDate, Orders.RequiredDate, Orders.ShippedDate
FROM Customers INNER JOIN Orders ON Customers.CustomerID = Orders.CustomerID
```

The Resync Command property would look like this:

```
SELECT Orders.CustomerID, Customers.CompanyName, Customers.ContactName,
Customers.ContactTitle, Orders.OrderID, Orders.EmployeeID,
Orders.OrderDate, Orders.RequiredDate, Orders.ShippedDate
FROM Customers INNER JOIN Orders ON Customers.CustomerID = Orders.CustomerID
WHERE Customers.CustomerID = ?
```

Building Access Data Project Reports

The same guidelines that are true for forms are true for reports. The main thing to remember is that you want to bring over as little data as possible whenever possible. If you need to produce a report that contains aggregate data, you should always aggregate the data on the server. If you perform the aggregation on the client, Access will need to bring all of the necessary detail records over the network wire. On the other hand, if you use a view or stored procedure to aggregate the data, the server will aggregate the data and send only the aggregated results over the network wire.

Input Parameters

Just as a form has input parameters, so does a report. You use the input parameters for a report in the same way that you use input parameters for a form. When using input parameters, the report record source can be either a SQL statement with question marks embedded for the parameters or a stored procedure. The report called rptCustomers provides an example (see Figure 12.43).

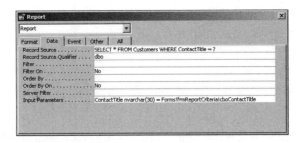

FIGURE 12.43   The report called rptCustomers includes an input parameter that is based on a combo box on the frmReportCriteria form.

Notice the record source:

```
SELECT * FROM Customers WHERE ContactTitle = ?
```

The input parameters property looks like this:

```
ContactTitle nvarchar(30) = Forms!frmReportCriteria!cboContactTitle
```

Notice that the input parameter references a combo box on a form called frmReportCriteria. The Open event of the report loads the frmReportCriteria form modally. It looks like this:

```
Private Sub Report_Open(Cancel As Integer)
    DoCmd.OpenForm "frmReportCriteria", WindowMode:=acDialog
End Sub
```

The cmdOK command button hides the form, therefore allowing report processing to continue.

```
Private Sub cmdOK_Click()
    Me.Visible = False
End Sub
```

Finally, the Close event of the report closes the criteria form.

```
Private Sub Report_Close()
    DoCmd.Close acForm, "frmReportCriteria"
End Sub
```

Server Filter by Form

A little earlier in this chapter, you learned about Server Filter by Form. You can use the filter established by the Server Filter by Form feature to limit the rows that appear on your reports. You simply bind the report to the same data source as the form. The form called frmServerFilterByForm and the report called rptCustomersServerFilterByForm provide an example. The form contains a command button with the following code:

```
Private Sub cmdPreview_Click()
    DoCmd.OpenReport "rptCustomersServerFilterByForm", acViewPreview
End Sub
```

The report's record source is the same as the form's record source (the Customers table). The code behind the Open event of the report looks like this:

```
Private Sub Report_Open(Cancel As Integer)
    Dim strServerFilter As String

    If IsLoaded("frmServerFilterByForm") Then
        strServerFilter = Forms!frmServerFilterByForm.ServerFilter
        Me.ServerFilter = strServerFilter
    Else
        MsgBox "No Data Meets the Filter Criteria", vbCritical, _
            "Canceling Report"
        Cancel = True
    End If
End Sub
```

It begins by ensuring that the frmServerFilterByForm form is open. It then sets the ServerFilter property of the report to a string containing the filter of the form.

The ServerFilter Property

The example in the previous section uses the Server Filter by Form feature to set the ServerFilter property of the report to a string containing the ServerFilter for the form. You may not like the Server Filter by Form feature. Furthermore, it is not always the most efficient way to limit the data returned from the server. You can always build your own criteria form and set the ServerFilter property of the report based on what is selected in your criteria form.

Basing Reports on SQL Server Functions

SQL Server 2000 introduced functions. SQL Server functions combine many of the benefits of stored procedures and views (for more details, see Chapter 8). Fortunately, Access 2002 allows you to base ADP reports on the result of a SQL Server function that returns a table. Consider the function called CustGetByTitle (created in Chapter 8):

```
CREATE FUNCTION dbo.CustGetByTitle
    (@Title nVarChar(30))
RETURNS Table
AS
RETURN SELECT CustomerID, CompanyName, ContactName, City, Region
FROM Customers WHERE ContactTitle = @Title
```

This function receives a parameter for the ContactTitle and returns a table containing CustomerID, CompanyName, ContactName, City, and Region. The report has no record source. The Open event of the report is responsible for populating the record source with the results of the function. It looks like this:

```
Private Sub Report_Open(Cancel As Integer)
    Dim strCriteria As String
    strCriteria = InputBox("Please Enter a Title")

    If Len(strCriteria) = 0 Then
        MsgBox "You must enter a title", vbCritical, "Canceling Report"
Else
        Me.RecordSource = "SELECT * FROM CustGetByTitle('" & strCriteria & "')"
    End If
End Sub
```

The code prompts the user for a title. It then sets the RecordSource property of the report to a SELECT statement that selects the results of the CustGetByTitle function. Notice that the title that the user entered is passed as a parameter to the function.

ADP Gotchas

The important thing to remember when dealing with ADP files is that there is no local storage and there are no local queries. No local storage means that you must place temp tables and lookup tables on the server. No local queries means that all of the queries in your application need to be rewritten as views, stored procedures, and functions. This can all take some getting used to.

Another important gotcha involves security. Access ADP files do not offer user-level security. This means that if you are accustomed to assigning your users different rights to different objects, you will not be able to duplicate this behavior with ADP files. The only security alternatives are to compile the project as an ADE or to place a password on the module code. Although both of these options protect your code from being viewed or modified by unauthorized individuals, they do not provide the differential security afforded by MDB files.

Another major security issue involves the updateability of data within ADP forms. If you want to bind the ADP forms to stored procedures and have Access automatically propagate data changes back to the server, you will need to provide users of the forms with insert, update, and delete rights for the tables underlying the forms. This is because Access uses the `sp_executeSQL` stored procedure to update the data on the server. The `sp_executeSQL` stored procedure requires that the user executing the statement has the appropriate rights to the tables referenced in the SQL statement.

Summary

Two main techniques are available for building client/server applications. The first employs the use of linked tables within a standard database file (.mdb). This method can be quite successful if you build the application so that a minimal amount of data travels over the network wire. The alternative to this technique is to use an Access Project. With an Access Project, you establish a direct connection to the client/server database, and no linked tables are involved. Regardless of the technique employed, the objective is to minimize the data that travels over the network wire. You reduce traffic by ensuring that only the data that the user specifically requests is returned. Techniques that achieve this goal include not requesting data until the user clicks the tab containing that data.

This chapter showed you how to create ADP files. It then walked you through the process of administering a SQL Server database from an ADP file. Finally, it showed you how to design ADP forms and reports that keep network traffic to a minimum.

13

Building Unbound Applications

Why This Chapter Is Important

Sometimes Access introduces unnecessary overhead into an application. When this occurs, you might decide to control everything yourself. An unbound form uses *no* linked tables. With an unbound form, you must do everything yourself. You must write the code to connect to the database, populate the form with data, and save any changes to disk. The process generally involves a combination of ActiveX data object (ADO) code, pass-through queries, and SQL Server stored procedures. The text that follows covers specific techniques involved.

The Benefits of Unbound Applications

The goal of an unbound application is to bring back as little data as possible over the network wire and to connect to the database for as short a period as possible. With an unbound application, you can control exactly what happens to your SQL Server database and when. Unbound applications are more scalable than bound applications, meaning that you can deploy them to much larger groups of users. Furthermore, it is easy to move unbound applications to a three-tier architecture, as discussed in Chapter 14, "Building *N*-Tier Applications."

The Unbound Form

The form used in the first example utilizes a public ADO connection object. This object initializes when the form loads and remains in memory as long as the application is running. You will need to evaluate whether it is more efficient to re-establish the connection repeatedly or to maintain the public connection. Generally, if there are fewer users, the approach shown in this example (a public connection) is more efficient. This is because Access does not need to connect to the server repeatedly. As the number of users increases, you may find that the public connection utilizes excessive server resources. You would then modify the code to have each event routine establish its own local connection.

The code in Listing 13.1 uses the Open method of the Connection object to establish a connection to the NorthWind database on the 5000Alison server. Notice that the code supplies the user ID and password. As an alternative, you could use integrated security to establish the connection.

LISTING 13.1   The Form Load Event

```
Private Sub Form_Load()

    Set gcnn = New ADODB.Connection

    'Open the connection
    gcnn.Open "Provider=SQLOLEDB.1;" & _
            "Data Source=(local); Initial Catalog=NorthWind;" & _
            "User ID='SA';Pwd="

End Sub
```

NOTE

To keep thingssimple, the examples in this chapter are devoid of error handling. In a real-life application, particularly an unbound application, fastidious use of error handling is necessary. Many things can go wrong: The server may not be available, the row that you are inserting may be invalid (for example, it may lack required data), or the rows that you are attempting to delete may have child rows associated with them. Chapter 8, "Designing SQL Server Stored Procedures, User-Defined Functions, and Triggers," and Chapter 10, "ADO and SQL Server," cover the process of handling errors in your stored procedures and the application code that calls them.

As an alternative, you could use integrated security to establish the connection as shown in Listing 13.2.

LISTING 13.2   An Alternative Form Load Event That Uses Integrated NT Security

```
Private Sub Form_Load()

    Set gcnn = New ADODB.Connection

    'Open the connection
    gcnn.Open "Provider=SQLOLEDB.1;" & _
            "Data Source=(local); Initial Catalog=NorthWind;" & _
            "Integrated Security = SSPI"

End Sub
```

Figure 13.1 shows the form. The user types a CustomerID in the header of the form. He then clicks Retrieve. The customer's information displays. The user can then modify the information and click Save. The code commits the changes to disk. The user clicks Add to clear the form. Once the user enters the data for the new record, he clicks Save. As you will see, the Save button handles an edit or add, as appropriate.

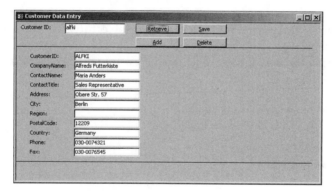

FIGURE 13.1   An unbound data entry form.

Populating the Form with Data

Because the form is unbound, it is necessary that you write the code to populate the controls on the form with data from the underlying database. The code under the Retrieve command button, shown in Listing 13.3, first calls the GetCustomer routine. The GetCustomer routine retrieves the data for the customer designated in the txtCustomerID text box. After calling the GetCustomer routine, the Click event of the cmdRetrieve command button loops through each control on the form. If the type of the control is a text box, it sets the locked property of the control to False. It also sets the module-level flag called AddMode to False.

LISTING 13.3   The Code Under the cmdRetrieve Command Button

```
Private Sub cmdRetrieve_Click()
    Dim ctl As Control

    'Call the routine to retrieve the customer
    Call GetCustomer

    'Loop through each control on the form
    'If it is a text box, set its Locked property to False
    For Each ctl In Me.Controls
        If ctl.ControlType = acTextBox Then
            ctl.Locked = False
        End If
    Next ctl

    'Set the Add Flag to False
    Me.AddMode = False
End Sub
```

The `GetCustomer` routine, shown in Listing 13.4, is responsible for retrieving the data for the designated customer. It uses a `Recordset` object to accomplish its work. The code first evaluates to ensure that the user entered a CustomerID in the txtCustomerID text box. If the user entered a CustomerID, it continues. Otherwise, it displays a message to the user.

LISTING 13.4   The `GetCustomer` Routine

```
Sub GetCustomer()
    Dim rst As ADODB.Recordset
    Dim ctl As Control
    Dim fld As Field

    'If the user has filled in the CustomerID text box,
    'open a recordset with that customer's data
    If Not IsNull(Me.txtCustomerID) And _
        Not Me.txtCustomerID = "" Then

        Set rst = New ADODB.Recordset
        With rst
            .CursorType = adOpenKeyset
            .LockType = adLockReadOnly
            .Source = "SELECT CustomerID, CompanyName, ContactName, " & _
```

LISTING 13.4   Continued

```
                "ContactTitle, Address, City, Region, PostalCode, " & _
                "Country, Phone, Fax " & _
                "FROM Customers " & _
                "WHERE CustomerID = '" & Me.txtCustomerID & "'"
            .ActiveConnection = gcnn

            .Open Options:=adCmdText

            'Loop through the resulting recordset,
            'populating the controls on the form with the
            'values in the fields in the recordset
            If Not .EOF Then
                For Each fld In .Fields
                    Me(fld.Name).Value = fld.Value
                Next fld

            'If the customer was not found, display a message to the user
            Else
                MsgBox "Customer Not Found"
            End If

        End With

    Else
        MsgBox "You must enter a CustomerID " & _
            "before proceeding", _
            vbCritical, "Error"

    End If
End Sub
```

If the user entered a CustomerID, the code sets four properties of the Recordset object. It sets the CursorType property to adOpenKeyset, indicating a key-set type of cursor. It sets the LockType property to adLockReadOnly, indicating that the recordset is read-only. It sets the Source property to a SQL statement that retrieves data from the customer designated in the txtCustomerID text box. Finally, it sets the ActiveConnection property to a connection string stored in a public constant called gcnn.

After setting properties of the Recordset object, the code under the cmdRetrieve command button opens the recordset. If the recordset contains data, the code loops through each field in the `fields` collection of the resulting recordset. It sets the control with the same name as the field to the value of the field. If the `Open` method of the `Recordset` object returned no data, the code displays a message to the user indicating that the customer was not found.

Adding a Record

The code to add a record is quite simple (see Listing 13.5). It first calls the `ClearControls` routine, passing it `False`. The `ClearControls` routine clears the values in the text boxes and unlocks the controls. The code under the `Click` event of the `cmdAdd` command button then sets the `AddMode` flag to `True`.

LISTING 13.5   The Code to Add a Record

```
Private Sub cmdAdd_Click()
    'Clear the form controls
    Call ClearControls(False)

    'See Add Flag to True
    Me.AddMode = True
End Sub
```

The `ClearControls` routine, shown in Listing 13.6, loops through each control on the form. If the control is a text box, the value is set to a zero-length string and the `locked` property is set to the value received as a parameter (in this case, `False`).

LISTING 13.6   The `ClearControls` Routine

```
Public Sub ClearControls(boolLocked As Boolean)
    Dim ctl As Control

    'Loop through each control on the form
    'If it is a text box, set its value to
    'a zero-length string and its locked property
    'to the value passed in as a parameter
    For Each ctl In Me.Controls
        If ctl.ControlType = acTextBox Then
            ctl.Value = ""
            ctl.Locked = boolLocked
        End If
    Next ctl
End Sub
```

Saving Data

The code under the `Click` event of the cmdSave command button (see Listing 13.7) is responsible for saving data whether the user is editing an existing record or adding a new record. It begins by ensuring that the user entered a CustomerID and Company Name. If not, the code displays a message to the user and exits the subroutine.

If the user did enter the CustomerID and Company Name, the code evaluates the `AddMode` flag to determine whether the user is adding or editing data. It builds the appropriate SQL statement, `INSERT INTO` or `UPDATE`, depending on the task that the user is performing. It then uses the `Execute` method of the public `Connection` object to execute the SQL statement.

Finally, if the `AddMode` flag is set to `True`, the code sets the value of the txtCustomerID text box to the value in the CustomerID data entry control and resets the `AddMode` flag to `False`.

LISTING 13.7   The Code Under the `Click` Event of the cmdSave Command Button

```
Private Sub cmdSave_Click()

    Dim strSQL As String
    Dim lngRowsAffected As Long

    With gcnn

        'If the user has not filled in the CustomerID
        'and Company Name, display a message and exit the subroutine
        If IsNull(Me.CustomerID) Or _
            IsNull(Me.CompanyName) Then

            MsgBox "CustomerID and CompanyName" & vbNewLine & _
                "Must be Filled In"
            Exit Sub

        'If the user has filled in the CustomerID text box,
        'build a SQL statement to Insert or Update the
        'customer data as appropriate
        Else
            If Me.AddMode Then
                strSQL = "INSERT INTO Customers " & _
                    "(CustomerID, CompanyName, ContactName, " & _
                    "ContactTitle, Address, City, Region, PostalCode, " & _
                    "Country, Phone, Fax) " & _
                    "VALUES ('" & _
```

LISTING 13.7 Continued

```
                    Me.CustomerID.Value & "', '" & _
                    Me.CompanyName.Value & "', '" & _
                    Me.ContactName.Value & "', '" & _
                    Me.ContactTitle.Value & "', '" & _
                    Me.Address.Value & "', '" & _
                    Me.City.Value & "', '" & _
                    Me.Region.Value & "', '" & _
                    Me.PostalCode.Value & "', '" & _
                    Me.Country.Value & "', '" & _
                    Me.Phone.Value & "', '" & _
                    Me.Fax.Value & "')"
            Else
                strSQL = "UPDATE Customers " & _
                    "SET CompanyName = '" & Me.CompanyName.Value & "', " & _
                    "ContactName = '" & Me.ContactName.Value & "', " & _
                    "ContactTitle = '" & Me.ContactTitle.Value & "', " & _
                    "Address = '" & Me.Address.Value & "', " & _
                    "City = '" & Me.City.Value & "', " & _
                    "Region = '" & Me.Region.Value & "', " & _
                    "PostalCode = '" & Me.PostalCode.Value & "', " & _
                    "Country = '" & Me.Country.Value & "', " & _
                    "Phone = '" & Me.Phone.Value & "', " & _
                    "Fax = '" & Me.Fax.Value & "'" & _
                    " WHERE CustomerID = '" & Me.txtCustomerID & "'"
            End If

            'Execute the SQL statement
            .Execute strSQL, lngRowsAffected

            'If adding a record, set the CustomerID text box
            'to the CustomerID associated with the new customer
            If Me.AddMode Then
                Me.txtCustomerID = Me.CustomerID
            End If

            'Turn the Add Flag to False
            Me.AddMode = False
        End If

    End With

End Sub
```

Deleting Data

The code under the `Click` event of the cmdDelete command button (see Listing 13.8) first evaluates the contents of the txtCustomerID text box. If the txtCustomerID text box is blank, the code displays a message to the user. Otherwise, it uses the `Execute` method of the public `Connection` object to execute a `Delete` statement that deletes the data for the customer entered in the txtCustomerID text box.

LISTING 13.8   The Code Under the `Click` Event of the cmdDelete Command Button

```
Private Sub cmdDelete_Click()
    Dim lngRecordsAffected As Long
    With gcnn

        'Ensure that the user has entered a CustomerID
        If Not IsNull(Me.txtCustomerID) And _
            Not Me.txtCustomerID = "" Then

            'Use the Connection object to execute a SQL statement
            'that deletes the customer designated in the txtCustomerID
            'text box
            .Execute "DELETE FROM Customers WHERE CustomerID = '" & _
                Me.txtCustomerID & "'", lngRecordsAffected
            MsgBox lngRecordsAffected
        End If

        'Clear the controls on the form
        Call ClearControls(True)

        'Unlock the txtCustomerID text box
        Me.txtCustomerID.Locked = False
    End With
End Sub
```

WARNING

As with the other examples, this code contains *no* error handling. If, for example, you try to delete a customer who has orders, a referential integrity error occurs, causing the code to fail. Chapter 8 and Chapter 10 cover the process of handling errors in your stored procedures and the application code that calls them.

The Unbound Form and Pass-Through Queries

The examples in the previous section all use ADO code and SQL statements to retrieve and update table data. An alternative is to use a stored pass-through query to accomplish the same results. Pass-through queries provide an efficient means of retrieving and updating SQL Server data. Pass-through queries require two pieces of information: They require the SQL statement that you want to execute and connection information for how to connect to the SQL Server.

Using a Pass-Through Query to Populate the Form with Data

The examples that follow use the frmCustomersPassThrough form located in the Chap13Ex database. To run the examples, you must have an ODBC datasource called NorthWind that points at the SQL Server NorthWind database. As with the previous examples, because the form is unbound, it is necessary that you write the code to populate the controls on the form with data from the underlying database. Listing 13.9 shows the code under the Retrieve command button. As you can see in Listing 13.9, this code is the same code that we used when we opened a recordset to retrieve the data.

LISTING 13.9   The Code Under the Pass-Through Version of the cmdRetrieve Command Button

```
Private Sub cmdRetrieve_Click()
    Dim ctl As Control

    'Call the routine to retrieve the customer
    Call GetCustomer

    'Loop through each control on the form
    'If it is a text box, set its Locked property to False
    For Each ctl In Me.Controls
        If ctl.ControlType = acTextBox Then
            ctl.Locked = False
        End If
    Next ctl

    'Set the Add Flag to False
    Me.AddMode = False
End Sub
```

The GetCustomer routine, shown in Listing 13.10, is responsible for retrieving the data for the designated customer. It differs from the example shown in the previous section. It uses a pass-through query to accomplish its work. The code first evaluates to ensure that the user entered a CustomerID in the txtCustomerID text box. If the user entered a CustomerID, it continues. Otherwise, it displays a message to the user.

If the user entered a CustomerID, the code sets three properties of the pass-through query. It sets the SQL property to a SQL statement that retrieves data from the customer designated in the txtCustomerID text box. It sets the Connect property to an Open Database Connectivity (ODBC) connection string that connects to the SQL Server database. Finally, it sets the ReturnRecords property to True, indicating that the pass-through query returns records.

After setting properties of the Recordset object, the code opens a recordset based on the results of executing the pass-through query. If the recordset contains data, the code loops through each field in the fields collection of the resulting recordset. It sets the control with the same name as the field to the value of the field. If the stored procedure returned no data, the code displays a message to the user indicating that the customer was not found.

LISTING 13.10   The GetCustomer Routine Used by the Pass-Through Version of the Code

```
Sub GetCustomer()
Dim rst As ADODB.Recordset
    Dim qdf As DAO.QueryDef
    Dim ctl As Control
    Dim fld As Field

    'If the user has filled in the CustomerID text box,
    'open a recordset with that customer's data
    If Not IsNull(Me.txtCustomerID) And _
       Not Me.txtCustomerID = "" Then

        'Set properties of the pass-through query
        Set qdf = CurrentDb.QueryDefs("qpassGeneric")

        qdf.SQL = "SELECT CustomerID, CompanyName, ContactName, " & _
                "ContactTitle, Address, City, Region, PostalCode, " & _
                "Country, Phone, Fax " & _
                "FROM Customers " & _
                "WHERE CustomerID = '" & Me.txtCustomerID & "'"
        qdf.Connect = "ODBC;DSN=NorthWind;UID=SA;Trusted_Connection=Yes"
        qdf.ReturnsRecords = True
```

LISTING 13.10   Continued

```
        qdf.Close

        'Set properties of the Recordset object and then
        'open a recordset based on results of executing the
        'pass-through query
        Set rst = New ADODB.Recordset
        With rst
            .ActiveConnection = CurrentProject.Connection
            .CursorType = adOpenForwardOnly
            .LockType = adLockReadOnly
            .Source = "qpassGeneric"
            .Open

            'If a row is returned, loop through each field
            'in the recordset, setting the values of the
            'controls on the form to the value of the associated field
            If Not .EOF Then
                For Each fld In rst.Fields
                    Me(fld.Name).Value = fld.Value
                Next fld
            Else
                MsgBox "Customer Not Found"
            End If
        End With

    Else
        MsgBox "You must enter a CustomerID before proceeding", _
            vbCritical, "Error"

    End If
End Sub
```

Adding a Record

The code to add a record is the same as that shown when we used the previous
methodology (see Listing 13.11).

LISTING 13.11   The Pass-Through Version of the Code to Add a Record

```
Private Sub cmdAdd_Click()
    'Clear the form controls
    Call ClearControls(False)

    'See Add Flag to True
    Me.AddMode = True
End Sub
```

Listing 13.12 shows the `ClearControls` routine. Again, this is the same routine that we worked with before.

LISTING 13.12   The Pass-Through Version Also Includes the `ClearControls` Routine

```
Public Sub ClearControls(boolLocked As Boolean)
    Dim ctl As Control

    'Loop through each control on the form
    'If it is a text box, set its value to
    'a zero-length string and its locked property
    'to the value passed in as a parameter
    For Each ctl In Me.Controls
        If ctl.ControlType = acTextBox Then
            ctl.Value = ""
            ctl.Locked = boolLocked
        End If
    Next ctl

End Sub
```

Saving Data

The code under the `Click` event of the cmdSave command button (see Listing 13.13) is responsible for saving data whether the user is editing an existing record or adding a new record. The routine begins by evaluating the contents of both the CustomerID and CompanyName controls. If either is blank, the code displays a message and exits the routine.

If the `AddMode` flag is set to `True`, the code builds an `INSERT INTO` statement. Otherwise, it builds an `UPDATE` statement. If the user entered the required data, the code sets three properties of the pass-through query. It sets the SQL property to a SQL statement that inserts or updates data for the customer designated in the

CustomerID text box. It sets the Connect property to an ODBC connection string that connects to the SQL Server database. Finally, it sets the ReturnRecords property to False, indicating that the pass-through query does not return records.

LISTING 13.13 The Pass-Through Version of the Code Under the Click Event of the cmdSave Command Button

```
Private Sub cmdSave_Click()

    Dim strSQL As String
    Dim qdf As DAO.QueryDef
    Dim cnn As ADODB.Connection


    With gcnn

        'Ensure that the user filled in both the CustomerID and
        'CompanyName fields. If not, display a message and exit
        'the subroutine
        If IsNull(Me.CustomerID) Or _
            IsNull(Me.CompanyName) Then

            MsgBox "CustomerID and CompanyName" & vbNewLine & _
                "Must be Filled In"
            Exit Sub
        Else

            'Build the appropriate SQL statement based on whether
            'we are adding or editing
            If Me.AddMode Then

                strSQL = "INSERT INTO Customers " & _
                    "(CustomerID, CompanyName, ContactName, " & _
                    "ContactTitle, Address, City, Region, PostalCode, " & _
                    "Country, Phone, Fax) " & _
                    "VALUES ('" & _
                    Me.CustomerID.Value & "', '" & _
                    Me.CompanyName.Value & "', '" & _
                    Me.ContactName.Value & "', '" & _
                    Me.ContactTitle.Value & "', '" & _
                    Me.Address.Value & "', '" & _
                    Me.City.Value & "', '" & _
                    Me.Region.Value & "', '" & _
                    Me.PostalCode.Value & "', '" & _
                    Me.Country.Value & "', '" & _
```

LISTING 13.13   Continued

```
                        Me.Phone.Value & "', '" & _
                        Me.Fax.Value & "')"
                Else
                    strSQL = "UPDATE Customers " & _
                        "SET CompanyName = '" & Me.CompanyName.Value & "', " & _
                        "ContactName = '" & Me.ContactName.Value & "', " & _
                        "ContactTitle = '" & Me.ContactTitle.Value & "', " & _
                        "Address = '" & Me.Address.Value & "', " & _
                        "City = '" & Me.City.Value & "', " & _
                        "Region = '" & Me.Region.Value & "', " & _
                        "PostalCode = '" & Me.PostalCode.Value & "', " & _
                        "Country = '" & Me.Country.Value & "', " & _
                        "Phone = '" & Me.Phone.Value & "', " & _
                        "Fax = '" & Me.Fax.Value & "'" & _
                        " WHERE CustomerID = '" & Me.txtCustomerID & "'"
                End If


                'Set properties of the pass-through query
                Set qdf = CurrentDb.QueryDefs("qpassGeneric")

                qdf.SQL = strSQL
                qdf.Connect = "ODBC;DSN=NorthWind;UID=SA;Trusted_Connection=Yes"
                qdf.ReturnsRecords = False
                qdf.Close

                'Use the connection associated with the current project
                'to execute the pass-through query
                Set cnn = CurrentProject.Connection
                cnn.Execute "qpassGeneric", Options:=adCmdStoredProc

                'If in add mode, set the txtCustomerID text box to
                'the CustomerID associated with the current record
                If Me.AddMode Then
                    Me.txtCustomerID = Me.CustomerID
                End If

        End If
    End With

    Me.AddMode = False
End Sub
```

Deleting Data

The code under the `Click` event of the cmdDelete command button (see Listing 13.14) evaluates the contents of the txtCustomerID text box. If the txtCustomerID text box is blank, the code displays a message to the user and exits.

If the user entered a CustomerID, the code builds a `DELETE` statement. It sets three properties of the pass-through query. It sets the `SQL` property to a SQL statement that retrieves data from the customer designated in the txtCustomerID text box. It sets the `Connect` property to an ODBC connection string that connects to the SQL Server database. Finally, it sets the `ReturnsRecords` property to `False`, indicating that the pass-through query does not return records.

LISTING 13.14   The Pass-Through Version of the Code Under the `Click` Event of the cmdDelete Command Button

```
Private Sub cmdDelete_Click()
    Dim qdf As DAO.QueryDef
    Dim cnn As ADODB.Connection

    'Ensure that the user has entered a CustomerID
    If Not IsNull(Me.txtCustomerID) And _
        Not Me.txtCustomerID = "" Then

        'Update the pass-through query to reflect
        'the correct connection information and a SQL
        'statement deleting the customer designated in the
        'txtCustomerID text box
        Set qdf = CurrentDb.QueryDefs("qpassGeneric")

        qdf.SQL = "DELETE FROM Customers WHERE CustomerID = '" & _
            Me.txtCustomerID & "'"
        qdf.Connect = "ODBC;DSN=NorthWind;UID=SA;Trusted_Connection=Yes"
        qdf.ReturnsRecords = False
        qdf.Close

        'Use the Connection object associated with the current database
        'to execute the pass-through query
        Set cnn = CurrentProject.Connection
        cnn.Execute "qpassGeneric", Options:=adCmdStoredProc

        'Clear the controls on the form
        Call ClearControls(True)

        'Unlock the txtCustomerID text box
```

LISTING 13.14   Continued

```
        Me.txtCustomerID.Locked = False

    End If
End Sub
```

The Unbound Form and Stored Procedures

My favorite technique with unbound forms is to use stored procedures to retrieve, insert, update, and delete data. Whereas the first two techniques covered in this chapter include the SQL statements required to manipulate the data, the code in this section simply executes stored procedures that retrieve, insert, update, and delete the data. The process of using stored procedures has the following benefits:

- Stored procedures help you to separate the client application from the structure of the database.

- Stored procedures help you to simplify client coding.

- Stored procedures process at the server (reducing required bandwidth).

- Stored procedures allow you to create reusable code.

- Stored procedures allow you to perform error handling at the server.

- Stored procedures facilitate the security of data.

- Because stored procedures are precompiled, they execute more quickly.

- Stored procedures improve the stability of the application.

- Stored procedures reduce network locking.

- When you build a stored procedure, a query plan is created. This query plan contains the most efficient method of executing the stored procedure given available indexes and so on.

As you can see, the benefits of using stored procedures in an unbound application are many. There are really no downsides, except that you have to be familiar enough with SQL Server to write the T-SQL required for the data manipulation that you want to perform.

NOTE

You must create the stored procedures that the example, use *before* running the examples. Chapter 8 covers the process of creating the stored procedures.

Populating the Form with Data

Once again we must write the code to populate the controls on the form with data from the underlying database. You can find the code used for the examples in the frmCustomersStoredProc form within the Chap13Ex sample database. The code under the Retrieve command button, shown in Listing 13.15, is the same code shown for the other two models.

LISTING 13.15   The Code Under the Stored Procedure Version of the cmdRetrieve Command Button

```
Private Sub cmdRetrieve_Click()
    Dim ctl As Control

    'Call the routine to retrieve the customer
    Call GetCustomer

    'Loop through each control on the form
    'If it is a text box, set its Locked property to False
    For Each ctl In Me.Controls
        If ctl.ControlType = acTextBox Then
            ctl.Locked = False
        End If
    Next ctl

    'Set the Add Flag to False
    Me.AddMode = False
End Sub
```

The GetCustomer routine, shown in Listing 13.16, is responsible for retrieving the data for the designated customer. It uses a Command object and a Recordset object to accomplish its work. It first evaluates to ensure that the user entered a CustomerID in the txtCustomerID text box. If the user entered a CustomerID, it proceeds. Otherwise, it displays a message to the user and exits.

After validating the CustomerID, the code sets three properties of the Command object. It sets the CommandText property to the name of the stored procedure that it will execute. It sets the CommandType property to acCmdStoredProc, indicating that that CommandText property contains the name of a stored procedure. It sets the ActiveConnection property to a connection string stored in a public constant called gcnn.

After setting properties of the Command object, the code appends a parameter named @CustomerID to the Command object. It populates the parameter with the contents of the txtCustomerID text box. It then uses the Execute method of the Command object to execute the stored procedure named in the CommandText property. It places the resulting recordset in the Recordset object referred to as rst.

Finally, if the stored procedure returns a row, the code loops through each field in the fields collection of the resulting recordset. It sets the control with the same name as the field to the value of the field. If the stored procedure returned no data, the code displays a message to the user indicating that the customer was not found.

LISTING 13.16   The Stored Procedure Version of the GetCustomer Routine

```
Sub GetCustomer()
    Dim cmd As ADODB.Command
    Dim rst As ADODB.Recordset
    Dim ctl As Control
    Dim fld As Field


    'If the user entered a CustomerID, proceed as planned.
    'Otherwise, display a message and don't continue
    If Not IsNull(Me.txtCustomerID) And _
        Not Me.txtCustomerID = "" Then

        'Instantiate a Command object and set its properties
        Set cmd = New ADODB.Command
        With cmd
            .CommandText = "procCustomerGet "
            .CommandType = adCmdStoredProc
            .ActiveConnection = gcnn

                'Append a parameter containing the value entered
                'in the txtCustomerID text box
                .Parameters.Append .CreateParameter( _
                    "@CustomerID", adChar, adParamInput, 5, _
                    Me.txtCustomerID.Value)

                'Use the Execute method of the Command object to
                'return a result into the rst object variable
                Set rst = .Execute

                'If a row is returned, loop through the row,
                'populating the controls on the form with the data returned
                If Not rst.EOF Then
```

LISTING 13.16 Continued

```
                For Each fld In rst.Fields
                    Me(fld.Name).Value = fld.Value
                Next fld
            Else
                'If no data was returned, display a message to the user
                MsgBox "Customer Not Found"
            End If
        End With
    Else
        MsgBox "You Must Enter a Customer Before Proceeding", _
            vbCritical, "Error"
    End If
End Sub
```

The procCustomerGet stored procedure, shown in Listing 13.17, receives the
@CustomerID input parameter. It selects the requested fields from the Customers table
where the CustomerID field matches the value received as an input parameter.

LISTING 13.17 The procCustomerGet Stored Procedure

```
CREATE PROCEDURE dbo.procCustomerGet(@CustomerID nchar(5))
AS SELECT    CustomerID, CompanyName, ContactName, ContactTitle,
Address, City, Region, PostalCode, Country, Phone, Fax
FROM         dbo.Customers
WHERE        (CustomerID = @CustomerID)
```

Adding a Record

The code to add a record is the same code shown in the previous examples. It
appears in Listing 13.18.

LISTING 13.18 The Stored Procedure Version of the Code to Add a Record

```
Private Sub cmdAdd_Click()
    'Clear the form controls
    Call ClearControls(False)

    'See Add Flag to True
    Me.AddMode = True
End Sub
```

The `ClearControls` routine, shown in Listing 13.19, is once again the same routine used with the previous techniques.

LISTING 13.19 The Stored Procedure Version of the `ClearControls` Routine

```
Public Sub ClearControls(boolLocked As Boolean)
    Dim ctl As Control

    'Loop through each control on the form
    'If it is a text box, set its value to
    'a zero-length string and its locked property
    'to the value passed in as a parameter
    For Each ctl In Me.Controls
        If ctl.ControlType = acTextBox Then
            ctl.Value = ""
            ctl.Locked = boolLocked
        End If
    Next ctl

End Sub
```

Saving Data

The code under the `Click` event of the cmdSave command button (see Listing 13.20) is responsible for saving data whether the user is editing an existing record or adding a new record. It begins by declaring and instantiating a `Command` object. It then sets the `ActiveConnection` property of the `Command` object to the value stored in the public constant gcnn. It sets the `CommandType` property of the `Command` object to `acCmdStoredProc`, indicating that the value in the `CommandText` property is the name of a stored procedure.

The routine evaluates the contents of both the CustomerID and CompanyName controls. If either is blank, the code displays a message and exits the routine. Otherwise, the code appends several input parameters, one for each control on the form. Each input parameter corresponds with a field in the database. The code sets the value of the parameter to the value contained in the appropriate text box.

Finally, if the AddMode flag is set to `True`, the code sets the `CommandText` property to procCustomerAdd. If the AddMode flag is set to `False`, the code sets the `CommandText` property to procCustomerEdit. The code uses the `Execute` method of the `Command` object to execute the appropriate stored procedure and resets the AddMode flag to `False`.

LISTING 13.20   The Code Under the Stored Procedure Version of the `Click` Event of
the cmdSave Command Button

```
Private Sub cmdSave_Click()

    Dim cmd As ADODB.Command

    'Ensure that the user filled in both the CustomerID and
    'CompanyName fields. If not, display a message and exit
    'the subroutine
    If IsNull(Me.CustomerID) Or _
        IsNull(Me.CompanyName) Then

        MsgBox "CustomerID and CompanyName" & vbNewLine & _
            "Must be Filled In"
        Exit Sub

    Else

        'Instantiate a command object and set its properties
        Set cmd = New ADODB.Command
        With cmd
            .ActiveConnection = gcnn
            .CommandType = adCmdStoredProc

                'Append one parameter for each parameter in the
                'add and edit stored procedures
                .Parameters.Append .CreateParameter( _
                    "@CustomerID", adChar, adParamInput, 5, _
                    Me.CustomerID.Value)
                .Parameters.Append .CreateParameter( _
                    "@CompanyName", adVarChar, adParamInput, 40, _
                    Me.CompanyName.Value)
                .Parameters.Append .CreateParameter( _
                    "@ContactName", adVarChar, adParamInput, 30, _
                    Me.ContactName.Value)
                .Parameters.Append .CreateParameter( _
                    "@ContactTitle", adVarChar, adParamInput, 30, _
                    Me.ContactTitle.Value)
                .Parameters.Append .CreateParameter( _
                    "@Address", adVarChar, adParamInput, 60, _
                    Me.Address.Value)
                .Parameters.Append .CreateParameter( _
                    "@City", adVarChar, adParamInput, 15, _
```

LISTING 13.20 Continued

```
                    Me.City.Value)
                .Parameters.Append .CreateParameter( _
                    "@Region", adVarChar, adParamInput, 15, _
                    Me.Region.Value)
                .Parameters.Append .CreateParameter( _
                    "@PostalCode", adVarChar, adParamInput, 10, _
                    Me.PostalCode.Value)
                .Parameters.Append .CreateParameter( _
                    "@Country", adVarChar, adParamInput, 15, _
                    Me.Country.Value)
                .Parameters.Append .CreateParameter( _
                    "@Phone", adVarChar, adParamInput, 24, _
                    Me.Phone.Value)
                .Parameters.Append .CreateParameter( _
                    "@Fax", adVarChar, adParamInput, 24, _
                    Me.Fax.Value)
                .Parameters.Append .CreateParameter( _
                    "@ResultMessage", adVarChar, adParamOutput, 20)

            'Set the name of the stored procedure to execute
            'as appropriate
            If Me.AddMode Then
                .CommandText = "procCustomerInsert "
            Else
                .CommandText = "procCustomerUpdate "
            End If

            'Use the Execute method of the Command object to
            'execute the stored procedure
            .Execute

            'Display the number of rows affected in a message box
            MsgBox .Parameters("@ResultMessage").Value

            'Turn the Add flag off
            Me.AddMode = False


        End With

    End If
End Sub
```

The procCustomerInsert stored procedure (see Listing 13.21) receives several input parameters, one corresponding to each control on the data entry form. It has an output parameter that it populates with a status message.

The routine inserts into the designated fields of the Customers table the values that come in as input parameters. It populates the @ResultMessage output parameter with a string containing the number of rows affected by the insert.

LISTING 13.21   The procCustomerInsert Stored Procedure

```
CREATE PROCEDURE procCustomerInsert
@CustomerID char(5),
@CompanyName nvarchar(40),
@ContactName nvarchar(30) = Null,
@ContactTitle nvarchar(30) = Null,
@Address nvarchar(60) = Null,
@City nvarchar(15) = Null,
@Region nvarchar(15) = Null,
@PostalCode nvarchar(10) = Null,
@Country varchar(15) = Null,
@Phone varchar(24) = Null,
@Fax varchar(24) = Null,
@ResultMessage varchar(20) = Null Output
AS
INSERT INTO Customers
(CustomerID, CompanyName, ContactName, ContactTitle,
Address, City, Region, PostalCode, Country, Phone, Fax)
VALUES
(@CustomerID, @CompanyName, @ContactName, @ContactTitle,
@Address, @City, @Region, @PostalCode, @Country, @Phone, @Fax)
SELECT @ResultMessage = Convert(varchar(20),  @@RowCount) + ' Records Affected'
```

The procCustomerUpdate stored procedure (see Listing 13.22) receives several input parameters, one corresponding to each control on the data entry form. It has an output parameter that it populates with a status message.

The routine updates the Customers table, setting the values for the designated fields to the values that come in as input parameters for the customer whose CustomerID matches the value in the @CustomerID input parameter. The routine populates the @ResultMessage output parameter with a string containing the number of rows affected by the update.

LISTING 13.22   The Stored Procedure Version of the procCustomerUpdate Stored Procedure

```
CREATE PROCEDURE procCustomerUpdate
@CustomerID char(5),
@CompanyName nvarchar(40),
@ContactName nvarchar(30) = Null,
@ContactTitle nvarchar(30) = Null,
@Address nvarchar(60) = Null,
@City nvarchar(15) = Null,
@Region nvarchar(15) = Null,
@PostalCode nvarchar(10) = Null,
@Country varchar(15) = Null,
@Phone varchar(24) = Null,
@Fax varchar(24) = Null,
@ResultMessage varchar(20) = Null Output
AS
Update Customers
Set CompanyName = @CompanyName,
    ContactName = @ContactName,
    ContactTitle = @ContactTitle,
    Address = @Address,
    City =@City,
    Region = @Region,
    PostalCode = @PostalCode,
    Country = @Country,
    Phone = @Phone,
    Fax = @Fax
    WHERE CustomerID = @CustomerID
SELECT @ResultMessage =
    Convert(varchar(20),  @@RowCount) +
    ' Records Affected'
```

Deleting Data

The code under the Click event of the cmdDelete command button (see Listing 13.23) first declares and instantiates a Command object. It sets the CommandText property of the Command object to procCustomerDelete and sets the CommandType property of the Command object to adCmdStoredProc, indicating that CommandText contains a stored procedure name. The code sets the ActiveConnection property of the Command object to the connection string stored in the gcnn public constant.

Next, the code evaluates the contents of the txtCustomerID text box. If the txtCustomerID text box is blank, the code displays a message to the user. Otherwise, it appends parameters to the Command object.

LISTING 13.23   The Stored Procedure Version of the Code Under the `Click` Event of the cmdDelete Command Button

```
Private Sub cmdDelete_Click()
    Dim cmd As ADODB.Command

    'If the txtCustomerID text box is filled in, proceed
    If Not IsNull(Me.txtCustomerID) And _
        Not Me.txtCustomerID = "" Then

        'Instantiate a Command object and set its properties
        Set cmd = New ADODB.Command
        With cmd
            .CommandText = "procCustomerDelete "
            .CommandType = adCmdStoredProc
            .ActiveConnection = gcnn

                'Append parameters for the CustomerID input parameter
                'and the Result Message output parameter
                .Parameters.Append .CreateParameter( _
                    "@CustomerID", adChar, adParamInput, 5, _
                    Me.txtCustomerID.Value)
                .Parameters.Append .CreateParameter( _
                    "@ResultMessage", adVarChar, adParamOutput, 20)

                'Use the Execute method of the Command object to
                'execute the stored procedure
                .Execute

                'Display the result message in a message box
                MsgBox .Parameters("@ResultMessage").Value

                'Clear the controls on the form
                Call ClearControls(True)

                'Unlock the txtCustomerID text box
                Me.txtCustomerID.Locked = False

        End With

    End If

End Sub
```

The procCustomerDelete stored procedure appears in Listing 13.24. It deletes a row from the Customers table where the CustomerID equals the CustomerID received as a parameter.

LISTING 13.24   The procCustomerDelete Stored Procedure

```
CREATE PROCEDURE procCustomerDelete
@CustomerID char (5),
@ResultMessage varchar(20) = Null Output
AS
DELETE FROM Customers
WHERE CustomerID = @CustomerID
SELECT @ResultMessage =
    Convert(varchar(20),   @@RowCount) +
    ' Records Affected'
```

Summary

At times, you might want to disable the default record movement and add, edit, or delete functionality from a form and code all the functionality yourself. You might want to perform these actions if you are going against client/server data and want to execute additional control over the data-entry environment. You also might want to use these techniques when you are developing applications for both the Access and Visual Basic environments and are striving for maximum code compatibility. Regardless of your reasons for using the aforementioned techniques, it is a good idea to know how to assign a Recordset object to a form and then use the form's underlying recordset to display and modify data.

14

Building N-Tier Applications

Why This Chapter Is Important

Chapter 13, "Building Unbound Applications," covered the process of building unbound forms. Even an unbound form does not afford you with the maximum amount of scalability. Furthermore, you cannot share with multiple applications the business logic you place in an Access application. For these reasons, you might opt to build an *n*-tier application. This chapter shows you how to build both logical and physical three-tier applications. It also shows you how to turn a logical three-tier application into a physical three-tier application.

The Basics of *N*-Tier Development

With an *n*-tier application, you place only the code that is necessary to support the graphical user interface (GUI) within the Access application. You place all of the code that interacts with the database in middle-tier business objects, developed in an environment such as Microsoft Visual Basic and compiled as a Dynamic Link Library (.dll object). The advantages of this model are:

- Improved scalability

- Reusability

- Shortened testing cycle

- Improved maintainability

- Greater flexibility

An *n*-tier architecture offers improved scalability because you can place the DLL on multiple servers and have various groups of users access each DLL. In fact, you can place the DLL under the control of Microsoft Transaction Server (MTS) to further expand its scalability. The DLL can be used not only by your Microsoft Access application, but other Access applications, Visual Basic applications, Web applications, COM+ applications, and other applications can share it also. After you test the DLL fully with one application, you do not have to test it as extensively with other applications. Furthermore, when a change is necessary, you can make that change in one place, rather than having to make it in multiple applications. Finally, if you decide to change, for example, your data access technology, you can make that change in one place (the DLL). The change is transparent to all of the various front ends.

Access's Role in the *N*-Tier Model

Access used alone is a one-tier architecture. This means that if you build your forms and reports in Microsoft Access, and you store your data in the MDB file format as well, you are using a one-tier architecture. This is because one application handles both the presentation and the processing of data.

When you introduce SQL Server into the picture, you begin to work with a two-tier model. In the two-tier model, Access is responsible for presenting the data, and SQL Server is responsible for processing the data. This model generally adds a lot more efficiencies, particularly if you develop your application properly. This means that if you take advantage of SQL Server stored procedures, views, functions, and triggers, and you bring as little data over the network wire as possible, you can build a robust client/server application with linked tables.

Many people believe that an application cannot be scalable if you develop it with linked tables and bound forms. I have personal experience with numerous large corporate clients that can assure you that this is not the case. It is quite possible to build a powerful, scalable Access application using a calculated *combination* of linked tables, bound forms, SQL Server stored procedures, SQL Server views, SQL Server functions, and SQL Server triggers. The key is that you must use bound forms only where you can ensure that you are bringing limited data over the network wire. You use unbound forms, stored procedures, views, functions, and triggers where you need to limit connections, limit locking times, or ensure that you process large volumes of data on the server (for example, in a payment-posting process).

You might be wondering when the three-tier architecture comes into the picture. These days, I am developing more and more applications in which multiple developers must share business logic with Access applications, VB applications, Web front ends, and so on. In these cases, it does not make sense to write that business logic over and over again. Although you can copy a module from an Access module to a

VB module and then to an ASP file, you will experience the nightmare of maintaining all of these modules when the business logic changes. This is where the three-tier architecture comes into play. You use Access to do what it does best: display the data. You build business components (COM components) that your Access, Visual Basic, ASP, and other applications can share. The business components are responsible for communicating with your back end, such as Microsoft SQL Server.

Finally, what about *n*-tier? Well, components can call other components, creating in essence a layering of components. People often refer to this as the *n*-tier model.

Access and a Logical Three-Tier Model

Sometimes you might suspect that you will need to move to a true three-tier model in the future, but you are not ready to do so yet. Other times, you might want to take advantage of Access's rapid application development environment to perfect your three-tier architecture. In either case, you can build a model that is logically three-tier, while retaining all of the application components within Microsoft Access. The process involves moving all data access logic into class modules and ensuring that the application forms contain no data access logic. The sections that follow illustrate this process.

Populating the Form with Data

The example shown in this chapter is the same example shown in Chapter 13. Figure 14.1 shows the data entry form. The difference with the example shown in this chapter is that the data access code is no longer located in the Access user interface. Instead, I have moved it to a class module within the Access database.

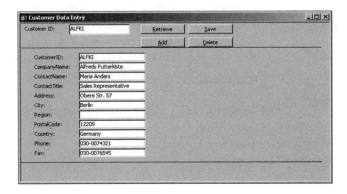

FIGURE 14.1   An unbound data entry form that utilizes the three-tier model.

The code under the `cmdRetrieve` command button in the `frmCustomers` form
(located in Listing 14.1) first calls the `GetCustomer` routine. The `GetCustomer` routine
is responsible for retrieving the data for the designated customer and populating the
form with that customer's data. After the `GetCustomer` routine executes, the code
loops through each control on the form. If the control is a text box, its locked property is set to `False`. Finally, the code sets the `AddMode` flag to `False`.

LISTING 14.1   The Code Under the `cmdRetrieve` Command Button

```
Private Sub cmdRetrieve_Click()
    Dim ctl As Control

    'Call the GetCustomer routine
    Call GetCustomer

    'Loop through all controls,
    'unlocking all of the text boxes
    For Each ctl In Me.Controls
        If ctl.ControlType = acTextBox Then
            ctl.Locked = False
        End If
    Next ctl

    Me.AddMode = False
End Sub
```

The `GetCustomer` routine, also in `frmCustomers`, appears in Listing 14.2. After ensuring that the user filled in the txtCustomerID text box, it calls the `Retrieve` method
of the `Customer` object, passing it the txtCustomerID text box value. The `Retrieve`
method returns a recordset with the data for the designated customer. The
`GetCustomer` routine loops through the field's collection of the returned recordset,
populating the form controls with the data from the recordset.

LISTING 14.2   The `GetCustomer` Routine

```
Sub GetCustomer()
    Dim rst As ADODB.Recordset
    Dim objCustomer As Customer
    Dim ctl As Control
    Dim fld As Field

    If Not IsNull(Me.txtCustomerID) And _
        Not Me.txtCustomerID = "" Then

        Set objCustomer = New Customer
```

LISTING 14.2   Continued

```
        Set rst = objCustomer.Retrieve(Me.txtCustomerID.Value)

        'Loop through each field in the resulting recordset.
        'Set the control with the same name as the field
        'equal to the value in the field
        If Not rst.EOF Then
            For Each fld In rst.Fields
                Me(fld.Name).Value = fld.Value
            Next fld
        Else
            MsgBox "Customer Not Found"
        End If
    End If
End Sub
```

The Retrieve method is located in the class called Customer. It appears in Listing 14.3. The Retrieve method receives a string with the CustomerID as an input parameter, and it returns a recordset. The method then uses a Command object to execute the stored procedure called procCustomerGet.

LISTING 14.3   The Retrieve Method of the Customer Object

```
Public Function Retrieve(strCustomerID As String) As Recordset

    Dim cmd As ADODB.Command
    Dim rst As ADODB.Recordset
    Set cmd = New ADODB.Command

    'Retrieve the customer entered in the text box
    With cmd
        .CommandText = "procCustomerGet "
        .CommandType = adCmdStoredProc
        .ActiveConnection = GCONN
        .Parameters.Append .CreateParameter( _
                "@CustomerID", adChar, adParamInput, 5, _
                strCustomerID)
        Set rst = .Execute
    End With

    Set Retrieve = rst
End Function
```

Notice the constant GCONN, which is used for the ActiveConnection property. GCONN is located in the basVariable module. It looks like this:

```
Public Const GCONN = "Provider=SQLOLEDB.1;" & _
            "Data Source=(local); Initial Catalog=NorthWind;" & _
            "Integrated Security = SSPI"
```

The procCustomerGet procedure is a parameterized stored procedure that receives the CustomerID as an input parameter. It returns a recordset that the code places in the rst variable. The code returns a reference to the rst variable from the method to the calling procedure. Listing 14.4 shows the procCustomerGet stored procedure.

LISTING 14.4　The procCustomerGet Stored Procedure

```
CREATE PROCEDURE dbo.procCustomerGet(@CustomerID nchar(5))
AS SELECT    CustomerID, CompanyName, ContactName, ContactTitle,
Address, City, Region, PostalCode, Country, Phone, Fax
FROM         dbo.Customers
WHERE        (CustomerID = @CustomerID)
```

NOTE

If you followed along with Chapter 13, you already created this stored procedure and it's not necessary for you to create it again.

Adding a Record

The code under the cmdAdd command button is quite simple. It calls the ClearControls subroutine to clear all of the controls on the form, and then sets the AddMode property to True (see Listing 14.5).

LISTING 14.5　The Code to Add a Record

```
Private Sub cmdAdd_Click()

    'Clear and unlock all text boxes
    Call ClearControls(False)

    'Set Add flag to true
    Me.AddMode = True
End Sub
```

The `ClearControls` routine (see Listing 14.6) loops through each control in the controls collection of the form, setting its `Value` property to a zero-length string and its `Locked` property equal to the value that is received as a parameter (in this case, `False`).

LISTING 14.6   The `ClearControls` Routine

```
Public Sub ClearControls(boolLocked As Boolean)
    Dim ctl As Control

    'Loop through all controls on the form,
    'setting their value and locking or unlocking them
    'as appropriate
    For Each ctl In Me.Controls
        If ctl.ControlType = acTextBox Then
            ctl.Value = ""
            ctl.Locked = boolLocked
        End If
    Next ctl

End Sub
```

Saving Data

The code under the `cmdSave` command button (see Listing 14.7) is responsible for calling the routine that saves an added or edited record to the underlying database. The code first evaluates the `CustomerID` and `CompanyName` controls to ensure that they contain values. It then calls the `Save` method of the `Customer` object, passing all of the form values to the method. The code also passes a flag to the `Save` method, indicating whether the user is in Add mode or Edit mode. The `Save` method saves the data to disk and returns a string with status information.

LISTING 14.7   The Code Under the `Click` Event of the `cmdSave` Command Button

```
Private Sub cmdSave_Click()

    Dim objCustomer As Customer
    Dim strResultMessage As String

    'If the CustomerID or CompanyName are null,
    'display a message and exit the subroutine
    If IsNull(Me.CustomerID) Or _
        IsNull(Me.CompanyName) Then

        MsgBox "CustomerID and CompanyName" & vbNewLine & _
```

LISTING 14.7   Continued

```
                "Must be Filled In"
        Exit Sub

    'If the CustomerID and CompanyName are filled in,
    'pass the text box values to the Save method of the
    'Customer object
    Else

        Set objCustomer = New Customer
        strResultMessage = objCustomer.Save( _
                Me.CustomerID.Value, _
                Me.CompanyName.Value, _
                Me.ContactName.Value, _
                Me.ContactTitle.Value, _
                Me.Address.Value, _
                Me.City.Value, _
                Me.Region.Value, _
                Me.PostalCode.Value, _
                Me.Country.Value, _
                Me.Phone.Value, _
                Me.Fax.Value, _
                Me.AddMode)
    End If

    MsgBox strResultMessage

    'Set flag indicating that we are not adding
    Me.AddMode = False
End Sub
```

WARNING

As with the other examples, this code contains *no* error handling. This means that if, for example, you try to add a customer who already exists, a primary key violation error occurs, causing the code to fail. Chapters 8, "Designing SQL Server Stored Procedures, User-Defined Functions, and Triggers," and 10, "ADO and SQL Server," cover the process of handling errors in your stored procedures and the application code that calls them.

The Save method of the Customer class appends parameters to the Command object. It executes either the procCustomerAdd or procCustomerEdit stored procedure, depending on the value of the AddMode flag. Finally, it returns the value of the @ResultMessage parameter to its caller. Listing 14.8 shows the Save method of the Customer object.

LISTING 14.8   The Save Method of the Customer Object

```
Public Function Save(strCustomerID As String, _
    strCompanyName As String, _
    strContactName As String, _
    strContactTitle, _
    strAddress As String, _
    strCity As String, _
    strRegion As String, _
    strPostalCode As String, _
    strCountry As String, _
    strPhone As String, _
    strFax As String, _
    boolAddMode As Boolean) _
    As String

    Dim cmd As ADODB.Command
    Dim intRowsAffected As Integer

    Set cmd = New ADODB.Command

    With cmd
        .ActiveConnection = GCONN
        .CommandType = adCmdStoredProc

        'Create a parameter for each field.  Set the parameter
        'value equal to the appropriate function parameter
        .Parameters.Append .CreateParameter( _
            "@CustomerID", adChar, adParamInput, 5, _
            strCustomerID)
        .Parameters.Append .CreateParameter( _
            "@CompanyName", adVarChar, adParamInput, 40, _
            strCompanyName)
        .Parameters.Append .CreateParameter( _
            "@ContactName", adVarChar, adParamInput, 30, _
            strContactName)
        .Parameters.Append .CreateParameter( _
            "@ContactTitle", adVarChar, adParamInput, 30, _
            strContactTitle)
```

LISTING 14.8 Continued

```
            .Parameters.Append .CreateParameter( _
                "@Address", adVarChar, adParamInput, 60, _
                strAddress)
            .Parameters.Append .CreateParameter( _
                "@City", adVarChar, adParamInput, 15, _
                strCity)
            .Parameters.Append .CreateParameter( _
                "@Region", adVarChar, adParamInput, 15, _
                strRegion)
            .Parameters.Append .CreateParameter( _
                "@PostalCode", adVarChar, adParamInput, 10, _
                strPostalCode)
            .Parameters.Append .CreateParameter( _
                "@Country", adVarChar, adParamInput, 15, _
                strCountry)
            .Parameters.Append .CreateParameter( _
                "@Phone", adVarChar, adParamInput, 24, _
                strPhone)
            .Parameters.Append .CreateParameter( _
                "@Fax", adVarChar, adParamInput, 24, _
                strFax)

            'Call the appropriate stored procedure depending on
            'if we are adding or editing
            If boolAddMode Then
                .CommandText = "procCustomerAdd "
            Else
                .CommandText = "procCustomerEdit "
            End If

            .Execute

            Save = .Parameters("@ResultMessage").Value
        End With

End Function
```

The `procCustomerInsert` stored procedure (see Listing 14.9) receives several input parameters—one corresponding to each control on the data entry form. It has an output parameter that it populates with a status message.

LISTING 14.9   The procCustomerInsert Stored Procedure

```
CREATE PROCEDURE procCustomerInsert
@CustomerID char(5),
@CompanyName nvarchar(40),
@ContactName nvarchar(30) = Null,
@ContactTitle nvarchar(30) = Null,
@Address nvarchar(60) = Null,
@City nvarchar(15) = Null,
@Region nvarchar(15) = Null,
@PostalCode nvarchar(10) = Null,
@Country varchar(15) = Null,
@Phone varchar(24) = Null,
@Fax varchar(24) = Null,
@ResultMessage varchar(20) = Null Output
AS
INSERT INTO Customers
    (CustomerID, CompanyName, ContactName, ContactTitle,
    Address, City, Region, PostalCode, Country, Phone, Fax)
VALUES
    (@CustomerID, @CompanyName, @ContactName, @ContactTitle,
    @Address, @City, @Region, @PostalCode, @Country, @Phone, @Fax)
SELECT @ResultMessage = Convert(varchar(20),  @@RowCount) + ' Records Affected'
```

The routine inserts the values that come in as input parameters into the designated fields of the Customers table. It populates the @ResultMessage output parameter with a string that contains the number of rows affected by the insert.

The procCustomerUpdate stored procedure (see Listing 14.10) receives several input parameters, one corresponding to each control on the data entry form. It has an output parameter that it populates with a status message.

LISTING 14.10   The procCustomerUpdate Stored Procedure

```
CREATE PROCEDURE procCustomerUpdate
@CustomerID char(5),
@CompanyName nvarchar(40),
@ContactName nvarchar(30) = Null,
@ContactTitle nvarchar(30) = Null,
@Address nvarchar(60) = Null,
@City nvarchar(15) = Null,
@Region nvarchar(15) = Null,
@PostalCode nvarchar(10) = Null,
```

LISTING 14.10   Continued

```
@Country varchar(15) = Null,
@Phone varchar(24) = Null,
@Fax varchar(24) = Null,
@ResultMessage varchar(20) = Null Output
AS
Update Customers
Set CompanyName = @CompanyName,
       ContactName = @ContactName,
       ContactTitle = @ContactTitle,
       Address = @Address,
       City =@City,
       Region = @Region,
       PostalCode = @PostalCode,
       Country = @Country,
       Phone = @Phone,
       Fax = @Fax
 WHERE CustomerID = @CustomerID
SELECT @ResultMessage =
       Convert(varchar(20),  @@RowCount) +
       ' Records Affected'
```

The routine updates the Customers table, setting the values for the designated fields to the values that come in as input parameters for the customer whose `CustomerID` matches the value in the `@CustomerID` input parameter. The routine populates the `@ResultMessage` output parameter with a string that contains the number of rows affected by the update.

Deleting Data

The code that is under the `cmdDelete` command button instantiates a `Customer` object. The code then calls the `Delete` method of the `Customer` object, passing the value in the txtCustomerID text box. The `Delete` method of the `Customer` object is responsible for deleting the designated customer. The code then calls the `ClearControls` routine, clearing the controls on the form. Finally, the code sets the `Locked` property of the `txtCustomerID` control to `False`. Listing 14.11 shows the code under the `cmdDelete` command button.

LISTING 14.11   The Code Under the `cmdDelete_Click` Event

```
Private Sub cmdDelete_Click()
    Dim objCustomer As Customer
```

LISTING 14.11   Continued

```
    Dim strReturnValue As String

    Set objCustomer = New Customer

    strReturnValue = objCustomer.Delete(Me.txtCustomerID)
    MsgBox strReturnValue

    Call ClearControls(True)
    Me.txtCustomerID.Locked = False
End Sub
```

The Delete method, found in the Customer class, receives a string with the CustomerID of the designated customer. The Delete method then instantiates a Command object. The code uses the Command object to execute the procCustomerDelete stored procedure. The procCustomerDelete stored procedure receives the CustomerID as an input parameter and then outputs a string with a status message. Listing 14.12 shows the code for the Delete method.

LISTING 14.12   The Delete Method of the Customer Object

```
Public Function Delete(strCustomerID As String) As String
    Dim cmd As ADODB.Command
    Set cmd = New ADODB.Command
    Dim intRowsAffected As Integer

    'Execute the procCustomerDelete stored procedure,
    'Deleting the customer designated as the parameter
    With cmd
        .CommandText = "procCustomerDelete "
        .CommandType = adCmdStoredProc
        .ActiveConnection = GCONN
        .Parameters.Append .CreateParameter( _
            "@CustomerID", adChar, adParamInput, 5, _
            strCustomerID)
        .Parameters.Append .CreateParameter( _
            "@ResultMessage", adChar, adParamOutput, 20)
        .Execute


        Delete = .Parameters("@ResultMessage").Value
    End With
End Function
```

Building the Middle-Tier Component

To move an application to the *n*-tier model, you must remove all data access code from the user interface and place it in a DLL. Here are the steps involved:

1. Launch Visual Basic.

2. Indicate that you want to create an ActiveX DLL (see Figure 14.2) and click Open. The Visual Basic environment appears as in Figure 14.3.

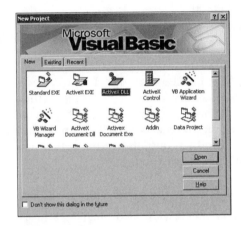

FIGURE 14.2   Launch Visual Basic and create an ActiveX DLL project.

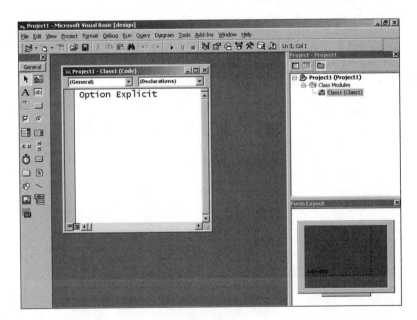

FIGURE 14.3   The Visual Basic environment after creating an ActiveX DLL project.

3. Return to the Access VBE and right-click the Customer class.

4. Select Export File. The Export File dialog box appears (see Figure 14.4).

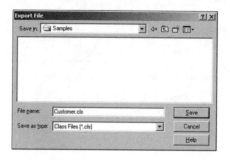

FIGURE 14.4 The Export File dialog box allows you to export an Access module or class module to a text file.

5. Enter Customer.cls as the name of the file you are exporting and click Save. Access exports the class to a text file.

6. Perform the same steps to export the basVariables module to basVariables.bas.

7. Return to Visual Basic.

8. Select the project in the Project Explorer and click Properties. The Properties window appears (see Figure 14.5).

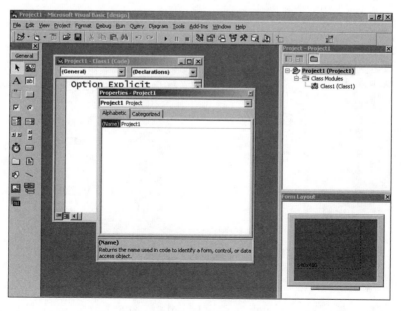

FIGURE 14.5 Use the Properties window to change project properties.

9. Click the Name property and rename the project to Customers. The project should appear as in Figure 14.6.

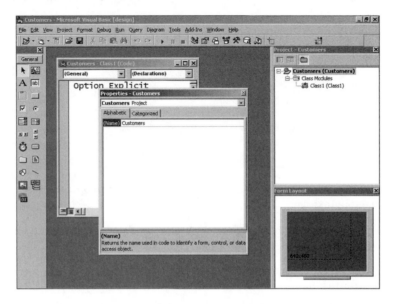

FIGURE 14.6   Change the name of the project to Customers.

10. Right-click Class1 and select Remove Class1 (see Figure 14.7). Click No when asked if you want to save the file.

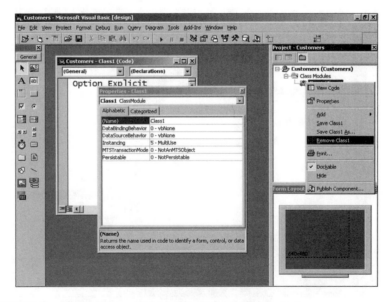

FIGURE 14.7   Right-click to remove Class1 from the project.

11. Right-click the project and select Add, Class Module (see Figure 14.8). The Add Class Module dialog box appears.

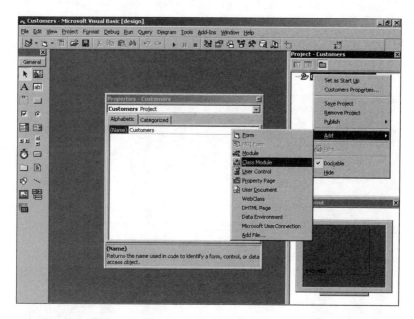

FIGURE 14.8 Right-click the project and select Add, Class Module to add a new class module to the project.

12. Click the Existing tab and locate the class module that you exported in step 5 (see Figure 14.9).

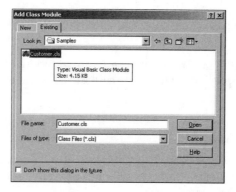

FIGURE 14.9 Click the Existing tab and locate the class module that you exported in step 5.

TIP

An alternative to steps 11 and 12 is to use the Ctrl+D keystroke combination. Ctrl+D invokes the Add File dialog box, allowing you to easily add a new object to the project.

13. Click Open. The `Customer` class module should now appear as part of the project (see Figure 14.10).

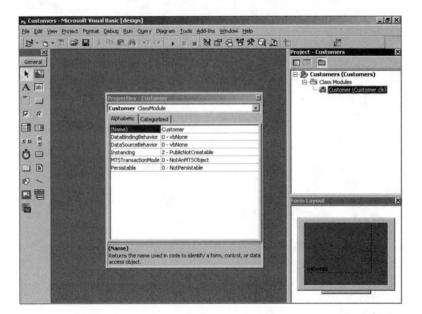

FIGURE 14.10   After adding the class module, it appears as part of the project.

14. Right-click the project and select Add, Module. The Add Module dialog box appears.

15. Click the Existing tab and locate the standard module (`basVariables`) that you exported in step 6. Click Open. Visual Basic adds the `basVariables` module to the project.

16. Select the `Customer` class and change the `Instancing` property of the class to MultiUse (see Figure 14.11).

17. Unlike Access, Visual Basic does not automatically create a reference to the ADO object library. Use Project, References to add a reference to the Microsoft ActiveX Data Objects type library.

18. Select File, Make Customers.dll. The Make Project dialog box appears.

19. Click OK to make the DLL. This process creates the DLL and registers it on your machine.

20. Close Visual Basic and save the project and any modules if prompted.

FIGURE 14.11 Change the `Instancing` property of the class to MultiUse.

You are now ready to modify the Access application so that it uses the DLL rather than the Customers class module that is part of the database.

Access and a Physical Three-Tier Model

To move an application to an *n*-tier model, all data access code must be removed from the user interface and placed in the .dll. You must reference the business object from the Access application. If you built your application with a logical three-tier model, your application will require only minor modifications. Otherwise, you must modify the front end to instantiate the business object and execute its methods. As with the logical three-tier model, you must pass necessary information, such as the values of text boxes, to the methods on the back end.

Preparing the Access Database for a Physical Three-Tier Model

You must take two steps to prepare the Access database to utilize the DLL that you built. First, you must remove the `Customer` class and the `basVariables` module from the database. Then you must reference the Customers DLL that you just created. Here are the specific steps involved:

1. Return to Microsoft Access and open the database containing the `Customers` class and the `basVariables` module.

2. Delete both objects from the project.

3. Go to the Access VBE.

4. Use Tools, References to open the References dialog box.

5. Click to create a reference to the Customers DLL that you just built (see Figure 14.12).

6. Click OK to close the dialog box.

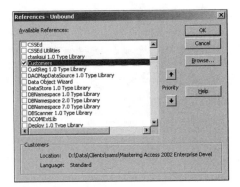

FIGURE 14.12   In the References dialog box, click to create a reference to the Customers DLL that you just built.

Populating the Form with Data

The remainder of the example shown in this part of the chapter is the same example shown in the logical three-tier section of the chapter. The difference is that the data access code is no longer located in the Access user interface. Instead, it is included in the `Customers.dll` object.

The code under the `cmdRetrieve` command button is the same code shown in the logical three-tier example. It appears in Listing 14.13.

LISTING 14.13   The Code Under the `cmdRetrieve_Click` Event in the Physical Three-Tier Model

```
Private Sub cmdRetrieve_Click()
    Dim ctl As Control

    'Call the GetCustomer routine
    Call GetCustomer

    'Loop through all controls,
    'unlocking all of the text boxes
    For Each ctl In Me.Controls
        If ctl.ControlType = acTextBox Then
            ctl.Locked = False
        End If
    Next ctl

    Me.AddMode = False
End Sub
```

The `GetCustomer` routine appears in Listing 14.14. It is also identical to its logical three-tier counterpart. It uses the `Retrieve` method of the `Customer` object to retrieve information for the specified customer.

LISTING 14.14   The GetCustomer Routine in the Physical Three-Tier Model

```
Sub GetCustomer()
    Dim rst As ADODB.Recordset
    Dim objCustomer As Customer
    Dim ctl As Control
    Dim fld As Field

    If Not IsNull(Me.txtCustomerID) And _
        Not Me.txtCustomerID = "" Then

        Set objCustomer = New Customer
        Set rst = objCustomer.Retrieve(Me.txtCustomerID.Value)

        'Loop through each field in the resulting recordset.
        'Set the control with the same name as the field
        'equal to the value in the field
        If Not rst.EOF Then
            For Each fld In rst.Fields
                Me(fld.Name).Value = fld.Value
            Next fld
        Else
            MsgBox "Customer Not Found"
        End If
    End If
End Sub
```

The `Retrieve` method of the `Customer` object appears in Listing 14.15. It is identical to its logical three-tier counterpart, except for one significant difference. It is now located in the Visual Basic project.

LISTING 14.15   The Retrieve Method of the Customer Object

```
Public Function Retrieve(strCustomerID As String) As Recordset

    Dim cmd As ADODB.Command
    Dim rst As ADODB.Recordset
    Set cmd = New ADODB.Command

    'Retrieve the customer entered in the text box
```

LISTING 14.15   Continued

```
With cmd
    .CommandText = "procCustomerGet "
    .CommandType = adCmdStoredProc
    .ActiveConnection = GCONN
    .Parameters.Append .CreateParameter( _
            "@CustomerID", adChar, adParamInput, 5, _
            strCustomerID)
    Set rst = .Execute
End With

Set Retrieve = rst
End Function
```

Adding a Record

The code under the `cmdAdd` command button is identical to the code in the logical three-tier example. The code appears in Listing 14.16.

LISTING 14.16   The Code Under the `cmdAdd` Command Button in the Physical Three-Tier Model

```
Private Sub cmdAdd_Click()

    'Clear and unlock all text boxes
    Call ClearControls(False)

    'Set Add flag to true
    Me.AddMode = True
End Sub
```

The code in the `ClearControls` routine is also unchanged. It appears in Listing 14.17.

LISTING 14.17   The `ClearControls` Routine in the Physical Three-Tier Model

```
Public Sub ClearControls(boolLocked As Boolean)
    Dim ctl As Control

    'Loop through all controls on the form,
    'setting their value and locking or unlocking them
    'as appropriate
```

LISTING 14.17   Continued

```
For Each ctl In Me.Controls
    If ctl.ControlType = acTextBox Then
        ctl.Value = ""
        ctl.Locked = boolLocked
    End If
Next ctl

End Sub
```

Saving Data

The code under the cmdSave command button is responsible for calling the routine that saves an added or edited record to the underlying database. It appears in Listing 14.18 and is identical to the code in the logical three-tier example.

LISTING 14.18   The Code Under the cmdSave Command Button in the Physical Three-Tier Example

```
Private Sub cmdSave_Click()

    Dim objCustomer As Customer
    Dim strResultMessage As String

    'If the CustomerID or CompanyName is null,
    'display a message and exit the subroutine
    If IsNull(Me.CustomerID) Or _
        IsNull(Me.CompanyName) Then

        MsgBox "CustomerID and CompanyName" & vbNewLine & _
            "Must be Filled In"
        Exit Sub

    'If the CustomerID and CompanyName are filled in,
    'pass the text box values to the Save method of the
    'Customer object.
    Else

        Set objCustomer = New Customer
        strResultMessage = objCustomer.Save( _
                Me.CustomerID.Value, _
                Me.CompanyName.Value, _
```

LISTING 14.18   Continued

```
                Me.ContactName.Value, _
                Me.ContactTitle.Value, _
                Me.Address.Value, _
                Me.City.Value, _
                Me.Region.Value, _
                Me.PostalCode.Value, _
                Me.Country.Value, _
                Me.Phone.Value, _
                Me.Fax.Value, _
                Me.AddMode)
        End If

        MsgBox strResultMessage

    'Set flag indicating that we are not adding
    Me.AddMode = False
End Sub
```

The Save method is now part of the `Customers.dll` object. It appears in Listing 14.19.

LISTING 14.19   The Save Method as Part of the `Customers.dll` Object

```
Public Function Save(strCustomerID As String, _
    strCompanyName As String, _
    strContactName As String, _
    strContactTitle, _
    strAddress As String, _
    strCity As String, _
    strRegion As String, _
    strPostalCode As String, _
    strCountry As String, _
    strPhone As String, _
    strFax As String, _
    boolAddMode As Boolean) _
    As String

    Dim cmd As ADODB.Command
    Dim intRowsAffected As Integer

    Set cmd = New ADODB.Command

    With cmd
```

LISTING 14.19 Continued

```
.ActiveConnection = GCONN
.CommandType = adCmdStoredProc

'Create a parameter for each field.  Set the parameter
'value equal to the appropriate function parameter
.Parameters.Append .CreateParameter( _
    "@CustomerID", adChar, adParamInput, 5, _
    strCustomerID)
.Parameters.Append .CreateParameter( _
    "@CompanyName", adVarChar, adParamInput, 40, _
    strCompanyName)
.Parameters.Append .CreateParameter( _
    "@ContactName", adVarChar, adParamInput, 30, _
    strContactName)
.Parameters.Append .CreateParameter( _
    "@ContactTitle", adVarChar, adParamInput, 30, _
    strContactTitle)
.Parameters.Append .CreateParameter( _
    "@Address", adVarChar, adParamInput, 60, _
    strAddress)
.Parameters.Append .CreateParameter( _
    "@City", adVarChar, adParamInput, 15, _
    strCity)
.Parameters.Append .CreateParameter( _
    "@Region", adVarChar, adParamInput, 15, _
    strRegion)
.Parameters.Append .CreateParameter( _
    "@PostalCode", adVarChar, adParamInput, 10, _
    strPostalCode)
.Parameters.Append .CreateParameter( _
    "@Country", adVarChar, adParamInput, 15, _
    strCountry)
.Parameters.Append .CreateParameter( _
    "@Phone", adVarChar, adParamInput, 24, _
    strPhone)
.Parameters.Append .CreateParameter( _
    "@Fax", adVarChar, adParamInput, 24, _
    strFax)

'Call the appropriate stored procedure depending on
'if we are adding or editing
```

```
    If boolAddMode Then
        .CommandText = "procCustomerAdd "
    Else
        .CommandText = "procCustomerEdit "
    End If

    .Execute

    Save = .Parameters("@ResultMessage").Value
End With


End Function
```

Deleting Data

The code under the `cmdDelete` command button is unchanged from the logical three-tier example. It appears in Listing 14.20.

LISTING 14.20   The Code Under the `cmdDelete` Command Button in the Physical Three-Tier Model

```
Private Sub cmdDelete_Click()
    Dim objCustomer As Customer
    Dim strReturnValue As String

    Set objCustomer = New Customer

    strReturnValue = objCustomer.Delete(Me.txtCustomerID)
    MsgBox strReturnValue

    Call ClearControls(True)
    Me.txtCustomerID.Locked = False
End Sub
```

The `Delete` method is part of the `Customers.dll` business object. It appears in Listing 14.21.

LISTING 14.21   The Delete Method as Part of the Customers.DLL Business Object

```
Public Function Delete(strCustomerID As String) As String
    Dim cmd As ADODB.Command
    Set cmd = New ADODB.Command
    Dim intRowsAffected As Integer

    'Execute the procCustomerDelete stored procedure,
    'Deleting the customer designated as the parameter
    With cmd
        .CommandText = "procCustomerDelete "
        .CommandType = adCmdStoredProc
        .ActiveConnection = GCONN
        .Parameters.Append .CreateParameter( _
            "@CustomerID", adChar, adParamInput, 5, _
            strCustomerID)
        .Parameters.Append .CreateParameter( _
            "@ResultMessage", adChar, adParamOutput, 20)
        .Execute


        Delete = .Parameters("@ResultMessage").Value
    End With
End Function
```

Summary

Although Access can be an excellent player in the client/server arena, it does not always offer as much scalability as your environment requires. Using unbound forms and the *n*-tier model, you can scale your Access applications to largescale enterprise models. Furthermore, moving your business logic to middle-tier components allows you to maximize the reuse of your business logic. This makes your application more easily maintainable and reduces development costs.

This chapter showed you how to build both logical and physical three-tier applications. You learned how to move your business logic and data access code to class modules within an Access application (a logical three-tier model) and then how to move the class modules to a separate Visual Basic DLL (a physical three-tier model).

15

Configuring, Maintaining, and Tuning SQL Server

Why This Chapter Is Important

The most attractive application can be extremely frustrating to use if its performance is less than acceptable. As a developer, you must try to ensure that the SQL Server is as lean and efficient as possible.

This chapter focuses on several techniques for improving performance. Probably one of the easiest ways to improve performance is to modify the hardware and software environment within which SQL Server operates. You'll begin by learning how the hardware that you select influences the performance of your application.

By following the guidelines covered in this chapter, you can help ensure that you are not inadvertently introducing bottlenecks into your database and, therefore, your application. Although any one of the suggestions included in this chapter might not make a difference by itself, the combined effect of these performance enhancements can be quite dramatic.

Hardware Selection and Tuning

Your choice of hardware can greatly affect the performance of your server. Areas of particular concern are the amount of memory, processor speed, and hard disk configuration. The network architecture is also an important factor. The sections that follow cover the details of each of these items.

Memory—The More RAM, the Better!

SQL Server uses memory (RAM) to hold all data pages, index pages, and log records. It also uses memory to hold compiled queries and stored procedures. Needless to say, that memory is vital to the performance of the server.

Clients are always asking me how much memory they should purchase for their server. My answer is, the more, the better. In fact, RAM is the best investment that you can make for your SQL Server. That aside, here are some guidelines. A bare minimum amount of RAM for any server is 256MB. SQL Server 2000 can take advantage of 2GB of RAM on Windows NT 4.0 and 3GB of RAM on Windows NT 4.0 Enterprise. Running under Windows 2000, SQL Server 2000 can benefit from up to 8GB of RAM. Finally, Windows 2000 Datacenter Server can take advantage of up to 64GB of RAM!

Processor

Although it's not as important as RAM, more processing power never hurts. Under Windows 2000, SQL Server can take advantage of multiple processors. Running under Windows 2000, SQL Server 2000 can take advantage of up to 4 processors, and SQL Server 2000 Enterprise can take advantage of up to 32 processors. In fact, SQL Server 2000 Enterprise is capable of processing a single query over several processors! Despite the advantages of multiple processors, if limited funds force a choice between more RAM and multiple processors, more RAM is the most cost-effective choice.

Disks

Because SQL Server stores all of your data on disk, the type and layout of disks that you use are both important factors. Small Computer System Interface (SCSI) disks are faster than Integrated Drive Electronics (IDE) disks. It is also effective to use multiple SCSI disks, each with its own disk controller. This allows SQL Server to distribute the workload across several disks and several controllers.

The system and transaction log files should both be duplexed. This means that they should be mirrored and on separate SCSI controllers wherever possible. You can use mirrored disk stripes or RAID disk arrays. Mirrored disk stripes are more expensive, but any disk in the system can be lost with no effect on performance. RAID stands for Redundant Array of Inexpensive Disks. RAID arrays are less expensive than mirrored disk stripes, but their downside is that performance suffers if any one disk fails.

Network

Both the network card in the SQL Server and the network bandwidth are important factors in the performance of your application. The server should contain a 32- or 64-bit bus-mastering network card. You should use 100MB versus 10MB Ethernet network cards whenever possible. You can also consider other fast networking technologies. The bottom line is that the best hardware and the best designed database do you no good on a slow, overtaxed network.

SQL Server Configuration and Tuning

If you do not configure the server properly, all of the hardware in the world and the best designed database mean nothing. Processor options, memory options, I/O options, and query and index options all allow you to designate the most appropriate server configuration for you. Although most of the time you will leave these options at their default values, it is useful to know what configuration options are available to you.

Processor Options

You can configure the way in which SQL Server uses your server's processors. The configuration options available include:

- You can configure the relative priority of the SQL Server process.
- You can determine which of the server's CPUs SQL Server will use.
- You can designate the total number of operating system threads that SQL Server can use on your computer.
- You can set the maximum number of CPUs used by parallel query operations.

To modify the processor-related properties:

1. Right-click the server you want to affect, and select Properties.
2. Click the Processor tab (see Figure 15.1).
3. Modify the options as desired.

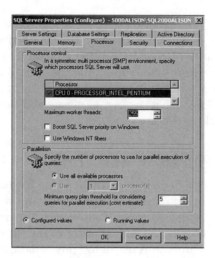

FIGURE 15.1   The Processor tab of the SQL Server Properties dialog box allows you to set processor options.

Memory Options

You can designate the minimum and maximum memory used by SQL Server. You can also specify the minimum memory allocated to each user for each query run. You should generally not modify any of the memory options. This is because SQL Server does an excellent job of allocating and deallocating memory on its own. The only time you would want to modify these options is if you are running SQL Server on the same machine as another highly memory-intensive application, such as Microsoft Exchange Server. I recommend running SQL Server on a dedicated machine when this is not a problem. If you must modify the SQL Server memory options, here's the process:

1. Right-click the server you want to affect, and select Properties.

2. Click the Memory tab (see Figure 15.2).

3. Modify the options as desired.

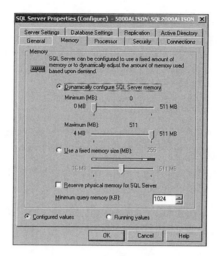

FIGURE 15.2   The Memory tab of the SQL Server Properties dialog box allows you to set memory options.

I/O Options

Versions of SQL Server prior to SQL 2000 offered I/O options. SQL Server 2000 eliminated these options. It always automatically starts the needed threads to issue I/O to the operating system. Although there are no configurable I/O options, you can improve I/O by spreading your data across multiple disks with multiple controllers.

Database Maintenance

Most companies store mission-critical information on their SQL Servers. If your data is important to you, it is imperative that you properly maintain your databases. Database maintenance generally includes backing up your database and auditing database access. It is also important that you understand how to restore a database in the case of a failure.

Backing Up Your Databases

Think of backing up your database like brushing your teeth. It is something that you don't think about; you just do it unequivocally each and every day, *without exception*! Four types of backups are available:

- **Full database backups**—Back up the entire database and portions of the log.

- **Differential database backups**—Back up data modified since the last backup.

- **Transaction log backups**—Back up the transaction log.

- **File or filegroup backups**—Back up data located in a designated filegroup.

You need to decide which backup option is appropriate for you. This depends on how much information is changed each day as well as how critical the information is to you. For example, if the data is changed throughout the day and is mission-critical, you will want to perform a full database backup daily and then back up the transaction log hourly.

SQL Server offers three recovery models:

- **Full**—Offers full protection. With this option, you are able to restore all committed transactions. The database and the log are both backed up.

- **Bulk Logged**—Offers *minimal* data recovery. With this option, logging is minimal. You get the best performance and use the least amount of memory.

- **Simple**—In the case of failure, loses all data modified since the last backup. With this option, you can recover data only as of the last backup.

To select a recovery model:

1. Right-click the database for which you want to establish the recovery model and select Properties. The Properties dialog box appears.

2. Click the Options tab.

3. Open the Model drop-down list and select the appropriate recovery model (see Figure 15.3).

4. Click OK to close the Properties dialog box and save your changes.

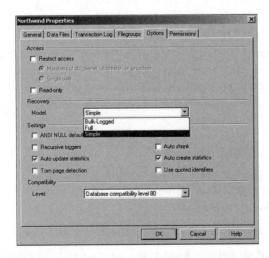

FIGURE 15.3   The Model drop-down list on the Options tab allows you to select the appropriate recovery model.

To perform a backup:

1. Right-click the database that you want to back up, and select All Tasks, Backup Database. The SQL Server Backup dialog box appears (see Figure 15.4).

2. Designate which database you want to back up, the name for the backup, and an optional description for the backup.

3. Use the Backup option buttons to indicate whether you want to perform a full or a differential backup.

4. Click Add or Remove to designate the filename and location for the backup.

5. Designate whether you want to append to or overwrite the existing media.

6. Click the Schedule check box to schedule the backup, if desired.

7. Click the Options tab to designate additional backup options (see Figure 15.5). For example, you can designate whether you want SQL Server to verify the backup on completion.

8. Click OK to complete the process.

FIGURE 15.4   The SQL Server Backup dialog box allows you to designate information about the backup.

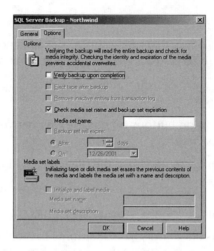

FIGURE 15.5 The Options tab of the SQL Server Backup dialog box allows you to designate additional backup options.

Restoring a Database

Restoring a database is similar to backing it up. You can restore a database to itself (overwrites the existing database), to another existing database, or to a new database. To restore a database:

1. Right-click the database that you want to restore and select All Tasks, Restore Database. The Restore Database dialog box appears (see Figure 15.6).

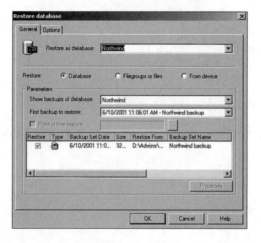

FIGURE 15.6 The Restore Database dialog box allows you to designate information about the restore process.

2. Designate whether you want to restore a database, filegroups, or files, or whether you want to restore from a device.

3. If you click From Device, the dialog box in Figure 15.7 appears. Here, you can designate whether you want to perform a complete or differential restore, or whether you want to restore the transaction log, a filegroup, or a file.

FIGURE 15.7   The Restore Database dialog box with From Device selected.

4. Click the Options tab to designate the restore options (see Figure 15.8).

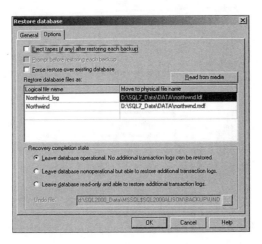

FIGURE 15.8   The Options tab of the Restore Database dialog box allows you to designate additional restore options.

5. Designate whether you want to force restore over an existing database. If you do not select this option and you attempt to restore to an existing database, SQL Server will return an error.

6. Designate the logical and physical filenames for the database and the log file. If you are restoring from one machine to another and the machines have different directory structures, you will need to change the physical filename to reflect the appropriate directory structure.

7. Indicate the recovery completion state.

8. Click OK to perform the restore process.

NOTE

It is important to be aware of who has rights to your database and what rights they have. You should periodically review users and their rights to ensure that only authorized individuals can access the database and that they can perform only the intended and necessary tasks.

The Database Maintenance Plan Wizard

SQL Server 2000 ships with an awesome wizard that can assist you with the process of establishing a database maintenance plan. Here's the process:

1. Right-click a database and select All Tasks, Maintenance Plan. The Database Maintenance Plan Wizard appears (see Figure 15.9).

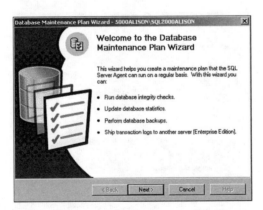

FIGURE 15.9   The Database Maintenance Plan Wizard makes it easy for you to create a maintenance plan.

2. The first step of the wizard prompts you to select the database(s) for which you want to create maintenance plans (see Figure 15.10). You can opt to include all databases, just system databases, just user databases, or selected databases. Make your selection and click Next.

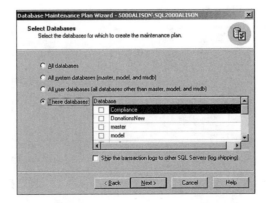

FIGURE 15.10   Select the database(s) for which you want to create maintenance plans.

3. The next step prompts you to select the optimizations that you want SQL Server to perform (see Figure 15.11). You can opt to have SQL Server reorganize data and index pages, update statistics used by the query optimizer, and remove unused space. Make your selection and click Next.

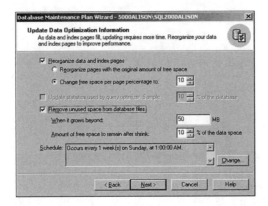

FIGURE 15.11   Select the optimizations that you want SQL Server to perform.

4. The wizard asks you to select the database integrity checks that you want SQL Server to perform (see Figure 15.12). You can include or exclude indexes, and you can designate whether you want SQL Server to perform the checks before backing up the databases. Make your selections and click Next.

5. The next step of the wizard prompts you to specify information about the backup plan (see Figure 15.13). You can designate whether you want the backup performed as part of the maintenance plan and whether you want SQL Server to verify the backup. You can also designate whether the backup will go to tape or disk. Finally, you can select a schedule for the backup. Make your choices and click Next.

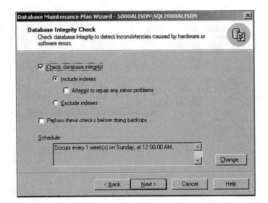

FIGURE 15.12   Select the database integrity checks that you want SQL Server to perform.

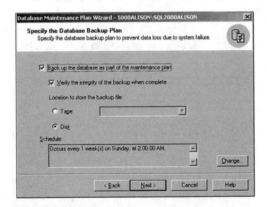

FIGURE 15.13   Specify information about the backup plan.

6. In the next step of the wizard, you designate location information for the backup (see Figure 15.14). Notice that you can have each database backup appear in a separate subdirectory. You can indicate a time period after which SQL Server deletes the backup, and you can specify a file extension. Make your selections and click Next.

7. The following step asks you whether you want to back up the log file (see Figure 15.15). If you do opt to back up the log file, you can designate whether the backup will go to tape or disk. Finally, you can select a schedule for the backup. Make your choices and click Next.

8. In the next step of the wizard, you designate location information for the log file. Notice that you can have each log backup appear in a separate

subdirectory. You can indicate a time period after which SQL Server deletes the backup, and you can specify a file extension. Make your selections and click Next.

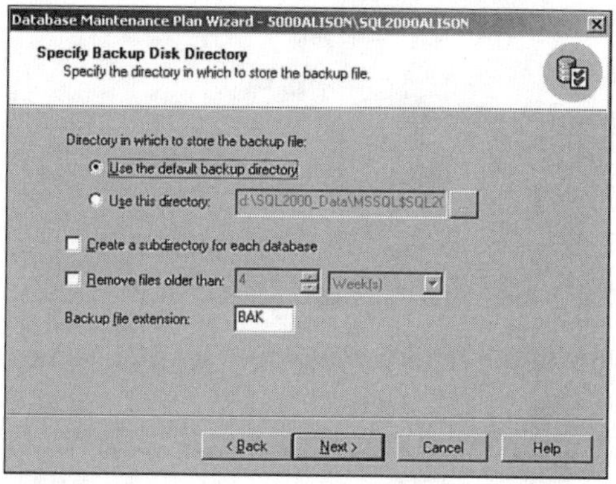

FIGURE 15.14   Designate location information for the backup.

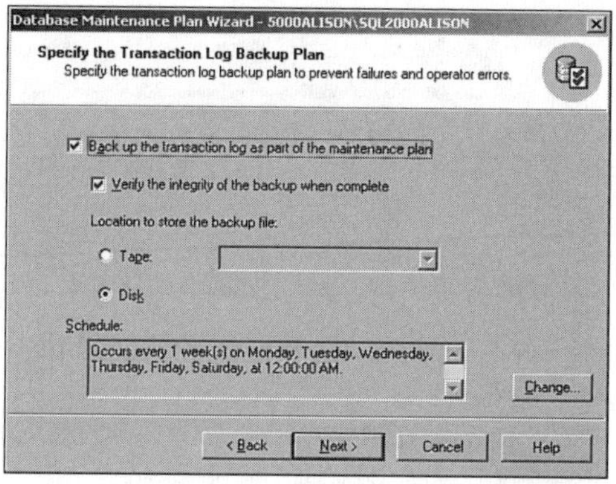

FIGURE 15.15   Indicate whether you want to back up the log file.

9. The wizard prompts you to designate the reports that you want SQL Server to generate (see Figure 15.16). Notice that you can send an e-mail report to an operator. Make your choices and click Next.

10. The wizard asks you to specify information about the maintenance plan history (see Figure 15.17). Designate whether you want history written to the msdb.dbo.sysdbmaintplan_history table on the server. You can also indicate a maximum number of rows for the table. If desired, you can write the history to a remote server. Make your selections and click Next.

11. SQL Server displays the designated options in a dialog box (see Figure 15.18). Click Finish to create the maintenance plan.

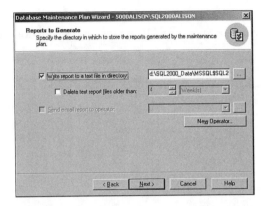

FIGURE 15.16   Designate the reports that you want SQL Server to generate.

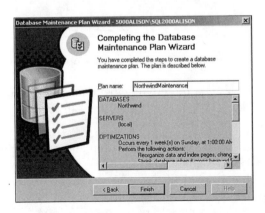

FIGURE 15.17   Specify information about the maintenance plan history.

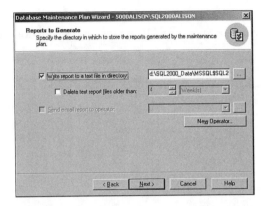

FIGURE 15.18   The last step of the wizard displays information about the selected options.

Table and Object Maintenance

You should periodically perform certain audits on the tables and other objects in your database. The main things that you should keep track of are the record count and who has access to an object.

Generally, the amount of data that a table should contain is fairly predictable. It's usually a good idea to keep an eye on the number of records in each table. If the number of records exceeds your limit, you should consider archiving the extra data.

Just as it is important to keep an eye on who has been granted access to the database, it is important to keep track of what permissions users and roles have for each object.

Job Maintenance

It is not enough to run the Database Maintenance Plan Wizard, set up several jobs, and then let things run. Once you establish jobs, it is important that you:

- **Monitor job status**—Review the success or failure of each job.

- **Review job schedules**—Review each job for both schedule and frequency.

- **Review job durations**—Review how long it took to run the job.

- **Review job outputs**—Review log files, backup files, and so on from each job.

To review the success or failure of a job:

1. From within Enterprise Manager, select the Jobs subnode under the SQL Server Agent mode.

2. Right-click the job in the right pane whose status you want to monitor, and select View Job History. The Job History dialog box appears (see Figure 15.18A). Here, you can see information about the success or failure of the job.

3. Click the Show Detail Steps check box to view details of the steps that make up the job (see Figure 15.18B).

4. Click Close to close the dialog box when done.

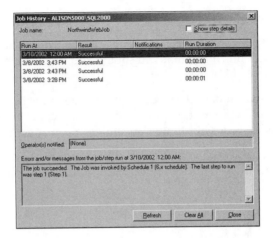

FIGURE 15.18A   The Job History dialog box allows you to monitor the history of a job.

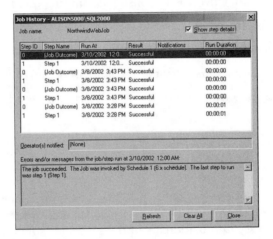

FIGURE 15.18B   Click the Show Detail Steps check box to view details of the steps that make up the job.

To review a job for schedule and frequency:

1. From within Enterprise Manager, select the Jobs subnode under the SQL Server Agent mode.

2. Right-click the job in the right pane whose status you want to monitor, and select Properties. The Job Properties dialog box appears.

3. Click the Schedules tab to view the schedule (see Figure 15.18C).

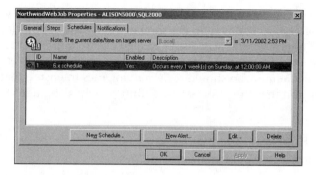

FIGURE 15.18C   The Schedules tab allows you to view the schedule for a job.

4. Click Edit to modify the job schedule. The Edit Job Schedule dialog box appears (see Figure 15.18D).

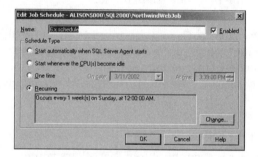

FIGURE 15.18D   The Edit Job Schedule dialog box allows you to modify the schedule for a job.

5. Click Change to change the recurrence of the job. The Edit Recurring Job Schedule dialog box appears.

6. Click OK three times to close the dialog boxes and return to the Enterprise Manager when done.

To determine how long it took for a job to run:

1. From within Enterprise Manager, select the Jobs subnode under the SQL Server Agent mode.

2. Right-click the job in the right pane whose status you want to monitor, and select View Job History. The Job History dialog box appears.

3. The Run Duration column of the dialog box shows you how long it took for the job to run.

4. Click Close to close the dialog box when done.

The process to review job outputs differs depending on the type of job that was run. For example, after a backup is run, you should look at the appropriate folder, tape, or other medium to ensure that SQL Server created the backup file. You should also perform a test restore to ensure that the restore process will complete successfully in case of an actual failure. You should review all log files to ensure that they are being written to disk and that the information within them is complete and accurate.

Performance Monitoring

Performance problems can be due to the following:

- Application problems
- Problems with the logical or physical design of the database
- Problems with the server configuration options
- Problems with the hardware configuration

Although SQL Server offers tools to diagnose and correct problems, you must look at all of these as potential causes of the performance problems that you encounter. The tools available for performance monitoring include the SQL Server Profiler and the System Monitor (Performance Monitor). The following sections cover each of these tools in detail.

The SQL Server Profiler

The SQL Server Profiler is a graphical tool that allows you to:

- Monitor SQL Server performance
- Identify and diagnose slow-running queries
- Capture a series of SQL statements in a test file so that you can replay them on a test server
- Step through and debug stored procedures
- Audit and record security activities, such as the success and failure of login attempts

Before you learn how to use the profiler, it is important that you understand some important terms:

- **Trace**—Records SQL Server activity.
- **Template**—Defines the data that you want to collect.

- **Event**—Action generated by the SQL Server engine.

- **Event category**—A group of similar events.

- **Filter**—Allows you to designate what events are monitored and what data you want to collect.

As mentioned, SQL Server groups events into categories:

- Cursors

- Database

- Errors and Warnings

- Locks

- Objects

- Performance

- Scans

- Security Audit

- Sessions

- Stored Procedures

- Transactions

- TSQL

- User Configurable

When you create a new trace, SQL Server automatically adds five categories of events to the trace. You can leave them as is or remove them as desired. The five categories of events are:

- Audit Login Event

- Audit Logout Event

- ExistingConnection

- RPC:Completed

- SQL:BatchCompleted

To create a new trace:

1. Launch SQL Profiler either from the SQL Server program group or by selecting Tools, SQL Profiler.

2. Click the New Trace tool on the toolbar. The Connect to SQL Server dialog box appears (see Figure 15.19).

FIGURE 15.19   The Connect to SQL Server dialog box allows you to supply connection information.

3. Supply the connection information and click OK. The Trace Properties dialog box appears (see Figure 15.20).

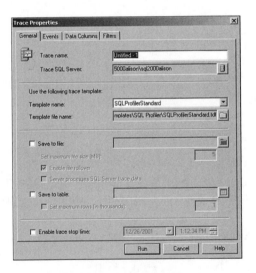

FIGURE 15.20   The Trace Properties dialog box allows you to enter the specifics of the trace.

4. Enter the name of the trace in the Trace Name text box.

5. Select a template from the Template Name drop-down.

6. Designate whether you want to save the trace to a file or to a table.

7. Click the Events tab (see Figure 15.21). This is where you add events to the trace or remove them from the trace. Notice that the event classes contain individual events.

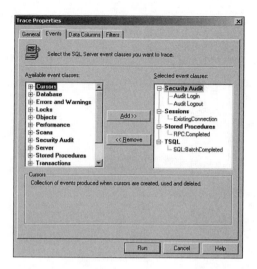

FIGURE 15.21 The Events tab is where you add events to the trace or remove them from the trace.

8. Click the Data Columns tab (see Figure 15.22) to designate the data columns that you want the trace to capture.

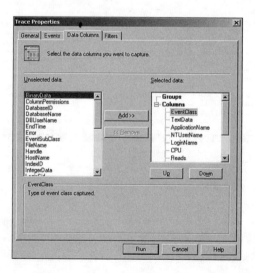

FIGURE 15.22 The Data Columns tab allows you to designate the data columns that you want the trace to capture.

9. Click the Filters tab (see Figure 15.23) to filter the data that you include in the trace. For example, you can trace only events associated with a particular database.

FIGURE 15.23   The Filters tab allows you to filter the data that you include in the trace.

10. Click Run to run the trace. The running trace appears (see Figure 15.24).

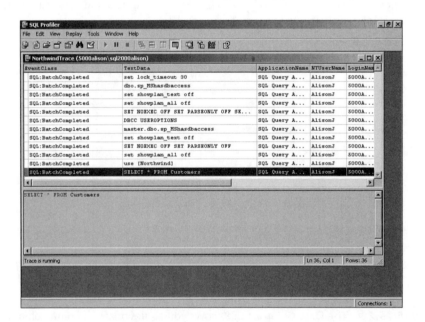

FIGURE 15.24   The running trace shows all the activities for the selected events.

11. To stop the trace when you are done, click Stop Selected Trace.

The System Monitor

The Windows NT Performance Monitor is called the System Monitor in Windows 2000. Many people still refer to it as the Performance Monitor, though. The Performance Monitor is an operating system tool that intercepts network traffic and monitors applications. Although the Performance Monitor is a Windows utility, when you install SQL Server, it adds counters to the Performance Monitor. These counters allow you to use the Performance Monitor as a monitoring tool for SQL Server. The counters include:

- SQL Server I/O

- SQL Server memory usage

- SQL Server user connection

- SQL Server locking

- Replication activity

You can launch the Performance Monitor either from the Start Menu or from the Profiler. From the Profiler, select Tools, Performance Monitor. The Performance Monitor appears as in Figure 15.25.

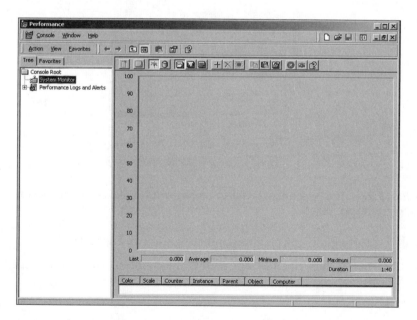

FIGURE 15.25   The Performance Monitor is an operating system tool that intercepts network traffic and monitors applications.

To use the Performance Monitor:

1. Right-click the chart area and select Add Counters. The Add Counters dialog box appears (see Figure 15.26).

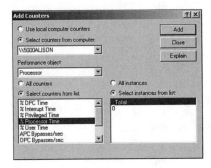

FIGURE 15.26   The Add Counters dialog box allows you to designate the specifics of what you want to monitor.

2. Select the appropriate performance object from the Performance Object drop-down list (see Figure 15.27).

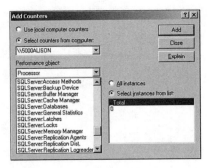

FIGURE 15.27   The Performance Object drop-down list allows you to select the appro-priate performance object.

3. Select the appropriate counters and click Add (see Figure 15.28).

4. Click Close when you are done adding the counters. The Performance Monitor appears with the running counters (see Figure 15.29).

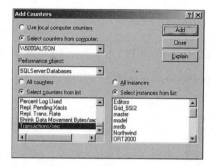

FIGURE 15.28 Click Add to add the appropriate counters.

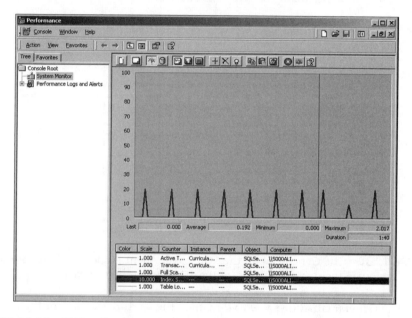

FIGURE 15.29 The Performance Monitor shows you the activity associated with the running counters.

The SQL Server Agent

The SQL Server Agent is the SQL Server tool that is responsible for running system tasks at specified intervals. You can configure the SQL Server Agent to alert certain people when a specific condition exists. It is also the tool responsible for handling replication tasks. The SQL Server Agent is divided into three parts:

- **Jobs**—Objects consisting of one or more steps that you want SQL Server to perform.

- **Alerts**—Actions that you want SQL Server to take when specific events occur.

- **Operators**—People who can receive alerts via e-mail, a pager, or a net send network command.

To configure the SQL Server Agent:

1. Return to Enterprise Manager and expand the Management node for the server.

2. Right-click the SQL Server Agent subnode and select Properties. The SQL Server Agent Properties dialog box appears (see Figure 15.30).

FIGURE 15.30   The General tab of the SQL Server Agent Properties dialog box allows you to designate the startup account for the SQL Server Agent service.

3. The General tab allows you to designate the startup account for the SQL Server Agent service. You can also specify a mail profile for mail that the agent sends and the name of the error log file.

4. The Advanced tab lets you designate whether you want to autostart SQL Server or SQL Server Agent if they stop unexpectedly (see Figure 15.31). Here, you can also opt to forward events to another server.

5. The Alert System tab (see Figure 15.32) lets you specify address formatting options.

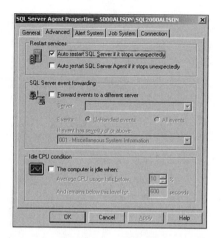

FIGURE 15.31   The Advanced tab lets you designate whether you want to autostart SQL Server or autostart SQL Server Agent if they stop unexpectedly.

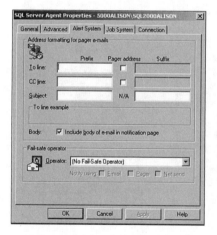

FIGURE 15.32   The Alert System tab lets you specify address formatting options.

6. The Job System tab (see Figure 15.33) lets you designate job history log and job execution information.

7. Finally, the Connection tab (see Figure 15.34), as its name implies, prompts you to enter information about the SQL Server connection.

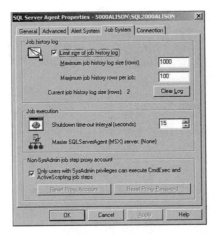

FIGURE 15.33   The Job System tab lets you designate job history log and job execution information.

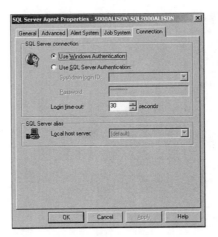

FIGURE 15.34   The Connection tab, as its name implies, prompts you to enter information about the SQL Server connection.

The Create Job Wizard helps you to easily create a SQL Server job. It works like this:

1. Select Tools, Wizards. The Select Wizard dialog box appears.

2. Select Create Job Wizard from the Management node. Click OK.

3. Click Next to bypass the starting screen.

4. Designate the job command type (see Figure 15.35).

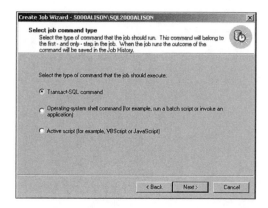

FIGURE 15.35   The Create Job Wizard allows you to designate the job command type.

5. The next step varies depending on the selected job command type. If you select Transact-SQL statement and click Next, the next step of the wizard appears, as in Figure 15.36.

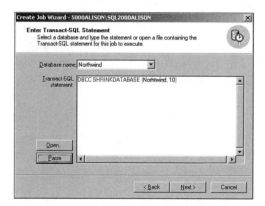

FIGURE 15.36   If you select Transact-SQL Statement, you must select the appropriate database and type the Transact-SQL statement for the job to execute.

6. Select the appropriate database and type the Transact-SQL statement for the job to execute. Click Next.

7. The next step of the wizard prompts you to schedule the job (see Figure 15.37). Make your selection and click Next.

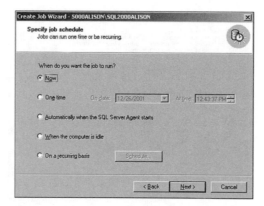

FIGURE 15.37   The next step of the wizard prompts you to schedule the job.

8. Designate information about the job notifications (see Figure 15.38) and click Next.

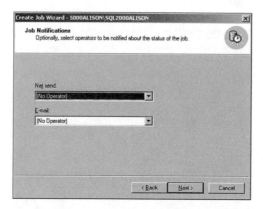

FIGURE 15.38   The next step of the wizard prompts you to designate information about the job notifications.

9. Review the job information and name the job (see Figure 15.39). Click Finish to complete the process.

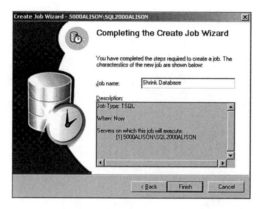

FIGURE 15.39   The final step of the wizard allows you to review the job information and name the job.

Summary

The best-designed system will fail to meet users' needs if it performs poorly. The first line of attack when attempting to optimize performance is to ensure that the hardware on which SQL Server runs is adequate for the job at hand. When all the proper hardware is in place, you must determine that you have properly configured the SQL Server software. After you configure your hardware and the SQL Server software, you must make sure that you take all of the steps to properly maintain the server. You must implement and test a backup and restore procedure, as well as take steps to complete other maintenance tasks such as performing database integrity checks. The Database Maintenance Plan Wizard helps you quickly and easily set up a maintenance plan for both your system and user databases. If performance bottlenecks still occur, the SQL Server Profiler and the Windows Performance Monitor can help you to identify those difficult-to-diagnose performance problems.

PART II

Access Enterprise Techniques

IN THIS PART

16

Transaction Processing

Why This Chapter Is Important

Transaction processing refers to the grouping of a series of changes into a single batch. The entire batch of changes is either accepted or rejected as a group. One of the most common implementations of transaction processing is a bank automated teller machine (ATM) transaction. Imagine that you go to the ATM to deposit your paycheck. In the middle of processing, a power outage occurs. Unfortunately, the bank recorded the incoming funds before the outage, but the funds had not yet been credited to your account when the power outage occurred. You would not be very pleased with the outcome of this situation. Transaction processing would prevent this scenario from occurring. With transaction processing, the whole process succeeds or fails as a unit.

A group of operations is considered a transaction if it meets the following criteria:

- **It is atomic**—The group of operations should complete as a unit or not at all.

- **It is consistent**—The group of operations, when completed as a unit, retains the consistency of the application.

- **It is isolated**—The group of operations is independent of anything else going on in the system.

- **It is durable**—After the group of operations is committed, the changes persist, even if the system crashes.

If your application contains a group of operations that are atomic and isolated, and if, to maintain the consistency of your application, all changes must persist even if the system crashes, you should place the group of operations in a transaction loop. With Access 2002, the primary benefit of transaction processing is data integrity. As you will see in the next section, with versions prior to Access 95, transaction processing also provided performance benefits.

Understanding the Benefits

In Access 2.0, there were many marginal benefits of added transaction processing because Access 2.0 did no implicit transaction processing itself. Listing 16.1 shows code that, when run in Access 2.0, writes the data to disk each time the Update method occurs in the loop. These disk writes were costly in terms of performance, especially if the tables were not located on a local machine.

LISTING 16.1   Transaction Processing Using Access Basic as Seen in Access 2.0

```
Sub IncreaseQuantity()

    On Error GoTo IncreaseQuantity_Err
    Dim db As DATABASE
    Dim rst As Recordset

    Set db = CurrentDb
    Set rst = db.OpenRecordset("Select OrderId, _
            Quantity From tblOrderDetails", _
            dbOpenDynaset)

    'Loop through recordset increasing Quantity field by 1
    Do Until rst.EOF
        rst.Edit
        rst!Quantity = rst!Quantity + 1
        rst.UPDATE
        rst.MoveNext
    Loop

IncreaseQuantity_Exit:
    Set db = Nothing
    Set rst = Nothing
    Exit Sub

IncreaseQuantity_Err:
    MsgBox "Error # " & Err.Number & ": " & Error.Description
    Resume IncreaseQuantity_Exit
End Sub
```

The same code found in Listing 16.1 performs much differently when run in Access 2002. In addition to any explicit transaction processing that you might implement for data-integrity reasons, Access 2002 does its own behind-the-scenes transaction processing. Access 2002 does this implicit transaction processing solely to improve the performance of your application. As the processing loop in the IncreaseQuantity routine executes, Access buffers and then periodically writes the data to disk. In a multiuser environment, Jet (implicitly) commits transactions every 50 milliseconds, by default. Access optimizes this period of time for concurrency rather than performance. If you feel that it is necessary to sacrifice concurrency for performance, you can modify a few Windows Registry settings to achieve the specific outcome that you want. The next section covers these settings.

Although implicit transaction processing, along with the modifiable Windows Registry settings, generally gives you better performance than explicit transaction processing, it is not a cut-and-dried situation. Many factors influence the performance benefits gained by both implicit and explicit transaction processing:

- Amount of free memory

- Number of columns and rows being updated

- Size of the rows being updated

- Network traffic

If you plan to implement explicit transaction processing solely to improve performance, you should make sure that you benchmark performance using both implicit and explicit transactions. It is critical that your application-testing environment be as similar as possible to the production environment in which the application will run.

Modifying the Default Behavior

Before you learn how to implement transaction processing, take a look at what you can do to modify the default behavior of the transaction processing built into Access 2002. Three Registry settings affect implicit transactions in Access 2002: ImplicitCommitSync, ExclusiveAsnycDelay, and SharedAsyncDelay. These keys are located in the \HKEY_LOCAL_MACHINE\SOFTWARE\Microsoft\Jet\4.0\Engines\Jet 4.0 Registry folder.

> **TIP**
>
> You can access the Windows Registry using the RegEdit utility. To utilize RegEdit, select the Run option from the Start menu. Then type **RegEdit**.

The `ImplicitCommitSync` setting determines whether the system waits for a commit to finish before proceeding with application processing. The default is `No`. This means that the system will proceed without waiting for the commit to finish. You generally won't want to change this setting; using `No` dramatically improves performance. The danger of accepting the value of `No` is that you will increase the amount of time during which the data is vulnerable. Before Access flushes the data to disk, the user might turn off the machine, compromising the integrity of the data.

The `ExclusiveAsyncDelay` setting specifies the maximum number of milliseconds that elapse before Jet commits an implicit transaction when the user or application code opens a database for exclusive use. The default value for this setting is 2000 milliseconds. This setting does not in any way affect databases that are open for shared use.

The `SharedAsyncDelay` setting is similar to the `ExclusiveAsyncDelay` setting. It determines the maximum number of milliseconds that elapse before Jet commits an implicit transaction when the user or code opens a database for shared use. The default value for this setting is `50`. The higher this value is, the greater the performance benefits are reaped from implicit transactions, but the higher the chances are that concurrency problems will result. The section titled "Using Transaction Processing in a Multiuser Environment," later in this chapter, discusses concurrency issues in detail.

In addition to the settings that affect implicit transaction processing in Access 2002, an additional Registry setting affects explicit transaction processing. The `UserCommitSync` setting controls whether Access completes explicit transactions synchronously or asynchronously. With the default setting of `Yes`, control doesn't return from a `CommitTrans` statement until Access writes the transactions to disk, resulting in synchronous transactions. When you change this value to `No`, Access queues the series of changes, and control returns before the changes are complete.

You can modify the values of these Registry settings and other Jet settings by using Regedit.exe (the Registry Editor) for Windows 95/98 or RegEdt32.exe for Windows NT. Changes to this section of the Registry affect all applications that use the Jet 4.0 Engine. If you want to affect only your application, you can export the Microsoft Jet portion of the Registry tree and import it into your application's Registry tree. You then can customize the Registry settings for your application. To force your application to load the appropriate Registry tree, you must set the `INIPath` property of the `DBEngine` object.

A much simpler approach is to set properties of the ActiveX Data Objects (ADO) Connection object; you can specify new settings at runtime for all the previously mentioned Registry entries as well as additional entries. A further advantage of this approach is that it will modify (temporarily) Registry entries for any machine under which your application runs. Any values that you change at runtime temporarily override the Registry values that are set, enabling you to easily control and maintain specific settings for each application. This code illustrates how you modify the ExclusiveAsyncDelay and SharedAsyncDelay settings using properties of the Connection object:

```
Sub ChangeOptions()
    Dim cnn As ADODB.Connection
    Set cnn = CurrentProject.Connection

    cnn.Properties("JET OLEDB:Exclusive Async Delay") = 1000
    cnn.Properties("JET OLEDB:Shared Async Delay") = 50
End Sub
```

Implementing Explicit Transaction Processing

Now that you are aware of the settings that affect transaction processing, you are ready to learn how to implement transaction processing. Three methods of the Connection object (covered in *Alison Balter's Mastering Access 2002 Desktop Development*) control transaction processing:

- BeginTrans
- CommitTrans
- RollbackTrans

The BeginTrans method of the Connection object begins the transaction loop. The moment the code encounters BeginTrans, Access begins writing all changes to a log file in memory. Unless you issue the CommitTrans method on the Connection object, Access never actually writes the changes to the database file. When you issue the CommitTrans method, Access permanently writes the updates to the database object. If the code encounters a RollbackTrans method of the Connection object, Access releases the log in memory. Listing 16.2 shows an example of how transaction processing works under Access 2002. Compare this to Listing 16.1.

LISTING 16.2   Transaction Processing in Access 2002 Using BeginTrans, Logging, CommitTrans, and RollbackTrans

```
Sub IncreaseQuantityTrans()
    On Error GoTo IncreaseQuantityTrans_Err
    Dim cnn As ADODB.Connection
    Dim rst As ADODB.Recordset
    Dim boolInTrans As Boolean

    boolInTrans = False
  Set rst = New ADODB.Recordset

    Set cnn = CurrentProject.Connection
    rst.ActiveConnection = cnn
    rst.CursorType = adOpenKeyset
    rst.LockType = adLockOptimistic
    rst.Open "Select OrderId, Quantity From tblOrderDetails"

    'Begin the Transaction Loop
    cnn.BeginTrans
        boolInTrans = True
        'Loop through recordset increasing Quantity field by 1
        Do Until rst.EOF
            rst!Quantity = rst!Quantity + 1
            rst.UPDATE
            rst.MoveNext
        Loop
        'Commit the Transaction; Everything went as Planned
    cnn.CommitTrans
    boolInTrans = False

IncreaseQuantityTrans_Exit:
    Set cnn = Nothing
    Set rst = Nothing
    Exit Sub

IncreaseQuantityTrans_Err:
    MsgBox "Error # " & Err.Number & ": " & Err.Description
    'Rollback the Transaction; An Error Occurred
    If boolInTrans Then
        cnn.RollbackTrans
    End If
    Resume IncreaseQuantityTrans_Exit
End Sub
```

This code uses a transaction loop to ensure that everything completes as planned or not at all. Notice that the loop that moves through the recordset, increasing the Quantity field in each record by 1, is placed in a transaction loop. If all processing in the loop completes successfully, the CommitTrans method executes. If the error-handling code is encountered, the code issues the RollbackTrans method, ensuring that none of the changes is written to disk. The code uses the boolInTrans variable to determine whether the code is within the transaction loop. This ensures that the error handler performs the rollback only if an error occurs within the transaction loop. If the code encounters a CommitTrans or RollbackTrans method without an open transaction, an error occurs.

Looking at Transaction Processing Issues

Before you decide that transaction processing is the best thing since sliced bread, you should keep in mind several issues concerning transaction processing. This section outlines these issues.

Realizing That Transactions Occur in a Workspace

Transactions exist in the context of a Connection object. The BeginTrans, CommitTrans, and RollbackTrans methods affect all operations on the specific connection. If you want simultaneous, unrelated transactions to be in effect, you must create separate Connection objects in which the transactions are applied. Whereas data access objects (DAO) supported transactions that spanned multiple databases, ADO transactions are limited to a specific data source because they exist in the context of a connection.

Making Sure That the Data Source Supports Transactions

Not all data sources support transaction processing. Excel and dBase files, for example, do not support transaction processing. Neither do certain back-end Open Database Connectivity (ODBC) database servers. When in doubt, you can use the Transaction DDL property of the Connection object to determine whether the data source supports transaction processing. If the Transaction DDL property exists and is nonzero, the data source supports transaction processing. To determine whether the property exists, query its value. If the property is nonexistent, an error occurs. Listing 16.3 shows an example of how to determine whether an object supports transaction processing.

LISTING 16.3   Determining Whether a Connection Supports Transaction Processing

```
Sub SupportsTransCurrentDB()
    On Error GoTo SupportsTrans_Err
    Dim cnn As ADODB.Connection
    Dim rst As ADODB.Recordset
    Dim boolSupportsTrans As Boolean
    Dim vntValue As Variant

    boolSupportsTrans = False

    Set cnn = CurrentProject.Connection

    Set rst = New ADODB.Recordset
    rst.ActiveConnection = cnn
    rst.CursorType = adOpenKeyset
    rst.LockType = adLockOptimistic
    rst.Open "tblOrderDetails"

    'Begin the Transaction Loop Only if Recordset
    'Supports Transaction
    On Error Resume Next
    vntValue = cnn.Properties.Item("Transaction DDL")
    If Not Err.Number And _
        cnn.Properties.Item("Transaction DDL").Value <> 0 Then
        boolSupportsTrans = True
        cnn.BeginTrans
    End If
    On Error Goto SupportsTrans_Err

    'Loop through recordset increasing Quantity field by 1
    Do Until rst.EOF
        rst!Quantity = rst!Quantity - 1
        rst.UPDATE
        rst.MoveNext
    Loop

    'Issue the CommitTrans if Everything went as Planned
    'and Recordset Supports Transactions
    If boolSupportsTrans Then
        cnn.CommitTrans
    End If

SupportsTrans_Exit:
```

LISTING 16.3   Continued

```
    Set cnn = Nothing
    Set rst = Nothing
    Exit Sub

SupportsTrans_Err:

    MsgBox "Error # " & Err.Number & ": " & Err.Description

    'Rollback the Transaction if An Error Occurred
    'and Recordset Supports Transactions
    If boolSupportsTrans Then
        cnn.RollbackTrans
    End If
    Resume SupportsTrans_Exit

End Sub
```

The code uses a Boolean variable called boolSupportsTrans to track whether the connection supports transactions. Notice the statement On Error Resume Next. The code evaluates the Transaction DDL property of the Connection object. If it does not exist, an error occurs. The next statement tests for a nonzero error number and a nonzero property value. Only if the Transaction DDL property for the Connection object exists and is nonzero does the code issue the BeginTrans method and set the boolSupportsTrans variable to True. The code evaluates the boolSupportsTrans variable two different times in the remainder of the routine. It issues the CommitTrans method only if boolSupportsTrans evaluates to True. The error-handling routine issues the RollbackTrans method only if the boolSupportTrans variable is equal to True.

Listing 16.4 shows an example in which the data source, an Excel spreadsheet, does not support transactions. Notice that the code uses a data source that references the Excel spreadsheet. It opens a recordset using the Connection object. It then determines whether the connection supports transactions.

NOTE

To test the example in Listing 16.4, you will need to create an ODBC data source called TestXLS. To run the example, export the Northwind Customers table to an Excel spreadsheet. Then use the ODBC Manager to create the TestXLS data source and point it to the exported spreadsheet.

LISTING 16.4 Determining Whether a Connection Based on a Non-Access Data Source Supports Transaction Processing

```
Sub SupportsTransOtherDB()
    On Error GoTo SupportsTrans_Err
    Dim cnn As ADODB.Connection
    Dim rst As ADODB.Recordset
    Dim boolSupportsTrans As Boolean
    Dim vntValue As Variant

    boolSupportsTrans = False

    Set cnn = New ADODB.Connection

    cnn.Open "DSN=TestXLS;UID=;PWD=;"

    Set rst = New ADODB.Recordset

    With rst
        .ActiveConnection = cnn
        .CursorType = adOpenKeyset
        .LockType = adLockOptimistic
        .Open "Customers"
    End With

    'Evaluate to determine if the Recordset
    'supports transactions

    On Error Resume Next
    vntValue = cnn.Properties.Item("Transaction DDL")
    If Not Err.Number And _
        cnn.Properties.Item("Transaction DDL").Value <> 0 Then
        boolSupportsTrans = True
        MsgBox "Supports Transactions!"
    Else
        MsgBox "Warning, this Provider does NOT support transactions!"
    End If

SupportsTrans_Exit:
    Set cnn = Nothing
    Set rst = Nothing
```

LISTING 16.4   Continued

```
    Exit Sub

SupportsTrans_Err:

    MsgBox "Error # " & Err.Number & ": " & Err.Description

    Resume SupportsTrans_Exit
End Sub
```

CAUTION

When dealing with an application that contains links to a data source that does not support transactions, the Transaction DDL property will not evaluate properly. Because when dealing with linked tables the connection that you use is that of the Access database, the Transaction DDL property will appear to support transactions. Access exhibits this same behavior if your code uses the Jet Provider to connect to the data source. In either case, no error will occur when the code executes the BeginTrans, CommitTrans, or RollbackTrans methods. Instead, the process will appear to complete successfully. If the code issues a RollbackTrans, no rollback occurs and Access retains all changes!

Nesting Transactions

Another issue to be aware of with transactions is that you can nest transactions. The hierarchy for nesting is FIFO (first in, first out). The inner transactions always must be committed or rolled back before the outer transactions. After a CommitTrans occurs, you cannot undo changes made to that transaction unless you nest it in another transaction that is itself rolled back. The BeginTrans method returns a value indicating the level of nesting. It returns 1 for a top-level transaction, 2 for a second-level transaction, and so on.

NOTE

Some OLE DB providers do not support nested transactions through the ADO interface. If the provider does not support nested transactions, the following message appears:

```
Run-time error '-2147168237 (8004d013)':
Only one transaction can be active on this session
```

Neglecting to Explicitly Commit Transactions

When a transaction loop is executing, Access writes all updates to a log file in memory. If your code never executes a CommitTrans, Access essentially rolls back all changes. In other words, a RollbackTrans is implicit if your code never explicitly writes the changes to disk with the CommitTrans method. This generally works to your advantage. If the power is interrupted or the machine hangs before your code executes the CommitTrans, Access implicitly rolls back all changes. This behavior can get you into trouble if you forget the CommitTrans method, however. If you close the connection without executing the CommitTrans method, Access flushes the memory log and implicitly rolls back the transaction.

Checking Available Memory

Another gotcha with transactions occurs when the transaction log exhausts the physical memory on the computer. Access 2002 first attempts to use virtual memory. The transaction log is written to the temporary directory specified by the TEMP environment variable of the user's machine. This method dramatically slows down the transaction process. If the transaction process exhausts all memory and the TEMP disk space, an error 2004 results. You must issue a rollback at this point. Otherwise, you are in danger of violating the integrity of the database.

> **CAUTION**
>
> If your code attempts to commit the transaction after a 2004 error has occurred, the Jet Engine commits as many changes as possible, leaving the database in an inconsistent state. You find the 2004 error using the SQLState property of the Errors collection of the Connection object.

Using Forms with Transactions

Access handles its own transaction processing on bound forms. You cannot control this transaction processing in any way. If you want to use transaction processing with forms, you must create unbound forms or run code with no form interface.

Using Transaction Processing in a Multiuser Environment

In a multiuser environment, transaction processing has implications beyond the protection of data. By wrapping a process in a transaction loop, you ensure that you are in control of all records involved in the process. The cost of this additional control is reduced concurrency for the rest of the users of the application. Listing 16.5 illustrates this scenario.

LISTING 16.5   A Safe Way to Do Transactions in a Multiuser Environment That Sacrifices Concurrency

```
Sub MultiPessimistic()
    On Error GoTo MultiPessimistic_Err
    Dim cnn As ADODB.Connection
    Dim rst As ADODB.Recordset
    Dim intCounter As Integer
    Dim intChoice As Integer
    Dim intTry As Integer
    Dim boolInTrans As Boolean


    boolInTrans = False
    Set rst = New ADODB.Recordset
    Set cnn = CurrentProject.Connection

    rst.ActiveConnection = cnn
    rst.CursorType = adOpenKeyset
    rst.CursorLocation = adUseServer
    rst.LockType = adLockPessimistic
    rst.Open "Select OrderId, ProductID, UnitPrice " & _
        "From tblOrderDetails Where ProductID > 50"

    'Begin the Transaction Loop
    cnn.BeginTrans
        boolInTrans = True
        'Loop through recordset increasing UnitPrice
        Do Until rst.EOF
            'Lock Occurs Here for Each Record in the Loop
            rst!UnitPrice = rst!UnitPrice * 1.1
            rst.UPDATE
            rst.MoveNext
        Loop
        'Commit the Transaction; Everything went as Planned
        'All locks released for ALL records involved in the Process
    cnn.CommitTrans
    boolInTrans = False
    Set cnn = Nothing
    Set rst = Nothing
    Exit Sub


MultiPessimistic_Err:
```

LISTING 16.5   Continued

```
   Select Case cnn.Errors(0).SQLState
       Case 3260
       intCounter = intCounter + 1
       If intCounter > 2 Then
           intChoice = MsgBox(Err.Description, _
               vbRetryCancel + vbCritical)
           Select Case intChoice
               Case vbRetry
                   intCounter = 1
               Case vbCancel
                   'User Selected Cancel, Roll Back
                   Resume TransUnsuccessful
           End Select
       End If
       DoEvents
       For intTry = 1 To 100: Next intTry
       Resume
       Case Else
           MsgBox "Error # " & Err.Number & ": " & Err.Description
   End Select

TransUnsuccessful:
   If boolInTrans Then
       cnn.RollbackTrans
   End If
   MsgBox "Warning: Entire Process Rolled Back"
   Set cnn = Nothing
   Set rst = Nothing
   Exit Sub

End Sub
```

The `MultiPessimistic` routine uses pessimistic locking. This means that each time the code edits the data within a record, it locks the edited record. If all goes well and no error occurs, the code releases the lock when it reaches the `CommitTrans`. The error-handling code traps for a 3260 error. This error means that another user locked the record. The code gives the user running the transaction processing the opportunity to retry or cancel. If the user chooses Retry, the code again tries to edit the data within the record. If the user chooses Cancel, a rollback occurs. This cancels the changes made to all the records involved in the process.

I want to highlight two key points about the `MultiPessimistic` routine. First, as this routine executes, the code locks each record involved in the process. This potentially means that all other users will be unable to edit a large percentage, or even any, of the records until the transaction process finishes. This is wonderful from a data-integrity standpoint, but it might not be practical in an environment where users must update data on a frequent basis. It therefore is a good idea to keep transaction loops as short in duration as possible. Second, if any of the lock attempts are unsuccessful, the code cancels the entire transaction. Again, this might be what you want or need from a data-integrity standpoint, but it might require that all users refrain from editing data while an important process completes.

With optimistic locking, the lock attempt occurs when the code issues the `Update` method rather than when the code edits the data. This does not make much of a difference; all the records involved in the transaction remain locked until the `CommitTrans` or `RollbackTrans` occurs. The main difference is in the errors for which you must trap. Listing 16.6 shows the code for using optimistic locking in a multiuser environment.

LISTING 16.6   Optimistic Locking in a Multiuser Environment

```
Sub MultiOptimistic()
    On Error GoTo MultiOptimistic_Err
    Dim cnn As ADODB.Connection
    Dim rst As ADODB.Recordset
    Dim intCounter As Integer
    Dim intChoice As Integer
    Dim intTry As Integer
    Dim boolInTrans As Boolean

    boolInTrans = False
    Set rst = New ADODB.Recordset
    Set cnn = CurrentProject.Connection

    rst.ActiveConnection = cnn
    rst.CursorType = adOpenKeyset
    rst.CursorLocation = adUseServer
    rst.LockType = adLockOptimistic
    rst.Open "Select OrderId, ProductID, UnitPrice " & _
        "From tblOrderDetails Where ProductID > 50"

    'Begin the Transaction Loop
    cnn.BeginTrans
        boolInTrans = True
        'Loop through recordset increasing UnitPrice
```

LISTING 16.6   Continued

```
        Do Until rst.EOF
            rst!UnitPrice = rst!UnitPrice * 1.1
            'Lock Occurs Here for Each Record in the Loop
            rst.UPDATE
            rst.MoveNext
        Loop
        'Commit the Transaction; Everything went as Planned
        'All locks released for ALL records involved in the Process
    cnn.CommitTrans
    boolInTrans = False
    Set cnn = Nothing
    Set rst = Nothing
    Exit Sub

MultiOptimistic_Err:
    Select Case cnn.Errors(0).SQLState
        Case 3197   'Data Has Changed Error
            If rst.EditMode = adEditInProgress Then
                intChoice = MsgBox("Overwrite Other User's Changes?", _
                vbYesNoCancel + vbQuestion)
                Select Case intChoice
                    Case vbCancel, vbNo
                        MsgBox "Update Canceled"
                        Resume TransNotSuccessful
                    Case vbYes
                        rst.UPDATE
                        Resume
                End Select
            End If
        Case 3186, 3260   'Locked or Can't be Saved
            intCounter = intCounter + 1
            If intCounter > 2 Then
                intChoice = MsgBox(Err.Description, _
                            vbRetryCancel + vbCritical)
                Select Case intChoice
                    Case vbRetry
                        intCounter = 1
                    Case vbCancel
                        'User Selected Cancel, Roll Back
                        Resume TransNotSuccessful
                End Select
```

LISTING 16.6   Continued

```
            End If
            DoEvents
            For intTry = 1 To 100: Next intTry
            Resume
        Case Else
            MsgBox "Error # " & Err.Number & ": " & Err.Description
    End Select

TransNotSuccessful:
    If boolInTrans Then
        cnn.RollbackTrans
    End If
    MsgBox "Warning: Entire Process Rolled Back"
    Set cnn = Nothing
    Set rst = Nothing
    Exit Sub

End Sub
```

Notice that, in the `MultiOptimistic` routine, the lock occurs each time the code issues the `Update` method. The code releases all of the locks when it executes the `CommitTrans` method. Furthermore, the error handling checks for a 3197 (data has changed) error. The 3197 occurs when another user changes the data between the time the code issues the `Edit` method and just before it issues the `Update` method.

Using Transaction Processing in a Client/Server Environment

When dealing with transactions in a client/server environment, you must consider several additional issues: when and how transactions occur, what types of transactions the server supports, and what types of problems can occur. When using Access in a client/server environment, it is always best to implement transaction processing on the server rather than in your ADO code. Chapter 8, "Designing SQL Server Stored Procedures, User-Defined Functions, and Triggers," covers transaction processing on the server. This means that if all of your update code is in a stored procedure, and the stored procedure contains transaction processing, you can roll back the transaction at the server level and then pass a status message to the client indicating that things went awry. No data is updated on the server.

Implicit Transactions

When explicit transactions are not used, the way in which transactions are committed on the database server depends on what types of commands your code executes. In general, every line of code has an implicit transaction around it. This means that there is no way to roll back an action because it is committed immediately on the database server. The exceptions to this rule are any SQL statements issued that modify data. These SQL statements (UPDATE, INSERT, and APPEND) are executed in batches; a transaction loop is implicitly placed around the entire statement. If Access cannot successfully update any records involved in the SQL statement, it rolls back the entire UPDATE, INSERT, or APPEND.

Explicit Transactions

When you use explicit transactions, ODBC translates the BeginTrans, CommitTrans, and RollbackTrans methods to the appropriate syntax of the back-end server and the transaction processes as expected. The main exception to this rule is when the specific back end that you are using does not support transactions. Listing 16.7 shows an example of transaction processing with a SQL Server back end. To run this example, you will need to set up an ODBC DSN (data source) pointing at the PUBS database.

LISTING 16.7   Transaction Processing with a SQL Server Back End

```
Sub TransSQLServer()
    Dim cnn As ADODB.Connection
    Dim cmd As ADODB.Command
    Dim boolInTrans As Boolean

    boolInTrans = False
    Set cnn = New ADODB.Connection
    Set cmd = New ADODB.Command

    cnn.ConnectionString = "Provider=SQLOLEDB; Data Source=Alexis; " & _
        "Initial Catalog=Pubs; User ID=SA; Password="
    cnn.Open

    cnn.BeginTrans
        boolInTrans = True
        cmd.ActiveConnection = cnn
        cmd.CommandText = "UPDATE sales Set qty = qty + 1 " & _
            "Where Stor_ID = '7067';"
        cmd.CommandType = adCmdText
        cmd.Execute
```

LISTING 16.7   Continued

```
        cmd.CommandText = "Update titles Set price = price + 1 " & _
            "Where Type = 'Business'"
        cmd.CommandType = adCmdText
        cmd.Execute
    cnn.CommitTrans
    boolInTrans = False

TransSQLServer_Exit:
    Set cnn = Nothing
    Set cmd = Nothing
    Exit Sub

TransSQLServer_Err:
    MsgBox "Error # " & Err.Number & ": " & Err.Description
    If boolInTrans Then
        cnn.Rollback
    End If
    Resume TransSQLServer_Exit
End Sub
```

The `TransSQLServer` routine begins by creating both `Connection` and `Command` object variables. Next, it executes the `BeginTrans` method on the connection. It creates a temporary query definition. The `ConnectionString` property of the `Connection` object is set to point to a SQL Server database called Pubs. The `Open` method of the `Connection` object opens the connection. The code uses the `BeginTrans` method of the `Connection` object to initiate the transaction loop. Several properties are set for the `Command` object, including the `ActiveConnection`, `CommandText`, and `CommandType` properties. After the code sets these properties, it executes the temporary query. It modifies the `CommandText` property of the query definition and executes the query again. If both `Execute` methods complete successfully, the code issues the `CommitTrans` method on the `Connection` object. If any error occurs during processing, it issues the `RollbackTrans` method.

TIP

Listing 16.7 provides an example of using transactions when going against data stored in Microsoft SQL Server. Using ADO recordsets to update client/server data is very inefficient. It is almost always preferable to update client/server data using stored procedures and to place the transaction handling within those stored procedures.

Lock Limits

A potential pitfall when dealing with client/server databases involves lock limits. Many database servers impose strict limits on how many records can be locked concurrently. As you saw in Listings 16.2 and 16.3, a transaction loop can potentially lock a significant number of records. It is important to consider the maximum number of locks supported by your back end when using transaction loops in your VBA code. Using stored procedures to update your client/server data eliminates this problem.

Negative Interactions with Server-Specific Transaction Commands

You should never use the server-specific transaction commands when building pass-through queries. These server-specific commands can conflict with the `BeginTrans`, `CommitTrans`, and `RollbackTrans` methods, causing confusion and potential data corruption.

Practical Examples: Using Transaction Processing to Improve the Integrity of Your Applications

As you continue to develop your own applications, you might find it necessary to use VBA code to accomplish certain tasks. These tasks might require that several processes complete successfully or not at all. As these situations arise, you should consider placing them in a transaction loop. An example of such a situation is the frmArchivePayments form, as shown in Figure 16.1. frmArchivePayments enables the user to specify a date range. The code uses this date range as the criterion to determine what data it sends to the tblPaymentsArchive table and removes from the tblPayments table. When the user runs the process, you want to ensure that the process runs in its entirety or not at all. Listing 16.8 shows transaction loop code suitable for this situation.

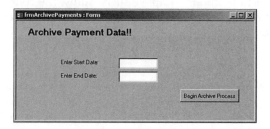

FIGURE 16.1   The frmArchivePayments form enables the user to specify a date range of payments to be archived.

LISTING 16.8   A Transaction Loop Suitable for the Time and Billing Application

```
Sub cmdArchivePayments_Click()
    On Error GoTo Err_cmdArchivePayments_Click

    Dim cnn As ADODB.Connection
    Dim strSQL As String
    Dim boolInTrans As Boolean

    boolInTrans = False

    Set cnn = CurrentProject.Connection

    cnn.BeginTrans
        boolInTrans = True
        strSQL = "INSERT INTO tblPaymentsArchive" & _
            " SELECT DISTINCTROW tblPayments.* " & _
            " FROM tblPayments " & _
            " WHERE tblPayments.PaymentDate Between #" & _
            Me!txtStartDate & _
            "# And #" & _
            Me!txtEndDate & "#;"
        cnn.Execute strSQL
        strSQL = "DELETE DISTINCTROW tblPayments.PaymentDate " & _
            "FROM tblPayments " & _
            " WHERE tblPayments.PaymentDate Between #" & _
            Me!txtStartDate & _
            "# And #" & _
            Me!txtEndDate & "#;"
        cnn.Execute strSQL
    cnn.CommitTrans
    boolInTrans = False

Exit_cmdArchivePayments_Click:
    Exit Sub

Err_cmdArchivePayments_Click:
    MsgBox Err.Description
    If boolInTrans Then
        cnn.RollbackTrans
    End If
    Resume Exit_cmdArchivePayments_Click

End Sub
```

This routine uses the `BeginTrans` method of the `Connection` object to initiate a transaction loop. It builds a SQL statement, using the values of the `txtStartDate` and `txtEndDate` controls on the form as criteria. This SQL statement adds all records in the specified date range to the tblPaymentsArchive table. The code applies the `Execute` method to the `Connection` object, using the SQL string as an argument. It then modifies the SQL string to build a statement that deletes all records in the specified date range from the tblPayments table. If both SQL statements execute successfully, the code executes the `CommitTrans` method, committing both transactions. If an error occurs, it rolls back the whole transaction.

Summary

If you use transactions properly, you can gain many benefits from them. Transactions help ensure that all parts of a logical piece of work complete successfully or not at all. In some situations, they also can improve performance. You must be aware of several issues when using transactions. The potential pitfalls vary, depending on whether you are issuing a transaction in a multiuser Access environment or in a client/server environment. If you take all mitigating factors into account, you can ensure that transactions provide you with the data integrity that you expect from them.

17

Access Replication Made Easy

Why This Chapter Is Important

Access 95 was the first desktop database that included built-in replication capabilities. Replication has further matured with the introduction of each subsequent version of Access; it's a powerful feature that is becoming increasingly important in today's world of mobile and distributed computing. This chapter teaches you about replication and how to implement it through both the user interface and code.

Uses of Replication

Data replication is the capability of a system to automatically make copies of its data and application objects in remote locations. You can easily propagate any changes to the original or data changes to the copies to all the other copies. Data replication allows users to make changes to data offline at remote locations. Access synchronizes changes to either the original data or the remote data with other instances of the database.

We refer to the original database as the *design master*. You can make changes to definitions of tables or other application objects only at the design master. You use the design master to make special copies called *replicas*. Although there is only one design master, replicas can make other replicas. We refer to the process of the design master and replicas sharing changes as *synchronization*. The design master and replicas that participate in the synchronization process are collectively referred to as a *replica set*.

To see an example of data replication at work, let's say that you have a team of sales-people who are out on the road all day. At the end of the day, each salesperson logs on to one of the company's Windows NT servers through Dial-Up Networking (DUN) or Remote Access Services (RAS). The replication process sends each salesperson's transactions to the server. If necessary, the process sends any changes from the server data to the salesperson. In addition to allowing data to be replicated, if the developers in the organization are busily adding forms, reports, and modules to the database's master copy, any changes to the application components are also updated in the remote copies as users log on to the system.

This example illustrates just one of the several valuable uses of replication. In a nutshell, data replication is used to improve the availability and integrity of data throughout an organization or enterprise. The practical uses of data replication are many; we can categorize them into five general areas, explained in the following sections.

Sharing Data Among Offices

In today's global economy, it's the norm for companies to have many offices distributed throughout the country or even the world. Before Access 95, it was difficult to implement an Access application that would support sharing data among several offices. However, with replication, each office can have a replica of the database. Periodically throughout the day, each office can synchronize its changes with corporate headquarters. How often the synchronization happens depends on the frequency required for data at each location to be current at any given moment.

Sharing Data Among Dispersed Users

The salesperson example used earlier provides an example of sharing data among dispersed users. This implementation of replication generally involves mobile users who connect to the network after modifying data out on the road. Because only incremental changes are transferred from the design master (the original) to the replicas (the copies) and from the replicas to the design master, this form of replication makes the mobile computing scenario economically feasible.

Reducing Network Load

Replication can be very effective in reducing network traffic loads. You can replicate the design master onto one or more additional servers. Distributed users can then make changes to one of the additional servers, which significantly improves performance by distributing the processing load throughout the network. You can synchronize changes made to the data on the additional servers with the main server periodically during the day. The frequency of the synchronization depends on the need for data to be current at any moment in time.

Distributing Application Updates

Replication is an excellent vehicle for distributing application updates. Access allows you to make design changes only to the design master; therefore, as users throughout the organization log on to synchronize with the design master, any structural changes to the application are sent to the user. This is much more efficient and effective than giving every user an entirely new copy of the application database each time you make a minor change to the application's schema.

Backing Up the Data in Your Application

Many people don't think of replication as a means of backing up application data, but replication is extremely well suited for this task. Ordinarily, to back up an Access database, everyone must log off the system, but that's not necessary with replication. The synchronization process can occur periodically during the day while users are still logged on to the system and all changes are replicated. Not only is this more efficient than backing up the entire database, but it also ensures that you can quickly be up and running on a backup server if there's a problem on a server.

Understanding When Replication Isn't Appropriate

Despite the many positive aspects of replication, it is not appropriate in a few situations, such as when data consistency is critical. If an application requires that data be current at every given moment, it isn't a good candidate for replication. Replication is also not effective when many different users modify a large volume of existing records throughout the day. In a situation such as this, resolving conflicts that happen when multiple users update the same record isn't practical. Furthermore, you cannot utilize replication if you are using Visual SourceSafe to manage the development process. Finally, you cannot rename or move design masters, and a design master that becomes corrupted can be difficult to recover.

Understanding the Implementation of Replication

The following steps compose the replication process:

1. Making a database replicable
2. Creating and distributing replicas
3. Synchronizing replicas with the design master
4. Resolving conflicts

These steps can be done in the following ways:

- Through the Access user interface
- By using the Replication Manager
- By using ActiveX Data Objects (ADO) code

This chapter covers the steps needed for the replication process and the alternatives for performing each step. The sections that follow provide an overview of each alternative.

The Access User Interface

The Access user interface gives you a series of menu items that allow you to perform all the steps of the replication process. The Tools, Replication Create Replica, Synchronize Now, Partial Replica Wizard, Resolve Conflict, and Recover Design Master. This chapter covers these menu options.

The Replication Manager

The Replication Manager is a sophisticated tool that's part of Microsoft Office XP Developer. It's a mandatory player in the replication process when you're managing many replicas. Besides providing basic replication functionality, the Replication Manager lets you schedule the synchronization of replicas. In fact, the Replication Manager allows you to manage and intricately control all aspects of the replication process. The section "Using the Replication Manager" later in this chapter covers the Replication Manager in detail.

ADO Code

You can also perform most aspects of the replication process using ADO code, which can make a database replicable, create, and synchronize replicas, as well as get and set properties of a replicable database. You can easily integrate ADO with the other methods of replication. Although it requires the most time and effort on your part, ADO code lets you base replication on events rather than time and gives your users a custom user interface for the replication process.

Programs That Support Replication Using ADO

Visual Basic 4.0 and higher, Excel for Windows 95 and higher, and Visual C++ all support replication using DAO. You can't perform replication with these products by using Microsoft Office Developer, however, so it's easier to manage the replication process on a machine that has Access installed.

Understanding the Replication Architecture: What Makes Replication Tick?

Now that you know what replication is and what alternatives you have for implementing it, you're ready to learn about what makes it happen. Five components are responsible for the replication process:

- Tracking Layer
- Microsoft Replication Manager
- Synchronizer
- File System Transport
- Registry Entries

The Tracking Layer

The Tracking Layer refers to the part of the Jet Engine that's capable of tracking and recording all the changes made to the design master and to each of the replicas. It's responsible for making sure that changes are available to be transmitted to other replicas.

The Microsoft Replication Manager

The Replication Manager gives you the tools needed to support the replication process. You can also use it to generate reports on synchronization activity.

The Synchronizer

If you use the Access user interface to manage the replication process, Jet handles the exchange of information between the replicas. If you use the Replication Manager to manage the replication process, the Synchronizer is responsible for monitoring the changes and handling the exchange of data between replicas.

When you're using the Replication Manager, it assigns each replica to a Synchronizer. The Synchronizer performs either direct or indirect synchronization between the members of a replica set. When you initiate synchronization, the Synchronizer tries to make a direct connection with the target member of the replica set. If the Synchronizer can open both members of the replica set simultaneously, direct synchronization occurs, which means that it applies changes from one member of the replica set directly to the other member.

If the Synchronizer determines that the target replica set member isn't available, indirect synchronization takes place. The target replica set member might be unavailable for many reasons; some possible reasons why the Synchronizer can't establish a direct connection include the following:

- The network server where the replica resides is down.

- The computer containing the other replica is logged off the network.

- The other member is currently involved in another synchronization.

- The other member is not in a shared folder.

Regardless of the cause of an indirect synchronization, the Synchronizer for the first member of the replica set leaves a message for the Synchronizer assigned to the member of the unavailable replica set. This message is stored in a shared folder on the network that acts as a drop-box location for the target member. All messages sent while a member of the replica set is unavailable are stored in the drop-box location.

> **NOTE**
>
> If you need to determine whether a direct or indirect synchronization occurred, you can browse the MSysExchangeLog system table. The section of this chapter titled "System Tables Added to the Database" covers this table that is included only in replicated databases.

The Synchronizer is configured through the Replication Manager user interface and is covered in more detail in the section "Using the Replication Manager," later in this chapter.

The File System Transport

The File System Transport is responsible for supplying messaging services to the Synchronizer.

The Registry Entries

Several Windows Registry entries are responsible for helping with the replication process; Figure 17.1 shows a couple of these Registry entries. Notice the Transporter subkey under the `HKEY_LOCAL_MACHINE\SOFTWARE\Microsoft\Jet\4.0` key. This entry contains important path information used by the Replication Manager and the Synchronizer.

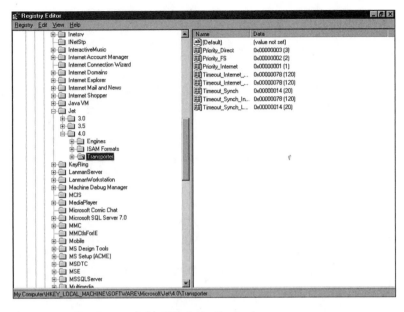

FIGURE 17.1   Replication and the Windows Registry.

Understanding Replication Topologies

The topology for data synchronization determines which replicas synchronize with each other. The *topology* is essentially a blueprint for how the changes are merged between the members of the replica set. Different topologies are used for different situations, and the topology that you choose is determined by your business needs and your organization's design. The synchronization topologies are star, ring, fully connected, linear, and hybrid. (See Figure 17.2.)

Star Topology

With the star topology, a single hub periodically synchronizes with the rest of the replicas. The two biggest advantages of this topology are simplicity and ease of programming. Another advantage is that data doesn't have to travel very far. Each replica synchronizes with only one other database, the hub. However, this isn't particularly reliable. If the controlling replica is damaged or unavailable, the synchronization process can't take place. Another disadvantage of the star topology is that the first replica to synchronize with the hub gets no data from the other replicas, but the last replica to synchronize with the hub receives all the data from the others. Issuing two rounds of synchronization can circumvent this problem. Finally, you can't use the star topology with a large number of replicas because the entire load is placed on the hub.

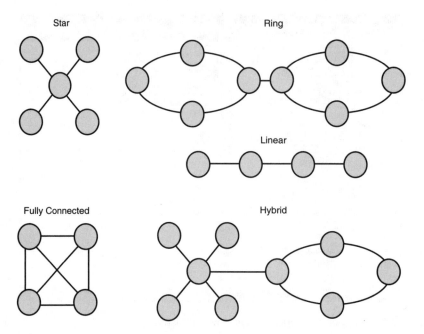

FIGURE 17.2   Examples of replication topologies.

NOTE

The design master must never be a hub. If you designate it as the hub, it's possible for someone to accidentally synchronize partial design changes to the rest of the replicas. Instead, place the design master on one of the satellite machines and synchronize design changes with the controlling replica whenever they're complete and fully tested.

Ring Topology

With the ring topology, each computer synchronizes with the next computer in the replication chain. There's no central point of synchronization in this scenario. The major advantage of the ring topology is that it distributes the load throughout the satellite machines. The primary disadvantage is that it might take a long time for changes to be distributed throughout the replicas because there's no central point of synchronization. Furthermore, if one of the replicas in the chain is damaged or unavailable, the replication process stops, but you can handle this using code that senses the problem and bypasses the unavailable machine.

Fully Connected Topology

When the fully connected topology is used, every replica synchronizes with every other replica. This topology offers several advantages. Its strongest point is that it makes sure that data is the most current at any given moment because with this topology you send data directly from each replica to all the other replicas in the replica set. For this reason, it's the best solution when the data must be as current as possible. Another benefit of the fully connected topology is its high level of redundancy. This means that the same data exists in multiple places. Also, because of the low level of *latency* (which means that at any given moment, it's likely that the data isn't current) in the fully connected topology, the effect of any one of the replicas failing is minimal. The fully connected topology does have disadvantages, however. It requires the most overhead of any of the topologies because of the network traffic generated as each replica in the set synchronizes with all the others. Furthermore, the replication schedules must be staggered; otherwise, collisions will probably happen as more than one replica tries to synchronize with the same replica.

Linear Topology

The linear topology is similar to the ring topology except that the chain is never completed. For this reason, the linear topology has the highest level of latency. The biggest advantage of the linear topology is the low level of network traffic generated; however, this topology isn't practical for most applications because it takes more time for changes to reach all the replicas in the set.

Hybrid Topology

A hybrid topology is any combination of the other topologies. In a complex application, it's usually not appropriate to use a single topology by itself. By combining the topologies, you can get exactly the results you need. Figure 17.2 illustrates just one example of a hybrid topology—a ring connected with a star. You should experiment with the different configurations to see which topology best balances processing load, network traffic, and data latency.

Changes That Replication Makes to Your Database

Replication makes several changes to the database, but they're necessary to manage the demands of the replication process. Access makes the following changes to a database when it's replicated:

- It adds fields to each replicated table.
- It adds several system tables to the database.
- It adds properties to the database document objects.
- It changes sequential AutoNumber fields to random AutoNumber fields.
- The size of the database increases.

Fields Added to Each Replicated Table

During the replication process, the Jet Engine determines whether each table has a field with an AutoNumber data type and a ReplicationID field size. If it doesn't find a field meeting these criteria, it adds a field called s_Guid to the table that uniquely identifies each record. It's identical across replicas.

The Jet Engine also adds three additional fields to each table in the database: s_Lineage, s_ColLineage, and s_Generation. The s_Lineage field stores the IDs of replicas that have updated a record and the last version created by those replicas; the s_Generation field stores information about groups of changes. These fields are visible only if you opt to view system objects (use Tools, Options).

System Tables Added to the Database

The Jet Engine also adds several tables to your database that track conflicts, errors, and exchanges made between the replica databases. MSysSideTables and MSysExchangeLog are the most useful of these tables; they can be viewed if you have chosen to view system objects (using Tools, Options).

MsysSidetable tracks tables that have experienced a conflict during the synchronization process. It stores the name of the side table that has the conflicting records.

MSysErrors tracks all unresolved synchronization errors. It's empty when all errors have been resolved. You can find this table in all the replicas.

MSysSchemaProb identifies errors that happened while synchronizing a replica's design. It's visible only if a design conflict has occurred between the user's replica and another replica in the set.

MSysExchangeLog is a local table that stores information about synchronizations that have taken place between the local replica and other members of the replica set.

Properties Added to the Database Objects

Access adds several new properties to a replicable database, some of which are available only in VBA code. The database's `Replicable` property is set to `True`. You cannot modify this property after it has been set to `True`. The `ReplicaID` property is a unique ID assigned to each replica. The `DesignMasterID` property can transfer the design master status to another database, which you generally do only if the original master becomes irreparably damaged.

In addition to the properties that apply to the database, you can apply two properties to the tables, queries, forms, reports, macros, and modules in the database: the `KeepLocal` and `Replicable` properties. The `KeepLocal` property, applied to an object before you replicate the database, prevents anyone from copying the object to the other replicas in the set. The `Replicable` property, which you use after you replicate a database, indicates that you will replicate the object.

Changes to Sequential AutoNumber Fields

Another important change made to your tables when replicating a database is that Access changes all the AutoNumber fields from incremental to random. Existing records aren't affected, but Access generates new keys randomly because that reduces conflicts when you synchronize the databases. If all the copies generate sequential keys, you can see that conflicts will happen when you try to merge changes. By randomly generating primary keys, this conflict is much less likely to take place.

Changes to the Size of the Database

When you replicate a database, its size increases because of the added fields and tables. Generally, this increase isn't a problem. If disk space is at a premium, you should consider this aspect of replication before you decide to build replication into your application.

Making a Database Replicable

A replicable database is simply a database whose `Replicable` property has been set to `True`. If a database hasn't been marked as replicable, you can't replicate it. However, when you flag a database as replicable, the Jet Engine makes several changes to it to render it replicable. Until the Jet Engine makes these changes, Access doesn't recognize the database as part of a replication set and you can't synchronize it with other databases.

When you're ready to replicate a database, you should take the following steps:

1. Flag any objects in the database that you don't want replicated as local by setting their `KeepLocal` property to `True`.

2. Make a replication design master by setting the database's `Replicable` property to `True`.

3. Make copies of the design master, called replicas.

You can make a database replicable by using the Access user interface, using the Replication Manager, or writing code. The following section covers using the Access user interface. Making a database replicable by using the Replication Manager is covered in the section "Using the Replication Manager"; using code is covered in the section "Implementing Replication Using Code," both later in this chapter.

Rendering a Database Replicable with the Access User Interface

To render a database replicable with the Access user interface, choose Tools, Replication, Create Replica. Microsoft Access gives you a warning that it must close the database before proceeding. (See Figure 17.3.)

FIGURE 17.3   This dialog box warns you that Access must close the database before converting it to a design master.

After selecting Yes, you see another dialog box asking whether you want Access to make a backup of the original database before continuing. (See Figure 17.4.) It's always a good idea to back up a database before replicating it because you can't return a database to its nonreplicable state after it has been flagged as replicable.

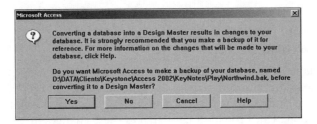

FIGURE 17.4   This dialog box prompts you to have Access create a backup of the database before it's replicated.

Next, Access prompts you for the name and location of your new replica in the Location of New Replica dialog box. (See Figure 17.5.) After you click OK, Access creates the new replica and the process is finished.

FIGURE 17.5   The Location of New Replica dialog box allows you to specify a location and name for the replica.

Your original database is converted to a design master, and the replica is assigned the name and location specified in the Location of New Replica dialog box. If Access completes the replication process successfully, the dialog box shown in Figure 17.6 appears. Notice that only the design master can accept changes to the database structure (schema).

FIGURE 17.6   This dialog box appears after successful replication of a database.

Preventing Objects from Being Replicated

You might want to prevent specific objects in a replicable database from being replicated if, for example, certain data in your database is confidential or it's unnecessary for most users to see certain data. An employee salary table, for example, might be maintained and used in the master but isn't necessary for any of the replicas. The fewer objects that you replicate, the more effective the synchronization process is.

In the Access user interface, you can check the Make Replicable check box in the Save As dialog box when you create a new object, as shown in Figure 17.7 (if unchecked, the new object is local), or you can change the `Replicable` property of an existing object in its properties sheet, as shown in Figure 17.8. Access indicates replicated objects by an icon of a globe with rotating arrows in the objects lists, which are contained in the Database window.

FIGURE 17.7   Making a new object replicable in the Save As dialog box.

You can also change the `Replicable` property by using VBA code or the Replication Manager. To do this, set the `KeepLocal` property of the specific objects to `True`. When you try to set the `KeepLocal` property to `True` with VBA code, you get an error unless you have already appended the property onto the object. Therefore, you must include error handling in your code to handle this problem. The section "Replicating a Database with the Replication Manager" later in this chapter covers using the Replication Manager to flag an object as nonreplicable. The section "Implementing Replication Using Code" later in this chapter covers the code required to add the `KeepLocal` property to an object and set its value to `True`.

FIGURE 17.8   Changing an object's `Replicable` property in its properties sheet.

Creating Additional Replicas

After you have made one replica, you'll probably want to make more. These additional replicas are copies that you can distribute throughout the organization. You can create them using the Access user interface, the Replication Manager, or VBA code.

A sales organization, for example, might use multiple replicas for sales reps who take copies of the database along on their notebook computers. Each of these copies must be a replica created by the replication process rather than a copy made by the operating system. Otherwise, the work of each salesperson can't be synchronized with that of the others.

You can make replicas with any of the three methods mentioned, but you can also make additional replicas from any member of a replica set. Each replica set is independent from all other replica sets. You can't synchronize replicas from different sets.

To create additional replicas with the Access user interface, follow these steps:

1. Open the database that you want to replicate. You can open either the design master or any replica.

2. Choose Tools, Replication, Create Replica.

3. When prompted, supply a name for the new replica.

Synchronizing Replicas

Synchronizing replicas means reconciling all the changes between them. Modified records are changed in all the copies, deleted records are removed from all the replicas, and added records are appended to all the replicas.

The ability to synchronize is what makes data replication useful. Additions, modifications, and deletions are propagated among all the replicas in a set, which lets users see the changes other users made.

As with creating a replica, Access gives you three methods of synchronizing replicas: the Access user interface, the Replication Manager, and VBA code.

To perform synchronization with the Access user interface, follow these steps:

1. Choose Tools, Replication, Synchronize Now.

2. The Synchronize Database dialog box opens. (See Figure 17.9.) Select the database that you want to synchronize with and click OK.

3. You're prompted to allow Access to close the database prior to synchronization (see Figure 17.10). If you select Yes, Access closes and reopens the database for you.

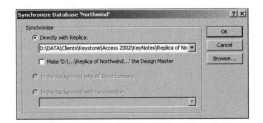

FIGURE 17.9   The Synchronize Database dialog box lets you select the database that you want to synchronize with.

FIGURE 17.10   This dialog box confirms that you will allow Access to close the database prior to synchronization.

Resolving Replication Conflicts

When the Jet Engine tries to synchronize two databases, it might find that the same row has been changed in both databases, resulting in a conflict that must be handled. The rule is that the database in which the row has changed most often wins. If both rows have changed the same number of times, Access chooses the winner randomly. This might sound frightening, but it isn't as bad is it seems because you can let the user know which changes were rejected.

You must know whether two members of the replica set contain conflicting information. Two users out in the field might have entered different information about a sale or a customer, so it's important that the program identify these inconsistencies and have a method for handling them.

If there are conflicts, Access warns you about them when you try to open the database that has the conflicts. (See Figure 17.11.) Here, you're given the choice of whether to resolve the conflicts.

FIGURE 17.11   This dialog box warns of synchronization conflicts.

If the user selects Yes, the Jet Engine tries to identify the conflicts. After identifying the conflicts, the Microsoft Replication Conflict Viewer dialog box, shown in Figure 17.12, appears. Notice that, in this example, the Jet Engine identified two conflicts in the Customers table. The user can either resolve the conflict or postpone the conflict resolution.

FIGURE 17.12   Use the Microsoft Replication Conflict Viewer dialog box to resolve conflicts between tables.

If the user clicks View, another Microsoft Replication Conflict Viewer dialog box opens. (See Figure 17.13.) This dialog box shows the user each record that has a conflict, providing the opportunity to keep existing data, keep revised data, overwrite with conflicting data, or overwrite with revised data.

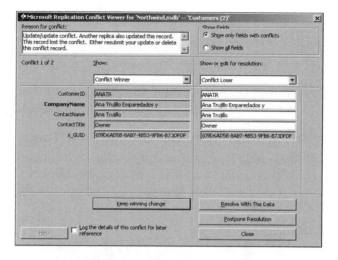

FIGURE 17.13   In this Replication Conflict Viewer dialog box, you view and resolve specific conflicts.

The user can log the details of the conflict for later reference. The user also can resolve or postpone the resolution of each conflict. After responding to all conflicts, Access returns the user to the Microsoft Replication Conflict Viewer dialog box.

NOTE

If you don't want to give your users this level of control over conflict resolution, you can write code to resolve conflicts in any way you want. The section "Synchronizing a Database Using Code" later in this chapter covers this process.

Using the Replication Manager

The Replication Manager is a powerful tool that lets you take full advantage of replication in Access 2002. It's included only with Microsoft Office XP Developer, as one of the Developer Tools. The Replication Manager's major benefits include the following:

- Lets you easily replicate a database

- Allows you to easily create additional replicas

- Gives you the ability to synchronize any replicas in the set

- Allows you to schedule automated synchronization

- Gives you the opportunity to view an object's replication history

- Lets you easily manage replication properties

- Offers a way to manage synchronization with replicas at remote sites

- Allows you to perform synchronization over a LAN, an intranet, or the Internet

Running the Replication Manager for the First Time

You can open the Replication Manager using a desktop shortcut or the Windows Start menu, where it is located in the Microsoft Office XP Developer program group. The first time you run the Replication Manager, the Configure Replication Manager Wizard appears. (See Figure 17.14.)

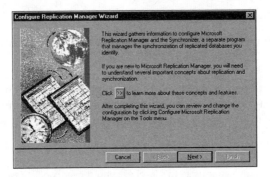

FIGURE 17.14   The Configure Replication Manager Wizard.

The Configure Replication Manager Wizard is a straightforward utility that allows you to easily configure replication of your database. The following steps depict how to utilize the Replication Manager Wizard interface to simplistically configure your database for replication:

1. Click Next to start the configuration process and launch the Configure Replication Manager Wizard.

2. This step of the Configure Replication Manager Wizard asks whether you want to support indirect synchronization (see Figure 17.15). With indirect synchronization, a Synchronizer for each of the two replicas opens its own replica locally. A desktop computer leaves changes in a drop box on the network. When the laptop connects to the network, the Synchronizer on the laptop finds the changes in its drop-box folder and applies them to the replica. The notebook leaves its changes in a drop-box folder of the desktop Synchronizer, which finds the changes and applies them. This is the preferred synchronization method for remote users who aren't always logged on to the network. Make your selection and click Next.

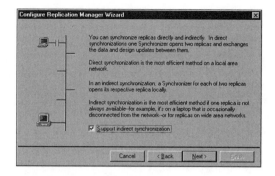

FIGURE 17.15   Selecting a form of synchronization.

3. If you choose to support indirect synchronization, the next step of the wizard gives you some information about synchronization types. After reading this, click Next. The wizard prompts you for a location for the drop-box folder. (See Figure 17.16.) Select a folder and click Next.

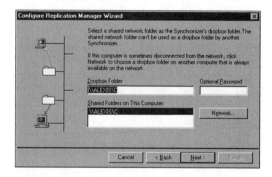

FIGURE 17.16   Selecting a location for the Synchronizer to store changes.

4. The wizard asks you whether the computer on which you're running the wizard is an Internet server. Make your selection and click Next.

5. If you indicate that the computer is an Internet server, the next step asks whether you want to use the Internet server to synchronize replicated databases. If you respond Yes and click Next, you're prompted for the name of the Internet server. Enter the name and click Next. (See Figure 17.17.) The next step asks you to provide a shared folder and shared name used when synchronizing over the Internet. Click Next, and you're prompted for an FTP alias name. Select the FTP alias name and click Next.

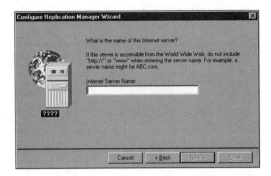

FIGURE 17.17   If your computer is an Internet server, here's the place to tell the wizard its partial URL.

6. The next step of the Configure Replication Manager Wizard prompts you to designate the order in which the synchronization methods are attempted. The example shown in Figure 17.18 shows that Access will attempt to perform indirect synchronization. If it does not succeed, Access will attempt direct synchronization. Finally, Access will attempt to perform Internet synchronization.

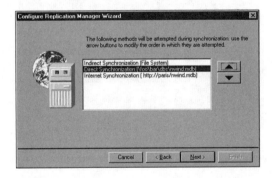

FIGURE 17.18   Select the order in which each synchronization method is attempted.

7. Select a location for the log file used to record significant events that happen during the synchronization process. (See Figure 17.19.) Click Next.

8. The next step of the wizard prompts you for a Synchronizer name. Access uses this name for an icon and as a descriptive name for the Synchronizer. This step of the wizard also asks whether you want to automatically start the Synchronizer when Windows starts. (See Figure 17.20.) The Synchronizer must be running for scheduled synchronization to take place, so you might want to select this option. Enter a Synchronizer name and indicate whether you want the Synchronizer to automatically start; then click Next.

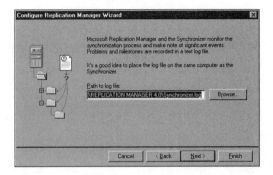

FIGURE 17.19   Selecting the name and location for the log file.

9. Click Finish to complete the process.

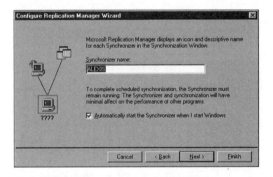

FIGURE 17.20   Selecting a name for the Synchronizer.

After the Configure Replication Manager Wizard is finished, you can either convert a database to a design master or create a new replica. (See Figure 17.21.) You can perform these tasks any time, so you should click Close.

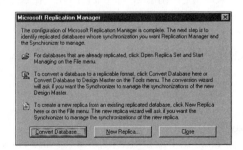

FIGURE 17.21   The Microsoft Replication Manager launches for the first time.

NOTE

If you opted to load the Synchronizer whenever you launch Windows and you decide that you don't want the Synchronizer to be launched automatically, you must remove the Synchronizer icon from the Windows Startup folder.

Replicating a Database with the Replication Manager

In addition to using the Access user interface to make a database replicable, you can use the Replication Manager. It offers additional options, such as designating an object as local. Here are the steps:

1. From the Replication Manager, click the Convert Database to the Design Master toolbar button or choose File, Convert Database to Design Master. The Database to Convert to the Design Master dialog box appears. (See Figure 17.22.)

FIGURE 17.22   Select the database that you want to convert to a design master.

2. Select a file to convert and click Open.

3. The Convert Database to Design Master Wizard appears. Click Next after reading the introductory information.

4. Indicate whether you want to make a backup of the database before converting it to a design master. Then click Next. It's always a good idea to keep a backup of the unreplicated database.

5. Enter a description for the new replica set and click Next. All replicas made from this design master will be members of the replica set you're creating. (See Figure 17.23.)

6. The wizard asks you whether you want to make all objects available to the replica set or flag some of them as local. (See Figure 17.24.) If you click Make Some Objects Available to the Entire Replica Set and click the Choose Objects button, the Select Replicated Objects dialog box opens so that you can designate selected objects as local. (See Figure 17.25.) To flag an object as local, clear its check box. Click OK when you're finished.

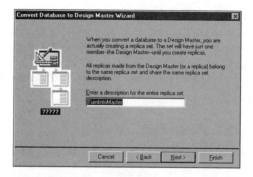

FIGURE 17.23   Entering a description for the replica set.

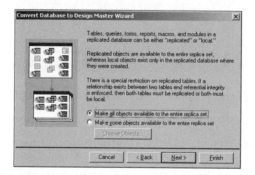

FIGURE 17.24   Designating whether you want all or just some objects to be replicated.

FIGURE 17.25   Flagging objects as local or replicated.

7. Next, indicate whether you want the replicas to be read-only. (See Figure 17.26.) The design master is the only place where you can make schema changes. If you want to limit data changes to the design master as well, select the option that makes all replicas read-only. In general, you should keep the default option of I Want to Be Able to Create Read/Write Replicas. Click Next after you a selection.

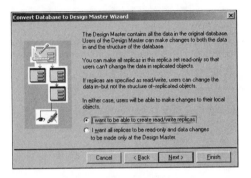

FIGURE 17.26   Indicating whether the database will allow read/write replicas to be created.

8. The next step of the wizard asks whether you want to manage synchronization of the design master with the Synchronizer found on the current machine. If you answer No, synchronization must originate by another managed member of the replica set. Make your selection and click Next.

9. Click Finish to complete the wizard; Access notifies you of success or warns you about any problems that happened during the conversion process.

NOTE

You cannot designate a table as local if it's involved in a relationship with a replicated table.

NOTE

When you have more than one replica set, you must use the Managed Replicas tool on the Replication Manager toolbar to view a different replica set. You can view only one replica set at a time.

Creating Replicas with the Replication Manager

Just as you can create replicas by using the Access user interface, you can create replicas with the Replication Manager. To do so, follow these steps:

1. Click New Replica on the toolbar; then click Next.

2. Select a source and destination for the replica. The source is the name of the database you're replicating, and the destination is the name of the replica. Click Next.

3. Indicate whether you want to be able to make data changes within the replica. Click Next.

4. Indicate whether you want the Synchronizer on the current machine to manage the replica. Click Next.

5. Click Finish.

NOTE

If you create a replica of a database managed by a different Synchronizer, you must use the Replication Manager on the other computer to configure the Synchronizer.

Synchronizing Replicas with the Replication Manager

Just as you can synchronize replicas with the Access user interface, you can use the Replication Manager by following these steps:

1. From the Replication Manager, click the Synchronize Now tool on the toolbar.

2. The Synchronize Now dialog box opens. (See Figure 17.27.) Here, you can designate details of the synchronization process. When you're finished, click OK to finish the synchronization process.

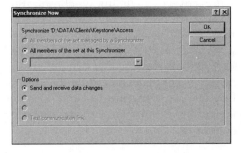

FIGURE 17.27   The Synchronize Now dialog box allows you to designate details of the synchronization process.

Remote Synchronizations

You might be surprised that the Replication Manager map shows only one machine, even though you have many replicas. One icon appears for each Synchronizer involved in the replica set. Figure 17.28 shows two Synchronizers involved in the replication process: 5000Alison and HOME1. The second site was set up by installing the Replication Manager on the second machine. Any replica from the local site can then be moved to the remote site by establishing a connection to the remote site and choosing File, Move Replica. You can locate the managed folder at the remote site and move the replica to the remote site's managed folder.

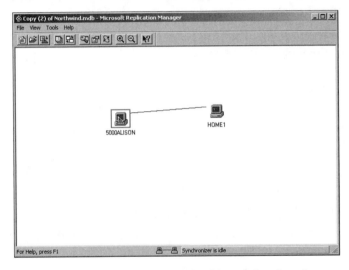

FIGURE 17.28   The Replication Manager map with two Synchronizers.

After both sites appear on the replication map, you can manage synchronizations by using the join line that connects them. You can right-click on the join line and select Synchronize Now or, to establish a schedule for synchronization, select Edit Schedule. The next section covers scheduling synchronization.

Scheduled Synchronizations

You can schedule synchronizations between replicas managed by the same Synchronizer or between replicas managed by two different Synchronizers. To schedule synchronization between replicas managed by the same Synchronizer, right-click on the icon representing the local Synchronizer and select Edit Locally Managed Replica Schedule. (See Figure 17.29.) From here, you can select the days and times when the replicas synchronize.

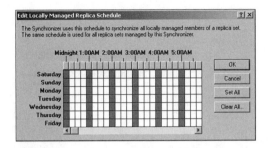

FIGURE 17.29   Use the Edit Locally Managed Replica Schedule dialog box to select the days and times when the replicas synchronize.

To schedule the synchronization process between two different Synchronizers, right-click on the join line and select Edit Schedule to open the Edit Schedule dialog box. Here you can schedule the specifics of the synchronization process between the two sites. The shading of each box indicates which Synchronizer initiates that exchange. If Access can't make the connection when the exchange is initiated, the drop-box folder keeps a temporary log of the changes. Every 15 minutes, it retries the connection until it's successful.

Reviewing the Synchronization History

The synchronization history can be very useful. Besides giving you an audit trail, it helps you analyze the effectiveness of the topology and synchronization schedule you have selected. The Replication Manager keeps three types of logs:

- The local synchronization history

- The remote synchronization history

- The Synchronizer log

To view the local synchronization history, right-click the local machine icon and select View Local Synchronization History. This opens the Synchronization History dialog box. (See Figure 17.30.) It shows you details about the exchange of information between the local replicas.

To view the remote synchronization history, select the line joining two Synchronizers and choose View, Synchronization History to open the Synchronization History dialog box. If you want more information about any of the log entries, click Details to open the Synchronization Details dialog box. (See Figure 17.31.)

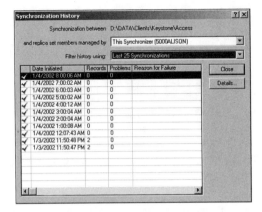

FIGURE 17.30   Viewing local synchronization history.

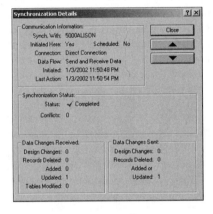

FIGURE 17.31   The Synchronization Details dialog box shows the details of a synchronization process.

Working with Synchronization Properties

You can also view properties of the selected Synchronizer. To do this, double-click the Synchronizer; the Replica Properties window appears. This tabbed dialog box gives you important information about the selected Synchronizer.

NOTE

Jet 4.0 and Access 2002 support synchronization over the Internet or over an intranet. You place a replica on a server and use the Replication Manager to synchronize, using a standard HTTP connection.

Using Partial Replication

Jet 3.5 and Access 97 introduced *partial replication*, meaning that you replicate only a subset of the data. This is useful, for example, when you have several salespeople and you want each salesperson to have just his or her own data. However, you want all the salespeople to be able to synchronize their changes with other databases on the network. You can create partial replicas using the Partial Replica Wizard, available via the Access user interface or by using VBA code. The procedure for using VBA code to create a partial replica is covered in the section "Creating a Partial Replica Using Code," later in this chapter. The text that follows covers the Partial Replica Wizard. To create a partial replica, follow these steps:

1. Within Microsoft Access, with the database that you want to replicate open, select Tools, Replication, Partial Replica Wizard. The Partial Replica Wizard appears.

2. Designate whether you want to create a new partial replica or modify an existing partial replica (see Figure 17.32). Click Next. The screen appears as in Figure 17.33.

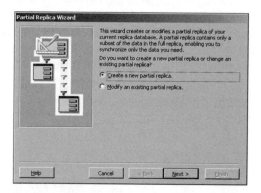

FIGURE 17.32   The Partial Replica Wizard prompts you to designate a name and location for the partial replica; indicate whether you want to create a global, local, or anonymous replica; and indicate whether you want to designate the replica as read-only or prohibit users from deleting records in the replica.

3. Designate a name and location for the partial replica, and indicate whether you want to create a global, local, or anonymous replica. This step also allows you to designate the replica as read-only or to prohibit users from deleting records in the replica. Designate your options and click Next.

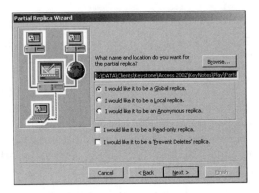

FIGURE 17.33   Designate whether you want to create a new partial replica or modify an existing partial replica.

4. Create a filter expression that limits the data contained in the partial replica. To do this, select the table whose data you want to filter. Next select the field that you want to use as criteria and select the operator appropriate for the expression. Click Paste. To complete the expression, enter for the expression the value that you want to use to limit the data contained in the partial replica. You can expand or refine the selection using And and Or, as appropriate. Figure 17.34 shows a filter expression that creates a partial replica with data only for customers in the region of California. Click Next.

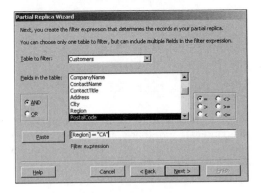

FIGURE 17.34   Designate the filter expression used to limit the data contained in the partial replica.

5. The next step of the Partial Replica Wizard is very important. It allows you to designate additional tables that you want to include within the partial replica. Tables that appear bold are related to the table whose criteria you are using to create the partial replica. You must deselect these tables so that only records

related to the records in your filter are included in the partial replica. Tables that are not bold are not related to the filtered table with referential integrity enforced. It is up to you whether you want to include the data within these unrelated tables. In Figure 17.35, the check marks have been removed from all the related tables, but the check mark remains for the unrelated table. This means that only related data is included for all the tables in which referential integrity is established, whereas the entire Customers1 table is included.

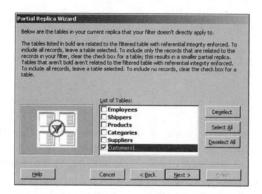

FIGURE 17.35 Designate what additional data is included in the partial replica.

6. Finally, you can designate whether you want Access to create a report with all the property settings that apply to the partial replica. Make your selection and click Finish.

Implementing Replication Using Code

You can implement most of the replication functions using code, but this isn't the easiest way to manage replication. However, sometimes you might want to implement aspects of the replication process with code so that you can better control the process and its interface from within your application.

NOTE

All the examples that follow require the use of the Jet Replication Objects (JRO) object library. To access the JRO object library, you must use Tools, References in the VBE to select the Microsoft Jet and Replication Objects 2.5 Library or above. The database that will use the JRO library must be open.

Making a Database Replicable by Using Code

 The routine shown in Listing 17.1, located in the Chap17Ex database, renders a
database replicable by using code.

LISTING 17.1   Making a Database Replicable

```
Sub MakeReplicable(strMaster As String)
    Dim rep As JRO.Replica

    Set rep = New JRO.Replica

    rep.MakeReplicable strMaster, True
    Set rep = Nothing
End Sub
```

This routine accepts the path to any database as a parameter. It first creates a JRO
Replica object. The code uses the MakeReplicable method of the Replica object to
convert the database to a design master. The MakeReplicable method receives the
name of the database that you want to convert to a design master and an optional
parameter that is used to designate whether you want the master to use column-level
tracking (discussed in the accompanying note).

NOTE

Before Access 2000, conflicts were generated at the record level. This means that if two users
made changes to different fields in the same record, Access generated a conflict. Access 2000
introduced column-level tracking. This means that if two users make changes to different
fields in the same record, a conflict does not occur. Conflicts occur only when two users make
changes to the same field in the same record. Column-level tracking is an optional feature
that Access turns on by default. Column-level tracking can be set only when the database is
made replicable.

Flagging an Object as Local

Unless you do something special, all objects in a database are included in the replication process. The code in Listing 17.2 illustrates how to flag a database object as
local.

LISTING 17.2   Flagging an Object as Local

```
Sub MakeLocal(strDatabase As String, _
    strName As String, _
```

LISTING 17.2   Continued

```
    strObjType As String)

    Dim rep As New JRO.Replica

    rep.ActiveConnection = strDatabase
    rep.SetObjectReplicability strName, strObjType, False

    Set rep = Nothing
End Sub
```

The code begins by declaring a JRO `Replica` object. The `ActiveConnection` property of the `Replica` object is set to point at the database whose object you want to flag as local. The code uses the `SetObjectReplicability` method of the `Replica` object to flag a database object as local. It receives the name of the object that you want to flag as local and the type of object you are flagging. Because the code sets the replicability to `False`, it flags the object as local.

Creating a Replica Using Code

You can use the `CreateReplica` method of the `Replica` object to create a new replica with code. The code appears in Listing 17.3.

LISTING 17.3   Making a Replica

```
Sub MakeReplica(strMaster As String, strReplica As String)
    Dim rep As JRO.Replica
    Set rep = New JRO.Replica

    rep.ActiveConnection = strMaster
    rep.CreateReplica strReplica, "Replica of " & strMaster
End Sub
```

This code accepts two parameters, the first containing the path and filename for the master, and the second containing the path and filename for the replica. The code executes the `CreateReplica` method on the `Replica` object. The first parameter of the `CreateReplica` method is the name of the replica you are creating. The second parameter is the name of the replica. Other optional parameters include the type of replica you want to create, the visibility of the replica, the priority for the replica, and the updateability of the replica.

Types of Replicas

When creating a replica, you can use the ReplicaType parameter to designate the type of replica created. You can designate a replica as a design master, a full replica, a partial replica, or a replica that is not replicable.

Visibility of Replicas

Access 2000 and JRO introduced a new property, Visibility, that you use to designate the visibility of a replica. The replica's visibility determines which replicas can synchronize with a given replica. You can set the visibility of a replica only when you create it. You designate a replica as global, local, or anonymous. A global replica can synchronize with any replica in its replica set. By default, all replicas are global.

A local replica can synchronize only with its parent. A parent can schedule synchronization with a local replica. The parent proxies replication conflicts and errors for the local replica. A local replica can create only other local replicas. The replicas created by a local replica share the same parent as the local replica. All other replicas are unaware of a local replica.

An anonymous replica can synchronize only with its parent. Anonymous replicas are appropriate when a replica rarely participates in the synchronization process. The anonymous replica proxies its identity for updates to the publishing replica. Anonymous replicas can create only other anonymous replicas. The child replicas share the same parent as the anonymous replica.

Priority for Replicas

You can use another new property of a replica, Priority, to indicate the priority of the replica during the synchronization process. If Access encounters conflicts during the synchronization process, the replica with the highest priority wins.

Updateability of Replicas

You can use the Updateability property of the replica to determine whether the data in the replica is updateable. By default, a replica's data is updateable. Setting this property to the constant value jrRepUpdReadOnly designates the data within the replica as read-only.

Creating a Partial Replica Using Code

You can also create a partial replica using VBA code, as appears in Listing 17.4.

LISTING 17.4   Creating a Partial Replica

```
Sub CreatePartialReplica()

    Dim repFull As New JRO.Replica
```

LISTING 17.4   Continued

```
Dim repPartial As New JRO.Replica

repFull.ActiveConnection = "c:\My Documents\MyMaster.mdb"
repFull.CreateReplica "c:\My Documents\CA Clients.mdb", _
    "Partial Replica of MyMaster", _
    jrRepTypePartial
Set repFull = Nothing

repPartial.ActiveConnection = "c:\My Documents\CA Clients.mdb"
repPartial.Filters.Append "tblClients", jrFilterTypeTable, _
    "State = 'CA'"
repPartial.Filters.Append "tblProjects", jrFilterTypeRelationship, _
  "ClientProjects"
repPartial.PopulatePartial "c:\My Documents\MyMaster.mdb"
Set repPartial = Nothing

End Sub
```

The code begins by establishing a connection to the master. It uses the
CreateReplica method of the Replica object to create a partial replica. It then
makes a connection to the replica. It appends two filters to the Replica object. It
uses the first filter to populate the tblClients table in the replica with all the clients
located in the state of California. It uses the second filter to populate the tblProjects
table with all the projects associated with clients in the state of California. It uses the
PopulatePartial method to populate the replica with the data designated in the
filters.

Synchronizing a Database Using Code

At times, you might want to finish the synchronization process by using VBA code.
The routine shown in Listing 17.5 synchronizes the two databases designated as
parameters. The constant jrSyncTypeImpExp indicates that you want to perform a
two-way synchronization. The constant jrSyncModeDirect indicates that the
synchronization mode is direct.

LISTING 17.5   Synchronizing Two Databases

```
Sub Synchronize(strDB1 As String, strDB2 As String)
    Dim rep As New JRO.Replica
    rep.ActiveConnection = strDB1
    rep.Synchronize strDB2, jrSyncTypeImpExp, jrSyncModeDirect
    Set rep = Nothing
End Sub
```

Handling Conflicts Using Code

You can also handle conflicts by using code (see Listing 17.6). What you do when a conflict is identified is determined by the business needs of your users.

LISTING 17.6   Identifying Conflicts Using Code

```
Sub IdentifyConflicts(strConflictDB)
    Dim rep As New JRO.Replica
    Dim rst As ADODB.Recordset

    rep.ActiveConnection = strConflictDB
    Set rst = rep.ConflictTables

    If rst.BOF And rst.EOF Then
        MsgBox "No Conflicts!!!"
    Else
        Do Until rst.EOF
            Debug.Print rst.Fields(0)
            rst.MoveNext
        Loop
    End If

End Sub
```

This routine goes through each table, determining whether something is in the table's ConflictTable property. If the ConflictTable property has something in it, it opens a recordset from the Conflict table. The routine loops through each record of the Conflict table, displaying the value of the first field in the debug window.

Practical Examples: Managing the Time and Billing Application with Replication

You must make a decision about whether it's necessary to implement replication in your applications. It could be very useful if, for example, you have many consultants who work in the field and need to enter client, project, billing, and expense information while on the road. Using what you've learned in this chapter, you can make sure that all changes made to each consultant's copy of the database are sent to the main server database each time the consultant dials into the office.

You can also use replication so that the data managed by your applications is backed up during the day, which minimizes the chance of data loss or downtime. Finally, you might want to implement replication in your applications to distribute the workload over a few servers in your organization.

The potential benefits of using replication with your applications are many. With what you have learned in this chapter, you must decide whether replication is appropriate for your application and how it can best be used in your organization.

Summary

Replication is a very complex and robust Access feature. You can use it at the most basic level to synchronize changes between two databases or, in an enterprise-wide application, to synchronize changes between many machines on a wide area network (WAN). The easiest but least robust way to implement replication is to use the Access user interface. However, with the Replication Manager, you can schedule and manage synchronization activity as well as handle the most complex of replication topologies. Finally, by using code, you can customize the behavior of your application's synchronization activities.

18

Taking Advantage of the Microsoft Office XP Developer

Why This Chapter Is Important

Microsoft Office XP Developer (MOD) is a version of Microsoft Office that includes all the components of Office XP Professional plus a rich set of developer tools and applications. MOD enables you to package and distribute professional-looking applications without requiring your users to purchase Access for each computer running the application. You also can add extra functionality to your applications using MOD. Additionally, MOD includes a set of tools that enhance the development environment (some of which had to be purchased separately in previous versions of Office).

What's in the Microsoft Office XP Developer

The Microsoft Office XP Developer includes the following:

- Access runtime

- Replication Manager

- Code Librarian

- Packaging Wizard

- VBA Code Commentor

- VBA Error Handler

- VBA String Designer

- Data Access Page Designer
- Digital Dashboards
- Integrated development environment
- Office Web components
- Workflow Designers
- Online documentation
- Smart Tag technology
- XML support

The Access Runtime

The royalty-free runtime license provided with MOD enables your users to take advantage of your application and all that it provides without owning their own copy of Access. When running your application with the Access runtime version, your users cannot directly create new database objects. Furthermore, they do not have access to the Database window, built-in toolbars, numerous menu items, and several other features that are part of the full Access product. In many situations, you don't want the user to have access to all these features. Instead, you want to provide your users with a very complete, fully integrated application that only you will be responsible for modifying. Furthermore, you want to provide all this to your users without requiring them to purchase Access for every computer running your application. The MOD, with its royalty-free runtime license, enables you to do exactly that.

Using Full Versions Versus Runtime Versions of Access

Many people have the misconception that using the Packaging Wizard and distributing your application using the Access runtime version somehow means that the application is compiled. This is not the case at all! In fact, if you do not properly secure the database, anyone can install his own copy of Access and modify the application's data and other objects, just as you can. Using the Packaging Wizard and distributing your application with the Access runtime version does not modify the database in any way. It simply gives you the license to freely distribute the engine required to run your application.

Actually, the engine is not even a modified version of the Access executable! The MSACCESS.EXE file that you distribute is the same as the MSACCESS.EXE file that you use to build your application. When you create installation disks for your users with the Packaging Wizard, the installation process copies the same MSACCESS.EXE file to the installation disks. So how can there be any difference between the retail and runtime versions of Access?

When the user installs your application, the installation process copies the MSAC-CESS.EXE file to the user's machine. During this process, the installation program checks a Windows Registry licensing key to see whether the user owns a copy of Access. If the licensing key indicates that the user does not own a copy of Access, or if the key does not exist, the licensing key (which is a set of numbers and letters) is updated to indicate that the user will be using the runtime version of the product. When Access executes and the runtime licensing key is found, the product launches in runtime mode.

When the runtime licensing key is found, Access behaves differently than it does when the full licensing key is found. If you are not aware of the differences, you will be quite surprised when certain aspects of your application no longer function as expected. The following is a list of the limitations of the runtime versions of the product:

- The Database window is hidden.

- Design views are hidden.

- Built-in toolbars are not supported.

- Some menu items are not available.

- Certain keys are disabled.

Hidden Database Window

When users launch your application using the runtime version of Access, the Database window is not visible. It's actually there, but it is hidden because its colors are set to the same colors as the Windows background color. This means that you can interact with the Database window using code, but the users of your application will be unable to interact with the Database window directly.

The fact that the Database window is hidden tends to be a double-edged sword. On one hand, it prevents most users from modifying the objects in your application. On the other hand, it puts the responsibility on you to build a complete interface for your application. Remember that, for you as a developer, the Database window is a starting point. You must provide a different starting point and navigational tools for your users to maneuver throughout your application.

Hidden Design Views

The users of your application won't have direct access to any design views, which means that they will be unable to create or modify tables, queries, forms, reports, macros, or modules. You still can get to all this functionality through code, though. You can build a wizard that enables your users to define all aspects of a query or some other object, for example, and then build the query (or other object) using ActiveX data objects (ADO) code. Again, this helps protect your application from novice users, but it puts the pressure on you to ensure that your application provides its users with all the functionality they need.

Built-In Toolbars Not Supported

All built-in toolbars are completely unavailable with the runtime version of Access, which means that you must design your own toolbars and attach them to your forms and reports as appropriate.

Unavailable Menu Items

Built-in toolbars are not supported at all when using the runtime version of Access. Menus are simply modified after the runtime key is found. Many menu items are hidden in the runtime version. These hidden menu items prevent users from making changes to your application.

Although many of the menu commands are hidden from the user, they can be accessed by using the DoMenuItem command. In other words, the functionality is there, but it is simply hidden from your users.

Disabled Keys

Several keystrokes are unavailable to your users when they run your application with the runtime version of Access. Table 18.1 lists these keystrokes.

TABLE 18.1   Disabled Keys

Keys	Function
Ctrl+Break	Halts macro and code execution
Shift (when opening the database)	Prevents execution of the AutoExec macro and ignores Startup properties
Alt+F1/F11	Displays the Database window
F12	Displays the Save As dialog box
Shift+F12	Saves a database object
Ctrl+G	Displays the Debug window
Ctrl+F11	Toggles between custom and built-in toolbars

As you can see, these are keys that you would rarely, if ever, want your users to use. You might consider the disabling of these keystrokes a positive side effect of using the runtime version of the product.

Preparing Your Database for Use with the Access Runtime Version

Several steps are required to prepare your database for use with the Access runtime version. Although many of these steps are mandatory when distributing your application with the runtime version, they also are good as a general practice when developing a polished application. To prepare your application for use with the Access runtime version, follow these steps:

1. Create the application.

2. Create Help files and associate the Help topics with the application's objects, if desired.

3. Test and debug the application.

4. Run and test the application with the /Runtime command-line argument.

5. Run the Packaging Wizard.

6. Deploy the application.

7. Package and distribute the application.

Creating the Application

You must be concerned about several things when designing an application for use with the Access runtime version. Although the following items are niceties in any application, they are a mandatory aspect of developing an application for use with the Access runtime version:

- Build the application around forms and menus.

- Build error handling into the application.

- Build custom menus and toolbars into the application.

- Set startup options for the application.

- Properly secure the application.

Building the Application Around Forms and Menus

The first step when creating the application with runtime distribution in mind is to build the application around forms and menus. This means that everything in the application needs to be form- and menu-driven. Your application generally should begin by displaying a Main Switchboard, or a startup form with a main menu. The user then can navigate from the Main Switchboard to additional switchboards, such as a Data Entry Switchboard, a Reports Switchboard, a Maintenance Switchboard, and so on.

An alternative is to display the most commonly used form when the application launches. Menu and toolbar items are used to navigate to other parts of your application. For example, if the application's main purpose is to maintain membership information for a union, the startup form could be the membership form. Other forms, such as the member payments form, could be accessed via a menu attached to the membership form. This second option is my personal favorite.

Building Error Handling into the Application

It is imperative that you build error handling into your application. If an error occurs when someone is using the runtime version of Access and no error handling is in place, an error message is displayed and the user instantly is returned to the Windows desktop. Therefore, it is crucial that you build error handling into all your routines.

You can call a *generic* error handler from every procedure in your application to respond to any type of error. A generic error handler prevents you from having to write specific error handling in each of your subroutines and functions. This enables you to invoke error handling throughout your application in the most efficient manner possible.

You can take many approaches to create a generic error handler. The error handler should give users information about the error, enable users to print this information, and log the information to a file. To research more information on creating a generic error handler to assist you with this task, you can find detailed information in my book, *Alison Balter's Mastering Access 2002 Desktop Development.*

Adding Custom Menus and Toolbars

As mentioned earlier in this chapter, limited versions of the standard Access menus are available under the Access runtime version, but toolbars are not available. You therefore must provide your users with whatever menu bar and toolbar functionality the application requires.

Setting Startup Options

Access 2000 and Access 2002 provide you with several startup options that enable you to control what happens to your application when it is loaded. Figure 18.1 shows the Startup dialog box, which includes the Advanced options. Table 18.2 lists each option in the Startup dialog box.

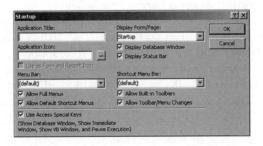

FIGURE 18.1   The Startup dialog box.

TABLE 18.2   Startup Options

Option	Function
Application Title	Sets the `AppTitle` property, which displays a custom title in the application title bar
Application Icon	Sets the `AppIcon` property, which displays a custom icon in the application title bar
Menu Bar	Sets the `StartupMenuBar` property, which specifies the custom menu bar displayed by default when the application is loaded
Allow Full Menus	Sets the `AllowFullMenus` property, which allows or restricts the use of Access menus
Allow Default Shortcut Menus	Sets the `AllowShortcutMenus` property, which allows or restricts the use of standard Access shortcut menus (menus accessed with a right-click)
Display Form/Page	Sets the `StartupForm` property, which specifies the form displayed when the application is loaded
Display Database Window	Sets the `StartupShowDBWindow` property, which determines whether the Database window is visible when the application is opened
Display Status Bar	Sets the `StartupShowStatusBar` property, which determines whether the status bar is visible when the application is opened
Shortcut Menu Bar	Sets the `StartupShortcutMenuBar` property, which specifies that a menu bar be displayed by default as the shortcut (right-click) menu bar
Allow Built-In Toolbars	Sets the `AllowBuiltInToolbars` property, which indicates whether built-in toolbars are available to your users
Allow Toolbar/Menu Changes	Sets the `AllowToolbarChanges` property, which determines whether your users can customize toolbars in the application
Use Access Special Keys	Sets the `AllowSpecialKeys` property, which determines whether the user can use keys such as F11 to display the Database window, Ctrl+F11 to toggle between custom and built-in toolbars, and so on

NOTE

Notice in Figure 18.1 that the Use as Form and Report Icon property is available when an application icon is designated. When this is checked, the icon designated as the application icon is used as the icon for forms and reports.

As you might have guessed, many of these options apply only when you are running the application under the full version of Access (as opposed to the runtime version). You do not need to set the Display Database Window option, for example, if your application will be running only under the runtime version of Access. The Database window is never available under the runtime version of the product, so Access ignores this property when the application is run under the runtime version. Nevertheless, I like setting these properties to ensure that the application behaves as I want it to under *both* the retail and runtime versions of the product.

All the properties can be set by using the Startup dialog box or by using code. If you use code, you must make sure that the property exists for the `Database` object before you set it. If the property does not exist, you must append the property to the `Database` object.

Only users with Administer permission for the database can modify the startup properties. If you want to ensure that certain users cannot modify the startup options of the database, you must make sure that they do not have Administer permissions.

As part of setting startup options for your database, you should determine what code, if any, is run when the application is loaded. You can accomplish this in one of two ways. You can start the application with an AutoExec macro and then issue a `RunCode` action to execute a VBA procedure. The other option is to designate a Startup form for the application and then call a custom routine from the `Open` event of the Startup form. I *always* use the second option because it provides more control and because error handling can be included in the code module behind the Startup form, whereas an AutoExec macro cannot contain error handling.

Securing the Application

Don't fool yourself! Remember that the runtime version of Access in no way secures your application. It simply provides you with royalty-free distribution. You must perform all the same measures to secure your application under the runtime version of Access that you perform under the retail version of the product. The bottom line is that you must take measures to secure your application if you want it and its data to be secure.

User-level security enables you to grant specific rights to users and groups in a workgroup. This means that each user or group can have different permissions on the same object. With this method of security, each user begins by entering a username and password. The Jet Engine validates the username and password and determines the permissions associated with the user. Each user maintains his own password, which is unrelated to the passwords of the other users.

In this method of security, users belong to groups. You can assign rights at the group level, the user level, or both. Users inherit the rights of their least restrictive group, which is highlighted by the fact that security is always on. By default, all users have rights to all objects because every user is a member of the group called Users. By default, this group is given all rights to all objects. If you have not implemented security, all users are logged on as the Admin user, who is a member of the Users group and the all-powerful Admins group. The Jet Engine determines that the Admin user has no password and does not display an opening logon screen. Because members of the Users and Admins groups get rights to all objects by default, it appears as though no security is in place.

With user-level security, you easily can customize and refine the rights to different objects. One set of users might be able to view, modify, add, and remove employee records, for example. Another set of users might be able to view only employee information. The last group of users might be allowed no access to the employee information, or it might be allowed access only to specific fields (such as name and address). The Access security model easily accommodates this type of scenario.

The major steps to implementing user-level security follow (each step is developed in detail later in the chapter):

1. Use the Workgroup Administrator to establish a new system database.

2. Start Access and change the Admin user's password to a non-Null password.

3. Create a new user who will be the administrator of the database.

4. Make the user a member of the Admins group.

5. Exit and restart Access, logging on as the new system administrator.

6. Remove the Admin user from the Admins group.

7. Assign a password to the new system administrator.

8. Open the database you want to secure.

9. Run the Security Wizard.

10. Create users and groups consisting of members of the workgroup defined by the system database.

11. Assign rights to users and groups for individual objects.

You can find more in-depth information about Access security in my book *Alison Balter's Mastering Access 2002 Desktop Development*. Distributing your application as an MDE (compiled database) provides an additional level of security while improving performance and decreasing the size of the database file.

Distributing Your Application as an MDE

The process of creating an MDE file compiles all modules, removes all source code from your database, and compacts the destination database. All code will run, but the user will be unable to modify forms, reports, and modules. Besides protecting the objects in your database, this process reduces the size of the database and some of the overhead associated with it, thereby improving application performance. Creating and distributing an MDE file is not as simple as it might appear at first glance. *Alison Balter's Mastering Access 2002 Desktop Development* covers the process of creating an MDE file and the important issues that surround this file format.

Adding Custom Help to the Application

To add polish to your application and ensure that the help you provide to your users applies to what they are looking at in your application, you must provide a custom Help file. In essence, adding help to your application involves first creating Help files. You then must add help to the various objects in your application. Many excellent tools are available to assist you in this, such as WinHelp or RoboHelp.

Testing and Debugging the Application

Before you even bother trying to run your application under the runtime version, you should fully test and debug the application under the retail version of the product. When you are fairly confident that you have all the kinks worked out of the application, you are ready to test it in the runtime environment.

Running and Testing the Application with the /Runtime Command-Line Switch

If you have the Microsoft Office 2002 Developer tools installed, Microsoft provides a very easy way to test an application and see how it will perform under the runtime version of Access without having to actually create distribution disks. You can do this by using the /Runtime command-line switch. The /Runtime switch forces Access to load in runtime mode. Here's how it works:

```
c:\program files\microsoft office\office\msaccess.exe c:\databases\MyDB.mdb /
➥runtime
```

After you load the application with the /Runtime switch, you should again test all aspects of the application. At times, you might want to test to see whether the application has been launched with the runtime or retail version of the product. You can accomplish this with the following code:

```
If Not SysCmd(acSysCmdRuntime) _
     And CurrentUser <> "Admin" Then
     MsgBox "You aren't allowed here"
End If
```

The SysCmd function, when passed the constant acSysCmdRuntime, checks to see whether the application was launched using the runtime version of Access. In this case, if the program was run with the retail version of Access and CurrentUser is not Admin, a message is displayed indicating that the user is not allowed. Of course, you easily could modify this routine to check for other users and to quit the application if an unauthorized person attempts to launch the application without the runtime version of the product.

TIP

If you want to simulate the runtime environment on the machine of a user who has Access installed, you must copy the file mso9rt.dll to the \program files\common files\microsoft shared\vba\vba6 directory on the user's machine.

The Replication Manager

The Replication Manager is a powerful tool that lets you take full advantage of replication in Access 2002. It's included only with Microsoft Office XP Developer, as one of the Developer Tools. Among the Replication Manager's major benefits, it enables you to:

- Easily replicate a database
- Easily create additional replicas
- Synchronize any replicas in the set
- Schedule automated synchronization
- View an object's replication history
- Easily manage replication properties
- Manage synchronization with replicas at remote sites
- Perform synchronization over a LAN, an intranet, or the Internet

Chapter 17, "Access Replication Made Easy," covers the Replication Manager in detail.

The Code Librarian

The Code Librarian helps you create reusable code. It accomplishes this by providing a centralized database that teams of developers share or that you can utilize for your own personal use. The VBA Code Librarian ships with a large database of prewritten code, and you can add code of your own to help you create standardized applications. You can even add entire databases of your own code libraries.

Using the Code Librarian

The VBA Code Librarian launches as a separate application. Follow these steps to use the Code Librarian:

1. Select Start, Programs, Microsoft Office XP Developer, Code Librarian. The Code Librarian launches within the Microsoft Development Environment (see Figure 18.2).

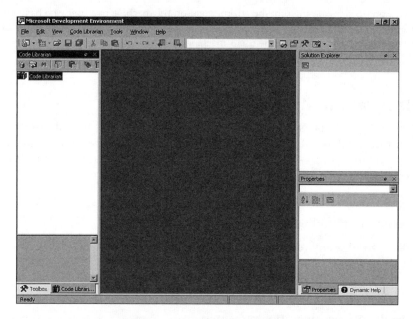

FIGURE 18.2   The Microsoft Development Environment with the Code Librarian.

2. To open a code library, select Code Librarian, Add, Existing Library. The Open dialog box appears (see Figure 18.3).

3. Select the library that you want to open, and click Open (codelib.clb is a code library that ships with the Microsoft Office XP Developer). The code library opens, and its contents are displayed in the Code Librarian window.

4. Click the + (plus) sign to view the contents of the library. As shown in Figure 18.4, the codelib.clb library contains categories of library functions.

FIGURE 18.3   The Open dialog box enables you to select the code library with which you want to work.

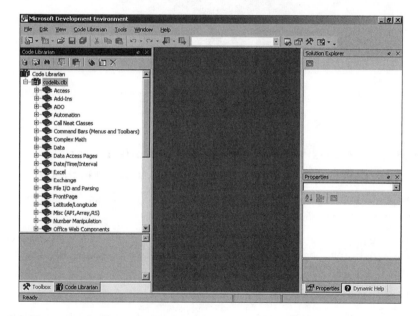

FIGURE 18.4   The codelib.clb code library ships with the MOD and contains a wealth of sample functions.

5. Click the + (plus) sign for a particular category to view the functions contained within the category. Figure 18.5 shows the Access category with its list of functions.

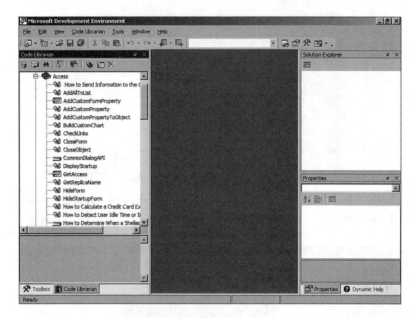

FIGURE 18.5   The Access category contains functions specifically relating to Microsoft Access.

Working with Existing Functions in the Code Library

Follow these steps to view and use functions already included in the code library:

1. Expand the node for the desired code category. The functions contained in the category appear.

2. Double-click to select the function whose code you want to view. The code for the function appears in the code window. Figure 18.6 shows the CheckLinks function selected.

3. Modify the function's code, if you want.

4. To insert the function's code into an Access module, select the Copy Code to Clipboard toolbar tool. Alternatively, select the function text and then right-click within the code window and select Copy.

5. Paste the code into your Access project at the desired position.

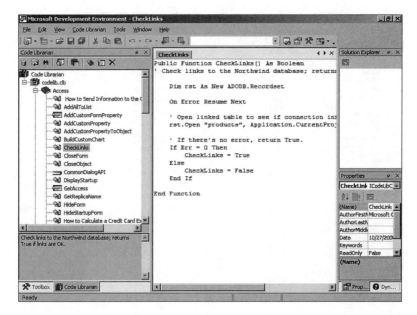

FIGURE 18.6   The code for the CheckLinks function appears in a separate window.

Creating New Code Libraries

In addition to working with existing code libraries, you will probably want to create new code libraries. Take the following steps to create a new code library:

1. Select Code Librarian, Add, New Library. The Save As dialog box appears.

2. Use the Save In drop-down list to select a location for the library.

3. Type the name of the library in the File Name text box.

4. Click Save to create the library.

Adding Functions to a Code Library

So far, we have discussed how to work with existing library functions. This section discusses how to create new library functions. To create a new library function, follow these steps:

1. Right-click the category to which you want to add the code and select New Code Item. The Code Librarian creates a new code item and allows you to supply a name (see Figure 18.7).

2. Enter a name for the function.

3. Add the code for the function in the large text box that appears to the right. A completed function appears in Figure 18.8.

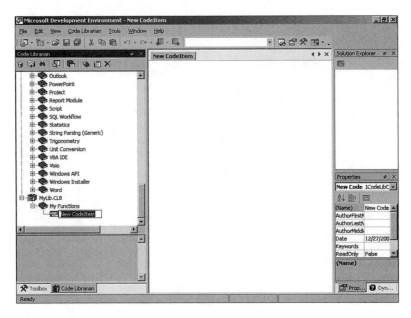

FIGURE 18.7   The Code Librarian allows you to supply a name for the new library function.

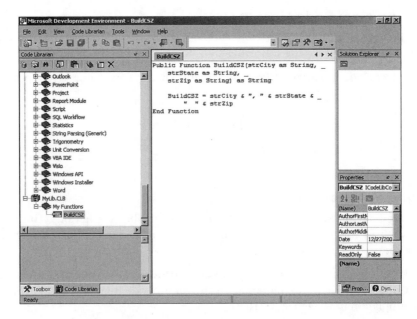

FIGURE 18.8   The function BuildCSZ has been added as a library function.

Adding a New Category for Your Library Functions

To help organize the functions in your library, you can categorize them and associate keywords with them. To add a library category, follow these steps:

1. Right-click the library or category under which you want the new category to appear. Select New Category. The Code Librarian creates a new category that you can rename (see Figure 18.9).

2. Supply a name for the new category.

3. Add new functions to the category, *or* drag and drop existing functions to place them within the new category.

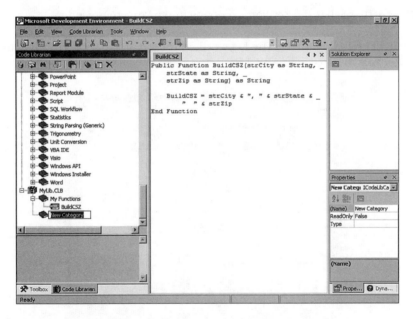

FIGURE 18.9   You can easily rename a category after you add it.

To associate keywords with a library function:

1. Select the function that you want to associate keywords with.

2. Click to select the Keywords property in the Properties window (see Figure 18.10).

FIGURE 18.10   Select the Keywords property in the Properties window.

3. Click the Build button. The Keyword Editor tab of the Property Pages dialog box appears (see Figure 18.11).

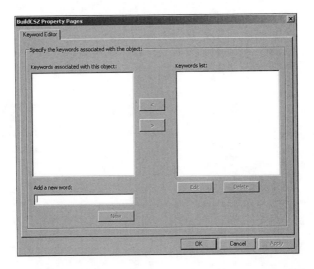

FIGURE 18.11   Use the Keyword Editor tab of the Property Pages dialog box to associate keywords with a function.

4. Type the name of the new keyword and click New. In Figure 18.12, the Addresses and Customers keywords have been added, and the Employees keyword is in the process of being added.

5. When you're finished adding new keywords, click OK. You are returned to the Microsoft Development Environment.

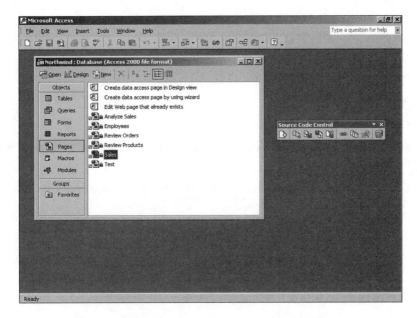

FIGURE 18.12   Click New to add new keywords to your library.

The Code Librarian Viewer

The Code Librarian Viewer is a royalty-free distributable that you can deploy to your users' computers. Using the Packaging Wizard, you can easily distribute your libraries and the Code Librarian Viewer to your users.

The Packaging Wizard

The Packaging Wizard enables you to easily create distribution disks containing all the files necessary to run your application. The Packaging Wizard creates a highly professional-looking setup program that your users will run when they want to install your application. Using the Packaging Wizard, they can customize what is included with your application. You can even provide your users with the familiar Standard, Compressed, and Custom options that they have come to know from installing other Microsoft products.

Loading the Packaging Wizard Add-In

Before you can use the Packaging Wizard, you must activate the Packaging Wizard add-in. To do this:

1. Activate the Visual Basic Development Environment (VBE) by clicking on Tools, Macro, and selecting Visual Basic Editor or by using the hotkey Alt+F11.

2. Select Add-In Manager from the Add-Ins menu. The Add-In Manager dialog box appears (see Figure 18.13).

3. Select Packaging Wizard.

4. Check the Loaded/Unloaded check box.

5. Check Load on Startup if you want the wizard to be loaded each time that you launch Access.

6. Click OK. The Packaging Wizard should now appear as an option under the Add-Ins menu (see Figure 18.14).

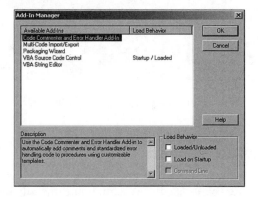

FIGURE 18.13   The Add-In Manager dialog box allows you to load the Packaging Wizard.

Running the Packaging Wizard

After you have fully tested and prepared your application for distribution, you are ready to run the Packaging Wizard. The Packaging Wizard walks you through all the steps required to build distribution disks that include all the components that your application needs to run.

1. To launch the Packaging Wizard from VBE, activate the VBE.

2. Select Packaging Wizard from the Add-Ins menu. The Packaging Wizard starting dialog box appears, as shown in Figure 18.15.

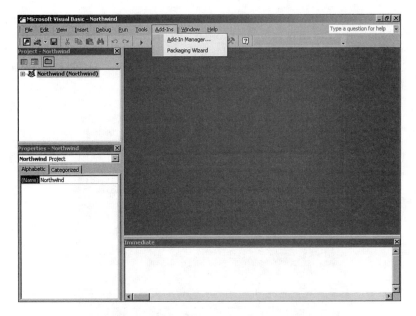

FIGURE 18.14 The Add-Ins menu after the Packaging Wizard add-in has been activated.

FIGURE 18.15 The Packaging Wizard welcome dialog box.

3. The Packaging Wizard starting dialog box provides you with an introduction to the Packaging Wizard and what it does. Click Next to proceed to the next step.

4. The first step of the wizard, show in Figure 18.16, gives you the opportunity to designate the file that you want to package, name the package that you are creating, and rename, delete, and duplicate packaging scripts. Identify the file that you want to package, and supply a package name (see Figure 18.16). Then click Next.

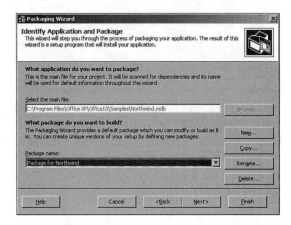

FIGURE 18.16   The first step of the Packaging Wizard allows you to designate the file that you want to package and to supply the package name.

5. The second step of the wizard, illustrated in Figure 18.17, allows you to specify application information. You must supply the application title, your company name, version information, and the setup language. Click Next when you're ready to continue.

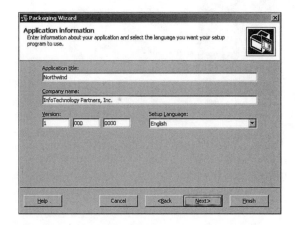

FIGURE 18.17   The second step of the Packaging Wizard allows you to supply information about the application you are creating.

6. The third step of the wizard, shown in Figure 18.18, enables you to designate all files that you want to scan for dependency information. This information is used to ensure that all necessary files are included in the package. Click Add File to add any additional files that you want to scan. Click Next when done.

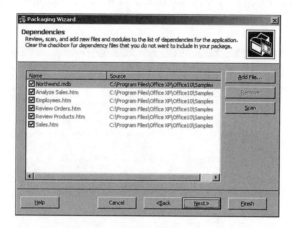

FIGURE 18.18   The third step of the Packaging Wizard allows you to designate all files that you want scanned for dependencies.

7. The fourth step of the Packaging Wizard (see Figure 18.19) allows you to designate where to install each file in the package. For each file, indicate where to place the file and whether it is shared by other applications. Click Next when done.

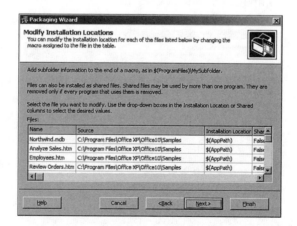

FIGURE 18.19   The fourth step of the Packaging Wizard allows you to designate where you want to install the application files.

8. The fifth step of the wizard, shown in Figure 18.20, enables you to determine whether the Access runtime is included with the packaged application. If you opt to include the Access runtime, you can designate whether you want to include system files and Internet Explorer 5.1. Finally, you can designate the language of the Access runtime that you want to include. Click Next to continue.

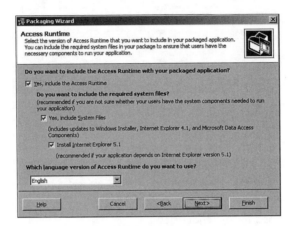

FIGURE 18.20   The fifth step of the Packaging Wizard allows you to specify whether you want to include the Access runtime with your installation.

9. The sixth step of the wizard enables you to select the database components that you want to include with your package (see Figure 18.21). Click to select the desired components and click Next.

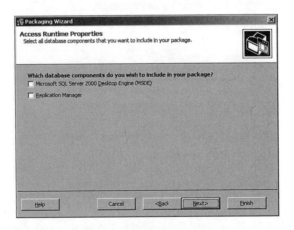

FIGURE 18.21   The sixth step of the Packaging Wizard allows you to select the database components for packages to include with the package.

10. In the seventh step of the Packaging Wizard, you can designate Start menu groups and items that are created during the installation process (see Figure 18.22). Click New Folder to create a new folder and New Shortcut to create a new shortcut. If you click a shortcut and click Properties, the Start Menu Item Properties dialog box appears (see Figure 18.23). Designate the name, command line, "start in" path, database information, and profile information for the item. Click OK to return to the Start Menu Shortcuts step of the wizard. Click a shortcut and click Remove to remove a shortcut. Click Next when you're finished designating all options.

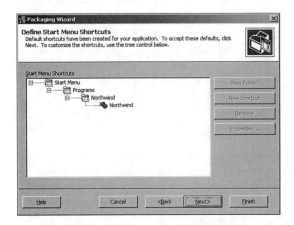

FIGURE 18.22 Selecting Start menu groups and items that are created during the installation process.

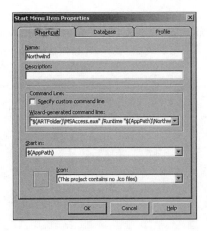

FIGURE 18.23 Specify the name, command line, and "start in" path for shortcut items that you create.

11. The eighth step of the Packaging Wizard allows you to specify a command to execute when the installation is complete (see Figure 18.24). For example, you can designate that you want Access to open a ReadMe file when the installation of the application is complete.

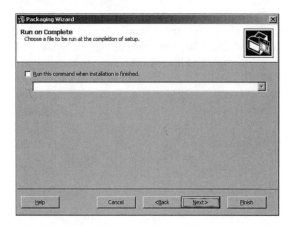

FIGURE 18.24   The eighth step of the Packaging Wizard allows you to designate a command to execute when the installation process is complete.

12. The final step of the Packaging Wizard prompts you either to build the setup program or to save the package script without building it. Select the appropriate option and click Finish (see Figure 18.25). Access notifies you of each step in the setup (see Figure 18.26) and then lets you know when the process is complete (see Figure 18.27).

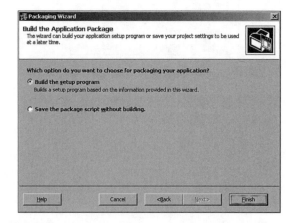

FIGURE 18.25   Designate whether you want to build the setup program or save the script to be run later.

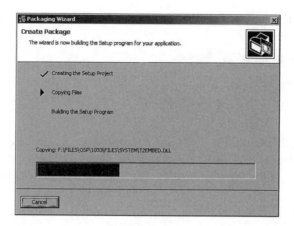

FIGURE 18.26   Access notifies you of each step during setup that it takes in completing the package.

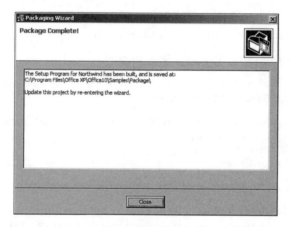

FIGURE 18.27   Access notifies you when the process is complete.

Deploying the Application

The Packaging Wizard creates a folder that contains all of the necessary installation files. To deploy the application, you simply place the installation files on a CD or on a network location where all of the users can access them. To install the application, the user simply double-clicks SETUP.EXE.

Distributing the Application

The most important thing you must do when packaging and distributing your application is test the application on a machine that has never had a copy of Access or any Access runtime application installed. This ensures that your application includes all required components for packages. I like to keep a "virgin" machine available for testing my application setups. Here's what I do:

1. Use Symantec Ghost to create an image of the operating system drive on the test machine.

2. Install the application.

3. Test the application.

4. Restore from the Ghost image.

By following these steps, I ensure that I always have a "clean" machine on which to test my application. Obviously, it is imperative that you test *all* aspects of your application on the machine on which you performed the installation from your setup disks.

TIP

Several third-party software packages are available to help you to back up and restore your Windows installation easily. My favorite program is Ghost, available from Symantec.

When you are ready to test the Setup process, follow these steps:

1. Select Run from the Windows Start menu.

2. In the Run dialog box, locate the setup files that the Packaging Wizard created, as shown in Figure 18.28. Click OK.

3. After you are notified of the setup's progress, the Application Setup dialog box appears, as shown in Figure 18.29.

4. Click OK to continue.

5. Select a location for the application installation (see Figure 18.30).

6. Click the Command button to install the application to the specified directory. The Choose Program Group dialog box appears. Select a program group and click Continue.

FIGURE 18.28   The Run dialog box appears after selecting Run from the Start menu.

FIGURE 18.29   The Application Setup welcome dialog box.

FIGURE 18.30   Selecting a location for the program installation.

The installation process is completed. If you opted during the Packaging Wizard process to create desktop shortcuts, they are created automatically when the Setup program is executed.

The Code Commentor and Error Handler Add-In

The Code Commentor and Error Handler Add-In enables you to quickly and easily add standardized comments and error handling to your programming code. To accomplish this, it provides customizable templates that you apply to your procedures. To use the Code Commentor and Error Handler Add-In, you must first activate it as an add-in using the Add-In Manager.

After you have loaded the Code Commentor and Error Handler Add-In, you are ready to use it.

1. Select Code Commentor and Error Handler Add-In from the Add-Ins menu. The Code Commentor and Error Handler Add-In dialog box appears (see Figure 18.31).

2. Click to designate whether you want to add comments to the current procedure, to all procedures in the current module, or to all procedures in the current project.

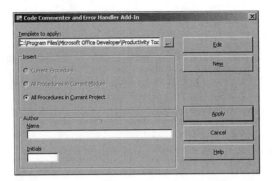

FIGURE 18.31   The Code Commentor and Error Handler Add-In dialog box enables you to designate the options that are used when comments and error handling are inserted into your code.

3. Enter the name of the template that you want to apply.

4. Provide the name and initials of the author.

5. Click Edit to view or edit the template, if you want. The Code Commentor and Error Handler Template Editor appears (see Figure 18.32). View or modify the template as desired. Close the window when you're done.

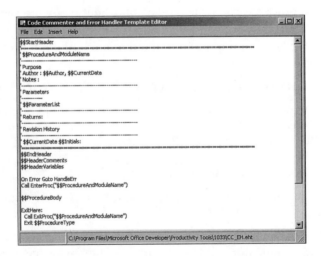

FIGURE 18.32   The Code Commentor and Error Handler Template Editor enables you to preview and modify the template to be used to comment and add error handling to your code.

6. Click Apply when you are ready to generate the comments and error-handling code. An example of comments entered by the Code Commentor and Error Handler Add-In appears in Figure 18.33. Remember that you can customize the template to modify the generated comments and error handling to your specific needs.

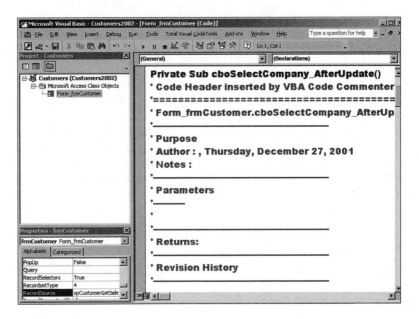

FIGURE 18.33   Comments and error handling inserted into your code vary depending on the template used.

The VBA String Editor

The VBA String Editor enables you to quickly and accurately build strings of text and variables for expressions of various kinds, including SQL statements and scripts. After you create them, you can easily embed these strings in your VBA code. To use the VBA String Editor, you must first activate it as an add-in using the technique described for the Code Librarian. After you have loaded the VBA String Editor, you are ready to use it. To use it, select String Editor from the Add-Ins menu. The VBA String Editor dialog box appears (see Figure 18.34).

FIGURE 18.34   The VBA String Editor helps you construct strings of text and variables for use in code.

The String Editor automatically puts quotation marks, spaces, carriage return constants, and other syntactical elements into strings, such as the strings displayed in message boxes or strings printed in the Immediate window by `Debug.Print` statements. Instead of worrying about getting the quotes, spaces, and constants just right, simply type the whole expression, omitting the syntactical elements, mark the variables with a toolbar button, and paste the expression into your code. All the parsing is done automatically, even inserting the `vbCrLf` carriage return and line-feed constant where you broke the line of text.

For example, if you type the following line and mark the variables using the Toggle to Non-String toolbar button:

strFirstName strLastName lived at strStreetAddress on dteOrderDate

the expression is transformed into:

```
strFirstName & " " & strLastName & " lived at " & strStreetAddress & _
" on " & dteOrderDate
```

Summary

Microsoft Office XP Developer contains a host of valuable tools. Some of these tools, such as the Access runtime, the Replication Manager, and ActiveX controls, provide runtime functionality. Others, such as Visual SourceSafe, the VBA Code Librarian, and the Code Commentor and Error Handler Add-In, assist with the development process. In this chapter, you learned the role of each tool in Microsoft Office XP Developer. After reading the chapter, you should be comfortable using the add-in tools available within the development environment.

19

Source Code Control

Why This Chapter Is Important

Visual SourceSafe, also known as VSS, is a tool you can use to manage the development of an Access application being worked on by a team of developers. After you place a database under SourceSafe control, you must check out each object before you modify it. After you make the changes to the object, you check it in so that other developers can see the changes. At any time, you can get the following information about the objects in the database:

- Which objects are checked out

- A history of everything that has happened to an object

- The differences between two versions of an object

Using Visual SourceSafe, you can easily revert an object to a previous version or merge different versions of an object. Visual SourceSafe is a tool not only for teams of developers, but also for an individual developer who wants to keep every version of each object in an application. It's a phenomenal tool that helps make Access a serious developer environment.

How Do I Install Visual SourceSafe?

You can use Visual SourceSafe only with the Microsoft Office 97 Developer Edition of Access, the Microsoft Office 2000 Developer, and the Microsoft Office XP Developer. Microsoft includes it with the Microsoft Office XP Developer as one of the developer applications. This source control tool is also included as part of the Enterprise edition of Visual Basic, or you can buy it as a standalone product. In fact, Visual SourceSafe isn't the only source-code control product that you can use with Office XP Developer. Instead, Office XP Developer supplies a software source-code control component that can integrate various source-code control products into Access. To integrate Visual SourceSafe or another version-control product into Access, you need to install both the Office XP Developer Tools and the client part of your version-control product.

To install Visual SourceSafe, use the SourceSafe CD included with the Microsoft Office XP Developer CD set. Follow the onscreen instructions to install VSS, selecting one of these three installation options:

- Shared database server

- Custom

- Standalone

In addition to installing VSS from the Microsoft Office XP Developer, you need the Source Code Control integration that is part of the Office XP Developer Tools software. If you installed the entire set of Developer Tools when installing Office XP Developer, you have this feature; otherwise, run Office XP Developer setup again and, on the Developer Tools setup screen, select Access Productivity Tools (this selection includes VSS integration). This sets up the Visual SourceSafe client. After you install Visual SourceSafe and the VSS integration tool, you'll see a SourceSafe entry under the Tools menu displaying the following options:

- Create Database from SourceSafe Project

- Add Database to SourceSafe

- Run SourceSafe

- Options

The Create Database from SourceSafe Project menu item allows you to create a local database from an existing Visual SourceSafe project. The Add Database to SourceSafe option creates a Visual SourceSafe project from the open database. The Run SourceSafe option runs the Visual SourceSafe Explorer. Finally, the Options menu item lets you configure different Visual SourceSafe options. The following sections cover each of these menu items.

Using Visual SourceSafe: An Overview

When you want to place a database under SourceSafe control, you create it from a SourceSafe project; this database becomes the master copy. Each developer works on a local copy of the database, and no one can modify objects in the database until the developer checks them out. When a developer checks out an object, Visual SourceSafe copies it into the local database. No other developers see changes made to the object until the developer checks it back in. When the developer checks the object back in, Visual SourceSafe copies it from the local database to the Visual SourceSafe project.

With the exception of modules, only one person can check out an object at a time. This means that two people can't make changes to any other types of objects under SourceSafe control simultaneously. Multiple developers, however, can check out modules. When you check a module back in, your changes are merged with any changes that other developers have made since you checked out the module.

The Logistics of Managing a Project with Visual SourceSafe

The first step you must take when you decide to place an object under SourceSafe control is to add the host database to SourceSafe. You can then begin to check objects in and out and to use the product's features. The following sections explain in more detail how to work with Visual SourceSafe.

Adding a Database to Visual SourceSafe

When you're ready to place an application under SourceSafe control, take the following steps:

1. If you are not already set up as a VSS user, run the Visual SourceSafe 6.0 Admin selection from the Microsoft Visual SourceSafe program group, and follow the onscreen instructions to add yourself as a user.

2. Choose Tools, SourceSafe, Add Database to SourceSafe.

3. A dialog box opens, indicating that Visual SourceSafe must close the database before you can place it under SourceSafe control. (See Figure 19.1.) Click Yes to continue.

FIGURE 19.1   This dialog box notifies you that you must close the database for it to be added to SourceSafe control.

4. The Visual SourceSafe Login appears. (See Figure 19.2.) Enter your login information for the user you just created, and click OK.

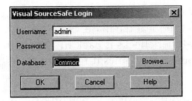

FIGURE 19.2   The VSS Login dialog box requires you to successfully log in before placing a database under SourceSafe control.

5. After you successfully log on, the Add to SourceSafe Project dialog box appears. (See Figure 19.3.) SourceSafe selects the name of the database as the name for the SourceSafe Project.

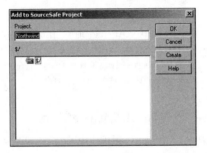

FIGURE 19.3   Use the Add to SourceSafe Project dialog box to select a project name.

6. Click OK to accept the project name. SourceSafe prompts you to create the project. (See Figure 19.4.)

FIGURE 19.4   The dialog box asks whether you want to create the project.

7. Click Yes to create the project; this opens the Add Objects to SourceSafe dialog box. (See Figure 19.5.) Here you can determine which database objects you want to place under SourceSafe control. By default, SourceSafe selects each object in the database. You can deselect specific objects or deselect all objects; then select just the objects you want. When you're finished, click OK.

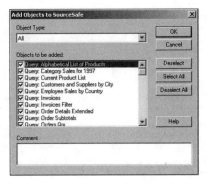

FIGURE 19.5   The Add Objects to SourceSafe dialog box lets you specify which objects you want to add to SourceSafe control.

8. SourceSafe notifies you as it exports each object. (See Figure 19.6.) When the export process is complete, the warning shown in Figure 19.7 tells you that you don't have the Data and Misc. objects checked out. This means that any changes you make to local tables are lost the next time you check out or get the latest version of these objects. You can prevent this by always checking the selection Other: Data and Misc. Objects when adding objects to a VSS project.

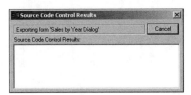

FIGURE 19.6   The dialog box showing the results of exporting an object from the host database.

FIGURE 19.7   This warning message tells you that you don't have the Data and Misc. objects checked out.

9. Click OK to complete the process. Looking at the Database window, you should see that each object has a lock that remains until you have checked out an object. (See Figure 19.8.)

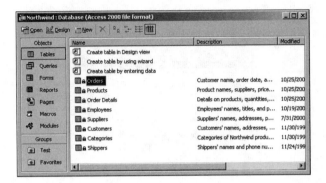

FIGURE 19.8   The Database window of a database under SourceSafe control with all objects locked.

After you add a database to SourceSafe control, the SourceSafe submenu expands to include many options needed to manage a SourceSafe project. (See Figure 19.9.) The remainder of this chapter covers these options.

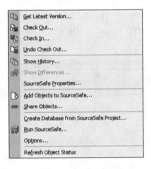

FIGURE 19.9   The Visual SourceSafe menu gives you several options for managing a Visual SourceSafe project.

Understanding the Objects Placed Under SourceSafe Control

Each query, form, report, macro, and module is stored as a separate text file in Visual SourceSafe. When you add an object to SourceSafe control, it's exported to a text file and copied into the Visual SourceSafe project. When you check out an object, it's copied to a temporary location on your machine and then imported into the Access database on your machine as a query, form, report, macro, or module.

All other database objects (tables, relationships, command bars, database properties, startup properties, import/export specs, VBA project references, the VBA project name, and conditional compilation arguments) are stored in one Access MDB file that Visual SourceSafe treats as a binary file. You can't check out these objects individually.

As mentioned, all queries, forms, reports, macros, and modules are stored as text files; the rest of the objects are stored in one binary file. Table 19.1 shows each object type and the extension that the object is stored with when you add it to Visual SourceSafe.

TABLE 19.1   File Extensions for Visual SourceSafe Files

Object	Extension
Queries	ACQ
Forms	ACF
Reports	ACR
Macros	ACS
Modules	ACM
Tables, relationships, and miscellaneous objects	ACB

Creating a Database from a SourceSafe Project

The developer who adds a database to SourceSafe can continue to work on the original copy. Other developers who want to work on the application must create their own local copies of the database. To do that, follow these steps:

1. Add each developer as a VSS user, using the Visual SourceSafe 6.0 Admin selection in the Microsoft Visual SourceSafe program group.

2. Log on to VSS (if necessary).

3. Make sure that you close the database that you wish to work with. Then, in the Visual SourceSafe 6.0 Admin Utility, choose Tools, SourceSafe, Create Database from SourceSafe Project from the menu to open the Create Local Project from SourceSafe dialog box. (See Figure 19.10.)

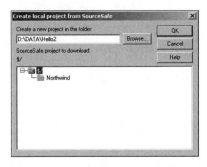

FIGURE 19.10   In the Create Local Project from SourceSafe dialog box, you select a project used to create a local database copy.

4. Select an existing project.

5. Select a folder in which to place the local database copy.

6. Click OK to create the database. If the path designated in Step 5 does not exist, SourceSafe prompts you to add it. During the process of creating the local database copy, the Source Code Control Results window keeps you apprised of the progress. (See Figure 19.11.) When SourceSafe is done creating the local objects, the Source Code Control Results window reads "Completed."

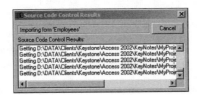

FIGURE 19.11   The Source Code Control Results window shows you the status of the database-creation process.

The Visual SourceSafe Toolbar

The VSS toolbar shown in Figure 19.12 gives you a selection of buttons that give you one-click access to various VSS features. These buttons let you add objects to SourceSafe, get the latest version of an object, check objects in and out, share objects, show the History or Differences windows, and run SourceSafe with the same functionality as using the menu commands, as described in the following sections.

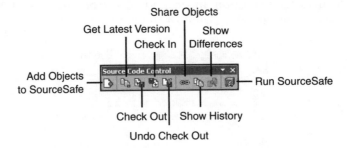

FIGURE 19.12   The Visual SourceSafe toolbar in floating mode.

Checking In and Checking Out Database Objects

After a database has been added to Visual SourceSafe, you can't modify any of the objects that you designated as controlled by SourceSafe without first checking them out. You check out the objects that you want to modify, make changes to them, and check them back in when you're finished. The easiest way to check out a single object is to right-click it and select Check Out. If you want to check out multiple objects, click Check Out on the VSS toolbar, or choose Tools, SourceSafe, Check Out; this opens the Check Out Object(s) from SourceSafe dialog box. (See Figure 19.13.) Here you can select all the objects you want to check out. When you return to the Database window, the objects that you checked out have a check mark next to them. (See Figure 19.14.)

FIGURE 19.13   Use the Check Out Objects from SourceSafe dialog box to designate which database objects you want to check out.

FIGURE 19.14   The Database window adds an icon to show which objects in a database have been checked out.

If you try to modify the design of an object that is not controlled by Visual SourceSafe, you don't get any error messages, so everything proceeds as usual. On the other hand, if you try to modify the design of an object that Visual SourceSafe controls but that no user has checked out, the error message in Figure 19.15 appears.

As you can see, Visual SourceSafe gives you the choice of checking out the object, opening the object as read-only and not checking it out, or canceling.

FIGURE 19.15   The error message you see when you try to modify the design of an object that hasn't been checked out.

You can check in one object or check in several objects simultaneously. To check in objects, right-click any object that's checked out and select Check In (or select the object and click Check In on the VSS toolbar); this opens the Check In Objects to SourceSafe dialog box. (See Figure 19.16.) Click to select any objects you want to check in, and then click OK. The objects that you checked in once again appear in the Database window with a padlock icon, indicating that you can't modify them without checking them out.

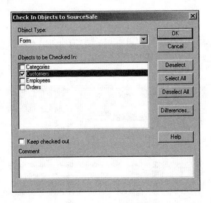

FIGURE 19.16   Use the Check In Objects to SourceSafe dialog box to designate which checked-out objects you want to check in.

TIP

If you check out an object and realize that you made a mistake, you can right-click the object and choose Undo Check Out to quickly check it back in.

Getting the Latest Version

While you're working on the database, the objects in your local copy might not reflect changes that other users have made to the objects. To see these changes, you must get the object's latest version from the SourceSafe project. To do this with one object, right-click the object and select Get Latest Version, or select the object and click Get Latest Version on the VSS toolbar; for multiple objects, choose Tools, SourceSafe, Get Latest Version. The Get Objects from SourceSafe dialog box appears, allowing you to select the objects you want.

Adding Objects to Visual SourceSafe

Depending on how you have configured Visual SourceSafe, you might be prompted to add new objects to SourceSafe control. If you add objects to your database and don't place them under SourceSafe control, you can always opt to add them later. To do this, choose Tools, SourceSafe, Add Object(s) to SourceSafe, or click Add Objects to SourceSafe on the VSS toolbar. The Add Objects to SourceSafe dialog box opens, showing you all the objects in your local database that you haven't placed under SourceSafe control.

> **TIP**
>
> To control whether new objects are automatically placed under SourceSafe control, choose Tools, SourceSafe, Options. Pick the option that you want from the Add Objects to Source Control When Adding Them to Microsoft Access drop-down list.

Refreshing an Object's Status

When looking at the Database window, you can't be sure that the icons indicating an object's status accurately reflect the object's current state. To refresh the icons in the Database window, choose Tools, SourceSafe, Refresh Object Status.

Leveraging the Power of Visual SourceSafe

Not only does Visual SourceSafe help to manage the process of several developers working on an application simultaneously, but it also helps you manage versions of your application. It does this by showing you the differences between the checked-out version of an object and the version stored in the Visual SourceSafe project, by allowing you to view an object's history, and by letting you revert to an object's previous version.

Showing Differences Between Modules

One of the most powerful aspects of Visual SourceSafe is its capability to show the differences between the checked-out version of an object and the version in the SourceSafe project. These differences show you what you've done since you checked out the object. To view the differences, choose Tools, SourceSafe, Show Differences. First the Difference Options dialog box opens, where you can select display options; then the Differences window opens, which lets you easily jump from difference to difference within the object. Deleted lines are blue, changed lines are red, and added lines are green.

Showing an Object's History

Often it helps to view everything that has transpired in an object; for example, you might want to see who checked out each object and when. To see an object's history, first click to select the object; then choose Tools, SourceSafe, Show History. First you get a History Options dialog box (see Figure 19.17), where you enter From, To, and User information. The From and To boxes accept dates, versions, or labels, and the User box accepts a valid VSS username.

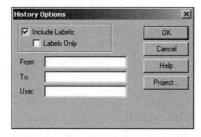

FIGURE 19.17   The History Options dialog box.

The History Options dialog box enables you to designate options for the history information that you view. VSS tracks changes by internal version, date, or user-designated labels. Labels generally are the most useful way to track changes because you can use meaningful phrases such as "2.01," "First Beta," or "Approved for Company-Wide Distribution."

Click OK after making your selections. The History of File dialog box opens, which shows you the versions of the object, who performed each action on the object, the date the action was performed, and what the action was (see Figure 19.18). From the History of File dialog box, you can do the following:

- View each version of the object.

- See the details of each action taken on the object.

- Get the object's current version from the Visual SourceSafe project.

- See the differences between two versions of the object.

- Pin a specific version of a file to the current project, ensuring that the file can't be changed when shared.

- Roll back to a previous version of the object.

- Get a report of everything that has transpired with the object.

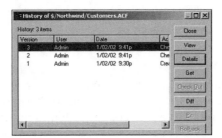

FIGURE 19.18   The History of File dialog box allows you to view just about everything that has happened to an object.

Reverting to an Object's Previous Version

Visual SourceSafe also enables you to roll back to previous versions of an object. This is particularly useful if things have gone seriously awry and you want to start over in a version in which conditions were more stable. You can revert to an object's previous version from the History of File dialog box. Select the version that you want to roll back to and click Rollback. Visual SourceSafe warns you that your actions are irreversible. If you select Yes, the object is rolled back to the selected version.

Changes Visual SourceSafe Makes to Access's Behavior

Visual SourceSafe alters Access's behavior; therefore, the following sections explain these changes so they don't take you by surprise.

The Compact Command

Before you distribute a database, you should always compact it. When you try to compact a database that's under SourceSafe control, SourceSafe asks whether you want to remove the database from SourceSafe control. When you respond Yes, Access goes through each object in the database and removes all SourceSafe properties.

Opening a Database

When you open a database that's under SourceSafe control, SourceSafe always opens it exclusively. This prevents more than one developer from modifying objects in the local database at a given time.

When you open a database, you can opt to have Access automatically refresh all objects from the SourceSafe project, you can have Access prompt you as to whether you want to refresh all objects, or you can opt not to have Access automatically refresh any objects. To modify this option, choose Tools, SourceSafe, Options and use the drop-down list named Get Latest Checked-In Version of Objects When Opening a Database to designate your choice.

Closing a Database

When closing a database, you can choose to have Access automatically check in all objects, to prompt you on for whether you want to check in all objects, or not to have Access check in any objects. This option is found under Tools, SourceSafe, Options. Use the drop-down list titled Check In Objects When Closing the Database to select your choice.

Opening an Object in Design View

Each time you check out an object, Access determines whether someone has already checked it out. If another user hasn't checked out the object, SourceSafe asks you whether you want to check it out. If you respond No, Access opens the object as read-only. If another user has checked out the object and it's a module, SourceSafe warns you that another user has the object checked out, and you get the option of checking the object out. SourceSafe merges your changes with the other user's changes later. If you try to check out any object other than a module and another user has already checked it out, SourceSafe warns you that you can just view the object as read-only in Design view.

Saving a New Object or Using Save As on an Existing Object

When you save a new object or choose File, Save As for an existing object, you can designate whether the new object is placed under SourceSafe control. Designating what happens when a new object is saved is accomplished by choosing Tools, SourceSafe, Options. You can have Access automatically place the object under SourceSafe control, you can have Access prompt you for your choice, or you can tell Access not to place the object under SourceSafe control. Use the drop-down list titled Add Objects to Source Control When Adding Them to Microsoft Access to make your selection.

Renaming an Object

When you rename an object that's under SourceSafe control, Access automatically reflects the name change in the source-control project. You cannot rename an object while another user has it checked out.

> **NOTE**
>
> If you want to rename tables, command bars, and other objects that are part of the binary file, you must first check out Data and Misc. objects because changes to the former objects will affect the latter.

Deleting an Object

When you delete an object, you can have Visual SourceSafe display a message box asking whether you want to remove the object from the SourceSafe project, you can have Access automatically remove the object from the SourceSafe project, or you can opt for Access not to remove the object from the SourceSafe project. This option can be configured by choosing Tool, SourceSafe, Options in the drop-down list titled Remove Objects from Source Control When Deleting Them from Microsoft Access.

> **NOTE**
>
> If you installed VSS Help as part of the MSDN Help Library that comes with Office XP Developer, you can open extensive Help books on VSS either from Help buttons on VSS screens or directly from the MSDN Help library.

Understanding the Limitations of Visual SourceSafe

Although Visual SourceSafe is a powerful product, it does impose some limitations that you should be aware of. User and group permissions can't be set when an object is under SourceSafe control. In fact, when you add a database to SourceSafe control, SourceSafe removes all user and group permissions! Furthermore, you can't put replicated databases under source-code control, and you can't move, rename, or copy the local version of the database and continue working with it under SourceSafe control. To move a database, you must first check in all objects, delete the local database, and then re-create the database in the new location.

Summary

Visual SourceSafe is a powerful product for both the individual developer and members of a development team. It helps you manage group development and versioning of the objects in a database. Furthermore, it integrates seamlessly with Microsoft Access 2002 and is fairly easy to use. In my opinion, you should place most, if not all, Access databases under SourceSafe control while you're developing them.

PART III

Access and the Internet

IN THIS PART

20

Publishing Data on the Web

Why This Chapter Is Important

No good course today is complete without a discussion involving the Web. At its most basic level, Web functionality includes the ability to produce static HTML documents. At a more sophisticated level, Web functionality incorporates the capability to publish Web pages dynamically. This chapter shows you how to save database objects as static HTML documents. You will also learn how to use both IDC and ASP files to publish Web pages dynamically.

Saving Database Objects as HTML

Probably one of the most basic but powerful features in Access is the capability to save database objects as Hypertext Markup Language (HTML) documents. You can publish table data, query results, form datasheets, forms, and reports as HTML. The following sections cover each of these objects.

HTML—A Primer

HTML is the language of the Web. It consists of a combination of formatting tags and text. HTML is *not* a programming language. Instead, it is a formatting language. The beauty of HTML is that it is platform- and operating system–independent. This means that machines running a large variety of operating systems can read Access-generated HTML documents.

Saving Tables as HTML

When saving table data to HTML, you can store it in the HTML file format so that you can easily publish it on the Web. Just follow these steps:

1. Click Tables in the Objects list of the Database window.
2. Click to select the table whose data you want to save as HTML.
3. Choose File, Export to open the Export Table dialog box.
4. Use the Save as Type drop-down list to select HTML documents.
5. Select a filename and location for the HTML document.
6. Click Export to finish the process.

Access exports the file to HTML so that any Web browser can display it. (See Figure 20.1.) You can also view the HTML source, as shown in Figure 20.2.

NOTE

To view the source in Internet Explorer, select Source from the View menu.

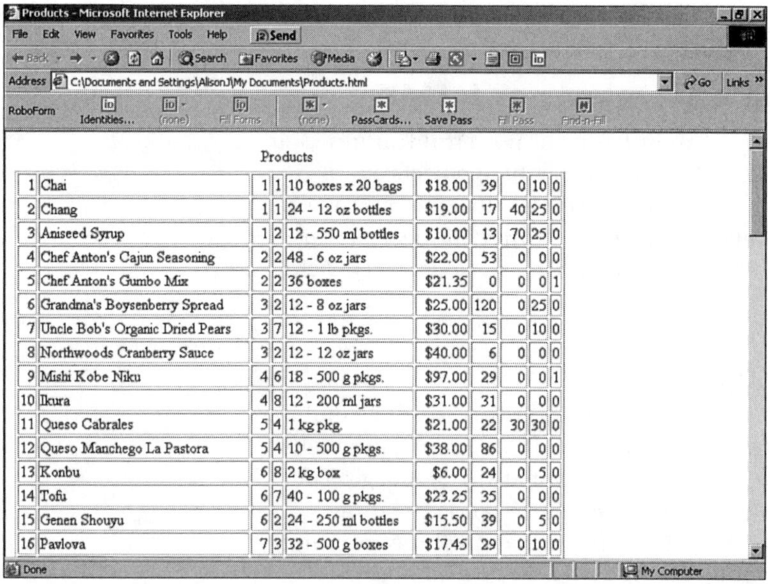

1	Chai	1	1	10 boxes x 20 bags	$18.00	39	0	10	0
2	Chang	1	1	24 - 12 oz bottles	$19.00	17	40	25	0
3	Aniseed Syrup	1	2	12 - 550 ml bottles	$10.00	13	70	25	0
4	Chef Anton's Cajun Seasoning	2	2	48 - 6 oz jars	$22.00	53	0	0	0
5	Chef Anton's Gumbo Mix	2	2	36 boxes	$21.35	0	0	0	1
6	Grandma's Boysenberry Spread	3	2	12 - 8 oz jars	$25.00	120	0	25	0
7	Uncle Bob's Organic Dried Pears	3	7	12 - 1 lb pkgs.	$30.00	15	0	10	0
8	Northwoods Cranberry Sauce	3	2	12 - 12 oz jars	$40.00	6	0	0	0
9	Mishi Kobe Niku	4	6	18 - 500 g pkgs.	$97.00	29	0	0	1
10	Ikura	4	8	12 - 200 ml jars	$31.00	31	0	0	0
11	Queso Cabrales	5	4	1 kg pkg.	$21.00	22	30	30	0
12	Queso Manchego La Pastora	5	4	10 - 500 g pkgs.	$38.00	86	0	0	0
13	Konbu	6	8	2 kg box	$6.00	24	0	5	0
14	Tofu	6	7	40 - 100 g pkgs.	$23.25	35	0	0	0
15	Genen Shouyu	6	2	24 - 250 ml bottles	$15.50	39	0	5	0
16	Pavlova	7	3	32 - 500 g boxes	$17.45	29	0	10	0

FIGURE 20.1 The tblCustomers table saved as HTML.

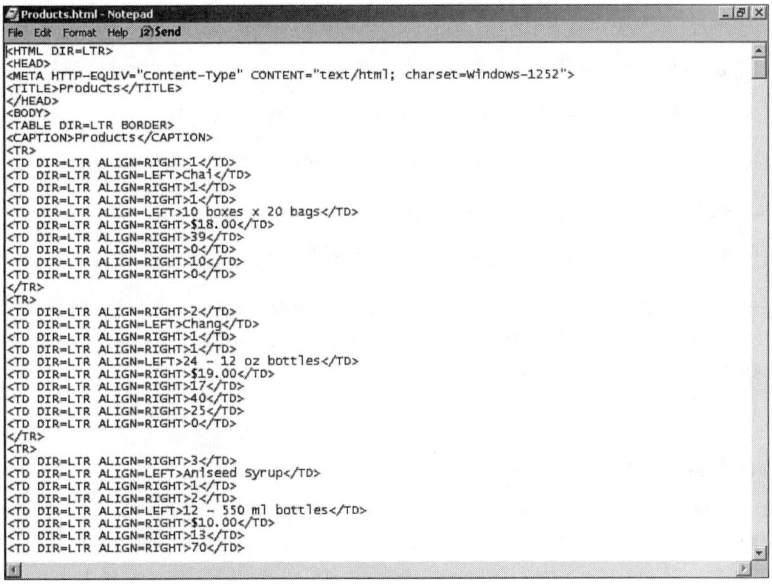

```
<HTML DIR=LTR>
<HEAD>
<META HTTP-EQUIV="Content-Type" CONTENT="text/html; charset=Windows-1252">
<TITLE>Products</TITLE>
</HEAD>
<BODY>
<TABLE DIR=LTR BORDER>
<CAPTION>Products</CAPTION>
<TR>
<TD DIR=LTR ALIGN=RIGHT>1</TD>
<TD DIR=LTR ALIGN=LEFT>Chai</TD>
<TD DIR=LTR ALIGN=RIGHT>1</TD>
<TD DIR=LTR ALIGN=RIGHT>1</TD>
<TD DIR=LTR ALIGN=LEFT>10 boxes x 20 bags</TD>
<TD DIR=LTR ALIGN=RIGHT>$18.00</TD>
<TD DIR=LTR ALIGN=RIGHT>39</TD>
<TD DIR=LTR ALIGN=RIGHT>0</TD>
<TD DIR=LTR ALIGN=RIGHT>10</TD>
<TD DIR=LTR ALIGN=RIGHT>0</TD>
</TR>
<TR>
<TD DIR=LTR ALIGN=RIGHT>2</TD>
<TD DIR=LTR ALIGN=LEFT>Chang</TD>
<TD DIR=LTR ALIGN=RIGHT>1</TD>
<TD DIR=LTR ALIGN=RIGHT>1</TD>
<TD DIR=LTR ALIGN=LEFT>24 - 12 oz bottles</TD>
<TD DIR=LTR ALIGN=RIGHT>$19.00</TD>
<TD DIR=LTR ALIGN=RIGHT>17</TD>
<TD DIR=LTR ALIGN=RIGHT>40</TD>
<TD DIR=LTR ALIGN=RIGHT>25</TD>
<TD DIR=LTR ALIGN=RIGHT>0</TD>
</TR>
<TR>
<TD DIR=LTR ALIGN=RIGHT>3</TD>
<TD DIR=LTR ALIGN=LEFT>Aniseed Syrup</TD>
<TD DIR=LTR ALIGN=RIGHT>1</TD>
<TD DIR=LTR ALIGN=RIGHT>2</TD>
<TD DIR=LTR ALIGN=LEFT>12 - 550 ml bottles</TD>
<TD DIR=LTR ALIGN=RIGHT>$10.00</TD>
<TD DIR=LTR ALIGN=RIGHT>13</TD>
<TD DIR=LTR ALIGN=RIGHT>70</TD>
```

FIGURE 20.2 Viewing the source of the Products table's HTML file.

Saving Query Results as HTML

The capability to save query results as HTML means that you don't need to save all fields and all records to an HTML file. In fact, you can even save the results of Totals queries and other complex queries as HTML. Saving the result of a query as HTML is similar to saving a table as HTML:

1. Click Queries in the Objects list of the Database window.
2. Click to select the query whose results you want to save as HTML.
3. Choose File, Export to open the Export Query dialog box.
4. Use the Save as Type drop-down list to select HTML documents.
5. Select a filename and location for the HTML document.
6. Click Export to finish the process.

Saving Forms as HTML

Because an HTML file is a static file, you can save a form's datasheet only as HTML. An HTML file doesn't change as the data in the database changes. Furthermore, the user cannot modify the data in the HTML document. To save a form's datasheet as HTML, follow these steps:

1. Click Forms in the Objects list of the Database window.

2. Click to select the form whose results you want to save as HTML.

3. Choose File, Export to open the Export Form dialog box.

4. Use the Save as Type drop-down list to select HTML documents.

5. Select a filename and location for the HTML document.

6. Click Export; this opens the HTML Output Options dialog box.

7. Select an optional HTML template that Access applies to the HTML document. By selecting an HTML template, you can easily maintain a consistent look for your Web publications. Click OK.

Saving Reports as HTML

You can save reports and their formatting as HTML. This provides an elegant way to publish data on an Internet or intranet site. To publish a report as HTML, just follow these steps:

1. Click Reports in the Objects list of the Database window.

2. Click to select the report whose results you want to save as HTML.

3. Choose File, Export to open the Save As dialog box.

4. Use the Save as Type drop-down list to select HTML documents.

5. Select a filename and location for the HTML document.

6. Click Export to open the HTML Output Options dialog box.

7. Select an optional HTML template that's applied to the HTML document. Click OK.

Figure 20.3 shows a report published as HTML. Because the report is a multipage report, Access generates several HTML files. Each page of the report is linked, and the user can easily navigate from page to page by using the First, Previous, Next, and Last hyperlinks automatically generated during the Export process.

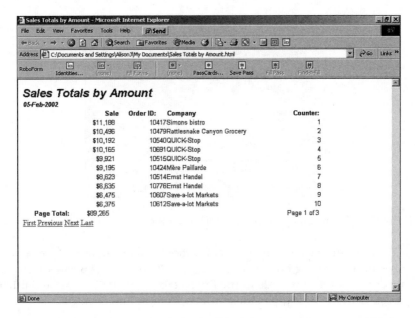

FIGURE 20.3   Viewing the Northwind Sales Totals by Amount report as HTML.

Linking to HTML Files

Just as you can link to dBase tables, Paradox tables, or ODBC data sources, you can link to HTML files by following these steps:

1. Right-click within the Database window and select Link Tables; this opens the Link dialog box.

2. Use the Files of Type drop-down list to select HTML documents.

3. Select the HTML file that you want to link to, and click Link. The Link HTML Wizard appears (see Figure 20.4).

4. In the wizard's first step, indicate whether the first row of data contains column headings. You can also see Access's proposed layout for the linked table.

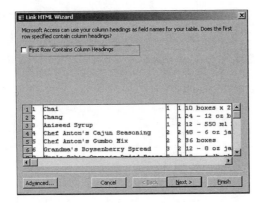

FIGURE 20.4   The first step of the Link HTML Wizard.

5. Click Advanced to designate specifics about the linked table. The Link Specification dialog box opens (see Figure 20.5). Here you can select which fields you want to include in the linked table, date delimiters, and other specifics of the linked file. Make your selections and click OK.

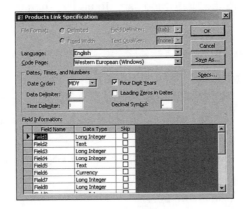

FIGURE 20.5   In the Link Specification dialog box, you designate specifics about the linked table.

6. Click Next to proceed with the Link HTML Wizard. In the next step, you select a field name and data type for each field in the HTML file. Make your selections and click Next.

7. In the wizard's last step, you supply a table name for the linked table. Make your selection and click Finish.

8. You then see a message that the table linked successfully. The table appears in the Database window with a special icon indicating that it's an HTML file (see Figure 20.6).

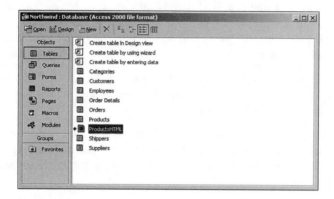

FIGURE 20.6   The Database window with a linked HTML document.

You can browse, query, and create reports on the linked HTML file just like any other table. However, you cannot modify any of the data in the linked file.

Importing HTML Files

You can import the data in an HTML file so that it becomes exactly like any other Access table; follow these steps to import an HTML file:

1. Right-click within the Database window and select Import; this opens the Import dialog box.

2. Use the Files of Type drop-down list to select HTML documents.

3. Select the HTML file that you want to import and click Import to open the Import HTML Wizard. This wizard is almost identical to the Link HTML Wizard.

4. In the wizard's first step, you indicate whether the first row of data contains column headings. You can also see Access's proposed layout for the imported table.

5. Click Advanced to designate specifics about the imported table. The Import Specification dialog box opens. Here you can select which fields you want to include in the imported table, date delimiters, and other specifics of the imported file. Make your selections and click OK.

6. Click Next to go to the next step. Here, you have the choice of importing the data into a new table or adding it to an existing table. Make your selection and click Next.

7. In the next step, select a field name and data type for each field in the HTML file. You can also designate whether you want Access to create an index for the field and even whether you want to exclude the field entirely. Make your selections and click Next.

8. Next, the wizard lets you designate a primary key for the imported table. If you prefer, you can have Access supply the primary key (see Figure 20.7). Make your selection and click Next.

9. In the wizard's last step, supply a table name for the linked table. If you're concerned about whether the imported table is normalized, you can have Access launch the Table Analyzer after the import is finished. Make your selections and click Finish.

10. You then see a message that the table imported successfully; it appears in the Database window just as any other Access table does.

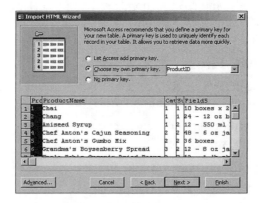

FIGURE 20.7   Designating a primary key for your new table.

Working with Hyperlinks

Hyperlinks in Access 2000 and Access 2002 are extremely powerful. They enable you to jump from your application to an Internet, intranet, or file location. Hyperlinks can be stored in table fields or placed directly on forms and reports.

Storing Hyperlinks in Tables

Using the Hyperlink field type, you can easily store URLs (addresses to Internet or intranet sites) and UNCs (addresses to files on a local area network or a local hard disk) in your tables' records. To create a Hyperlink field, select Hyperlink from the Data Type drop-down list while viewing a table's design. Access uses the data stored in the field as a hyperlink address.

Including Hyperlinks on Forms

Although the Hyperlink field type enables you to associate URLs and UNCs with each record in a table, the capability to place hyperlinks on forms and reports lets your users easily navigate from your forms and reports to other parts of your application and to URL and UNC locations. You can add hyperlinks to command buttons, labels, and image controls because each of these controls has a Hyperlink Address and Hyperlink SubAddress property (see Figure 20.8). The Hyperlink Address property contains the actual URL or UNC, and the Hyperlink SubAddress property specifies a particular location in the URL or UNC. For example, if the UNC points to an Access database, the Hyperlink SubAddress might point to a form in the database.

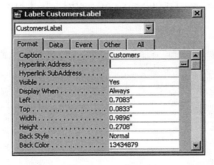

FIGURE 20.8   Command buttons, labels, and image controls have Hyperlink Address and Hyperlink SubAddress properties.

To add a hyperlink to a image control, follow these steps:

1. Click to select the control.

2. View the control's properties.

3. Select the Format tab of the Properties window.

4. Click in the Hyperlink Address property.

5. Click the Build button (the ellipsis) to open the Insert Hyperlink dialog box (see Figure 20.9).

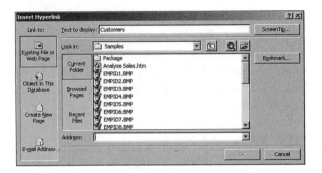

FIGURE 20.9   Establishing a link to a file or URL by using the Insert Hyperlink
dialog box.

6. With Existing File or Web Page selected as the Link To, you can enter a file
path or URL in the text box or click Current Folder to locate a file or Web page
in the current folder. You can also click to insert hyperlinks to browsed pages
or recent files. With Object in This Database selected as the Link To, you can
link to an object in the current database (see Figure 20.10). Select Create New
Page to create a new data access page, and select Email Address to link to an
e-mail address.

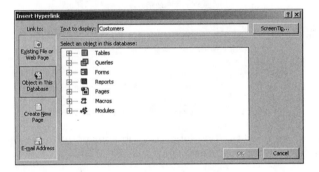

FIGURE 20.10   Setting the location within an Access database for your hyperlink.

7. Click OK to finish the process. The contents of the Link to File or URL combo
box become the Hyperlink Address, and the object name (if you designate one)
becomes the Hyperlink SubAddress (see Figure 20.11).

TIP

Using a hyperlink address to open an object in an Access database rather than using the
Click event of the command button and VBA code allows you to remove the class module
associated with the form (if that is the only procedure you need for the form), thereby opti-
mizing the form's performance.

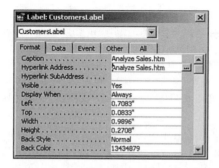

FIGURE 20.11   Hyperlink address defined for a label control.

Static Versus Dynamic Web Pages

Many people don't understand the differences between publishing static and dynamic data. *Static data* doesn't change. If you want to publish information that rarely, if ever, changes, you should create a static Web page; the text at the beginning of this chapter covers the techniques for doing so. The data output for each of the methods discussed so far is static and can be changed only by republishing the data and resubmitting it to the Web.

Dynamic data, on the other hand, does change. You should save your data in the dynamic format when you know that it will change frequently and your Web application needs to store and retrieve live data from your application by using a form. To publish dynamic Web data, you have several choices. Data access pages are one solution. Microsoft targeted data access pages toward intranet rather than Internet applications. For Internet applications, you can output the object to either the ASP file format or the HTX/IDC file format instead of an HTML file.

ASP stands for Active Server Page. Active Server is a component of Microsoft Internet Information Server (IIS) 3.0 and later versions. The .asp file contains the following:

- ODBC connection information, such as the data source name, user name, and password

- One or more queries in the form of SQL statements

- Template directives for layout of the resulting HTML file

- VBScript code containing references to Active Server controls

With an ASP file, you publish the object and install it. The Microsoft IIS, at the request of the Web browser, runs VBScript code and calls the Active Server controls. It then opens the database by using the ODBC driver and the .asp file, runs the queries stored in the .asp file, and merges the results and HTML tags in the .asp file into an HTML file. IIS then sends the HTML file back to the Web browser for display.

When you select the IDC/HTX file format, Access creates two files. The .htx file—an HTML extension file—has all the formatting tags and instructions needed so that the query's results can be formatted. The .idc file—an Internet Database Connector file—contains a SQL statement and other information needed by the Microsoft IIS so that it can connect to an ODBC data source, such as your Access database file (.mdb). The ODBC data source name, username, and password are all stored in the .IDC file, but no data is stored in it.

After you have published a database object and installed it on the Web by using a Web document publishing server, such as the Microsoft IIS, the server opens the Access database by using the ODBC driver and the .IDC information file on request from a Web browser. It runs the query stored in the .IDC file and merges the result and the .HTX file into an HTML file that's sent back to the Web browser for display.

Working with HTX/IDC Files

The following steps are required to output data to HTX/IDC files:

1. Select the database object that you want to export.

2. Select File, Export. The Export Table dialog box appears.

3. Select Microsoft IIS 1-2 from the Save as Type drop-down list and click Export. The HTX/IDC Output Options dialog box appears (see Figure 20.12).

4. Click Browse to select an HTML template, if desired.

5. Specify an ODBC data source. You must establish this data source in your operating system's Administrative Tools. The Web server uses the data source to access data within the Access database.

6. Designate the user and password under which IIS will make the connection.

7. Click OK to output the .htx and .idc files.

FIGURE 20.12   The HTX/IDC Output Options dialog box enables you to designate required options to output your database object in the HTX/IDC file format.

Working with Active Server Pages (.asp Files)

The following steps are required to output data to an ASP file:

1. Select the database object that you want to export.

2. Select File, Export. The Export Table dialog box appears.

3. Select Microsoft Active Server Pages from the Save as Type drop-down list. Click Save. The Microsoft Active Server Pages Output Options dialog box appears (see Figure 20.13).

4. Click Browse to select an HTML template, if desired.

5. Specify an ODBC data source. You must establish this data source in your operating system's Administrative Tools. The Web server uses the data source to access data within the Access database.

6. Designate the user and password under which IIS will make the connection.

7. Click OK to output the .asp file.

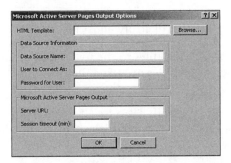

FIGURE 20.13   The Microsoft Active Server Pages Output Options dialog box enables you to designate required options to output your database object in the .asp file format.

Testing ASP and HTX/IDC Files

Because both the ASP format and the HTX/IDC file formats utilize server-side processing to output an HTML document, you must take the following steps to test the files on your Web server:

1. Install the appropriate software on the computer that will act as the Web server (for example, the Microsoft Internet Information Server).

2. Create a virtual directory under the root directory of the Web server (see Figure 20.14).

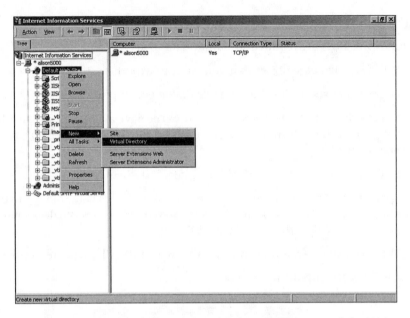

FIGURE 20.14   Create a virtual directory under the root directory of the Web server.

3. Copy the ASP or HTX/IDC files to the folder. Make sure that you copy any related files, such as graphics or linked files.

4. Define privileges for the folder. Make sure that you include Execute privileges for IIS 3.0 or Run Scripts privileges for IIS 4.0 and above (see Figure 20.15). The IIS Explorer appears as in Figure 20.16 when you are done.

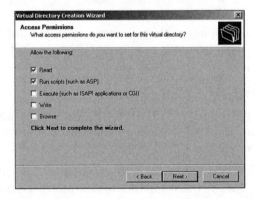

FIGURE 20.15   Make sure that you include Run Scripts privileges for the folder.

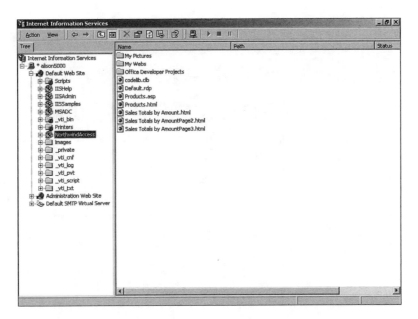

FIGURE 20.16 The IIS Explorer after you create a virtual directory called NorthwindAccess.

5. Define an ODBC data source that points to the database containing the data that you want to publish. Make sure that you define the data source as a System DSN on the Web server and that the data source name (DSN) matches the data source that you designated in the Microsoft Active Server Pages Output Options or HTX/IDC Output Options dialog boxes. Make sure that the username and password match the username and password entered in the User to Connect As and Password for User text boxes of the Microsoft Active Server Pages Output Options or HTX/IDC Output Options dialog boxes.

6. Because the ASP and HTX/IDC file formats both utilize server-side processing, you must use the HTTP protocol when testing them. Notice that in Figure 20.17, the HTTP protocol is used to process the Products.asp file. The Web address used within the browser to process the IDC file is
   `http://localhost/NorthwindAccess/Products.asp`.

NOTE

Although this chapter covers both the ASP and HTX/IDC file formats, they are not equally represented in current technologies. Whereas the ASP technology is being used more and is highly supported within Microsoft Visual InterDev 6.0, the HTX/IDC format is supported by Microsoft only for purposes of backward compatibility. You should carefully consider whether it is prudent to utilize the HTX/IDC technology.

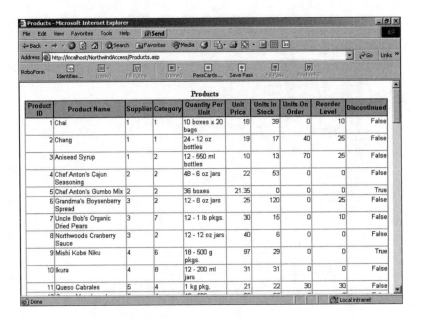

FIGURE 20.17   The HTTP protocolis used to access ASP and HTX/IDC files on a Web server.

Summary

It's easy to integrate Access with the Internet or with an intranet. Access enables you to easily publish database objects to the Web and import HTML data from the Web. In fact, you can even create dynamic Web pages! Using data access pages, covered in Chapter 22, "Data Access Pages," you can even build forms that display and update live data directly from a browser. Access 2002 helps bring your data to the continually evolving information superhighway—the possibilities are endless!

21

XML Support in Microsoft Access

Why This Chapter Is Important

Hypertext Markup Language (HTML) has one major limitation: It in no way separates data from the presentation of data. XML stands for Extensible Markup Language. Its main objective is to separate data and its structure from the presentation of the data. Furthermore, it provides a universal data format that can be read by a multitude of machines on a multitude of operating systems and platforms. It bridges the gap between the variety of systems that store data in a variety of disparate formats.

The Basics of XML

Whereas HTML includes predefined formatting tags such as the <B> tag, which bolds data, XML is composed of custom tags that define data. Using XML, you create your own set of tags. These tags focus on defining the data.

You should be aware of several terms when working with XML:

- **XML document**—Any document that follows XML syntax rules.

- **Element**—Unit of an XML document enclosed in a pair of tags: <tag>element</tag>.

- **Attribute**—A name="value" pair that follows the first tag name of an element: <tag attributename='attributevalue'>...</tag>.

- **XML header**—Optional component of an XML document that specifies the encoding method: <?xml version=1.0" encoding="UTF-8" ?>.

- **Well-formed**—An XML document that a parsing tool such as the MSXML parser included with Internet Explorer 5+ can display.

- **XML schema**—Metadata (data) that describes the structure of the XML document and the data it contains.

- **XML namespace**—Specifies standard elements and attributes for a software product. Usually consists of a URL.

- **XML style sheet**—The Extensible Stylesheet Language (XSLT) defines the presentation of the XML document and transforms one XML document into another XML or HTML document with a different structure.

The following is an example of a simple XML document generated by Microsoft Access. It is based on the NorthWind Shippers table:

```
<?xml version="1.0" encoding="UTF-8" ?>
 <dataroot xmlns:od="urn:schemas-microsoft-com:officedata">
 <Shippers>
  <ShipperID>1</ShipperID>
  <CompanyName>Speedy Express</CompanyName>
  <Phone>(503) 555-9831</Phone>
  </Shippers>
 <Shippers>
  <ShipperID>2</ShipperID>
  <CompanyName>United Package</CompanyName>
  <Phone>(503) 555-3199</Phone>
  </Shippers>
 <Shippers>
  <ShipperID>3</ShipperID>
  <CompanyName>Federal Shipping</CompanyName>
  <Phone>(503) 555-9931</Phone>
  </Shippers>
 </dataroot>
```

The first tag, `<?xml version="1.0" encoding="UTF-8">`, contains information about the XML document. It declares that the document is an XML document, that it conforms to the version 1.0 XML specification, and that it uses the UTF-8 character set. XML consists of three different types of tags: start tags, end tags, and empty tags. Start tags begin with a less-than symbol (<) and end with a greater-than symbol (>). End tags begin with a less-than symbol followed by a forward slash (</) and end

with a greater-than symbol (>). Empty tags begin with a less-than symbol (<) and end with a slash plus a greater-than symbol (/>). The names of the elements are enclosed within tags. You can name an element whatever you would like. Notice the tag that defines the Shippers table. Within that tag are subsets of elements or attributes that define the fields and data within the Shippers table. Viewed in Internet Explorer, the XML document appears as in Figure 21.1.

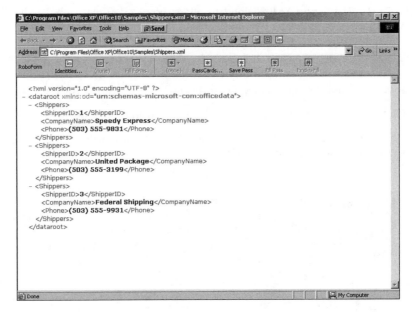

FIGURE 21.1   An XML document based on the NorthWind Shippers table, viewed in Internet Explorer.

Exporting Data to XML

Access makes it easy for you to export data to XML. To export an object to an XML file:

1. Right-click the object that you want to export, and select Export.

2. Select XML Documents from the Save As Type drop-down box.

3. Select the folder where you want Access to save the XML file, and click Export. The Export XML dialog box appears (see Figure 21.2).

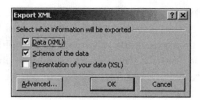

FIGURE 21.2   The Export XML dialog box allows you to designate what XML-related documents you want to create.

4. Select whether you want to export the data, the schema of the data, the presentation of the data, or any combination of the three. The sections that follow discuss the schema (XSD) and presentation (XSLT) files.

5. Click the Advanced button to designate additional options.

6. Click OK to create the XML document. Viewed in a browser, after you select the Presentation of Your Data option, the XML document appears as in Figure 21.3.

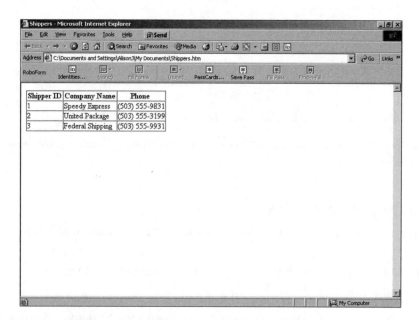

FIGURE 21.3   An XML document viewed in the browser after the Presentation of Your Data option is selected.

Working with XML Style Sheets (XSL or XSLT)

Style sheets, often referred to as XSL or XSLT documents, determine how data in an XML document is presented. XSLT stands for Extensible Stylesheet Language Transformation. XSLT files are combined with XML files by an XSLT processor, producing an output file. The output file can be in HTML, plain text, or a variety of other formats.

When you opt to produce an XML style sheet, Access generates the XSL file *and* an HTML document. The HTML document looks like this:

```
<HTML xmlns:signature="urn:schemas-microsoft-com:office:access">
<HEAD>
<META HTTP-EQUIV="Content-Type" CONTENT="text/html;charset=UTF-8"/>
</HEAD>

<SCRIPT event=onload for=window>
  objData = new ActiveXObject("MSXML.DOMDocument");
  objData.async = false;
  objData.load("Shippers.xml");
  if (objData.parseError.errorCode != 0)
    alert(objData.parseError.reason);

  objStyle = new ActiveXObject("MSXML.DOMDocument");
  objStyle.async = false;
  objStyle.load("Shippers.xsl");
  if (objStyle.parseError.errorCode != 0)
    alert(objStyle.parseError.reason);

  document.open("text/html","replace");
  document.write(objData.transformNode(objStyle));
</SCRIPT>

</HTML>
```

Notice that the HTML document contains a script block that references both the XML document and the XSL document. The MSXML parser loads the XML document and the XSL document. It then uses the XSL document to format the XML document. A portion of the XSL document for the Shippers table appears here. Notice that it defines things such as the width and format of each column.

```
<?xml version="1.0"?>
<xsl:stylesheet xmlns:xsl="http://www.w3.org/TR/WD-xsl" language="vbscript">
<xsl:template match="/">
<HTML>
```

```
<HEAD>
<META HTTP-EQUIV="Content-Type" CONTENT="text/html;charset=UTF-8" />
<TITLE>
Shippers
</TITLE>
<STYLE TYPE="text/css">
</STYLE>
</HEAD>
<BODY link="#0000ff" vlink="#800080">
<TABLE BORDER="1" BGCOLOR="#ffffff" CELLSPACING="0" CELLPADDING="0"><TBODY>

<xsl:for-each select="/dataroot/Shippers">
<xsl:eval>AppendNodeIndex(me)</xsl:eval>
</xsl:for-each>
<xsl:for-each select="/dataroot/Shippers">
<xsl:eval>CacheCurrentNode(me)</xsl:eval>
<xsl:if expr="OnFirstNode">
<TR><TH style="width: 0.802in">
Shipper ID
</TH>
<TH style="width: 1.1562in">
Company Name
</TH>
<TH style="width: 1in">
Phone
</TH>
</TR>
</xsl:if>
<TR><TD>
<xsl:eval no-entities="true">Format(GetValue("ShipperID", 3),"" ,"")</xsl:eval>
</TD>
<TD>
<xsl:eval no-entities="true">Format(GetValue("CompanyName", 202),"" ,"")</xsl:eval>
</TD>
<TD>
<xsl:eval no-entities="true">Format(GetValue("Phone", 202),"" ,"")</xsl:eval>
</TD>
</TR>
<xsl:if expr="OnLastNode">
</xsl:if>
<xsl:eval>NextNode()</xsl:eval>
</xsl:for-each>
</TBODY></TABLE>
</BODY>
</HTML>
```

This document has elements of both HTML and XML. In fact, this XSLT document combined with the XML document results in an HTML document. To see how the process works, you need to understand only one main rule: The XML processor sends anything that does not include xsl: within the tag directly to the output. The processor performs special processing on any tag prefixed with xsl:. The first of such tags in the example is:

```
<xsl:for-each select="/dataroot/Shippers">
```

This tag indicates the starting tag of a for-each element in the XSL namespace. The /dataroot/Shippers attribute of the element matches any Shippers element that is a child of the dataroot element in the XML document. One such element for each shipper is included in the XML document. The parser executes the code between the `<xsl:for-each select="/dataroot/Shippers">` and the `</xsl:for-each>` once for each occurrence of the Shippers element included in the XML file. As it processes each element, it outputs text (in this case, HTML). The XSL file shown previously loops through each shipper, creating a table header for the first row and then formatting the data for each data row into an HTML table. The formatted output appears in Figure 21.4.

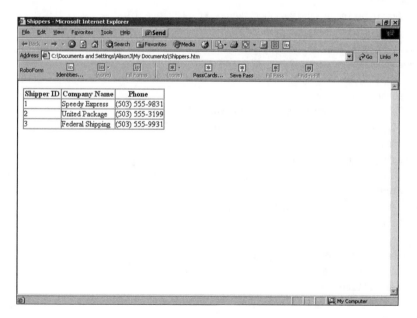

FIGURE 21.4   An XML document formatted by an XSL style sheet.

Working with XML Schemas—The XSD File

As mentioned previously, an XML schema document, known as the XSD file, defines the data stored in an XML document. Using an XSD file, you can supply the schema information for the data in the XML document. The following is the XML schema file generated for the Shippers table.

```
<?xml version="1.0" encoding="UTF-8"?>
<xsd:schema xmlns:xsd="http://www.w3.org/2000/10/XMLSchema"
xmlns:od="urn:schemas-microsoft-com:officedata">
<xsd:element name="dataroot">
<xsd:complexType>
<xsd:choice maxOccurs="unbounded">
<xsd:element ref="Shippers"/>
</xsd:choice>
</xsd:complexType>
</xsd:element>
<xsd:element name="Shippers">
<xsd:annotation>
<xsd:appinfo>
<od:index index-name="PrimaryKey" index-key="ShipperID "
primary="yes" unique="yes" clustered="no"/>
</xsd:appinfo>
</xsd:annotation>
<xsd:complexType>
<xsd:sequence>
<xsd:element name="ShipperID" od:jetType="autonumber"
od:sqlSType="int" od:autoUnique="yes" od:nonNullable="yes">
<xsd:simpleType>
<xsd:restriction base="xsd:integer"/>
</xsd:simpleType>
</xsd:element>
<xsd:element name="CompanyName" minOccurs="0" od:jetType="text"
od:sqlSType="nvarchar">
<xsd:simpleType>
<xsd:restriction base="xsd:string">
<xsd:maxLength value="40"/>
</xsd:restriction>
</xsd:simpleType>
</xsd:element>
<xsd:element name="Phone" minOccurs="0" od:jetType="text" od:sqlSType="nvarchar">
<xsd:simpleType>
<xsd:restriction base="xsd:string">
```

```
<xsd:maxLength value="24"/>
</xsd:restriction>
</xsd:simpleType>
</xsd:element>
</xsd:sequence>
</xsd:complexType>
</xsd:element>
</xsd:schema>
```

The XSD file begins with a reference to two namespaces. The xsd namespace is the proposed standard at the W3C's Web site. The od namespace is one that Microsoft developed to maintain information about the various Office data types.

```
<xsd:schema xmlns:xsd="http://www.w3.org/2000/10/XMLSchema"
xmlns:od="urn:schemas-microsoft-com:officedata">
```

The next part of the file defines the contents of the dataroot element. The dataroot element is complex, in that it contains multiple pieces of data. The xsd:choice tag, with its maxOccurs attribute of unbounded, indicates that the contents of the dataroot element can occur multiple times in the file that the XSD describes. The attribute ref="Shippers" indicates that Shippers is defined somewhere else in the XSD file.

```
<xsd:element name="dataroot">
<xsd:complexType>
<xsd:choice maxOccurs="unbounded">
<xsd:element ref="Shippers"/>
</xsd:choice>
</xsd:complexType>
</xsd:element>
```

The Shippers element provides information about the Shippers data type. This is where you can supply specific information about the Shippers element. Notice that the od tag provides information about the indexes within the Shippers table.

```
<xsd:element name="Shippers">
<xsd:annotation>
<xsd:appinfo>
<od:index index-name="PrimaryKey" index-key="ShipperID "
primary="yes" unique="yes" clustered="no"/>
</xsd:appinfo>
</xsd:annotation>
<xsd:complexType>
<xsd:sequence>
```

The remaining types define the fields within the Shippers table. Notice that the
`ShipperID` element is an autonumber field based on the int data type. It is unique
and allows numbers.

```
<xsd:element name="ShipperID" od:jetType="autonumber"
od:sqlSType="int" od:autoUnique="yes" od:nonNullable="yes">
<xsd:simpleType>
<xsd:restriction base="xsd:integer"/>
</xsd:simpleType>
</xsd:element>
```

The `CompanyName` element is an nvarchar field. It is 40 characters long.

```
<xsd:element name="CompanyName" minOccurs="0" od:jetType="text"
od:sqlSType="nvarchar">
<xsd:simpleType>
<xsd:restriction base="xsd:string">
<xsd:maxLength value="40"/>
</xsd:restriction>
</xsd:simpleType>
</xsd:element>
```

The `Phone` element is also an nvarchar field. It is 24 characters long.

```
<xsd:element name="Phone" minOccurs="0" od:jetType="text" od:sqlSType="nvarchar">
<xsd:simpleType>
<xsd:restriction base="xsd:string">
<xsd:maxLength value="24"/>
</xsd:restriction>
</xsd:simpleType>
</xsd:element>
```

The following element instructs the XML document to use the XSD file. It is found
in the Access-generated XML document when you opt to include a schema file with
the document that you are exporting.

```
<dataroot xmlns:od="urn:schemas-microsoft-com:officedata"
xmlns:xsi="http://www.w3.org/2000/10/XMLSchema-instance"
xsi:noNamespaceSchemaLocation="Customers.xsd">
```

Exporting Gotchas

A few gotchas exist in the export process. First, the Access-generated XML file is not
set up to automatically utilize the XSL document. One alternative is to use the

HTML file generated during the export process. The HTML file uses scripting to combine the XML and XSL files. The other alternative is to modify the XML file and instruct it to use the appropriate XSL file. The modified XML file looks like this:

```
<?xml version="1.0" encoding="UTF-8" ?>
<?xml-stylesheet type="text/xsl" href="Shippers.xsl"?>
 <dataroot xmlns:od="urn:schemas-microsoft-com:officedata">
 <Shippers>
  <ShipperID>1</ShipperID>
  <CompanyName>Speedy Express</CompanyName>
  <Phone>(503) 555-9831</Phone>
  </Shippers>
 <Shippers>
  <ShipperID>2</ShipperID>
  <CompanyName>United Package</CompanyName>
  <Phone>(503) 555-3199</Phone>
  </Shippers>
 <Shippers>
  <ShipperID>3</ShipperID>
  <CompanyName>Federal Shipping</CompanyName>
  <Phone>(503) 555-9931</Phone>
  </Shippers>
  </dataroot>
```

Notice the second line in the modified XML document:

```
<?xml-stylesheet type="text/xsl" href="Shippers.xsl"?>
```

This line instructs the parser to use the Shippers.xsl document to format the XML document.

It is also important to note that hyperlink fields display as straight text in the resulting XML document, and OLE object fields display as an ellipse (...). Furthermore, the Access-generated XML document is very basic and is usually meant only as a starting point. You will generally want to modify and enhance the file to better meet your specific needs.

Exporting Forms and Reports to XML

Earlier in this chapter, you saw how you can export a table as XML. You can also export forms and reports as XML.

1. Right-click the form or report that you want to export, and select Export.

2. Select XML Documents from the Save as Type drop-down box.

3. Select the folder where you want to save the XML file, and click Export. The Export XML dialog box appears.

4. Select whether you want to export the data, the schema of the data, the presentation of the data, or any combination of the three.

5. Click the Advanced button to designate additional options.

6. Click OK to create the XML document. Viewed in a browser, the results of a form that is exported to an XML document appear as in Figure 21.5. Figure 21.6 shows a report exported to an XML document.

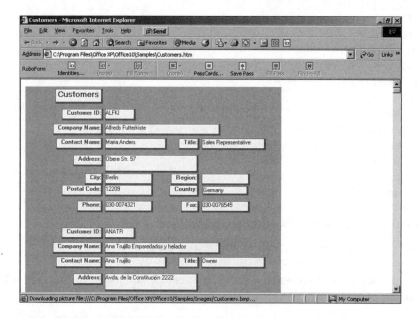

FIGURE 21.5   The Customers form from the NorthWind database exported as XML.

If the data is stored in SQL Server rather than Access, you can opt to export live *report* data as XML. Here are the steps involved:

1. Right-click the form or report that you want to export, and select Export.

2. Select XML Documents from the Save as Type drop-down box.

3. Select the folder where you want Access to save the XML file, and click Export. The Export XML dialog box appears.

4. Select whether you want to export the data, the schema of the data, the presentation of the data, or any combination of the three.

5. Click the Advanced button to designate additional options.

6. Click to select the Data tab.

7. Click the Live Data option button (see Figure 21.7).

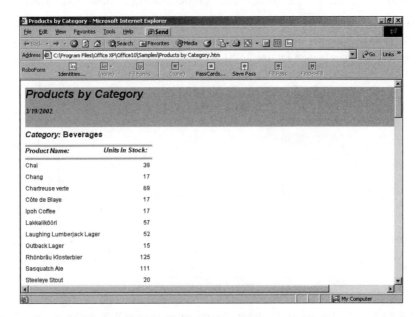

FIGURE 21.6   The Products by Category report from the NorthWind database exported as XML.

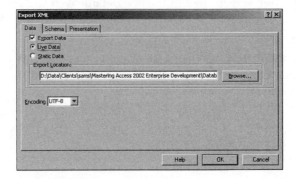

FIGURE 21.7   To designate that you want a report to be based on live data, click the Advanced button, select the Data tab, and click the Live Data option button.

8. Click OK to create the XML document.

To enable this feature, you will need to use the IIS Virtual Directory Management for SQL Server. Here are the steps involved:

1. Create a folder named Customers in your \Inetpub\wwwroot directory.

2. Add two subdirectories, one called template and the other called schema.

3. From the Windows Start menu, select Start, Programs, SQL Server, Configure SQL XML Support in IIS. The IIS Virtual Directory Management for SQL Server window appears (see Figure 21.8).

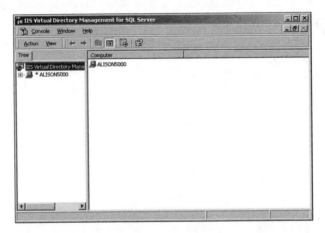

FIGURE 21.8   The IIS Virtual Directory Management for SQL Server window allows you to create a new virtual directory.

4. Expand the Web server; then right-click Default Web Site and select Create New Virtual Directory. The New Virtual Directory Properties dialog box appears (see Figure 21.9).

5. On the General tab, enter the name of the virtual directory (Customers, in this example). Enter the full path to the actual directory that the virtual directory is associated with (see Figure 21.9).

6. On the Security tab, select SQL Server as the account type. Then supply a login and password that has access to the database, or select Use Windows Integrated Authentication (see Figure 21.10).

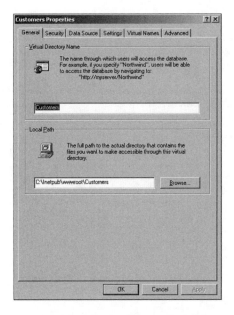

FIGURE 21.9   The New Virtual Directory Properties dialog box allows you to set the appropriate options.

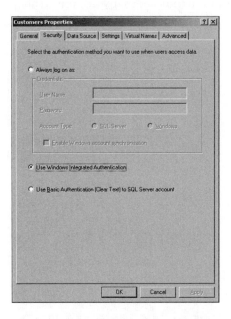

FIGURE 21.10   Designate the appropriate security information.

7. On the Data Source tab, enter the name of the server and the appropriate database name (see Figure 21.11).

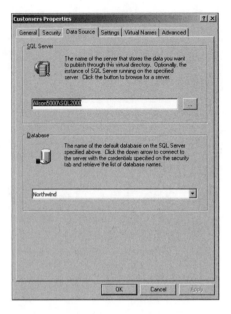

FIGURE 21.11   Designate information about the data source.

   8. Use the Settings tab to indicate that you want to allow URL queries, template
        queries, and XPath options (see Figure 21.12).

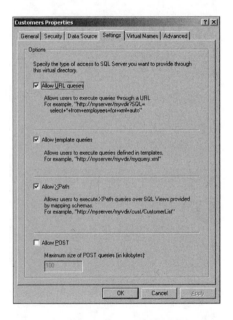

FIGURE 21.12   The Settings tab allows you to designate other important options.

9. Use the Virtual Names tab to create virtual names for the template and schema subdirectories. Select the Virtual Names tab and then click New. The Virtual Name Configuration dialog box appears (see Figure 21.13).

FIGURE 21.13 Use the Virtual Name Configuration dialog box to create virtual names for the schema and template folders.

10. Enter the virtual name, select the appropriate type, and designate the path to the folder (see Figure 21.13). Click Save. When you are done, the dialog box should appear as in Figure 21.14.

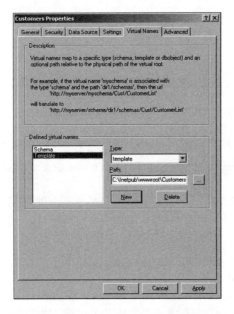

FIGURE 21.14 The Virtual Name Configuration dialog box after creating the virtual names.

11. Use your browser to verify that everything is working properly. Type the following SQL statement:

```
http://localhost/Customers?sql=SELECT * FROM Customers WHERE
➥CustomerID = 'ALFKI' FOR XML AUTO
```

The results appear in Figure 21.15. You are now ready to test your report based on live data.

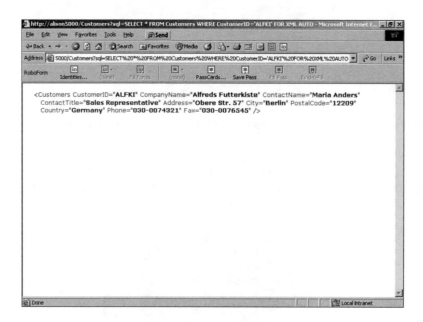

FIGURE 21.15   Verifying that the process was successful.

The following is the HTML generated when you opt to base a report on live data:

```
<HTML xmlns:signature="urn:schemas-microsoft-com:office:access">
<HEAD>
<META HTTP-EQUIV="Content-Type" CONTENT="text/html;charset=UTF-8"/>
</HEAD>

<SCRIPT event=onload for=window>
  objData = new ActiveXObject("MSXML.DOMDocument");
  objData.async = false;
  objData.load("http://ALISON5000\\SQL2000/Northwind?
  sql=SELECT+*+FROM+%22Products+by+Category%22+for+xml+auto,
  elements&root=dataroot");
  if (objData.parseError.errorCode != 0)
    alert(objData.parseError.reason);

  objStyle = new ActiveXObject("MSXML.DOMDocument");
```

```
    objStyle.async = false;
    objStyle.load("Products%20by%20Category.xsl");
    if (objStyle.parseError.errorCode != 0)
      alert(objStyle.parseError.reason);

    document.open("text/html","replace");
    document.write(objData.transformNode(objStyle));
</SCRIPT>

</HTML>
```

Notice that the `load` method points to the server on which SQL Server is running. The `sql` variable contains the SQL statement that underlies the report. The Access-generated XML file appears in the code that follows:

```
<?xml version="1.0" encoding="UTF-8"?>
<!DOCTYPE dataroot [
  <!ENTITY livedata SYSTEM "http://ALISON5000\SQL2000/Northwind?
sql=SELECT+*+FROM+%22Products+by+Category%22+for+xml+auto,elements">
]>
<dataroot xmlns:od="urn:schemas-microsoft-com:officedata"
xmlns:xsi="http://www.w3.org/2000/10/XMLSchema-instance"
  xsi:noNamespaceSchemaLocation="Products%20by%20Category.xsd">
&livedata;</dataroot>
```

Once again, note that the XML file contains the name of the server containing the SQL data. If you want to open the XML file directly and you want the XSL file to apply, you will need to insert a processor directive in the XML file. As an alternative, the Access-generated HTML file contains the information required to open the XML document using the XSL file for formatting.

Some aspects of forms and reports don't translate to XML. They include:

- Form and report captions do not appear in the resulting XML.

- Page headers and page footers appear only once per report.

- The `CanGrow` and `CanShrink` options are ignored.

- All forms are displayed as continuous forms with no navigation buttons.

- All combo boxes are converted to text boxes.

- Data in the browser is read-only.

- Code behind forms and reports is not exported.

- Controls based on expressions using VBA functions that are not available in VBScript do not translate.

- No aggregate functions are supported in XML.

Importing XML Data into Access

You can import an XML file into Access. The process is very simple but is also somewhat limited. To import an XML file:

1. Open the database that is to contain the XML file.

2. Right-click in the Database window, and choose Import.

3. Select XML Documents from the Files of Type drop-down box.

4. Select the folder where the XML file is located.

5. Select the XML file.

6. Click Import. The Import XML dialog box appears (see Figure 21.16).

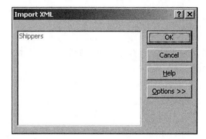

FIGURE 21.16   The Import XML dialog box allows you to specify the details of the
import process.

7. Click OK. Access imports the XML file.

Several problems and limitations are associated with the process of importing XML
data:

- Access can read only Access-generated XSD files. This means that unless an
  Access-generated XSD file is available, you have little control over the structure
  of the imported table.

- If the XML file is not syntactically correct, the Export process fails. In this case,
  Access generates an ImportErrors table.

- Access can read only an element-centric XML file, not an attribute-centric one.

- If the table name in the XML is dataroot, root, or schema, the export process
  fails, resulting in the generation of an ImportErrors table.

Programmatically Importing and Exporting XML Data

Access has ExportXML and ImportXML methods. You can use these methods to export data to XML and import data from XML, respectively. The ExportXML method of the Application object looks like this:

```
Application.ExportXML(ObjectType as AcExportXMLObjectType, _
    DataSource as String, _
    [DataTarget as String], _
    [SchemaTarget as String], _
    [PresentationTarget as String], _
    [ImageTarget as String], _
    [Encoding as AcExportXMLEncoding = acUTF8], _
    [OtherFlags as Long])
```

You use the ObjectType parameter to specify the type of object that you want to export. The ObjectType can be acExportForm, acExportFunction, acExportQuery, acExportReport, acExportServerView, acExportStoredProcedure, or acExportTable.

You use the DataSource parameter to designate the name of the object that you want to export. You can optionally specify the DataTarget, which is the name of the XML document that you want to export. Another optional parameter is the SchemaTarget, which is the name of the XSD file that you want to create. The PresentationTarget is the name of the XSLT file that you want to generate. The ImageTarget is the path that you want to use for exported images. You can designate acUTF16 for UTF-16 encoding or acUTF8 for UTF-8 encoding. Finally, the OtherFlags parameter allows you to designate a combination of constants that determine the behavior of the export. For example, the code that follows exports a table called Shippers. It creates an XML document, an XSD document, and an XSL document, all in the same folder as the current project.

```
Public Sub ExportXML()
    Application.ExportXML acExportTable, _
        "Shippers", _
        CurrentProject.Path & "\ShippersXML.XML", _
        CurrentProject.Path & "\ShippersXML.XSD", _
        CurrentProject.Path & "\ShippersXML.XSL"
End Sub
```

The ImportXML method looks like this:

```
Application.ImportXML(DataSource as String, _
    [ImportOptions as AcImportXMLOption = acStructureAndData])
```

The example that follows imports an XML document called ShippersXML into the path of the current project. The code imports both the structure and the data from the XML document.

```
Public Sub ImportXML()
    Application.ImportXML _
        CurrentProject.Path & "\ShippersXML.XML", acStructureAndData
End Sub
```

Using ADO Code to Work with XML

As an alternative, you can use ADO code to work with an XML document. The code that follows provides an example.

```
Public Sub ExportXMLADO(strTableName as String, strFileName as String)

    Dim rst As ADODB.Recordset

    On Error GoTo ExportXMLADO_Err

    Set rst = New ADODB.Recordset
    rst.Open strTableName, CurrentProject.Connection
    rst.Save CurrentProject.Path & "\" & strFileName, adPersistXML
    rst.Close

    Set rst = Nothing

ExportXMLADO_Exit:
    Exit Sub

ExportXMLADO_Err:
    MsgBox Err.Number & ": " & Err.Description
    Resume ExportXMLADO_Exit
End Sub
```

The code opens a recordset based on the table name received as the strTableName input parameter. It uses the Save method of the Recordset object to save the resulting recordset as an XML document within the current folder, with the name designated in the strFileName input parameter. The XML resulting document looks like this:

```
<?xml version="1.0" encoding="UTF-8"?>
<dataroot xmlns:od="urn:schemas-microsoft-com:officedata"
```

```
xmlns:xsi="http://www.w3.org/2000/10/XMLSchema-instance"
xsi:noNamespaceSchemaLocation="ShippersXML.XSD">
<Shippers>
<ShipperID>1</ShipperID>
<CompanyName>Speedy Express</CompanyName>
<Phone>(503) 555-9831</Phone>
</Shippers>
<Shippers>
<ShipperID>2</ShipperID>
<CompanyName>United Package</CompanyName>
<Phone>(503) 555-3199</Phone>
</Shippers>
<Shippers>
<ShipperID>3</ShipperID>
<CompanyName>Federal Shipping</CompanyName>
<Phone>(503) 555-9931</Phone>
</Shippers>
</dataroot>
```

Not only can you use ADO code to write an XML document, but you can also use it to import an XML document. Here's an example:

```
Public Sub ImportXMLADO(strSourceFile As String, _
    strDestinationTable As String)
    Dim rstSource As ADODB.Recordset
    Dim strPath As String
    Dim rstDestination As ADODB.Recordset
    Dim cat As ADOX.Catalog
    Dim tbl As ADOX.Table
    Dim col As ADOX.Column
    Dim fld As ADODB.Field

    On Error GoTo ImportXMLADO_Err

    'Open a recordset based on the XML document
    Set rstSource = New ADODB.Recordset
    strPath = CurrentProject.Path & "\" & strSourceFile
    rstSource.Open strPath, Options:=adCmdFile

    'Use the ADOX Catalog object to create a table
    'with the name designated as an input parameter
    Set cat = New ADOX.Catalog
```

```
Set cat.ActiveConnection = CurrentProject.Connection

Set tbl = New ADOX.Table
tbl.Name = strDestinationTable

'Add fields to the new table based
'on the fields in the XML Source
For Each fld In rstSource.Fields
    Set col = New ADOX.Column

    col.Name = fld.Name
    col.Type = fld.Type
    col.DefinedSize = fld.DefinedSize
    tbl.Columns.Append col
Next fld

'Append the table to the current database
cat.Tables.Append tbl

'Open a recordset to receive the data from
'the XML document
Set rstDestination = New ADODB.Recordset
rstDestination.Open strDestinationTable, _
    CurrentProject.Connection, _
    adOpenKeyset, _
    adLockOptimistic

'Loop through the XML document, adding rows
'to the new table
Do Until rstSource.EOF
    rstDestination.AddNew

    For Each fld In rstSource.Fields
        rstDestination(fld.Name).Value = _
            rstSource(fld.Name).Value
    Next fld

    rstSource.MoveNext

    rstDestination.Update
Loop

'Clean up
```

```
        rstSource.Close
        rstDestination.Close

        Set rstSource = Nothing
        Set rstDestination = Nothing
        Set cat = Nothing
        Set col = Nothing
        Set fld = Nothing
        Set tbl = Nothing

ImportXMLADO_Exit:
    Exit Sub

ImportXMLADO_Err:
    MsgBox Err.Number & ": " & Err.Description
    Resume ImportXMLADO_Exit

End Sub
```

The code begins by opening a recordset based on the XML document. It then uses an
ADOX catalog object to create a table with the name designated as the input parameter to the procedure. It adds fields to the table based on the elements in the XML
document. It then loops through the XML document, adding rows to the new table.

Summary

XML is proliferating throughout the computer world. Fortunately, Access provides
you with many ways that you can both import data from and export data to XML
documents. This chapter began by covering the basics of XML. It then showed you
how you can import and export XML data using both the user interface and
programming code.

22

Data Access Pages

Why This Chapter Is Important

Access 2000 introduced data access pages. Using data access pages, you can quickly and easily create a Web view of your data. Data access pages are extremely flexible and scalable. You can create the simplest data access page as easily as any Access form. On the other hand, using the Microsoft Script Editor (MSE), you can turn your data access pages into powerful Web pages. Probably the biggest downside of data access pages is that users must view them on a machine with Internet Explorer 5 and Microsoft Office installed. This makes data access pages an excellent candidate for intranet applications but not Internet applications.

> **TIP**
>
> You can run data access pages over an Internet or intranet if the client has IE5/Office Extensions.

Exploring the Uses of Data Access Pages

You can use data access pages to display, analyze, and modify data. Data access pages are strong in all of these areas.

Displaying Data

Data access pages allow you to display your application data in a browser. They offer an excellent alternative to Access reports. In fact, data access pages are more flexible and powerful than reports. For example, using a data access page, you can easily collapse and expand to view summary and detail information as required. An example is the data access page shown in Figure 22.1. The user can easily collapse and expand to view the products within a letter grouping.

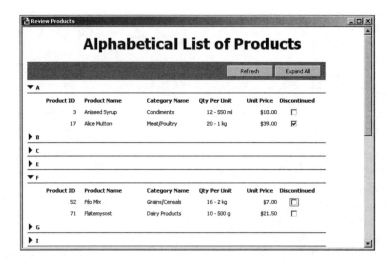

FIGURE 22.1   One important use of a data access page is to display data to the user.

Analyzing Data

Data access pages also provide you with an excellent means for analyzing data. You can include PivotTables and PivotCharts in the data access pages that you build, allowing the user to change the way he is viewing the data with a simple click and drag of the mouse. The data access page pictured in Figure 22.2 provides an example. Using the data access page shown in the illustration, the user can easily view and filter data to meet his specific analysis needs.

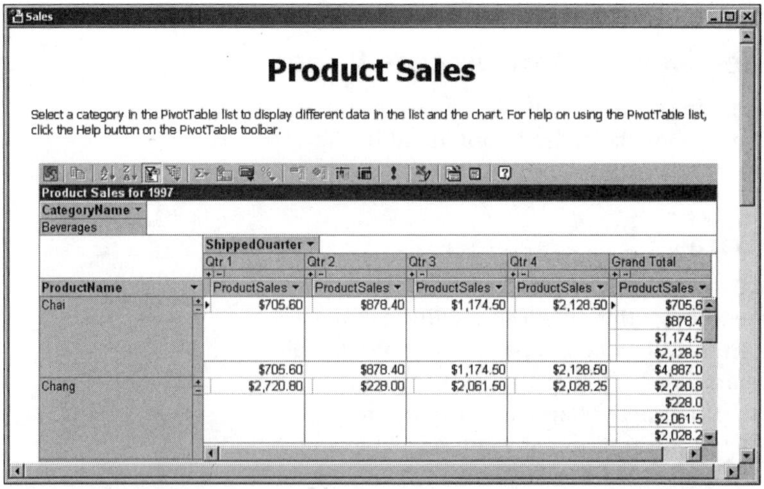

FIGURE 22.2   Data access pages provide an excellent means of analyzing data.

Modifying Data

In addition to acting as an excellent reporting mechanism, data access pages can be used to update data. In fact, using a data access page, users can easily update Access or SQL Server data from within their browsers, without ever loading Microsoft Access. Figure 22.3 provides an example. This form allows you to easily view and update employee information. The example shows the form within Microsoft Access. As you'll see later in this chapter, you can easily display the same form within the browser.

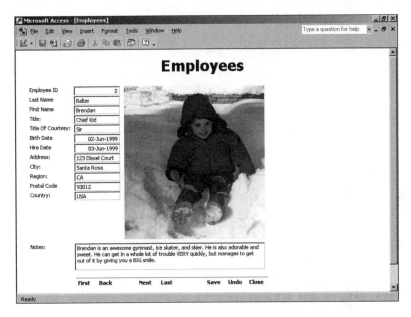

FIGURE 22.3   Using a data access page, users can modify Access or SQL Server data from within their browsers.

Creating a Simple Data Access Page

You can create data access pages in one of the following four ways:

- Using AutoPage
- Using a wizard
- From an existing Web page
- From scratch

Creating a Data Access Page Using the AutoPage Feature

To create a data access page using AutoPage, follow these steps:

1. Click Pages in the list of objects in the Database window.

2. Click the New button in the Database window. The New Data Access Page dialog box appears.

3. Choose the table or query on which you want to base the data access page.

4. Select AutoPage: Columnar from the list of options for creating a data access page (see Figure 22.4).

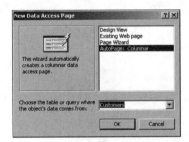

FIGURE 22.4   The New Data Access Page dialog box allows you to select the method that you want to use to create a data access page.

5. Click OK. Access creates the data access page (see Figure 22.5).

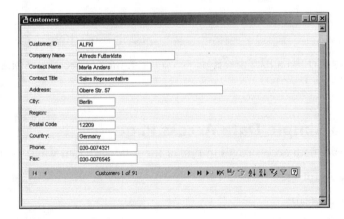

FIGURE 22.5   A data access page based on the NorthWind Customers table using the AutoPage feature.

Using a Wizard to Create a Data Access Page

To create a data access page using a wizard, follow these steps:

1. Click Pages in the list of objects in the Database window.

2. Double-click the Create Data Access Page by Using Wizard option. The Page Wizard appears (see Figure 22.6).

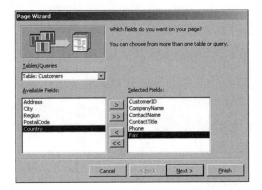

FIGURE 22.6   Selecting the table or query and the fields that you want to include in the data access page.

3. Select the table or query on which you want to base the data access page. In Figure 22.6, the Customers table is selected.

4. Select the fields that you want to appear on the data access page. In Figure 22.6, the CustomerID, CompanyName, ContactName, ContactTitle, Phone, and Fax fields are selected. Click Next to continue.

5. Add any desired grouping levels to the page (see Figure 22.7). Click Next to continue.

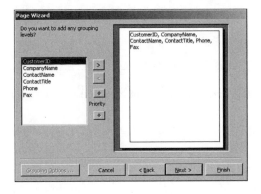

FIGURE 22.7   Adding grouping levels to a data access page.

6. Select a sort order for the records included on the page (see Figure 22.8). In the figure, the page is sorted by the ContactTitle field combined with the ContactName field. Click Next to continue.

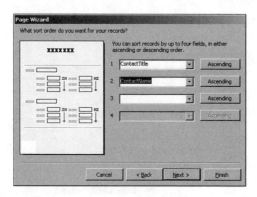

FIGURE 22.8   Selecting a sort order for the records on a page.

7. The last page of the wizard asks you for a title for the page. Enter the title and then designate whether you want to open the page or modify the page's design (see Figure 22.9). Click Finish to complete the process. Figure 22.10 shows the completed page in Design view. Figure 22.11 shows the completed page in Page view. (Use the View tool to switch to Page view.)

FIGURE 22.9   The last page of the wizard asks you for a title for the page.

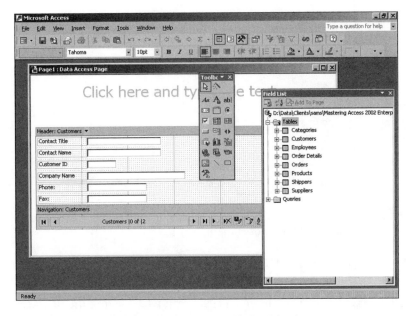

FIGURE 22.10   A completed data access page in Design view.

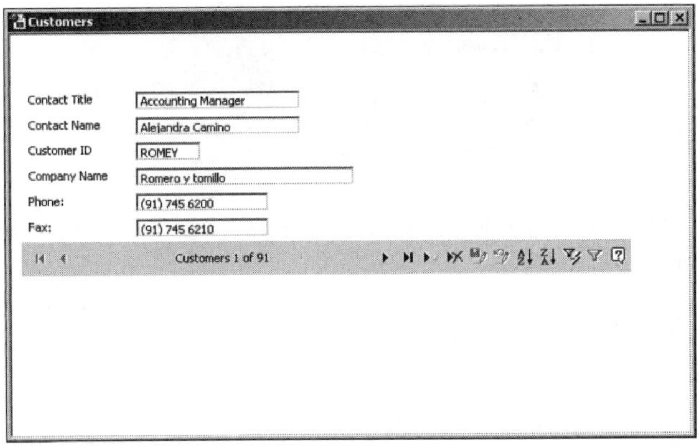

FIGURE 22.11   A completed data access page in Page view.

Access does not store data access pages in your database file or project. Instead, it saves the data access pages that you build as HTML files. To save a data access page, follow these steps:

1. Click Save on the toolbar. The Save as Data Access Page dialog box appears (see Figure 22.12).

FIGURE 22.12   The Save as Data Access Page dialog box allows you to select a name and location for the saved HTML document.

2. Enter the name of the HTML document. In the figure, the name is entered as Customers.htm.

3. Click Save. Unless you entered a UNC path when saving the file, Access prompts you with a warning indicating that the page may not be able to connect to data via the network (see Figure 22.13).

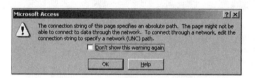

FIGURE 22.13   You must enter a UNC path for the page if you want to ensure that the page can connect to data via the network.

Although Access saves the data access page as a separate document, it appears in the Database window (see Figure 22.14).

Notice in the figure that a ToolTip appears, indicating the name and location of the saved HTML document. When you open the data access page from within Microsoft Access, it appears as a window within the Access environment. To view the page as it will appear in a browser, right-click the page in the Database window and select Web Page Preview. The page appears within the user's browser (see Figure 22.15).

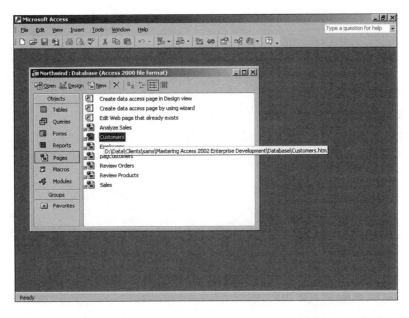

FIGURE 22.14   A completed data access page appears as an object in the Database window.

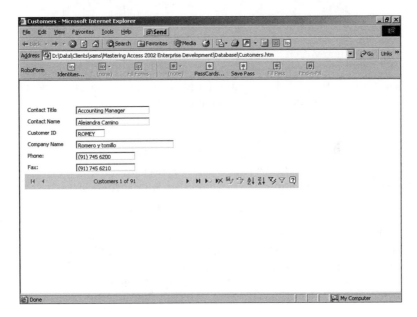

FIGURE 22.15   A completed data access page viewed in Internet Explorer.

Creating a Data Access Page from an Existing Web Page

You might already have an HTML document that you have created. Fortunately, Access 2000 and Access 2002 allow you to base a new data access page on an existing HTML document. To create a data access page from an existing Web page, follow these steps:

1. Click Pages in the list of objects in the Database window.

2. Double-click the Edit Web Page That Already Exists Wizard option. The Locate Web Page dialog box appears (see Figure 22.16).

FIGURE 22.16   The Locate Web Page dialog box allows you to open an existing HTML document for editing within the Access environment.

3. Select an existing HTML document and click Open. You can now edit the page right within the Microsoft Access environment.

Creating a Data Access Page from Scratch

Although the Data Access Page Wizard is very powerful, sometimes you will want to build a data access page from scratch. To do this, follow these steps:

1. Click Pages in the list of objects in the Database window.

2. Double-click the Create Data Access Page in Design View option. If your database is in the Access 2000 file format, you are warned that when you create a data access page in Access 2002, you cannot modify its design in Access 2000. Users can view it in Page view in Access 2000 if they have Microsoft Office XP Web Components installed.

3. Click OK. A blank data access page appears (see Figure 22.17).

4. Add controls to the data access page and set their properties.

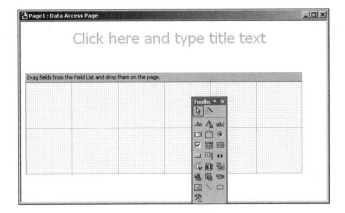

FIGURE 22.17   When the Create Data Access Page in Design View option is used, a blank data access page appears.

You might wonder how to associate a table from your database with a data access page that you build from scratch. The process differs somewhat from the process of associating a form with data. The process is as follows:

1. Click the Field List tool on the toolbar. The Field List window appears (see Figure 22.18).

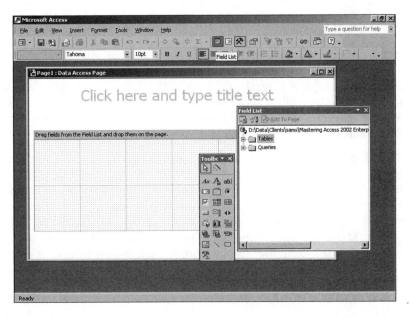

FIGURE 22.18   The Field List window allows you to easily add table and query fields to your data access pages.

2. Notice that the Field List window shows two expandable lists: one with the tables in the database and the other with the queries in the database (see Figure 22.19).

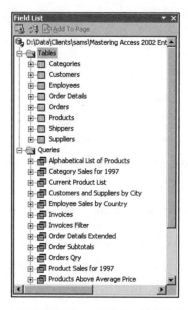

FIGURE 22.19   The expanded Field List window shows you all the tables and queries within the current database.

3. To add all fields from an existing table or query to the data access page, drag an entire table or query from the field list to the data access page. If you have the Control Wizards toolbox tool selected, the Layout Wizard appears asking if you want to add the controls in a Columnar, Tabular, PivotTable, PivotChart, or Office Spreadsheet format. Make your choice and click OK.

4. To add specific fields from a table or query to the data access page, expand the Field List window to display the desired table or query, and then drag and drop individual fields to the data access page. If you have the Control Wizards toolbox tool selected, the Layout Wizard appears asking if you want to add the controls in a Columnar, Tabular, PivotTable, PivotChart, or Office Spreadsheet format. Make your choice and click OK. In Figure 22.20, selected fields have been added in a Columnar format from the Employees table to the data access page.

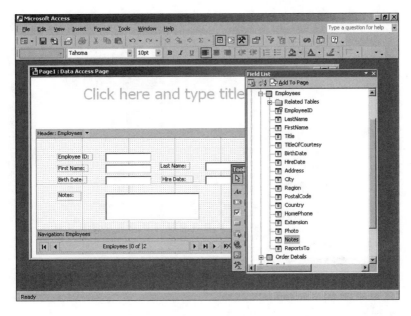

FIGURE 22.20   A data access page containing selected fields from the Employees table.

Notice that only one record appears at a time on the page. If you want to be able to view multiple records at a time, take the following steps:

1. Switch to Design view of the page.

2. Click the arrow in the group header (see Figure 22.21) and select Group Level Properties. The Group Level Properties window appears.

3. Change the DataPageSize property to the appropriate number. In Figure 22.22, the DataPageSize property is set to 3. This means that three employees will appear at a time when you display the page in Page view.

WARNING

If you base a data access page on a query and you do not include the primary key field from the table on the page, the data on the page will not be editable. In fact, if you add the primary key *after* you add other fields to the page, once again the data on the page will not be editable. If you add the primary key after you add other fields to the page, you must change the UniqueTable property to the name of the appropriate table to render the data on the page editable.

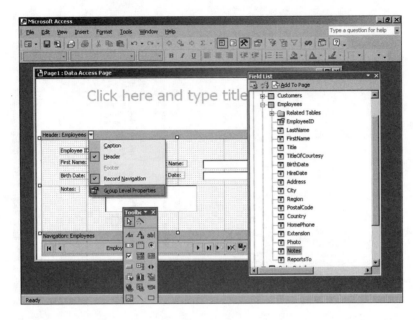

FIGURE 22.21   To modify the group-level properties, click the arrow in the group header and select Group Level Properties.

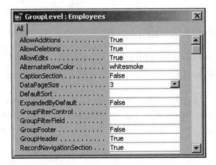

FIGURE 22.22   Setting the `DataPageSize` property to 3 means that three employees will appear at a time when you display the page in Page view.

NOTE

Because Access stores data access pages as separate HTML documents, it will not be able to locate the data access pages associated with a database if the pages are deployed to a different directory structure than the structure that existed when they were first created. You must write code to "fix" the links to the pages. The section of this chapter titled "Deploying Data Access Pages" addresses this problem.

Creating a Complex Data Access Page

So far, you have seen how to create simple data access pages. We will now delve into some more complex aspects of data access pages. These include grouping and using pages based on data from multiple tables.

Adding Groupings to Your Data Access Pages

It is easy to add groupings to the data access pages that you build. Here are the steps involved:

1. Select Pages in the list of objects.

2. Double-click to create a new page in Design view.

3. Click OK when prompted with the warning message.

4. Display the Field List, if it is not already visible.

5. Select the CustomerID, CompanyName, ContactName, ContactTitle, Phone, and Fax fields (see Figure 22.23).

FIGURE 22.23   Select the CustomerID, CompanyName, ContactName, ContactTitle, Phone, and Fax fields from the Field List.

6. Click and drag to add the fields to the form (see Figure 22.24). If you have the Control Wizards toolbox tool selected, the Layout Wizard appears asking if you want to add the controls in a Columnar, Tabular, PivotTable, PivotChart, or Office Spreadsheet format. Make your choice and click OK.

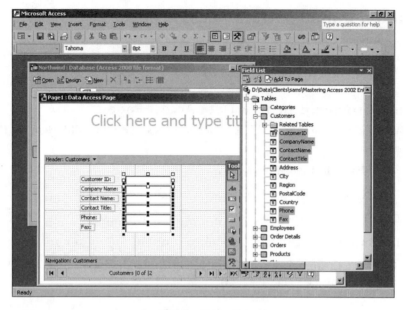

FIGURE 22.24   Click and drag to add the fields to the form.

7. Click and drag the City field above the Customers header, as shown in Figure 22.25. The result appears in Figure 22.26.

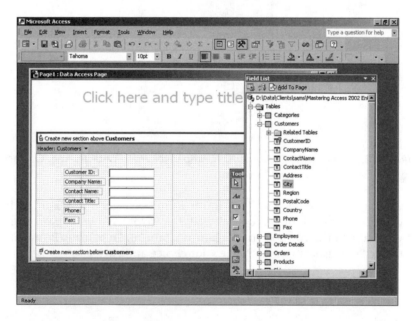

FIGURE 22.25   To add a grouping based on city, click and drag the City field above the Customers header.

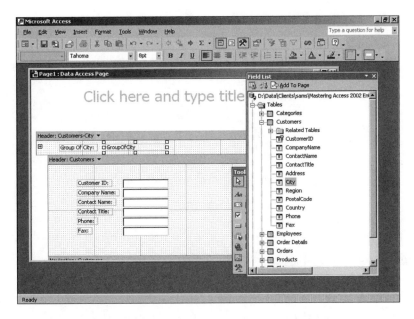

FIGURE 22.26 The result of adding a City header.

8. Switch to Page view. You will see that the data is now grouped by city (see Figure 22.27). You can click a plus sign to expand the list of customers within a city (see Figure 22.28).

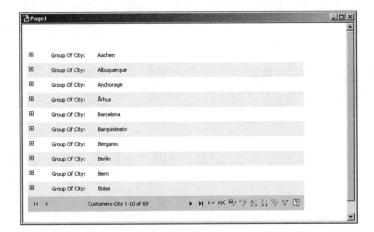

FIGURE 22.27 The data in the page is grouped by city.

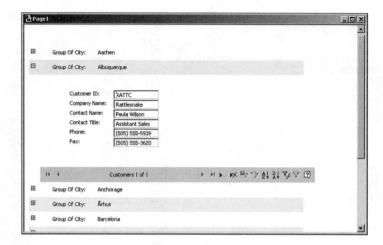

FIGURE 22.28   Click a plus sign to view the list of customers within a city.

9. Return to Design view.

10. Click and drag the Country field, and drop it above the City header (see Figure 22.29). The results appear in Figure 22.30.

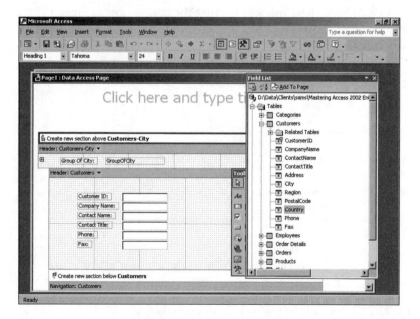

FIGURE 22.29   Click and drag the Country field, and drop it above the City header.

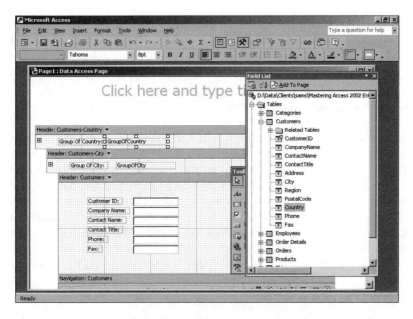

FIGURE 22.30 The results of adding a Country grouping.

11. Switch to Page view. The data is now grouped by country and within a country by city (see Figure 22.31).

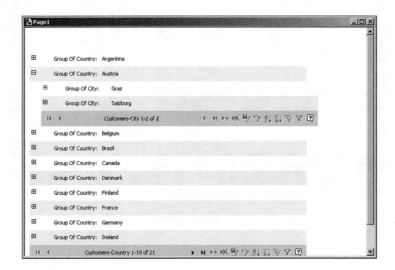

FIGURE 22.31 A data access page grouped by country and city.

Basing Data Access Pages on Multiple Tables

The examples in the previous section showed a data access page based on data from one table. At times, you will want to include data from more than one table. You can either base the data access page on a query that includes data from more than one table, or you can drag and drop fields from more than one table onto the page. We will cover both techniques here.

Data Access Pages Based on a Query That Includes Data from More Than One Table

Basing data access pages on a query that includes data from more than one table is similar to basing a data access page on a table. An example is the data access page shown in Figure 22.32. The page is based on a query called qryCustomersWithOrders. Notice that the page includes the CustomerID, CompanyName, ContactName, and ContactTitle fields from the Customer table. It includes the OrderID, OrderDate, ShipVia, and Freight fields from the Orders table. Figure 22.33 shows the page in Page view. Notice that it appears as if the page is displaying data from one table.

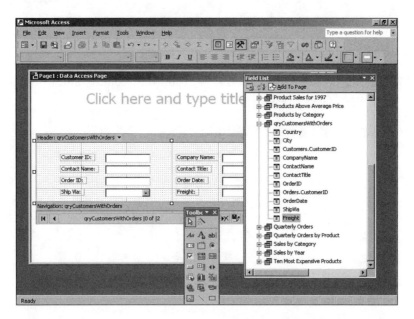

FIGURE 22.32   A data access page in Design view based on a query containing data from multiple tables.

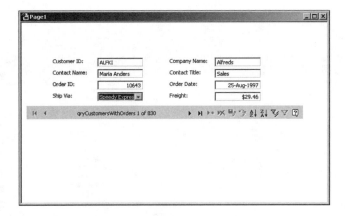

FIGURE 22.33   A data access page in Page view based on a query containing data from multiple tables.

Data Access Pages That Include Fields from More Than One Table
You can use data access pages to represent a one-to-many relationship between the tables in your database. Here's the process:

1. Select Pages in the list of objects.

2. Double-click to create a new page in Design view.

3. Click OK when prompted with the warning message.

4. Display the Field List if it is not already visible.

5. Select the OrderID, EmployeeID, OrderDate, ShipVia, and Freight fields from the Orders table.

6. Drag and drop the selected fields to the data access page. After selecting Columnar, the page appears as in Figure 22.34.

7. Click to expand the list of fields in the Customers table.

8. Select the CustomerID, CompanyName, ContactName, and ContactTitle fields.

9. Drag and drop them above the Orders header (see Figure 22.35). If you have the Control Wizards tool on the toolbar turned on, the Layout Wizard appears, asking you the type of data access page you want to create. If you select Columnar, the resulting data access page appears as in Figure 22.36.

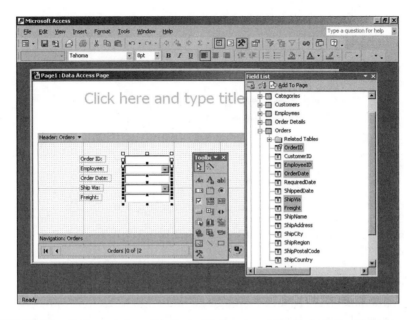

FIGURE 22.34 Drag and drop the OrderID, EmployeeID, OrderDate, ShipVia, and Freight fields from the Orders table onto the page.

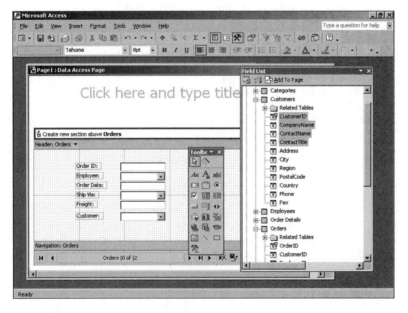

FIGURE 22.35 Drag and drop the CustomerID, CompanyName, ContactName, and ContactTitle fields above the Orders header.

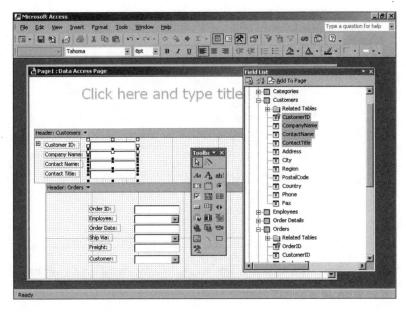

FIGURE 22.36   A data access page in Design view with customer and order information.

10. Switch to Page view. Notice that only the customer information displays (see Figure 22.37).

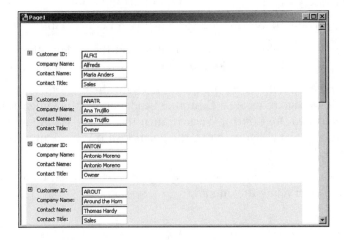

FIGURE 22.37   In Page view, only the customer information displays.

11. Click a plus sign to expand the detail for a customer. Notice that you can see the orders for that customer (see Figure 22.38). You should be able to make changes to both the customer and order information.

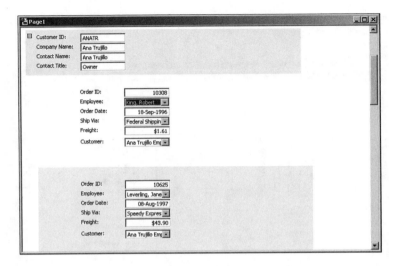

FIGURE 22.38   After clicking a plus sign to expand the detail for a customer, you can see the orders for that customer.

Because in the previous example you dragged and dropped fields from two related tables to the page, Access understood the relationship between them. If you drop a query and a table or two queries to the page, Access will need information about the relationship between them. Here's an example:

1. Build a query based on the NorthWind Customers table.

2. Build a second query based on the NorthWind Orders table.

3. Drag and drop fields from the query based on the Orders table onto the data access page, and select Columnar when the Layout Wizard appears.

4. Drag and drop fields from the query based on the Customers table onto the data access page to create a Customer header above the Order header. If you have activated the Control Wizards, then the Layout Wizard appears, prompting you to select a layout. Next, the Relationship Wizard appears (see Figure 22.39).

5. Click to select the field from each query that relates their data. Click OK. The page now can relate the queries.

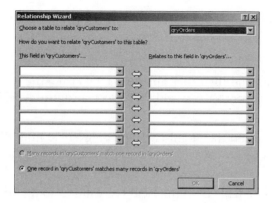

FIGURE 22.39   The Relationship Wizard allows you to select the field from each query that relates the data in one query to the data in the other query.

Working with Data Access Page Controls

Although the process of working with controls on data access pages is somewhat similar to that of working with form and report controls, you will find that some of the controls available for data access pages differ from those available for forms and reports. Furthermore, the process of manipulating controls on data access pages is not identical to that of manipulating controls on forms and reports. Finally, the properties available for data access page controls differ from those available for their form and report counterparts. For this reason, the section that follows covers data access page controls.

Adding Controls

The process for adding controls to a data access page differs depending on whether you are adding a bound or an unbound control. To add an unbound control, simply select it from the toolbox and then click and drag to place it on the page (the same process as for form and report controls). The easiest way to add a bound control is to drag and drop it from the field list directly onto the page. Unlike in forms and reports, the process of dragging and dropping a field from the field list onto the page links the page to its data source. Although one way to add a bound control to a page is to drag and drop it onto the page, several techniques are available. They include:

- Click and drag a field from the Field List window to the page.

- Click a field and then click the Add to Page button that appears at the top of the Field List window.

- Right-click a field and then select Add to Page from the context-sensitive menu.

- Double-click a field in the Field List window. Access adds it to the page.

- Click a control and then click and drag a field from the Field List window to the grid on the page. Access adds the selected control type, bound to the selected field.

- Click a control and then right-click and drag a field from the Field List window to the grid. A context-sensitive menu appears, allowing you to add the fields in a Tabular, Columnar, PivotTable, PivotChart, or OfficeSpreadsheet format.

- Click and drag a table from the Field List window to the page. Access displays the Layout Wizard (see Figure 22.40). The Layout Wizard allows you to add all the fields from the table in a Tabular or Columnar layout, or to add a PivotTable, PivotChart, or Office Spreadsheet to the page.

FIGURE 22.40   The Layout Wizard allows you to add all the fields from the table in a tabular or columnar layout, or to add a PivotTable, PivotChart, or Office Spreadsheet to the page.

- Right-click a table name from the Field List window and then click and drag to the grid. A context-sensitive menu appears with the Tabular, Columnar, PivotTable, PivotChart, and Office Spreadsheet choices.

- Right-click a table name from the Field List window and select Add to Page. Access displays the Layout Wizard.

NOTE

If the Layout Wizard does not appear, make sure that you select the Control Wizards tool in the toolbox.

Modifying Control Properties

To modify a control property, you must first select the control whose property you want to modify. You can then right-click the control and select Properties, or you can click the Properties tool on the toolbar. In either case, the Properties window appears. As you can see, the properties of data access page controls are not identical to those of their form and report counterparts (see Figure 22.41). For example, a form text box has a text and a value property, whereas a data access page text box has only the value property.

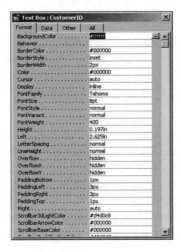

FIGURE 22.41   The properties of data access page controls differ from those of traditional controls.

You can use your Shift key to select multiple controls. You can then apply property settings to the group. As an alternative, you can lasso the objects that you want to select. You will find many of the familiar sizing and alignment options under the Format menu.

Getting to Know the Control Types

Just as properties of controls differ between data access pages and forms, so do the types of controls available. The following sections discuss the controls available in the data access page toolbox.

Label

The behavior of the data access page Label control is similar to that of a form Label control. The user cannot edit the contents of the Label control at runtime. You can change the caption of the Label control at design time by clicking to select it and clicking a second time to enter edit mode, or you can modify the InnerText property in the Properties window.

Text Box

The Text Box control is very similar to its form counterpart. You can easily bind this control to data. The results are fully editable.

Bound Span

You can bind the Bound Span control to data, but the user cannot edit the results. The Bound Span control is more efficient than the Text Box control discussed previously. You should therefore use the Bound Span control whenever it is not necessary for the user to modify the contents of data that you display.

Scrolling Text

The Scrolling Text control allows you to display text that scrolls. The control has properties that let you define the text to scroll, the speed of the scroll, the number of loops, and the direction. To bind a Scrolling Text control to data, first select the control in the toolbox and then drag a field from the Field List window onto the page.

Option Group and Option Button

An option group allows the user to select one button from a group of buttons. An Option Group control can contain only option buttons, each with a unique value. You bind an option group to data by first selecting the Option Group control and then simply clicking and dragging the desired field from the Field List control to the page. Unlike its Access counterpart, the data access page Option Group control allows you to use a text string within the value. The caveat is that the text string is case-sensitive.

List Boxes and Drop-Down Lists

List boxes and drop-down lists are similar to their form counterparts. You bind them to a data source and then store the selection in a field in one of the tables represented in the form.

Hyperlink

The Hyperlink control allows you to insert a link to another page, to insert a link to a bookmark on the existing page, or to supply e-mail information. When you insert a link on a page, the Insert Hyperlink dialog box shown in Figure 22.42 appears. Here you can modify the properties of the hyperlink.

FIGURE 22.42   The Insert Hyperlink dialog box allows you to modify the properties of the hyperlink.

Image and Image Hyperlink

The Image and Image Hyperlink controls allow you to display images on your pages. The Image Hyperlink control allows you to associate a hyperlink with the image so that the user navigates to a new location when he clicks the image. You can bind both the Image control and the Image Hyperlink control to a field containing a path to an image.

Record Navigation

When you create a data access page, Access automatically provides a Record Navigation control. If you are happy with the look and behavior of the control, you do not need to modify the control. Access provides you with the capability to customize the button images, to remove buttons from the control, to change the text shown in the record count information, or to eliminate the control entirely and to build the functionality into your own application. To modify properties of the control, right-click it and then select Navigation Buttons (see Figure 22.43). Notice that you can toggle buttons on and off as necessary.

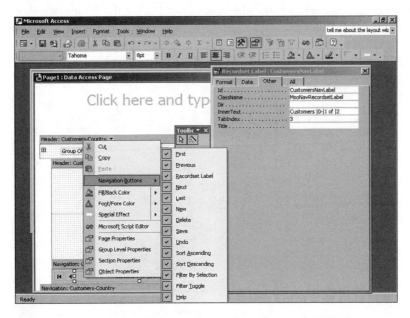

FIGURE 22.43   To modify properties of the control, right-click it and then select Navigation Buttons.

Modifying Page Properties

Just as many properties exist for a form, they also exist for a page. To view or modify form properties, simply right-click the title bar of the page and select Properties. The property sheet appears with the properties of the selected item. You can modify any of the properties as necessary.

Important page-level properties include `ConnectionFile`, `ConnectionString`, `DataEntry`, `MaxRecords`, and `RecordsetType`. You use the `ConnectionFile` property to specify the name of an Office Data Connection (ODS) or Universal Data Link (UDL) file containing data source and connection information for the page. The `ConnectionString` property contains a valid ActiveX data object (ADO) connection string. You use it to specify the data source and connection information for the page. Like its form counterpart, you use the `DataEntry` property to specify whether the page is used only for data entry. When set to `True`, the page allows the user to only enter new rows. The `MaxRecords` property specifies the maximum number of records that the connection will return to the local computer. Finally, like its form counterpart, you use the `RecordsetType` to designate the recordset returned to the page as a snapshot or an updateable snapshot.

Modifying Group Properties

Just as grouping levels on a form or report have properties, grouping levels on data access pages have properties. The easiest way to ensure that you are viewing the group properties is to simply use the drop-down list for the group (see Figure 22.44) and then select Group Level Properties. The Properties window appears with the properties of the selected group.

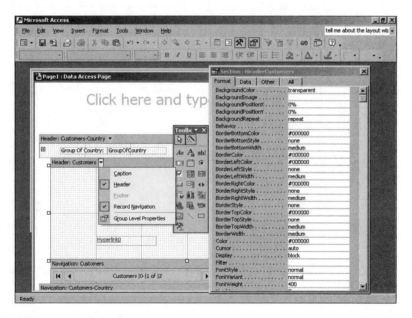

FIGURE 22.44   The easiest way to ensure that you are viewing the group properties is to simply use the drop-down list for the group.

Important group-level properties include `AllowAdditions`, `AllowDeletions`, `AllowEdits`, `DataPageSize`, `GroupHeader`, and `GroupFooter`. When the `AllowAdditions` property is set to `True` and the data in the page is editable, the user can add new records to that group. When the `AllowDeletions` property is set to `True` and the data in the page is editable, the user can delete rows from the group. You use the `DataPageSize` property to designate the number of rows that display when the section appears. The `GroupHeader` and `GroupFooter` properties, when set to `True`, display a group header and a group footer, respectively. You can use group headers and group footers to display special data, such as subtotals, for the grouping.

Deleting Data Access Pages

When you attempt to delete a data access page, Access prompts you with the dialog box that appears in Figure 22.45. Notice that you can delete the link and the files, delete the link only, or cancel. If you opt to delete the link and the files, Access deletes the link in the MDB or ADP, as well as the underlying HTML files. If you opt to delete the link only, Access deletes the link in the MDB or ADP file but leaves the HTML documents intact. Finally, selecting Cancel aborts the process without Access taking any action.

FIGURE 22.45   Dialog box that appears when you attempt to delete a data access page.

Deploying Data Access Pages

You must be concerned with two issues when deploying data access pages. The first issue involves how Access maintains links between the MDB or ADP file and the HTML documents. The second is how the HTML documents link to the appropriate data source. Unfortunately, Access hard-codes both the path from the MDB or ADP file to the HTML document, and the path from the HTML document to the data source. This means problems for you if someone moves the MDB, ADP, HTML documents, or data source.

The first thing that you need to be able to do is determine whether the link to the data access page is broken. The code in Listing 22.1 accomplishes this task.

LISTING 22.1   Determining Whether the Link to a Data Access Page Is Broken

```
Public Function CheckDataAccessPageLink(dap As AccessObject) As Boolean
    Dim strPageName As String
    Dim strPageToLocate As String

    On Error GoTo CheckDataAccessPageLink_Err
    'Compare the FullName property of the data access page
    'with the HTM filename. If they are the same, it means
    'that the HTM file is located in the same folder as
    'the MDB. It is then necessary to append the folder name
    'to the HTM filename before searching for the file.
    If StrComp(dap.FullName, GetFileName(dap.FullName), vbTextCompare) = 0 Then
        strPageToLocate = FixPath(CurrentProject.Path) & dap.FullName
    Else
        strPageToLocate = dap.FullName
    End If

    'Attempt to locate the file and return whether
    it is found
    CheckDataAccessPageLink = Len(Dir(strPageToLocate))

CheckDataAccessPageLink_Exit:
    Exit Function

CheckDataAccessPageLink_Err:
    CheckDataAccessPageLink = False
    Resume CheckDataAccessPageLink_Exit

End Function
```

You call the function like this:

```
CheckDataAccessPageLink(CurrentProject.AllDataAccessPages("Employees"))
```

The caller uses the `AllDataAccessPages` collection of the current project to pass a reference to the named data access page. The code compares the `FullName` property of the data access page (which contains the name and path) to the filename. If they match, the HTM file is in the same folder as the MDB. You must append the path to the HTM file name and then attempt to locate it with the `Dir` command. Otherwise, you can simply attempt to locate the HTM filename. In either case, if the `Dir` command locates the file, the link is okay. Otherwise, it is broken.

If a link is broken, you must re-establish it. The code in Listing 22.2 accomplishes the task.

LISTING 22.2   Re-establishing a Broken Link

```
Public Function ChangePageLink(dap As AccessObject, _
    strPagePath As String) As Boolean

    Dim strFileName As String
    Dim strOriginalFileName As String

    'Evaluate whether the page path is the same as the
    'path associated with the current project
    'If yes, store the HTM filename in a variable.
    'If no, store the HTM filename and the new path in a variable
    If StrComp(strPagePath, CurrentProject.Path) = 0 Then
        strFileName = GetFileName(dap.FullName)
    Else
        strFileName = FixPath(strPagePath) & GetFileName(dap.FullName)
    End If

    'Compare the data access page name with the contents of
    'the string variable
    'If they match, the link may already be correct
    'Check the link and exit if OK
    If StrComp(dap.FullName, strFileName, vbTextCompare) = 0 Then
        ChangePageLink = CheckDataAccessPageLink(dap)
        GoTo ChangePageLink_Exit
    End If

    'Store the full name of the data access page in a variable
    strOriginalFileName = dap.FullName

    'Select the data access page
    DoCmd.SelectObject acDataAccessPage, dap.Name, True

    'Set its FullName property to the filename
    'stored in the variable
    dap.FullName = strFileName

    'Check the link to make sure that it is okay now
    ChangePageLink = CheckDataAccessPageLink(dap)

ChangePageLink_Exit:
```

LISTING 22.2   Continued

```
    Exit Function

ChangePageLink_Err:
    MsgBox Err.Number & ": " & Err.Description
    Resume ChangePageLink_Exit
End Function
```

The code uses two helper functions. The first, called FixPath, adds a backslash to the pathname, if necessary. It appears in Listing 22.3.

LISTING 22.3   Add a Backslash to the Pathname, If Necessary

```
Public Function FixPath(strPathName As String) As String

    Dim strSlash As String

    'Evaluate whether the path is an HTTP or file path
'Store the appropriate type of slash in a variable
    If Left(strPathName, 4) = "HTTP" Then
        strSlash = "/"
    Else
        strSlash = "\"
    End If

    'Add the appropriate type of slash to the
    'filename, if necessary
If Len(strPathName) > 0 Then
        If Right(strPathName, 1) = strSlash Then
            FixPath = strPathName
        Else
            FixPath = strPathName & strSlash
        End If
    End If
End Function
```

The second function strips the filename out of a full path and filename. It appears in Listing 22.4.

LISTING 22.4 Extract the Filename Out of a Full Path and Filename

```
Public Function GetFileName(strFullPath As String) As String
    Dim strFileName As String
    Dim lngStartPos As String

    'Replace all slashes with backslashes to make
    'the code work with both file paths and HTTP
    'addresses
    strFileName = Replace(strFullPath, "/", "\")

    'Locate the last backslash
    lngStartPos = InStrRev(strFileName, "\")

    'If at least one backslash is found, extract
    'everything following the last backslash
    If lngStartPos > 0 Then
        strFileName = Mid(strFileName, lngStartPos + 1)
    End If

    GetFileName = strFileName
End Function
```

You call the `ChangePageLink` routine like this:

```
ChangePageLink(CurrentProject.AllDataAccessPages("Employees"), _
    "C:\Program Files\Office XP\Office10\Samples\")
```

The `ChangePageLink` routine evaluates whether the page path is the same as the path associated with the current project. If it is, the code stores the HTM filename in a variable. If it is not, the code stores the HTM filename and the new path in a variable. The code then compares the data access page name with the contents of the string variable. If they match, the link may already be correct. The code checks the link and exits the routine if the link is okay. The code stores the full name of the data access page in a variable. It then selects the data access page and sets its `FullName` property to the filename stored in the variable. Finally, it checks the link to ensure that it is intact.

Access stores the connection to a data source in the XML code underlying the page. Data access pages use the `DataSourceControl` ActiveX control to provide a link between the page and the data source. The XML referencing the control looks like this:

```
<OBJECT id=MSODSC tabIndex=-1
classid=CLSID:0002E553-0000-0000-C000-000000000046>
<PARAM NAME="XMLData" VALUE="
<xml xmlns:a=&quot;urn:schemas-microsoft-com:office:access&quot;>
&#13;&#10; <a:DataSourceControl>&#13;&#10;
<a:OWCVersion>10.0.0.2224 </a:OWCVersion>&#13;&#10;
<a:ConnectionString>Provider=Microsoft.Jet.OLEDB.4.0;
Password=&amp;quot;&amp;quot;;User ID=Admin;
Data Source=Northwind.mdb;
```

Two options exist for re-establishing the link. The first option involves basing your data access pages on a connection file. When the location of the data changes, you simply modify that file. The second option requires that you programmatically modify the connection string in each data access page.

With the first solution, you fill in the ConnectionFile property of the page and point it to the name of an Office Data Connection (.odc) or Microsoft Data Link (.udl) file. The ConnectionFile property always takes precedence over the ConnectionString property, so you don't need to be concerned if the ConnectionString property is filled in. If all of your pages share the same connection information, you can specify the name of the ODC or UDL file in the Pages tab of Tools, Options (see Figure 22.46). Simply check the Use Default Connection File option and then enter the name of the default connection file. If you move the data source to a different location, you simply open the ODC or UDL file and modify it.

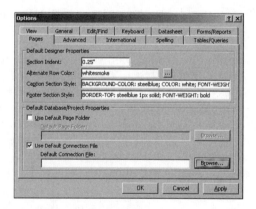

FIGURE 22.46   The Pages tab of Tools, Options allows you to specify a default ODC or UDL file to be used by all of your data access pages.

To create a new ODC or UDL file:

1. Select Tools, Options.

2. Click to select the Pages tab (refer to Figure 22.46).

3. Click the Browse button for the default connection file. The Select Data Source dialog box appears (see Figure 22.47).

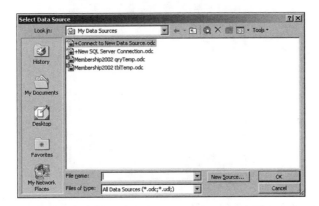

FIGURE 22.47   The Select Data Source dialog box allows you to select an existing ODC or UDL file, or to create a new one.

4. The Select Data Source dialog box allows you to select an existing ODC or UDL file, or to create a new one. ODC and UDL files are very similar. The ODC file is a plain text file that stores HTML that you can display in IE 5.0 and above. The UDL file is a text file that you can open in Notepad. Both files contain important connection information about the data source. Double-click Connect to a New Data Source. The Data Connection Wizard launches (see Figure 22.48).

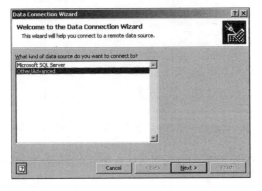

FIGURE 22.48   The first step of the Data Connection Wizard allows you to select the type of data source that you want to use.

5. Select the type of data source that you want to use, and click Next. The next step varies depending on the data source selected. If you select Other/Advanced, the dialog box appears as in Figure 22.49. Select an OLE DB provider and click Next.

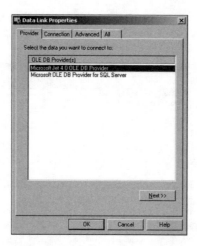

FIGURE 22.49   If you select Other/Advanced, you must select an OLE DB provider.

   6. Again, this step varies depending on the provider selected. If you select
      Microsoft Jet 4.0 OLE DB Provider, the next step appears as in Figure 22.50.

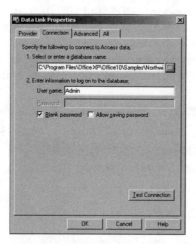

FIGURE 22.50   If you select Microsoft Access, you must select or enter a database name
and enter any required security information.

   7. Select or enter a database name, enter any required security information, and
      then click Test Connection. If the test succeeds, click OK to complete the
      process and close the dialog box. The Select Database and Table step of the

Data Connection Wizard appears (see Figure 22.51). Because you selected Microsoft Jet 4.0 OLE DB Provider, you cannot modify any information in this step of the process. Click Next to continue.

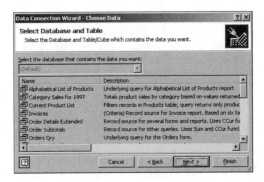

FIGURE 22.51   The Select Database and Table step of the Data Connection Wizard.

8. The final step allows you to type a name and description for the data source (see Figure 22.52). Enter the information and click Finish.

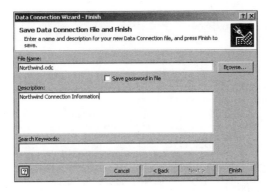

FIGURE 22.52   The final step allows you to type a name and description for the data source.

9. Click OK to close the Options dialog box. Viewed in a browser, the ODC file looks like Figure 22.53. Viewed in Notepad, it looks like Figure 22.54.

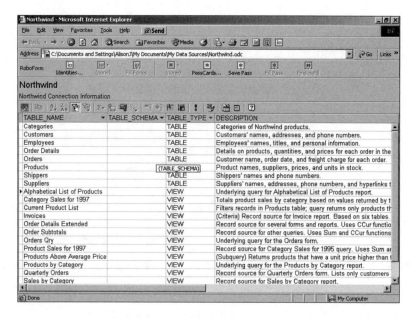

FIGURE 22.53   A ODC file viewed in a browser.

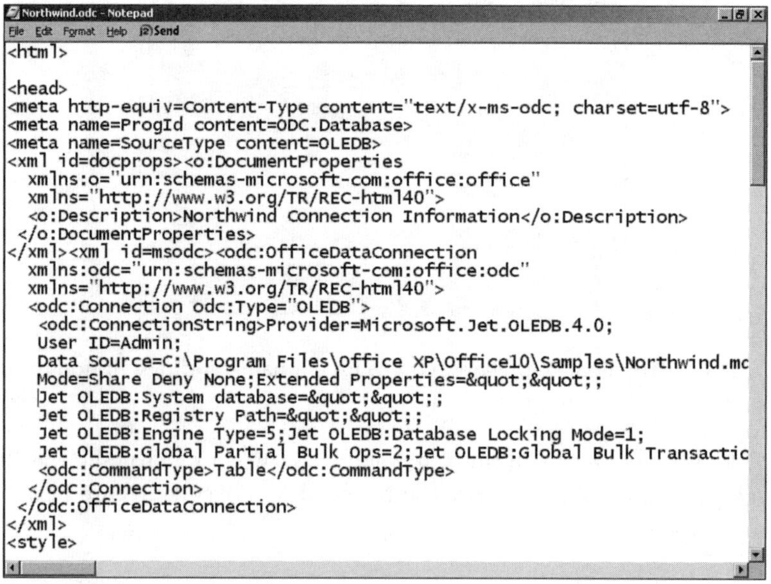

FIGURE 22.54   A ODC file viewed in Notepad.

The alternative is to use code to modify the connection information. Listing 22.5 provides an example.

LISTING 22.5   You Can Use Code to Modify the Connection Information

```
Public Function ChangeDataLink(dap As AccessObject, _
    strDataSource As String, _
    Optional strConnectionType As String) As Boolean

    On Error GoTo ChangeDataLink_Err
    Dim dapObject As DataAccessPage

    DoCmd.SetWarnings False

    'Open data access page in design view
    DoCmd.OpenDataAccessPage dap.Name, acDataAccessPageDesign

    'Point object variable at the data access page
    Set dapObject = DataAccessPages(dap.Name)

    'Set the appropriate connection string for the
    'object
    If strConnectionType = "String" Then
        dapObject.MSODSC.ConnectionString = _
            "Provider=Microsoft.Jet.OLEDB.4.0;" & _
            "Data Source=" & strDataSource
    Else
        dapObject.MSODSC.ConnectionFile = strDataSource
    End If

    'Close and save the data access page
    DoCmd.Close acDataAccessPage, dapObject.Name, acSaveYes

    ChangeDataLink = True

ChangeDataLink_Exit:
    On Error Resume Next
    Set dapObject = Nothing
    DoCmd.SetWarnings True
    Exit Function

ChangeDataLink_Err:
    MsgBox Err.Number & ": " & Err.Description
    ChangeDataLink = False
    Resume ChangeDataLink_Exit
End Function
```

This code receives a reference to a data access page, connection information, and an optional connection type as parameters. It opens the data access page in Design view. It then points an object variable at the data access page so that it can modify the connection string associated with the object. Finally, it closes and saves the data access page. You call the procedure like this:

```
ChangeDataLink(CurrentProject.AllDataAccessPages("Employees"),"c:\datalinks\
➥Northwind.odc")
```

Notice that the example uses the `AllDataAccessPages` collection of the `CurrentProject` object to locate the Employees data access page. The example passes in the name of an ODC file that the procedure uses for the connection information.

An Introduction to Scripting Data Access Pages

One of the powers of data access pages is the capability to customize them beyond what the data access page designer allows. The Microsoft Script Editor (MSE) allows you to create scripts that extend the functionality of your data access pages. Using the MSE, you create scripts behind the events of objects on the data access page.

To open the MSE and create script behind a data access page:

1. Create a data access page.

2. Use the Toolbox tool on the toolbar to display the toolbox.

3. Make sure that you deselect the Control Wizards tool. Then add a control, such as a command button, to the data access page. Use the ID property to rename the control, if desired.

4. Right-click the control and select Microsoft Script Editor (see Figure 22.55). The Microsoft Development Environment (MDE) appears (see Figure 22.56).

5. Locate the Document Outline window. You may need to select View, Other Windows, Document Outline; use the Ctrl+Alt+T keystroke combination; or click the Document Outline tab to activate the Document Outline window. When the Document Outline window is active, right-click the object for which you want to write code, and select View Client Script. The Script Editor writes a script block for the default event (see Figure 22.57).

6. Write code that executes in response to the event. In Figure 22.57, the `MsgBox` statement is used to display the message "Hello World" when someone clicks the `cmdHello` command button.

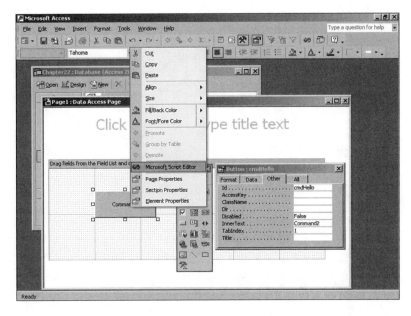

FIGURE 22.55   Right-click the control and select Microsoft Script Editor.

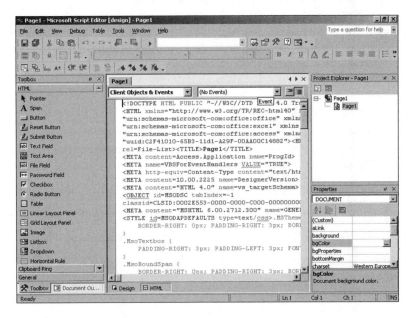

FIGURE 22.56   The Microsoft Script Editor allows you to write code in response to events generated within your data access pages.

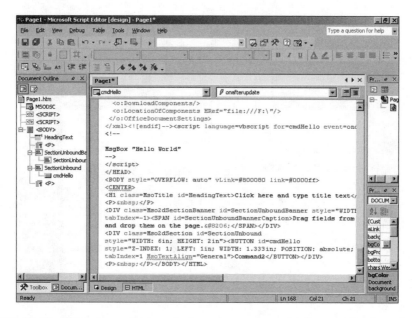

FIGURE 22.57   VBScript code that displays the message "Hello World" when the
`onclick` event of the `cmdHello` command button occurs.

7. To view the events associated with an object, select the object from the Object
   drop-down list and select the event from the Event drop-down list. The Script
   Editor creates the appropriate procedure for you.

VBScript Versus VBA

Because Internet Explorer 5.0 cannot interpret VBA, scripts that you write must be in
the VBScript language. VBScript is a subset of the VBA language. The following are
important differences between VBA and VBScript that you should be aware of:

- All variables are variants. This means that `Dim` statements cannot include types.

- Arguments (parameters) to subroutines and functions cannot have types.

- Many built-in functions available in VBA are not available in VBScript.

- Intrinsic constants such as `vbYesNo` are not available in VBScript. If you want to
  include constants in your code, you will have to declare them yourself.

VBScript Versus JavaScript

Scripts that you write behind your data access pages can be written in either VBScript or JavaScript. If you are accustomed to writing VBA code, you will probably find VBScript much easier to learn than JavaScript. On the other hand, if you are experienced at developing Web pages using JavaScript, you will probably want to continue writing your scripts in JavaScript. The following are some important differences between VBScript and JavaScript:

- VBScript is better supported by the data access page object model. This means that certain page events are not recognized if coded in JavaScript.

- JavaScript is case-sensitive, making it more difficult to write than VBScript.

Summary

Data access pages were a valuable addition to Access 2000. Access 2002 brought many enhancements and improvements to data access pages. Using data access pages, you can quickly and easily build HTML documents based on the data in your database. Users can display these pages on any machine running Internet Explorer 5 and Microsoft Office 2000 or Microsoft Office XP. As with forms and reports, you can quickly and easily build a data access page using a wizard. After you build a data access page, you can customize it to your needs. This customization can include adding VBScript or JavaScript that executes in response to events that occur for controls on the page.

23

SQL Server and the Internet

Why This Chapter Is Important

SQL Server 2000 is closely integrated with the Internet. Using the Web Assistant Wizard, you can quickly and easily generate HTML documents from your SQL Server data. In fact, you can use the Web Assistant Wizard to generate triggers that automatically update HTML documents each time the table data changes. In addition to having the capability to publish SQL Server data as HTML, you can generate XML from SQL queries. These and other Web features included with SQL Server 2000 make SQL Server a key player in the Internet world.

You might wonder why I am covering these techniques in an Access 2002 enterprise-development book. The reason is that, as you've discovered throughout this text, most enterprise applications require that data be stored in a SQL Server database. As an Access client/server developer, you may want to take advantage of the rich integration that SQL Server has with the Web. This chapter focuses on the SQL Server tools that you can use to generate Web pages from your application data.

The Web Assistant Wizard

The Web Assistant Wizard is a tool that helps you to quickly and easily publish SQL Server data as HTML. Here's how it works:

1. From within Enterprise Manager, select Tools, Wizards. The Select Wizard dialog box appears (see Figure 23.1).

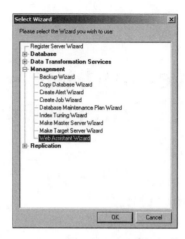

FIGURE 23.1   The Select Wizard dialog box includes the Web Assistant Wizard.

  2. Select the Web Assistant Wizard and click OK. The Web Assistant Wizard appears (see Figure 23.2).

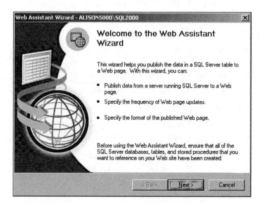

FIGURE 23.2   The Web Assistant Wizard helps you publish SQL Server data to a Web page.

  3. Click Next. The Select Database step of the wizard appears (see Figure 23.3).

  4. Select the database whose data you want to publish, and click Next. The Start a New Web Assistant Job step appears (see Figure 23.4).

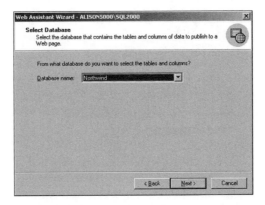

FIGURE 23.3   The Select Database step of the wizard allows you to select the database whose data you want to publish.

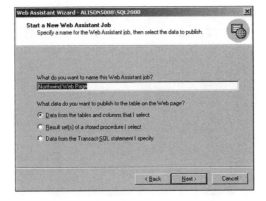

FIGURE 23.4   The Start a New Web Assistant Job step allows you to name the job and designate the data that you want to publish.

5. Name the Web Assistant job and designate whether you want to publish data from tables, the result set of a stored procedure, or the data returned from a Transact-SQL statement that you enter. Make your selection and click Next to continue. The next step varies depending on which option you select. Figure 23.5 shows the next step when you opt to publish data from tables and columns that you select.

6. Select the tables and columns whose data you want to publish. In Figure 23.5, CustomerID, CompanyName, ContactName, ContactTitle, Phone, and Fax are selected from the Customers table. Make your selection and click Next. The Select Rows step of the wizard appears (see Figure 23.6).

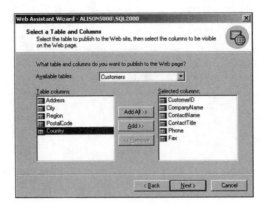

FIGURE 23.5   If you opt to publish data from tables and columns that you select, the wizard prompts you to select the tables and columns.

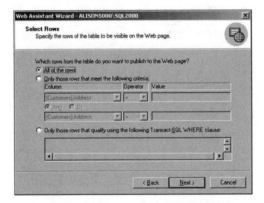

FIGURE 23.6   The Select Rows step of the wizard allows you to designate the rows that you want to publish.

7. In the Select Rows step of the wizard, you can opt to publish all rows from the specified table or to designate criteria for the rows that you want to publish. Make your selection and click Next. The Schedule the Web Assistant Job step of the wizard appears (see Figure 23.7).

8. You can opt to publish data one time, on demand, whenever the data changes, or at regularly specified intervals. If you opt to publish at regularly specified intervals and click Next, the wizard appears as in Figure 23.8.

9. Designate a schedule for the job and click Next. The Publish the Web Page step of the wizard appears (see Figure 23.9).

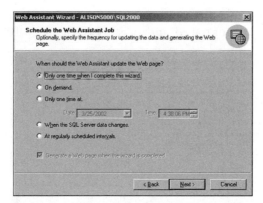

FIGURE 23.7   The Schedule the Web Assistant Job step of the wizard allows you to create a job that publishes data at specified intervals.

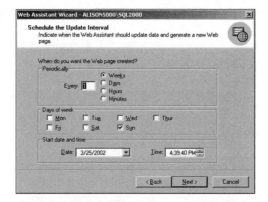

FIGURE 23.8   Schedule how often the HTML document is updated.

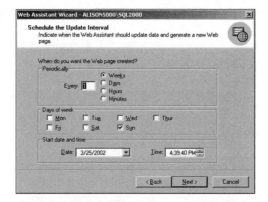

FIGURE 23.9   Provide a name and location for the HTML document.

10. Designate the name and location for the Web page, and click Next. The Format the Web Page step of the wizard appears (see Figure 23.10).

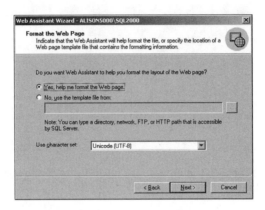

FIGURE 23.10   Designate whether you want the wizard to help you to format the page.

11. Select the desired option and click Next. If you opt to have the wizard help you format the page, the Specify Titles dialog box appears (see Figure 23.11).

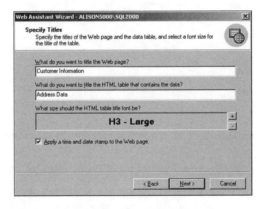

FIGURE 23.11   Designate title text and size information.

12. Enter titles for the Web page and the table containing the data. Designate the table title font and click Next. The Format a Table step of the wizard appears (see Figure 23.12).

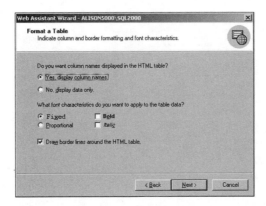

FIGURE 23.12   Designate formatting information.

13. Designate formatting information and click Next. The Add Hyperlinks to the Web Page step of the wizard appears (see Figure 23.13).

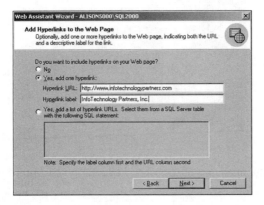

FIGURE 23.13   Designate hyperlinks that you want to add to the page.

14. Designate what hyperlinks you want to add to the page, and click Next. The Limit Rows step of the wizard appears (see Figure 23.14).

15. Indicate whether you want to return all rows of data. Also specify whether you want all the returned data to appear on one scrolling page or multiple linked pages. In Figure 23.14, only 10 rows will appear on each page. Click Next to continue. The final step of the wizard appears (see Figure 23.15).

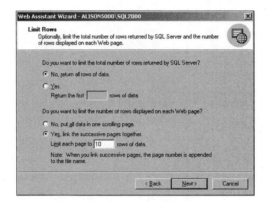

FIGURE 23.14   Designate formatting information.

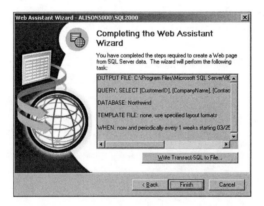

FIGURE 23.15   The final step of the wizard allows you to write the Transact-SQL to a file.

16. Click Write Transact-SQL to File if you want to generate a file containing Transact-SQL that you can run at any time. Click Finish when done. SQL Server notifies you that the process completed successfully.

Editing a Web Job

If you selected any of the scheduling options when you ran the Web Assistant Wizard, SQL Server created a Web job. To view or modify the wizard-generated Web jobs, you must locate the job under the SQL Server Agent node (see Figure 23.16).

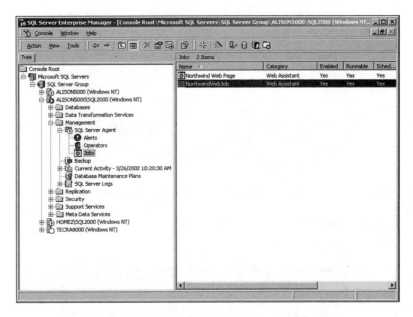

FIGURE 23.16   To view or modify the wizard-generated Web jobs, you must locate the job under the SQL Server Agent node.

To modify a Web job:

1. Right-click the job and select Properties. The Web Job Properties dialog box appears (see Figure 23.17). The General tab allows you to modify general information about the job, such as the job name.

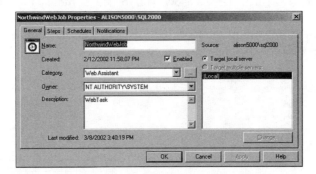

FIGURE 23.17   The General tab in the Web Job Properties dialog box allows you to modify general information about the job.

2. Click the Steps tab to view or modify the steps included in the job (see Figure 23.18). The Steps tab allows you to add and remove steps as well.

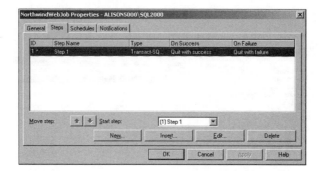

FIGURE 23.18   The Steps tab allows you to view or modify the steps included in the job.

3. Click the Schedules tab to view or modify the schedule for the job (see Figure 23.19).

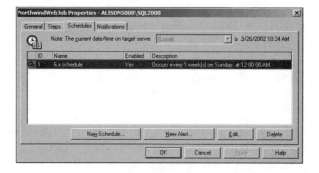

FIGURE 23.19   The Schedules tab allows you to view or modify the schedule for the job.

4. Click the Notifications tab to designate who is notified and under what conditions (see Figure 23.20).

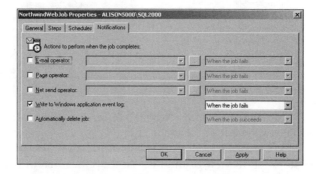

FIGURE 23.20   The Notifications tab allows you to designate who is notified and under what conditions.

NOTE

Chapter 15, "Configuring, Maintaining, and Tuning SQL Server," covers additional details about the SQL Server Agent.

Web Jobs and Triggers

The Web Assistant Wizard (covered earlier in the section of the chapter titled "The Web Assistant Wizard") asks you if you want to publish data one time—on demand—whenever the data changes, or at regularly specified intervals. If you opt to have SQL Server update the Web page each time that the SQL Server data changes (see Figure 23.21), SQL Server presents you with a step of the wizard that asks you which tables and fields you want to monitor (see Figure 23.22). As you can see in the figure, I have opted to monitor changes to the CompanyName, ContactName, ContactTitle, City, Country, Phone, and Fax fields. To perform the updates, SQL Server creates triggers on the tables that you select.

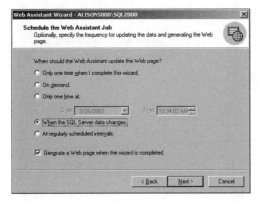

FIGURE 23.21   You can ask SQL Server to update the Web page each time that the data changes.

The process of selecting fields from the Customers table, as in Figure 23.22, created three triggers on the Customers table (see Figure 23.23). The wizard created an insert trigger, an update trigger, and a delete trigger. Notice the update trigger shown in Figure 23.24. It executes when someone changes the data in the CompanyName, ContactName, ContactTitle, City, Country, Phone, or Fax fields. Notice that it executes a stored procedure called sp_runwebtask. In the example, the sp_runwebtask stored procedure receives the task Northwind Automatic Update as the name of the Web task to run. The section that follows discusses the sp_runwebtask stored procedure.

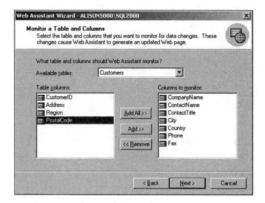

FIGURE 23.22   SQL Server presents you with a step of the wizard that asks you which tables and fields you want to monitor.

FIGURE 23.23   The process of selecting fields from the Customers table creates three triggers on the Customers table.

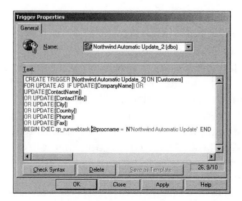

FIGURE 23.24   The update trigger generated by selecting fields from the Customers table.

Take a better look at the code in the update trigger. It responds to the user modifying data in any of the fields selected in the wizard. If the user updates any of those fields, the trigger executes the sp_runwebtask stored procedure, passing it the name of the stored procedure responsible for selecting the data that comprises the Web page.

```
CREATE TRIGGER [Northwind Automatic Update_2] ON [Customers]
FOR UPDATE AS   IF UPDATE([CompanyName])
OR UPDATE([ContactName])
OR UPDATE([ContactTitle])
OR UPDATE([City])
OR UPDATE([Country])
OR UPDATE([Phone])
OR UPDATE([Fax])
BEGIN EXEC sp_runwebtask @procname =  N'Northwind Automatic Update'  END
```

Notice the code in the insert trigger. It is almost identical to that of the update trigger. Again, it responds to the user updating any of the selected fields during the insert process. It also executes the sp_runwebtask stored procedure, passing it the name of the stored procedure responsible for generating the data underlying the Web page.

```
CREATE TRIGGER [Northwind Automatic Update_1] ON [Customers]
FOR INSERT AS   IF UPDATE([CompanyName])
OR UPDATE([ContactName])
OR UPDATE([ContactTitle])
OR UPDATE([City])
OR UPDATE([Country])
OR UPDATE([Phone])
OR UPDATE([Fax])
BEGIN EXEC sp_runwebtask @procname =  N'Northwind Automatic Update'  END
```

Notice the code in the delete trigger. It responds to someone deleting a row from the Customers table. When someone deletes a row, the sp_runwebtask stored procedure runs, regenerating the Web page without the deleted row.

```
CREATE TRIGGER [Northwind Automatic Update_4] ON [Customers]
FOR DELETE AS
BEGIN EXEC sp_runwebtask @procname =  N'Northwind Automatic Update'  END
```

Web-Related Stored Procedures

A few stored procedures are involved in the process of generating and updating Web pages with SQL Server data. They are sp_makewebtask, sp_runwebtask, and sp_dropwebtask. The sections that follow cover the details of each of these very powerful stored procedures.

sp_makewebtask

sp_makewebtask is a system stored procedure that receives a multitude of input parameters. This stored procedure is responsible for generating a Web task that publishes XML data. If you review the Transact-SQL file created in the final step of the Web Assistant Wizard, you will see that it executes the sp_makewebtask stored procedure. All of the options that you selected in the wizard appear as parameters to the stored procedure (see Figure 23.25). Furthermore, if you opted to update the HTML file each time the user updates, deletes, or inserts data, SQL Server creates triggers as well (discussed in the previous section).

FIGURE 23.25   Transact-SQL generated if you opted to write the Transact-SQL to a file.

sp_runwebtask

Whereas the sp_makewebtask stored procedure is responsible for generating the Web task, the sp_runwebtask stored procedure is responsible for running it. It is the sp_runwebtask stored procedure that the wizard-generated triggers execute. You call the sp_runwebtask stored procedure like this:

```
sp_runwebtask
    @procname = 'procname'
    @outputfile = 'outputfile'
```

For example, the update trigger for the Customers table calls the `sp_runwebtask` stored procedure like this:

```
sp_runwebtask @procname = N'Northwind Automatic Update'
```

This code executes `sp_runwebtask`, passing it the Web job called Northwind Automatic Update. The Web Assistant Wizard created a stored procedure that looks like this:

```
CREATE PROCEDURE [Northwind Automatic Update]  AS
SELECT [CustomerID], [CompanyName], [ContactName],
[ContactTitle], [City], [Country], [Phone], [Fax]
FROM [Customers]
```

Notice that the stored procedure simply selects data from the Customers table. In summary, the update trigger for the Customers table runs the `sp_runwebtask` stored procedure, passing it the name of the stored procedure to execute—in this case, Northwind Automatic Update. The `sp_runwebtask` stored procedure then generates the requested HTML file. An example of a completed Web page appears in Figure 23.26.

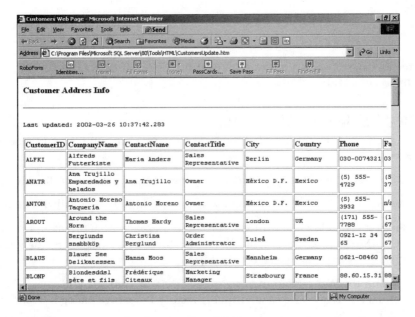

FIGURE 23.26   An example of a completed Web page based on data from the Customers table.

```
sp_dropwebtask
```

The `sp_dropwebtask` stored procedure drops both the Web task and the associated Web page. It looks like this:

```
sp_dropwebtask
    @procname = 'Northwind Automatic Update'
    @outputfile = 'C:\Program Files\Microsoft SQL Server\80\Tools\' & _
        'HTML\CustomersUpdate.htm'
```

This example drops the stored procedure called Northwind Automatic Update. It also deletes the triggers and the CustomerUpdate.htm file.

Generating XML from SQL Queries

SQL Server allows you to access its data via a uniform resource locator (URL) over HTTP. The query looks like this:

```
http://YourServerName/CustomerData?sql=SELECT+*+FROM+Customers+FOR+XML+AUTO
```

> **NOTE**
>
> You must replace the reference to *YourServerName* with the name of your server.

Before you can run such a query, you must first set up Internet Information Server (IIS) to accept a URL.

Setting Up IIS for SQL Server

Several steps must be fastidiously followed before you can submit a URL request to SQL Server:

1. Create a folder named Customers in your \Inetpub\wwwroot directory.

2. Add two subdirectories, one called template and the other called schema.

3. From the Windows Start menu, select Start, Programs, SQL Server, Configure SQL XML Support in IIS. The IIS Virtual Directory Management for SQL Server dialog box appears (see Figure 23.27).

4. Expand the Web server; then right-click Default Web Site and select Create New Virtual Directory. The New Virtual Directory Properties dialog box appears (see Figure 23.28).

5. On the General tab, enter the name of the virtual directory (Customers, in this example). Enter the full path to the actual directory that the virtual directory is associated with (see Figure 23.28).

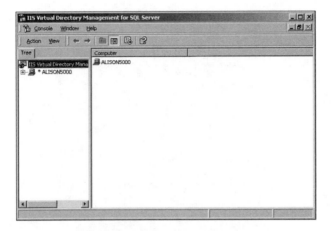

FIGURE 23.27   The IIS Virtual Directory Management for SQL Server dialog box allows you to create a new virtual directory.

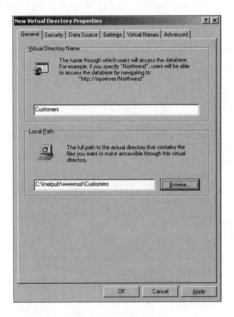

FIGURE 23.28   The New Virtual Directory Properties dialog box allows you to set the appropriate options.

6. On the Security tab, select SQL Server as the account type. Supply a login and password that has access to the database (see Figure 23.29).

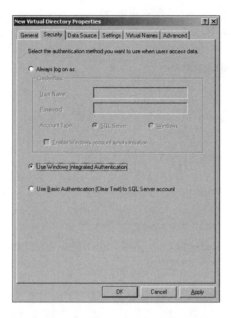

FIGURE 23.29 Designate the appropriate security information.

7. On the Data Source tab, enter the name of the server and the appropriate database name (see Figure 23.30).

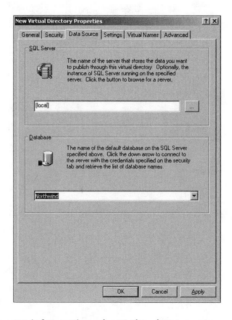

FIGURE 23.30 Designate information about the data source.

8. Use the Settings tab to indicate that you want to allow URL queries, template queries, and XPath options (see Figure 23.31).

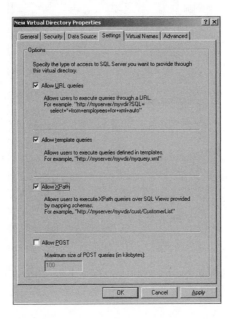

FIGURE 23.31 The Settings tab allows you to designate other important options.

9. Use the Virtual Names tab to create virtual names for the template and schema subdirectories. Select the Virtual Names tab and then click New. The Virtual Name Configuration dialog box appears (see Figure 23.32).

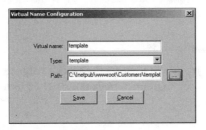

FIGURE 23.32 Use the Virtual Name Configuration dialog box to create virtual names for the schema and template folders.

10. Enter the virtual name, select the appropriate type, and designate the path to the folder (see Figure 23.32). Click Save. When you are done, the dialog box should appear as in Figure 23.33.

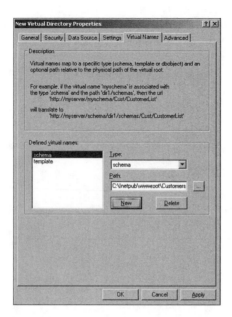

FIGURE 23.33   The Virtual Name Configuration dialog box after creating the virtual names.

Accessing SQL Server Data with a URL

Now that you have successfully set up the SQL Server to receive URL queries, you are ready to attempt to access it with a URL. Launch your browser and type the following SQL statement in the address:

```
http://YourServerName/Customers?sql=SELECT * FROM Customers WHERE
➥CustomerID = 'ALFKI' FOR XML AUTO
```

The results appear in Figure 23.34.

When retrieving results from a SQL Server over the Internet, you must specify the XML mode as Raw, Auto, or Explicit. The sections that follow discuss each of these options and their implications.

Raw Mode

When you use FOR XML RAW, SQL Server returns a <row> tag for each row in the record set. It specifies each column with an attribute tag with the name of the SQL Server column. This option does not take advantage of XML's capability to describe structured data. Consider the following SQL statement:

```
SELECT Customers.CustomerID, Customers.CompanyName,
Orders.OrderID, Orders.OrderDate
FROM Customers INNER JOIN ORDERS ON Customers.CustomerID = Orders.CustomerID
ORDER BY Customers.CustomerID
FOR XML RAW&root=ROOT
```

Notice that the results, shown in Figure 23.35, do not adequately represent the data structure.

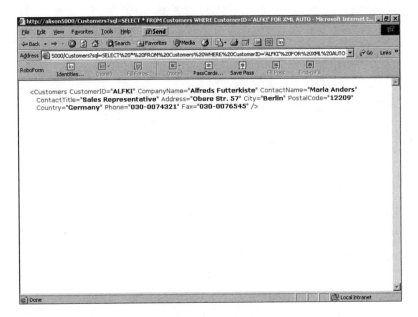

FIGURE 23.34   Verifying that the process was successful.

Auto Mode

When you use FOR XML AUTO, SQL Server names and structures the data based on the underlying table structures. Consider this example:

```
SELECT Customers.CustomerID, Customers.CompanyName,
Orders.OrderID, Orders.OrderDate
FROM Customers INNER JOIN ORDERS ON Customers.CustomerID = Orders.CustomerID
ORDER BY Customers.CustomerID
FOR XML AUTO&root=ROOT
```

As you can see in Figure 23.36, the row tag is eliminated. Furthermore, you can easily identify the relationship between the tables included in the SELECT statement.

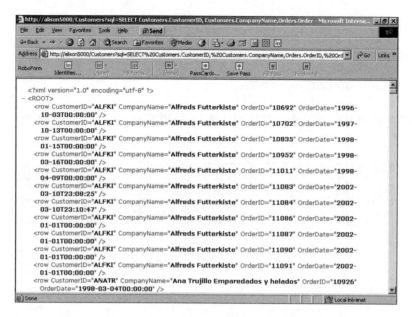

FIGURE 23.35   The results of executing a query with XML RAW.

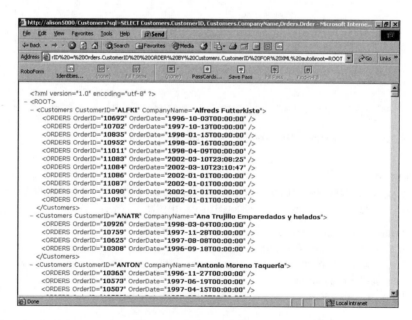

FIGURE 23.36   The results of executing a query with XML AUTO.

Using FOR XML Explicit

The FOR XML EXPLICIT syntax allows you to specify the structure and naming scheme of the resulting XML. Furthermore, it provides directives that you can use to improve the performance of the query. Unfortunately, it is extremely cumbersome to work with. SQL Server Books Online provides some information about XML EXPLICIT.

Summary

SQL Server 2000 contains powerful Web features that make it a key player in the Internet world. Using the Web Assistant Wizard, you can easily publish data to the Web. Furthermore, you can return SQL Server data as XML within a browser. This chapter focused on how you can take advantage of SQL Server 2000's rich integration with the Internet to publish your application's data to the Internet or to an intranet site.

Index

Symbols

How can we make this index more useful? Email us at indexes@samspublishing.com

How can we make this index more useful? Email us at indexes@samspublishing.com

C

How can we make this index more useful? Email us at indexes@samspublishing.com

E

H

How can we make this index more useful? Email us at indexes@samspublishing.com

DECLARE, variables, 246

DISTINCT, table columns, 174-175

library functions, 601-602

Keywords property, selecting in Properties window, 601-602

L

Label control, data access pages, 703

labels

controls, defining hyperlink addresses, 645

Hyperlink Address and SubAddress properties, 643

Labels, stored procedures, 250-253

languages. *See also* **HTML; SQL; XML**

DDL (data definition language), definition, 77

XSLT (Extensible Stylesheet Language Transformation), 652-657

launching

Packaging Wizard from VBE (Visual Basic Environment), 604

Profiler (SQL Server), 117-118

Query Analyzer, 114

layers, Tracking Layer (data replication), 551

Layout Wizard, 688, 702

.LDB file, 63

LEFT

function (T-SQL), 193

JOIN (tables), 220

LEN function (T-SQL), 195

less-than symbol (<), tags, 652-653

less-than symbol with forward slash (</), end tags, 652

levels, grouping (adding to data access pages), 681

leveraging power of VSS (Visual SourceSafe), objects, 627-629

libraries, 12, 463, 595-603

licenses, 586-587

Limit Rows step (Web Assistant Wizard), 729-730

linear topology (data replication), 555

Link

Specification dialog box, 640

Tables dialog box, 349-350, 364

Link HTML Wizard, 639-640

linked HTML (Hypertext Markup Language) documents, 641

linked servers (Enterprise Manager tree), 112

Linked Table Manager, 380

linked tables. *See* **tables, linked**

links. *See* **hyperlinks**

LinkTables routine, 33-34, 37

list boxes, 381-382, 704

listings. *See* **code**

lists

customers, viewing by cities, 693-694

drop-down, data access pages, 704

Field List, selecting fields, 691

functions in Access category, 597-598

Orders header or table, dragging and dropping fields, 697-698

Performance Object, 514

Live Data button, 663

load method, 669

loading Packaging Wizard add-in, 603-604

local query issues, ADO (ActiveX Data Objects) files, 433

local storage issues, ADO (ActiveX Data Objects) files, 433

local tables, 379-381

Locate Web Page dialog box, 686

locating. *See* **finding**

Location of New Replica dialog box, 558

locations

application installations, selecting, 612-613

cursors, code, 323-324

log files, 566-567

M

N

How can we make this index more useful? Email us at indexes@samspublishing.com

P

How can we make this index more useful? Email us at indexes@samspublishing.com

How can we make this index more useful? Email us at indexes@samspublishing.com

How can we make this index more useful? Email us at indexes@samspublishing.com

W

X-Y-Z

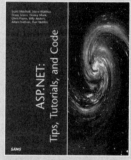

What's on the CD-ROM

The companion CD-ROM contains all the examples developed in the book, software resources, and training resources.

Windows Installation Instructions

1. Insert the CD-ROM disc into your CD-ROM drive.

2. From the Windows desktop, double-click on the My Computer icon.

3. Double-click on the icon representing your CD-ROM drive.

4. Double-click on start.exe. Follow the on-screen prompts to finish the installation

NOTE

If you have the AutoPlay feature enabled, start.exe will be launched automatically whenever you insert the disc into your CD-ROM drive.